The Book of Unveiling

The Institute of Ismaili Studies
Shi'i Heritage Series, 11

Editorial Board: Farhad Daftary (general editor), Maria De Cillis (managing editor), Gurdofarid Miskinzoda (managing editor), Mohammad-Ali Amir-Moezzi, Hermann Landolt, Andrew Newman, Sabine Schmidtke, Paul E. Walker

Previously published titles:

1. Daftary, Farhad. *A History of Shiʿi Islam* (2013).
2. Daftary, Farhad, and Gurdofarid Miskinzoda, ed. *The Study of Shiʿi Islam: History, Theology and Law* (2014).
3. Mir-Kasimov, Orkhan. *Words of Power: Ḥurūfī Teachings Between Shiʿism and Sufism in Medieval Islam* (2015).
4. Asatryan, Mushegh. *Controversies in Formative Shiʿi Islam: The Ghulat Muslims and their Beliefs* (2017).
5. De Cillis, Maria. *Salvation and Destiny in Islam: The Shiʿi Ismaili Perspective of Ḥamīd al-Dīn al-Kirmānī* (2018).
6. Mir-Kasimov, Orkhan, ed. *Intellectual Interactions in the Islamic World: The Ismaili Thread* (2019).
7. Hermann, Denis, and Matthieu Terrier, ed. *Shiʿi Islam and Sufism: Classical Views and Modern Perspectives* (2019).
8. Esots, Janis. *Patterns of Wisdom in Safavid Iran: The Philosophical School of Isfahan and the Gnostic of Shiraz* (2021).
9. Daftary, Farhad, and Janis Esots, ed. *The Renaissance of Shiʿi Islam: Facets of Though and Practice* (2022).
10. Amir-Moezzi, Mohammad Ali. *The Proof of God: Shiʿi Mysticism in the Work of al-Kulayni (9th-10th centuries)*, tr. Maria De Cillis and Orkhan Mir-Kasimov (2023).

The Book of Unveiling

Early Fatimid Ismaili Doctrine in the Kitāb al-Kashf, *attributed to Jaʿfar b. Manṣūr al-Yaman*

by
Fârès Gillon

I.B. TAURIS
in association with
The Institute of Ismaili Studies
LONDON, 2024

I.B. TAURIS
Bloomsbury Publishing Plc
50 Bedford Square, London, WC1B 3DP, UK
1385 Broadway, New York, NY 10018, USA
29 Earlsfort Terrace, Dublin 2, Ireland

In association with The Institute of Ismaili Studies
Aga Khan Centre, 10 Handyside Street, London N1C 4DN
www.iis.ac.uk

First published in Great Britain 2024

A catalogue record for this book is available from the British Library.

A catalog record for this book is available from the Library of Congress.

ISBN: HB: 978-0-7556-5386-7
PB: 978-0-7556-5387-4
ePDF: 978-0-7556-5389-8
eBook: 978-0-7556-5388-1

Series: Shiʿi Heritage Series

Typeset by RefineCatch Limited, Bungay, Suffolk
Printed and bound in Great Britain

The Institute of Ismaili Studies

The Institute of Ismaili Studies has an extensive programme of multilingual research and publications dating back to 1977. It endeavours to make available scholarly works of a high academic standard related to Islam in its historical and contemporary contexts, with a particular focus on Shiʿi and Ismaili heritage, Qurʾanic studies, and expressions of Islam's diverse devotional, literary and esoteric traditions. The IIS also publishes engaging and accessible works exploring the relationship of religious faith and practice to broader dimensions of society, culture and modernity. IIS publications fall into a number of categories, including monographs of original research and analysis; critical editions and translations of important primary texts; conference proceedings; catalogues of manuscripts and bibliographies; works of reference; and works on Ismaili history, literature and thought. Authors of the Institute's publications express a range of views which, as such, are not necessarily those of the Institute itself.

A full list of the publications of the Institute of Ismaili Studies can be found on our website at: https://www.iis.ac.uk/publications-listing/.

Shiʿi Heritage Series

Shiʿi Muslims, with their rich intellectual and cultural heritage, have contributed significantly to the fecundity and diversity of the Islamic traditions throughout the centuries, enabling Islam to evolve and flourish both as a major religion and also as a civilisation. In spite of this, Shiʿi Islam has received little scholarly attention in the West, in medieval as well modern times. It is only in recent decades that academic interest has focused increasingly on Shiʿi Islam within the wider study of Islam.

The principal objective of the *Shiʿi Heritage Series*, launched by The Institute of Ismaili Studies, is to enhance general knowledge of Shiʿi Islam and promote a better understanding of its history, doctrines and practices in their historical and contemporary manifestations. Addressing all Shiʿi communities, the series also aims to engage in discussions on theoretical and methodological issues, while inspiring further research in the field.

Works published in this series will include monographs, collective volumes, editions and translations of primary texts, and bibliographical projects, bringing together some of the most significant themes in the study of Shiʿi Islam through an interdisciplinary approach, and making them accessible to a wide readership.

Contents

List of Abbreviations xiii
Note on Transliteration and Usage xv
Acknowledgements xvii

INTRODUCTION
1. Historical and Intellectual Context 6
2. Transmission: Manuscripts, Editions, and Reception 28
3. The Problematic Authorship of the *Kitāb al-Kashf*: Some Remarks on the Corpus Attributed to Jaʿfar b. Manṣūr al-Yaman 43
4. The Six Treatises of the *Kitāb al-Kashf* and their Contents 60
5. Between Chaos and Order: The Art of Compilation and Structure in the *Kitāb al-Kashf* 63

Notes on the Translations and Commentaries 68

TREATISE I

Treatise I Translation 74
Treatise I Commentary 120
1. The Divine Trust (*amāna*), *walāya* and the covenant 121
2. The *daʿwa*, an esoteric family 128
3. God's 'Order' (*amr*) and its continuity 134
4. The continuity of antagonism: the enemies of the Imam 147
5. *Musūkhiyya*: from literal to metaphoric metamorphosis 154
6. The Mahdī and his Return 162

Conclusion 166

TREATISE II

Treatise II Translation 170
Treatise II Commentary 184
1. Divine transcendence 185
2. The Throne, the Footstool and the problem of anthropomorphism 189
3. The alphabetic cosmogony 195
Conclusion 205

TREATISE III

Treatise III Translation 209
Treatise III Commentary 248
1. Identifying the 'Sage' (*al-ḥakīm*) and dating *Treatise III* 252
2. The *daʿwa*: an organization and its enemies 256
3. The Orphan: evolution of a concept, from *ghuluww* to Fatimid Ismailism 272
4. Salmān, a Shiʿi figure in support of the Fatimid reform 286
5. The 'Bearer of the Sword' and the *rajʿa* 293
Conclusion 299

TREATISE IV

Treatise IV Translation 302
Treatise IV Commentary 308
1. Several *ḥadīth* fragments 308
2. A *ḥadīth* on language 311
Conclusion 316

TREATISE V

Treatise V Translation 322
Treatise V Commentary 384
1. The Imam and his Proof, the *ʿAyn* and the *Fāʾ* 390
2. The rejection of antinomianism 408
3. Organizing the *daʿwa*: instruction to the missionaries and refutation of the false Mahdī 419
Conclusion 424

TREATISE VI

Treatise VI Translation 429
Treatise VI Commentary 448
1. God's choice challenged by human caprice 450
2. ʿAlī and Aaron as Books of God 458
3. Proofs and Summoners 463
Conclusion 471

GENERAL CONCLUSION 473

Bibliography 483
Index of Qur'anic Verses 497
Index of Names and Places 507
Index of Technical Terms 511

List of Abbreviations

BSOAS	Bulletin of the School of Oriental and African Studies
EI1	*Encyclopedia of Islam*, 1st edition
EI2	*Encyclopedia of Islam*, 2nd edition
EI3	*Encyclopedia of Islam*, 3rd edition
EIr	*Encyclopaedia Iranica*
EIs	*Encyclopaedia Islamica*
EQ	*Encyclopaedia of the Qur'ān*
JAOS	*Journal of the American Oriental Society*
JQS	*Journal of Qur'anic Studies*
JSAI	*Jerusalem Studies in Arabic and Islam*
SSR	*Shi'i Studies Review*

Note on Transliteration and Usage

The system of transliteration follows *EI3* with some minor exceptions.

Acknowledgements

The journey leading to the publication of this monograph has been a long and, at times, painful one. More than once, I was on the verge of getting lost in this labyrinth that the Ismaili tradition transmits under the deceptive title: *Book of Unveiling*. If I finally found my way out, it is only thanks to the help of colleagues, friends and family, and it is a pleasant duty to express my deepest gratitude to them.

This book originates in my PhD dissertation, which I presented in 2017 at the École Pratique des Hautes Études in Paris, under the supervision of Profs. Mohammad Ali Amir-Moezzi and Daniel De Smet. I must therefore start by acknowledging my immense debt to these two leading scholars in the fields of Shiʿi and Ismaili studies, not only for their academic contributions, which paved the way for the present research, but also for their guidance, insightful comments and kind advice throughout my doctoral years. I must also extend my appreciation to the other members of my Ph.D. committee – Carmela Baffioni, Michel Boivin and Thierry Zarcone.

The English version of the book was prepared during my delightful years at the Institute of Ismaili Studies, between 2019 and 2022. I am grateful to Dr Farhad Daftary, co-director of the IIS at the time, for his constant encouragements, confidence in my work and enthusiasm to see it published. I am also grateful to the new co-director of the IIS, Prof. Zayn Kassam, for seeing the project through. The IIS provided an ideal and thriving environment for my research, thanks to the knowledgeability and kindness of its scholars. I wish to mention in particular Toby Mayer, Omar Ali-de-Unzaga, Orkhan Mir-Kasimov, Hasan al-Khoee, Aslisho Qurboniev, Reza Shah-Kazemi, David Bennett, Alessandro Cancian, Karen Bauer, Wafi Momin, and the late Janis Esots whose memory will remain vivid. I am grateful to these friends for their availability for the informal, yet stimulating, chats which are essential in the life of a scholar. I am also thankful to Julia Kolb and Naushin Premji for their helpfulness.

Over my years working on the *Kashf*, I have benefited from feedback and comments from several scholars and friends during academic events or private conversations. Among them, may Mushegh Asatryan, Wissam Halawi, Edmund Hayes, David Hollenberg, Paul Neuenkirchen, Michael Noble, Christian Sahner, Mathieu Terrier and Gregory Vandamme find here a token of my deep appreciation.

I wish to thank the editors of the Shiʿi Heritage Series, Maria De Cillis and Gurdofarid Miskinzoda, for welcoming the monograph in their series and providing helpful feedback, as well as Tara Woolnough for her active involvement in the publication process. I am also grateful to Russell Harris for his meticulous and thorough copyediting of the typescript.

The two anonymous reviewers of the manuscript have provided suggestions and, at times, corrections, which tremendously contributed to the improvement of the text. Any remaining mistakes and shortcomings are of course my own.

Last, but not least, I owe my family all my gratitude for their patience and support throughout these past years – my parents, Jean-Yves and Nada, my brother, Jihâd, and especially my wife, Sterenn, and our children, for their love and the joy and courage they have inspired in me.

INTRODUCTION

Since it was first edited by Rudolf Strothmann in 1952, the *Book of Unveiling* (*Kitāb al-Kashf* or *Kashf*) has sparked the interest of several generations of scholars.[1] The scarcity of publicly accessible Ismaili material at that time and for several decades, as well as the fact that it was rightly deemed one of the oldest Ismaili compositions to have reached the present day, have made it a central source on Ismailism in Western scholarship.

[1] See W. Ivanow, *A Guide to Ismaili Literature* (London, 1933), p. 36, XI no. 50; idem, *Ismaili Literature: A Bibliographical Survey* (Tehran, 1963), p. 21, no. 13; P. Kraus, 'La bibliographie ismaëlienne de W. Ivanow', *Revue des Etudes Islamiques*, 6 (1932), pp. 486–487; I.K. Poonawala, *Biobibliography of Ismāʿīlī Literature* (Malibu, 1977), p. 73, no. 5. The main studies dedicated to the *Kashf* are the following: H. Feki, *Les Idées religieuses et philosophiques de l'ismaélisme fatimide, Organization et doctrine* (Tunis, 1978), pp. 17, 93–94, 175, 295; W. Madelung, 'Das Imamat in der frühen ismailitischen Lehre', *Der Islam*, 37 (1961), pp. 52 ff; H. Halm, *Kosmologie und Heilslehre der frühen Ismāʿīlīya: Eine Studie zur islamische Gnosis* (Wiesbaden, 1978), pp. 18–52; 149–156, 165–168; idem, 'Das "Buch der Schatten": Die Mufaḍḍal-Tradition der Ġulāt und die Ursprünge des Nuṣairiertums. II. Die Stoffe', *Der Islam*, 58 (1981), pp. 83–84; idem, 'The Cosmology of the Pre-Fatimid Ismāʿīliyya', in F. Daftary, ed, *Mediaeval Isma'ili History and Thought* (Cambridge, 1996), pp. 75–83, esp, pp. 79–80; I.K. Poonawala, 'Ismāʿīlī *ta'wīl* of the Qur'an', in A. Rippin, ed, *Approaches to the History of the Interpretation of the Qur'an* (Oxford, 1988), pp. 220–221; M.M. Bar-Asher, 'Outlines of Early Ismāʿīlī-Fātimid Qur'an Exegesis', *Journal Asiatique*, 296/2 (2008), pp. 262–263, 277, 286, 288–289; F. Gillon, 'Une version ismaélienne de *ḥadīṯs* imāmites. Nouvelles perspectives sur le traité II du *Kitāb al-Kašf* attribué à Ǧaʿfar b. Manṣūr al-Yaman (Xe s.)', *Arabica*, 59/5 (2012), pp. 484–509; idem, 'Aperçus sur les origines de l'ismaélisme à travers le *Kitāb al-Kašf* attribué au dāʿī Ǧaʿfar b. Manṣūr al-Yaman', *Ishraq: Islamic Philosophy Yearbook*, 4 (2013), pp. 90–111; idem, 'Lumière et théophanie dans l'ismaélisme fâtimide: le cas du traité I du *Kitāb al-Kašf*', *Chronos*, 32 (2015), pp. 141–155; D. Hollenberg, *Beyond the Qur'an. Early Ismāʿīlī Ta'wīl and the*

At first glance, one may wonder how this source of unclear authorship, transmitted in only two available manuscripts and hardly ever quoted in later Ismaili sources, has come to be considered as such an emblematic Ismaili text. Apart from the early origin of the text, the reason for this is the richness and the variety of the material found in the *Kashf*, which is mostly of exegetical nature. It is not only specialists of Ismailism that were attracted to the *Kashf*, but also, more widely, scholars working on various trends of early Shiʿi Islam or Islamic thought. The *Kashf* is indeed a witness of the Shiʿi doctrines that circulated before their institutionalization, either through Twelver Shiʿi orthodoxy as formed during the Buyid period (945–1055), or Ismaili orthodoxy as formed by the Fatimids (909–1171). But it is also a valuable source on the early Fatimid attempts to normalize and reform the Ismaili doctrine. The presence of both trends — the generally Shiʿi and the Ismaili — in a single work thus illustrates the anchorage of early Ismailism in a common pool of Shiʿi doctrines. In sum, not only does the *Kitāb al-Kashf* provide valuable information on both pre-Fatimid and early Fatimid periods of Ismailism, but it also echoes both the 'moderate' Shiʿism of 10th c. Twelver Shiʿi *ḥadīth* collections, and the *ghuluww* — the so-called 'exaggerating' Shiʿism — teachings. The connection with this heritage of the *ghulāt* further explains why the *Kashf* also resonates with Nuṣayrī sources which have kept with the doctrinal orientations of the *ghulāt*. In addition, the *Kashf* displays several examples of Qurʾanic interpretations that are in line with what M.M. Bar-Asher has labelled the Imami 'pre-Buwayhid

Secrets of the Prophets (Columbia, NY, 2016), pp. 45–46; M. Asatryan, *Controversies in Formative Shiʿi Islam. The Ghulat Muslims and their Beliefs* (London, 2017), pp. 38–39; idem, 'Early Ismailis and Other Muslims: Polemics and Borrowing in *Kitāb al-Kashf*', in O. Mir-Kasimov, ed, *Intellectual Interactions in the Islamic World. The Ismaili Thread* (London, 2020), pp. 273–298; J. Velji, *An Apocalyptic History of the Early Fatimid Empire* (Edinburgh, 2018), pp. 42–60; R. Adem, 'Early Ismailism and the Gates of Religious Authority: Genealogizing the Theophanic Secret of Early Esoteric Shiʿism', in R. Adem and E. Hayes, eds, *Reason, Esotericism and Authority in Shiʿi Islam* (Leiden, 2021), pp. 24–72.

school of exegesis'.[2] This privileged situation at the crossroads of several Shiʿi and Ismaili trends makes the *Kitāb al-Kashf* an essential source, and an excellent introduction to both Shiʿi and Ismaili doctrines and debates at the beginning of the 10th century.

Yet, in spite of its widely acknowledged importance, the *Kitāb al-Kashf* has not benefited from a complete study until now, due to the many challenges such a study presents. Indeed, the *Kashf* is composed of six treatises quite different in style, content and structure. Therefore, one is to make sense of the collection by attempting to give consistency to the diversity displayed by the treatises, yet without overlooking the specificity of each treatise.

Among the difficulties presented by the *Kashf* is the fact that the two available manuscripts are late, compared to the supposed time of composition of the text, and that they are the result of a flawed transmission. Indeed, the text is corrupted in several places and contains countless grammatical and syntactical mistakes. Several sentences are illegible beyond any possibility of recovering their meaning, while some arguments are so elusive that it seems parts of sentences, or even whole paragraphs, are missing.

The poor quality of the text only adds to the general elusiveness of the *Kashf*. Indeed, the various parts, sections, textual units are seldom connected to each other by logical markers, and the text almost never explicitly refers to the historical context during which it was composed. As will be shown, it has likely been composed following a kind of 'scattering of knowledge' (*tabdīd al-ʿilm*) technique, which has effects not only on the overall structure of the *Kashf*, but also on the structure of each treatise (particularly Treatises I, III, V and VI).

Taking all these issues into account, it will come as no surprise that dating the text is not a straightforward process. In his major study on the Imamate in early Ismaili doctrine, W. Madelung had reached the conclusion that the *Kitāb al-Kashf* was a collection of pre-Fatimid texts that were probably rearranged and amended in the early Fatimid period. According to him, if Jaʿfar b. Manṣūr al-Yaman, a Fatimid Ismaili *dāʿī* active in the first half of the 10th century, was indeed

[2] M.M. Bar-Asher, *Scripture and Exegesis in Early Imāmī Shiʿism* (Leiden, Boston and Jerusalem, 1999).

involved in the *Kashf*, he was but the editor of earlier texts he had brought with him from Yemen when he emigrated to North Africa to join the Fatimid court.[3] Madelung's hypothesis that the *Kitāb al-Kashf* is essentially a pre-Fatimid work was accepted by later scholars.[4]

In the present study, however, I will attempt to revise this hypothesis and to demonstrate that the *Kitāb al-Kashf* should be fully considered as an early Fatimid composition, although it evidently draws on pre-Fatimid material. This does not exactly contradict Madelung's findings; rather, I seek to emphasize the Fatimid features of the *Kashf*. Madelung believed the *Kashf* was *edited* during the reign of the second Fatimid caliph, Abū al-Qāsim al-Qā'im bi-Amr Allāh (r. 322–334/934–946), but in the light of my research, I will suggest that it was rather *composed* at this time — and maybe even earlier, under the reign of the first Fatimid caliph, ʿAbd Allāh al-Mahdī (r. 296–322/909–934).

Besides attempting to date the *Kashf*, the major focus of this study is to present the *Kashf* as a work in which the *formation* of the early Fatimid Ismaili doctrine can be observed. After the Fatimids accessed power, they sought to reform the earlier, pre-Fatimid, Ismaili doctrine. The *Kashf* is a rare testimony of the very first stages of this endeavour, prior to the more elaborate efforts under the caliphate of the fourth Fatimid caliph, al-Muʿizz li-Dīn Allāh (r. 341–368/953–975). It is an attempt to mobilize pre-Fatimid material to support the new Fatimid claims, and thus to justify a lasting dynastic rule in place of the eschatological expectations the pre-Fatimid *daʿwa* had nurtured. In this capacity, it is a precious witness of both periods, as it illustrates the anchorage of early Ismailism in Shiʿi Islam as it was before the Major Occultation (328–329/940–941) — that is, prior to its 'rationalization' and institutionalization.

Indeed, while Madelung had focused on the *Kashf* as an Ismaili text, Heinz Halm, for his part, although also studying the Ismaili features of the *Kashf* in his monograph *Kosmologie und Heilslehre der frühen*

---

[3] W. Madelung, 'Das Imamat', pp. 52 ff. On Jaʿfar's life and works, see discussion below, pp. 43 ff.

[4] See e.g. H. Halm, *Kosmologie*, p. 169; idem, 'The Cosmology of the Pre-Fatimid Ismāʿīliyya', p. 79; F. Daftary, *The Ismāʿīlīs. Their History and Doctrines*, 2nd edition (Cambridge, 2007), p. 98; D. Hollenberg, 'Interpretation after the End of Days: The Fatimid-Ismāʿīlī Taʾwīl (interpretation) of Jaʿfar ibn Manṣūr al-Yaman (d. ca. 960)' (University of Pennsylvania, 2006), p. 59; idem, *Beyond the Qur'an*, p. 45.

Ismāʿīlīya, paid some attention to the many *ghulāt* traits that the work contains.[5] The present research will provide further evidence in favour of these origins of the text (pre-Fatimid, early Fatimid Ismaili and *ghulāt*), adding to it the Shiʿi origin, particularly in relation to the 'pre-Buwayhid school of exegesis'. The Shiʿi historiography of the succession of the Prophet Muḥammad, and its 'anti-Sunni tendency',[6] are indeed very present in the *Kashf*. However, this historiography becomes part of the Fatimid official rhetoric, and serves legitimation purposes: in the *Kashf* particularly, it is not so much directed to actual 'Sunnis', as it is to direct enemies of the Fatimid state, whether internal or external.

In order to contextualise the *Kashf* both intellectually and historically, I will begin with a discussion of *ghuluww* within Shiʿi Islam, before providing a few relevant landmarks of early Ismaili history. The proper introduction of the *Kashf* will then tackle the transmission of the text and the complex matter of the authorship of the works attributed to Jaʿfar b. Manṣūr al-Yaman. The general contents of each treatise and the structure of the *Kashf* will then be briefly examined.

I have provided here the first full translation of the *Kitāb al-Kashf* into English. In order to help the reader appreciate the specificity of each treatise, I have dedicated a chapter to each. The translation of each treatise will thus be preceded by a brief summary of its main themes and an outline of its structure, and will be followed by a detailed, yet not necessarily linear, commentary. The commentaries do not claim exhaustiveness; indeed, I am convinced that the progress in our knowledge of Fatimid Ismaili thought, and particularly of the corpus transmitted under the name of Jaʿfar b. Manṣūr al-Yaman, will bring some new insights on this difficult and complex work — as will the discovery of new manuscripts of the *Kashf*. The aim here is to provide some of the main keys to a major source of early Fatimid Ismailism.

---

[5] It is true, however, that Halm did not 'fully acknowledge the pentadist elements of Ismailism', as noted by R. Adem, 'Early Ismailism and the Gates of Religious Authority', esp. pp. 26–28, 63–64.

[6] See M.M. Bar-Asher, *Scripture and Exegesis*, pp. 82–86, where the 'extreme anti-Sunnī tendency and hostile attitude to the Companions of the Prophet' are one of the four characteristics of early Shiʿi *tafsīr*. Of course, the use of the term 'Sunni' for a 9th/10th c. context is anachronistic. I will occasionally use it nevertheless, as a convenient way to designate the non-Shiʿi part of the Muslim community, or the 'proto-Sunni' community.

1. Historical and Intellectual Context

i. *Shiʿi Islam and the problem of* ghuluww

Islamic studies in Western academia have long suffered from the methodological bias of minoritarian trends of Islam being studied through the lenses of majoritarian ones: thus, Shiʿism was first approached from a Sunni perspective. In the past decades, however, progress in Shiʿi studies has helped temper this fact. Similarly, the study of Christian gnostic groups had long been dependent on the accounts of hostile heresiographers, admittedly due to a lack of sources, but probably also due to the dominance of 'orthodox' viewpoints held by institutional churches. The development of Shiʿi studies benefits, not only from greater attention being paid, and access, to Shiʿi sources, but also from a renewal of the historical perspective with greater attention given to minorities. However, the same tendency arises again, as the diversity of Shiʿi movements is approached from the perspective of majoritarian, institutionalized, Twelver Shiʿism. So-called Shiʿi 'heresies' are measured against a Twelver 'orthodoxy' that has labelled them 'exaggerating' or 'extremist' (*ghulāt*), in an a posteriori reconstruction. Thus, while these 'heresies' in fact seem to predate the construction of Shi'i orthodoxy, they are seen as going astray from the 'original' doctrine. As in Christianity, and despite the obvious differences in the process (since there are no ecumenical councils in Islam), orthodoxy in Islam is not a given from the outset and 'heretics' are not historically those who deviate from a predefined orthodoxy; rather, they are those whom orthodoxy rejects, and it is precisely this act of rejection that constitutes orthodoxy as such. The definition of orthodoxy emerges through a process of negative selection; an apophatic one, one might say. In this regard, Heinz Halm writes: 'Just as the theology of the Christian Church could only emerge in a struggle against the ancient gnosis, so too Imamite orthodoxy only developed against the backdrop of the *ġulāt* teachings, in disagreement with them and confrontation.'[7]

---

[7] H. Halm, 'Das 'Buch der Schatten'', II, p. 86: 'Wie die Theologie des christlichen Hochkirche erst im Kampf gegen die ältere Gnosis entstanden ist, so hat sich auch die imamitische Orthodoxie erst vor dem Hintergrund der *ġulāt*-Lehren, in der Auseinandersetzung mit ihnen und in ihrer Bekämpfung, herausgebildet.'

Indeed, from the second half of the 10th century, after the Major Occultation (329/941) and the coming to power of the Buyid viziers in Baghdad (334/945), Twelver Shiʿis embarked on a process of theological rationalization, and thus of the gradual filtering of a number of doctrines and traditions labelled as 'exaggerations' by heresiographs. Traditions of an esoteric and occult nature, attributing supernatural powers to the Imams, became progressively toned down, if not purely and simply excluded from *ḥadīth* collections. Amir-Moezzi is to be credited with several studies on this question which have helped distinguish clearly between the esoteric tradition of ancient Imamism and its later juridico-rationalist evolutions. Relying on the oldest collections of Imami *ḥadīths*, he has shown that the most 'esoteric' *ḥadīths* were gradually removed from the great Shiʿi collections, beginning with Ibn Bābawayh (d. 381/991).[8]

[8] See M.A. Amir-Moezzi, *Le Guide divin dans le shīʿisme originel. Aux sources de l'ésotérisme en islam* (Paris, 1992), esp. pp. 39–45; English trans. by D. Streight, *The Divine Guide in Early Shiʿism. The Sources of Esotericism in Islam* (Albany, 1994), pp. 15–19; idem, 'Remarques sur les critères d'authenticité du ḥadīth', esp. pp. 5–25; idem and C. Jambet, *Qu'est-ce que le shîʿisme ?* (Paris, 2004), esp. pp. 181–194. See also M.M. Bar-Asher, *Scripture and Exegesis*, pp. 39–45. Note that Amir-Moezzi's research has led him to surmise a 'porosity' of the boundaries between the various Shiʿi groups. Given that, as Amir-Moezzi shows, doctrines and themes considered as typical of *ghuluww* nevertheless find their way into the institutionalized Twelver Shiʿi corpus, it should be concluded that the distinction between 'moderates' and 'exaggerators' is largely artificial. Several modern scholars of Shiʿism disagree with this view, and hold that the *ghulāt* movements were only a late development (3rd/9th c.) within Shiʿism, which is otherwise fundamentally 'moderate' and alien to any form of 'extremism'. See H. Modarressi, *Crisis and Consolidation in the Formative Period of Shīʿite Islam: Abū Jaʿfar ibn Qiba al-Rāzī and his Contribution to Imāmite Shīʿite Law* (Princeton, 1993); T. Bayhom-Daou, 'The Second-Century Šīʿite Ġulāt, were they really Gnostic?', *Journal of Arabic and Islamic Studies*, 5 (2003), pp. 13–61; W. Madelung, 'Early Imāmī Theology as Reflected in the *Kitāb al-kāfī* of al-Kulaynī', in F. Daftary and G. Miskinzoda, eds, *The Study of Shiʿi Islam. History, Theology and Law* (London, 2014), pp. 465–474. The latter thus writes that 'the explicit adoption of rationalist Muʿtazili doctrine by the leading Imāmī scholars in the Būyid age (. . .) can no longer be viewed as a sudden radical break with the early Imāmī theological tradition during the presence of the Imams' (ibid., pp. 467–468). See also M.A. Amir-Moezzi's review of H. Modarressi's book, in *Bulletin Critique des Annales Islamologiques*, 14 (1997), pp. 53–57. Whatever may be the nature of the original teachings of the Imams, and

From the first Occultation (260/874) on, the urgency of the situation had already prompted the soon-to-become 'Twelver' Shiʿis to produce a literature aimed at distancing themselves from 'exaggerating' currents and at refuting them: works of *Radd ʿalā al-ghulāt* (*Refutation of the ghulāt*),[9] *Firaq* (enumerations of the various sects),[10] *Rijāl* (prosopographical works, allowing the classification of Shiʿi personalities as orthodox or heterodox), as well as *ḥadīth* collections were all composed in the perspective of this ideological battle — compiling *ḥadīth*s indeed implies a selection, and therefore a theological orientation. Shiʿism became the scene of a struggle for spiritual legitimacy between exotericist and esotericist Shiʿis, between supporters of the *sufarāʾ* and supporters of the *abwāb*. The *sufarāʾ* are the four intermediaries who, according to official Twelver Shiʿism, ensured the link between the twelfth Imam and his followers between the Minor and the Major Occultations.[11] As for the *abwāb* (sg. *bāb*, 'Gate' or 'Threshold'), they were charismatic disciples of the Imams whom the so-called *ghulāt* held to be initiates of higher rank and 'gates'

even though I tend to agree more with Amir-Moezzi's approach (which seems more in line with what we know of the process of institutionalization and the fact that orthodoxy is almost systematically a construction after the fact — the initial fact being 'heresy'), all sides must agree that the period between the two Occultations was a key moment in the definition of Shiʿi identities. The 'rationalist' school, whether rationalism was indeed a novelty in Shiʿi thought, as Amir-Moezzi has it, or not, as advocated by Modarressi and Madelung, nevertheless strove to differentiate itself from 'esotericists', labelled as *ghulāt*, in the aftermath of the Occultations.

[9] See W. al-Qāḍī, 'The Development of the Term Ghulāt in Muslim Literature with Special Reference to the Kaysāniyya', in A. Dietrich, ed, *Akten des VII. Kongresses für Arabistik und Islamwissenschaft* (Göttingen, 1976); repr. in E. Kohlberg, ed, *Shīʿism* (Aldershot, 2003), pp. 316–317, for a list of Shiʿi authors of works bearing this title. Most are no longer extant.

[10] Among these, the most famous and still extant are the *Firaq al-shīʿa* by al-Nawbakhtī and the *Kitāb al-Maqālāt wa'l-firaq* by al-Qummī, who were both active at the beginning of the 10th century; on this literature, see W. Madelung, 'Bemerkungen zur imamatischen Firaq-Literatur', *Der Islam*, 43 (1967), pp. 37–52, esp. p. 40, regarding the claim that al-Nawbakhtī's and al-Qummī's probable source was Hishām b. al-Ḥakam (end of 8th c.). This claim was questioned through a new analysis of the texts by T. Bayhom-Daou, 'The Second Century Šīʿite Ġulāt', pp. 22–46.

[11] On the representatives of the Imam during Occultation and the construction of the doctrine of the *sufarāʾ*, see now E. Hayes, *Agents of the Hidden Imam: Forging Twelver Shiʿism 850–950 CE* (Cambridge, 2022).

of access to the Imam's esoteric knowledge.[12] These *abwāb* were often close disciples of the Imams whom the subsequent rationalized Twelver Shiʿi tradition either rejected or included, which illustrates the ambiguous treatment they received. Mufaḍḍal al-Juʿfī (d. after 183/799) was thus an important transmitter of many *ḥadīths* from the Imams Muḥammad al-Bāqir (d. 115/732) and Jaʿfar al-Ṣādiq (d. 148/765), but also the tutelary figure of several *ghulāt* currents who gave rise to a 'Mufaḍḍalian tradition' which has been masterfully studied by Heinz Halm.[13] This tradition found particular expression in Nuṣayrism, the Islamic tradition par excellence for the preservation of the texts and doctrines of *ghuluww*. But the latter in fact permeates the whole of Shiʿism, including Ismailism as the *Kashf* illustrates.

The term *ghuluww* derives from two Qurʾānic verses stating: '*Do not exaggerate in your religion*' (*lā taghlū fī dīnikum*).[14] In the Qurʾan, this recommendation is directed to the 'People of the Book', and in Q. 4:171, it applies more specifically to those who claim that Jesus was the son of God. In later periods however, the Islamic tradition mostly applied these verses to the 'extremist' or 'exaggerating' Shiʿis, and to a set of doctrines, including belief in the divinity of the Imam or some of his disciples, the transmigration of the souls (*tanāsukh*, *maskh*), and antinomianism (*ibāḥa*). In other words, *ghuluww* is a polemical designation meant for some specific groups — who were often also political rebels, and not merely theological dissidents — and to exclude them from what was considered the true religion.[15]

---

[12] See ibid., esp. pp. 148–159; M. Asatryan, *Controversies in Formative Shiʿi Islam*, Ch. 3: 'Polemics and Authority in the 3rd/9th Century', pp. 79–121, esp. pp. 80–82, 111–116.

[13] H. Halm, 'Das 'Buch der Schatten': Die Mufaḍḍal-Tradition der Ġulāt und die Ursprünge des Nuṣairiertums. I. Die Überlieferer der häretischen Mufaḍḍal-Tradition', *Der Islam*, 55 (1978), pp. 219-266; idem, 'Das 'Buch der Schatten'', II. On Mufaḍḍal, see also L. Capezzone, 'La questione dell'eterodossia di Mufaḍḍal b. ʿUmar al-Juʿfī nel *Tanqīḥ al-maqāl* di al-Māmqānī', in R. Tottoli, ed, *Ḥadīth in Modern Islam*, special issue of *Oriente Moderno*, 21 n.s. 82/1 (2002), pp. 147–157; M. Asatryan, 'Heresy and Rationalism in Early Islam: The Origins and Evolution of the Mufaḍḍal-Tradition' (New Haven, CT, 2012), esp. pp. 12–62; idem, *Controversies in Formative Shiʿi Islam*, esp. pp. 43–61; idem, 'Mofażżal al-Joʿfi', *EIr*.

[14] Q. 4:171 and 5:77.

[15] See De Smet, D., 'Exagération', in *Dictionnaire du Coran*, ed. M.A. Amir-Moezzi (Paris, 2007), pp. 292–295; S. Anthony, 'Ghulāt (extremist Shīʿīs)', *EI3*.

In fact, and especially as far as ʿIrāq is concerned, *ghuluww* overlaps de facto with Shiʿism for the period preceding the Minor Occultation. According to H. Halm, what was later labelled as *ghuluww* by the heresiologists was then 'die ursprüngliche Form des Šīʿa' ('the original form of Shiʿism').[16] Indeed, a number of doctrines attributed to the *ghulāt* are found either as they are, or in an attenuated form, in the ancient canonical collections of Twelver *ḥadīths*.[17] In this regard, Hodgson states that the *ghulāt* represented 'a distinctive speculative tendency within the general Shīʿī political orientation', with these speculations forming 'a reservoir of ideas from which many later Shīʿī movements drew their main inspiration'.[18]

Heresiologists often present ʿAbd Allāh b. Saba' (1st/7th c.) as the forefather of *ghuluww*. He was considered so because of his refusal to accept ʿAlī's death, and his belief in the latter's triumphant return (*rajʿa*) as the Mahdī, after a period of occultation (*ghayba*). As is well known, both notions were later integrated into official Twelver Shiʿism, which illustrates the ambiguity of the charge of *ghuluww*: how are the so-called *ghulāt* to be branded as 'exaggerators', when their doctrines were eventually adopted by orthodoxy? The *rajʿa* was particularly favoured among the *ghulāt* who understood this notion as the historical return of a Mahdī before the Resurrection. It could be conceived either as the return of an Imam-in-occultation, or as his resurrection proper.[19] The success of this notion, no doubt, was due in part to its political applicability: many movements offered political and earthly hope to the Alids, who were persecuted by the Umayyads (41–132/661–750) and then betrayed by the Abbasids

[16] H. Halm, 'Das "Buch der Schatten"', II, p. 86.

[17] This is the argument of several publications by M.A. Amir-Moezzi: see M.A. Amir-Mozzi, *Guide divin*, passim; idem, *La Religion discrète*, Ch. 3 to 6, pp. 89–175; idem, *Le Coran silencieux et le Coran parlant*, Ch. 4: 'Avènement de la gnose. Une monographie sur la connaissance par al-Saffâr al-Qummî', pp. 127–158; idem, 'Note sur deux traditions °hétérodoxes" imāmites'.

[18] M.G.S. Hodgson, 'Ghulāt', *EI2*.

[19] E. Kohlberg, 'Radjʿa', *EI2*. On the emergence and early evolutions of the concept of *rajʿa*, see also A. A. Sachedina, *Islamic Messianism, the idea of the Mahdi in Twelver Shiʿism* (Albany, 1981), pp. 166–179; J. Van Ess, *Theology and Society in the Second and Third Centuries of the Hijra. A History of Religious Thought in Early Islam*, English trans. by J. O'Kane, (Leiden and Boston, 2017), vol. 1, pp. 330–357.

(132–656/750–1258). Among several groups, the *raj'a* accompanied a historicizing exegesis of the Qur'anic verses referring to the Day of Judgement: some interpreted the 'Return' (*ma'ād*) of the Qur'an as a *raj'a*, i.e. as a resurrection or the reappearance of the Mahdī, before the actual final Resurrection. Accounts predicting the Mahdī's deeds and sayings upon his return are found in several *ḥadīth*s from canonical collections.[20] Treatise I of the *Kashf* contains a tradition of this type.[21] It is noteworthy that Jābir al-Ju'fī, a disciple of the fifth Imam suspected of *ghuluww*, is said to have been a promoter of the *raj'a*;[22] his name also appears in Treatise I.[23]

Besides their belief in various forms of *raj'a*, the *ghulāt* were also characterized by a tendency to anthropomorphism. Al-Mughīra b. Sa'īd is thus said to have described God in the form of a man.[24] It is against these kinds of propositions that one must understand the many chapters devoted to the affirmation of God's transcendence and unicity (*tawḥīd*) in Twelver *ḥadīth* collections and works bearing this title, such as Ibn Bābawayh's *Kitāb al-Tawḥīd*; several *ḥadīth*s thus feature the Imam asserting God's absolute transcendence in response to a question that tends to subject him to the limitations (notably

---

[20] See e.g. the study dedicated to one such tradition as reported by Muḥammad Bāqir al-Majlisī, in C. Turner, 'The "Tradition of Mufaḍḍal" and the Doctrine of the *Raj'a*: Evidence of *Ghuluww* in the Eschatology of Twelver Shi'ism?', *Iran: Journal of the British Institute of Persian Studies*, 44 (2006), pp. 175–195.

[21] Ja'far b. Manṣūr al-Yaman, *Kitāb al-Kashf*, ed. R. Strothmann (London, New York, Bombay, Calcutta, Madras, 1952), I, pp. 32–35, §§ 68–73. Henceforth, all references to the *Kitāb al-Kashf* will be noted in an abbreviated form: *Kashf*, followed by the number of the treatise, the page number in Strothmann's edition and the paragraph number in my translation. Where a page number appears alone, it refers to the numbering of the present monograph.

[22] W. Madelung, 'D̲j̲ābir al-D̲j̲u'fī', *EI2*; J. Van Ess, *Theology and Society*, vol. 1, pp. 341–345.

[23] *Kashf* I, p. 18, § 14.

[24] A disciple of the Imam Muḥammad al-Bāqir until the latter's death in 114/732, he was at the head of a Shi'i revolt in Kūfa in 119/737. He seems to have described God with human features and professed the creation of men as 'shadows' (*aẓilla*), starting with Muḥammad and 'Alī. On him, see W. Madelung, 'Mughīriyya', *EI2*; W.F. Tucker, *Mahdis and Millenarians. Shī'ite Extremistes in Early Muslim Iraq.* (New York, 2008), pp. 52–70; J. Weaver, 'Mughīriyya', *EI3*.

temporal and spatial) of creatures. As for the tendency to deify the Imams, this was gradually discarded or tempered, and while the Twelver *ḥadīth* collections still bear traces of such beliefs (in ʿAlī's mystical sermons, for instance),[25] it was preserved explicitly only in currents such as Nuṣayrism or, later, Druzism.

The divinization of the Imams goes hand in hand with the doctrine of metempsychosis (*naskh*), or 'metemphotosis', according to the expression proposed by M.A. Amir-Moezzi to account for the transmigration of light from Imam to Imam.[26] According to such views, the names and attributes of God are thus epiphanized in a succession of Imams. A certain docetism, also prized among the *ghulāt*, is attached to this idea of a manifestation of a divine nature, the *lāhūt*, in successive luminous forms corresponding to the successive Imams; the latter are not born through natural ways, they are not subject to death, nor to the normal needs of humans with bodies, for their divine nature is clothed in a subtle, or 'glorious', body, and not a material one.[27]

It is not just the souls of the Imams who can transmigrate, but also others: either the souls of their disciples who, from reincarnation to reincarnation, refine their essence, or the souls of their enemies, who, according to a dualistic conception, are the representatives of an

---

[25] See M.A. Amir-Moezzi, *La Religion discrète*, Ch. 3: 'Remarques sur la divinité de l'imâm', pp. 89–108 (English trans., *Spirituality of Shiʿi Islam*, Ch. 3: 'Some Remarks on the Divinity of the Imam', pp. 103–131.

[26] M.A. Amir-Moezzi, *Guide divin*, p. 109 (English trans., *Divine Guide*, pp. 42–43).

[27] On docetism among the *ghulāt*, see H. Corbin, 'Epiphanie divine et naissance spirituelle dans la gnose ismaélienne', in idem, *Temps cyclique et gnose ismaélienne* (Paris, 1982), pp. 116–131; H. Halm, *Die islamische Gnosis: Die extreme Schia und die ʿAlawiten* (Zurich and Munich, 1982), index s.v. 'Doketismus'; D. De Smet, 'Eléments chrétiens dans l'ismaélisme yéménite sous les derniers Fatimides. Le problème de la gnose ṭayyibite', in M. Barrucand, ed, L'Égypte *fatimide, son art et son histoire*, ed. (Paris, 1999), pp. 45–53, esp. pp. 48–52; idem, 'La valorisation du féminin dans l'ismaélisme ṭayyibite. Le cas de la reine yéménite al-Sayyida Arwā (1048–1138)', *Mélanges de l'Université Saint-Joseph*, 58 (2005), pp. 107–122; idem, 'Crucifixion', in M.A. Amir-Moezzi, ed, *Dictionnaire du Coran* (Paris, 2007), pp. 197–199; idem, 'La naissance miraculeuse de l'Imam ismaélien: nourritures célestes et corps camphré', in C. Cannuyer and C. Vialle, eds, *Acta Orientalia Belgica*, 28 (2015), pp. 323–333; idem, 'Les racines docétistes de l'imâmologie shiʿite', in M.A. Amir-Moezzi et al, eds, *L'ésotérisme shiʿite, ses racines et ses prolongements* (Turnhout, 2016), pp. 87–112.

ontological Evil prior to the creation of humans, and opposed to Good from and for all eternity. Thus, the first two Muslim caliphs, Abū Bakr and ʿUmar, are said to be manifested in the features of the enemies of the earlier prophets (the Pharaoh, typically, but also the anonymous adversaries of Noah, etc.). The enemies of the Imams can be reincarnated as animals (monkeys, dogs, swine, foxes...): this metamorphosis into a lower form is called *maskh*. From the *Kitāb al-Haft wa'l-aẓilla*, a famous work from the *ghulāt* attributed to Mufaḍḍal al-Juʿfī,[28] to the Twelver *ḥadīth* collections, the *maskh*, a transmigrationist concept, becomes a punishment in the hereafter. This is also the case in the *Kitāb al-Kashf*: the transmigrationist meaning of the term *musūkhiyya* is implicitly discarded in favour of an initiatory and eschatological interpretation.

Finally, antinomianism is considered a characteristic thesis of the *ghulāt*, if not the 'exaggerating' doctrine par excellence. Abū'l-Khaṭṭāb,[29] a disavowed disciple of Jaʿfar al-Ṣādiq, is thus accused of having given a licentious teaching, authorising his followers to engage in fornication, sodomy, theft, alcohol, and allowing them to abandon the religious duties prescribed to the common Muslim (prayer, almsgiving, fasting, pilgrimage). Ritual obligations were indeed seen as metaphors for men whose 'friendship' (*walāya*) should be sought and sins symbolized men from whom one should disassociate (*tabarraʾa*).[30] Interpreting Q. 4:28: *'God desires to reduce your [obligations]'*, the Khaṭṭābiyya apparently claimed that their obligations were 'reduced' on the authority of Abū'l-Khaṭṭāb, and that anyone who knew the Prophet or the Imam could dispense of the religious prescriptions.[31] According to Abū Manṣūr al-ʿIjlī, another figure of the

---

[28] See the textual analysis of this work in M. Asatryan, *Controversies in Formative Shiʿi Islam*, pp. 13–42.

[29] On Abū'l-Khaṭṭāb and the Khaṭṭābiyya, see B. Lewis, 'Abu'l-K͟haṭṭāb', *EI2*; W. Madelung, 'K͟haṭṭābiyya', *EI2*; H. Ansari, 'Abū al-Khaṭṭāb', *EIs*; M.A. Amir-Moezzi, 'K͟aṭṭābiya', *EIr*; H. Halm, *Die islamische Gnosis*, pp. 199–217; R.P. Buckley, 'The Imām Jaʿfar al-Ṣādiq, Abū'l-Khaṭṭāb and the Abbassids', *Der Islam*, 79 (2002), pp. 118–140.

[30] This is based on the Shiʿi opposition between *walāya* and *barāʾa*, discussed in the commentary of *Kashf* I, pp. 129 ff., 147 ff.

[31] Al-Nawbakhtī, *Firaq al-Shīʿa*, ed. H. Ritter (Istanbul, 1931), pp. 38–39, 59; al-Qummī, *Kitāb al-Maqālāt wa'l-firaq*, ed. M.J. Mashkūr (Tehran, 1963), pp. 51–53, 81.

ghulāt, religious duties were to be understood as symbolizing historical persons (*ashkhāṣ*), be they friends or enemies of God, and religion consisted in identifying them as such.[32]

One might argue that antinomianism may have been a polemical accusation used by the so-called orthodox heresiologists — i.e. rationalist Twelver Shiʿis — to disqualify their adversaries, whom they labelled as 'exaggerators' (*ghulāt*). Nonetheless, antinomian positions are attested in several sources of the so-called *ghulāt*.[33] Among many other examples, the *Kitāb al-Haft wa'l-aẓilla* explicitly states that whoever reached a certain rank of initiation and 'elevation' (*taraqqī*) may abandon their religious duties: 'Whoever knows this esoteric [knowledge] is exempt from the fulfilment of the exoteric' (*man ʿarafa hādhā al-bāṭin fa-qad saqaṭa ʿanhu ʿamal al-ẓāhir*).[34]

The esoteric — and 'personalized' — interpretation of religious duties is consistent with an essential early Shiʿi belief according to which 'religion is knowledge of men' (*al-dīn maʿrifat al-rijāl*). This expression appears in a letter from Jaʿfar al-Ṣādiq to his disciple Mufaḍḍal b. ʿUmar al-Juʿfī, in which he asserts this fundamental principle, while firmly rejecting its potential antinomian

[32] Abū Manṣūr al-ʿIjlī was a disciple of Muḥammad al-Bāqir from the region of Kūfa. He declared himself to be his successor. He claimed he had seen God and that he possessed the knowledge of *ta'wīl*. On him, see H. Halm, *Die islamische Gnosis*, pp. 86–89; W. Madelung, 'Manṣūriyya', *EI2*; W.F. Tucker, *Mahdis and Millenarians*, pp. 71–87, esp, pp. 80–81.

[33] See e.g. H. Halm, 'Courants et mouvements antinomistes dans l'islam medieval', in *La notion de liberté au Moyen Age. Islam, Byzance, Occident*, ed. G. Makdisi, D. Sourdel and J. Sourdel-Thomine, (Paris, 1985), pp. 135–141, esp. pp. 137–139; M.M. Bar-Asher and A. Kofsky, *The Nuṣayrī -ʿAlawī Religion. An Enquiry into its Theology and Liturgy* (Leiden, 2002), pp. 66–67; M. Asatryan, *Controversies in Formative Shiʿi Islam*, pp. 93–96, 157–161; idem, 'Of Wine, Sex, and Other Abominations: The Meanings of Antinomianism in Early Islamic Iraq', *Global Intellectual History*, forthcoming. Antinomianism will also be discussed in the commentary of *Kashf* V, pp. 408–419.

[34] Mufaḍḍal al-Juʿfī, *Kitāb al-Haft wa'l-aẓilla*, ed. ʿĀrif Tāmir and Ignace-A. Khalifé (Beirut, 1960), Ch. 13, p. 45.

consequences.[35] Although it is apparently not found elsewhere in Shiʿi literature, it is emblematic of Shiʿi Islam and its Imam-centred theology. This personalized approach of religion is one of the key features of early Shiʿi *tafsīr*, especially in the interpretative tradition based on what M.A. Amir-Moezzi has labelled, in regard to al-Ḥibarī's *Tafsīr*, 'commentaire coranique personnalisé'.[36] This technique consists in interpreting a number of Qurʾanic verses in relation to historical individuals from the origins of Islam, in order to support the Shiʿi historiography of early Islam. More specifically, a 'personalized commentary' of the Qurʾan is geared towards a testimony of ʿAlī b. Abī Ṭālib's divine election as Muḥammad's rightful successor. This exegesis thus resides in the identification of Qurʾanic allusions to ʿAlī and/or his descendants. Of course, this technique is closely related to the Shiʿi concept of *walāya* and the obligation for the faithful to acknowledge, follow, and love the Imam. Hence, 'religion is knowledge of men' means that religion consists in the recognition of the rightful Imam. Inasmuch as *walāya* goes hand in hand with *barāʾa*, that is the

---

[35] Al-Ṣaffār al-Qummī, *Baṣāʾir al-darajāt fī faḍāʾil āl Muḥammad*, ed. Muʾassasat al-Imām al-Mahdī (Qom, n.d.), pp. 939–950. For recent discussions of this letter, see H. Ansari, *L'Imamat et l'occultation selon l'imamisme: Etude bibliographique et histoire des textes* (Leiden, 2016), pp. 245–247; M.A. Amir-Moezzi, 'Les Imams et les Ghulāt. Nouvelles réflexions sur les relations entre imamisme "modéré" et shiʿisme "extrémiste"', *SSR*, 4 (2020), pp. 5–38; M. Asatryan, 'Of Wine, Sex, and Other Abominations'; idem, 'The Heretic Talks Back: Feigning Orthodoxy in al-Ṣaffār al-Qummī's *Baṣāʾir al-darajāt* (d. 902–3)', *History of Religions*, 61/4 (2022), pp. 362–388.

[36] See M.A. Amir-Moezzi, *Le Coran silencieux et le Coran parlant*, Ch. 3: 'Nécessité de l'herméneutique. Autour du commentaire coranique d'al-Ḥibarī', pp. 101–125 (English trans., *The Silent Qurʾan and the Speaking Qurʾan*, Ch. 3: 'The Necessity of Hermeneutics: On the Qurʾanic Commentary of al-Ḥibarī', pp. 75–96); idem, 'ʿAlī et le Coran (Aspects de l'imamologie duodécimaine XIV)', *Revue des Sciences Philosophiques et Théologiques*, 98 (2014), pp. 681–685; idem, '*Al-Durr al-ṯamīn* attribué à Rağab al-Bursī. Un exemple des "commentaires coraniques personnalisés" šiʿites (Aspects de l'imamologie duodécimaine XVI)', *Le Muséon*, 130/1–2 (2017), pp. 207–240. The 'personalized commentary' is a Shiʿi literary genre illustrated by several works throughout the history of Shiʿi Islam; see the lists provided by M.A. Amir-Moezzi in these articles. See also commentary of *Kashf* I below, pp. 148 ff.

disavowal of the Imam's enemies,[37] 'knowledge of men' also comprises recognition of the impostors the true believer must not follow.

This fundamentally personalized approach to faith has manifested itself in various ways in many Shiʿi trends. It explains the struggle for legitimacy between various protagonists claiming to represent the Imams, before and after the Minor Occultation. Indeed, if religion consists in the knowledge of men, this knowledge also extends to persons who are initiated (or claim to have been initiated and appointed) by the Imam and thus benefit from his spiritual prestige. In addition to political and financial factors,[38] it is within this doctrinal framework that one may understand the claims of various *bābs* to represent the Imams — a claim that on occasions went as far as claiming the Imamate itself. And, as we will see, this framework also allows one to understand the *daʿwa* hierarchy as the Ismaili interpretation of the common Shiʿi principle that 'religion is knowledge of men' or 'persons' (*ashkhāṣ*).

As we have seen above, the personalized approach was extended to the interpretation of Islamic religious duties by some groups, which led to antinomianism. Indeed, if these ritual obligations have an exoteric (*ẓāhir*) meaning, referring to their actual performance by the believers, and an esoteric (*bāṭin*) meaning, referring to 'a man', 'an individual' or 'a person' (*rajul, shakhṣ*), there then arises the temptation to declare the obsolescence of the exoteric in favour of the esoteric. Ismailism was not new to this problematic, since it also developed a personalized interpretation of religious duties, as attested by several sources. Treatise V of the *Kitāb al-Kashf* thus understands the pilgrimage to the Kaʿba as meeting the Imam of the time. The *Riḍāʿ fi'l-bāṭin*, another work attributed to Jaʿfar b. Manṣūr al-Yaman, is almost entirely dedicated to such 'personalized' interpretations of ablutions (*wuḍū'*), prayer (*ṣalāt*), fasting (*ṣiyām*), alms-giving (*zakāt*) and pilgrimage (*ḥajj*), the various parts of which are identified with

[37] E. Kohlberg, '*Barā'a* in Shīʿi doctrine', JSAI, 7 (1986), pp. 139–175; M.A. Amir-Moezzi, *La Religion discrète*, Ch. 7: 'Note à propos de la *walāya* imamite', pp. 177–207 (English trans.: *The Spirituality of Shiʿi Islam*, Ch. 7: "Notes on Imami Walāya", pp. 231–275); M. Massi Dakake, *The Charismatic Community: Shiʿite Identity in Early Islam* (Albany, 2007), pp. 65–67.

[38] On these, see E. Hayes, *Agents of the Hidden Imam*.

Muḥammad, ʿAlī, the Mahdī or the ranks of the *daʿwa*.[39] The *Taʾwīl al-zakāt*, also attributed to Jaʿfar b. Manṣūr al-Yaman, barely addresses alms-giving at all, despite its title, and focuses again on the *daʿwa* and its ranks.

However, contrary to *ghulāt* sources, Fatimid Ismaili works emphasize the necessity of actually performing the external rites, even when their esoteric meaning is known: 'Both knowledge and action remain obligations as long as the spirit and the body coexist.'[40] The *Taʾwīl al-zakāt* even goes as far as to state that 'the esoteric taken alone is heresy towards the signs of God' (*ilḥād fī āyāt Allāh*), and that whoever 'believes in abandoning his [exoteric] obligations must be killed' (*qutila man iʿtaqada isqāṭ farāʾiḍihi*).[41] This harshness may be explained by the fact that the Fatimids were confronted with antinomian outbursts from within their ranks on several occasions in their history.

As previously said, although these doctrines are generally associated with *ghuluww*, Amir-Moezzi has shown that many nevertheless found their way into Twelver Shiʿi compositions, sometimes in attenuated form, sometimes not. Amir-Moezzi understands this as a demonstration that the Imams in fact adhered to these doctrines to a certain extent, while their definition of *ghuluww* only embraced antinomianism, that is, the abandoning of Islamic religious duties justified by the access to their true meaning via esoteric interpretation (*taʾwīl*). It is indeed the only doctrine of the *ghulāt* that is not found in

---

[39] On this work and its interpretation of prayer in relation to the general Shiʿi personalized approach to religion, see F. Gillon, 'Ismaili *Taʾwīl* of Religious Rites: Interpretation of Obligatory Prayer in Jaʿfar b. Manṣūr al-Yaman's *Riḍāʿ fī l-Bāṭin*', *SSR*, 6 (2022), pp. 224–252.

[40] *Kashf* V, p. 112, § 39.

[41] Jaʿfar b. Manṣūr al-Yaman, *Taʾwīl al-zakāt*, ed. Ḥ. Khaḍḍūr (Salamiyya, 2018), p. 97. The text goes on to explain that the esoteric meaning of 'killing' (*qatl*) is 'to be cut off from the ranks (*ḥudūd*) and to refrain from opening the influx (*mawādd*) of divine assistance (*taʾyīd*) and knowledge to the Respondents (*mustajībīn*) (. . .) so as to become dead, without spirit.' However, it is unclear whether this esoteric meaning of 'killing' renders its exoteric meaning obsolete — particularly when the point is to assert the necessity of the *ẓāhir*! The Respondents are the neophytes who begin their initiation within the *daʿwa*.

Twelver Shiʿi literature.[42] Whether the Imams indeed advocated such a strict definition of *ghuluww* or not, it is nevertheless clear that there seems to be a wide consensus in the sources to consider antinomianism as an 'exaggeration' — while things are not as clear-cut when it comes to the other 'typical' *ghulāt* doctrines.

Indeed, in the literature claiming orthodoxy, one often finds what appears to be *fragments* of teachings that are more fully displayed in so-called *ghulāt* literature, as if they were taken from the ideological system in which they made sense to be integrated into a system where they are only understood metaphorically. I have briefly discussed the example of animal metamorphosis, which is present in Twelver collections, but in isolation from the cosmogony wherein it makes full sense. In the *Kitāb al-Kashf*, as will be seen, metamorphosis is also present but understood in a metaphorical sense only. Moreover, traces of the cosmology of the *ghulāt* can be found in isolated texts: the primordial 'shadows' (*aẓilla*) or 'forms' (*ashbāḥ*) of *ghulāt* works such as the *Kitāb al-Haft wa'l-aẓilla* or others, are thus mentioned in many Twelver Shiʿi *ḥadīths*.[43]

The presence of such traces of *ghulāt* doctrines in a corpus claiming orthodoxy (be it Twelver Shiʿi or Fatimid Ismaili) begs the question: are these fragments the result of an adaptation, of a 'toning down' of certain doctrines, or are they indications of the actual beliefs of the

---

[42] See M.A. Amir-Moezzi, 'Les Imams et les Ghulāt'.

[43] See e.g. the *ḥadīths* cited in M.A. Amir-Moezzi, *Guide divin*, pp. 81 ff (English trans.: *Divine Guide*, pp. 32 ff); see also idem, 'Cosmogony and cosmology, V. In Twelver Shīʿism', *EIr*. On *ghulāt* works discussing primordial 'shadows', see H. Halm, 'Das 'Buch der Schatten'', I and II; L. Capezzone, 'Il *Kitāb al-Ṣirāṭ* attribuito a Mufaḍḍal b. 'Umar al-Ǧuʿfī. Edizione del ms. unico (Paris, Bibliothèque nationale) e studio introduttivo', *Rivista degli Studi Orientali*, 69 (1995), pp. 295–416; M. Asatryan, 'Shiite Underground Literature Between Iraq and Syria: "The Book of Shadows" and the History of the Early Ghulat', in T. Langermann and R. Morrison, eds, *Texts in Transit in the Medieval Mediterranean* (University Park, MD, 2016), pp. 128–161; idem, 'An Early Shīʿi Cosmology, *Kitāb al-Ashbāḥ wa'l-aẓilla* and its Milieu', *Studia Islamica*, 110 (2015), pp. 1–80; idem, *Controversies in Formative Shiʿi Islam*, pp. 64–78, 138–145 and index s.v. 'apparitions', 'shadows'; idem, 'An Agenda for the Study of early Shiʿi cosmologies', in G.W. Trompf, G.B. Mikkelsen and J. Johnson, eds, *The Gnostic World* (London and New York, 2020), pp. 321–327, esp. pp. 324–327.

authors? In other words, is the curbing of *ghulāt* doctrines into more consensual ones sincere, or is it an effect of *taqiyya*? Indeed, *taqiyya* is an essential tenet of Shiʿi faith — as demonstrated for instance by *ḥadīths* such as the following: 'God's Rule is keeping the Secret [i.e. *taqiyya*]'; 'Whoever does not keep the Secret is devoid of Faith'.[44] What, then, is the object of *taqiyya* in Shiʿi discourses, particularly in the discourses of the 'rationalist' Shiʿis? It may be considered that rationalist theologians were convinced of the falsity of so-called 'irrational' doctrines about the Imams. But it is also possible to consider that for some, rationalistic Shiʿism, far from opposing its esoteric counterpart, was a way to hide and protect it so as to become its exoteric aspect. Esotericists could thus consider that the rationalistic approach was the one that should be held in public in order to hide their more intimate beliefs.

The problem of intentions arises with regard to the Imams themselves: the sources mention that some disciples were publicly disavowed by their Imam. Should one understand these excommunications as *taqiyya* and consider that the *ghulāt* were not rejected for the doctrines they professed, but only because they professed them publicly and without the Imam's permission?[45] At any rate, this is what some of the *ghulāt* allege, interpreting the opprobrium

---

[44] Cited in M.A. Amir-Moezzi, *Guide divin*, p. 311 (English trans.: *Divine Guide*, p. 129). On *taqiyya*, see also E. Kohlberg, 'Some Imāmī Shīʿī views on *taqiyya*', *JAOS*, 95 (1975), pp. 395–402; idem, '*Taqiyya* in Shīʿi Theology and Religion', in H.G. Kippenberg and G.C. Stroumsa, eds, *Secrecy and Concealment* (Leiden, New York and Cologne, 1995), pp. 345–380; D. De Smet, 'La pratique de *taqiyya* et *kitmān* en islam chiite: compromis ou hypocrisie?', in M. Nachi, ed, *Actualité du compromis: la construction politique de la différence* (Paris, 2011), pp. 148–161; idem, 'La *taqiyya* et le jeûne du Ramadan: quelques réflexions ismaéliennes sur le sens ésotérique de la charia', *Al-Qanṭara*, 34/2 (2013), pp. 357–386; M.A. Amir-Moezzi, 'Dissimulation tactique (*taqiyya*) et scellement de la prophétie (*khatm al-nubuwwa*) (Aspects de l'imamologie duodécimaine XII)', *Journal Asiatique*, 302/2 (2014), pp. 411–438.

[45] See M.A. Amir-Moezzi, *Guide divin*, pp. 313–316 (English trans.: *Divine Guide*, pp. 129–130); idem, *La Religion discrète*, pp. 166–168 (English trans.: *Spirituality of Shiʿi Islam*, pp. 216–219), where the following *ḥadīth* attributed to Jaʿfar al-Ṣādiq is quoted after the *Kitāb al-Ghayba* by al-Nuʿmānī: 'It happens that I confer a teaching to someone; then he leaves me and reports it exactly as he heard it from me. Because of this, I declare that it is lawful to curse him and dissociate oneself from him.'

cast by the Imam as a blessing and an investiture, by virtue of a perhaps excessive understanding of *taqiyya*.

The notion of *ghuluww* must therefore be handled with great caution. In the first place, and with the possible exception of antinomianism, the elements considered characteristic of 'exaggeration' are not fundamentally opposed to what is found in the earliest *ḥadīth* collections — and they are even sometimes incorporated as they are, as illustrated by the *raj'a*, considered a typical feature of *ghuluww* in the first century of Islam, which became 'orthodox' after the Great Occultation. Secondly, the importance of *taqiyya* in Shi'i Islam may influence the propensity to publicly condemn or incompletely expound doctrines to which one secretly adheres. Finally, it is a polemical category designed to undermine the influence of the supporters of the *abwāb* for the benefit of a ruling Shi'i elite which gained further power as early as 945, thanks to the Buyid viziers. Pursuing this political track, we also realise that other elements considered to be 'exaggerating', but less emblematic of *ghuluww*, seem to have been discarded for reasons more diplomatic than theological. Thus, the Shi'i thesis of the falsification of the Qur'an was discarded by the rationalizing Twelver orthodoxy, and the reason is clearly the concern to adopt a more consensual position vis-à-vis the Muslim majority. In the same vein, some *ghulāt* seem to have been labelled such only because of their political activism and the revolts they led. Insofar as revolutionary movements were often based on *ghulāt* doctrines, it is not always clear how to separate political *ghuluww* from theological *ghuluww*.

However, I believe the term can be used as an approximate category: provided we are aware of its limitations, it remains useful inasmuch as there is a general understanding — both in the sources and in modern scholarship — of the type of doctrines covered by the term. Rather than searching for an illusory absolute meaning of the term, it should be accepted that it only has a relative meaning, in the sense that *ghuluww* relates to a set of doctrines that came to be seen as falling outside the 'orthodox' consensus. While the boundaries seem quite clear regarding antinomianism, they prove more blurred when it comes to other *ghulāt* doctrines, as we have seen. However, borderline cases do not demonstrate, in my opinion, the futility of the category. They are rather an invitation to keep it flexible, and to avoid giving it a rigid definition.

ii. A brief overview of the Ismaili *daʿwa*, from its origins to the founding of the Fatimid caliphate

Given the huge progress made in Ismaili and Fatimid studies over recent decades, it is not necessary to synthesize here the early history of the Ismailis and the Fatimids, as the reader can be referred to this growing literature. However, a few aspects need to be recalled to shed light on the context of the composition of the *Kitāb al-Kashf*. This context is all the more important since the *Kashf* itself does not provide clear indications as to the circumstances that prompted its composition; it is therefore for the reader to join the dots and to clarify the obscure allusions of the *Kashf* by examining the certain historical context and finding to which events and debates this or that passage of the *Kashf* might be a response — although this exercise is not without risk and can bear no certainties.

There are three periods in the early history of Ismailis that are relevant to the study of the *Kitāb al-Kashf*: the origins (in the aftermath of Ismāʿīl b. Jaʿfar's death, in the mid-8th century); the clandestine pre-Fatimid *daʿwa* (until the proclamation of al-Mahdī in 899); and, the early Fatimid years (covering the reigns of the first two Fatimid caliphs, from the proclamation to 946). On the first two periods, however, the information is scant. As a clandestine movement, the Fatimid *daʿwa* did not produce any internal chronicles, and external observers could not provide accounts about this secret organization. As a result, information regarding the history or Ismailism preceding the foundation of the Fatimid caliphate is only accessible through the screen of the Fatimid institutionalized rewriting of the events, mainly by al-Qāḍī al-Nuʿmān (d. 363/974) and his *Iftitāḥ al-daʿwa*,[46] or through the reports of non-Ismaili authors, either late and/or hostile.

As noted by Farhad Daftary, for 'the opening stage of the Ismāʿīlī movement (. . .), the accounts of the early Imamī heresiographers al-Ḥasan b. Mūsā al-Nawbaḫtī (died between 300 and 310/912–922) and Saʿd b. ʿAbd Allāh al-Ašʿarī al-Qummī (d. 301/913–4), who are

[46] Al-Qāḍī al-Nuʿmān, *Iftitāḥ al-daʿwa*, ed. W. al-Qāḍī, (Beirut, 1970); al-Qāḍī al-Nuʿmān, *Iftitāḥ al-daʿwa*, ed. F. Dachraoui (Tunis, 1975); English trans.: H. Haji, *Founding the Fatimid State. The Rise of an Early Islamic Empire* (London, 2006).

well-informed about the Šīʿī divisions, in fact provide our main sources of information'.[47] According to these accounts, the death of Imam Jaʿfar al-Ṣādiq was followed by a crisis of succession, and the community of his followers were divided into six groups, two of which can be considered 'proto-Ismailis'.[48] Of these latter two groups, it is the one named the Mubārakiyya that benefits from the longest reports by al-Nawbakhtī and al-Qummī.[49] Most of these reports is in fact dedicated to Abū'l-Khaṭṭāb, as well as to the subdivisions of his disciples, the Khaṭṭābiyya, and their beliefs. It thus seems that in this earliest stage of Ismaili history, there was a strong connection between the radical Shiʿi movements (the so-called *ghulāt*) of the time, and Ismāʿīl, the son of Jaʿfar al-Ṣādiq who would have succeeded him had he not predeceased his father.[50]

These reports sparked a debate in modern scholarship to determine to what extent the proto-Ismailis may have actually been Khaṭṭābis or deeply influenced by Khaṭṭābī beliefs. On the one hand, scholars such as Madelung and Daftary argued that the beliefs and doctrines attributed to the Khaṭṭābiyya were entirely different from those appearing in later Ismaili texts — not to mention that Abū'l-Khaṭṭāb is explicitly disavowed in Fatimid Ismaili texts.[51] On the other hand, Massignon and Corbin held that it was plausible for Ismailism to have had Khaṭṭābi roots.[52] For this discussion, the *Kitāb al-Kashf* is a key document — especially due to the many *ghulāt* resonances found in Treatise I, and also in several passages in Treatises III and V where a form of response to *ghulāt* doctrines can be perceived. The *Kashf*, as the present study aims to show, precisely illustrates the fact that

[47] F. Daftary, 'The Earliest Ismāʿīlīs', *Arabica*, 38/2 (1991), p. 215.

[48] Al-Nawbakhtī, *Firaq al-shīʿa*, pp. 57–67; al-Qummī, *Maqālāt*, pp. 79–89. See also F. Daftary, 'The Earliest Ismāʿīlīs', pp. 219–222; idem, *The Ismāʿīlīs*, pp. 88–90.

[49] Al-Nawbakhtī, *Firaq al-shīʿa*, pp. 58–64; al-Qummī, *Maqālāt*, pp. 81–86.

[50] F. Daftary, 'The Earliest Ismāʿīlīs', pp. 225 ff.

[51] See e.g. al-Qāḍī al-Nuʿmān, *Daʿāʾim al-islām*, ed. A.A.A. Fyzee (Cairo, 1963), vol. 1, pp. 49–50 (English trans.: *The Pillars of Islam: "Daʿaʾim al-Islam" of Qadi al-Nuʿman*, trans. A.A.A. Fyzee, rev. and annot. I.K. Poonawala (New Delhi, 2002), vol. 1, pp. 65–66).

[52] For a recent overview of this debate and new arguments in favour of the Khaṭṭābi-Ismaili connection, a great part of which is based on the *Kitāb al-Kashf*, see R. Adem, 'Early Ismailism and the Gates of Religious Authority'.

Ismailism is not unrelated to the Khaṭṭābī heritage, even when refuting it. As we shall see, it appears that part of the *ghulāt* teachings of the pre-Nuṣayri tradition provided the material for nascent Ismailism. While no clear and direct intellectual filiation can be established between the many movements of early Shiʿism, on the one hand, and Ismailism, on the other hand, it is clear that the latter was born in an intellectual environment coloured by *ghuluww*.

Indeed, the ground in which proto-Ismailism was formed is linked to the figure of Jaʿfar al-Ṣādiq in two respects: firstly, although little is known about his son Ismāʿīl, it can be said that he and his entourage could not have been strangers to the proliferation of esoteric sects around Jaʿfar al-Ṣādiq. Ismailism is clearly anchored in the dynamic of speculative *ghuluww*, even if it later sought to distance itself from it. Moreover, the fact that it wanted to distance itself from *ghuluww* can be read as an indication of its initial proximity to the *ghulāt* currents. Secondly, the massacre of Abū'l-Khaṭṭāb and his followers originated in an attempted revolt on their part — one of the many revolts with religious claims after the first century of Islam. It is reasonable to think that this politico-esoteric agitation — the exact nature of which is unfortunately unknown — had some connection with the betrayal of Shiʿi hopes raised by the Abbasid revolution, on the one hand, and with Jaʿfar al-Ṣādiq's resolute political quietism, on the other hand.[53] It could therefore be argued that Ismailism was the heir to Abū'l-Khaṭṭāb in the sense that it stemmed from a refusal to abandon the political aspect of Shiʿism — in addition to the messianic and speculative aspects of Abū'l-Khaṭṭāb's mission. But again, to establish these links is not to establish a filiation. It cannot be asserted with any certainty that Ismailism emerged directly from the Khaṭṭābiyya; yet, it is clear that it emerged from an intellectual and political environment on which the Khaṭṭābiyya and similar groups had left their mark.

The second stage of early Ismaili history, that of the clandestine *daʿwa* which would eventually blossom in the founding of the Fatimid caliphate, is, as one would expect, obscure. The *daʿwa* appears to date back to the preaching of a certain ʿAbd Allāh, nicknamed al-Akbar by his Fatimid descendants. While there is a consensus of sources, both

[53] See R.P. Buckley, 'The Imām Jaʿfar al-Ṣādiq, Abū'l-Khaṭṭāb and the Abbassids'.

internal and external to Ismailism, on this point, as well as on his appearance in ʿAskar Mukram in Khūzistān, his identity is at the heart of the dispute over Fatimid genealogy. Forced to flee ʿAskar Mukram because of his preaching, and after a short stay in Baṣra, ʿAbd Allāh al-Akbar settled in Salamiyya, Syria, disguised as a merchant. From there, he began sending missionaries to Iraq and Iran to preach the coming of the Mahdī. Salamiyya would thenceforth be the centre of the Ismaili organization until the founding of the Fatimid caliphate.[54] Almost nothing is known of his son, Aḥmad, who took over the leadership of the organization, except that he had two sons: al-Ḥusayn and Muḥammad. It was apparently under the leadership of the latter, the younger of the two, that the underground activity of the *daʿwa* began to bear fruit. Having no son, Muḥammad b. Aḥmad, nicknamed Abū al-Shalaghlagh, appointed as his successor his nephew, Saʿīd, the son of al-Ḥusayn, and the future founder of the Fatimid dynasty who would become known as ʿAbd Allāh al-Mahdī (d. 322/934).[55]

It is not necessary to dwell on the progress of the *daʿwa* and the adventures of the various missionaries.[56] A few words must be said, however, about Abū ʿAbd Allāh al-Shīʿī, the architect of the founding of the Fatimid caliphate in Ifrīqiya. Sent to Mecca by Ibn Ḥawshab, the father of Jaʿfar b. Manṣūr al-Yaman, he met members of the Berber tribe of the Kutāma. He accompanied them to their homeland, the mountains of Little Kabylia, in 280/893, settled there and recruited several Berber chiefs and other notables, who converted to Ismailism. Eventually, in 289/902, he was able to confront the Aghlabids, the local dynasty of Arab emirs, who had been in power since the year 800. In 296/909, Abū ʿAbd Allāh made his entry into Raqqāda, and

---

[54] On ʿAbd Allāh al-Akbar, see H. Halm, *The Empire of the Mahdi, The Rise of the Fatimids*, Eng. trans. by M. Bonner (Leiden, New York and Cologne, 1996), pp. 5–14.

[55] Ibid., p. 14–15.

[56] See the very complete overviews by H. Halm, *The Empire of the Mahdi*, esp. pp. 22–57; F. Daftary, *The Ismāʿīlīs*, pp. 58–116. For the methods of recruitment of the early *dāʿīs*, see H. Halm, 'Methods and forms of the earliest Ismāʿīlī daʿwa', in E. Kohlberg, ed, *Shīʿism* (Aldershot, 2003), pp. 277–290; on the methods and symbols of the *daʿwa*, see D. Hollenberg, *Beyond the Qurʾān*, pp. 53–78.

then Qayrawān. He was then able to organize a government with a view to bringing ʿAbd Allāh al-Mahdī to Ifrīqiya.[57]

In 899, upon the death of the leader of the *daʿwa*, Muḥammad Abū al-Shalaghlagh, who had apparently presented himself until then as the representative, the 'Proof' (*ḥujja*) of the Imam, he was succeeded by his nephew ʿAlī (or Saʿīd, which must be his pseudonym). He then claimed to be the expected Mahdī, a change of doctrine which troubled several of the missionaries of the *daʿwa*. Among the most important of them, Ibn Ḥawshab (in Yemen) and Abū ʿAbd Allāh al-Shīʿī (in Ifrīqiya) admitted this reform of the status of the head of the *daʿwa*. But ʿAbdān (in Iraq), al-Jannābī (eastern coast of the Arabian Peninsula), and Ibn Ḥawshab's companion, ʿAlī b. al-Faḍl, refused to recognise ʿAbd Allāh al-Mahdī and continued to wait for the return of Muḥammad b. Ismāʿīl. The Yemeni *daʿwa* did not survive its dissensions, and we shall see later what happened after the death of Ibn Ḥawshab. As for the *daʿwa* of eastern Arabia, it took on its independence, and despite diplomatic efforts in this direction, never recognized the Fatimid caliph as Imam. It gave rise to a state, that of the Qarmatians, named after one of the founders of the Iraqi *daʿwa*, Ḥamdān Qarmaṭ, ʿAbdān's brother-in-law.[58]

---

[57] On Abū ʿAbd Allāh al-Shīʿī, the main source is the *Iftitāḥ al-daʿwa* by al-Qāḍī al-Nuʿmān. See F. Dachraoui, *Le califat fâtimide au Maghreb: Histoire politique et institutions, 296–362/909–973* (Tunis, 1981), pp. 58–132; P.E. Walker, 'Abū ʿAbdallāh al-Shīʿī', *EI3*.

[58] On this schism in the *daʿwa*, and the events following the proclamation of his eschatological status by ʿAbd Allāh al-Mahdī, see W. Madelung, 'Das Imamat', pp. 59–65; idem, 'The Fatimids and the Qarmaṭīs of Baḥrayn', in F. Daftary, ed, *Mediaeval Ismaʿili History and Thought* (Cambridge, 1996), pp. 21–73; S.M. Stern, 'Ismāʿīlis and Qarmaṭians', in idem, *Studies in Early Ismāʿīlism* (Jerusalem and Leiden, 1983), pp. 289–298; F. Daftary, 'A Major Schism in the Early Ismāʿīlī Movement', *Studia Islamica*, 77 (1993), pp. 123–139; idem, *The Ismāʿīlīs*, pp. 116–126. Michael Brett developed an alternative view on this 'schism', claiming that the various Ismaili movements did not have an organizational unity and that this unity was merely the result of a posteriori Fatimid historiography. F. Daftary, W. Madelung, and Omert J. Schrier have argued against this thesis: see M. Brett, *The Rise of the Fatimids; the World of the Mediterranean and the Middle East in the Fourth Century of Hijra, Tenth Century CE* (Leiden, 2001), pp. 29–48; F. Daftary, Review of M. Brett, *The Rise of the Fatimids* (2001), *BSOAS*, 65/1 (2002), pp. 152–153; W. Madelung, Review of M. Brett, *The Rise of the Fatimids* (2001), *Journal of Islamic Studies*, 13/2 (2002), pp. 202–204; O.T. Schrier, 'The Prehistory of the Fatimid Dynasty: Some Chronological and Genealogical Remarks', *Die Welt des Orients*, 36 (2006), pp. 143–191.

ʿAbd Allāh al-Mahdī chose to join his followers in the Maghreb, where Abū ʿAbd Allāh al-Shīʿī had been strengthening his position for years. In 909, the city of Qayrawān was taken by Abū ʿAbd Allāh. A few months later, in January 910, ʿAbd Allāh al-Mahdī made his triumphal entry into Raqqāda and was officially proclaimed caliph.

Soon after his enthronement in 297/910, ʿAbd Allāh al-Mahdī relegated Abū ʿAbd Allāh al-Shīʿī to the background. This political disappointment was further aggravated by one of a spiritual nature: expected to be the central figure of eschatological events, al-Mahdī proved incapable of performing any miracles. His taste for pomp and luxury shocked the very sober and ascetic Abū ʿAbd Allāh, who reproached the new caliph for corrupting the austere morals of the Kutāma warriors. Encouraged by his brother Abū'l-ʿAbbās, who also held important positions in the *daʿwa*, Abū ʿAbd Allāh began to doubt the quality of the man who presented himself — and whom he himself had presented to the Kutāma — as the Mahdī. As a result, a conspiracy to overthrow the new caliph emerged among several leaders of the *daʿwa*. ʿAbd Allāh al-Mahdī gained intelligence of this and had Abū ʿAbd Allāh and his accomplices executed in Jumāda II 298/February 911.[59] This event stirred up great discontent and turmoil. Led by a certain Kādū b. Muʿārik al-Māwaṭī, a faction of the Kutāma warriors rebelled against Fatimid rule in 300/912, a year after Abū ʿAbd Allāh al-Shīʿī's execution. Interestingly, the rebels are said to have believed in the latter's messianic return; according to al-Qāḍī al-Nuʿmān (d. 363/974) and the much later historian Ibn ʿIdhārī (fl. second half of the 7th–first half of 8th/13th–14th century), their leader claimed to be a prophet and a *mahdī*, who would create a new religion and authorize illicit sexual practices and 'other forbidden things', thereby causing confusion.[60]

---

[59] F. Dachraoui, *Le Califat Fatimide au Maghreb*, pp. 127–132; H. Halm, *The Empire of the* Mahdi, pp. 159–168; P.E. Walker, 'Abū ʿAbd Allāh al-Shīʿī', *EI3*.

[60] Al-Qāḍī al-Nuʿmān, *Iftitāḥ al-daʿwa*, ed. W. al-Qāḍī, (Beirut, 1970), p. 273; al-Qāḍī al-Nuʿmān, *Iftitāḥ al-daʿwa*, ed. F. Dachraoui (Tunis, 1975), pp. 324–325; Abū l-ʿAbbās Aḥmad b. Muḥammad Ibn ʿIdhārī al-Marrākushī, *Kitāb al-Bayān al-mughrib fī akhbār al-Maghrib*, ed. G.S. Colin and É. Lévi-Provençal (Leiden, 1948), vol. 1, pp. 166–167; F. Dachraoui, *Le Califat Fatimide au Maghreb*, pp. 134–135; H. Halm, *The Empire of the Mahdi*, pp. 172–174; M. Brett, *The Rise of the Fatimids*, pp. 108–111. Another episode shows ʿAbd Allāh al-Mahdī confronting the excessive enthusiasm of

It was on this occasion that ʿAbd Allāh al-Mahdī is said to have officially designated his successor. Naming his son Muḥammad b. ʿAbd Allāh after the Prophet himself, al-Mahdī attempted to divert the messianic hopes raised by the *daʿwa* onto himself. Placed at the head of the army, Abū'l-Qāsim Muḥammad b. ʿAbd Allāh, the soon-to-be second Fatimid caliph al-Qāʾim bi-Amr Allāh, was charged with crushing the revolt. His mission was crowned with success as he took the false Mahdī and his lieutenants prisoners; they were then publicly executed in Raqqāda.[61] The fact that al-Qāʾim's official designation as heir is directly connected to the repression of a rival messianic and antinomian movement, is of great importance. Having this in mind is essential to our understanding of the *Kitāb al-Kashf* — and of Treatise V in particular, as we will see, since this treatise explicitly names al-Qāʾim and contains a refutation of antinomianism and of an unnamed 'false Mahdi'. It is also noteworthy that during the entire reign of al-Mahdī, al-Qāʾim has already taken on major political and military responsibilities.

This episode illustrates that the Fatimid caliphate was highly unsettled in its early years, plagued by revolts and defections. This may explain the many allusions of the *Kitāb al-Kashf* to 'those who knew the truth' and yet turned away from it. It also explains the constant need to justify the Fatimid reign, threatened on all sides, both by internal revolts and external enemies, namely the Umayyads, to the west, and the Abbasids, to the east. After the death of al-Mahdī in 322/934, al-Qāʾim succeeded him. He had been in office as heir for some twenty years, and had gained political as well as military experience (having led several unsuccessful campaigns in Egypt, among other things). It was at the end of his reign that a revolt broke out, led by the Kharijite Abū Yazīd, which almost led to the caliphate's downfall. When al-Qāʾim died (334/946), his son and successor al-Manṣūr (r. 334–341/946–953) hid the news and officially declared himself caliph only after Abū Yazīd had been defeated. The caliphate

---

some of his followers and having several of his own missionaries executed for antinomian practices, such as drinking alcohol and eating pork during Ramaḍān; see al-Qāḍī al-Nuʿmān, *Iftitāḥ al-daʿwa*, ed. W. al-Qāḍī, p. 276; al-Qāḍī al-Nuʿmān, *Iftitāḥ al-daʿwa*, ed. F. Dachraoui, pp. 328–329; Ibn ʿIdhārī, *Kitāb al-Bayān al-mughrib*, vol. 1, pp. 185–186; H. Halm, *The Empire of the Mahdi*, pp. 247–250.

[61] Halm H., *The Empire of the Mahdi*, p.173–174.

was now firmly established and would subsequently be consolidated under the rule of al-Muʿizz (r. 341–365/953–975), whose generals finally succeeded in occupying Egypt, which had been in their sights for several years.[62]

2. Transmission: Manuscripts, Editions, and Reception

The *Kashf* has been transmitted down to the present day by the Ṭayyibī *daʿwa*, as indicated by the manuscript tradition, as well as by the rare quotations of the text in Ismaili literature — all found in Ṭayyibī sources, as we will see.

Only two publicly available manuscripts of the *Kashf* have come down to us.[63] These are the two manuscripts on which Rudolf Strothmann based his 1952 edition of the text.

The first one, labelled 'manuscript A' by Strothmann, has been preserved in the Staatsbibliothek in Berlin since 1928, under the code Or. add. Oct. 2768.[64] It consists of 164 numbered folios, with 11 lines per page. The writing is clear and neat. Red ink is used for some words.[65] The copy is dated 28 Muḥarram 1135 (8 November 1722). Strothmann notes that the name of the copyist is 'unclear' (*ghayr wāḍiḥ*), but that it 'resembles Yasir b. Māwlā'.[66] Unlike manuscript B, manuscript A does not mention the name of the *dāʿī* under whose authority the copy was made. The colophon translates as follows:

> 'Completed on the 28th of the month of Muḥarram, in the year 1135 with the help of God, the King, the Highest, copied by his wretched and humble servant, who is in need of the forgiveness of God, his Summoner and Friend, Yasir b. Māwlā

---

[62] For detailed accounts of the beginnings of the Fatimid caliphate, see F. Dachraoui, *Le califat fatimide au Maghreb*; H. Halm, *The Empire of the Mahdi*; M. Brett, *The Rise of the Fatimids*.

[63] I.K. Poonawala lists seven more manuscripts of the *Kashf* in private libraries, but these were not accessible to me; see I.K. Poonawala, *Biobibliography*, p. 73.

[64] Available at the following URL: https://digital.staatsbibliothek-berlin.de/werkansicht/?PPN=PPN627485588, consulted on 22 February 2023.

[65] This is particularly the case of the words cyphered in the secret alphabet; on this alphabet, see below, pp. 35–38.

[66] *Kashf*, p. 179, n. 1.

> Luṭf Allāh, in about 167 folios, 2,400 lines (*bayt*), each line comprising 50 letters.'[67]

Manuscript B is preserved at the University of Bombay under the code Fyz 21, indicating that it is from the collection of the Ismaili scholar Ali Asghar Fyzee.[68] It consists of 130 folios, with about 15 lines per page. The writing is sloppy and hasty, resulting in numerous grammatical and spelling errors, as well as terms erroneously replacing others. This could also be due to the copyist's poor command of Arabic. The copy is dated 20 Dhū al-Ḥijja 1130 (14 November 1718), and was made by ʿAbd al-Raḥīm b. Ṭayyib Khān, under the authority of the '*dāʿī al-duʿāt*' ('Chief Summoner') in India, Sindh and Yemen, our master Badr al-Dīn al-Shaykh Ismāʿīl Jī".[69] The colophon is significantly longer than that of manuscript A:

> 'Copied by the weak, wretched and humble, servant of servants, ʿAbd al-Raḥīm b. Ṭayyib Khān. I have read this book and had it sealed by our master Badr al-Dīn al-Shaykh Ismāʿīl Jī son of Salīl, our master Ṣafī al-Dīn al-Shaykh Ādam.[70] May God lengthen his life and the light of his summons, in the name of Muḥammad and his family, the pure — may God bless them all.

[67] There is a discrepancy of three folios between the number of folios in the manuscript that has come down to us and the count of the copyist. Also, the number of 2400 lines seems excessive (164 folios X 11 lines = 1804 lines).

[68] See M. Goriawala, *A Descriptive Catalogue of the Fyzee Collection of Ismaili Manuscripts* (Bombay, 1965), p. 15, no. 21. Goriawala mistakenly states, however, that the name of the copyist does not appear in the manuscript. The Fyzee collection also contains another manuscript of the *Kashf*, under the code Fyz 22, which, according to Goriawala, is the manuscript of Strothmann's edition sent to the print, since it includes footnotes and an introduction. I have not been able to consult directly the Bombay manuscript, but a copy was kindly provided to me by a private source who wished to remain anonymous.

[69] 38th Indian Dāwūdī *dāʿī*, d. 1150/1737. The copy is dated 1130/1718, which is the year of the death of his predecessor, Nūr Muḥammad Nūr al-Dīn b. Mūsā Kalīm al-Dīn; see F. Daftary, *The Ismāʿīlīs*, p. 511, no. 38, where he is mentioned under the name Ismāʿīl Badr al-Dīn b. Shaykh Ādam Ṣafī al-Dīn.

[70] Shaykh Ādam Ṣafī al-Dīn b. Ṭayyibshāh, d. 1030/1621, was the 28th *dāʿī* of the Dāwūdī and ʿAlawī branches of Ṭayyibī Ismailism; see F. Daftary, *The Ismāʿīlīs*, pp. 511–512; I.K. Poonawala, 'Shaykh Ādam', *EI2*.

> Praise be to God, the One, the Forgiving, the Creator of night and day, the Creator of the heavens, the earth and the seas, the Creator of the flocks, the birds and the trees, who bestows upon Creation all the colours and fruits. Our master, the Summoner of the Summoners in India, Sindh and Yemen, our master Badr al-Dīn al-Shaykh Ismāʿīl Jī, gifted with forbearance, knowledge and power, has granted us certainty (*al-yaqīn*); gifted with eloquence and nobility, he has granted us the faithful Spirit, the way of salvation, the means for creatures to be saved from matter to reach the Abode of Purity, in the highest of ʿIliyyīn [Q. 83:18], in the name of our master Muḥammad and all his family.
>
> I have completed this book on the date of the 20th of the glorious month of Dhū al-Ḥijja, in the year 1130 of the *hijra* of the chosen Prophet Muḥammad. May God pray upon our master Muḥammad, the Messenger of God, and upon his family, the pure.'

Both manuscripts thus date from the beginning of the 18th century, which is late considering the supposed time of composition of the work (early Fatimid period). This is however a common issue with Ismaili manuscripts. Although manuscript A is later than manuscript B, the latter is not the model for the former. Indeed, Ms B contains many mistakes, several of which are not found in Ms A. However, there are also cases where both manuscripts transmit similar errors (which can be recognized as such by comparing the text with other sources, be they Ismaili or Twelver Shiʿi), which suggests that even if they do not both rely on the same copy, they at least belong to the same manuscript tradition. Ms A is the more reliable, and it is essentially on this one that Strothmann based his edition.

This edition was published without Strothmann's *imprimatur*,[71] as indicated, for instance, by a note in Henry Corbin's handwriting on the title page of his personal copy.[72] In the final pages of his edition of the *Kitāb al-Haft wa'l-aẓilla*, Muṣṭafā Ghālib provides facsimiles (of

---

[71] Inasmuch as Strothmann disavowed the 1952 edition, it is only out of convenience that I will refer to it as 'Strothmann's edition' throughout this study.

[72] 'Edition provisoire sans 'Imprimatur''. I would like to thank Christian Jambet for allowing me to consult this copy.

rather poor quality) of three letters in French he received from Strothmann. They are unfortunately undated and not always perfectly legible. Nevertheless the following lines can be deciphered in one of the letters:

> 'My dearest colleague, I am glad to have received your correspondence (?). You requested the *Kitāb al-Kashf* from me. I have you sent *(sic)* by post (. . .) a copy, but against my will; the edition has many mistakes (*ghalṭāt*) and typographical errors. I had sent my manuscript to Islamic Research Association in 1939. It was printed in Bombay, Cairo and Calcutta and edited in 1952 without my having had the opportunity to read the proofs!'[73]

A new edition of the text would therefore be necessary, particularly in the light of the results of the present study and the quotations of and parallels to the *Kashf* I have found in other sources. However, this task must be reserved for a future publication: I have preferred to provide a study of the contents of the work rather than a new edition. It seemed more urgent to examine the meanings, aims and spirit of the *Kitāb al-Kashf*, than to establish its precise text. Also, in the absence of new manuscripts, a new edition might not be so useful, especially since the 1952 edition remains overall satisfactory — at least sufficiently so to be translated with the occasional recourse to manuscripts or other sources for the faultiest passages. Finally, the text of the *Kashf* itself is well-known to scholars who have devoted several partial studies to it. What is lacking today is not so much access to the text, but a study that endeavours, inasmuch as possible, to provide a broader historical contextualization of it, as well as a detailed commentary of some of its essential features.

---

[73] 'Mon très cher collègue, je suis heureux d'avoir reçu votre correspondance (?). Vous me demandez le كتاب الكشف. J'ai vous envoyé *(sic)* par poste (. . .) une copie, mais contre mon gré; l'édition a beaucoup de غلطات et fautes typographiques. J'avais envoyé mon manuscrit à Islamic Research Association en 1939. Il a été imprimé à Bombay, le Caire et Calcutta et édité en 1952 sans que j'aie eu l'occasion de lire les épreuves!'; see Mufaḍḍal b. ʿUmar al-Juʿfī, *Al-Haft al-sharīf*, ed. M. Ghālib (Beirut, 1977), p. [204].

There exists a second edition of the *Kashf*, published in 1984 by Muṣṭafā Ghālib.[74] In the introduction to his edition, he describes the conditions under which he came to edit this text: in 1954, while visiting Pakistan for a series of lectures organized by the Ismaili Society, Ghālib met in Hyderabad a certain Dr. ʿAzīz ʿAlī, who had a great interest in 'esoteric studies' (*al-dirāsāt al-bāṭiniyya*). Moreover, as the head of the highest local Ismaili council he granted Muṣṭafā Ghālib access to his personal library which contained rare Ismaili manuscripts: 'Fortunately, the *Kitāb al-Kashf* was among them.'[75] With the manuscript now in his possession, Ghālib sought another copy of this text in order to produce an edition. In 1958, he received a letter from Rudolf Strothmann in which the latter stated that he had established the text of the *Kashf* as early as 1939 for the Islamic Research Association in Bombay. This edition was based on manuscript no. 2768 in the Staatsbibliothek in Berlin. Apart from the mention of the Berlin manuscript, this corresponds to the data in the letter from which a passage was reproduced above.

Unfortunately, Ghālib goes on, the *dāʿī* Ṭāhir Sayf al-Dīn (d. 1965)[76] objected to the publication of the *Kitāb al-Kashf* and demanded that the Indian authorities should confiscate the copies even before they left the printing house. According to Ghālib, Strothmann then proposed to him that he should re-edit the *Kashf* in the light of the manuscript Ghālib possessed, especially since Strothmann had claimed that the manuscript on which he had relied for the first edition was of poor quality and contained many typographical errors and mistakes. Ghālib says he then asked for the printed text to be sent to him, but Strothmann died in 1960 before he could sent it to Ghālib. Having searched in vain for another manuscript, he had to resort to editing the text on the basis of the only manuscript available to him.

Ghālib then provides a description of his manuscript: 132 folios, 14 lines per page and 11 words per line on average, nice legible

---

[74] Jaʿfar b. Manṣūr al-Yaman, *Kitāb al-Kashf*, ed. M. Ghālib (Beirut, 1984).

[75] Ibid., p. 18.

[76] 51st Indian Dāwūdī *dāʿī*, d. 1385/1965; see F. Daftary, *The Ismāʿīlīs*, p. 512, no. 51, where he is mentioned under the name Ṭāhir Sayf al-Dīn b. Muḥammad Burhān al-Dīn.

handwriting, titles and symbols in red ink. The copy is dated Thursday 6 Rajab 1073 (14 February 1663), and the name of the copyist is ʿAbd al-ʿAzīz b. al-Shaykh Ādam b. Ṣafī al-Dīn al-Yamanī al-Ḥarrazī, under the authority of the *dāʿī* al-Shaykh ʿAlī b. Sulaymān b. Jaʿfar.

Several aspects of this account are questionable and perplexing. First, it is surprising — although not entirely impossible — that Ghālib was not aware of the edition of the *Kitāb al-Kashf* until 1958, that is, six years after its publication, even though he and Strothmann maintained a correspondence. Moreover, Ghālib was apparently not aware that Strothmann had relied on a second manuscript (the one from the Fyzee collection) since he does not mention it at any point. Worse, the claim that the Berlin manuscript was faulty does not hold; Ghālib obviously confused the two manuscripts used by Strothmann, and applied to manuscript A the characteristics of manuscript B. Such confusion suggests that he had not consulted Strothmann's edition (although his own was published in 1984, 24 years after Strothmann's death!) or read its introduction. Yet a comparison of the two editions, despite some inconsequential variations, regularly makes it clear that, in spite of what he says, Ghālib was inspired by his predecessor and correspondent. In many cases, he seems to have merely reproduced in the body of the text the suggestions for correction indicated by Strothmann in the footnotes of his own edition or in his table of errors. Either Ghālib edited the *Kitāb al-Kashf* without consulting the 1952 edition, or he consulted it while claiming not to have done so. Whatever the case, this lack of clarity is hardly compatible with a scholarly approach, and it is therefore questionable whether the 1984 edition is critical. Furthermore, there is no evidence that the Hyderabad manuscript Ghālib claims to have used for his edition actually existed, since Ghālib does not provide facsimiles of a few pages of the manuscript, contrary to what he usually did in his editions. Incidentally, it is unclear whether this manuscript ended up in Ghālib's library, or whether he worked on a copy.

The names of the copyist and the *dāʿī* are also problematic. According to the description provided by Ghālib[77] and the colophon

[77] Jaʿfar b. Manṣūr al-Yaman, *Kitāb al-Kashf*, ed. M. Ghālib, p. 19.

of the manuscript reproduced at the end of his edition,[78] the manuscript was copied by a certain ʿAbd al-ʿAzīz b. al-Shaykh Ādam b. Ṣafī al-Dīn, under the authority of the *dāʿī* al-Shaykh "ʿAlī b. Sulaymān b. Jaʿfar". Now, while there is indeed a Sulaymānī *dāʿī* named ʿAlī b. Sulaymān — in office at the supposed time of the copy (1073/1663) since he died in 1088/1677[79] — the name Jaʿfar seems wrong. Indeed, the first *dāʿī* of the Sulaymānī branch of Ṭayyibī Ismailism was named Sulaymān b. Ḥasan: as his son, the *dāʿī* ʿAlī should be named ʿAlī b. Sulaymān b. *Ḥasan*. However, ʿAlī did not immediately succeed Sulaymān b. Ḥasan: from 1597 to 1640, he was preceded by his brother, Jaʿfar b. Sulaymān, which perhaps explains the confusion. But it is unlikely that the copyist ignored the name of his *dāʿī*.

As for the copyist, ʿAbd al-ʿAzīz b. al-Shaykh Ādam b. Ṣafī al-Dīn, his name indicates that he was a son of Shaykh Ādam Ṣafī al-Dīn (d. 1030/1621), 28th *dāʿī* of the Dawūdī and ʿAlawī branches of Ṭayyibī Ismailism — and therefore a brother of the 38th Dawūdī *dāʿī* under whose authority manuscript B was copied, Ismāʿīl Badr al-Dīn b. al-Shaykh Ādam Ṣafī al-Dīn. Should we infer from this that the copyist, although coming from a line of Dawūdī *dāʿīs*, worked on behalf of a Sulaymānī *dāʿī*? Although not entirely impossible, this is unlikely.

These elements suggest the need to approach Ghālib's edition with caution. For the present study, however, it has been occasionally consulted in the hope of clarifying difficult passages. Apart from a few cases, indicated in the footnotes to the present translation, Ghālib's edition proved not to be of much help in general.[80]

It is impossible to venture into final conclusions regarding the manuscript tradition of the *Kashf* based on two manuscripts only. Yet, these manuscripts can provide some indications as to the history of the

---

[78] Ibid., p. 153.

[79] See F. Daftary, *The Ismāʿīlīs*, p. 512, n. 29.

[80] It should be added that, in 2010, a third 'edition' of the *Kashf* was printed by Alwarrak publishers (London, Beirut and Baghdad). In fact, this so-called edition merely reproduces Strothmann's 1952 edition without any emendations, which only adds more confusion to a difficult text by creating a third pagination for the *Kashf*. The new 'edition' does not refer to the previous editions and lacks scholarly value. I have not used this reprint, since its only merit is to provide easier commercial access to the *Kashf*.

Kashf's transmission — especially when this information may be augmented by a survey of the quotations of the *Kashf* in Ismaili literature. It appears that the *Kashf* was mainly transmitted through the Yemeni Ṭayyibī tradition. In the case of manuscript B, the colophon is sufficient to reach this conclusion.

Things are trickier in the case of manuscript A, however, since the colophon does not provide any names. One possible way to infer the Ṭayyibī origin of manuscript A, despite this dearth of information, could be its use of secret alphabets, which are also found in manuscript B. These secret characters are used to encrypt certain terms, proper names (particularly those of the enemies of the Imams) and curses (see **Figures 1 and 2**, see overleaf). However, this use is not systematic throughout the volume, since, for instance, the name of Abū Bakr is sometimes cyphered, sometimes not. Strothmann also encountered these alphabets in his edition of the Ismaili manuscript preserved in the Biblioteca Ambrosiana in Milan under the code H 75.[81] For the purpose of identifying the tradition to which the *Kashf* belongs, the secret alphabets are of importance, since, as noted by Daniel De Smet, they seem to appear only in 'the Arabic manuscripts transmitted by the Ṭayyibī branch'. While this is not enough to state categorically that these alphabets are a specifically Ṭayyibī feature, it is nevertheless a strong indication in favour of this hypothesis. Another clue invoked by D. De Smet is that these alphabets also appear in manuscripts of the *Risāla al-Jāmiʿa*, which, according to De Smet, 'played a considerable role in the Ismaili assimilation of the doctrine of the Ikhwān [al-Ṣafā']'.[82] Indeed, this Ismaili assimilation of the famous encyclopaedia and its attribution to a pre-Fatimid Imam was precisely carried out by

[81] See R. Strothmann, *Gnosis-Texte der Ismailiten. Arabische Handschrift Ambrosiana H 75* (Göttingen, 1943), esp. pp. 60–61 of the introduction, and p. 178 for the equivalence table between the two secret alphabets and the Arabic alphabet. See also the discussion of the 'secret writing' (*al-kitāba al-sirriya*) and the equivalence table in Strothmann's introduction to his edition of the *Kashf*. As noted by Daniel De Smet, these two tables present several differences; see D. De Smet, 'L'alphabet secret des Ismaéliens ou la force magique de l'écriture', in *Charmes et sortilèges. Magie et magiciens*, ed. R. Gyselen (Bures-sur-Yvette, 2002), pp. 51–60, esp. p. 52.

[82] See D. De Smet, 'L'alphabet secret des Ismaéliens', pp. 53–54.

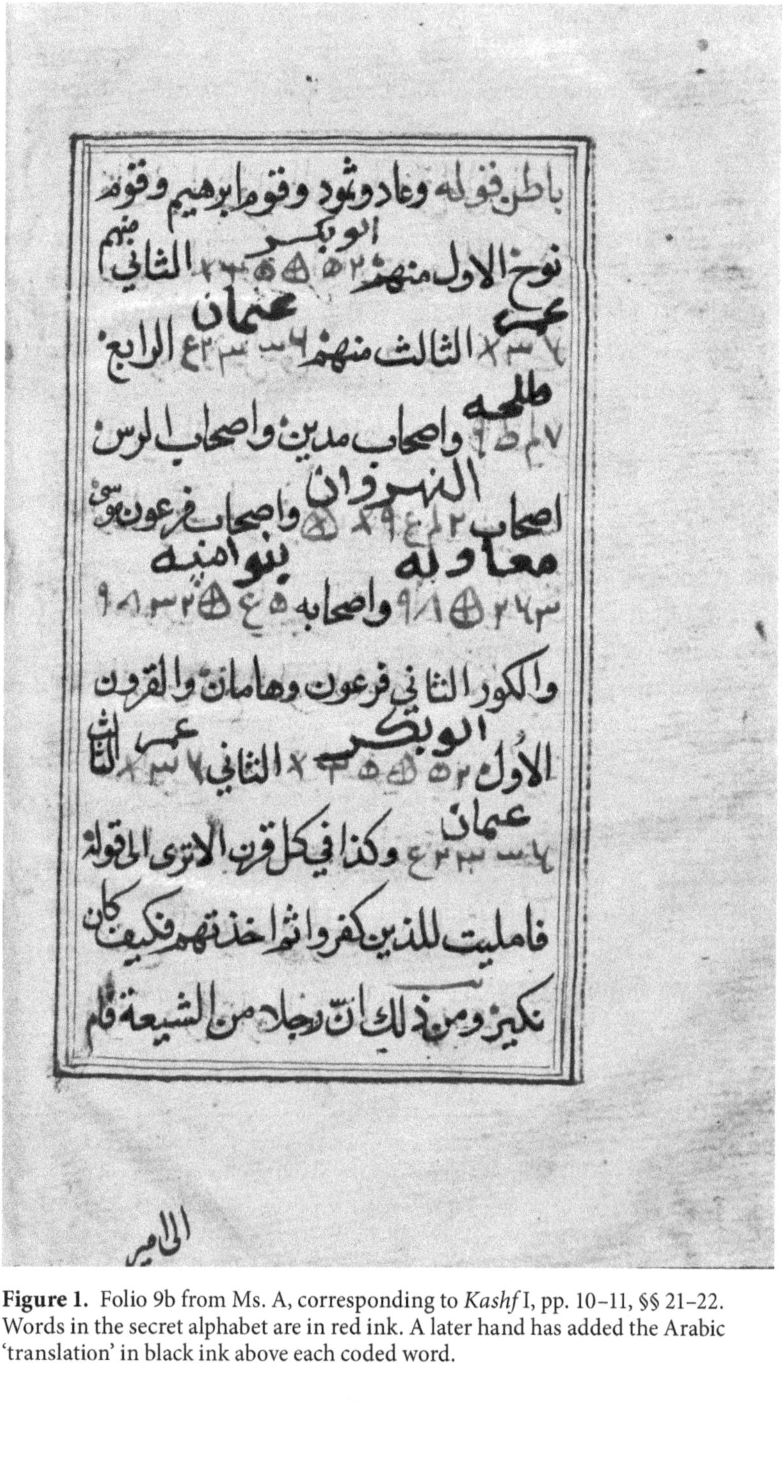
باطن قوله وعاد وثمود وقوم ابرهيم وقوم
ابو بكر منهم
نوح الاول منهم الثاني
عمر عثمان
الثالث منهم الرابع
طلحه
واصحاب مدين واصحاب الرس
النهروان
اصحاب واصحاب فرعون موسى
معاويه بنو امية
واصحابه
والكور الثاني فرعون وهامان والقرون
ابو بكر عمر
الاول الثاني الثالث
عثمان
وكذا في كل قرن الاترى الى قوله
فامليت للذين كفروا ثم اخذتهم فكيف كان
نكير ومن ذلك ان رجلا من الشيعة قام
الى امير

Figure 1. Folio 9b from Ms. A, corresponding to *Kashf* I, pp. 10–11, §§ 21–22. Words in the secret alphabet are in red ink. A later hand has added the Arabic 'translation' in black ink above each coded word.

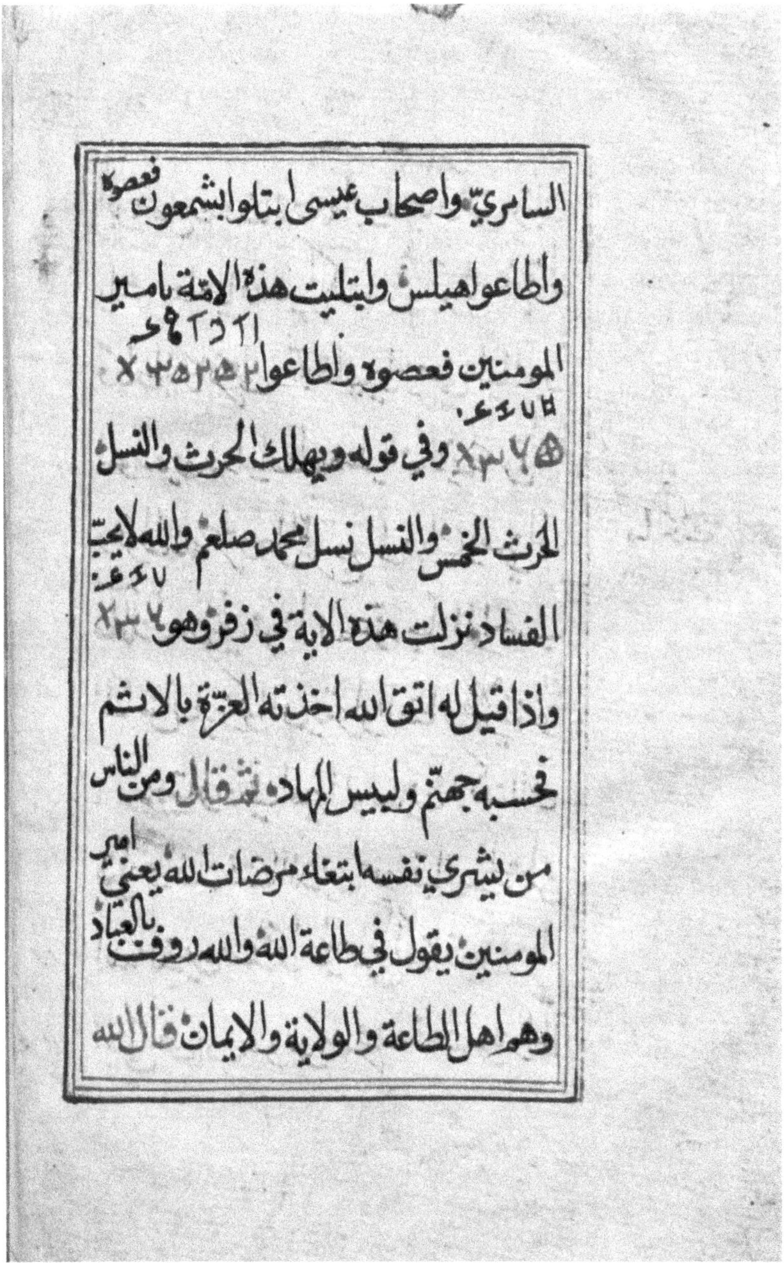
السامري واصحاب عيسى ابتلوا بشمعون فعصوه
واطاعوا اهيلس وابتليت هذه الامة بامير
المومنين فعصوه واطاعوا
وفي قوله ويهلك الحرث والنسل
الحرث الخمس والنسل نسل محمد صلعم والله لا يحب
الفساد نزلت هذه الاية في زفر وهو
واذا قيل له اتق الله اخذته العزة بالاثم
فحسبه جهنم ولبيس المهاد ثم قال ومن الناس
من يشري نفسه ابتغاء مرضات الله يعني امير
المومنين يقول في طاعة الله والله رءوف بالعباد
وهم اهل الطاعة والولاية والايمان قال الله

Figure 2. Folio 27b from Ms. A, corresponding to *Kashf* I, p. 31, §§ 65–66. Here, a second secret alphabet has been used in black ink, above the words in the first alphabet in red ink.

Ṭayyibī authors, around the 13th century.[83] Yet, the origin of this alphabet and whether it was created by Ṭayyibī Ismaili authors, or merely borrowed by them from the *Risāla al-Jāmiʿa* remains an open question.[84]

Further evidence of the Ṭayyibī transmission of the *Kashf* is to be sought in the attestations of the work in Ismaili literature. In light of our current knowledge of the latter, the mentions of the *Kashf* in other works would seem to indicate that it benefited from the Ṭayyibī interest in Fatimid texts, and that before that it was a rather a secondary text in the works attributed to Jaʿfar b. Manṣūr al-Yaman.[85] Indeed, I have found no mentions of it prior to the Ṭayyibī *dāʿī* Idrīs ʿImād al-Dīn (d. 872/1468).[86] In his *Zahr al-maʿānī*, an exposition of 'esoteric truths' (*ḥaqāʾiq*), reporting many *ḥadīth*s of a spiritual nature, he quotes Jaʿfar b. Manṣūr al-Yaman on several occasions, although he does not always indicate from which work the quotations are taken.[87] At times, Idrīs does not even present them as quotations: such is the case in a page of the *Zahr al-maʿānī* that repeats elements of Treatise I of the *Kashf*.[88] There are, however, two explicit mentions of the *Kitāb al-Kashf* in the *Zahr al-maʿānī*, and it is indeed attributed to Jaʿfar b.

---

[83] See D. De Smet, 'L'auteur des *Rasāʾil Ikhwān al-Ṣafāʾ* selon les sources ismaéliennes ṭayyibites', *SSR*, 1 (2017), pp. 151–166.

[84] On this, see D. De Smet, "Alī b. Abī Ṭālib et l'alphabet himyarite ou l'invention de l'écriture secrète ismaélienne', in *Acta Orientalia Belgica*, 36 (2023), ed. S. Holvoet and R. Veymiers, pp. 347–358.

[85] As opposed to a text such as the *Riḍāʿ fī'l-bāṭin* which seems to have served as a handbook of *taʾwīl*, as suggested by the fact that al-Qāḍī al-Nuʿmān mentions it, and that it was a major source of the anti-Ismaili work of the Zaydī author al-Daylamī; on the former, see below, pp. 45 ff, section on Jaʿfar b. Manṣūr al-Yaman, on the latter, see al-Daylamī, *Bayān madhhab al-bāṭiniyya wa-buṭlānihi, manqūl min Kitāb Qawāʿid ʿaqāʾid āl Muḥammad (Die Geheimlehre der Bāṭiniten nach der Apologie "Dogmatik des Hauses Muḥammed")*, ed. R. Strothmann (Istanbul, 1939), index s.v. *Riḍāʿ fī'l-bāṭin*.

[86] On him, see T. Qutbuddin, 'Idrīs ʿImād al-Dīn', *EI3*.

[87] See e.g. Idrīs ʿImād al-Dīn, *Zahr al-maʿānī*, ed. M. Ghālib (Beirut, 1991), pp. 195–196, where a passage attributed to Jaʿfar b. Manṣūr al-Yaman is indeed a quotation of the latter's *Taʾwīl al-zakāt*, pp. 163–164.

[88] Compare Idrīs ʿImād al-Dīn, *Zahr al-maʿānī*, p. 171 and *Kashf* I, p. 11, §§ 23–24; p. 30, § 63; pp. 37–39, § 80.

Manṣūr al-Yaman. The first of these mentions precedes lengthy quotations from Treatise II, which prove useful in clarifying certain passages poorly transmitted by the manuscript tradition of the *Kitāb al-Kashf*.[89] The second explicit mention of the *Kashf* precedes a quotation from Treatise V.[90]

To my knowledge, there are only two more attestations attributing the *Kitāb al-Kashf* to Jaʿfar b. Manṣūr al-Yaman: one is found in the *Fihrist* of al-Majdūʿ (d. 1183/1769), a much later directory of works. Al-Majdūʿ arranges his lists of works by topic, not by author, and without following a chronological order; as a result, the books attributed to Jaʿfar b. Manṣūr al-Yaman are scattered here and there.[91] It seems that al-Majdūʿ did not have direct access to the *Kitāb al-Kashf* since he does not dedicate a specific note to it. He only mentions it within a note on the *Majmūʿ al-ḥaqāʾiq*, an anonymous compilation of thematically arranged Ismaili texts, mainly containing excerpts from works by Jaʿfar b. Manṣūr al-Yaman, as well as by two other important Fatimid authors, Ḥamīd al-Dīn al-Kirmānī and al-Muʾayyad fīʾl-Dīn al-Shīrāzī.[92] This is clearly a Ṭayyibī compilation since it contains quotations attributed to Imam al-Ṭayyib and extracts from the *Risāla al-Jāmiʿa*. It is divided into seven chapters: according to al-Majdūʿ, it is in chapters 5 and 6, respectively devoted to the 'sources of religion' (*uṣūl al-dīn*) and the eschatological 'return' (*maʿād*), that excerpts from the *Kashf* are found.[93] Unfortunately, this work was not accessible to me.

The *Kashf* is also quoted and attributed to Jaʿfar b. Manṣūr al-Yaman in at least one other compilation. François de Blois reports an allusion

---

[89] Compare Idrīs ʿImād al-Dīn, *Zahr al-maʿānī*, pp. 127–131 and *Kashf* II, pp. 42–48, §§ 7–22. Note that the quotation of the *Kashf* by Idrīs is not continuous but interrupted several times by glosses. Some passages of *Kashf* II are not quoted.

[90] Compare Idrīs ʿImād al-Dīn, *Zahr al-maʿānī*, p. 217 and *Kashf* V, pp. 103–104, §§ 26–27.

[91] See al-Majdūʿ, *Fihrist al-Kutub waʾl-Rasʿāʾil*, ed. ʿAlīnaqī Manzavī (Tehran, 1966), index *s.n.* 'Jaʿfar b. Manṣūr al-Yaman'.

[92] See I.K. Poonawala, *Biobibliography*, p. 329, no. 83; W. Ivanow, *Guide to Ismaili Literature*, p. 79, n. 417; idem, *Ismaili Literature*, p. 98, no. 391.

[93] For a summary of the contents of the *Majmūʿ al-ḥaqāʾiq*, see al-Majdūʿ, *Fihrist*, pp. 257–260, and pp. 259, 260 for the mentions of the *Kashf*.

to a passage from the *Kitāb al-Kashf* in his description of a manuscript from the Hamdani collection held at the Institute of Ismaili Studies and bearing the number 1496.[94] This manuscript contains four treatises: 1) the *Ghāyat al-Mawālīd* by al-Khaṭṭāb (d. 533/1138), a Yemeni tribal leader who was a key supporter of the Ṭayyibī *daʿwa* in its struggle for independence from the Fatimid caliphate;[95] 2) an assemblage of several extracts from the works of Jaʿfar b. Manṣūr al-Yaman, al-Qāḍī al-Nuʿmān, al-Kirmānī and al-Muʾayyad. It is here that we find a brief reference to the 'seventy forms (*haykal*)' mentioned in a passage from *Kashf* V;[96] 3) the *Risāla* by Abū ʿĪsā al-Murshid, edited by S.M. Stern from another manuscript;[97] 4) an extract from the

---

[94] F. De Blois, *Arabic, Persian and Gujarati Manuscripts: The Hamdani Collection* (London and New York, 2011), pp. 103–105, esp. p. 104.

[95] On al-Khaṭṭāb, see F. Daftary, *The Ismāʿīlīs*, pp. 264–265, and references p. 608, n. 84. On the *Ghāyat al-Mawālīd*, see also D. De Smet, 'Une femme musulmane ministre de Dieu sur terre? La réponse du *dāʿī* ismaélien al-Ḫaṭṭāb', *Acta Orientalia Belgica*, 15 (2001), pp. 155–164; idem, 'La valorisation du féminin dans l'ismaélisme Ṭayyibite. Le cas de la reine yéménite al-Sayyida Arwā (1048–1138)', *Mélanges de l'Université Saint-Joseph*, 58 (2005), pp. 107–122; K. Bauer, 'Spiritual Hierarchy and Gender Hierarchy in Fatimid Ismāʿīlī Interpretations of the Qurʾan', *Journal of Qurʾanic Studies*, 14/2 (2012), pp. 29–46, esp. pp. 40–42.

[96] See IIS MS 1496, f. 63, which refers to *Kashf* V, pp. 102–103, § 24. It should be noted that the theme of the 'seventy forms', or seventy *maqāms*, seems to have been reused by the Ismailis from earlier Shiʿi speculations — as indicated for instance by the existence of a *Kitāb al-Sabʿīn* among *ghulāt* works; see M. Asatryan, *Controversies in Formative Shiʿi Islam*, p. 181. While the interest in it progressively diminished during the Fatimid period, it apparently regained importance in the Ṭayyibī *daʿwa*; in the *Kanz al-walad*, a founding work of Ṭayyibī doctrine, the author mentions the 'seventy *haykals*' in reference to Jaʿfar b. Manṣūr al-Yaman and identifies the *haykals* with the Speaking-Prophets, their Legatees and their Completer Imams, from Adam to the Qāʾim, through the Fatimid caliphs, Imam al-Ṭayyib and the seven 'substitutes' (*abdāl*) from the latter's progeny — thus illustrating the adaptation to Ṭayyibī doctrine of an earlier tradition; see Ibrāhīm b. al-Ḥusayn al-Ḥāmidī, *Kanz al-walad*, ed. M. Ghālib (Beirut, 1970), pp. 207–208; compare to Jaʿfar b. Manṣūr al-Yaman, *Kitāb al-Riḍāʿ fīʾl-bātin*, ed. Ḥ. Khaḍḍūr (Salamiyya, 2018), pp. 185–187. As for the term *haykal*, it means 'temple', but has wider symbolic connotations; it is a receptacle of sacredness, as well as a place of epiphany. To avoid confusion with *ṣūra*, usually translated as 'form', and to emphasize this sacredness, I translate it as 'sacred form'. On *haykal* in the *Kashf*, see index s.v.

[97] See S.M. Stern, 'The earliest cosmological doctrines of Ismāʿīlism', in idem, *Studies in Early Ismāʿīlism*, pp. 3–29.

Risāla al-Mudhhiba, attributed to al-Nuʿmān.[98] This compilation is obviously a typical product of the Ṭayyibī tradition as indicated not only by the presence of a Ṭayyibī text, the *Ghāyat al-Mawālīd* but also by its deference towards Fatimid intellectual heritage.

These are the only explicit references to the *Kashf* that I was able to find in later Ismaili literature. However, there are other hints that, along with several other Fatimid texts, the *Kashf* was an important source in the Ṭayyibī context. Indeed, several concepts found in the *Kashf* (and apparently nowhere else in Fatimid literature) have been incorporated in Ṭayyibī sources. The notion of *haykal* is an example of this Ṭayyibī revival of early Shiʿi and Ismaili concepts that had been seemingly neglected during the Fatimid period; in the framework of such a revival of themes that lean towards *ghuluww*,[99] the *Kashf* must have played a role as a witness of the *ghulāt* origins of Ismailism. Other illustrations of the influence that the *Kashf* may have had on the Ṭayyibī *daʿwa* include the abovementioned direct quotations of the *Kashf* in the *Zahr al-maʿānī*, but also some less direct hints. For instance, the *Zahr al-maʿānī* makes use of the rare expression *al-ʿayn al-ʿaẓīma*, found in Treatise V of the *Kashf*.[100] Another rare expression, the 'Greater Mary' (*Maryam al-kubrā*), also appears in another major Ṭayyibī source, the *Kanz al-walad*.[101]

In another passage of the *Zahr al-maʿānī*, the author relates miracles performed by the Fatimid Imam-Caliph al-Mustanṣir bi'llāh (d. 487/1094). Among these miracles is the Imam's appearance 'in the forms (*ṣuwar*) of the ten Imams, the domes of light' (*ẓahara bi-ṣuwar*

---

[98] On the *Risāla al-Mudhhiba*, see Y. Marquet, 'La pensée philosophique et religieuse du Qāḍī al-Nuʿmān à travers la *Risāla Muḏhiba*', *Bulletin d'Etudes Orientales*, 39/40 (1987–1988), pp. 141–181; D. De Smet, 'The *Risāla al-Muḏhiba* attributed to al-Qāḍī al-Nuʿmān', in *Fortress of the Intellect, Ismaili and Other Islamic Studies in Honour of Farhad Daftary*, ed. O. Ali-de-Unzaga (London and New York, 2011), pp. 59–79.

[99] On the new orientations of the Ṭayyibī *daʿwa*, see D. De Smet, 'Eléments chrétiens dans l'ismaélisme yéménite', pp. 45–53.

[100] See Idrīs ʿImād al-Dīn, *Zahr al-maʿānī*, pp. 130, 167, 193, 211, 217; cf. *Kashf* V, p. 97, § 13; p. 102, §23; p. 103, § 26. See also commentary of *Kashf* V, pp. 395–408.

[101] See Ibrāhīm b. al-Ḥusayn al-Ḥāmidī, *Kanz al-walad*, p. 212; cf. *Kashf* V, p. 97, § 13.

al-a'imma al-'ashara qubāb nūr); the text does not elaborate further on these 'domes'. The 'ten domes of light' are also mentioned by a much earlier Ṭayyibī *dā'ī*, the prolific 'Alī b. Muḥammad b. al-Walīd (d. 612/1215).[102] In a work which contains several quotations of Ja'far b. Manṣūr al-Yaman's works (but not the *Kashf*), the expression appears in a *ḥadīth* attributed to 'Alī b. Abī Ṭālib, and the domes are identified with the first ten Fatimid caliphs who precede 'the veiling of the son of our master al-Āmir', i.e. al-Ṭayyib.[103] It seems, therefore, that a *ḥadīth* of the ten domes was popular among Ṭayyibī authors — and well-known to them if we consider that it is alluded to only in these texts. But I have not been able to find any version of it, nor any other mention of it, except for the *ḥadīth* quoted in Treatise I, where Ja'far al-Ṣādiq speaks of his vision of 'ten domes of light'.[104] I will return to this *ḥadīth* — specifically to its relationship with *ghulāt* and Nuṣayri speculations.[105] What matters here is the reception of the *Kashf* in Ṭayyibī context and the hypothesis that the *Kashf* was a valuable resource for Ṭayyibī speculations, although, in the current state of our knowledge, it is not possible to evaluate the extent of its importance precisely.

In any case, one may state that the *Kashf* has survived down to the present day thanks to the Ṭayyibī transmission. The importance of this fact in the history of the *Kitāb al-Kashf* is not to be underestimated. Although the hypothesis that Ja'far b. Manṣūr al-Yaman indeed intervened on the *Kashf*, at least as an editor, is quite plausible, the possibility that the Ṭayyibī transmitters of the collection were responsible for some of the editorial arrangements should not be ruled out. Some of these arrangements may also date from a later Fatimid period — as is the case in other works by Ja'far b. Manṣūr al-Yaman which bear marks of successive reworkings, such as the *Fatarāt wa'l-qirānāt al-'ashar*.[106] But this should not lead us to dismiss the *early*

[102] On him, see I.K. Poonawala, "Alī b. al-Walīd', *EI3*.

[103] Alī b. Muḥammad b. al-Walīd, *Risālat tuḥfat al-murtād wa ghuṣṣat al-aḍdād*, in R. Strothmann, *Gnosis-Texte der Ismailiten*, p. 169.

[104] *Kashf* I, p. 7, §12.

[105] See commentary of *Kashf* I, pp. 139–142.

[106] See H. Halm, 'Zur Datierung des ismā'īlitischen "Buches der Zwischenzeiten und der zehn Konjunktionen" (Kitāb al-fatarāt wal-qirānāt al-'ašara) HS Tübingen Ma VI 297', *Die Welt des Orients*, 8/1 (1975), pp. 91–107.

Fatimid origin and the authenticity of the *Kashf* altogether. In spite of possible Ṭayyibī or Fatimid interventions (in the structure of the collection as a whole, or in specific treatises — particularly Treatise V), there is in fact no decisive argument causing us to doubt that most of the text was composed sometime under the reigns of the first two Fatimid caliphs — which corresponds to the time of activity of the Ismaili scholar Jaʿfar b. Manṣūr al-Yaman. As a matter of fact, I will present several arguments in favour of this hypothesis in the present study.

3. The problematic authorship of the *Kitāb al-Kashf*: some remarks on the corpus attributed to Jaʿfar b. Manṣūr al-Yaman

The attribution of the *Kashf* to Jaʿfar b. Manṣūr al-Yaman is based on the manuscript tradition, on the one hand, and on the scarce testimonies of much later sources, on the other hand. Yet, in spite of the late nature of the available evidence, the contents of the *Kashf* are consistent with Fatimid orientations such as the rejection of antinomianism. They are also consistent with other works attributed to Jaʿfar, as I will show occasionally in this study and in the footnotes to the translation. However, while this study aims at confirming that, for its main part, the *Kashf* is an early Fatimid composition, I will leave aside the question of the authorship until the rest of the corpus attributed to Jaʿfar b. Manṣūr al-Yaman is better known. Nevertheless, a brief presentation of this author and the corpus transmitted under his name is in order, to situate the *Kitāb al-Kashf* in relation to this literature — and to understand why the attribution of the text must remain an open question for now.

Jaʿfar b. Manṣūr al-Yaman was the son of Ibn Ḥawshab Manṣūr al-Yaman, the conqueror of Yemen on behalf of the Salamiyyan *daʿwa*. Abū al-Qāsim Ḥasan Ibn Ḥawshab, was an Iraqi Shiʿi from Kūfa. It is important to note that he was a learned man, having studied the Qurʾan, *ḥadīth* and *fiqh*. As he was walking on the banks of the Euphrates, distraught by the occultation of the Imam in 874, he met mysterious figures who captivated him with their esoteric knowledge of the Qurʾan, while holding out the promise of a meeting with the 'Imam of the Age'. They were Ismaili missionaries.

After taking the oath and joining the *daʿwa*, he was sent to Yemen in 881 by Muḥammad Abū al-Shalaghlagh, accompanied by another, younger, Yemeni *dāʿī*, ʿAlī b. al-Faḍl. His mission was to create a *dār al-hijra*, an 'emigration abode', on the model of the community founded by the Prophet Muḥammad when he left Mecca for Medina. It was in fact a territory to be placed under the authority of Salamiyya and preparing for the rise of the Mahdī. Ibn Ḥawshab managed to take several fortresses, a success which earned him the nickname of Manṣūr al-Yaman, 'the One Assisted (by God) for the conquest of Yemen'.[107]

After the death of Ibn Ḥawshab in 302/914–5, the Fatimids appointed as head of the Yemeni *daʿwa* a certain ʿAbdallāh b. ʿAbbās al-Shāwirī, thus overlooking Ibn Ḥawshab's sons. It is Ibn Mālik who reports the consequences this had for the Yemeni *daʿwa*, whereas Idrīs ʿImād al-Dīn only mentions that Jaʿfar b. Manṣūr al-Yaman eventually left Yemen to join the Imam.[108] According to Ibn Mālik, Abū al-Ḥasan Manṣūr, the eldest of Ibn Ḥawshab's sons travelled to the Fatimid court in Ifrīqiyā to plead his cause, but the messenger sent to appoint al-Shāwirī as *dāʿī* had already left. Enraged by what he considered an act of usurpation, and despite Jaʿfar's attempts to preserve the unity of the Ismaili community, Abū al-Ḥasan murdered ʿAbdallāh b. ʿAbbās and recovered his father's conquests, renouncing Ismailism and his allegiance to the Fatimids. Jaʿfar was the only one of his siblings to remain loyal to them, and apparently the only one to survive the period of turmoil that started with the revolt of Abū al-Ḥasan Manṣūr, who was subsequently assassinated. Jaʿfar therefore left Yemen, as the situation there had become too unstable. The exact date of his departure is not known. Both Ibn Mālik and Idrīs ʿImād al-Dīn, state that Jaʿfar left Yemen to join the Imam in Ifrīqiyā. Ibn Mālik situates

---

[107] On Ibn Ḥawshab, see H. Halm, 'Die Sīrat Ibn Ḥaušab': die ismailitische daʿwa im Jemen und die Fatimiden', *Die Welt des Orients*, 12 (1981), pp. 107–135; idem, 'Ebn Ḥawšab, Abu'l-Qāsim Ḥasan', *EIr*; W. Madelung, 'Manṣūr al-Yaman', *EI2*.

[108] Compare Ibn Mālik, *Kashf asrār al-bāṭiniyya wa-akhbār al-qarāmiṭa*, ed. M.Z. al-Kawtharī (Cairo, 1939), p. 40; Idrīs ʿImād al-Dīn, *ʿUyūn al-akhbār*, ed. Y.S. Faṭṭūm (London, Beirut, Damascus, Amman, 2008), vol. 5, p. 74; ed. A.F. Sayyid, vol. 7, p. 8. Note that in both passages, Idrīs ʿImād al-Dīn claims that it was Ibn Ḥawshab himself who appointed ʿAbdallāh b. ʿAbbās al-Shāwirī as his successor.

this departure within the conflict over Ibn Ḥawshab's succession. He further adds that Jaʿfar 'left to join (*kharaja ilā*) the son of ʿUbayd [the first Fatimid caliph] who was named al-Qāʾim [bi-Amr Allāh]'.[109] Several scholars assumed that Jaʿfar went to Ifrīqiyā under the reign of al-Qāʾim, that is, between 322/934 and 334/946.[110] This would imply that he stayed some twenty years in Yemen after his father died, in spite of the less than favourable circumstances. It seems more likely that Jaʿfar attached himself to the service of al-Qāʾim before the latter became a caliph in his own right. Al-Qāʾim held important functions within the Fatimid state as early as 912: he was then appointed as the official successor of ʿAbd Allāh al-Mahdī and charged with the suppression of the Kutāma revolt, which was a reaction to the execution of Abū ʿAbd Allāh al-Shīʿī the previous year. It is therefore possible that the information provided by Ibn Mālik is to be interpreted differently: Jaʿfar b. Manṣūr al-Yaman travelled to North Africa sometime after al-Qāʾim had become the second strongman of the Fatimid caliphate, but before he became the new Imam-Caliph. The many allusions in the *Kashf* to al-Qāʾim (not to mention the fact that he is explicitly mentioned), the meaning given to the notion of Proof (*ḥujja*),[111] and the fact that I deem the *Kashf* to have been composed under the reigns of the first two Fatimid caliphs, seem to be in line with this interpretation — provided, of course, we admit that the *Kitāb al-Kashf* is for the most part correctly attributed to Jaʿfar b. Manṣūr al-Yaman, for which I see no strong counter-argument.

In any case, Jaʿfar is then seen taking part in the war against the Kharijite rebel Abū Yazīd which nearly ended the Fatimid caliphate.[112] This rebellion occupied the last two years of al-Qāʾim's reign, and the first of his successor's, al-Manṣūr biʾllāh (r. 334–341/946–953). Jaʿfar is said to have participated in the fighting and several fragments of his

---

[109] Ibn Mālik, *Kashf asrār al-bāṭiniyya*, p. 40.

[110] See e.g. Madelung, 'Das Imamat', p. 81, n. 197; Poonawala, *Biobibliography*, p. 70; Halm, 'D̲j̲aʿfar b. Manṣūr al-Yaman', *EI2*; Haji, 'Jaʿfar b. Manṣur al-Yaman', *EIr*.

[111] Particularly in Treatise V. See commentary below, pp. 390–408.

[112] On this episode, see H. Halm, *The Empire of the Mahdi*, pp. 298–325; M. Brett, *The Rise of the Fatimids*, pp. 165–175.

poetry on the military campaign and the Fatimid victories have been preserved.[113]

His dates of birth and death are uncertain. James W. Morris believes that Jaʿfar was born around the year 270/883,[114] and that he must have died before al-Qāḍī al-Nuʿmān wrote the *Iftitāḥ al-daʿwa* around 346/957.[115] For his part, in the introduction to his edition of the *Kitāb al-Kashf*, Musṭafā Ghālib gives the year 270 H. as the approximate date of birth, and 347 H. as the date of death.[116] This corresponds to the estimate of Morris, but Ghālib provides no explanation nor sources for

---

[113] For Jaʿfar b. Manṣūr al-Yaman's biography, the main sources are Ibn Mālik's *Kashf asrār al-bāṭiniyya wa akhbār al-qarāmiṭa*, Jaʿfar's partially preserved poetry which attests his presence at the Fatimid court at the time of Abū Yazīd's rebellion, and an anecdote involving him at the beginning of al-Muʿizz's reign and reported in the *Sīrat al-ustadh Jawdhar*. According to James W. Morris, Jaʿfar's presence can also be deduced during certain episodes of his father's life as reported by al-Qāḍī al-Nuʿmān in his *Iftitāḥ al-daʿwa*: on several occasions, al-Nuʿmān bases his account on the direct testimony of an unnamed witness who is close to Ibn Ḥawshab, and whom Morris deems to be Jaʿfar himself; for an overview of what is known of Jaʿfar's life, see J.W. Morris, *The Master and the Disciple. An Early Islamic Spiritual Dialogue* (London and New York, 2001), pp. 22–27; D. Hollenberg, 'Interpretation after the End of Days', pp. 48–56. See also H. Halm, 'Dja̱ʿfar b. Manṣūr al-Yaman', *EI2*; idem, *The Empire of the Mahdi*, pp. 286–288; S.M. Stern, 'Jaʿfar Ibn Mansūr al-Yaman's Poems on the Rebellion of Abū Yazīd', in idem, *Studies in Early Ismāʿīlism*, pp. 146–152; H. Haji, 'Jaʿfar b. Manṣūr al-Yaman', *EIr*.

[114] If we accept with Morris that the direct testimony on which al-Nuʿmān bases his report of the departure of ʿAbdallāh al-Shīʿī to Ifrīqiya in 280/893 is indeed that of Jaʿfar; see J.W. Morris, *The Master and the Disciple*, pp. 23–24 and related footnotes. See also previous footnote.

[115] See J.W. Morris, *The Master and the Disciple*, p. 24: 'It seems quite likely (although this is only one possible hypothesis) that al-Qāḍī al-Nuʿmān's massive but unacknowledged 'borrowing' from Jaʿfar's *Sīrat Ibn Ḥawshab* presupposes that he was already dead at the time of its writing (ca. 346/957).' Like D. Hollenberg, 'Interpretation after the End of Days', p. 54, I am not convinced by this conjecture and find more convincing Abbas Hamdani's remark that Jaʿfar is not named among the notables who accompanied the Imam-caliph al-Muʿizz to Egypt in 362/973, which prompts him to estimate that Jaʿfar must have lived 'somewhere between 270/883 and 360/970'; see A. Hamdani, 'An Early Fatimid Source on the Time and Authorship of the *Rasāʾil Iḫwān al-Ṣafāʾ*', *Arabica*, 26/1 (1979), p. 65; cited by J.W. Morris, *The Master and the Disciple*, p. 53 note 46.

[116] Jaʿfar b. Manṣūr al-Yaman, *Kitāb al-Kashf*, ed. M. Ghālib, p. 13.

these dates. In the introduction to his edition of the *Sarāʾir wa-asrār al-nutaqāʾ*, another work by Jaʿfar, he admits that he was unable to establish a date of birth, but gives, 'according to some Ismaili manuscripts', the year 380/990 as the date of death...[117] It is difficult to explain this inconsistency, especially since both editions were published in the same year (1984). Morris further points out that in the introduction to his edition of Ibrāhīm al-Ḥamīdī's *Kanz al-Walad* (1971), Ghālib gives the dates as 240 H. to 347 H.[118] In all likehood, Jaʿfar b. Manṣūr al-Yaman died early in the reign of al-Muʿizz (r. 341–365/953–975), as Morris believes, and not towards the end of that reign, as suggested by Madelung based on a passage in the *Taʾwīl al-zakāt* that he interprets as an allusion to the problematic succession of that al-Muʿizz.[119] D. Hollenberg has proposed a date of death of ca. 348/960, 'for the sake of convention', since, he argues, 'most of the works ascribed to him were composed during the rule of al-Muʿizz li-Dīn Allāh'.[120]

The reception of Jaʿfar b. Manṣūr al-Yaman's intellectual contribution is somewhat ambiguous. On the one hand, the Ṭayyibī tradition has considered him one of the major Fatimid authors of works of 'esoteric truths' (*ḥaqāʾiq*), alongside Ḥamīd al-Dīn al-Kirmānī and al-Muʾayyad fīʾl-Dīn al-Shīrāzī. A few references to his work during Fatimid times indicate that his writings (or those transmitted under his name) were essential in the initiatory training of the members of the *daʿwa*. Indeed, al-Qāḍī al-Nuʿmān refers to his *Kitāb al-Riḍāʿ fīʾl-bātin* as a landmark in the initiatory progression of the Ismaili neophytes, but without naming its author.[121]

Later, in a chapter in which he lists the Ismaili works one should read before delving into his *Rāḥat al-ʿaql*, Ḥamīd al-Dīn al-Kirmānī

---

[117] Jaʿfar b. Manṣūr al-Yaman, *Sarāʾir wa-asrār al-nutaqāʾ*, ed. M. Ghālib (Beirut, 1984), p. 8.

[118] See Ibrāhīm b. al-Ḥusayn al-Ḥāmidī, *Kanz al*-walad, p. 43, n. 1; cited by J.W. Morris, *The Master and the Disciple*, p. 53, n. 46.

[119] See W. Madelung, 'Das Imamat', p. 96, n. 282; J.W. Morris, *The Master and the Disciple*, p. 51, n. 42.

[120] See D. Hollenberg, 'Interpretation after the End of Days', p. 54.

[121] As noted by I.K. Poonawala, 'The Chronology of al-Qāḍī al-Nuʿmān's Works', *Arabica*, 65/1–2 (2018), p. 145. See al-Qāḍī al-Nuʿmān, *Asās al-taʾwīl*, ed. ʿĀ. Tāmir (Beirut, 1960), p. 316

first mentions 'books on the exoteric aspect of worship', naming three of al-Qāḍī al-Nuʿmān's compositions. Turning to the 'books of exegesis' (*kutub al-ta'wīl*) dealing with the 'esoteric worship that is attached to knowledge' (*al-ʿibāda al-bāṭiniyya al-mutaʿalliqa bi'l-ʿilm*), he then mentions 'the books of Jaʿfar b. Manṣūr al-Yaman, and other masters (*shuyūkh*) of the *daʿwa* who are known for the appropriateness of their method (*bi-sadād al-ṭarīqa*), such as Abū Ḥātim al-Rāzī, Muḥammad b. Aḥmad b. al-Nakhshabī [i.e. al-Nasafī] and Abū Yaʿqūb al-Sijzī [i.e. al-Sijistānī]'.[122] This indicates that at the time of al-Kirmānī, Jaʿfar's works still held importance.

Yet, as noted by D. Hollenberg, 'it is likely that [Jaʿfar b. Manṣūr al-Yaman's] stature in the later Ismāʿīlī tradition was greater than his importance in his own day'.[123] There are two main reasons for this statement: first, he is rarely mentioned in contemporary or near-contemporary Fatimid sources. Second, strangely enough, al-Qāḍī al-Nuʿmān never seems to mention him directly, although they both 'supposedly lived in the caliphal capital' at the same time,[124] and both were intellectuals of the Fatimid court. The nature of al-Qāḍī al-Nuʿmān's non-doctrinal works (i.e. his chronicles and works of history such as the *Iftitāḥ al-daʿwa* or the *Majālis wa'l-musāyarāt*) would indeed allow us to expect at least one mention of Jaʿfar b. Manṣūr al-Yaman, an author whom the subsequent Ismaili tradition held in such high esteem. Yet, there seems to be none. Hollenberg goes on to suggest a reason for this: 'This could be explained by the fact that from [al-Qāḍī al-Nuʿmān's] and Jaʿfar's point of view the true "author" of such *ta'wīl*, was, after all the Imam al-Muʿizz li-dīn Allāh, not the *dāʿī* himself.'[125]

While this hypothesis is not to be dismissed, I believe, however, that al-Nuʿmān's odd silence regarding Jaʿfar, and more generally, the relative silence surrounding his works during the Fatimid period, could be further explained by a combination of two additional factors,

[122] Ḥamīd al-Dīn al-Kirmānī, *Rāḥat al-ʿaql*, ed. M. Kāmil Ḥusayn and M. Muṣṭafā Ḥilmī (Cairo, 1953), p. 22; ed. M. Ghālib (Beirut, 1983), p. 109.

[123] D. Hollenberg, 'Interpretation after the End of Days', p. 49.

[124] Ibid., p. 55.

[125] Ibid., p. 65.

that I propose as hypotheses: 1) the existence of a rivalry between al-Nuʿmān and Jaʿfar; 2) the fact that towards the end of his life, Jaʿfar, who had been very close to the Imam-Caliphs al-Qāʾim and al-Manṣūr, was less favoured by the new caliph, al-Muʿizz, who preferred al-Nuʿmān.

These two hypotheses are based on my interpretation of two of the rare anecdotes transmitted by the sources on Jaʿfar. The first of these appears in the *Sīrat al-ustadh Jawdhar* where he is shown as being financially supported by the Imam while he was about to be forced out of his house in al-Manṣūriyya. Although the Imam of the time, al-Muʿizz, gives the order to help Jaʿfar and to settle his debt, he also manifests some irritation towards Jaʿfar for putting himself in that difficult situation and exhorts him not to do it again.[126] It appears that the respect Jaʿfar had earned in his many years of faithful service to the dynasty prompted the Imam to support him. Yet, the tone of al-Muʿizz's letter and the exasperation he expresses seem to point to the fact that at that time, towards the end of Jaʿfar's life, the latter's prestige was fading, and that he was deemed somewhat out of date. One might also question the intentions of Jawdhar in reporting this episode; it can be suspected that, had Jaʿfar enjoyed the full favour of the Imam, Jawdhar may have been more hesitant to show him in such a shameful position.

The second anecdote appears in a much later source than the *Sīrat al-ustadh Jawdhar* and should not be taken at face value as it bears quite obvious marks of embellishment. In his *ʿUyūn al-akhbār*, Idrīs ʿImād al-Dīn (d. 872/1468) briefly presents the virtues of Jaʿfar b. Manṣūr al-Yaman, in an effort to portray him as a *dāʿī* from a higher level than al-Nuʿmān, whom Idrīs had just been praising in the preceding section. According to Idrīs, al-Nuʿmān once complained to the Imam that Jaʿfar did not visit him while he was sick. As a response, the Imam handed him books by Jaʿfar, and al-Nuʿmān then understood that his rank was lower than that of Jaʿfar whom the Imam refers to as 'your master' (*mawlāk*). After that, al-Nuʿmān ran to Jaʿfar's house and threw himself at his feet, 'without disdain nor pride, and without jealousy for the loftiness of his position' (*ghayr mustankif wa-lā*

---

[126] See H. Haji, *Inside the Immaculate Portal. A History from Early Fatimid Archives* (London and New York, 2012), pp. 139–140 (Arabic: pp. 146–147).

mustakbir wa-lā ḥāsid lahu ʿalā ʿuluww maqāmihi). The implicit meaning of the story, as intended by Idrīs, is that the *bātin* (represented by Jaʿfar) is superior to the *ẓāhir* (represented by al-Nuʿmān). What is interesting here is the conciliatory intentions of the text, which clearly attempts to reconcile Jaʿfar and al-Nuʿmān while establishing a hierarchy between them at the same time, as if Idrīs were taking sides. But why would they need to be reconciled if there was no tension between them to begin with? Although the veracity of the story is questionable, it bears some accents of authenticity — especially in the final paragraph of the anecdote where, notwithstanding the happy ending, Idrīs's very choice of words suggests that the problem may indeed have been one of 'pride' and 'jealousy'.[127]

Al-Qāḍī al-Nuʿmān was younger than Jaʿfar and although he had been in the service of the Fatimid caliphs from the beginning, it was apparently not until the reign of al-Muʿizz that he became a major figure of the Fatimid intellectual milieu. His fortune under the dynasty, as well as that of his descendants who occupied high positions in the Fatimid state for several generations, may explain why Jaʿfar b. Manṣūr al-Yaman was progressively relegated to the background, although his works continued to be studied by the Ismaili *dāʿīs*, as attested by al-Kirmānī's testimony.

Ismail K. Poonawala has listed some fifteen[128] works attributed to Jaʿfar b. Manṣūr al-Yaman, based on known manuscripts or attestations

---

[127] See Idrīs ʿImād al-Dīn, *ʿUyūn al-akhbār*, ed. M. Fākhūrī and M. Kamāl (London, Beirut, Damascus, Amman, 2007), vol. 6, pp. 68–70.

[128] I.K. Poonawala, *Biobibliography*, pp. 70–75. Not all fifteen are 'works' in the strict sense: no. 15 is merely 'a chapter by (*faṣl ʿan*) (. . .) Jaʿfar b. Manṣūr al-Yaman'. Poonawala does not provide a description of the contents of this *faṣl*. No. 13 refers to Jaʿfar's poetry, but only fragments are extant, and they may not have been part of a single written and composed *qaṣīda* or *dīwān*. H. Feki provided another list of Jaʿfar's works, which does not include Jaʿfar's poetry or the abovementioned *faṣl*, nor the *Adilla wa'l-shawāhid*, the *Ta'wīl sūrat al-nisā'* and the *Ta'wīl al-ḥurūf al-muʿjam* (for brief presentations of these works and references, see below). He nevertheless reaches a number of twelve works by counting the *Kitāb al-Rushd wa'l-hidāya* (although he ascribes it to Ibn Ḥawshab), as well as a *al-Tawārīkh wa'l-siyar*, which Feki claims is mentioned in the *Kanz al-walad* and the *ʿUyūn al-akhbār*; see H. Feki, *Les Idées religieuses et philosophiques de l'ismaélisme fatimide*, pp. 16–19; for the *Tawārīkh wa'l-siyar*, see ibid., p. 16, no. 1. However, it seems Feki has mistaken an expression used by

in Ismaili literature, since this list is nowhere to be found in its entirety in Ismaili literature. The corpus transmitted under Jaʿfar b. Manṣūr al-Yaman's name remains largely understudied and has not yet been thoroughly examined until now, in spite of a handful of scholarly studies.[129] Recently, David Hollenberg has provided the first monograph focusing on a corpus he labelled '*daʿwa* literature' and which comprises most of Jaʿfar b. Manṣūr al-Yaman's works; this marked tremendous progress in our knowledge of this corpus, its symbols and exegetical techniques.[130] Yet, much remains to be done to fully apprehend it. This would require critical editions of the works of the corpus to begin with. So far,five works attributed to Jaʿfar have received a full edition, but only two are critical ones, namely the editions of the *Kitāb al-Kashf* and the *Kitāb al-ʿĀlim wa'l-ghulām*.[131] A

---

the author of the *Sarā'ir al-nuṭaqā'* and the *Ta'wīl al-zakāt* for a book title; the expression 'the people of stories and biographies' (*ahl* or *aṣḥāb al-tawārīkh wa'l-siyar*) actually refers to the 'exoteric' historical literature, as opposed to the esoteric teachings of the *daʿwa*, particularly with regard to prophetic stories. For an attempt to organize chronologically the works attributed to Jaʿfar, see D. Hollenberg, 'Interpretation after the End of Days', pp. 59–61. Hollenberg does not include the poetry, the *faṣl*, and the pseudo-*Tawārīkh wa'l-siyar*. He still reaches a number of 14 works by counting the *Sarā'ir al-nuṭaqā'* and the *Asrār al-nuṭaqā'* as two separate works, and by adding a title unknown to Poonawala and Feki: the *Uṣūl al-dīn bi-maʿrifat al-ta'wīl*. On the latter work, see below.

[129] I will refer to these in the footnotes to the list of Jaʿfar's works below.

[130] D. Hollenberg, *Beyond the Qur'an. Early Ismāʿīlī Ta'wīl and the Secrets of the Prophets* (Columbia, SC, 2016), esp. list of sources, pp. 45–49. The list includes most of the works generally attributed to Jaʿfar b. Manṣūr al-Yaman's works, as well as the *Kitāb al-Rushd wa'l-hidāya* by Ibn Ḥawshab, the *Asās al-ta'wīl* and the *Risāla al-mudhhiba* by al-Qāḍī al-Nuʿmān.

[131] Edition and English translation by J.W. Morris, *The Master and the Disciple*. See also al-Majdūʿ, *Fihrist*, pp. 134–135; W. Ivanow, *Guide to Ismaili literature*, p. 36, XI no. 42; idem, *Ismaili literature*, p. 18, no. 10; P. Kraus, 'La bibliographie ismaëlienne de W. Ivanow', p. 486; M. Goriawala, *A Descriptive Catalogue*, p. 13, no. 18; I.K. Poonawala, *Biobibliography*, pp. 74–75, no. 14; H. Feki, *Les Idées religieuses et philosophiques de l'ismaélisme fatimide*, p. 17, no. 5; A. Gacek, *Catalogue of Arabic Manuscripts in the Library of the Institute of Ismaili Studies* (London, 1984), vol. 1, p. 3, no. 6; F. de Blois, *Arabic, Persian and Gujarati Manuscripts*, pp. 5–9; D. Cortese, *Ismaili and other Arabic Manuscripts. A Descriptive Catalogue of Manuscripts in the Library of the Institute of Ismaili Studies* (London and New York, 2000), p. 33, no. 52/1013; D. Hollenberg,

precise analysis of these works and those unpublished is still needed, for instance, to ascertain their authorship and/or to date them — which could be effected by comparing the doctrines, exegeses and technical vocabulary used in these works, and paying close attention to the differences between them, thus possibly highlighting evolutions in Fatimid Ismaili doctrine. This corpus is indeed central for the production of a history of Fatimid thought.

Indeed, while there is little question that this corpus is to be dated to the Fatimid period, it should be possible to propose a more precise dating, since Ismaili doctrine evolved during this period[132] — as exemplified by Madelung's study on the Ismaili doctrine of the Imamate.[133] Setting aside Jaʿfar b. Manṣūr al-Yaman's poetry,[134] his biography of his father Ibn Ḥawshab,[135] the *Kitāb al-ʿĀlim*

Beyond the Qur'an, p. 46. See also the studies by W. Ivanow, 'The Book of the Teacher and the Pupil', in W. Ivanow, *Studies in Early Persian Ismailism*, (Leiden, 1948), pp. 85–113; H. Corbin, 'L'initiation ismaélienne ou l'ésotérisme et le Verbe', *Eranos Jahrbuch*, 39 (1970), pp. 41–142; reed. in idem, *L'Homme et son Ange. Initiation et chevalerie spirituelle* (Paris, 1983), pp. 81–205; idem, 'Un roman initiatique ismaélien', *Cahiers de civilisation médiévale*, 15/57 (1972), pp. 1–25; 15/58 (1972), pp. 121–142.

[132] As previously mentioned, such an attempt was made by D. Hollenberg, 'Interpretation after the End of Days', pp. 59–61, but the reasons for the proposed chronological classification are not detailed for all the works.

[133] W. Madelung, 'Das Imamat'.

[134] I.K. Poonawala, *Biobibliography*, p. 74, no. 13. Extracts of Jaʿfar's poems have been preserved by Idrīs ʿImād al-Dīn in his *ʿUyūn al-akhbār*. S.M. Stern had collected them for a work on the genealogy of the Fatimids, which he prefaced with biographical data on Jaʿfar b. Manṣūr al-Yaman. He did not have time to complete this work before his demise, and the fragments were posthumously collected in chapter 7 of his *Studies in Early Ismāʿīlism*. These poems were composed during the military campaign against the Khārijite rebel Abū Yazīd; see S.M. Stern, 'Jaʿfar Ibn Mansūr al-Yaman's Poems on the Rebellion of Abū Yazīd'.

[135] W. Ivanow, *Ismaili literature*, p. 21, no. 23; I.K. Poonawala, *Biobibliography*, p. 74, no. 12. This work, presumably composed by Jaʿfar b. Manṣūr al-Yaman, is lost. H. Halm partially reconstructed its contents, thanks to three later sources that relied directly on it. Two of them are Ismaili (the *Iftitāḥ al-daʿwa* by al-Qāḍī al-Nuʿmān, and the *ʿUyūn al-akhbār* by Idrīs ʿImād al-Dīn), while the third is the *Kashf asrār al-bāṭiniyya wa akhbār al-qarāmiṭa*, a polemical anti-Ismaili work by the Sunni author Muḥammad b. Mālik; see H. Halm, 'Die Sīrat Ibn Ḥaušab', pp. 107–135.

wa'l-ghulām,[136] and the *Ta'wīl al-Ḥurūf al-mu'jam min-hā*[137], and focusing on the exegetical corpus transmitted under his name, it seems that it should be divided in at least two groups, depending on whether the works contain Neoplatonic features and technical vocabulary and whether they refer to a certain cosmology or not.

The first group of works generally develops classical Shi'i themes such as the distinction between *ẓāhir* and *bāṭin*, or the role of the Imam in enforcing the latter and, therefore, in transmitting and teaching the true interpretation (*ta'wīl*) of the revelation (*tanzīl*). It contains Qur'anic exegeses close to, if not common with, those found in what M.M. Bar-Asher has identified as the (proto-)Twelver Shi'i 'pre-Buwayhid school of exegesis'. It also makes use of the 'personalized commentary', a traditional Shi'i hermeneutical technique which identifies elements mentioned in the Qur'an with Good or Evil as

[136] The authorship and origin of this work are uncertain. As an initiatory tale staging the conversion of a young neophyte and his village to Ismailism, its literary style stands out in the corpus attributed to Ja'far b. Manṣūr al-Yaman. J.W. Morris' introduction to the edition and translation of the text barely discusses its attribution and seems to take it for granted. Such a discussion may be found in F. De Blois, *Arabic, Persian and Gujarati Manuscripts*, pp. 5–9, esp. p. 7, where it is suggested that 'the book is very likely to be an anonymous work from the pre-Fatimid or early Fatimid period which the tradition subsequently ascribed, now to Ja'far, and now to his father'. Other scholars have noticed the unique style of the *Kitāb al-'Ālim wa'l-ghulām*: H. Feki thus writes that 'ni le fond ni la forme ne ressemblent à ce que nous connaissons par ailleurs de Ja'far [b. Manṣūr al-Yaman]'; see H. Feki, *Les Idées religieuses et philosophiques de l'ismaélisme fatimide*, p. 17. Before him, P. Kraus stated the following: 'Il semble certain que cet ouvrage représente une phase plus ancienne de la littérature ismaélienne que tous les autres écrits conservés dans les collections Dâwûdiya.'; see P. Kraus, 'La bibliographie ismaëlienne de W. Ivanow', p. 486. This statement may be excessive, but it nevertheless points to the uniqueness of the work when compared to Ja'far's other books. The debate on its attribution therefore remains open.

[137] See al-Majdū', *Fihrist*, p. 153; W. Ivanow, *Ismaili Literature*, p. 22, no. 21; I.K. Poonawala, *Biobibliography*, p. 73, no. 10; A. Gacek, *Catalogue*, vol. 1, p. 118, no. 141; D. Cortese, *Arabic Ismaili Manuscripts. The Zāhid 'Alī Collection* (London and New York, 2003), pp. 182–183, no. 166; D. Hollenberg, *Beyond the Qur'an*, p. 46; idem, '*Anta anā wa- anā minka* ("You are me, and I am from you"): A Quasi-Nuṣayrī Fragment on the Intellect in the Early Ismā'īlī Treatise *Kitāb Ta'wīl ḥurūf al-mu'jam*', in *Arabic Humanities, Islamic Thought. Essays in Honor of Everett K. Rowson*, ed. J. E. Lowry and S. M. Toorawa (Leiden, 2017), pp. 50–66.

protagonists of the beginnings of Islam;[138] the use of this type of interpretation illustrates that the Ismailis had fully adopted the Shiʿi historiography of the succession of the Prophet Muḥammad, according to which ʿAlī's right to rule and guide the Islamic community was usurped by the first three caliphs of Islam. All these themes are found in the *Kitāb al-Kashf*.

Obviously, this first group of works also contains specifically Ismaili features. Thus, the classical form of 'personalized commentary' which interprets Qur'anic terms as allusions to historical persons is adapted to Ismaili orientations: rather than being merely referred to historical protagonists from the beginnings of Islam, Qur'anic verses are also understood as referring to ranks of the Ismaili *daʿwa* hierarchy, such as the Proof (*ḥujja*) or the Summoner (*dāʿī*). Also, the art of *ta'wīl* extends 'beyond the Qur'an', to Islamic rituals (e.g. the meaning of prayer) and natural elements (e.g. water, sky, earth, etc.). In general, exegeses revolving around *daʿwa*-related themes, and the corollary theme of initiation, are characteristic features of early Ismailism. One should also mention the importance of the Mahdī/Qā'im figure, which was always an essential feature of Ismaili doctrine even after the rise to power of the Fatimids, which was based on messianic claims that were subsequently toned down.

The first group includes the following works:

Kitāb al-Kashf;
Kitāb al-Riḍāʿ fi'l-bātin;[139]
al-Shawāhid wa'l-bayān;[140]

[138] On the notion of 'personalized commentary', an expression forged by M.A. Amir-Moezzi, see above, pp. 15 ff and below, commentary of *Kashf* I, pp. 148 ff.

[139] This work has been uncritically edited by Ḥusām Khaḍḍūr. See also al-Majdūʿ, *Fihrist*, pp. 138–139; W. Ivanow, *Guide to Ismaili literature*, p. 36, XI no. 46; idem, *Ismaili literature*, p. 22, no. 20; M. Goriawala, *A Descriptive Catalogue*, p. 16, no. 23; I.K. Poonawala, *Biobibliography*, p. 73, no. 7; H. Feki, *Les Idées religieuses et philosophiques de l'ismaélisme fatimide*, p. 18, no. 9; D. Hollenberg, *Beyond the Qur'an*, p. 48. A. Gacek, *Catalogue*, p. 48, no. 57; D. Cortese, *Arabic Ismaili Manuscripts*, pp. 79–80, no. 63; F. Gillon, 'Ismaili Ta'wīl of Religious Rites'.

[140] This work remains unedited, but I wish to thank Arzina Lalani who has been working on an edition of the text and has kindly provided me with a draft version of her work. See al-Majdūʿ, *Fihrist*, pp. 190–191; W. Ivanow, *Guide to Ismaili literature*,

Kitāb al-Farā'iḍ wa-ḥudūd al-dīn.[141] In all known manuscripts, the *Farā'iḍ* is followed by an extract of a *Kitāb al-Adilla wa'l-shawāhid* attributed to Jaʿfar b. Manṣūr al-Yaman, which seems otherwise lost.[142]

While all works attributed to Jaʿfar b. Manṣūr al-Yaman more or less fit the description above, the second group contains extra features, absent from the works of the first group:[143] a cosmological system influenced

---

p. 36, XI no. 49; idem, *Ismaili literature*, p. 21, no. 16; M. Goriawala, *A Descriptive Catalogue*, pp. 16–17, no. 24; I.K. Poonawala, *Biobibliography*, pp. 71–72, no. 1; idem, 'Ismāʿīlī *ta'wīl* of the Qur'an'; H. Feki, *Les Idées religieuses et philosophiques de l'ismaélisme fatimide*, p. 18, no. 8; A. Gacek, *Catalogue*, pp. 118–119, no. 142; D. Cortese, *Arabic Ismaili Manuscripts*, pp. 170–171, no.153; F. de Blois, *Arabic, Persian and Gujarati Manuscripts*, pp. 11–12; D. Hollenberg, *Beyond the Qur'an*, p. 47.

141 This work reproduces the letter sent by the first Fatimid caliph ʿAbd Allāh al-Mahdī to the Ismaili community in Yemen in order to assert the legitimacy of his claim to the caliphate, mainly through genealogical arguments. Apart from this letter, edited by H. Hamdani, the work remains unedited; on this letter, see H. Hamdani, *On the Genealogy of Fatimid Caliphs (Statement on Mahdī's Communication to the Yemen on the Real and Esoteric Names of his Hidden Predecessors)* (Cairo, 1958); A. Hamdani and F. De Blois, 'A Re-examination of al-Mahdī's Letter to the Yemenites on the Genealogy of the Fatimid Caliphs', *Journal of the Royal Asiatic Society*, 115 (1983), pp. 173–207; M. Brett, *The Rise of the Fatimids*, pp. 36–38, 112–116. On the *Farā'iḍ*, see also al-Majdūʿ, *Fihrist*, pp.187–188; W. Ivanow, *Guide to Ismaili literature*, p. 36, XI no. 45; id, *Ismaili literature*, p. 22, no. 19; P. Kraus, 'La bibliographie ismaëlienne de W. Ivanow', p. 486; M. Goriawala, *A Descriptive Catalogue*, p. 14, no. 20; I.K. Poonawala, *Biobibliography*, p. 73, no. 6; idem, 'Ismāʿīlī *ta'wīl* of the Qur'an'; H. Feki, *Les Idées religieuses et philosophiques de l'ismaélisme fatimide*, p. 19, no. 12; A. Gacek, *Catalogue*, p. 42, no. 49; D. Cortese, *Ismaili and other Arabic Manuscripts*, p. 34, no. 53/928; eadem, *Arabic Ismaili Manuscripts*, pp. 68–69, no. 53; M.M. Bar-Asher, 'Outlines of Early Ismāʿīlī-Fātimid Qur'an Exegesis', pp. 263, 272; F. de Blois, *Arabic, Persian and Gujarati Manuscripts*, p. 13; D. Hollenberg, *Beyond the Qur'an*, pp. 46–47.

142 Al-Majdūʿ, *Fihrist*, p. 188; P. Kraus, 'La bibliographie ismaëlienne de W. Ivanow', p. 487; W. Ivanow, *Ismaili Literature*, p. 22; M. Goriawala, *A Descriptive Catalogue*, p. 14, no. 20; I.K. Poonawala, *Biobibliography*, p. 72, no. 4; A. Gacek, *Catalogue*, p. 42, no. 49; F. de Blois, *Arabic, Persian and Gujarati Manuscripts*, pp. 13–14.

143 With some minor exceptions. See e.g. the occurrence of the term *jārī* ('flow'), which goes hand in hand with the cosmological system found in the second group, in *Kashf* II, p. 48, § 21; see commentary of *Kashf* II, p. 198. Another example is the 'philosophical' paragraph in *Kashf* V, pp. 111–112, § 39. However, inasmuch as these passages stand as exceptions within the *Kashf*, the latter can hardly be included in the

by Greek philosophy (*al-ʿaql/al-nafs*: the Intellect/the Soul), and the use of philosophical vocabulary, by which I mean the Arabic technical vocabulary that resulted from the movement of translation of Greek philosophical works, such as the pairs *biʾl-quwwa/biʾl-fiʿl* (in potentiality/in actuality) or *rūḥanī/jismānī* (spiritual/bodily), or the notions of *jawhar* (substance), *kawn wa-fasād* (generation and corruption), etc.

The second group of works includes the following:

Sarāʾir al-nutaqāʾ;[144]
Taʾwīl al-zakāt;[145]

---

second group where the use of philosophical concepts is not anecdotical but is fully part of the intellectual system. Such traces of a vocabulary specific to the second group may indicate that the *Kashf* was slightly reworked or marginally corrected at a later stage.

[144] The *Sarāʾir* has been edited with the *Asrār al-nutaqāʾ* as a single work by Muṣṭafā Ghālib: Jaʿfar b. Manṣūr al-Yaman, *Sarāʾir wa-asrār al-nutaqāʾ*. More recently, D. Hollenberg has critically edited and translated the prologue of the *Sarāʾir*; see D. Hollenberg, 'Interpretation after the End of Days', pp. 211–239. I leave out the *Asrār al-nutaqāʾ* here, because I agree with D. Hollenberg's conclusion that it was not composed by the same author as the *Sarāʾir*; while both works date from al-Muʿizz's reign, the *Asrār* is slightly later than the *Sarāʾir*, between fifteen and thirty years after Jaʿfar's supposed date of death; see the discussion by D. Hollenberg, 'Interpretation after the End of Days', pp. 61–66. I would add that the *Asrār* does not contain either clear Neoplatonic features, or most of the characteristic features of the first group of works as I have defined them above. On these two works, see also al-Majdūʿ, *Fihrist*, p. 278; W. Ivanow, *Guide to Ismaili literature*, p. 36, XI no. 43 and 44; idem, *Ismaili literature*, p. 21, nos. 14 and 15; I.K. Poonawala, *Biobibliography*, p. 72, nos. 2 and 3; H. Feki, *Les Idées religieuses et philosophiques de l'ismaélisme fatimide*, p. 19, nos. 10 and 11; A. Gacek, *Catalogue*, p. 8, no.11 and p. 111, no. 138; D. Cortese, *Ismaili and other Arabic Manuscripts*, pp. 32–33, no. 51/984; eadem, *Arabic Ismaili Manuscripts*, pp. 24–25, no. 13 and p. 159, no. 144; F. de Blois, *Arabic, Persian and Gujarati Manuscripts*, pp. 9–11; D. Hollenberg, *Beyond the Qurʾan*, pp. 48, 79–99, 109–125; idem, 'Interpretation after the End of Days', passim.

[145] This work has been uncritically edited by Ḥusām Khaḍḍūr: see Jaʿfar b. Manṣūr al-Yaman, *Kitāb Taʾwīl al-zakāt*, ed. Ḥ. Khaḍḍūr (Salamiyya, 2018). Note that an earlier incomplete 'edition' of this text was initially published by Khaḍḍūr under the title of *al-Riḍāʿ fīʾl-bāṭin*. I would like to thank Shafique Virani for providing me with a copy of this 'second print' of the pseudo-*al-Riḍāʿ fīʾl-bāṭin*. Probably realising his mistake, Khaḍḍūr then published the *Riḍāʿ* and the *Taʾwīl al-zakāt* as separate books in the following reprints — although I was not able to verify at which point in the reprints the correction was made.

Kitāb al-Fatarāt wa'l-qirānāt.[146]
Ta'wīl sūrat al-nisā'.[147]

Even though all these works contain Neoplatonic vocabulary, the *Fatarāt* and the *Ta'wīl sūrat al-nisā'* differ from each other and from the other two. The *Sarā'ir al-nutaqā'* and the *Ta'wīl al-zakāt*, on the other hand, share much: the style of writing, the concepts, the stories narrated are similar, and there are many parallels between them.[148]

These corrected editions seem approximately conform to the manuscripts of these texts held at the Institute of Ismaili Studies. See also al-Majdūʿ, *Fihrist*, p. 260; W. Ivanow, *Guide to Ismaili Literature*, p. 36, XI no. 40; idem, *Ismaili Literature*, p. 21, no. 17; I.K. Poonawala, *Biobibliography*, p. 73, no. 8; H. Feki, *Les Idées religieuses et philosophiques de l'ismaélisme fatimide*, p. 18, no. 7; A. Gacek, *Catalogue*, p. 129, no.155; D. Cortese, *Ismaili and other Arabic Manuscripts*, pp. 34–35, no .54/1028; eadem, *Arabic Ismaili Manuscripts*, p. 186, no.171; D. Hollenberg, *Beyond the Qur'an*, p. 47.

[146] This work has been uncritically edited by Ḥusām Khaḍḍūr: see Jaʿfar b. Manṣūr al-Yaman, *Kitāb al-Fatarāt wa'l-qirānāt*, ed. Ḥ. Khaḍḍūr (Salamiyya, 2021). The prologue has been critically edited and translated to English: see D. Hollenberg, 'Interpretation after the End of Days', pp. 97–143, and ibid., pp. 143–211 for an analysis of the contents; idem, 'Neoplatonism in pre-Kirmānīan Fatimid doctrine: A critical edition and translation of the prologue of the *Kitāb al-fatarāt wa-l-qirānāt*', *Le Muséon*, 122/1–2 (2009), pp. 159–202. There are two other studies of this work: H. Halm, 'Zur Datierung. . .'; E. Orthmann, '*Ẓāhir* und *bāṭin* in der Astrologie: Das *Kitāb al-Fatarāt wa-l-qirānāt al-ʿašara*', in *Differenz und Dynamik im Islam. Festschrift für Heinz Halm zum 70. Geburstag*, ed. H. Biesterfeldt and V. Klemm (Würzburg, 2012), pp. 337–358. See also al-Majdūʿ, *Fihrist*, pp. 265–269; W. Ivanow, *Guide to Ismaili Literature*, p. 36, XI no. 41; idem, *Ismaili Literature*, p. 21, no. 18; P. Kraus, 'La bibliographie ismaëlienne de W. Ivanow', p. 486; M. Goriawala, *A Descriptive Catalogue*, pp. 13–14, no.18–19; I.K. Poonawala, *Biobibliography*, pp. 73–74, no. 11; H. Feki, *Les Idées religieuses et philosophiques de l'ismaélisme fatimide*, pp. 17–18, no. 6; A. Gacek, *Catalogue*, p. 42, no. 50; D. Cortese, *Arabic Ismaili Manuscripts*, pp. 69–70, no. 54; D. Hollenberg, *Beyond the Qur'an*, p. 49.

[147] This work remains unedited. See al-Majdūʿ, *Fihrist*, p. 190; W. Ivanow, *Guide to Ismaili literature*, p. 36, XI no. 47; idem, *Ismaili literature*, p. 22, no. 22; I.K. Poonawala, *Biobibliography*, p. 73, no. 9; D. Cortese, *Arabic Ismaili Manuscripts*, pp.185–186, no. 170; D. Hollenberg, *Beyond the Qur'an*, pp. 47–48, 72–73.

[148] To enumerate the many parallels and similarities between the *Sarā'ir al-nutaqā'* and the *Ta'wīl al-zakāt* would however be beyond the scope of the present study. I will address this matter in a future publication. For our purpose here, suffice it to say that these two works stand apart from the rest of the corpus attributed to Jaʿfar and that we have established here that they have the same author.

Furthermore, there is solid evidence that they should be attributed to a single author: in both works, the author refers to another book he presents as one of his own: the *Uṣūl al-dīn bi-maʿrifat al-taʾwīl* or *Uṣūl al-dīn fī maʿrifat al-taʾwīl*, apparently no longer extant,[149] which allows us to ascribe with certainty these two works to a single author — be he Jaʿfar or not.

In addition, the 'voice', so to speak, of the author of the *Sarāʾir al-nutaqāʾ* and the *Taʾwīl al-zakāt* is very particular. It has a hint of individualism, generally absent from earlier *daʿwa* books such as the works of the first group, which are quite impersonal. Therefore, it is legitimate to wonder: is it possible that these two works were also written by Jaʿfar b. Manṣūr al-Yaman, when their tone is so different than the works of the first group? And how is one to interpret the sudden appearance of Neoplatonic vocabulary in the works of an author whose previous compositions were totally devoid of it? If we are not to admit that there is a minimum of two (in fact, probably more) 'Jaʿfars', we should at least postulate that there were two stages in his career, corresponding more or less to the abovementioned groups of works — with the reign of al-Muʿizz as a turning point.[150]

---

[149] Hollenberg has previously noticed this reference in the *Sarāʾir al-*nutaqā, which allowed him to add the *Uṣūl al-dīn* to his list of works attributed to Jaʿfar; see D. Hollenberg, 'Interpretation after the End of Days', p. 61, where the author refers to Jaʿfar b. Manṣūr al-Yaman, *Sarāʾir wa-asrār al-nutaqāʾ*, p. 79. The *Uṣūl al-dīn* is also mentioned by Jaʿfar in ibid., p. 76, although Ghālib mistakenly transcribed it as *Rusūm al-dīn ilā maʿrifat al-taʾwīl*. As it appears, the *Uṣūl al-dīn* is also named in the *Taʾwīl al-zakāt* as another composition of the latter's author; see Jaʿfar b. Manṣūr al-Yaman, *Taʾwīl al-zakāt*, p. 85.

[150] Indeed, the *Taʾwīl al-zakāt* refers explicitly to al-Muʿizz; see Jaʿfar b. Manṣūr al-Yaman, *Taʾwīl al-zakāt*, p. 152. As for the *Sarāʾir*, it mentions Muḥammad b. Ismāʿīl, which, according to Hollenberg, based on Madelung's analysis, is characteristic of the reform of the Fatimid genealogy under al-Muʿizz; see Jaʿfar b. Manṣūr al-Yaman, *Sarāʾir wa-asrār al-nuṭaqāʾ*, p. 39; W. Madelung, 'Das Imamat', pp. 86–101; D. Hollenberg, 'Interpretation after the End of Days', pp. 58, 64. Another feature pointing to al-Muʿizz is precisely the Neoplatonic vocabulary and doctrines found in several works produced during his reign. The process of the adoption of Neoplatonism by the Fatimid court is still under discussion among specialists, but it would seem that it occurred under the reign of al-Muʿizz and that this doctrinal shift had to do with the relation between the Fatimids and the Eastern *dāʿīs* forming what Madelung had labelled 'the Persian School'; see W. Madelung, 'Das Imamat', p. 101.

However, the hypothesis of multiple 'Ja'fars' seems more plausible. D. Hollenberg thus writes: 'I would speculate that many of the works ascribed to Ja'far were, in fact, works noted by custodians of the tradition to be of a similar type, and thus ascribed to the tradition.'[151] What matters, he adds, is that these works 'were composed during the reigns of Abū'l-Qāsim, al-Manṣūr, and al-Mu'izz, and that they represented official Fatimid doctrine in their time'.[152] Yet, a closer look at the corpus transmitted under Ja'far's name might lead to further discoveries and more precise classifications. It is hoped that this will be progressively accomplished in the future, but in the current situation, no conclusion can be reached regarding the authorship of any of these works (except, as established above, that the *Sarā'ir* and the *Ta'wīl al-zakāt* are by a single author). To use de Blois's words when contesting Kraus's contention that the *'Ālim wa'l-ghulām* is unique in its content: 'It seems to me that this question must be deferred until a time when all the works ascribed to Ja'far have been published and studied.'[153] This also applies to the matter of the *Kashf*'s authorship: in the absence of complete critical editions, as well as in-depth and comparative studies of all the works attributed to Ja'far, it is not possible to conclude whether the *Kitāb al-Kashf* is his or not — and it may never be decided conclusively. I have however indicated a few parallels between the *Kashf* and other works ascribed to Ja'far throughout this study and in the footnotes to the translation, but these

---

Unfortunately, this complex issue is beyond the scope of the present study, as Neoplatonic features are almost absent from the *Kashf*. On the ambiguous relation of the Fatimids to Neoplatonism, and the presence of Neoplatonism in Fatimid works before al-Kirmānī, see D. Hollenberg, 'Interpretation after the End of Days', which deals with this matter at length, esp. pp. 87–96, where the author reviews the scholarship on this topic (up to 2006). In addition to the references given there, see D. De Smet, 'Les bibliothèques ismaéliennes et la question du néoplatonisme ismaélien', in Cristina d'Ancona, ed, *The Libraries of the Neoplatonists*, (Leiden and Boston, 2007), pp. 481–492; idem, 'The *Risāla al-Muḏhiba*'; D. Hollenberg, 'Neoplatonism in pre-Kirmānīan Fatimid doctrine', pp. 159–202; idem, 'The Empire Writes Back: Fatimid Ismaili *Ta'wīl* (Allegoresis) in the Mysteries of the Ancient Greeks', in F. Daftary and G. Miskinzoda, eds, *The Study of Shi'i Islam*, pp. 135–147.

151 D. Hollenberg, 'Interpretation after the End of Days', p. 65.

152 Ibid.

153 F. De Blois, *Arabic, Persian and Gujarati Manuscripts*, p. 7.

occasional comparisons do not claim to be exhaustive. Furthermore, such parallels do not necessarily prove that two works are to be ascribed to a single author, since symbols and interpretations were shared by all Ismaili intellectuals of the time — hence the parallels with al-Qāḍī al-Nuʿmān's *Asās al-taʾwīl*, for instance.

This study is intended as a contribution to the necessary effort of deciphering a corpus that is essential for the history of Fatimid and Ismaili thought. It is an attempt to shed light on one of the works of this corpus. As for its attribution, it will remain an open question. In this regard, I can only say that the composition of the *Kitāb al-Kashf* took place at a period consistent with that of Jaʿfar's activity, and that, in addition to the parallels I have found with other works of his, this makes it plausible that the historical Jaʿfar was indeed involved in the authorship of *Kitāb al-Kashf*.

4. The Six treatises of the *Kitāb al-Kashf* and their contents

The *Kitāb al-Kashf* consists of six treatises of varying lengths, styles and structure. Detailed commentaries and analyses of the treatises will be found in the relevant sections. Here, I will only briefly present the contents and some essential features of each one.

Treatise I appears as a patchwork of *ḥadīth*s, exegeses and various fragments from the *ghulāt*, proto-Nuṣayrī and pre-Buyid Shiʿi traditions, interwoven with Fatimid and Ismaili glosses. Similarly to Treatise III, it transmits Qurʾanic exegeses that are in line with the methods of the 'pre-Buyid school of exegesis' — particularly regarding the 'anti-Sunni' stance. Although traces of the *ghulāt* tradition appear elsewhere in the *Kashf* — particularly in Treatises III and V — Treatise I contains significantly more in this regard, as it displays the characteristic vocabulary of the 'Mufaḍḍalian' tradition. However, the text also bears some clear, although occasional, traces of an Ismaili intervention. It is as if an Ismaili author had gathered Shiʿi exegetical fragments, at times slightly adapted to Ismaili doctrine, and occasionally either inserted glosses to reorient the meaning of the text,[154] or introduced a few

---

[154] *Kashf* I, pp. 8–9, § 17; p. 12, § 25.

typically Ismaili passages such as the incipit,[155] the one mentioning the 'Completer Imams' in the context of an exegesis of Qur'an 7:142,[156] or the one dealing with Joseph and the initiatory interpretation of the episode involving his master's wife.[157] Interestingly, it is precisely in the treatise that bears the clearer marks of the influence of the *ghulāt* that one finds an explicit condemnation of the said *ghulāt*.[158] The treatise also contains several lists of names: enemies of the Imams, Proofs and 'Orphans'. It ends with three long *ḥadīth*s dealing with three major themes: 1) the return of the Qā'im; 2) the luminous pre-eternal creation of Muḥammad, ʿAlī, Fāṭima, Ḥasan and Ḥusayn; and 3) ʿAlī's ability to resurrect the dead (which hints at the esoteric meaning of resurrection as access to esoteric knowledge).

Treatise II is very different and two-thirds of it consist of *ḥadīth*s found in Twelver collections of *ḥadīth*s, particularly in chapters devoted to *tawḥīd*. The first *ḥadīth* deals with the absolute transcendence of God, while the second is devoted to the rejection of anthropomorphism, in the context of speculations on the divine Throne and Footstool. The third and final section of the treatise is for the most part an alphabetical cosmogony, the exposition of which is, however, heavily corrupted and difficult to understand. At the end of the treatise, we briefly see the appearance of properly Ismaili notions, hitherto totally absent. The common themes of the three parts of the treatise are the two entities of the divine Throne and Footstool. Treatise II is the only treatise of the *Kashf* that dwells on cosmological considerations.

According to Heinz Halm, Treatise III is, just like Treatise I, built on a core stemming from the *ghulāt* tradition.[159] However, this tone is not as evident as it is in Treatise I, and Halm himself does not provide much evidence to support this claim. I have tried to demonstrate that we are actually dealing with an Ismaili composition, most likely from the early Fatimid period. 'Personalized commentary', especially in its

---

155 *Kashf* I, pp. 2–3, §§ 2–4.

156 *Kashf* I, pp. 15–16, §§ 32–35.

157 *Kashf* I, pp. 26–27, §§ 57–59.

158 *Kashf* I, pp. 7–8, § 13.

159 H. Halm, 'Das 'Buch der Schatten'', II, pp. 83–84.

negative species, is very much in evidence: the treatise appears to have been composed at least in part against enemies of the *daʿwa*, but their identity can only be the subject of speculation. Several exegeses, if not all, are attributed to a 'Sage' (*al-ḥakīm*) who must be an Imam of Salamiyya, and more precisely the predecessor of the Fatimid caliph ʿAbd Allāh al-Mahdī at the head of the *daʿwa*, as suggested by Wilferd Madelung.[160] But again, typical Ismaili doctrines do not appear at first sight, except for the passages concerning the Return of the Resurrector. The treatise focuses on the Imamate of ʿAlī, the faithfulness of his Proofs, the hostility of his enemies, and the Qur'anic verses are interpreted in this sense. Note, however, that about halfway through the treatise, a passage appears to justify a reform, the nature of which is not specified but which one suspects is the reform of the *daʿwa* by ʿAbd Allāh al-Mahdī. The treatise also presents us with a rare example of an Ismaili interpretation of two entire sūras, 89 and 107.

Treatise IV is very brief, but nevertheless difficult as it is corrupted beyond understanding. It contains two parts. The first part consists of three fragments of *ḥadīth*s found in Twelver sources and dedicated to *tawḥīd*, knitted together in a rather haphazard manner. The second part reproduces an entire chapter from the *Kitāb al-Haft wa'l-aẓilla*, a well-known proto-Nuṣayri *ghulāt* work. Structurally, Treatise IV recalls Treatise II, since it consists of a first part that has parallels in chapters of Twelver Shiʿi collections devoted to *tawḥīd*, and a second part belonging to a pre-Fatimid Ismaili tradition in the case of Treatise II, and to a *ghulāt* tradition in Treatise IV. The latter contains no identifiable trace of Ismaili doctrine.

Treatise V is more satisfying in this respect since it is clearly a Fatimid Ismaili text. Two Ismaili figures are named: Muḥammad b. Aḥmad, the 'sage' to whom several exegeses are attributed here and in Treatise III, and the second Fatimid caliph, al-Qā'im bi-Amr Allāh. Moreover, several passages opposed to antinomianism reflect official Fatimid doctrine on the *sharīʿa*. This treatise is the longest in the collection. On the surface, and according to its stated purpose, it is an epistle on pilgrimage. But a whole part of the treatise abandons this topic completely in favour of speculations relating to prophetology.

---

[160] W. Madelung, 'Das Imamat', pp. 55–56.

The reason for this is that the actual subject of the treatise is not so much pilgrimage in its exoteric sense as the necessity to acknowledge the Imam of the time, who is the true Kaʿba in the esoteric sense, as well as his representatives, who are thus conceived of as places of epiphany (or 'Houses'). Despite the partial persistence of a vocabulary derived from *ghulāt* doctrines, the treatise is undoubtedly Ismaili — which illustrates the proximity between early Fatimid Ismailism and *ghulāt* doctrines, even though the latter are reinterpreted and adapted to Ismaili doctrine.

Treatise VI is devoted to the demonstration of ʿAlī b. Abī Ṭālib's Imamate based on the interpretation of Qurʾanic verses. It revolves around the opposition between divine election and human choice, between the vertical investiture of an Imam elected by God, and the horizontal investiture of a man chosen by other men 'following their passions'. Inserted into this discussion and as if camouflaged, are some passages devoted to the Summoners (*duʿāt*) and the Proofs (*ḥujaj*). The final paragraphs of the treatise link the necessity of obeying ʿAlī and the representatives of the Imam, namely the Proofs and the Summoners.

Each of the treatises has its own literary, lexical, and even doctrinal, peculiarities overall, which makes it difficult to situate them chronologically in relation to each other. While some of them can be compared — Treatises III and V in particular — they nevertheless retain significant differences in style, in the organization of the subject matter and in the vocabulary. For example, Treatise III is especially fond of the nicknames of ʿAlī's opponents, namely Abū Bakr, ʿUmar and ʿUthmān; with the exception of ʿUmar's nickname, they are not found anywhere else in the collection.

5. Between chaos and order: the art of compilation and structure in the *Kitāb al-Kashf*

Structure plays an important role in the *Kitāb al-Kashf*, not only in the collection as a whole, but also in each of the treatises. An essential aim of the present study is to attempt to highlight these various layers of structure in a collection that seems to lack it completely. Indeed, the first impression gained by the reader is of being in the presence of a patchwork of unrelated paragraphs, which, although all revolving around similar themes, do not form a coherent whole, but rather a chaotic jumble of *ḥadīths* and exegetical fragments.

Yet, behind this apparent chaos, there is order, and, as far as the flawed transmission allows one to see, a deliberate composition. Before turning to some features of the internal structure of each treatise, we must note how the summary of the *Kitāb al-Kashf*'s contents in the previous section highlights the arrangement of the treatises. The three most important treatises, in terms of size as well as contents, are Treatises I, III and V. In between, the editor of the *Kitāb al-Kashf* has interspersed shorter treatises: Treatises II and IV, which both have similar structures and contents. Treatise VI, which closes the volume, is also quite short, but its contents are more or less in line with Treatise I, III and V, due to its Shiʿi passages on the analogy between ʿAlī and Aaron, on the one hand, and its distinctive Ismaili passages displaying Ismaili symbols and *daʿwa* ranks, on the other hand. Treatises II and IV contain nothing of the sort — although the case of Treatise II is more ambiguous since it does refer to the 'seven Speaking-Prophets' and the 'seven Imams' in its penultimate paragraph, and its alphabetical cosmogony echoes other Ismaili texts where we find similar plays with the letters of the alphabet. By their styles, contents and structure, Treatises II and IV nevertheless stand out in the collection, and it seems that the main reason they are found in the *Kashf* is to serve as interludes between the core treatises. Their independence vis-à-vis the other treatises is such that it would not be unreasonable to think that they do not belong in the same period as the rest of the *Kashf*. I have mentioned the possibility that the *Kashf* in the form in which it has reached us may well owe something to the Ṭayyibīs who have transmitted it. The insertion of Treatises II and IV could be one possible result of a Ṭayyibī intervention. Yet, again, the case of Treatise II is a little trickier because it tallies well with the notion that we are dealing with a pre-philosophical (or even counter-philosophical) Ismaili cosmology that should therefore be dated from either the pre-Fatimid or early Fatimid period.[161] As for Treatise IV, given the terrible state of corruption in which the text has reached the present day, it is impossible to reach any conclusion about it — apart from the mere

[161] See commentary of *Kashf* II, esp. pp. 190–191, 196–198, 205.

observation that it reproduces fragments of texts that are found in other sources, and that one of these sources is the *Kitāb al-Haft wa'l-aẓilla*, a famous *ghulāt* work. How did this fragment find its way into both the *Kashf* and the *Haft* is unclear, particularly since it bears no specifically *ghulāt* doctrines — or none that can be identified in the current state of preservation of this fragment.

Among the reasons for considering Treatises I, III, V, as well as VI to a lesser extent, as 'core treatises', is the subtle play of echoes from one treatise to another, as if there is a discrete, yet never explicitly acknowledged, connection between them — with one exception, to which I shall return. This network of internal resonances is a strong argument in favour of the consistency of the *Kitāb al-Kashf* as a unified book, rather than a random assortment of textual fragments. Furthermore, it suggests that the collection was composed according to the principle of 'scattering of knowledge' (*tabdīd al-ʿilm*), a literary technique common in esoteric circles, which consists in separating the complete exposition of a secret doctrine into several parts which are then scattered throughout a work or several.[162] The use of this

[162] It should however be noted that my use of the expression 'scattering of knowledge' is merely due to its convenience, as it describes adequately the way the author of the *Kashf* spins a web of concepts resonating with one another across the collection. This method is not named as such in Ismaili sources, as far as I know. In fact, while the method is widely spread in esoteric circles of various times and spaces, the expression *tabdīd al-ʿilm* itself comes from the writings of the alchemist Jābir b. Ḥayyān, with Paul Kraus being one of the first Western scholars to signal its use in the Jābirian corpus; see P. Kraus, *Jābir Ibn Ḥayyān. Contribution à l'histoire des idées scientifiques dans l'islam, vol. 1: Le corpus des écrits jābiriens* (Cairo, 1943), pp. XXVII–XXXI. See also H. Corbin, *Alchimie comme art hiératique* (Paris, 1986), pp. 183–184 and n. 84; P. Lory, *Dix traités d'alchimie* (Paris, 1983), pp. 126 ff. M.A. Amir-Moezzi suggests that this technique is also used in Twelver Shiʿi collections of *ḥadīth*; see M.A. Amir-Moezzi, *Guide divin*, pp. 124, n. 241; 307–308 and n. 679 (English trans.: *Divine Guide*, pp. 127, 175, n. 241, 229–230 note 679). See also idem, *La Preuve de Dieu. La mystique shi'ite à travers l'œuvre de Kulaynī IXᵉ-Xᵉ siècle* (Paris, 2018), pp. 257–258; R. Vilozny, *Constructing a Worldview. Al-Barqī's Role in the Making of Early Shīʿī Faith* (Turnhout, 2017), pp. 185, 208; O. Mir-Kasimov, 'The Word of Descent and the Word of Ascent in the Spectrum of the Sacred Texts in Islam', in *Controverses sur les écritures canoniques de l'islam*, ed. D. De Smet and M.A. Amir-Moezzi (Paris, 2014), p. 347, n. 1; idem, *Words of Power. Ḥurūfī Teachings between Shiʿism and Sufism in Medieval Islam* (London and New York, 2015), pp. 33 ff.

technique is noticeable on two levels, as previously said: from one treatise to another, and within one treatise.

The fact that the treatises echo each other is only partly due to the inevitable proximity between texts presenting the same doctrines and belonging to the same tradition, or simply to the editor's intervention and endeavour to unify the whole collection. Indeed, several examples seem to indicate an intention to 'scatter' the teaching. It is thus striking to find in Treatise III a long passage devoted to the torture of Abū Bakr upon the Return of the Resurrector,[163] whereas the torture of Abū Bakr and 'Umar — who remain unnamed in this passage — is barely hinted at in the long *ḥadīth* of Treatise I devoted to the return of the Mahdī.[164] This is particularly striking given that in other 'Shi'i apocalypses', the punishment of Abū Bakr and 'Umar is dealt with at length.[165] In the same passage of Treatise III, Abū Bakr's seventy thousand deaths are interpreted as the seventy dignitaries of the esoteric hierarchy who will accompany the Resurrector, each of whom will have an army of 'a thousand men and more';[166] these seventy dignitaries appear again in Treatise V.[167]

Another example is the opening of Treatise III, with two paragraphs devoted to the theme of the 'mosques and houses of God' which in fact represent the dignitaries of the *da'wa*.[168] Strangely enough, the 'houses' do not appear again in this treatise, but turn out to be the focal point of Treatise V. One may also mention a passage in Treatise III which briefly discusses the figures of Moses and Aaron as analogues of Muḥammad and 'Alī,[169] when it is in fact in Treatise VI that the analogy is treated at greater length.

Again, the play of echoes from one treatise to another could appear as a coincidence, but it is too constant to be completely unintentional. These echoes build a network of cross-references in the *Kashf*, connecting the treatises to one another — with some more connected

---

163 *Kashf* III, pp. 87–88, §§ 77–81.
164 *Kashf* I, p. 34, § 72.
165 See commentary of *Kashf* I, pp. 164–166.
166 *Kashf* III, p. 87, § 79.
167 *Kashf* V, pp. 102–103, § 24.
168 *Kashf* III, pp. 52–53, §§ 1–2.
169 *Kashf* III, p. 75, § 52.

than others. I already highlighted that Treatises II and IV stand out as the odd ones in the collection, and are reminiscent of each other in structure. Treatises I and III, on the other hand, particularly resonate together because of the emphasis they both put on naming the enemies of ʿAlī.[170] Treatises I and V also appear to be connected when the *ḥadīth* of ʿAlī resurrecting the dead in Treatise I finds its explanation in the passage of Treatise V dealing with the symbolic meaning of life as esoteric knowledge.[171] The presence of *ghulāt*-related vocabulary also strongly connects these two treatises, even though this vocabulary differs, and the styles and structure of the two treatises are very different. Among the features of this '*ghulāt*-connection' is the mention of Muḥammad b. Abī Bakr in both treatises, which is very unusual in Ismaili texts (but much more common in Nuṣayri literature).[172]

Finally, the passages on metamorphosis (*maskh* or *musūkhiyya*) present the most explicit argument for the composition of the collection by a careful and meticulous editor: the issue is addressed in Treatises I, III and V.[173] In Treatises III and V, the author explicitly states that the question of metamorphosis has already been discussed. In Treatise III, the passage ends as follows: 'And this has partly been explained previously', while in Treatise V, we read: 'This is the meaning of metamorphosis (*musūkhiyya*), as previously explained.' These two sentences are the only explicit internal references indicating that the collection was conceived as a coherent whole.

In addition to these inter-treatise cross-references, which can be interpreted as a method of 'scattering knowledge', there are other examples within the treatises themselves. I shall limit myself to one specific type of 'scattering', which consists of interrupting the exegesis of a verse with one or several more or less unrelated paragraphs, only to resume it afterwards — a method which, when applied to the *Kashf*,

170 See below, index, s.n, Abū Bakr, ʿUmar, ʿUthmān, Ṭalḥa, people of the Camel, people of Nahrawān, Muʿāwiya, Taym, ʿAdī, Makhzūm, Umayyads, ʿAmr b. al-ʿĀṣ, al-Mughīra b. Shuʿba, Khālid b. al-Walīd. Except for Abū Bakr, who is also mentioned in Treatise V, these names only appear in Treatises I and III.

171 *Kashf* I, pp. 37–39, § 80; V, p. 98, § 15.

172 *Kashf* I, p. 14, § 30; p. 24, § 52; V, pp. 94–95, §§ 7–8; p. 152, §103.

173 *Kashf* I, pp. 4–5, §§ 6–7; III p. 88, § 81; V, pp. 96, §§ 9–10; p. 135, § 72.

only complicates the reading of a book that generally suffers from a lack of logical connectors, as I have said earlier. This practice appears in Treatises I and III, but governs the structure of Treatise V in its entirety. In Treatise I, the exegesis of Q. 14:24–30 is thus interrupted by a series of digressions.[174] In Treatise III, the exegesis of Q. 25:45–46, where the word 'shadow' is identified with the Imam, is interrupted at length: the text then tackles Q. 77:30 which refers to a 'three-branched shade', the word 'shadow' or 'shade' (*ẓill*) justifying the passage of the exegesis from one verse to another, by association of ideas, as it were. The 'three branches' are then the pretext for an important development on Salmān, Abū Dharr and al-Miqdād. Immediately afterwards, the text resumes the exegesis of Q. 25:45–46.[175] This method is repeated over and over in Treatise V, the whole structure of which is organized around the interrupted and resumed interpretations of four main verses.[176]

These are just a few examples illustrating that the appearance of chaos in the *Kashf* may not only be due to a flawed transmission of the text — although this also has consequences — but is, at least in part, intentional. The chaos, when looked at more closely, reveals a carefully disorganized puzzle, manifesting an *art of compilation*. This study will be an attempt to put some of the pieces of the puzzle together, in order for patterns, themes and doctrines, to emerge. Yet, this puzzle is in itself an essential feature of the *Kashf*, and this is the reason why I have preferred to deal with each treatise individually, rather than to organize the study according to a thematic approach. In doing so, I hope to be attentive to the specific features of each treatise, yet without neglecting their connections.

Notes on the translations and commentaries

The translation is based on Rudolf Strothmann's 1952 edition which is currently the best available one, in spite of its shortcomings and

[174] The exegesis begins in *Kashf* I, pp.18–20, §§ 40–42, and resumes pp. 21–22, §§ 46–47.

[175] The exegesis begins in *Kashf* III, p. 69, § 42, and resumes pp. 73–74, § 50.

[176] See plan of Treatise V below, pp. 319–321.

mistakes (see my discussion of the editions above). I have therefore used the pagination of this edition, indicating the end of each of its pages between square brackets in bold **[. . .]**.

Although this volume aims at presenting a translation of the *Kitāb al-Kashf*, and not a critical edition, I have referred to the manuscripts on several occasions. This has been the case particularly for very corrupted passages when I have not followed the readings of the previous editors, and/or corrected the latter based on either the meaning or other sources. I have not mentioned the manuscript variants that I did not deem significant or those corrected by previous editors.

I have used <. . .> for variants that only appear in one manuscript or one edition, as well as for problematic passages and sentences that I have reconstructed, particularly on the basis of other sources.

The general contents of each treatise have been dealt with in their respective commentaries. However, I have occasionally attempted to clarify difficult and unclear passages in the footnotes to the translation.

One of the main features of this translation is the identification of the textual units forming each treatise. As a result, I have rearranged the paragraphs found in the previous editions. Also, I have identified main sections containing several paragraphs within each treatise and gave them titles between square brackets in order to clarify the convoluted structure of the *Kashf*.

All Qur'anic translations are mine, but I have benefited from the available English translations, particularly those by Arberry, Pickthall and Yusuf Ali.

I have tried to translate technical Arabic terms consistently throughout. On some occasions, however, I had to diverge from my usual translation, because a single English word can translate multiple Arabic terms (e.g. 'Proof', by which I generally translate *ḥujja*, but also use for *burhān*), or, in reverse, because a single Arabic term can have multiple meanings (e.g. *amr*, which I generally translate as 'order', but is better translated otherwise in certain contexts). In such cases, I have indicated the Arabic original in parentheses to avoid any confusion.

The underlined terms correspond to those that are cyphered in a 'secret alphabet' in the manuscripts.

The commentaries following the translations of each treatise are not linear and do not claim to be exhaustive. The *Kitāb al-Kashf* is a rich and complex work, and there is no way to exhaust all of its implications here. Only the most salient features and the most important themes have been addressed. Since the themes of the treatises often overlap, themes that appear in several treatises have sometimes been brought together in a single section. The theme of transmigration, for example, is addressed only in the commentary to Treatise I, although it also appears in Treatises III and V. Similarly, the notion of Proof has been dealt with in the commentary to Treatise V, although it appears in almost all the treatises.

TREATISE I

The first treatise of the *Kashf* is probably the most challenging because it intertwines fragments of various doctrinal origins, that is, Shiʿi in the broader sense (i.e. common to most Shiʿi trends), as well as passages that are clearly affiliated with *ghuluww*, all recombined to fit an Ismaili agenda. The main themes are of propaedeutic nature as they cover initiation, the pacts between God and humans and between the Imam and his followers, the Shiʿi historiography of the Prophet's succession, the necessity of the Imamate and its continuity, and the return of the Qāʾim-Mahdī. The text can be confusing as it seems, at first sight, to be a disorganized collection of fragments of texts. By the following breaking-down of its parts, we hope to show the treatise as a skilfully composed patchwork of fragments. Despite the apparent, and probably voluntary, disconnection of the various textual units, they may be regrouped under common themes and convey an overall coherent doctrine. What follows is an attempt to organize the treatise, and to highlight its structure and recurring themes.

1) Introduction: *daʿwa*, secrecy and loyalty

    [§ **1**] Introductive eulogy
    [§§ **2–5**] A pact of secrecy with the reader: the necessity of *kitmān*
    [§§ **6–11**] Meaning of metamorphosis: exegesis of Q. 2:6–9

2) Two *ḥadīth*s and their commentary

    [§ **12**] *Ḥadīth*: Jaʿfar al-Ṣādiq and his vision of ten domes of light
    [§ **13**] Commentary on the *ḥadīth*: a refutation of the *ghulāt*
    [§§ **14–16**] *Ḥadīth*: A mystical sermon by ʿAlī b. Abī Ṭālib
    [§ **17**] Commentary on the *ḥadīth*: the continuity of God's Order

3) Ranks of the *daʿwa*

[§ **18**] *Ḥadīth*: exegesis of Q. 70:40
[§§ **19–20**] Exegesis of Q. 52:1–8

4) The enemies

[§§ **21–22**] Enumeration of enemies of Prophets and Imams
[§§ **23–24**] *Ḥadīth*: ʿAlī b. Abī Ṭālib and the ancient communities
[§ **25**] Commentary on the *ḥadīth*: the continuity of God's Order

5) *Rajʿa*: the Return

[§ **26**] The Master of the Age: the Resurrector
[§ **27**] *Ḥadīth*: Jaʿfar al-Ṣādiq on retribution

6) Enumerations of names and ranks

[§§ **28–29**] Enumeration of the Gates and Proofs
[§§ **30–31**] Enumeration of the Orphans and their 'fathers'
[§§ **32–35**] The Completer Imams and the nights of Ramadan

7) The light of the Imamate

[§§ **36–39**] Exegesis of the verse of Light

8) *Walāya* and its adversaries

[§§ **40–42**] The 'good tree' and the 'bad tree': exegesis of Q. 14:24–27
[§ **43**] The path and the *walāya*
[§ **44**] The Speaking-Imam: exegesis of Q. 6:59

9) ʿAlī and the 'Imams of misguidance'

[§ **45**] Exegesis of Q. 2:1–3, 5
[§§ **46–47**] Exegesis of Q. 14:28–30
[§§ **48–50**] Exegesis of Q. 2:165–167
[§ **51**] Exegesis of Q. 44:41–45, 52–54, 57
[§ **52**] Exegesis of Q. 95
[§ **53**] Exegesis of Q. 67:30

10) Ranks of the *daʿwa*

[§ **54**] The Bees: exegesis of Q. 16:68–69

11) *Raj‘a*: the Return

 [§§ **55–56**] The Resurrector

12) Initiation and the *da‘wa*

 [§§ **57–59**] Joseph and initiation

13) The enemies of ‘Alī: crimes and punishment

 [§ **60**] Abū Bakr and the Return
 [§ **61**] Abū Bakr and his claim to the Divine Trust
 [§ **62**] The enemies and the Return
 [§§ **63–64**] Abū Bakr, ‘Umar: the Return and the continuity of enmity
 [§ **65**] Abū Bakr, ‘Umar and the continuity of enmity
 [§ **66**] ‘Umar, enemy of ‘Alī

14) *Raj‘a*: the Return

 [§ **67**] *Ḥadīth*: the etymology of *mahdī*
 [§§ **68–73**] *Ḥadīth*: the Return of the Resurrector

15) The light of the Imamate

 [§ **74**] Muḥammad and the Imams as light: exegesis of Q. 24:40
 [§ **75**] Legatee and Prophet: exegesis of Q. 22:45
 [§§ **76–79**] *Ḥadīth*: the creation of the Five and Adam

16) ‘Alī’s life and death

 [§ **79**] *Ḥadīth*: Ja‘far al-Ṣādiq on ‘Alī’s murder
 [§ **80**] *Ḥadīth*: ‘Alī’s power to resurrect the dead

17) [§ **81**] *Ḥadīth*: on the vision of God
18) Conclusion

 [§ **82**] *Ḥadīth*: *walāya* and *shirk*
 [§ **83**] End

Treatise I Translation

In the name of God, the Merciful, the Compassionate from whom we seek our help

1. Praise be to God who created (*faṭara*) His worshippers according to His nature (*fiṭraṭihi*). He weakens tongues in their attempt to describe and qualify Him, intellects are blunted in their attempt to grasp His essence and His magnitude. *'Praise be to God who created the heavens and the earth, and made the shadows and the light; yet those who disbelieve* [1] *ascribe equals to their Lord'* [Q. 6:1]. There is no god but God alone, without a partner. I bear witness that Muḥammad is His servant and Messenger — may God's blessings and peace be upon him and his family. There is no strength except in God the High, the Sublime.

[Introduction: a pact with the reader]

2. The first thing a believer needs concerning his religion and knowledge of the Truth and its people, is loyalty (*amāna*) to God and His Friends (*awliyā'*), for He has said — He is Mighty and Sublime (*'azza wa-jalla*): *'We presented the Trust* (*amāna*) *to the heavens and the earth and the mountains, but they refused to carry it and were afraid of it; and man carried it. Surely he is unjust and a fool'* [Q. 33:72]. As for me, brother, I bind you to God's Covenant (*'ahd*) and His Pact (*mīthāq*), the most firm Covenant and Pact to which He has always bound His Prophets and Messengers. God has forbidden His Prophets, His Messengers, His Gates (*abwāb*) and His Proofs (*ḥujaj*) — as well as your father who gave you drink and your brother who suckled (*raḍi'a*) with you from the same source —[1] [to eat items] such as

[1] 'Father' and 'brother' may be understood in the symbolic sense here; see commentary of *Kashf*, p. 128–134.

carrion, blood and swineflesh,[2] and similarly I forbid you to divulge [what follows], to let anyone but you read it or to speak it to one of the sons of Adam — '*the prime nature* (fiṭra) *on which God has created* (faṭara) *man*' [Q. 30:30].[3] Do not also write it **[2]** to anyone, unless they deserve it and are a true believer. If you transgress this, if you do other than what I have ordered you and should you divulge [what follows], God, His Messenger and the latter's Legatee will disassociate themselves (*barī'*) from you; God will submit you to the sword of Truth and will carry out His judgement against you, '*however much the associationists may be averse*' [Q. 9:33].[4]

3. Indeed, a report has come from the Friends (*awliyā'*), who received it from the Legatees (*awṣiyā'*), who received it from the Summoners (*du'āt*), who received it from the Chiefs (*nuqabā'*), who received it from the Nobles (*nujabā'*), who received it from the Gates (*abwāb*), who received it from the Proofs (*ḥujaj*):[5] 'Tell the people of Friendship (*walāya*): "Conceal our secret, obey our command, do not circulate our word, and we shall make you the elite of creation. There have been people before you from past communities who fulfilled what was entrusted to them, concealed the secret and did what they were ordered, and so God made them Messengers to His trustworthy ones, and Gates for[6] His Friends".'[7]

---

[2] This is an allusion to the following verses: '*He Has forbidden for you carrion and blood and swineflesh*' [Q. 2:173; 16:115]; '*Forbidden unto you are carrion and blood and swineflesh*' [Q. 5:3]. On this passage, and its potential esoteric meaning, see below pp. 127–128, n. 191.

[3] This could be an allusion to the tax named *fiṭra* which was due by the newly initiated believer, according to Ibn Rizām; cited by D. Hollenberg, *Beyond the Qur'an*, p. 14; see also ibid., p. 60. On initiation and *fiṭra* in a similar sense in an Ismaili source, see Ja'far b. Manṣūr al-Yaman, *Ta'wīl al-zakāt*, pp. 256–257.

[4] Also Q. 61:9.

[5] This chain of transmission, which is highly unusual as it is composed of ranks rather than names, also poses problems as to which is the highest rank. It seems that the rank of the Legatee has been misplaced.

[6] The text reads: *ilā*, 'to', which would make the 'Friends' the 'destination' of those who go through the Gates. I choose to understand 'Friends' as a synonym of 'believers' rather than referring to high ranks of the hierarchy — which seems to correspond to the 'chain of transmission' above, given the correction suggested in the previous footnote.

[7] A similar, though slightly longer, version of this *ḥadīth* is quoted and commented on in Ja'far b. Manṣūr al-Yaman, *Ta'wīl al-zakāt*, pp. 163–164, where it is attributed to Ja'far al-Ṣādiq. See also Idrīs 'Imād al-Dīn, *Zahr al-ma'ānī* (Beirut, 1991), pp. 195–196, who quotes this passage from the *Ta'wīl al-zakāt*.

4. By God, by God brother! Do not expose yourself to the wrath of God. Without what I have understood from you and what I know about the degree you have reached, I would not have unveiled this chapter. I make God your surety (*kafīl*).[8]

5. The words of the Greatest Master (*al-sayyid al-akbar*)[9] — may God's blessings be upon him — [also refer to this point]: 'Communities have perished only **[3]** because they did not consider this, did not reflect and because they divulged the secret.'[10] Whoever divulges the secret rejects the Truth after having known it.[11] There is no strength except in God the High, the Sublime.

[The metamorphosis (*musūkhiyya*): exegesis of Q. 2:6–9]

6. On God's words — He is Mighty and Sublime: '*As for the disbelievers, it is the same to them whether you warn them or do not warn them, they*

---

[8] This is an allusion to Q. 16:91: '*Fulfil God's convenant ('ahd), when you make covenant, and do not break your oaths after confirming them, and after you have made God your surety (kafīl).*'

[9] This unusual epithet designates the Prophet Muḥammad. It seems to characterise certain *ghulāt* groups, as we find it, for instance, in the *Kitāb al-Ṣirāṭ*, ff. 88b, 92b, 99b, 126b. L. Capezzone notes that, in his *Rijāl*, al-Kashshī says that Iṣḥāq. al-Aḥmar uses this expression. However, M. Asatryan is not convinced that this is sufficient evidence to attribute the *Kitāb al-Ṣirāṭ* to Iṣḥāq al-Aḥmar (d. 286/899), a *ghulāt* heresiarch (on him, see M. Asatryan, *Controversies in Formative Shiʿi Islam*, index s.n. 'Iṣḥāq al-Aḥmar', s.v. 'Iṣḥāqiyya'; idem, 'Esḥāq Aḥmar al-Nakaʿī', *EIr*). Asatryan actually refers to this passage of the *Kashf* to illustrate that the expression is not specific to one author, but rather to a certain trend. See L. Capezzone, 'Il *Kitāb al-Ṣirāṭ*', p. 304; M. Asatryan, 'Heresy and Rationalism', p. 68, n. 225; p. 77, n. 258. As a matter of fact, the expression is also found in Nuṣayri texts; see e.g. al-Ṭabarānī, *Majmūʿ al-aʿyād*, ed. R. Strothmann, *Der Islam*, 27 (1946), p. 13; idem, *Kitāb al-maʿārif*, ed. M.M. Bar-Asher and A. Kofsky (Leuven, Paris and Walpole, 2012), pp. 67, 70.

[10] Similar *ḥadīth*s appear in Sunni sources. See e.g. Ibn Māja, *Sunan*, ed. M.F. ʿAbd al-Bāqī (Cairo, 1952), *muqaddima*, *bāb* 10, p. 33, where the 'previous communities' have 'perished' because they did not agree with the doctrine of *qadar*.

[11] The rejection of faith after having embraced it is a Qur'anic theme (see e.g. 16:91). In a Shiʿi context, it is of course applied to those who followed the Prophet Muḥammad but then refused to acknowledge ʿAlī, that is, the *muslimūn*, as opposed to the *mu'minūn*. In the *Kashf*, it is also a recurring theme, due to the Shiʿi nature of the text, but it might also allude to renegade *duʿāt*.

will not believe' [Q. 2:6], [Jaʿfar] al-Ṣādiq — peace be upon him — said: 'He means the antagonists (*aḍdād*), and those who follow them.' '*God has set a seal on their hearts and on their hearing, and on their eyes is a covering, and they will have a painful torment*' [Q. 2:7], that is, in metamorphosis and the taking on of composite bodies in the painful layers of Hell (*bi'l-musūkhiyya wa'l-tarākīb bi'l-ṭabaqāt bi-alīm al-adrāk*).[12] They are objects of [God's] wrath, they have gone astray, and they rejected the Truth after knowing it, even though they knew it was the Truth. This shows that he refers to those who entered the Summons of Truth (*daʿwat al-ḥaqq*), then were driven out of it by one of the Gates of faithlessness (*nakth*) and hypocrisy in following the whisperings of Satan. They are consequently denied the benefits of knowledge, the degrees of religion and the substance of their visions and certainty. They become like beasts who profess no religion because they have been removed from where they were, by objecting to the Truth and <. . .>[13] of Falsehood (*al-bāṭil*). They have removed themselves from the Truth they had entered. Their visions have faded away, and so they do not see the Truth [anymore] and they are deprived from its benefits. They **[4]** do not hear them [the benefits], and '*He has set a seal on their hearts*' [Q. 2:7]. This is what deprivation is. '*They do not understand*' what guides them.

7. This is also the meaning of God's words — He is Mighty and Sublime: '*We created man in the fairest stature, and then We reduced him to the lowest of the low*' [Q. 95:4–5]. This means that he was guided to the straight path with God's approval, and that he was raised through this to the degrees of the pious worshippers who believe in Him. But when he broke (*nakatha*) [the Pact] and changed [path] by not observing adequately the Truth that reached him, he was deprived of worship and the benefit was not renewed (*tajdīd al-ifāda*). He was then in '*the lowest of the low*', which is the position of the people of ignorance. Indeed, the one who does not know is more forgivable than the one who knows and yet does not retain what he knows and does

[12] On the interpretation of this sentence, see M. Asatryan, 'Early Ismailis and Other Muslims: Polemics and Borrowing in Kitāb al-Kashf', in O. Mir-Kasimov, ed, *Intellectual Interactions in the Islamic World. The Ismaili Thread* (London and New York, 2020), p. 278, n. 19.

[13] Ms. A: *wa-karh*; ms. B: *wa-kasr*. Strothmann: blank; Ghālib: *wa-karh*.

not profit from it. The Loser is in the lowest abyss of misguidance as he received guidance and yet was not among the guided ones. This is the correct meaning of the allusion to metamorphosis (*al-musūkhiyya*).

8. '*Of the people, there are some who say: "We believe in God and the Last Day", but they are not believers. They think to beguile God and those who believed, and they beguile none save themselves, but they are not aware*' [Q. 2:8–9]. He means by this the Shiʿis who fall short (*al-shīʿa al-muqaṣṣira*) from knowing the Truth and who say: **[5]** '*We believe in God and the Last Day*'. The Last Day is the Mahdī, the Master of the Age (*ṣāḥib al-zaman*) — may God's blessings be upon him. God — He is Mighty and Sublime — made manifest what they kept secret in their words and said: '*They are not believers. They think to beguile God and those who believed.*' Those who believed are those who know this Law (*sharīʿa*).

9. '*When it was said to them: "Believe as the people believe", they say: "Shall we believe as fools believe?" Truly, they are the fools, but they do not know*' [Q. 2:13]. He means by this the First of the iniquitous, the Second[14] and those who believe in the two of them and follow them both. The 'people' (*al-nās*) are those who know and acknowledge the people of Truth. God has revealed this knowledge to His most venerable Messenger.

10. God has said: '*Truly, they are the workers of corruption, but they are not aware*' [Q. 2:12]. '*These are they who have bought misguidance at the price of guidance, and their trade has not profited them, and they are not right-guided*' [Q. 2:16]. He means by this the followers of the Pharaohs.

11. '*O Man! What has deluded you as to your generous Lord, who created you, then fashioned, you, and proportioned you?* [Q. 82:6–7]. The man who forgets what he has contracted with his Friend (*walī*) is

---

[14] Abū Bakr and ʿUmar: the use of the terms 'First' and 'Second' to designate them is a common code of Shiʿi exegesis. See e.g. I. Goldziher, 'Spottnamen der ersten Chalifen bei den Schīʿiten', *Wiener Zeitschrift für die Kunde des Morgenlandes*, 15 (1901), pp. 323; E. Kohlberg, 'Some Imamī Shīʿī views on the *Ṣaḥāba*', *JSAI*, 5 (1984), p. 165; M.M. Bar-Asher, *Scripture and Exegesis in Early Imamī Shiʿism* (Leiden, Boston and Jerusalem, 1999), p. 114, 118. See also *Kashf* I, p. 22, § 48; p. 24, § 52; p. 28, § 60; III, p. 58, §§ 12–13; V, p. 95, § 7. The sources sometimes mention the 'Third', that is, ʿUthmān.

the one 'deluded as to his generous Lord' to [the extent of opposing] God. [The Lord] is the Prince of the Believers. This is [stated in] a [clear] Bedouin Arabic language.[15] **[6]**

[Jaʿfar al-Ṣādiq and the domes of light]

12. Al-Ṣādiq — may God's blessings be upon him — said: 'I was contemplating the verse: *"God is the light of the heavens and the Earth"* [Q. 24:35], when these verses manifested ten domes of light (*qubāb min nūr*), approaching <the high nobility (*al-sharaf*)>.[16] Around them were a thousand [other] domes of light, until they reached <the Highest Nobility (*al-sharaf al-akbar*)>.[17] It was surrounded by [all the] creatures, and it was as if I heard it preaching its world.' A man stood up and said: 'Tell us more, may God hve mercy upon you.' [The Imam] said: 'The ten domes of light include the seven Speaking-Prophets (*nuṭaqāʾ*), and the [other] three are the*kālī*,[18] the Guardian (*raqīb*)[19] and the Gate (*bāb*). These are the ten domes of light. Whoever knows them knows God, and whoever rejects them rejects God.'

[Commentary of the vision]

13. By the 'domes', he only means that they are a covering (*sutra*) to the hidden knowledge of God. He referred to them by this name, but it is not in the sense that the Christians (*al-naṣārā*) say that Jesus' body is a sacred form (*haykal*) in which God descended on

---

[15] Correcting Strothmann's edition which reads *gharība* instead of *ʿarabiyya*. The meaning of the sentence might be that what has just been said is clear.

[16] Mss. A, B: *al-sharaf*; Ghālib (p. 28): *al-sharq*.

[17] Mss. A, B: *al-shahr al-akbar*; Ghālib (p. 28): *al-mashhad al-akbar*. Strothmann suggests replacing *al-shahr* by *al-shuraf*, but this word in plural would not bode well with the singular adjective. I correct into: *al-sharaf*, based on the occurrence of the term in the previous sentence.

[18] This term does not appear elsewhere in Ismaili literature, except for another occurrence in *Kashf* I, p. 10, § 20. Rather, we find it in Nuṣayrī texts. Its meaning is unclear, and its occurrences in Nuṣayrī literature do not give any indication in this regard; see al-Ṭabarānī, *Kitāb al-Maʿārif*, p. 107; idem, *Majmūʿ al-aʿyād*, p. 10. In the latter text, the *kālī* seems identified with 'Salsal', that is, Salmān al-Fārisī.

[19] Again, this is not an Ismaili technical term.

earth to walk among His servants; God is highly exalted above that! Similar is what the exaggerators (*ghulāt*) among the Muslims say about the Imams and the Messengers, as they also say that their bodies are forms (*hayākil*) with which the Creator covers (*yastajinn*) Himself to descend on earth. [Their bodies] are thus his domes, that is, sacred places (*maqāmāt*) that contain Him on His earth. He would be in the body of each one of them in his time. Glory to God, may He be exalted above what the iniquitous say! He has forbidden this in His Book, saying: *'O People of the Book, do not exaggerate (lā taghlū) in your religion and say not* [7] *as to God but the truth, etc.'* [Q. 4:171]. No one says such a thing, except the ignorant. We take refuge in God from ignorance after knowledge, and from doubt after certainty.

[A mystical sermon by ʿAlī b. Abī Ṭālib]

14. Jābir b. Yazīd al-Juʿfī[20] said: 'I heard my lord and master, Abū Jaʿfar al-Bāqir Muḥammad b. ʿAlī — may God's blessings be upon him — relating this tradition from the Prince of the Believers through his forefathers: "He stood on the pulpit in Kūfa and said: 'People! I am the Messiah (*al-masīḥ*)[21] who heals the blind and the leper, who creates the birds[22] and spreads the clouds'" — this means that he is the second Messiah. "'I am him and he is me.'"

---

[20] A disciple of Muḥammad al-Bāqir (d.114/733) who transmitted *ḥadīth* that were highly appreciated in *ghulāt* circles; see W. Madelung, 'Dj̲ābir al-Dj̲uʿfī', *EI2*. Note that Ms. A reads 'Zayd' instead of 'Yazīd' (Ms. B simply reads Jābir b. al-Juʿfī). We find the same mistake in other Ismaili sources; see e.g. Idrīs ʿImād al-Dīn, *Zahr al-maʿānī*, p. 215; al-Majdūʿ, *Fihrist*, p. 271. This may indicate that this mistake was common in the Ṭayyibī context.

[21] This refers to Jesus, as also indicated by the rest of the sentence in which ʿAlī claims attributes that are specific to Jesus in Islam.

[22] This alludes to Q. 3:49: *'I come unto you with a sign from your Lord: I fashion for you out of clay the likeness of a bird, and I breathe into it, and it becomes a bird by God's leave'* (quoted in *Kashf* V, p. 98, § 15). See also Q. 5:110: *'Jesus, son of Mary (. . .) you created out of clay the likeness of a bird — by My leave. Then you breathed into it, and it became a bird — by My leave. And you healed the blind and the leper — by My leave. And you brought the dead forth — by My leave, etc.'* This power of resurrecting the dead is also attributed to ʿAlī in the final pages of *Kashf* I; see *Kashf* I, pp. 37–39, § 80.

15. A man rose to him and said: "O Prince of the Believers, is the Torah non-Arabic (*aʿjamiyya*) or Arabic?" He answered: "It is non-Arabic, but its exegesis (*taʾwīl*) is Arabic."[23]

16. The Messiah is the One who rises with Truth (*al-qāʾim biʾl-ḥaqq*), the King of this world and the hereafter, as it is attested by the words of God — He is Mighty and Sublime: *'Peace be upon me the day I was born, and the day I die, and the day I am raised up alive'* [Q. 19:33]. "Jesus son of Mary is from me and I am from him. He is the Supreme Word of God (*kalimat Allāh al-kubrā*). <I am the contemplator, and I am the contemplated>."[24]

[Gloss on the notion of God's Order (*amr*)]

17. This is from the sayings of the Prince of the Believers — may God's blessings be upon him — namely that that God's Order is continuous (*amr Allāh muttaṣil*), from the first of His Prophets, Messengers and

---

[23] This passage on the exegesis of the Torah seems interpolated, as its connexion with the rest of the sermon is not clear. It might have something to do with the messianic doctrine according to which the true and esoteric meaning of previous revelations will be unveiled when the Mahdī comes. Therefore, ʿAlī's traditional role as 'master of the exegesis' would be a consequence of his status as the Messiah.

[24] Ms. A: *huwa al-shāhid wa-anā al-mashhūd ʿalā al-ghāʾibāt*; ms. B: *huwa al-shāhid wa-anā al-mashhūd ʿalā al-luʿanāʾ*. The Arabic text is not clear and is probably corrupted. Corrected to: *anā al-shāhid, anā al-mashhūd*, after a version of the *khuṭbat al-bayān* in which ʿAlī declares: 'I am the Contemplator, I am the Contemplated', which is more intelligible; see Jaʿfar Kashfī, *Tuḥfat al-mulūk*, cited in M.A. Amir-Moezzi, *La Religion discrète*, p. 107 (Eng. trans.: *Spirituality of Shiʿi Islam*, p. 129). This sentence is a reference to Q. 85:3: *wa-shāhid, wa-mashhūd*. H. Corbin translates the uncorrected version of the *Kashf* as follows: 'Il est le Témoin attestant les mystères et j'en suis l'attesté'; see H. Corbin, 'De la gnose antique à la gnose ismaélienne', in idem, *Temps cyclique et gnose ismaélienne*, p. 202. The expression *al-shāhid al-mashhūd* appears in Jaʿfar b. Manṣūr al-Yaman, *Sarāʾir wa-asrār al-nutaqāʾ*, p. 117, in another of ʿAlī's mystical sermons. See also R. Strothmann, *Esoterische Sonderthemen bei den Nusairi. Geschichten und Traditionen von den Heiligen Meistern aus dem Prophetenhaus* (Berlin, 1958), Arabic text p. 17, § 66, where the Imam Ḥasan al-ʿAskarī declares: 'We are the comtemplator, and we are the contemplated for one who desires it' (*naḥnu al-shāhid waʾl-mashhūd li-ṭālibihi*). On the literary genre of the mystical sermons attributed to ʿAlī, see M.A. Amir-Moezzi, *La Religion discrète*, Ch. 3: 'Remarques sur la divinité de l'Imam', pp. 89–108 (Eng. trans.: *Spirituality of Shiʿi Islam*, Ch. 3: 'Some Remarks on the Divinity of the Imam', pp. 103–131). See also *Kashf* I, p. 11, §§ 23–24.

Imams of His religion to the last of them: whoever obeys the last of them, it is as if he obeyed the first of them, because of the continuity of God's Order from the first of them, to the ones after him, and up to the last of them.[25] Whoever obeys **[8]** the first, his obedience will guide and lead him to the last. The 'Order of God' is that which He establishes with each one (*qā'im*)[26] of them in his era, and which then reaches his successor. It is *'the cable of God'* [Q. 3:103] that cannot be severed, and *'the firm handhold which will never break'* [Q. 2:256].[27] By this, God severs the words of the misguided misguiders who *'sever what God has ordered to be joined (yūṣal)'* [Q. 2:27]. They claim the sacred stations (*maqāmāt*) in favour of the iniquitous antagonists (*aḍdād*) in every era and every age (*fī kull 'aṣr wa-zamān*), and they invalidate the testamentary dispositions (*al-waṣāyā*) by which the Messengers designate their Legatees (*awṣiyā'*), and the Imams designate the Imams after them. God speaks the Truth, and He guides to the path through His Guidance and His trustworthy and chosen ones — may God bless them all.

[Exegesis of Q. 70:40]

18. *'I swear by the Lord of the Easts and the Wests'* [Q. 70:40]. <He says[28] that God has>[29] thirty-nine Easts, thirty-nine Wests, and thirty-nine cities other than yours, who have all taken the Covenant and the Pact to know us.[30] It was taken with *'the Jibt and the Ṭāghūt'* [Q. 4:51][31] in

---

[25] H. Corbin has translated most of the previous *ḥadīth*, as well as its explanation until this point; see H. Corbin, 'De la gnose antique à la gnose ismaélienne', in idem, *Temps cyclique et gnose ismaélienne*, pp. 201–202.

[26] In this paragraph of a distinct Fatimid stance, the term *qā'im* does not bear any eschatological connotation, and therefore cannot be translated by 'Resurrector' as is usually the case. On this particular meaning of the term, see commentary of *Kashf* III, pp. 290–293. Cf. also *Kashf* I, p. 12, § 25, where, within another distinctly Fatimid passage on God's Order, the Imam of the time is called *qā'im bi-amr Allāh*.

[27] Cf. *Kashf* III, p. 56, § 9; V, p. 99, §18; p. 122, § 55.

[28] The *Kitāb al-Kashf* contains numerous occurrences of *qāla* or *yaqūl* refering to anonymous interpreters.

[29] This only appears in M. Ghālib's edition, p. 28.

[30] Despite the absence of a chain of transmission, this paragraph is a *ḥadīth*. Therefore, 'us' refers to the Imams.

[31] Idols. They are often identified with Abū Bakr and 'Umar in a Shi'i context, as can be seen below in *Kashf* I, p. 22, § 48.

each city with every warner (*nadhīr*). I said: 'May I be your ransom! Explain to me the thirty-nine.' [The Imam] said: '[There are] twelve months, each having a Demonstrator (*mubarhin*), which makes twenty-four. [Then there are] seven heavens and a similar number on earth, which makes thirty-nine,[32] the number of the Easts as well as the Wests. As for the cities, they are the Gates (*abwāb*), the Proofs (*ḥujaj*), the Demonstrators (*mubarhinūn*) and the Wings (*ajniḥa*).[33] Do you understand?' I said: 'Yes master, may I be your ransom!' **[9]**

[Exegesis of Q. 52:1–8]

19. About His words — He is Mighty and Sublime: *'When the heaven is rent asunder, and it becomes red like ointment. . .'* [Q. 55:37], he[34] said: 'It is as if I am looking at the One who establishes the Truth (*al-qā'im bi'l-ḥaqq*); the Order of the Speaking-Prophets will be rent asunder, he will appear to his world and the horizon will shine for him. Then, the affliction (*al-hā'i'a*) will fall on the heretics (*ahl al-ilḥād*); this is the *'chastisement about to fall, it is ineluctable'* [Q. 52:7–8].'

[32] The count is wrong: twelve months, twelve 'Demonstrators', seven heavens and seven earths bring to a total of thirty-eight — not thirty-nine.

[33] The term *mubarhin* does not appear in other Ismaili texts, to the best of my knowledge. As for the 'Wings', they are indeed a rank of the Ismaili hierarchy, generally identified with the rank of the 'Summoners' (*du'āt*); see e.g. Ja'far b. Manṣūr al-Yaman, *Sarā'ir wa-asrār al-nutaqā'*, pp. 26, 159, 160; idem, *Ta'wīl al-Zakāt*, pp. 123, 228; al-Sijistānī, *Tuḥfat al-mustajībīn*, in 'Arif Tāmir, ed, *Khams rasā'il ismā'īliyya* (Salamiyya, 1956), p. 154; Idrīs 'Imād al-Dīn, *Zahr al-ma'ānī*, p. 247, etc. See also H. Feki, *Les Idées religieuses et philosophiques*, pp. 157–159, 223, 243; H. Corbin, *Trilogie ismaélienne*, index *s.v. ajniḥa*, esp. pp. 35–36 note 35; F. Daftary, *The Ismā'īlīs. Their History and Doctrines*, index *s.v. janāḥ*. It is noteworthy that al-Sijistānī explains that the 'Wings' are thus called because 'they fly (*yaṭīrūn*) to spread the two *da'was*, both the exoteric and the esoteric' (al-Sijistānī, *Tuḥfat al-mustajībīn*, p. 154), which is related to the symbolic identification of the birds to the Summoners; on the latter identification, see *Kashf* VI, p. 171, §30, and related footnote. The term 'Wings' may also have to do with the identification of members of the *da'wa* with angels; see e.g. *Kashf* III, p. 62, § 20 and related footnote; V, p. 154, §105, as well as my remarks in the commentary of *Kashf* V, pp. 413–414.

[34] Although the author of the exegesis is not specified, this 'he' must refer to an Imam.

20. This is the esoteric meaning of His words: *'By the Mount (al-ṭūr), by a Book inscribed, in a parchment unrolled, by the House frequented, and the roof exalted, and the sea swarming. Surely your Lord's chastisement is about to fall, it is ineluctable'* [Q. 52:1–8]. The 'Mount' is the Speaking-Prophet; the 'Book inscribed' is the knowledge; the 'parchment unrolled' is the Proof (*ḥujja*) — may God's blessings be upon him; the 'House frequented' is the progeny;[35] the 'roof exalted' is the *kālī*;[36] the 'sea swarming' is the Gate; the 'chastisement about to fall' is the Resurrector (*qāʾim*), whose coming is 'ineluctable'.[37]

[Enumeration of the enemies]

21. The knowledge of the esoteric meaning of His words concerning the people of ʿĀd and Thamūd,[38] and the people of Abraham and

---

[35] That is, the Imams from the progeny of Muḥammad and ʿAlī.

[36] See above, *Kashf* I, p. 7, §12.

[37] See the version of the *khuṭbat al-bayān* as transmitted by Jaʿfar Kashfī in his *Tuḥfat al-mulūk*; translated and transcribed in M.A. Amir-Moezzi, *La Religion discrète*, pp. 105–108 (English trans.: *Spirituality of Shiʿi Islam*, pp. 126–131): there, ʿAlī identifies himself with each of the elements mentioned in Q. 52:1–6. As we see, the exegesis of the *Kashf* is more precise. Similar interpretations of these verses are also found in later Ismaili sources: in one of his sermons, the fourth Fatimid caliph, al-Muʿizz, declares that the Imams are the Gates to God's 'House frequented' and 'roof exalted', which, if authentic, gives an idea of how the exegesis of theses verses has evolved, from the *ghulāt* origins of the *Kashf* (here attested by the use of the term *kālī*) to the official rhetoric of the Fatimid state; see P.E. Walker, *Orations of the Fatimid Caliphs: Festival Sermons of the Ismaili Imams* (London and New York, 2009), p. 136 (Arabic: p. 41). See also D. De Smet, *Les Épîtres sacrées des Druzes.* Rasāʾil al-Ḥikma. *Volumes 1 et 2. Introduction, édition critique et traduction annotée des traités attribués à Ḥamza b. ʿAlī et à Ismāʿīl at-Tamīmī* (Leuven, 2007), Epistle 33, p. 398, where Ḥamza b. ʿAlī identifies himself with the 'Mount', the 'Book inscribed', the 'House frequented' and the 'Master of Resurrection and the Last Day'. In the *Kashf*, the exegesis of sūra 52 outlines the historical transmission of divine knowledge from the last Speaking-Prophet, Muḥammad, to the Qāʾim ("the inevitable punishment"), through the Proof (probably ʿAlī), his descendants, the enigmatic *kālī*, and the Gate (who is most likely the Gate of the Qāʾim).

[38] ʿĀd and Thamūd are people mentioned several times in the Qurʾan where they are given as examples of past infidel communities who did not listen to the warnings of their prophets — these were respectively Hūd and Ṣāliḥ; see F. Buhl, "ʿĀd', *EI2*; I. Shahid, 'Thamūd', *EI2*; R. Tottoli, "ʿĀd', *EQ*; R. Firestone, 'Thamūd', *EQ*.

Noah: the first of them is Abū Bakr, the second is ʿUmar,[39] the third is ʿUthmān, the fourth is Talha.[40] The people of Madyan[41] and the people of Rass[42] are the people of the Camel[43] and the people of Nahrawān.[44] The companions of the Pharaoh of Moses are Muʿāwiya,[45] **[10]** and his companions, the Umayyads.

22. The second cycle (*al-kawr al-thānī*)[46] [is that of?] Pharaoh, Hāmān and Korah,[47] who are respectively the First Abū Bakr, the

---

[39] See *Kashf* III, pp. 57–58, §§ 12–13, where ʿĀd and Thāmūd are similarly identified with Abū Bakr and ʿUmar. See also al-Qummī, *Tafsīr*, ed. Ṭ. Al-Mūsawī al-Jazāʾirī (Najaf, 1386–7 [1966–7]), vol. 2, p. 263; ed. Muʾassasat al-Mahdī (Qom, 1435 [2014]), vol. 3, p. 920, a pre-Buyid Shiʿi source where ʿĀd and Thāmūd are identified with 'Quraysh' (*hum quraysh*).

[40] Ṭalḥa b. ʿUbayd Allāh was a Qurayshī and a cousin of Abū Bakr. Together with Zubayr b. al-ʿAwwām, he led a coalition against ʿAlī, and they were both defeated and killed at the Battle of the Camel in 36/656; see W. Madelung, 'Talḥa b. ʿUbayd Allāh', *EI2*; idem, 'Talḥa b. ʿUbayd Allāh', *EI3*; L. Veccia Vaglieri, 'al-Djamal', *EI2*; N.I. Haider, 'Camel, Battle of the', *EI3*.

[41] The Qurʾan refers to the people of Madyan who were preached to by the prophet Shuʿayb; see e.g. Q. 7:85; 9:84. Just like the people of ʿĀd and Thāmūd — with whom they are mentioned in Q. 9:70 — they are an example of an impious community from the past who refused God's warnings through His prophets; see F. Buhl and C.E. Bosworth, 'Madyan Shuʿayb', *EI2*; A. Rippin, 'Shuʿayb', *EI2*.

[42] The Qurʾan mentions the people of Rass twice, within enumerations also comprising the people of Noah, ʿĀd and Thāmūd; see Q.25:38; 50:12. No further information is given about them; see A.J. Wensick, 'Aṣḥāb al-Rass', *EI2*.

[43] The Battle of the Camel in 36/656 brought into conflict ʿAlī and a coalition led by Ṭalḥa b.ʿUbayd Allâh and Zubayr b. al-ʿAwwām; see L. Veccia Vaglieri, 'al-Djamal', *EI2*; N.I. Haider, 'Camel, Battle of the', *EI3*; L. Veccia Vaglieri, "Alī b. Abī Ṭālib', *EI2*; R. Gleave, "Alī b. Abī Ṭālib', *EI3*.

[44] The Battle of Nahrawān in 38/658 brought into conflict ʿAlī and those among his partisans who defected him after the Battle of Ṣiffīn, that is, the Khārijites; see L. Veccia Vaglieri, "Alī b. Abī Ṭālib', *EI2*; R. Gleave, "Alī b. Abī Ṭālib', *EI3*.

[45] ʿAlī's opponent in the Battle of Ṣiffīn, and founder of the highly despised — among the Shiʿis — Umayyad dynasty; see M. Hinds, 'Muʿāwiya I', *EI2*.

[46] *Kawr* has the same meaning as *dawr*, 'cycle'. The text is obviously corrupted here, but we gather that it is about demonstrating the continuity of the opposition to the prophets and the Imams; 'in every era and every age', as the *Kashf* puts it insistently, the same archetypes of adversity take new forms. See commentary of *Kashf* I, pp. 147–154.

[47] These three adversaries of Moses are named together in the Qurʾan in 29:33 and 40:24. On Korah, who is dealt with at more lenght, see Q. 28:76–82. On Hāmān, Pharaoh's intendant, see Q. 28:6–8; 40:36.

Second 'Umar and the Third 'Uthmān.[48] So it is in every epoch. Have you not seen the words of God: *'I respited the disbelievers, then I seized them, and how terrible was My rejection!'* [Q. 22:44].[49]

[*Ḥadīths* by ʿAlī b. Abī Ṭālib]

23. Related to this [is the report of] a Shiʿi man who stood before the Prince of the Believers while he was preaching in Kūfa, and said: 'O Prince of the Believers, how did you find this community (*umma*)?' He said: 'By Him who splits the seed and blows the breeze, I have found more in the ancient communities than I have in this one!' According to these words, it is necessary that he is the First and the Last.[50]

24. This is verified by God's words: *'I swear by the planets (al-khunnas),*[51] *that pass and hide'* [Q. 81:15–16]. The Prince of the Believers said: 'The Legatees are from me, and I am from them. We

[48] Pharaoh, Hāmān and their armies are identified with Abū Bakr, 'Umar and their followers in other Shi'i sources; see E. Kohlberg, 'Some Imamī Shīʿī views on the *Ṣaḥāba*', p. 164.

[49] This sentence appears in a context where previous communities who have denied the prophets are mentioned — among them the people of ʿĀd, Thāmūd, Madyan and Moses.

[50] Since he is able to compare the past communities to the present one. This is an allusion to ʿAlī's divinity and to a doctrine of transmigration.

[51] *Khunnas* is usually translated thus. The following exegesis plays on the meaning of the verb *khanasa*, 'to stay back, to recede, to retire, to remain behind', which applies to the planets inasmuch as they 'retire' at dawn. The exegesis alludes to the concealment of the Imamate — its 'retirement' — until the Resurrector comes. In the *Kitāb al-Iṣlāḥ*, the *khunnas* are the five ontological principles: *ʿaql / nafs / jadd / fatḥ / khayāl*; see Abū Ḥātim al-Rāzī, *Kitāb al-Iṣlāḥ*, ed. H. Mînûchehr and M. Moḥaghegh (Tehran, 2004), pp. 128–129. In his *Maqālīd al-malakūtiyya*, al-Sijistānī uses the term *khunnas* to designate the five planets corresponding to the five 'Masters of Laws' (*aṣḥāb al-sharāʾiʿ*) — as opposed to the first and the last 'Masters of Cycles' (*aṣḥāb al-adwār*) who do not bring forward a *sharīʿa*; see al-Sijistānī, *Kitāb al-Maqālīd al-malakūtiyya*, ed. I.K. Poonawala (Tunis, 2011), p. 246. In this interpretation of the term, the fact that the planets who 'retire' refer to the 'Masters of Laws' is probably an allusion to the fact that the Law brought by each one of them is abrogated by the following *nāṭiq*. For another Ismaili interpretation of Q. 81:15–16, see Idrīs 'Imād al-Dīn, *Zahr al-maʿānī*, p. 211.

recede (*nukhnis anfusanā*), we pass and hide from our enemy, until the Durdūr'[52] — which is the sword of the Resurrector.[53] **[11]**

[The continuity of God's Order (*amr*)]

25. The explanation of this is what has been mentioned before, that is, that in every era, there is a Proof of God, whether it is a messenger prophet (*nabī mursal*)[54] or a chosen Imam. Each of them has an enemy in his era, as God — He is Mighty and Sublime — said: '*Thus have We appointed to every prophet an enemy among the sinners*' [Q. 25:31]. The prophet is similar to [another] prophet, and the enemy is similar to [another] enemy. Therefore, every enemy to a prophet is also an enemy to the prophets before and after him, because they have shown enmity to God's Order. Whoever rises against [a prophet] is the enemy [of God's Order]. Thus is the guidance to God's Order, [one prophet] after another in every era and every age. God's Order is one; His Order does not change, and His Will does not turn. Thus, whoever showed enmity towards Ishmael, son of Abraham, who was Abraham's Legatee, is also an enemy to ʿAlī b. Abī Ṭālib, Muḥammad's Legatee — may God bless him and his family — and to Aaron, the Legatee of Moses

[52] This rare term means 'eddy, whirlpool, vortex'. I have found only one occurrence of it in classical Shiʿi literature, in a *ḥadīth* attributed to Jaʿfar al-Ṣādiq: while a Jew was in prayers, he saw two children abusing a cock. Because he did not interrupt his prayer to stop the children, God ordered the earth to swallow him, and 'he fell in the Durdūr' for eternity; see Majlisī, *Biḥār al-anwār, juz'* 100, *abwāb al-amr bi'l-maʿrūf wa'l-nahī ʿan al-munkar, bāb* 1: *wujūb al-amr bi'l-maʿrūf wa'l-nahī ʿan al-munkar wa-faḍluhumā* (Qom, 2008), vol. 21, p. 228, no 67.

[53] See Idrīs ʿImād al-Dīn, *Zahr al-maʿānī*, p. 171, where §§ 23—24 are reproduced quasi literally — except for the quotation of Q. 81:15–16. The latter verse is quoted and interpreted quite differently in ibid., p. 211.

[54] Both mss. read: *nabī wa-mursal*, but this is probably a mistake for *nabī mursal*, an expression found in the famous Shiʿi *ḥadīth*: 'Our Order is difficult, considered difficult, and it cannot be supported by anyone, except *a messenger prophet*, an angel of proximity or a believer whose heart has been tested by God for faith' (*inna amrana ṣaʿb mustaṣʿab, lā yaḥtamiluhu illā malāk muqarrab aw nabī mursal aw ʿabd mu'min imtaḥana Allāh qalbahu li'l-īmān*); see al-Ṣaffār al-Qummī, *Baṣā'ir al-darajāt*, pp. 57–70; al-Kulaynī, *Uṣūl al-Kāfī, k. al-ḥujja, bāb fī mā jā'a anna ḥadīthahum ṣaʿb mustaṣʿab*, ed. ʿA.A. Ghaffārī (Tehran, 1955), vol. 1, pp. 401–402, no. 1–2, 4–5. Also quoted in Jaʿfar b. Manṣūr al-Yaman, *Ta'wīl al-zakāt*, p. 56.

during his lifetime. The words of the Prince of the Believers — 'I found more in the ancient communities, etc.' — means that he establishes God's Order (*al-qā'im bi-amr Allāh*), which the ancient communities had denied when the Legatees established it after their prophets. This is an allusion to what the people of Moses did to Aaron, and what the people of Jesus did to Simon: they all denied God's Order that [the Legatees] had established, which is one. Thus, Muḥammad — may God bless him and all His prophets; the guidance is through His Order — said: 'Alī is in relation to me as Aaron was to Moses'.[55] And God — He is Mighty and Sublime — said: '*The community of your father Abraham*' [Q. 22:78].[56] This explanation is a demonstration of this matter, as was the previous explanation; it is sufficient, and it contains healing. **[12]**

[On the Master of the Age]

26. '*Of what do they question one another? Of the mighty Tiding, on which they are in disagreement*' [Q. 78:1–3]. He said:[57] The 'Tiding' is the Sign (*al-āya*), and what is 'mighty' is what God almighty has made so — there is no god but Him. The Sign is the mark, and the mark is the name, and the name is the tiding, the Master of the Age, who answers the people of the Heavens and the Earths when a calamity hits them. He is the One who establishes the Truth (*qā'im al-ḥaqq*), and from whom the wretched (*mankūs*) Creation turns away, as verified by His words — may He be exalted: '*It is a mighty Tiding, from which you are turning away*' [Q. 38:67–68], and : '*Nay, rather it is clear signs in the breasts of those who have been given knowledge*' [Q. 29:49]. The latter are the people of Friendship (*ahl al-walāya*) who know [the Tiding] and

---

[55] Also quoted in *Kashf* VI, p. 159, § 6; p. 161, § 9.

[56] The relation of the *ḥadīth* and the Qur'anic verse to what precedes is unclear. The author is apparently attempting to illustrate the continuity and unity of 'God's Order' by placing it under the patronage of Abraham, archetype of the monotheist prophet. Q. 22:78 is quoted again in the commentary of the verse of Light below; see *Kashf* I, pp. 17–18, §§ 36–39. See also *Kashf* V, where the 'sacred station of Abraham' (*maqām Ibrāhīm*) is central, esp. pp. 93–95, §§ 5–7; p. 111, § 37.

[57] Again, this indicates that the following exegesis is a *ḥadīth* attributed to an unknown Imam.

look down from it (*al-nāẓirūn minhu*)[58] — may blessings be upon them. It is the reason for God's words — He is Sublime and High: '*None rejects Our signs except every ungrateful disbeliever*' [Q. 31:32]. He means by this those who reject the Resurrector (*al-qā'im*) — may God's blessings be upon him.

[A *ḥadīth* on retribution]

27. Al-Ṣādiq Jaʿfar b. Muḥammad — may God's blessings be upon him — said: 'O Mufaḍḍal,[59] whoever worked yesterday reaps today, and whoever works today reaps tomorrow, retribution for retribution, good for good and evil for evil; your Lord is not iniquitous to anyone. O Mufaḍḍal, do you not see how the Glorious Kingdom (*mulk*) becomes settled (*yastawī*) when its King (*malik*) comes, **[13]** and is unsettled when he leaves? It is just at the beginning and becomes unjust at the end.' Then he recited [the verse]: '*[Not one soul shall be wronged anything;] even it be the weight of one grain of mustard-seed, We shall produce it, and sufficient are We for reckoning*' [Q. 21:47], and what He said about the unbelievers: '*Do We ever retribute any but the unbeliever?*' [Q. 34:17]. He then applied this to the Creation (*jaʿalahu jāriyan fī'l-khalq*): retribution for retribution. The meaning of this is that the one who begins is the most iniquitous; it is he the iniquitous one, not the one who retributes.

[Enumeration of the Gates, Proofs and Orphans]

28. The names of the Gates: the Gate of Adam was Seth, his Proof; the Gate of Noah was Shem, his Proof; the Gate of Abraham was Ismael, his Proof; the Gate of Moses was Joshua, his Proof;[60] and the Gate of Jesus was Simon, his Proof.

---

[58] R. Strothmann, p. 13, n. 1, suggests that this enigmatic expression might allude to Q. 57:13: '*On the day when the hypocritical men and the hypocritical women will say unto those who believe: "Look on us (unẓurūnā) that we may borrow from your light!".*' It could also allude to Q. 2:50: '*And when We brought you through the sea and rescued you, and drowned the folk of Pharaoh while you were beholding (wa-antum tanẓurūn).*'

[59] Mufaḍḍal b. Jābir al-Juʿfī, a disciple of Jaʿfar al-Ṣādiq and a figure of the *ghulāt*; see introduction, p. 9 and references provided there.

[60] On Joshua (Shuʿayb) as Proof of Moses, see also *Kashf* V, p. 97, § 12. Compare with other passages where Aaron is the Proof of Moses: *Kashf* I, p. 12, § 25; III, p. 75, § 52; VI, p. 162, § 12.

29. The Proof of Muḥammad was ʿAlī; <the Proof of ʿAlī was Ḥasan>,[61] the Proof of Ḥasan was Ḥusayn, the Proof of Ḥusayn was ʿAlī son of Ḥusayn, the Proof of ʿAlī son of Ḥusayn was his son Muḥammad al-Bāqir, the Proof of al-Bāqir was Abū ʿAbd Allāh Jaʿfar al-Ṣādiq son of Muḥammad. And so on with the Imams after Jaʿfar b. Muḥammad, his sons succeeding one another until the Resurrector comes — may God's blessings be upon them all.

30. The names of the Orphans:[62] Abū Dharr [Jundab b. Junāda al-Ghifārī],[63] al-Miqdād [b. al-Aswad al-Kindī],[64] ʿAmmār [b. Yāsir],[65] Dāwud,[66] Muḥammad [b. Abī Bakr?],[67] ʿAbd Allāh [b. Rawāḥa

---

[61] Missing in both manuscripts.

[62] On the notion of Orphan and for a discussion of the following passage, see commentary of *Kashf* III, pp. 272–279.

[63] One of the first converts to Islam, he is greatly revered in Shiʿi Islam as one of the closest companions of ʿAlī, along with Salmān al-Fārisī and al-Miqdād. On him, see J. Robson, 'Abū <u>Dh</u>arr', *EI2*; A. Asfaruddin, 'Abū Dharr al-Ghifārī', *EI3*; A.J. Cameron, *Abû Dharr al-Ghifârî. An examination of his image in the hagiography of Islam* (London, 1982). He is one of Salmān's five Orphans in Nuṣayrī doctrine; see R. Dussaud, *Histoire et religion des Noṣairîs* (Paris, 1900), pp. 68 ff.; Y. Friedman, *The Nuṣayrī-ʿAlawīs, An Introduction to the Religion, History and Identity of the Leading Minority in Syria* (Leiden, 2009), pp. 90 ff. See also *Kashf* III, pp. 70–71, § 46; V, p. 100, § 22.

[64] One of the first converts to Islam and a partisan of ʿAlī against Muʿāwiya. He is one of Salmān's five Orphans in Nuṣayrī doctrine; see R. Dussaud, *Histoire et religion des Noṣairîs*, pp. 68 ff..; Y. Friedman, *The Nuṣayrī-ʿAlawīs*, pp. 90 ff. See also *Kashf* III, p. 70, § 45.

[65] One of the first converts to Islam, he participated in all the battles led by the Prophet Muḥammad and was one of the heroes of the Battle of Badr. As a governor of Kūfa since ʿUmar's caliphate, he contributed in rallying its population to ʿAlī before the Battle of the Camel, in which he participated. He was therefore one of ʿAlī's most trusted men. He died at the Battle of Siffīn; see H. Reckendorf, "Ammār b. Yāsir', *EI2*. According to Nuṣayrī doctrine, he is one of the Orphans of Safīna, who himself was the *bāb* of the Imam Ḥasan.

[66] Like H. Halm, I was not able to identify him; see H. Halm, *Kosmologie* p. 154.

[67] He was the son of Abū Bakr, but never really knew his father who died when he was only three years old. His mother went on to marry ʿAlī who became fond of him and raised him. He was a salient figure of the opposition to ʿUthmān, and, according to some reports, participated in his assassination. A supporter of ʿAlī after the latter became the caliph, he fought alongside him during the Battle of the Camel. He then governed Egypt on ʿAlī's behalf before ʿAmr b. al-Āṣ took over and had him horribly tortured and killed; on him, see G.R. Hawting, 'Muḥammad b. Abī Bakr', *EI2*; M.

al-Ansārī ?],[68] al-ʿAbbās [b. ʿAbd al-Muṭṭalib],[69] Jaʿfar [b. al-Ḥārith],[70] **[14]** Ḥamza [b. ʿAbd al-Muṭṭalib],[71] Ḥanẓala [b. Asaʿd al-Shibāmī],[72] Aswad[73] and Shuʿayb[74] are Orphans.

Yazigi, 'Defense and Validation in Shi'i and Sunni Tradition: The Case of Muḥammad b. Abī Bakr', *Studia Islamica*, 98/99 (2004), pp. 49–70. In the present passage, the *Kitāb al-Kashf* does not specify the identity of this Muḥammad, which is probably why H. Halm refrains from identifying him with Muḥammad b. Abī Bakr; see H. Halm, *Kosmologie*, p. 155. It is true that the *Kashf* presents him as the Orphan of Ibn Abī Zaynab, i.e. Abū'l-Khaṭṭāb, which is anachronistic. However, as Muḥammad b. Abī Bakr is mentioned several times in the collection (see *Kashf* I, p. 24, § 52; V, pp. 94–95, §§ 7–8; p. 152, § 103), and because, just like ʿAmmār b. Yāsir, he is considered one of Safīna's five Orphans in the Nuṣayrī tradition, I am inclined to believe that he must be identified with the Muḥammad of the present list.

[68] On him, see A. Schaade, "Abd Allāh b. Rawāḥa', *EI2*; S. Mirza, "Abd Allāh b. Rawāḥa', *EI3*. Again, the *Kashf* does not specify the identity of this ʿAbd Allāh, and H. Halm refrains from identifying him; see H. Halm, *Kosmologie*, p. 155. However, it is likely that we are dealing with ʿAbd Allāh Rawāḥa al-Ansārī, since he is considered as one of Salmān's five Orphans in the Nuṣayrī tradition; see R. Dussaud, *Histoire et religion des Noṣairîs*, p. 68 ff.; Y. Friedman, *The Nuṣayrī-ʿAlawīs*, p. 90 ff.

[69] He was Muḥammad and ʿAlī's uncle, and fought against the Muslims at the Battle of Badr, before converting when they marched on Mecca in 8/630. He was on bad terms with ʿUmar; see W. Montgomery Watt, 'al-ʿAbbās b. ʿAbd al-Muṭṭalib', *EI2*.

[70] A grandson of ʿAbd al-Muṭṭalib. The Nusayrīs list him among the Prophet Muḥammad's Orphans; see H. Halm, *Kosmologie*, p. 155; M.M. Bar-Asher and A. Kofsky, *The Nuṣayrī -ʿAlawī Religion*, p. 190 (Arabic: p. 215).

[71] Another of Muḥammad and ʿAlī's uncles, he was very close to the former. He fought heroically during the battle of Badr and died the following year at the battle of Uḥud, which the Muslims lost to Quraysh; see G.M. Meredith-Owens, 'Ḥamza b. ʿAbd al-Muṭṭalib', *EI2*.

[72] I follow H. Halm's suggestion of identification, which he bases on a Nuṣayri text where Ḥanẓala b. Saʿd (*sic*) al-Shibāmī sacrifices himself for Ḥusayn in Karbalāʾ, thus allowing Ḥusayn to enter in occultation; see H. Halm, *Kosmologie*, p. 155 and p.155 note 70; R. Strothmann, *Esoterische Sonderthemen*, p. 10 (Arabic text, p. 13, § 45).

[73] According to H. Halm, he was a close companion to the fourth Imam, ʿAlī Zayn al-ʿĀbidīn; see H. Halm, *Kosmologie*, p. 155.

[74] According to H. Halm, he was considered as a 'client' (*mawlā*) of the fourth Imam, ʿAlī Zayn al-ʿĀbidīn, by the Nuṣayris; see H. Halm, *Kosmologie*, p. 155.

31. The father of the first two is Salmān,[75] and the father of the next two is <. . .>.[76] Muḥammad and ʿAbd Allāh's father is Ibn Abī Zaynab,[77] ʿAbbās and Jaʿfar's father is Safīna,[78] Ḥamza and Ḥanẓala's father is Rushayd al-Hajarī,[79] Aswad and Shuʿayb's father was Abū Khālid [ʿAbd Allāh b. Ghālib al-Kābulī].[80] These are the Orphans and their fathers.

[The Completers: exegesis of Q. 7:142]

32. *'We appointed for Moses thirty nights, and We completed them with ten; thus was completed the time appointed by his Lord of forty nights'* [Q. 7:142]. By these thirty, he means the Proofs, because the nocturnal Proof is the Master of the confidential speech (*najwā*)[81] and the covenant,

---

[75] A famous companion of Muḥammad and ʿAlī, a considerable literature was devoted to him, notably with regard to his importance in esoteric Shiʿism. He holds an eminent position in the Nuṣayri system, as third member of the trinity *maʿnā / ism / bāb*; see G. Levi Della Vida, 'Salmān al-Fārisī', *EI2*; L. Massignon, 'Salmān Pāk et les prémices spirituelles de l'Islam iranien', in idem, *Opera Minora*, ed. Y. Moubarac (Beirut, 1963), vol. 2, pp. 443–483; R. Dussaud, *Histoire et religion des Noṣairîs*, pp. 63–67; Y. Friedman, *The Nuṣayrī-ʿAlawīs*, index *s.v.* Salmān, etc. See also *Kashf* III, pp. 71–73, §§ 47–48.

[76] The name is lost; both manuscripts read *yatīm*, 'orphan'.

[77] As noted by Halm, this is Abū'l-Khaṭṭāb al-Asadī (d. 755), the famous founder of the sect of the Khaṭṭābiyya, who was excommunicated by Jaʿfar al-Ṣādiq; see H. Halm, *Kosmologie*, p. 155; idem, 'Das 'Buch der Schatten'', II, p. 83. The Nuṣayris consider him as the *bāb* of the seventh Imam, Mūsa al-Kāẓim; see Y. Friedman, *The Nuṣayrī-ʿAlawīs*, p. 287.

[78] Abū ʿAbd al-Raḥmān Qays b. Warqā' al-Riyāḥī, whose nickname was Safīna, was an emancipated slave of Muḥammad. The Nuṣayris consider him as the *bāb* of the second Imam, al-Ḥasan b. ʿAlī; see Y. Friedman, *The Nuṣayrī-ʿAlawīs*, p. 287.

[79] A quite obscure character, he suffered martyrdom for his loyalty to ʿAlī, according to several sources. Hence his special status in Shiʿi historiography. It seems he denied ʿAlī's death and believed in his *rajʿa*, in the manner of the Saba'iyya; see S. Anthony, *The Caliph and the Heretic*, pp. 213–218. The Nuṣayris consider him as the *bāb* of the third Imam, al-Ḥusayn b. ʿAlī; see Y. Friedman, *The Nuṣayrī-ʿAlawīs*, p. 287.

[80] The Nuṣayris consider him as the *bāb* of the fourth Imam, ʿAlī Zayn al-ʿĀbidīn; see Y. Friedman, *The Nuṣayrī-ʿAlawīs*, p. 287.

[81] Originally a Qur'anic term, *najwā* came to designate a tax paid by those who attended the *majālis al-ḥikma*, that is, the learning sessions held during the Fatimid period. This, as well as the present passage, suggest that the term was adopted by the Ismailis to designate initiation. On initiatory taxes, such as *najwā* or *fiṭra*, see H. Halm,

while the diurnal Proof is the Master of the sword and the evident proof (*burhān*), as God — may He be exalted — mentioned: '. . .*apparent cities. . .*' (*qurā ẓāhira*) [Q. 34:18]. The apparent [cities] are the Masters of the swords, while the hidden (*bāṭina*) [cities] are the Masters of the confidential talk.[82]

33. Between two Speaking-Prophets, there are six Completers (*atimmā'*); thus, from Adam to Noah, there were six, and so on until Aḥmad, that is, Muḥammad the Messenger of God[83] — may God's blessing and peace be upon him and his family. Six times five[84] equal thirty Completers by whom the Legacy is completed. And so, His words: '*We appointed for Moses thirty nights. . .*' [refer to] the thirty Completers from Adam to Muḥammad. When Aḥmad appeared, spoke the Revelation (*naṭaqa bi'l-tanzīl*) and summoned (*daʿā*)

'The Ismaʿili oath of allegiance (*ʿahd*) and the 'sessions of wisdom' (*majālis al-ḥikma*) in Fatimid times', in F. Daftary, ed, *Mediaeval Ismaʿili History and Thought* (Cambridge, 1996), pp. 103–104. See also D. Hollenberg, *Beyond the Qur'ān*, p. 14, although the author does not mention the *najwā*. The tax was abolished by the caliph al-Ḥākim bi-Amr Allāh; see M. Canard, 'al-Ḥākim bi-Amr Allāh', *EI2*; H. Halm, 'Der Treuhänder Gottes: Die Edikte des Kalifen al-Ḥākim', *Der Islam*, 63 (1986), pp. 41–42; P.E. Walker, 'The Ismaili Daʿwa in the Reign of the Fatimid Caliph Al-Ḥākim', *Journal of the American Research Center in Egypt*, 30 (1993), p. 174 and p. 174, n. 88. On the payments made in exchange for access to esoteric knowledge, see P. Walker, 'Techniques for guarding and restricting esoteric knowledge in the Ismaili daʿwa during the Fatimid period', in Popovič, M. et al, eds, *Sharing and Hiding Religious Knowledge in Early Judaism, Christianity, and Islam* (Berlin, 2018), pp. 186–197, esp. pp. 192–194. On the *majālis al-ḥikma*, see H. Halm, 'The Ismaʿili oath of allegiance'; idem, *The Fatimids and their Traditions of Learning* (London, 1997).

[82] For a similar distinction between the 'twelve nocturnal Proofs, Masters of the Exegesis' and the 'twelve diurnal Proofs, Masters of the Exoteric of the Revelation', see e.g. Jaʿfar b. Manṣūr al-Yaman, *Sarā'ir wa Asrār al-nutaqā'*, p. 42.

[83] The Prophet Muḥammad is named Aḥmad in reference to Q. 61:6, where Jesus announces a '*Messenger to come after me and whose name shall be Aḥmad*'. Here, the use of the name Aḥmad is aimed at distinguishing him from another Muḥammad, mentioned a few lines further, who is presumably the Mahdī. It is not clear, however, whether the Mahdī is called Muḥammad because of the traditional idea that he will bear the same name as the Prophet (i.e. Muḥammad b. ʿAbd Allāh), or if the text is referring to Muḥammad b. Ismāʿīl.

[84] There are five Speaking-Prophets before Muḥammad: Adam, Noah, Abraham, Moses and Jesus.

[people] to it, he abrogated the Laws (*nasakha al-sharāʾiʿ*) of the prophets who spoke before him: this is why **[15]** he established the month of Ramaḍān making it an obligation for everyone who settles in the community of Aḥmad to fast [during this month]. This is because each day [of fasting] corresponds to a Completer, and fasting, in the esoteric sense, is silence. When Aḥmad spoke, he broke the fasting of the fasters by his speaking of the Revelation.

34. *'And We completed them with ten'*: to be complete, the [number of] Proofs from Aḥmad to Muḥammad is eight. They are the bearers of the Throne; the Throne is knowledge, and knowledge is the exegesis (*al-ʿilm huwa al-taʾwīl*). *'We completed them with ten; thus was completed the time appointed by his Lord of forty nights'*: [the time is completed with] the eight Completers, to which are added Aḥmad and Muḥammad, which completes the ten — may God's blessings be upon them all.[85]

35. In this [verse], Moses represents Aḥmad, and the 'time' [referred to] is the Speaking-Prophet of Speaking-Prophets (*nāṭiq al-nuṭaqāʾ*).[86] The words of the Prophet — may God bless him: 'Fast when you see [the crescent of the moon], and break your fast when you see it',[87] mean: 'Stay silent on the knowledge of Truth'. 'Do not break your fast'[88] means: 'Do not talk before the appearance of the Speaking-Prophet of the cycle or an Imam.'

---

[85] Same interpretation in Jaʿfar b. Manṣūr al-Yaman, *Kitāb al-Farāʾiḍ wa-ḥudūd al-dīn*, IIS MS 1406, ff. 175–176. In contrast, the interpretation of Q. 7:142 in other works by Jaʿfar b. Manṣūr al-Yaman is quite different: see Jaʿfar b. Manṣūr al-Yaman, *Taʾwīl al-zakāt*, pp. 70–71, 131–132; idem, *Sarāʾir wa Asrār al-nutaqāʾ*, pp. 83, 217. In the latter source, each Speaking-Prophet is followed by a Legatee *and* six Completers — instead of six Completers only in the *Kashf*.

[86] That is, the Mahdī who is the seventh and the last of the Speaking-Prophets.

[87] This *ḥadīth* can be found in most Sunni collections; see e.g. al-Bukhārī, *Al-Jāmiʿ al-ṣaḥīḥ*, *k. al-ṣawm*, *bāb* 11, ed. M.D. al-Khaṭīb (Cairo, 1400/1979), no. 1909, vol. 2, p. 33.

[88] According to a variant of the same *ḥadīth*; see e.g. al-Bukhārī, *Ṣaḥīḥ*, *k. al-ṣawm*, *bāb* 11, no. 1906, vol. 2, p. 32: 'Do not fast before you see the crescent of the moon, and do not break fast before you see it.'

[The verse of Light: exegesis of Q. 24:35][89]

36. God — may He be exalted, glorified and praised — says: '*God is the Light of the heavens and the earth*' [Q. 24:35]. His Light in the heavens [**16**] is His guidance, and His light in the earth is the Imams through whom one is rightly guided. '*The similitude of His Light*' on earth '*is a niche wherein is a Lamp*': a niche (*mishkāt*), in the language of the Ethiopians, is a recess with an aperture.[90] [God] gives it as a similitude (*ḍarabahā mathalan*) of Fāṭima al-Zahrā', daughter of Muḥammad, who has no imperfection — may God bless them both.

37. '*[A niche] wherein is a Lamp*', that is, Ḥusayn — peace be upon him. '*The Lamp is in a Glass*', [refers to] when [Ḥusayn] was in her womb. '*The Glass is as it were a glittering star*' refers to Fāṭima — may God's blessings be upon her — who is like a glass due to her qualities, and whose elevation above other women is like that of a glittering, that is a radiant, star.

38. '*[The lamp] is kindled from a Blessed Tree*', which is Abraham, the intimate friend of the Merciful One — may God's blessings be upon him. '*An Olive Tree*' refers to Abraham; after He called him a tree, [He now specifies] that it is an olive tree. 'Olive tree' is among the names of the Imams and Messengers, while 'fig tree' is among the names of the Legatees and the Proofs.[91] Hence, it is said that [the lamp]

[89] The following exegesis of Q. 24:35 has several identical or close features with others: see al-Furāt al-Kūfī, *Tafsīr*, ed. M. al-Kāẓim (Tehran, 1990), pp. 281–282, 286; al-Qummī, *Tafsīr*, ed. Ṭ. Al-Mūsawī al-Jazā'irī, vol. 2, pp. 102–103; ed. Mu'assasat al-Mahdī vol. 2, p. 707; al-Kulaynī, *Uṣūl al-Kāfī, k. al-ḥujja, bāb anna al-a'imma nūr Allāh*, vol. 1, p. 195, no. 5; Ibn Bābawayh, *Kitāb al-Tawḥīd, bāb* 15, ed. Hāshim al-Ḥusaynī al-Tihrānī (Tehran, 1398/1978), pp. 157–159, no. 3–4; al-Sijistānī, *Al-Maqālīd al-malakūtiyya*, 52nd *iqlīd*, pp. 238–242. For a brief comparison of al-Sijistānī's *ta'wīl* of this verse with the *Kashf*'s, see I.K. Poonawala, 'Ismā'īlī ta'wīl of the Qur'an', pp. 220–221. It should be noted however that most of the *Kashf*'s interpretation builds on earlier Shi'i traditions, and is thus closer to the latter than to al-Sijistānī's interpretation. For a more clearly Ismaili exegesis of the verse of Light, see Ja'far b. Manṣūr al-Yaman, *Al-Shawāhid wa'l-bayān*, IIS MS. 734, ff. 88–89.

[90] This is indeed the case; see A. Jeffery, *The Foreign Vocabulary of the Qur'ān* (Baroda, 1938, repr. Leiden-Boston, 2007), p. 266.

[91] Same identification of the 'fig tree' with the Proofs and the 'olive tree' with the Imams in Ja'far b. Manṣūr al-Yaman, *al-Riḍā' fi'l-bātin*, p. 62. Such a distribution of roles with, on the one hand, the Messengers (*rusul*) and the Imams, and, on the other

is rooted in a Speaking-Prophet. Then, [God] says: *'Neither eastern, nor western'*, which means that the community is Abraham's — peace be upon him — his community being neither eastern, that is, Christian (*naṣrāniyya*), similar to the community of Jesus, nor western, that is, Jewish, similar to the community of Moses. Thus, God — may He be exalted — speaks of *'the community of your father Abraham, who named you* **[17]** *Muslims aforetime'* [Q. 22:78], and said: *'Abraham was neither Jewish nor Christian (naṣrāniyyan), but he was a ḥanīf and a Muslim'* [Q. 3:67].

39. Then He says: *'[A tree] whose oil would almost illuminate'* [Q. 24:35], which means that Ḥusayn — may God bless him — almost spoke of his Imamate while still in [Fāṭima's] womb, before she gave birth to him. This is [what] His words [mean]: *'[It would almost illuminate] though no fire touched it'*. He says: though he was not appointed by an Imam [yet]. *'Light upon Light'* is about his intelligence and his [spiritual] wealth; he guides and is guided by his Imam. *'God guides to His Light whom He wills'* among His creatures. He says[92] that, through their loyalty (*walāya*) [to the Imam], [God] guides them to the loyalty (*walāya*) to the Imams of his progeny. *'God strikes similitudes for men, and God knows all thing.'*

[The good tree and the corrupt tree: exegesis of Q. 14:24–27]

40. [God] — He is Mighty and Sublime — said: *'A good word is like a good tree'* [Q. 14:24]. The 'word' (*kalima*) is Muḥammad the Messenger of God — may God bless him and his family — [because] the Messengers are words. Have you not heard the words of God: *'[God] verifies the Truth by His Words'* [Q. 42:24] — that is, by His Messengers? *'Like a good tree'* means Fāṭima, who is good. *'. . .whose root is firm'* [Q. 14:24] means Muḥammad — may God bless him and his family. *'Its branches reach into heaven, it gives its produce every season by*

---

hand, the Legatees (*awṣiyā'*) and the Proofs (*ḥujaj*) can be found in other passages of the *Kashf*; see *Kashf* III, p. 80, § 64; V, pp. 126–127, § 62; p. 153, § 104. It seems characteristic of early Fatimid doctrine and designed to establish an analogy between prophethood and (Fatimid) Imamate.

[92] Again, it is not clear whether this 'he' refers to God or to the interpreter of the verse.

permission **[18]** *of its Lord*' [Q. 14:24–25]: this is the sacred station (*maqām*) of the succession of Imams from [Fāṭima's] progeny.

41. '*God strikes similitudes for men, in order that they may reflect. And the similitude of a corrupt word is as a corrupt tree*' [Q. 14:25–26]. This is Zufar[93] in the revelation (*tanzīl*), that is, Satan in the esoteric sense.[94] '*As a corrupt tree*' means the Umayyads.[95] '*Uprooted from the*

---

[93] One of ʿUmar's nicknames in Shiʿi literature. According to E. Kohlberg, it has no pejorative connotation and is used because it rimes with ʿUmar; see E. Kohlberg, 'Some Imamī Shīʿī views on the *Ṣaḥāba*', pp. 162, 163, n. 107. However, M.A. Amir-Moezzi indicates that the term means 'a beast loaded with heavy weights', that is, a donkey; see M.A. Amir-Moezzi, 'Review of *Scripture and Exegesis in Early Imâmî Shiism* by Meir M. Bar-Asher', *Studia Islamica*, 92 (2001), p. 209. See also M.M. Bar-Asher, *Scripture and Exegesis*, p. 119, n. 132, for further references in the pre-Buyid *Tafsīrs* of al-ʿAyyāshī and al-Qummī.

[94] In the pre-Buyid Shiʿi exegetical tradition, certain Qurʾanic mentions of Satan (Q. 2:208, 14:22) are identified with ʿUmar, either alone or together with Abū Bakr; see M.M. Bar-Asher, *Scripture and Exegesis*, pp. 84, 109, and 43–44 for the omission of this identification in the printed and some manuscript versions of *Tafsīr al-Qummī*. See also al-ʿAyyāshī, *Tafsīr*, ed. Muʾassasat al-Biʿtha (Qom, 2000), vol. 1, pp. 213, 214; vol. 2, p. 404. In the latter passage, it is said that every mention of 'Satan' in the Qurʾan should be understood as the 'Second', i.e. ʿUmar. The same hermeneutic key is found in a *ghulāt* source; see Mufaḍḍal al-Juʿfī, *Kitāb al-Haft waʾl-aẓilla*, Ch. 37, p. 77. Similar statement in *Kashf* I, p. 27, § 60, but 'anything concerning Satan in the Qurʾan' is referred to Abū Bakr. For an Ismaili example of the identification of Satan with ʿUmar, see Jaʿfar b. Manṣūr al-Yaman, *Sarāʾir wa-asrār al-nuṭaqāʾ*, p. 86. See also *Kashf* I, p. 30, § 63, and references there for the identification of the Qurʾanic couple 'man'/'Satan' with Abū Bakr and ʿUmar.

[95] In what Bar-Asher has labelled the 'pre-Buwayhid school of exegesis', both the 'cursed tree' from Q. 17:60 and the 'corrupt tree' from Q. 14:26 are commonly identified with the Banū Umayya, as opposed to the 'good tree' from verse 14:24; see M.M. Bar-Asher, *Scripture and Exegesis*, pp. 207–208. This exegetical tradition then flourished in Ismailism: see e.g. al-Qāḍī al-Nuʿmān, *al-Majālis waʾl-musāyarāt*, ed. H. al-Faqī et al. (Tunis, 1978), p. 116; al-Sijistānī, *Kitāb al-Iftikhār*, ed. I.K. Poonawala (Tunis, 2000), pp. 173 ('Umayyads'), 227 ('Yazīd'); al-Naysābūrī, *Ithbāt al-imāma*, in A. Lalani, ed. and trans., *Degrees of Excellence: A Fatimid Treatise on Leadership in Islam* (London and New York, 2010), pp. 47–48, §§ 26–27 (Arabic text, pp. 25–26). In the latter source, Q. 14:24–26 is used as an illustration of the distinction between plants that are good and useful to men, and others are bad and harmful; the former are the Imams, while the latter are the 'Imams of the people of exotericism' (*aʾimmat ahl al-ẓāhir*), who are not named. On Q. 17:60, see also Idrīs ʿImād al-Dīn, *Zahr al-maʿānī*, p. 193.

earth, having no stability', that is, from the higher hell (*min a'lā jahannam*).[96] The earth is similar to the Legatee from whom one is saved from hell. They are 'uprooted' from the Legatee, which means that they are separated [from him]. '*Having no stability*' means that it is not adequately attached to religion and the world.

42. '*God confirms those who believe by a firm saying in the worldly life*' — <. . .>[97] who places the exegesis above the revelation[98] — '*and in the hereafter*' [Q. 14:27], that is, the Recurrence (*al-karra*).[99] '*God misguides the iniquitous*' who rejected the Friendship (*walāya*) of the Prince of the Believers and claimed the Affair (*al-amr*) after the Messenger. '*God does what He wills*' [Q. 14:27]: He forgives whom He wills, for He is the Forgiver and the Merciful. '*God admits into His Mercy whom He wills*' [Q. 48:25], that is, into the Friendship (*walāya*) of 'Alī. '*If they are separated*', that is, if they are hypocrites, '*then We will punish* **[19]** *those from them who disbelieved*' in the Friendship (*walāya*) of the Prince of the Believers, '*with a painful punishment*' [Q. 48:25], that is, [a] sore [punishment].

[The path and the *walāya*: exegesis of Q. 47:1]

43. God — He is Mighty and Sublime — said: '*Those who disbelieve and bar from God's Path, God will send their deeds astray*' [Q. 47:1]. He[100] said that the clear Path (*al-sabīl al-wāḍiḥ*) is the Prince of the

---

[96] The text is ambiguous here as it seems to draw an equivalence between the 'earth', further identified with 'Alī, and the 'higher hell'. Of course, one should understand that whoever is 'uprooted' *is* in Hell.

[97] Ms. A: *wa-huwa 'inda al-nasla fī'l-tazwīj ya'nī*. . .; ms. B: *'inda al-mas'ala fī'l-tazwīj*. Neither is intelligible. Strothmann leaves a blank space until *al-ta'wīl*. See following footnote.

[98] Ms. A: *min awjuh al-ta'wīl bi'l-tanzīl*; ms. B: *min mazāwij awjuh al-ta'wīl bi'l-tanzīl*. I translated the version of ms. A, although the first part of the sentence is missing. See previous footnote.

[99] *Karra* would normally translate as 'return'. However, to differentiate it from the term *raj'a* or *ma'ād*, I will at times translate it by 'recurrence' — which also presents the advantage of highlighting the transmigrationist connotations of *karra*. The term was indeed used in this sense by certain *ghulāt*, which the *Kashf* clearly echoes, particularly in Treatise I.

[100] Once more, it alludes to an anonymous exegete of the verse, most probably an Imam.

Believers — may God's blessings be upon him. He is the '*straight Way (al-ṣirāṭ al-mustaqīm)*' [Q. 1:6].[101] Thus, whoever disbelieves in his Friendship (*walāya*) and meets God in this state, then God will frustrate his deed, send his effort astray and make it as '*scattered dust*' [Q. 25:23]. He will cast their faces into the Fire and do justice to every man among them on the Day of Resurrection. Even if he has [accomplished] works as [lofty as] the firm mountains (*al-jibāl al-rawāsī*), if he does not meet God in the Friendship (*walāya*) of the Prince of the Believers, his work will profit him nothing.[102] God — He is Mighty and Sublime — said: '*We shall turn unto the work they did and make it scattered dust*' [Q. 25:23].

[Exegesis of Q. 6:59]

44. God — He is Mighty and Sublime — said: '*Not a leaf falls but He knows it*' [Q. 6:59]. He said that the 'leaf' is the drop [of sperm] that enters the womb. '*Not a grain amid the darkness of the earth*': the 'grain' is the child, and the darkness of the earth is the mother. '*Nor anything fresh or dry*', that is, neither living nor dead, '*but it is in a Book Manifest*' [Q. 6:59], because of His words: '*[No affliction befalls in the earth or in yourselves] before We bring it into being*' [Q. 57:22]. He is saying that the manifest has manifested itself [through] the Speaking Imam (*al-Imam al-nāṭiq*) — may God's blessings be upon him and his family.

[Exegesis of Q. 2:1–3; 5]

45. '*Alif Lām Mīm. This is the Book wherein is no doubt*' [Q. 2:1–2]. He says that '*Alif Lām Mīm*' is Muḥammad — may God's blessings be upon him — and [the Book] opens by addressing him. The 'Book Manifest' is the Prince **[20]** of the Believers, ʿAlī b. Abī Ṭālib — may God's blessings be upon him. '*[The Book] wherein is no doubt*' means 'wherein there is no uncertainty'. The '*guidance for the godfearing*'

---

[101] The identification of ʿAlī, and the Imams in general, with the Qurʾanic terms *sabīl* and *ṣirāṭ* is common in pre-Buwayhid Shiʿi exegesis, particularly in the 'personalized commentaries'; see e.g. M.A. Amir-Moezzi, *Le Coran silencieux et le Coran parlant*, p. 96; idem, *La Religion discrète*, pp. 95, 183 (English trans.: *Spirituality of Shiʿi Islam*, pp. 112, 240); idem, '*Al-Durr al-ṯamīn* attribué à Rağab al-Bursī', pp. 221, 225; M.M. Bar-Asher, *Scripture and Exegesis*, p. 202. See also index s.v. *sabīl*, *ṣirāṭ*.

[102] This sentence is reminiscent of *1 Corinthians*, 13:2–3.

[Q. 2:2] is the Imam of the believers who sought protection in the Friendship (*walāya*) of ʿAlī b. Abī Ṭālib and fear the friendship (*walāya*) of *'the Jibt and the Ṭāghūt'* [Q. 4:51] and the Imams of misguidance. *'Those who believe in the mystery (ghayb)'* — that is, the mystery of what they know through the knowledge of the Imamate — *'and those who perform the prayer and spend of what We have provided them'* [Q. 2:3] — the prayer is Ḥusayn and the Imams of his progeny. *'They spend of what We have provided them'* refers to the alms that they convey to those to whom it belongs. *'Those are upon guidance from their Lord'* — that is, upon knowledge from their Imam — *'and those are the successful'* [Q. 2:5]; He says they are those who are saved in the hereafter.

[Exegesis of Q. 14:28–30][103]

46. God — He is Mighty and Sublime — said: *'Have you not seen those who exchange the grace of God for disbelief?'* [Q. 14:28]. The grace of God is the Friendship (*walāya*) of the Prince of the Believers, and their 'exchanging' is their rejection of his Friendship (*walāya*). They are the people of Taym, ʿAdī, <Makhzūm and Umayya>.[104] *'They have caused their people to descend to the abode of loss (dār al-bawār)'* (Q. 14:28). <. . .>[105] <light>[106] <of the Kingdom; they will never have any part in the Kingdom>[107], [as] God — He is Mighty and Sublime — said: *'You are a people lost (qawman būran)'* [Q. 48:12]. As for the Umayyads, [their fate] has been delayed **[21]** until the Day of Resurrection (*qiyāma*), which is the apparition of the Speaking-Prophet and his rising (*qiyāma*) — may God's blessings be upon him. In the hereafter, [there will be] *'Gehenna wherein they are roasted, a terrible abode'* [Q. 14:29].

47. *'They give equals to God to mislead [people] from His Path'* [Q. 14:30]: this refers to the leaders (*aʾimma*) they appoint apart from

---

[103] The following paragraphs continue the exegesis started above, pp. 18–20, §§ 40–42.

[104] Ms. A: blank space. All these clans are branches of Quraysh: Taym is the clan of Abū Bakr and Ṭalḥa ibn ʿUbayd Allāh, ʿAdī is the clan of ʿUmar, Makhzūm is the clan of Khālid b. al-Walīd — all of them enemies of the Shiʿa.

[105] Ms. A: blank space; ms. B: illegible words in secret alphabet.

[106] Ms. A: missing.

[107] Mss. A, B: *min al-mulk lā yakūn fīhim min al-mulk abadan.*

God. They obey them as the Friends (*awliyā'*) of God obey the Imam, that is, the Prince of the Believers — may God bless him. '*Say*', Muḥammad: '*Take your joy*', for their joy in diverging from you and the Imams from your progeny will bring them '*to the Fire*' [Q. 14:30].

[Exegesis of Q. 2:165–167]

48. He said — He is Mighty and Sublime: '*Yet there be men who take to themselves equals to God, apart from God*' [Q. 2:165], that is, leaders (*a'imma*) apart from God, '*and they love them as God is loved*', that is, as the Friends (*awliyā'*) of God love the Imam whom God — He is Mighty and Sublime — has chosen — may God's blessings be upon whom God choses. '*And those who believe*', that is, [those who believe] in His Messenger — may God bless him — and accept the Friendship (*walāya*) of ʿAlī — may God bless him — '*love [God] more ardently*' because they have for the one chosen by God the love those have for their *Jibt* and their *Ṭāghūt*. By '*the Jibt and the Ṭāghūt*' [Q. 4:51], he means the First and the Second.[108] 'If only you could see, Muḥammad, '*those who have been iniquitous*'[109] to the Prince of the Believers, that is, ʿAlī — peace be upon him — '*when they see the torment*' on the day the Resurrector rises (*yawma qiyām al-qā'im*), [they would see that] '*the power altogether belongs to God entirely, and that God is terrible in punishment*' [Q. 2:165].

49. To the enemies of the Prince of the Believers, He says: '*When those who are followed disown (tabarra'a) those who followed them, [when] they see the punishment* **[22]** *and the links*' of the Friendship (*walāya*) they gave to the one they took as a friend (*man tawallūhu*) '*are cut off*' [Q. 2:166], '*those who followed will say: "If only we might return (karra), and disown them as they have disowned us!"*' [Q. 2:167]. To return is to come back (*al-karra al-rajʿa*).[110] The follower and the

[108] Abū Bakr and ʿUmar. The *Jibt* and the *Ṭāghūt* are thus interpreted in Shiʿi sources such as the *Tafsīr al-ʿAyyāshī*; see M.M. Bar-Asher, *Scripture and Exegesis*, p. 109 and p. 109, n. 88. All mentions of these two Qur'anic terms in the *Kashf* are to be understood in reference to this hermeneutical key.

[109] The text has: *law tarā*, instead of the Qur'anic *law yarā*. Here, the subject is Muḥammad and the direct object is the 'iniquitous', while in the Qur'an, the latter are the subject.

[110] On the *rajʿa*, see commentary of *Kashf* I, pp. 162–166.

one followed will both be in the Fire, whatever effort, worshipping or good deed they have accomplished. *'Thus will God show them their deeds as anguish for them, and never shall they issue from the Fire'* [Q. 2:167].

50. He said that the All-Knowing is[111] *'God, the Creator, the Maker, the Shaper'* [Q. 59:24]. He is Powerful over everything, and He does what He wills.

[Exegesis of Q. 44:41–45; 52–54; 57]

51. God — He is Mighty and Sublime — said: *'The Day no protector can avail nothing a client, and they will not be helped, save those upon whom God has mercy'* [Q. 44:41–42]. This means that the Prince of the Believers and his partisans (*shīʿa*) have the Mercy of God. *'He is the Mighty (al-ʿazīz), the Wise'* [Q. 44:42].[112] This means that the Legatee transcends all likeness (*ʿazīz ʿan al-mathal*) and that he is wise in his action. *'Indeed, the tree of Zaqqūm is the food of the sinful. Like molten brass, it will boil in their bellies'* [Q. 44:43–45]. The *'sinful'* stands for every antagonist (*ḍidd*) and his followers. *'Surely, those who fear [God] (muttaqīn)'*, that is, those who fear the Friendship (*walāya*) of *'the Jibt and the Ṭāghūt'* [Q. 4:51], and seek refuge in the the Friendship (*walāya*) of the Prince of the Believers, *'shall be in a safe station (maqām)'* [Q. 44:51], in God's proximity, safe from terror, *'amid gardens and watersprings, wearing silk and brocade, facing one another. And we shall wed them to wide-eyed houris'* [Q. 44:52–54]. *'This is the supreme triumph'* [Q. 44:57]. **[23]**

[Exegesis of Q. 95:1–8]

52. God — He is Mighty and Sublime — said: *'By the fig and the olive'* [Q. 95:1], meaning Ḥasan and Ḥusayn. *'By Mount Sinai'* [Q. 95:2], that is, Muḥammad — peace be upon him — the Master of the Messengers (*sayyid al-mursalīn*). *'And this land secure'* [Q. 95:3] means the Prince of the Believers, ʿAlī. *'We indeed created man in the fairest stature'* [Q. 95:4] means the First because he had greater knowledge (*maʿrifa*) than

---

[111] Or: 'the savant said: He is God. . .' (*qāla al-ʿālim huwa Allāh*).

[112] The text reads *al-ḥakīm*, 'the Wise', instead of the Qur'anic *al-raḥīm*, 'the Merciful'.

the Second.[113] *‘Then we reduced him to the lowest of the low, save those who believe and do righteous deeds’* [Q. 95:5–6], that is, the deeds of those who obey the Imam whom they obey; they are Muḥammad b. Abī Bakr and <Hāshim>[114] b. ʿUtba b. Abī Waqqāṣ, and those who came after them among the righteous of their children. *‘They will have an unfailing reward. What can contradict you as to the judgement after this?’* [Q. 95:6–7]: O Muḥammad, who can argue with you as to the Friendship (*walāya*) of the Prince of the Believers? *‘Is not God the justest of judges?’* [Q. 95:8].

[Exegesis of Q. 67:30]

53. Concerning the words of God — He is Mighty and Sublime: *‘Say: What think you? If your water were to disappear into the earth, who then would bring you gushing water?’* [Q. 67:30], he says that it refers to the Prince of the Believers ʿAlī b. Abī Ṭālib — may God’s blessings be upon him. God made water as an example for him vis-à-vis his family, for just as He keeps the living alive by water, He brings the world (*al-ʿālam*) to life by the knowledge (*al-ʿilm*) which comes from the Savant (*al-ʿālim*). The ‘gushing water’ refers to the Resurrector from the family of Muḥammad — may God bless him. **[24]**

[The Bees: exegesis of Q. 16:68–69][115]

54. And from God’s words — He is Mighty and Sublime — [is the following verse]: *‘Your Lord revealed to the bees, saying: Take unto yourselves houses of the mountains and of the trees’* [Q. 16:68]. The ‘bees’ (*al-naḥl*) are the Imams who receive (*munḥalūn*) God’s knowledge. They are the depositaries (*mustawdaʿūn*) of God’s Guidance and Light.

---

[113] The ‘First’ and the ‘Second’ are respectively Abū Bakr and ʿUmar, as previously seen. This distinction between the first two caliphs sometimes appears in Shiʿi literature; Abū Bakr is thus portrayed as being under the evil influence of ʿUmar in usurping ʿAlī’s right to rule. Therefore, he is less to blame than ʿUmar. The same distinction appears in another passage of this treatise; see *Kashf* I, p. 30, § 63, and related footnotes; see also *Kashf* III, pp. 85–86, § 69. On the ‘satanic’ influence of ʿUmar over Abū Bakr, see also *Kashf* V, p. 95, § 7.

[114] Both manuscripts read ‘Hishām’ instead of ‘Hāshim’. He was a companion of ʿAlī b. Abī Ṭālib who died in the Battle of Ṣiffīn.

[115] For a discussion of this paragraph, see commentary of *Kashf* III, pp. 259–261.

The mountains are the Summoners[116] who belong to the sacred station (*maqām*) of the Proofs. *'And of the trees'*: they are the Summoners who are below the Proofs.[117] *'And of what they build'* [Q. 16:68], that is, of what they give birth to. God tells the Imams: *'Eat of all fruits, and follow the paths of your Lord in humility'* [Q. 16:69]. The 'fruits' are the knowledge (*'ilm*), and the 'paths' are the deeds (*'amal*). *'Then comes there forth out of their bellies a drink of diverse hues wherein is healing for men'* [Q. 16:69], that is, a decree (*ḥukm*) that discriminates between people and on which there is no disagreement. *'Surely in that is a sign'*: He means the demonstration of the Proof.

[The Resurrector]

55. And God's words — He is Mighty and Sublime: *'When the trumpet is sounded'* [Q. 74:8] are for the manifestation of the Imam when he rises. *'That day will be a harsh day for those who disbelieved'* [Q. 74:9–10] in the Friendship (*walāya*) of the Prince of the Believers, 'Alī — may God's blessings be upon him — *'it will not be easy'* [Q. 74:10].

56. Concerning God's words — He is Mighty and Sublime: *'Is He not who answers the compelled one, when he calls unto Him, and removes the evil and appoints you lieutenants (khulafā') in the earth?'* [Q. 27:62], he says that the one who answers is God — may He be exalted — and that the one who is 'compelled' is the Resurrector. When the night comes during which he will set out, **[25]** he will rise at night and will call God in fear of the beginning and the delay (*al-bad' wa'l-ta'khīr*). And [by the time] the dawn tears [the night], he will have set out.[118]

[Joseph and initiation][119]

57. About God's words — He is Mighty and Sublime: *'She desired him, and he would have desired her, had he not seen a proof (burhān) from his*

---

[116] On this equivalence, see *Kashf* VI, pp. 169–171, §§ 27–30.

[117] Here, the term *'dā'ī'* is to be understood in a broad sense, as it applies to both the Proofs and the actual Summoners under the authority of the Proofs.

[118] The text is unclear here and seems corrupted.

[119] As noted by M.M. Bar-Asher, 'Outlines of Early Ismā'īlī-Fāṭimid Qur'an Exegesis', p. 272, n. 51, the following passage, which rejects the exoteric interpretation of Joseph's seduction by his master's wife, has parallels in other Ismaili texts; see esp, al-Qāḍī al-Nu'mān, *Asās al-ta'wīl*, pp. 141–143. See also Ja'far b. Manṣūr al-Yaman, *Ta'wīl al-zakāt*, p. 173.

Lord. Thus have We turned away evil (al-sū') and turpitude (al-faḥshā') from him' [Q. 12:24], they said that he desired her to the point that he unfastened [her] drawers and laid with her as a man lies with a woman. He said: 'They lied; may God curse them!' Someone asked:[120] 'What is the proof (*burhān*) that he saw?' He said: 'The Proof (*ḥujja*) came upon him.'

58. One of the exoteric interpretations of this has that she desired him to come to her, while he desired to kill her and wanted to slaughter her '*had he not seen a proof from his Lord*'. He knew by what God taught him that it was not necessary to slaughter her, nor was he obliged towards her. '*Thus have We turned away evil and turpitude from him.*' The 'evil' is what he wanted, that is, to slaughter her although that was not necessary, and the 'turpitude' is what she wanted. This [explanation] is better than what the people of exotericism say, and closer to the esoteric meaning.[121]

59. The esoteric meaning is that the wife of al-ʿAzīz[122] alludes to one of [al-ʿAzīz's] ministers who had a longing for Truth and had heard Joseph's elucidation — may God bless him — and the excellence (*ḥusn*) of his explanation.[123] The exoteric meaning of this is his beauty; the 'excellence' by which he is described is his beauty. In the esoteric [sense], however, the excellence is that of elucidation and explanation.[124] The minister thus desired Joseph to summon him and placed himself under his direction, longing [for his knowledge]. **[26]** Indeed, the Summons (*al-daʿwa*) is analogous to coitus (*al-nikāḥ*) in the esoteric order.[125] Seeing [the minister's] longing, his faculty of understanding and the covetousness of his demand, Joseph desired to take the covenant upon him, '*had he not seen a proof from his Lord*', said God

---

[120] Ms.B: *qultu*, 'I asked'.

[121] That is: this explanation, albeit of exoteric nature, is better than the first explanation which interpreted the verse in an exclusively sexual sense; see commentary of *Kashf* I, pp. 131–132.

[122] Potiphar, Joseph's master, is thus named in the Qur'an.

[123] This refers to Joseph's interpretation of Pharaoh's dream in Qur'an 12:43–49.

[124] Same explanation in Jaʿfar b. Manṣūr al-Yaman, *Riḍāʿ fī al-Bāṭin*, p. 54.

[125] See *Kashf* III, p. 78–79, § 60; V, p. 114, § 41; p. 123, § 57; VI, p. 166, § 23, and commentary of *Kashf* I, pp. 130–134.

— He is Mighty and Sublime. This means that considering God's Order (*amr Allāh*) and the ranks (*ḥudūd*) of His religion, [Joseph concluded] that he was not to answer to the minister's demand for knowledge, nor to unveil it to him before the covenant was taken upon him. Yet, the covenant can only [be taken] by the Imam who takes it in person or has his Proofs and Summoners take it on his behalf. In that time, Joseph was not free (*muṭlaq*)[126] to take a covenant, nor to mention his sacred station (*maqām*), nor to unveil the esoteric aspects of his knowledge. Therefore, he refrained [from unveiling his knowledge] (*amsaka*) due to the proof (*burhān*) that was granted to him from the proofs of the ranks (*ḥudūd*) of God — may He be exalted. '*Thus have We turned away evil and turpitude from him.*' The 'evil' is the transgression of the ranks (*ḥudūd*) of God — may He be exalted — by taking the covenant before he was free to do so (*qabl an yuṭlaq lahu dhalik*). The 'turpitude' is the unveiling of the knowledge to someone upon whom the covenant has not been taken, and such was the case of the minister to whom Joseph — may God bless him — was about to unveil his knowledge.

[Abū Bakr and the Resurrector: exegesis of Q. 75:20–25; 29–34]

60. About God's words — He is Mighty and Sublime: '*No indeed! But you love the hasty life, and neglect the hereafter. That day will faces be resplendent, looking (nāẓira) towards their Lord*' [Q. 75:20–23], that is, illuminating (*mushriqa*).[127] '*Looking towards their Lord*' means [towards] the Prince of the Believers — may God's blessings be upon him. '*And that day faces that day shall be scowling*' [Q. 75:24], that is,

---

[126] The use of this term is probably an allusion to the rank of the *ma'dhūn muṭlaq*, that is, a preacher who has 'full permission' to take covenants, recruit new members to the *da'wa* and display the esoteric teachings — as opposed to the *ma'dhūn maḥdūd* who has 'limited permission'. According to a text attributed to al-Sijistānī, the *ma'dhūn muṭlaq* is appointed by the *dā'ī/janāḥ* and is given the freedom (*aṭlaqa lahu*) to preach to whomever he wants within a given region (*ṣuq'*), while the *ma'dhūn maḥdūd* has permission to preach to only one, two, three or four persons. Also, the latter's activity is more limited geographically; see al-Sijistānī, *Tuḥfat al-mustajībīn*, p. 154.

[127] See Ibn Bābawayh, *Kitāb al-Tawḥīd*, *bāb* 8, p. 116, no. 19, where *nāẓira* from the same verse is similarly glossed as *mushriqa*.

[27] gloomy, '*in the thought that some great disaster is about to fall on them*' [Q. 75:25]: this refers to the exemplary [punishment] (*al-mathla*) during the Recurrence (*karra*). '*But nay! When it reaches the clavicles*' [Q. 75:26]; he says [that this refers to] the exemplary [punishment] by the hand of the Resurrector — may God bless him — upon those who did not believe (*yuṣaddiq*) in him and did not accept the Friendship (*muwālāt*) of the Prince of the Believers before the manifestation [of the Resurrector]. The First[128] and his followers think that the Resurrector will not rise (*lā qiyāma li'l-qā'im*) until the Resurrection during the Return (*qiyāma al-ba'th fi'l-ma'ād*). '*And when leg is intertwined with leg, upon that day unto your Lord shall be the driving*' [Q. 75:29–30]: he says this is about the Gathering (*al-ḥashr*). '*For he neither believed (la ṣaddaqa), nor did he pray*' [Q. 75:31]: he did not believe in the Gathering and did not pray to God before the Recurrence (*al-karra*) in [its] esoteric [sense] (*fi'l-bāṭina*).[129] Prayer is obedience to the Prince of the Believers and the Imams whom God has chosen from among his sons. '*Instead, he denied and turned away*' [Q. 75:32], that is, he denied the word of the Messenger [concerning his succession] and turned away from the Prince of the Believers. [The verse:] '*Then he went to his household arrogantly. Woe to you, woe!*' [Q. 75:33–34] was revealed about him, just like anything concerning Satan in the Qur'an; he is the companion of those who forge lies.

[Abū Bakr and his claim to the Divine Trust: exegesis of Q. 33:72–73]

61. About God's words — He is Mighty and Sublime: '*Indeed, we offered ('araḍnā) the Trust (al-amāna) to the heavens and the earth and the mountains, and they refused to bear it and were afraid of it. But man (insān) bore it; indeed, he is iniquitous and ignorant, and God will punish the hypocrites*' [Q. 33:72–73]. The Trust is the rank (*martaba*) of the Prince of the Believers 'Alī b. Abī Ṭālib — may God's blessings be

[128] Abū Bakr.

[129] The author is making a distinction between an exoteric meaning of eschatology, i.e, the Resurrection in the afterlife, on the one hand, and an esoteric meaning, which refers to the 'Return' of the Imamate through the sons of 'Alī. In other words, eschatology is reoriented toward an initiatory approach.

upon him. God presented (*'araḍa*)[130] the Friendship (*walāya*) to the people of heavens, and to the people of earth, and to the Angels of the mountains. They accepted **[28]** his Friendship (*walāya*) and acknowledged his grace (*faḍl*). None of them imitated his sacred station (*maqām*), nor did they claim his rank (*martaba*), afraid to place themselves in a place where God and His Messenger had not placed them. '*But man bore it; indeed, he is iniquitous and ignorant*': this means Abū Bakr — may God curse him[131] — who claimed the rank of the Prince of the Believers and his lieutenancy (*khilāfa*) to the Messenger of God — may God bless him — although [this] had not been granted to him by God nor by his Messenger. '*God will punish the hypocrites, men and women*' — they are those who were iniquitous to the family of Muḥammad and are well-known for their iniquity — '*and those who associate [to God], men and women*', who associated to the Friendship (*walāya*) those to whom it did not belong. '*God forgives the believers, men and women*' [Q. 33:73]: He will cover their sins, for He is Forgiving, Merciful.

[The Resurrector]

62. About His word — He is Mighty and Sublime: '*Woe be to those who associate, who pay not the alms (al-zakāt) and disbelieve in the hereafter*' [Q. 41:6–7], he says that the alms have been imposed upon the people of prayer (*ahl al-ṣalāt*), but not upon those who associate. This verse was revealed about whoever directs the Friendship (*walāya*) [due] the Prince of the Believers to someone else (*ashraka*), and conveys the alms to the one appointed by his Satan who claims to be

---

[130] The exegesis takes advantage of the polysemy of the verb *'araḍa*, which, in the case of verse 33:72, is usually understood as meaning 'to offer' or 'to propose'. However, the term also means 'to present', 'to show'. Thus, instead of the traditional understanding of the verse, according to which God is somehow searching for a creature to bear the trust, here, the verse is understood in the sense that God is 'presenting' the trust for the Creation to worship and acknowledge. The verb *'araḍa* also appears in the sense of 'to present' in verse 2:31, where God 'presents' the creatures to the Angels, daring them to name them. The choice made by the exegete here allows for the interpretation that follows.

[131] On the identification of the Qur'anic 'man' (*insān*) with Abū Bakr, see *Kashf* I, p. 30, § 63, and references there; see also *Kashf* III, p. 59, § 16; pp. 62–63, § 21.

an Imam from God. '*They disbelieve in the hereafter*': he says they disbelieve in the Recurrence (*al-karra*) meaning they deny the Return. The Return is the manifestation of the Resurrector — may God bless him and his family — by which God returns **[29]** the assault of his enemy in favour of the family of Muḥammad. God will then give authority '*to the Truth over the False, He destroys it, and behold, the False disappears*' [Q. 21:18].

[Abū Bakr and 'Umar, enemies of 'Alī: exegesis of Q. 25:27–31; 50]

63. About God's words — He is Mighty and Sublime: '*The day that the iniquitous will bite his hands and say: Oh, would that I had taken a path with the Messenger!*' [Q. 25:27]. This refers to Abū Bakr — may God curse him. He will say: '*Alas for me! Would that I had not taken So-and-so (fulān)*[132] *for a close friend! He indeed led me astray from the remembrance (dhikr), after it had come to me*' [Q. 25:28–29],[133] that is, after the Messenger of God — may God bless him. '*Satan leads man astray*' [Q. 25:29]. 'Satan' means 'Umar — may God curse him — and 'man' the First.[134] '*The Messenger says: 'O my Lord! My people have taken*

---

[132] *Fulān* is usually a code used in Shi'i exegesis to allude to the first three caliphs of Islam (*fulān wa-fulān wa-fulān*) or to their family (*Banū Fulān*), as noted by E. Kohlberg. When used alone, it generally refers to Abū Bakr, (as seems to be the case in another occurrence of this verse in *Kashf* III, p. 71, § 46); see E. Kohlberg, 'Some Imamī Shīʿī views on the *Ṣaḥāba*', p. 164; M.M. Bar-Asher, *Scripture and Exegesis*, p. 118. However, in this particular case, it refers to 'Umar.

[133] The identification of *dhikr*, 'remembrance', with the Imams is common in Shiʿi literature; see e.g. al-Ṣaffār al-Qummī, *Baṣā'ir al-darajāt*, pp. 87–97, where the Imams are identified with the Qur'anic expression *ahl al-dhikr*. See also *Kashf* III, pp. 71, § 46; p. 79, § 62; VI, p. 158, § 3.

[134] That is, Abū Bakr. The author of the present treatise seems to have gathered here several interpretations based on the equivalence between the Qur'anic *insān* and Abū Bakr; see above, *Kashf* I, p. 29, § 61. The hermeneutical equivalence between *insān*/*shayṭān* and Abū Bakr/'Umar is rooted in early Shiʿism; for an almost identical interpretation of Q. 25:27–29, see al-Qummī, *Tafsīr*, ed. Ṭ. al-Mūsawī al-Jazā'irī, vol. 2, p. 113; ed. Mu'assasat al-Mahdī vol. 2, p. 721; see also Mufaḍḍal al-Juʿfī, *Kitāb al-Haft wa'l-aẓilla*, Ch. 37, p. 77. The same equivalence is found in other Ismaili sources, in relation to Q. 25:27–29 or to Q. 59:16: '*. . .like Satan, when he said to man: "Disbelieve", then, when he disbelieved, he said: "I am quit of you."*'; see W. Madelung and P. Walker, *An Ismaili heresiography. The 'Bāb al-šayṭān' from Abū Tammām's* Kitāb al-shajara (Leiden, Cologne and Boston, 1998), pp. 20–22, 71 (Arabic: pp. 2–4, 71); Jaʿfar b.

this Qur'an as a thing to be shunned' [Q. 25:30]. The 'Qur'an' means 'Alī — may God's blessings be upon him — whom they took as 'a thing to be shunned' (*mahjūr*) by them.[135]

64. *'We have made for every prophet an enemy among the criminals'* [Q. 25:31]. The enemy of Adam enemy was his son Cain; the enemies of Noah were the people of the Flood; the enemy of Abraham was Nimrod, son of Canaan; the enemy of Moses son of 'Imrān was Korah; the enemies of Jesus were the priests of the Children of Israel; the enemies of Muḥammad — may God bless him — were the two enemies from Quraysh: Abū Jahl son of Hishām and his uncle Abū Lahab. Muḥammad, *'your Lord suffices as a guide and as a helper'* [Q. 25:31]. *'And the disbeliever is ever a partisan against his Lord'* [Q. 25:55], that is, [against] 'Alī, the Prince of the Believers — may God's blessings be upon him — and the Imams of his progeny. **[30]** The word of God — He is Mighty and Sublime: *'Return to your Lord'* [Q. 12:50] means [return] to your Master (*mālik*).

[Abū Bakr and 'Umar, enemies of 'Alī: exegesis of Q. 29:1–3]

65. About God's word — He is Mighty and Sublime: *'Alif Lām Mīm. Do the people reckon that they will be left to say: "We believe" and will not be tried?'* [Q. 29:1–2], [the Imam] says that they are tested through the Prince of the Believers. Similarly, He says: *'We tried their predecessors, and God knows those who speak the Truth and those who lie'* [Q. 29:3]. [The Imam says] that the people of Moses were thus tested through Aaron, but they rebelled against him and obeyed the Sāmirī.[136] And

Manṣūr al-Yaman, *Sarā'ir wa-asrār al-nutaqā'*, pp. 48, 111; idem, *Ta'wīl al-zakāt*, p. 255; idem, *Al-Shawāhid wa'l-bayān*, IIS MS. 734, ff. 138–139. On this distinction, with a particular focus on the *Kashf* and on Abū Tammām's approach, see now D. De Smet, 'The Demon in Potentiality and the Devil in Actuality: Two Principles of Evil according to 4th/10th Century Ismailism', *Arabica*, 69 (2022), pp. 601–625.

[135] On 'Alī as 'a thing to be shunned' (Q. 25:30), see also Idrīs 'Imād al-Dīn, *Zahr al-ma'ānī*, p. 171, and references to *Tafsīr al-Qummī* and *Kitāb al-shajara* in previous footnote.

[136] A mysterious protagonist to whom the Qur'an, unlike the Torah, attributes the cult of the golden calf. By disculpating Aaron from this fault, the Qur'an paves the way to the Shi'i interpretation which sees in Aaron the Legatee of Moses. On the Sāmirī, see Q. 20:85–87. See also *Kashf* VI, p. 162, § 12, and commentary of *Kashf* I, pp. 147–154.

the people of Jesus were tested with Simon, but they rebelled against him and obeyed <Pilate>.[137] And this community was tested with the Prince of the Believers, but they rebelled against him and obeyed Abū Bakr and ʿUmar.

['Umar, enemy of ʿAlī: exegesis of Q. 2:205–207]

66. About His words: *'He destroys the crops and the lineage (nasl)'* [Q. 2:205]. The 'crops' are one fifth (*khums*), and the 'lineage' is the lineage of Muḥammad — may God's blessings and peace be upon them. *'And God loves not corruption'* [Q. 2:205]: this verse was revealed concerning Zufar, who is ʿUmar. *'If it is said to him: "Fear God", pride takes him to sin. Hell shall be enough for him — how evil a cradling!'* [Q. 2:206]. Then He said: *'Amongst the people, there are those who sell themselves seeking God's pleasure'* [Q. 2:207]. This refers to the Prince of the Believers. Concerning obedience to God, He says: *'God is kind to His worshippers'* [Q. 2:207]. They are the people of obedience and Friendship (*walāya*) and faith. God — may He be exalted — said: *'O you who believe, enter into peace altogether,* **[31]** *and follow not the footsteps of Satan, he is an avowed enemy to you'* [Q. 2:208]. He means ʿUmar — may God curse him.[138]

[*Ḥadīth* on the etymology of 'Mahdī']

67. He says: 'I asked Abū ʿAbd Allāh [Jaʿfar al-Ṣādiq] — may God's blessings and peace be upon him — about the Mahdī,[139] and why he is called the Mahdī.' He said: 'This is because he "guides" (*hadā, yahdī*) to the hidden Order.'[140]

---

[137] Both mss. read 'Haylas', a probable error for 'Bīlāṭus'.

[138] In the *Tafsīr al-ʿAyyāshī*, the 'footsteps of Satan' are 'the *walāya* of *fulān wa-fulān*' or 'of the First and the Second'; see al-ʿAyyāshī, *Tafsīr*, vol. 1, p. 213, 214.

[139] This is only the second occurrence of the term in this treatise (see the first one on p. 6, § 8), which rather opts for the term *qāʾim*.

[140] The same explanation is given by al-Nuʿmānī in his *Kitāb al-Ghayba*; cited by M.A. Amir-Moezzi, *Guide divin*, p. 291 and n. 643 (English trans.: *Divine guide*, pp. 120, 225, n. 643).

[*Ḥadīth* on the Return of the Resurrector][141]

68. He will emerge in anger from the sanctuary of God. When he is a *barīd*[142] away, supplicants (*ṣarīkh*) from Mecca will come to him. He will say: 'What is with you?' They will answer: 'This and that.' He will leave a lieutenant (*khalīfa*) with them and go. But as soon as we will have left the houses behind him, <the messenger will catch up with him and say>:[143] 'Your lieutenant has been killed.' He will return in anger, and he will recite the verse: '*If they fight you, slay them — such is the reward of the disbelievers*' [Q. 2:191].

69. Gabriel — peace be upon him — will appear to them in an aura of light, on a black and white horse with a golden saddle. He will be wearing an armour of light, an iron helm and will hold a spear of light, standing on ʿAqaba.[144] Victory is at the tip of his spear, Terror (*ruʿb*)[145] is in its middle, triumph is in its inferior iron part (*zujj*), and its handle is made from the light of the Throne. When the Resurector rises, [Gabriel] will recognise him.[146] **[32]** He will unsheathe his sword, will

---

[141] For a full German translation of this *ḥadīth*, as well as the paragraph that precedes, see H. Halm, *Kosmologie*, pp. 29–30. I have benefited from some of Halm's corrections and interpretations of the text.

[142] A unit of measurement equal to four *farsakh* (parasangs), which is about 24 kilometres. See H. Halm, *Kosmologie*, p. 29 note 58.

[143] Ms. A: *yaqūl al-rasūl*; ms. B: *laḥiqahu al-rasūl*. I translate the corrected text as suggested by Strothmann: *laḥiqahu al-rasūl yaqūl*.

[144] A locality between Mekka and Minā where Muḥammad received oaths of allegiance; see W.M. Watt, "Aḳaba', *EI2*. However, this could also allude to the pass (*ʿaqaba*) of Harshā, where, according to some Shiʿi reports, the Prophet was ambushed by several companions the night following the proclamation of Ghadīr Khumm, that is, in the Shiʿi narrative, after the Prophet had publicly appointed ʿAlī as his successor; on this alleged plot, see E. Kohlberg, 'Some Imamī Shīʿī views on the *Ṣaḥāba*', pp. 152–156. See also *Kashf* III, p. 84, §74, where we find a reference to 'the people of *ʿaqaba*'.

[145] On 'Terror' as an entity auxiliary to the Mahdī, see M.A. Amir-Moezzi, *Guide divin*, pp. 293–294, n. 647 (English trans., *Divine Guide*, pp. 121, 226, n. 647). See also below, *Kashf* I, p. 33, § 70.

[146] Compare with the Mufaḍḍal al-Juʿfī, *Kitāb al-Haft waʾl-aẓilla*, Ch. 65, p. 131, where the Resurrector will appear from 'God's sacred house' (*bayt Allāh al-ḥarām*) and Gabriel will be the first to swear his allegiance to him, along with all the Angels — which is reminiscent of the Angels bowing before Adam.

put it on his shoulder and will proclaim: 'You are "*the people whom God loves and who loves God, humble towards the believers, stern towards the disbelievers, striving in the path of God*" [Q. 5:54] "*as they ought to. He has chosen you, and he has laid no impediment upon you in religion*" [Q. 22:78].' He will call for the weapons to be unsheathed and will enter Mecca with the Resurrector. He will stain his sword with blood[147] amongst the Quraysh for seven months, until they say: 'If this one was from the Banū Hāshim, he would take our kinship into consideration!' Then, Gabriel will attack Medina with his spear, but the Resurrector will sheath his sword: '*God (. . .) heals the breasts of a people who believes and removes the rage from their hearts. God forgives whom He wills.*' [Q. 9:14–15].

70. Then, every time a banner of the Resurrector turns to a city, the Terror (*ruʿb*) in his hand will precede him at a distance of one month.[148] He will guide the people of no city unless they are guided by God. Whoever rejects [this guidance], God will make stones of sulphur fall on them, until He brings them all back to His guidance and they all surrender to Him.

71. [The Resurrector] will break the cross, destroy the churches (*biyaʿ*) and slaughter the pig.[149] The Summons of association (*daʿwat al-shirk*)[150] [to God] will be terminated, and the Summons of joy (*daʿwat al-faraj*) will be manifested. The Summons of religion (*al-daʿwa bi-dīn Allāh*) will rise **[33]**, faithful to God. This is the promise God made to His Prophet in His words — He is Mighty and

[147] I follow H. Halm's correction of *yaṣrakh* to *yaḍraj*; see H. Halm, *Kosmologie*, p. 29, n. 60.

[148] See M.A. Amir-Moezzi, *Guide divin*, pp. 293–294, n. 647 (English trans., *Divine Guide*, p. 226, n. 647), particularly the *ḥadīth* quoted there from al-Nuʿmānī's *Kitāb al-Ghayba*: 'And the Terror will march ahead of him [i.e. the Mahdī] at a distance of one month, behind him, on his right and on his left.'

[149] Classical features of messianic narratives in Islam. See e.g. Bukhārī, *Ṣaḥīḥ*, *k. al-buyūʿ*, *bāb* 102, no. 2222, vol. 2, p. 119. For other examples in Ismaili literature, see also the references given in H. Halm, *Kosmologie*, p. 30, n. 61. Halm notes that the expression: 'to break the cross' also appears in the Mufaḍḍal al-Juʿfī, *Kitāb al-Haft wa'l-aẓilla*, Ch. 48, p. 103.

[150] Ms. A: *al-tark*. I translate the variant from ms. B.

Sublime: *'[It is He who sent His Messenger with the Guidance and the Religion of Truth] to make it prevail over all religion, however averse the associationists may be'* [Q. 9:33]. God — He is Mighty and Sublime — will fulfil [this promise] by the hand of the Resurrector — may God's blessings be upon him. At that time, the bull and the lion will drink from the same pool, and the shepherd will entrust his sheep to the wolf.[151]

72. The Resurrector will enter Medina and he will ascend the pulpit, full of awe and dignity. He will be a young man of great longanimity and yellowish complexion. He will be wearing the Messenger's coat of mail and the turban 'al-Saḥāb' (*'amāmat al-saḥāb*)[152] and carrying his sword, Dhū al-Fiqār.[153] He will be surrounded by his partisans (*shī'a*) among the believers; their hearts will be stronger than iron, and they will pronounce the *takbīr* in a single voice, making the heart of every hypocrite and every enemy (*munāṣib*)[154] to shudder. On that day, the glory will be to God, to His Messenger and to the believers. [The Resurrector] will pronounce a sermon — peace be upon him — that will last from the morning prayer until the noon prayer, then he will rise and pray both prayers,

---

[151] This is reminiscent of Isaiah 11:6 and 65:25.

[152] This is the nickname of the Prophet's turban in the Shi'i tradition. According to various reports, Muḥammad is said to have put it on 'Alī's head, which symbolises his designation as the Prophet's Legatee. An illustration of this can be found further in this very treatise; see *Kashf* I, p. 38, § 80. On this turban in Shi'i tradition, see S. Anthony, *The Caliph and the Heretic: Ibn Saba' and the Origins of Shī'ism* (Leiden, 2011), pp. 229–231. According to Anthony, who refers to Imamī reports, the belief of some *ghulāt* groups in 'Alī's presence 'in the clouds' (*fi'l-saḥāb*) was due to a confusion between the name of the turban and that of the actual clouds. Yet, see the section on 'Alī's ability to ride the clouds in al-Ṣaffār al-Qummī, *Baṣā'ir al-darajāt*, pp. 739–740. H. Feki claims that a similar description (youth, longanimity, yellow complexion, coat of mail and turban) of the *qā'im* is found in Ja'far b. Manṣūr al-Yaman, *Kitāb al-Fatarāt wa'l-qirānāt al-'ashara*; cited in H. Feki, 'Deux traités du Dâ'î Yéménite Ismaélien 'Alî Ibn Moḥammad Ibn Al-Walīd (VIIe/XIIIe siècle)', *Annuaire de l'EPHE*, 78 (1969), pp. 380–381. I have not been able to find this description in Khaḍḍūr's edition of the *Fatarāt*.

[153] Name of 'Alī's sword.

[154] The root *n-ṣ-b* is often used in Shi'i context to designate 'Alī's adversaries. See also the more common expression, *ahl al-naṣb*, which occurs in *Kashf* V, p. 134, § 72.

each with its own two calls (*bi-adhānayn* wa-*iqāmatayn*).[155] Then he will go to the [Prophet's] grave and will destroy its wall until nothing is left but the grave itself. The one [lying] there will rise; they will inform him and he will order them both to be crucified.[156] Then *'the vain-doers shall lose'* [Q. 45:27].[157] Then all the people <. . .>[158]

73. He will put down the sword, and all **[34]** of their matters (*umūr*) will be unveiled, and all their innovations will be extinguished and wiped out. The right (*al-ḥaqq*) will be returned to those to whom it belongs,[159] in order for man to return as he was when he was born and for the people of Friendship (*walāya*) to know what they had adhered to.

[The divine Light of the Imams: exegesis of Q. 24:40]

74. God — He is Mighty and Sublime — says: *'Whoever God does not give Light, then he has no Light'* [Q. 24:40]. He says that God — He is Mighty and Sublime — created Muḥammad and the Imams of his progeny as a Light for those who follow them, guiding those who turn to them. He made praise (*al-ḥamd*) a garment to those who cleave to them. To whomever God gives no Imam, *'then he has no Light'*. This is the meaning of *'Whoever God does not give Light, then he has no Light'*.

[Exegesis of Qur'an 22:45]

75. God — He is Mighty and Sublime — says: *'A deserted well and a lofty castle'* [Q. 22:45]. The 'deserted well' is the Prince of the Believers, and the 'lofty castle' is the Messenger of God[160] — may God's blessings and peace be upon him. God — He is Mighty and Sublime — said: *'We granted them a true tongue of nobility'* [Q. 19:50]. He says [this refers to] a Legatee rising (*waṣī qā'im*) after the prophets, judging between them,

---

[155] Each prayer is traditionally preceded by two calls, the *adhān* and the *iqāma*.

[156] The sentence is very allusive, but the likely meaning is that the Prophet will be resurrected, and after being told of Abū Bakr and 'Umar's betrayal, he will order their crucifixion. See also *Kashf* III, pp. 86–87, §§ 79–80, where the torture of Abū Bakr, although of a different nature, is also linked with the Resurrector. See commentary of *Kashf* I, pp. 162–166.

[157] This could also be an approximate quotation of Q. 40:78.

[158] The rest is unintelligible in both manuscripts. Strothmann leaves a blank space.

[159] That is, the Imams.

[160] For a similar interpretation, see Idrīs 'Imād al-Dīn, *Zahr al-ma'ānī*, p. 223.

following their ways. And the Imams inherit this [tongue of nobility] one after another.

[Creation of the Five and Adam]

76. Abū ʿAbd Allāh [Jaʿfar al-Ṣādiq] — peace be upon him — said: 'God created veils (*ḥujub*) from the Light of His Face and named each one after one of His names. <The Praise (*al-ḥamd*) is His>[161] and He named His Prophet after it. He is the All-High (*al-ʿalī*) and the Prince of the Believers is ʿAlī. '*To Him belong the beautiful names* (*al-asmāʾ al-ḥusnā*)' [Q. 17:110],[162] and from these He derived the names of Ḥasan and Ḥusayn. And He is '*the Creator (fāṭir) of the heavens and the earth*' [Q. 6:14],[163] and from these He derived the name of Fāṭima.[164] When He created them, he set them to the right of the Throne. **[35]**

77. Then He created the angels, and when they looked at [these Five], they glorified their quality and learned from them to glorify [God] (*al-tasbīḥ*); thus, their glorification became the angels' glorification. Abū ʿAbd Allāh — may God's blessings be upon him — said: 'And this is [the meaning of] the word of God — He is Mighty and Sublime: '*We are verily ranged in ranks, and we are verily those who hymn His Glory (al-musabbiḥūn)*' [Q. 37:165–166]. This refers to the Five who were created as spiritual beings (*rūḥāniyyīn*) from the Light of His Face. He named [the angels] after [the Five], and He granted them His favour (*faḍḍalahum*) as He had granted it to [the Five] with the light from the Light of His Face.

78. Then God created Adam, and when he looked at them on the right of the Throne, he said: "Lord, who are these five?" He said: "Adam, these are my elect and my elite (*ṣafwatī wa-khāṣṣatī*). I created them from My Light and gave them names derived from Mine." He said: "Lord, by their right over You, and Your right over them, teach me." God said: "Adam, you have a secret of mine. Do not show it to anyone unless I ask you about it and permit you to do so." Adam said: "Yes Lord." God said: "Adam, take a covenant with Me on this." God took the covenant

[161] Mss. A, B: *huwa al-ḥamd*. Corrected to: *lahu al-ḥamd*.

[162] Also Q. 20:8 and 59:24.

[163] Also Q. 12:101; 14:10; 35:1; 39:46; 42:11.

[164] The same explanation of the names of the 'Five of the cloak' (*ahl al-kisāʾ*) is found in Twelver Shiʿi sources; see e.g. M.A. Amir-Moezzi, *Guide Divin*, pp. 78–79 (English trans., *Divine Guide*, p. 31). See also F. Daftary, '*Ahl al-Kisāʾ*', *EI3*.

from him and taught him the names and numbers [of the creatures]. *'Then He presented ('araḍa) them to the angels'* [Q. 2:31], having not [yet] taught none of them [the names and numbers]. *'He said: Inform me of the names of these, if you are Truthful. They said: Glory be to you! We have no knowledge save what you have taught us. Surely, you are the Knower,* [**36**] *the Wise. God said: Adam, inform them of their names'* [Q. 2:31–33]. The angels thus knew that Adam was a depository (*mustawda'*), and that he was favoured over them (*mufaḍḍal 'alayhim*) by the knowledge that God — may He be exalted — had given him. When they came to know this, He summoned them to prostrate [before Adam]. Their prostration before Adam was an act of worship to God, because it was [a act of] obedience for them and [a sign of] Adam's nobility. *'[They prostrated] except for Iblīs'* [Q. 2:34] the vicious, who *'refused'* to prostrate, and refused to accept Adam's favour (*faḍl*) [over him]. God asked him: *'What prevents you from prostrating when I have ordered you to? He replied: I am better than him'* [Q. 7:12]. God said: "I favoured him over you when he acknowledged the favour (*faḍl*) of the Five, over whom I have not given you any power, nor over those who follow them." This is the meaning of God's words [when Iblīs says]: *'[I shall pervert them] except Your devoted worshippers'* [Q. 15:40], and His words — may He be exalted: *'You have no power over my worshippers'* [Q. 15:42]: they are the partisans (*shī'a*) of the Prince of the Believers.

[A *ḥadīth* on 'Alī's murder]

79. [Ja'far al-Ṣādiq] — may God bless him — was once asked: 'Was there a sign for the murder of 'Alī b. Abī Ṭālib?' He said: 'Yes, not a single stone in the Sacred House (*al-bayt al-maqdis*) could be lifted without fresh blood being found underneath it.'

[*Ḥadīth* on 'Alī's power to resurrect the dead]

80. [Ja'far al-Ṣādiq] — may God bless him and his family — narrated the following: 'A group of priests came to the Messenger of God — may God bless him —and one of them said: "God spoke to Moses in person." Another one said: "God took Abraham as his intimate friend." And a third said: "God gave Jesus the Holy Spirit. So, what has He given to you, O Muḥammad?" [The Messenger] — may God bless him and his family — heaved a sigh, [**37**] and the people thought he was angry. He lingered a moment while revelation (*al-waḥī*) came to him. Then he raised his head and said: "God took Abraham as his intimate friend (*khalīl*), but He took me as his beloved (*ḥabīb*) and chose me. Adam and I are from one clay. And even though God spoke to Moses, He only spoke to him from behind a veil, whereas He spoke to me and I spoke to Him, and He saw me and I saw Him, and there was no veil between us. And God gave Jesus the Holy Spirit by which he revived the dead, and if you so wish, I shall revive your dead as well." The priests were pleased with him, and said: "Yes, we want this." He called ʿAlī b. Abī Ṭālib — may God's blessings be upon him — and he whispered and confided to him a supplication to utter (*yanṭuq*) to the dead in order to resurrect them. Then he called for his turban 'al-Saḥāb' and put it on [ʿAlī's] head. He put his head under ʿAlī's cloak and informed him. Then he made him bear his sword Dhū al-Fiqār and told him: "Take these people to [the cemetery of] al-Baqīʿ and revive for them whomever they will, with God's permission — may He be exalted." The Prince of the Believers went there with the group. When they reached the middle of [the cemetery of] al-Baqīʿ, his lips moved with what the Messenger of God — may God's blessings and peace be upon him — had ordered him, and the cemetery began to shake and burst open. When they saw this, they said to him: "Abū al-Ḥusayn! Forgive our false step!" He said — may God's blessings be upon him: "Is it not to me you have been insolent. It is to the Messenger of God that you have been insolent." They said: "Give us permission to go back to him." They went back and said: "Messenger of God, forgive our false step, may God forgive yours!" He said — may God's blessings be upon him **[38]** and his family: "Is it not to me you have been insolent, but to God. May He forgive your false steps!" Then he sent [them] to the Prince of the Believers and <they acknowledged that the Order was his>[165,166].

[165] *Thumma arsala ilā amīr al-muʾminīn fa-raddahu*: the last sentence of the *ḥadīth* is unintelligible. Some words seem to be missing. I reconstructed the probable meaning based on Idrīs ʿImād al-Dīn, *Zahr al-maʿānī*, p. 171. After alluding to this *ḥadīth*, Idrīs quotes another one containing the following sentence: 'He ordered him to give the Order back to the Prince of the Believers' (*amarahu an yarudda al-amr ilā amīr al-muʾminīn*).

[166] See Ibn Bābawayh, *Kitāb al-tawḥīd*, p. 423, where, among other tales of resurrections, a *ḥadīth* narrates — much more briefly than in the *Kashf* — how Muḥammad sends ʿAlī to the cemetery to revive the dead of Quraysh. In this *ḥadīth*, Q. 3:49 is explicitly referred to, while it is only implied here; it is quoted, however, in *Kashf* V, p. 98, § 15.

[A *ḥadīth* on the vision of God]

81. [Jaʿfar al-Ṣādiq] — may God bless him and his family — was once asked if Muḥammad had seen his Lord. 'Yes', he said, 'twice: once with his heart, and once with his eyes. Did you not hear him say: *'Indeed, he saw him yet another time'* until: *'His eye swerved not, nor did it stray'* [Q. 53:13–17]?'[167]

[On associating something to God]

82. [Jaʿfar al-Ṣādiq] — may God bless him and his family — [gave this interpretation of] the words of God — He is Mighty and Sublime: *'God forgives not that one should be associated with Him; less than that He forgives whomever He will'* [Q. 4:48]: 'They say about this that he is the association (*shirk*),[168] but it is not as they say. Association (*al-ishrāk*) in this context is to associate to the Friendship (*walāya*) of the Prince of the Believers and whomever has been appointed by God as a Friend (*walī*) and an Imam; [it is] thus to establish someone else alongside him, and to reject his Friendship (*walāya*), and therefore go totally astray. Association to God is therefore different from [what they say].' He said: *'Whoever associates [something] with God, then God will forbid Him the paradise, and his abode will be the Fire'* [Q. 5:72], and *'an evil destination'* [Q. 2:126]. May God preserve us and preserve you from associating anyone to the Friends of God, and from dissociating (*barāʾa*) from them. And tthese are two completely different matters.
83. The explanation has ended. **[39]**

---

[167] Compare with Ibn Bābawayh, *Kitāb al-tawḥīd*, *bāb* 8, p. 111, no. 9, where the commentary of the same verses in a *ḥadīth* attributed to ʿAlī al-Riḍā goes in the opposite direction, as it distinguishes between the vision of God and that of His signs. Indeed, Q. 53:18 does state: *'Verily he saw one of the greatest signs of his Lord'*. The *ḥadīth* also quotes Q. 42:11: *'Like Him there is naught'* (*laysa ka-mithlihi shay'*). In the same chapter, Ibn Bābawayh narrates several reports to the effect that the Prophet saw God with his heart, and not with his eyes. On this debate, see commentary of *Kashf* V, pp. 390–395. On the hermeneutical equivalence between the term 'sign' (*āya*) and the Imams, see *Kashf* III, p. 79, § 63, and related footnote.

[168] It is unclear to what or whom these pronouns refer to. Could this be an allusion to an anti-Shiʿi argument claiming that devotion to the Imam is *shirk*?

Treatise I Commentary

Despite its fragmented structure, the first treatise displays doctrinal unity. The reader is but compelled to observe the following paradox: on the one hand, the treatise leaves the reader with an impression of great confusion, as it does not contain any consistent argumentation, except in short passages that, in any case, are not formally and logically connected to each other. On the other hand, it cannot be denied that the text presents a certain coherence of content. The composition of the treatise is reminiscent of the technique of impressionist painters: it is only through a series of isolated touches, interspersed with an exegesis here, or an enumeration of names there, that a general picture progressively emerges. One is thus provided with fragments to reassemble the whole into a coherent doctrine — a method consistent with the technique of 'scattering of knowledge'.[169] That is to say, we are not dealing here with an actual 'treatise', in the sense of an organized and linear argumentation framed by an introduction and a conclusion, similar to what a philosophical or theological treatise would look like; the text is not systematic in its exposition. Rather, it manages to deliver its ideas through a play of passages echoing each other throughout the treatise. When examining the treatise closely, it appears that, far from being a chaotic collection of fragments more or less randomly combined, it must have been quite carefully composed — an assertion that may be extended to the whole *Kitāb al-Kashf*.

It is not only the structure that makes this treatise a difficult text, but also the variety of its doctrinal trends, which can be identified through the doctrines it displays, as well as its vocabulary. Indeed, at least three main trends can be detected. The first is Shiʿi in the broader sense;

[169] See Introduction, pp. 63–68.

some features of the text cannot be ascribed to a specific Shiʿi trend as they are common to several of them (e.g. the historiography of the succession to Muḥammad). The second, of course, is the Ismaili trend (e.g. the initiatory and messianic themes, the Ismaili conception of the continuity of the Imamate). However, the Ismaili trend is not as present as one might expect from a text stemming from the Ismaili tradition. The third trend, more surprisingly, is reminiscent of what is known of the *ghulāt*, both from external and internal sources. The themes, vocabulary and doctrines of the so-called 'Mufaḍḍal tradition' are overwhelmingly present in this treatise, when compared to others in the collection, even though the arrangement of the fragments was undoubtedly done by an Ismaili author or editor. We are thus dealing with a core formed by a text — or a cluster of texts — of mainly *ghulāt* origin, later adapted and reoriented in Ismaili fashion.

The following commentary will therefore attempt to reconstruct some of the intentions of the treatise by connecting its parts and occasionally connecting them with other passages of the *Kitāb al-Kashf*, as well as other sources (Ismaili, Imamī, Nuṣayri, etc.), thus highlighting both the origins of the various parts of the treatise and the way the latter were remodelled to fit the Ismaili orientations.

1. The Divine Trust (*amāna*), *walāya* and the covenant

The first pages are dedicated to the initiatory pact, which is grounded in the pre-eternal Pact between God and men. The author begins by defining the *amāna* as the first quality of the true believer. *Amāna* is a polysemic term with rich theological implications.[170] It means 'loyalty', 'fidelity', but also 'deposit' or 'trust' (i.e. something that is entrusted to someone),[171] as well as 'security pact'. Its root *a-m-n* — the same root as the word 'faith', *īmān* — points to notions of safety and confidence. In the Qur'an, the notion is either used in the sense of a trust one is exhorted to return to its legitimate owners — it then has to do with

[170] See D. Gril, 'Dépôt divin', in *Dictionnaire du Coran*, pp. 207–209.

[171] In this sense, the meaning of the term is close to *wadīʿa*. For the juridical aspects of the latter, see O. Spies, 'Wadīʿa', *EI1*.

loyalty to one's word[172] — or as a synonym of 'covenant' (*'ahd*).[173] However, in Q. 33:72, the term bears a cosmological sense, rather than a strictly social one.[174] *Amāna* thus has a double meaning: terrestrial and celestial, so to speak, or worldly and spiritual, which paves the way to its understanding in our treatise, that is, to the idea that the initiatory pact is but a reflection of the Covenant between God and men.

Amāna appears closely connected to several other important Shiʿi notions, namely *walāya*,[175] *amr* (the 'Cause', the 'Order' or the 'Affair' of the prophets and the Imams), as well as *taqiyya*. Much has been written on *walāya* in modern scholarship, and it is not necessary to elaborate on this here. Nevertheless, a few basic explanations are required. The root *w-l-y* expresses the idea of proximity, from which two series of meanings are derived: those related to friendship, and those related to governance and protection.[176] The term *walī* itself can

---

[172] See Q. 2:283: *'If someone entrusts something to another person, let him who is trusted to deliver what he is entrusted with'*; 4:58: *'God commands you to deliver trusts back to their owners.'*

[173] See Q. 23:8; 70:32; and 8:27 where the word *'ahd* does not appear but which nevertheless deals with a form of pact: *'Do not betray God and the Messenger, and do not betray your trusts.'* See quotation of the latter verse in *Kashf* V, pp. 147–148, § 95.

[174] *'We presented the Trust (amāna) to the heavens and the earth and the mountains, but they refused to carry it and were afraid of it; and man carried it. Surely he is unjust and a fool.'* Here, the Qur'an is obviously dealing with a form of alliance between God and men, which connects the *amāna* to other Qur'anic notions such as *'ahd* ('covenant') and *mīthāq*('pact', 'alliance'); see M. Ebstein, 'Covenant (religious) pre-eternal', *EI3*. God entrusts man with a sacred deposit, the nature of which is not clarified in this verse, but which can nevertheless be connected to the appointment of man as God's lieutenant on earth, as stated in Q. 2:30: *'Your Lord told the angels: I am setting in the earth a lieutenant (khalīfa).'*

[175] The *amāna* from Q. 33:72 is indeed identified with the '*walāya* of the Prince of the Believers'; see al-Kulaynī, *Uṣūl al-Kāfī, k. al-ḥujja, bāb fī-hi nikatun wa-nitafun min al-tanzīl fī'l-walāya'*, vol. 1, p. 413, no. 2.

[176] For a general overview of this Arabic root (which, however, does not discuss its Shiʿi connotations), see M. Chodkiewicz, *Le Sceau des saints: Prophétie et sainteté dans la doctrine d'Ibn Arabî* (Paris, 1986), pp. 30–35, esp. p. 33, where the author signals a Qur'anic play of echoes that allows us to connect *walāya* and *amāna*: Q. 10:62 mentions the *awliyā'*, the 'Friends' of God 'on whom there shall be 'no fear nor sorrow'. The same expression appears in Q. 2:38 as a promise to mankind after Adam's repentance, provided it follows God's guidance. Inasmuch as the 'man' of Q. 33:72 can

either have an active or a passive sense, that is to say that the *walī* can be either the protector or the protected. In a Shiʿi context, the *walāya* of the Imam, inasmuch as it denotes proximity to God, is what he derives his sanctity and authority from. By extension, it is therefore synonymous to these terms. As for the *walāya* of the believers, it consists of their acknowledgement of the spiritual and political legitimacy of the Imam, which implies a faithful commitment to the Imam's 'cause' as well as a spiritual love for him.

Insofar as the Imam is not only a historical person, but a theophany which pre-exists Creation,[177] the idea of *walāya* takes on a dimension which transcends the simple temporal and political recognition of this or that Imam, as it becomes an act of adherence to the Alliance between God and men, and a positive response to the question of Q. 7:172: *'Am I not your Lord?'* Consequently, *walāya* merges with the notion of 'divine deposit', the more so as, like the *amāna*, the *walāya* is in correspondence with the two aspects, pre-existent and worldly, of the Imam: it is through the metaphysical Imam, depositary of the Alliance, that God and mankind are connected, and the terrestrial Imam takes his legitimacy from the fact that he is but the reflection, the image of this metaphysical Imam.

According to the Islamic hierohistory of salvation, Prophets appear as successive reminders of a timeless, yet always forgotten, truth. This truth is the content of the divine deposit entrusted to Adam which humanity must preserve and which it still neglects; in the Shiʿi context,

---

be identified with Adam, it seems that the Qur'an itself establishes a link between the *walāya* and the covenant between God and mankind. On *walāya* in Shiʿism, see M.A. Amir-Moezzi, *La Religion discrète*, Ch. 7, 'Notes à propos de la *walāya* imamite', pp. 177–207 (English trans.: *Spirituality of Shiʿi Islam*, Ch.7: 'Notes on Imami *Walāya*', pp. 231–275); M. Massi Dakake, *The Charismatic Community*, pp. 33–69, 103–139, and ibid., pp. 15–31, for *walāya* in Islamic tradition; on *walāya* in the Ismaili corpus of al-Mu'ayyad fī'l-Dīn al-Shīrāzī, see also E. Alexandrin, *Walāyah in the Fāṭimid Ismāʿīlī Tradition* (Albany, 2017).

[177] See M.A. Amir-Moezzi, *Guide divin*, Ch. 2: 'La préexistence de l'imâm', pp. 73–154 (English trans.: *Divine Guide*, Ch. 2: 'The Preexistence of the Imam', pp. 29–59); idem, *La Religion discrète*, Ch. 4: 'La pré-existence de l'imâm', pp. 109–133 (English trans.: *Spirituality of Shiʿi Islam*, Ch. 4: 'The Pre-Existence of the Imam', pp. 133–168). An illustration of such pre-existence is found in the *Kashf*, in the cosmogony of the Five; see *Kashf* I, pp. 35–37, §§ 76–78.

this preservation is ensured by the men of God par excellence, the Imams. As al-Sijistānī puts it: 'The Sacred House is the Completer [Imam], the Master of the Age, because he is a house appointed to preserve the Trust for the community.'[178] According to a *ḥadīth* reported by al-Kulaynī, the non-Shiʿis are thus identified with 'traitors who have betrayed (. . .) their Repositories (*amānāt*)', because 'God's Book was given to them, and they falsified and changed it'.[179] This 'Book of God' can be interpreted more broadly, not only as the historical Qur'an, but also as the object of the Covenant between God and men. This may also be linked to an ancient Shiʿi exegetical key according to which the Qur'anic occurrences of the word 'Book' are a code-name for the Imam — a method amply illustrated in Treatise VI of the *Kitāb al-Kashf*, as we will see.[180]

With regard to the locus of the pact contracted between God and mankind, the guarantor and the conservator of this pact is the Imam, particularly ʿAlī ibn Abī Ṭālib, the Imam par excellence, as expressly stated in Treatise I: 'The Trust is the rank of the Prince of the Believers ʿAlī b. Abī Ṭālib.'[181] However, in the same passage, the 'man' from Q. 33:72 who agrees to bear the *amāna* is not Adam, but Abū Bakr, whose acceptance is interpreted as an illegitimate claim to a status that does not belong to him. To support this reading, the author confers to the verb *ʿaraḍa* in the verse a different meaning from that found in common exegeses. Rather than referring to the *proposal* that God makes to the various beings of Creation of the heavy burden of representing Him on earth, here, the exegesis is reminiscent of Q. 2:31 — cited at the end of the treatise, after the cosmogony of the Five[182] — where the same verb clearly has the meaning of *presentation*. In Q. 2:30–36, God announces to the angels that He will establish Adam as a lieutenant on earth. Faced with the doubts they express, God teaches *'all the names'* of beings to Adam, then *presents* (*ʿaraḍa*)

[178] Al-Sijistānī, *al-Maqālīd al-malakūtiyya*, pp. 310–311. The notion that the Imams are 'Houses' is a central point of *Kashf* V.

[179] Cited in M.A. Amir-Moezzi, *Guide divin*, p. 216 (English trans.: *Divine Guide*, p. 86).

[180] See commentary of *Kashf* VI, pp. 458–463.

[181] *Kashf* I, p. 28, § 61.

[182] *Kashf* I, pp. 36–37, § 78.

the latter to the angels, asking them to name them. Confessing their ignorance, the angels bow down to Adam. From this perspective, Q. 33:72 means that God *presents* (rather than offers) the Trust — that is to say the *maqām*, the sacred station, of ʿAlī b. Abī Ṭālib — to all beings. They all *'refused to carry it and were afraid of it'* [Q. 33:72], that is to say they refrained from claiming this eminent rank and they recognized its privileged status, just as the angels of Q. 2:34 had done when acknowledging Adam's rank.[183] The analogy between Satan who refuses to bow down to Adam and Abū Bakr who 'claimed the rank of the Prince of the Believers and his lieutenancy (*khilāfa*) to the Messenger of God'[184] is clear, although the author does not declare it explicitly.

Although based on the usual understanding of the verb *ʿaraḍa*, a similar interpretation of Q. 33:72 is reported by Abū Tammām, who, in his *Kitāb al-Shajara*, attributes it to the sect of the *mughīriyya*:

> He proposed (*ʿaraḍa*) to the heavens and the earth that they should prevent ʿAlī b. Abī Ṭālib from assuming the califate (*khilāfa*) and the imamate, but they refused. Next He proposed it to the mountains but they refused also. Then He proposed it to the people, whereupon ʿUmar went to Abū Bakr — both were at that moment still shadows (*aẓilla*) — and he ordered him to take upon himself preventing ʿAlī by both betraying him. Thereafter Abū Bakr did exactly that. All this is in God's statement, "*We did indeed offer the trust to the heavens and the earth and the mountains, but they refused to undertake it being afraid of it. But man undertook it; he was indeed unjust and foolish.*" Then ʿUmar said to Abū Bakr, "I will support you against ʿAlī, on him be peace, so that you can pass the caliphate to me after yourself."[185]

---

[183] It is worth noting that in the interpretation of Q. 33:72 found in the *Shawāhid wa'l-bayān*, the *amāna* is the 'sacred station of the Legatee' (*maqām al-waṣī*), who is ʿAlī, while the 'heavens', the 'earth' and the 'mountains' are respectively the Imams, the Proofs and the 'Chiefs' (*nuqabāʾ*). The 'man' is 'the first iniquitous one' (*al-ẓālim al-awwal*); see Jaʿfar b. Manṣūr al-Yaman, *Al-Shawāhid wa'l-bayān*, IIS MS. 734, ff. 228–231. Thus, the analogy between Adam and the angels prostrating to him, on the one hand, and ʿAlī and ranks of the *daʿwa*, on the other hand, highlights once more the symbolic equivalence between the 'angels' and members of the *daʿwa*; on this, see *Kashf* III, p. 62, § 20, and related footnote, as well as the commentary of *Kashf* V below, pp. 413–414.

[184] *Kashf* I, p. 29, § 61.

[185] W. Madelung and P. Walker, *An Ismaili heresiography*, pp. 70–71 (Arabic: p. 71).

From the fact that the episode takes place when Abū Bakr and ʿUmar were 'shadows', it is clear that the names of the protagonists refer to pre-eternal archetypes, rather than to historical individuals.[186] The latter are manifestations of pre-eternal entities at a particular time, and their conflict is a repetition of the conflict between Adam and Iblīs. Thus, there was, 'in every era and every age', an ʿAlī and an Abū Bakr, that is, the eternal entities ʿAlī and Abū Bakr appearing under different guises or forms. This will lead to the problem of metempsychosis, as well as the continuity of *amr*, 'God's Order', and the opposition it meets.[187] It is the background to passages such as the enumerations of the enemies of the prophets.[188]

Before tackling this notion of *amr* in detail, the practical application of *amāna* and *walāya* needs to be highlighted. In the treatise, *amāna* is immediately related to the initiation pact, and to what constitutes its prerequisite, that is, the pact of discretion. Since the author does not dwell on the idea of a pre-eternal pact, and confines himself to quoting Q. 33:72, it was necessary to show that the initiation covenant contracted between the author and the reader of the treatise is a reflection of the pre-eternal covenant, of which it is merely a particular illustration. The *ʿahd* which unites the disciple to the Imam in this world is based by the author of the treatise upon the *ʿahd* between God and humanity, and it is the latter that gives the initiatory pact its importance and status.

It is significant that the treatise begins by stating that: 'the first thing the believer needs concerning his religion and knowledge of the Truth and its people is loyalty (*amāna*) to God and His Friends'.[189] The rest of the text, in which the author goes without transition from the Covenant that 'God has always made with His prophets' to the pact of discretion, establishes a correspondence between *amāna* as a pre-eternal pact and the *amāna* which is due in this world. Now, the first definition of this second *amāna* is, as we can see next, *kitmān*, the silence that must be observed with regard to the teachings. Although

[186] Speculations on pre-eternal 'shadows' are a feature of *ghulāt* sources which have transpired in Twelver Shiʿi collections; see above, p. 18, n. 43.

[187] See esp. *Kashf* I, p. 12, § 25, and commentary of *Kashf* I, pp. 134–162.

[188] *Kashf* I, pp. 10–11, §§ 21–22.

[189] *Kashf* I p. 2, § 2.

the term does not appear in this treatise, it is indeed *taqiyya* we are dealing with. The first advice to the aspirant to the true religion is — with thinly veiled threats against their life! — to stay silent and preserve the secret teachings.[190] The author then assimilates this obligation to the Islamic food bans: revealing the secret to someone who is not worthy of it would be analogous to eating 'carrion, blood and pork' (*al-mayta wa'l-damm wa-laḥm al-khanzīr*).[191] This elevates *taqiyya* as

[190] In the prologue of his *Zahr bidhr al-ḥaqā'iq*, and after a series of eulogistic paragraphs, the third Ṭayyibī *dā'ī* Ḥātim b. Ibrāhīm al-Ḥāmidī (d. 596/1199) warns his reader in terms very similar to those found in the prologue of the *Kitāb al-Kashf*. He states that the *Zahr* is 'a trust on [the recipient's] neck' (*amāna fī ruqbatika*) and anyone 'who does not deserve it' (*man lā yastaḥiqquhā*) should not be allowed to lay eyes on it. The recipient will be held accountable for it when he meets God, His angels and His Friends. If he discloses the contents of the treatise, he and whoever reads it without deserving it will be 'disavowed by God' (*barī'ūn min Allāh*). This disavowal will take the transgressors from God's mercy to His wrath (*barā'a yakhruj bi-hā man fa'ala dhālik min raḥmat Allāh ilā ghaḍabi-hi*). Indeed, the author has 'unveiled' (*kashaftu*) matters that should not be unveiled but remain hidden and concealed (*kitmuhā wa-isrāru-hā*). Just as in the *Kashf*, Ḥātim also mentions the qualities of the recipient, justifiying the disclosure of the esoteric knowledge to him; see Ḥātim b. Ibrāhīm al-Ḥāmidī, *Zahr bidhr al-ḥaqā'iq*, in *Muntakhabāt ismā'īliyya*, ed. 'Ādil al-'Awwā (Damascus, 1958), p. 160. Another work from the same author, *al-Shumūs al-zāhira*, is similarly 'entrusted to the reader as an *amânat*'; see W. Ivanow, *Ismaili Literature*, p. 61. On Ḥātim b. Ibrāhīm al-Ḥāmidī, see ibid., pp. 61–68; W. Madelung, 'al-Ḥāmidī', *EI2*; I.K. Poonawala, *Bibliography*, pp. 151–155.

[191] *Kashf* I, p. 2, § 2. In a recent article, M. Asatryan suggests that this enumeration of forbidden things should be connected with the anti-*ghulāt* polemics in the *Kitāb al-Kashf*, since it is common, in heresiography works, to accuse the *ghulāt* of viewing carrion, blood and swineflesh as permitted to be eaten; see M. Asatryan, 'Early Muslims and Other Muslims: Polemics and Borrowings in *Kitāb al-Kashf*', in *Intellectual Interactions in the Islamic World: The Ismaili Thread*, ed. O. Mir-Kasimov (London, 2020), pp. 281–282. However, a more convincing explanation can be proposed in light of the specifically Ismaili *ta'wīl* of this unholy triad, as found in several other works: in Ja'far b. Manṣūr al-Yaman's *Riḍā' fi'l-bātin*, 'carrion (lit.: 'dead things'), blood and swineflesh' are respectively identified with 'the people of the exoteric' (*ahl al-ẓāhir*), 'doubt' (*shakk*) regarding 'God's Order', and the 'hypocrit' (*munāfiq*); see Ja'far b. Manṣūr al-Yaman, *Kitāb al-Riḍā' fi'l-bātin*, pp. 161–163. A similar interpretation appears in Ja'far b. Manṣūr al-Yaman, *Al-Shawāhid wa'l-bayān*, IIS MS. 734, ff. 187–188, and it is also reported by the Zaydī author al-Daylamī, who quotes it from an otherwise unknown *al-'Ilm al-maknūn wa'l-satr (sirr?) al-makhzūn*,

an essential prerequisite to accessing to the secret doctrine. Indeed, Shiʿi literature provides several *ḥadīths* asserting the centrality of *taqiyya* in Shiʿi faith: '*Taqiyya* is my religion and that of my fathers, thus says Jaʿfar al-Ṣādiq, and he who has no *taqiyya* has no religion';[192] 'Nine-tenths of religion consists of the Keeping of the Secret (*taqiyya*); those who do not practice it have no religion.'[193]

The primordial Covenant between God and Adam is the archetype of the initiatory pact which opens the *Kitāb al-Kashf*. However, this is only possible by virtue of a certain continuity in the transmission of the initial deposit, ensured by the succession of prophets and Imams. The primordial pact must be updated 'in every era and every age' through recognition of the 'Imam of the age'. By acknowledging this Imam, the Ismaili neophyte enters a new family, renouncing his bodily life and lineage, in favour of the spiritual life bestowed upon him by his masters, inasmuch as they provide him with the true esoteric knowledge. Symbolically, he exchanges his worldly affiliations in favour of a spiritual affiliation. To enter the *daʿwa* is to enter a new network of kinship.

2. The *daʿwa*, an esoteric family

One of the aims of the present study is to show how, drawing from general Shiʿi features, Ismailism constituted itself as a distinct trend with its own identity. What are the specific features of Ismailism, when compared to previous and contemporary Shiʿi movements? One of the

---

which he ascribes to Abū Yaʿqūb al-Sijistānī; see al-Daylamī, *Bayān madhhab al-bāṭiniyya wa-buṭlānihi*, p. 48. See also the *Mafātīḥ al-niʿma*, in W. Madelung and P. Walker, *Affirming the Imamate. Early Fatimid Teachings in the Islamic West* (London and New York, 2021), pp. 86–87 (Arabic: pp. 84–85), where a slightly different, yet overall similar, interpretation is provided. On these interpretations, see F. Gillon, 'Du *tafsīr* chiite au *ta'wīl* ismaélien, l'évolution du commentaire personnalisé négatif dans la *daʿwa*', in O. Mir-Kasimov and M. Terrier, eds, *Festschrift for M.A. Amir-Moezzi*, forthcoming.

192 A well-known and widely quoted *ḥadīth*; see references in M. A. Amir-Moezzi, *Guide divin*, p. 311 and p. 311, n. 682 (English trans.: *Divine Guide*, p. 129 and p. 230, n. 682).

193 See ibid., where this *ḥadīth* is quoted along with several others on *taqiyya*.

answers to this question is the notion of *daʿwa*, the 'Summons' — understood as a political clandestine organization whose hierarchy is built on a systematization of the initiatory themes of Shiʿi Islam. What separated early Ismailis from other Muslims, or from other Shiʿis at the time, is their belonging to such an organization. We will return to the *daʿwa* as such in another chapter, and focus here on one aspect of this organization, that is, its conceptualization as an alternative, spiritual, family — as opposed to the biological, natural, family.

The *Kitāb al-Kashf* contains several passages dealing with such a 'familial' symbolism, grounded on the implicit opposition between the biological, earthly family and the spiritual family — which is an ancient and well-known conception, as we find it, for instance, in the famous words of Jesus: 'He who loves his father or mother more than me is not worthy of me: and he who loves his son or daughter more than me is not worthy of me.'[194] At some point in the *ḥadīth* of Treatise I describing the return of the Mahdī,[195] the people of Banū Hāshim complain that the Mahdī has no regard for their kinship — the Mahdī, as a descendant of the Prophet, being also a Hāshimite. This expresses the idea that the love of truth must overcome any worldly attachments, family included. The 'esoteric family' entails two aspects, both of which symbolize the relation of the master and the disciple. According to one of these aspects, the master is symbolically male, while his disciple is female, and the initiation is therefore described as an 'esoteric marriage' or 'esoteric coitus' (*al-nikāḥ al-bāṭin*). From another point of view, the master is symbolically his disciple's father; as a result, all the disciples of a common master are brothers in true, esoteric, faith, which places Ismailism within a theoretical frame common to all initiatory brotherhoods. Of course, these two points of view are closely connected and complementary: the progressive initiation of the disciple, his coming to the esoteric life, is modelled on the whole process of birth and growth in the biological life.

This symbolic conception of the *daʿwa* as a new family is based on the interpretation of the notion that the Imams give life to the dead, as illustrated by the *ḥadīth* of Treatise I where ʿAlī is sent out to the

---

[194] Matt. 10:37.

[195] *Kashf* I p. 33, § 69.

cemetery to resurrect the dead.[196] This idea was also present in Imami circles.[197] The symbolic interpretation of this attribute of the Imams is that they dispense the spiritual and esoteric knowledge which is the life of the soul. The ability to give life to a body is thus a symbol of the ability to give spiritual life: 'The esoteric knowledge is a second life and a renewed creation' (*'ilm al-bāṭin huwa al-ḥayāt al-thāniya wa'l-khalqa al-mujaddada*).[198] In both the *Shawāhid wa'l-bayān* and the *Riḍā' fi'l-bāṭin*,[199] for instance, Q. 40:11: '*Our Lord, you have caused us to die twice and to live twice*', is interpreted with regard to this symbolism:

> The meaning of his words is that they were dead before the call to Islam, but he gave them life through Islam. Then, he concealed the esoteric (*katama al-bāṭin*) from them, and so they became dead with regard to the esoteric life. Then he gave them life through the knowledge of the esoteric. Such are their two deaths and their two lives.[200]

Several Ismaili texts from the early Fatimid period thus describe initiation and access to esoteric knowledge as 'rebirth' (*wilāda thāniya*),[201] as a 'second creation' (*khalq thānī*),[202] or a 'new creation' (*khalq jadīd*),[203] concepts with both initiatory and messianic implications. Henceforth, the analogy was taken further, in Ismaili doctrine as well as in Nuṣayrism, by expressing the process of the soul's coming to knowledge in terms borrowed from the biological process of life, thus drawing a strict analogy between the birth of a body and the (re-)birth of the soul, that is, access to the true esoteric knowledge. Insofar as bodies come to life through mating, and the soul comes to life through initiation, then initiation is strictly analogous to mating in the esoteric order. Thus, mating can be lawful — marriage,

---

196 *Kashf* I pp. 37–39, § 80.

197 See e.g. al-Ṣaffār al-Qummī, *Baṣā'ir al-darajāt*, pp. 480–489.

198 Ja'far b. Manṣūr al-Yaman, *Al-Shawāhid wa'l-bayān*, IIS MS. 734, f. 86.

199 Ibid., ff. 86–87; idem, *Al-Riḍā' fi'l-bāṭin*, p. 161.

200 Ja'far b. Manṣūr al-Yaman, *Al-Riḍā' fi'l-bāṭin*, p. 161.

201 See e.g. Ja'far b. Manṣūr al-Yaman, *Ta'wīl al-zakāt*, p. 113.

202 See e.g. ibid., pp. 87, 90.

203 The expression *khalq jadīd* appears in *Kashf* V, p. 97, § 13; p. 101, § 22; p. 149, § 97; p. 155, § 105. See also Ja'far b. Manṣūr al-Yaman, *Al-Shawāhid wa'l-bayān*, IIS MS. 734, ff. 71, 157, 223–224, 337–338; idem, *Ta'wīl al-zakāt*, p. 87.

that is, the covenant between the master and his disciple — or unlawful — adultery, that is, divulging secret teachings without permission. The new members of the *daʿwa* are thus 'married' to an initiator who, by 'fertilising' them with knowledge, is their symbolic 'husband', before he becomes their 'father'.

In this regard, one of the most interesting passages from Treatise I is the exegesis of the attempted seduction of Joseph by the wife of Potiphar (named 'al-ʿAzīz' in the Qur'anic account).[204] Several interpretations of this episode are given after the literal one is strongly rejected: according to the author, the story does not involve any sexual act (or refusal of such an act).[205] The usefulness and implications of the first interpretation are not quite clear, as one fails to grasp the meaning of Joseph's temptation to slaughter the wife of al-ʿAzīz — especially since it is presented as an exoteric interpretation.[206] It is likely that the main interest of this first interpretation is to introduce the idea that this seduction attempt should not be understood literally; this interpretation is thus 'better than what the people of exotericism say, and closer to the esoteric meaning'.[207] According to the second interpretation, presented as the esoteric one, the relationship in question here is of an initiatory, rather than sexual nature, because 'the Summons is analogous to coitus (*nikāḥ*) in the esoteric order'.[208] Consequently, the seduction attempt becomes a request for initiation and the sexual desire of Potiphar's wife is meant to be seen as a desire

---

[204] *Kashf* I, pp. 26–27, § 57–59.

[205] This recalls the prudishness of some Khariji opponents to the inclusion of Sūra 12 (*Yūsuf*) in the Qur'an because of its so-called licentious episodes. It may also be a remote echo of some so-called 'exaggerating' (*ghulāt*) beliefs denying any material corporeality to the Imams: according to these beliefs, the Imams do not feed, do not copulate, do not die, and even, are not born through natural ways.

[206] Although according to other Ismaili sources, the 'slaughter' (*al-dhabḥ*) symbolizes the taking of the initiatory oath; see e.g. Jaʿfar b. Manṣūr al-Yaman, *Al-Riḍāʿ fi'l-bāṭin*, pp. 169, 189–190. The author of the *Ta'wīl al-zakāt* further explains that to slaughter is to separate the head from the body, which symbolizes the fact that the neophytes separate themselves from their exoteric heads and chiefs who maintain them under the exoteric religion and reject the esoteric doctrine; see Jaʿfar b. Manṣūr al-Yaman, *Ta'wīl al-zakāt*, p. 110.

[207] *Kashf* I, p. 26, § 58.

[208] *Kashf* I, p. 27, § 59.

for knowledge. Joseph's refusal to be seduced symbolises his refusal to initiate a candidate deemed unsuitable to receive the esoteric knowledge; sexuality is understood only as a code for initiation. The very idea that the neophyte symbolically reaches a second birth when he is fully initiated presupposes a prior fertilization: for there to be a new-born, there must be sexual intercourse, therefore, symbolically, the master must fertilize the disciple in order for him to become a new man. In this relationship, the master is analogous to the male while the disciple is symbolically female.

The *Kitāb al-Kashf* contains several other occurrences of this symbolic identification of coitus with initiation, in Treatises III, V and VI.[209] In Treatise V, the idea that fornication means the unauthorized disclosure of esoteric doctrines appears in a passage aimed at organizing the *daʿwa* by giving instructions to the 'Summoners'. In Treatise VI, the same interpretation is found in a similar context. Several other Ismaili sources display the same symbolism and the general idea that the initiator, or master, is symbolically male, while the disciple is symbolically female:[210] 'Every instructor (*mufīd*) is in the place of the male, and every person instructed (*mustafīd*) is in the place of the female: indeed, the female receives what the male emanates to her, and through this reception, a child is manifested from her.'[211] The initiation itself is likened to mating (or marriage): 'Mating (*munākaḥa*) is the disclosure of the exegetical sciences and the esoteric wisdoms.'[212]

---

[209] *Kashf* III, p. 78, § 58; V, p. 114, § 41; p. 123, § 57; VI, p. 166, § 23.

[210] See K. Bauer, 'Spiritual Hierarchy and Gender Hierarchy in Fatimid Ismāʿīlī Interpretations of the Qurʾan', *Journal of Qurʾanic Studies*, 14/2 (2012), pp. 29–46, esp. pp. 34–40. This part of the article is based on the *Kitāb al-ʿĀlim waʾl-ghulām* by Jaʿfar b. Manṣūr al-Yaman, the *Asās al-taʾwīl* and the *Taʾwīl al-daʿāʾim* by al-Qāḍī al-Nuʿmān, as well as the *Majālis al-muʾayyadiyya* by al-Muʾayyad fīʾl-Dīn al-Shīrāzī. See also D. Hollenberg, *Beyond the Qurʾan*, Ch. 3: 'Rearing', pp. 53–78, esp. pp. 60, 72–73. In addition, see e.g. Jaʿfar b. Manṣūr al-Yaman, *Al-Riḍāʿ fīʾl-bāṭin*, pp. 51, 55; idem, *Taʾwīl al-zakāt*, pp. 113–114, 118; W. Madelung and P. Walker, *Affirming the Imamate*, p. 85 (Arabic: pp. 83–84). The same symbolism appears in the Druze writings, which suggests that the Ismaili *daʿwa* still used it at the time of the emergence of Druzism: see D. De Smet, *Épîtres sacrées des Druzes*, pp. 50–52; Epistle 8, pp. 187–188.

[211] Jaʿfar b. Manṣūr al-Yaman, *Taʾwīl al-zakāt*, p. 154.

[212] Jaʿfar b. Manṣūr al-Yaman, *Taʾwīl al-zakāt*, p. 118.

While this symbolic interpretation of sexuality apparently characterizes early Ismailism, it was probably drawn from earlier *ghulāt* doctrines, since it is also found in Nuṣayri sources, which have retained many elements of the *ghulāt* tradition.[213] In this literature, the notion that 'the pupil is in the place of the woman and the master (*sayyid*) is in the place of the husband' is a common idea.[214] This symbolism is perhaps not unrelated to the accounts of the Nuṣayri doctrine by Twelver Shiʿi heresiologists al-Nawbakhtī and al-Qummī, in which they accuse the founder of Nuṣayrism, Ibn Nuṣayr, of authorizing sodomy because it is 'an exercise of humility'.[215] Charges of sexual licentiousness are among the usual accusations against *ghulāt* groups to illustrate their antinomianism.[216] But it would seem that the reports transmitted in heresiographies were based on actual knowledge

---

[213] On Nuṣayri initiation as reported by al-Ṭabarānī, *Kitāb al-ḥāwī fī ʿilm al-fatāwī*, in *Silsilat al-turāth al-ʿalawī*, ed. Abū Mūsā and Shaykh Mūsā (Diyār ʿAql, 2006), vol. 3, pp. 45–116, see Y. Friedman, *The Nuṣayrīs-ʿAlawīs*, pp. 212–215; B. Tendler Krieger, 'Marriage, Birth and *bāṭinī ta'wīl*. A study of Nuṣayrī Initiation based on the *Kitāb al-Ḥāwī fī ʿilm al-fatāwī* of Abū Saʿīd Maymūn al-Ṭabarānī', *Arabica*, 58/1 (2011), pp. 53–75. There are three stages of initiation, the second being called the 'marriage' (*al-nikāḥ*), while the third is likened to breastfeeding. In this work, it is noteworthy that al-Ṭabarānī interprets several Qur'anic occurrences of *mu'mināt*, 'believing women', as a code for the neophytes. In another work of his, the *Kitāb al-Dalā'il fī'l-masā'il*, he explicitly states that since women are 'all blameworthy (. . .) therefore the mention of praiseworthy women in the Book of God, may He be exalted, are the students. The Gnostic is male and the one who seeks knowledge is female. The tongue of the Gnostic is the penis and the ear of the one who seeks knowledge is. . . the vulva'; cited in B. Tendler, 'Concealment and Revelation: a Study of Secrecy and Initiation among the Nuṣayrī-ʿAlawīs of Syria' (Princeton University, 2012), p. 66. On Nuṣayri initiation, see also R. Dussaud, *Histoire et religion des Noṣairîs*, pp. 104–119; M.M. Bar-Asher and A. Kofsky, *The ʿAlawī Religion: An Anthology* (Turnhout: 2021), pp. 149–167.

[214] Isḥāq al-Aḥmar, *Ādāb ʿAbd al-Muṭṭalib*, in *Silsilat al-turāth al-ʿalawī*, ed. Abū Mūsā and Shaykh Mūsā (Diyār ʿAql, 2006), vol. 6, p. 264.

[215] Al-Nawbakhtī, *Firaq al-shīʿa*, p. 78; al-Qummī, *Maqālāt*, pp. 100–101. See also M. Asatryan, *Controversies in Formative Shiʿi Islam*, p. 158, on the idea supported by Isḥāq al-Aḥmar according to which homosexuality has 'a blameworthy as well as a praiseworthy aspect', the latter being 'to seek the knowledge of *tawḥīd* from someone who is more knowledgeable than you'.

[216] See commentary of *Kashf* V, pp. 408–419.

of the sexual symbolism in Nuṣayri initiation,[217] although the teaching was misrepresented, probably intentionally, and understood literally.

3. God's 'Order' (*amr*) and its continuity

The polysemic term *amr* appears several times in Treatise I and in the *Kitāb al-Kashf* in general. The occurrences of the term in the *Kashf* do not refer — at least not directly — to the divine command *kun*, 'be', which brings beings into existence, and it bears no cosmological connotations. Speculations on a cosmological *amr* were engaged with by Ismaili authors, particularly among philosophers of the Neoplatonic tendency, who belong to the so-called 'Persian school'. In their texts, and especially in al-Sijistānī's works, it is a question of defining the relationship of God to Creation, and determining whether the creative imperative constitutes a separate hypostasis or whether it is consubstantial either to God or to Creation.[218] The *Kitāb al-Kashf* does not include comparable developments, and even the specifically Shiʿi reflections on the relationships between divine knowledge, power and imperative are absent, besides brief allusions in Treatise II[219] with regard to the first two.

Amr, here, must be understood in another, broader, sense. In the first place, *amr* is the command, the order, and to say that the Imam is

---

[217] Bella Tendler Krieger thus notes that the justification for these practices attributed to Ibn Nuṣayr by heresiologists suggests the latter may have known about the sexual symbolism of the Nuṣayri initiation; see B. Tendler Krieger, 'Marriage, Birth and *bāṭinī taʾwīl*', pp. 61–63.

[218] On this problem, see D. De Smet, 'Le verbe impératif dans le système cosmologique de l'Ismaélisme', *Revue des Sciences Philosophiques et Théologiques*, 73 (1989), pp. 397–412; P. Walker, *Early Philosophical Shiism, The Ismaili Neoplatonism of Abū Yaʿqūb al-Sijistānī* (New York, 1993), Ch. 6: 'Creation as command', pp. 81–86. See also C. Baffioni, '*Ibdāʿ*, Divine Imperative and Prophecy in the *Rasāʾil Ikhwān al-ṣafā*'', in O. Ali-de-Unzaga, ed, *Fortresses of the Intellect. Ismaili and other Islamic Studies in Honour of Farhad Daftary* (London-New York, 2011), pp. 213–226. The notion of *amr* has recently benefited from several studies: see M. Ebstein, *Mysticism and Philosophy in al-Andalus: Ibn Masarra, Ibn al-ʿArabī and the Ismāʿīlī Tradition* (Leiden and Boston, 2014), pp. 33–76; E. Krinis, *God's Chosen People: Judah Halevi's* Kuzari *and the Shīʿī Imām Doctrine* (Turnhout, 2014), index s.v. 'order', esp. pp. 189–223; O. Ghaemmaghami, *Encounters with the Hidden Imam in Early and Pre-Modern Twelver Shīʿī Islam* (Leiden and Boston, 2020), pp. 26–27; G.M. Schwarb, 'Amr', *EI3*.

[219] *Kashf* II, p. 41, § 4.

the holder of the *amr* (*ṣāḥib al-amr*) means that he is the holder of authority — whether spiritual, temporal, or both. This meaning is to be linked to the expression 'Prince of the Believers' (*amīr al-mu'minīn*), the official title of the head of the Islamic community which designates 'Alī b. Abī Ṭālib in particular in the Shi'i context.

But *amr* also bears a more general and vague meaning in Arabic: *amr* is the 'thing', the 'affair' or the 'matter'. It can also refer to the 'order', in the sense of 'command', but also as in 'system', 'organization' or 'hierarchized structure'. Just like the *amr* as divine imperative, this very general sense, anterior to any philosophical elaboration, appears in the collections of Shi'i *ḥadīth*s, where it designates the sacred 'cause', 'affair' or 'teaching' of the Imams — the Imams being the guarantors of the 'Affair' par excellence, that is, humanity's relationship to God — or even the divine 'Order' of which they are the emanations, the depositaries, and the guardians.[220] *Amr* is in fact 'a very commonly used term for *walāya*'.[221] In the passages of Treatise I dealing with *amr*, the emphasis is on the Order inasmuch as it is transmitted from Adam, from Prophet to Prophet, from Imam to Imam. The *amr* is to be identified with the divine trust, which is the content of the pre-eternal pact: the 'Order' is the transmission of the custody of this trust, from which the Imams derive their spiritual legitimacy.[222] It is as heirs of

[220] See e.g. the *ḥadīth* in which Ja'far al-Ṣādiq declares: 'Our *amr* is a secret within a secret, etc.', cited in M.A. Amir-Moezzi, *Guide divin*, p. 143 (English trans.: *Divine Guide*, p. 55), where it is translated as 'doctrine', and glossed as 'affair', 'cause' and 'order' in a footnote. See also the propositions '*res religiosa*' (idem, *Religion discrete*, p. 183 (English trans., *Spirituality of Shi'i Islam*, p. 240), and 'power', glossed as referring to the 'legitimate power', the 'succession of the Prophet' and the 'caliphate' (idem, *Le Coran silencieux et le Coran parlant*, p. 40, n. 47). See also idem, "La Nuit du *Qadr*' (Coran, sourate 97) dans le Shi'isme ancien (Aspects de l'imamologie duodécimaine XV)', *Mélanges de l'Institut dominicain d'études orientales* (*MIDEO*), 31 (2016), pp. 181–204, and its discussion of Shi'i commentaries of *amr* in Q. 97; the term is interpreted there in a sense that echoes its meaning in the *Kashf*.

[221] M.A. Amir-Moezzi, *La Religion discrète*, p. 203, n. 124 (English trans.: *Spirituality of Shi'i Islam*, pp. 270–271, n. 124); see also ibid., pp. 183, 193 (English trans: pp. 240, 255).

[222] In several Shi'i traditions, the pre-eternal pact contains four oaths: an oath of adoration to God, of *walāya* to Muḥammad, the Imams and the Mahdī; see M.A. Amir-Moezzi, *Guide divin*, pp. 86–87 (English trans.: *Divine Guide*, p. 34).

Adam and custodians of a knowledge that God reserves to them, that they are to be followed and obeyed. The 'Order' is the idea that the trust entrusted to man crosses the centuries and the men of God (Prophets and Imams), as a symbol of the Alliance and as the Threshold of access to esoteric knowledge. A *ḥadīth* reported by al-Kulaynī thus describes the passage of the Order from Adam to his legatee Imam and its transmission 'from the time of Adam until Muḥammad, who passed it on to his own Legatee'.[223]

Amr is explained twice in Treatise I, each time in passages following and commenting on mystical *ḥadīth*s by ʿAlī b. Abī Ṭālib. Since the second of these passages refers to the first,[224] they must belong to the same editorial layer, and it is likely that their author is also the editor of the treatise — to which other glosses and commentaries of *ḥadīth*s should also be attributed, particularly the anti-*ghulāt* passage commenting on a vision of Jaʿfar al-Ṣādiq.[225]

Following this latter passage, to which I will return, is a first *ḥadīth* attributed to ʿAlī, reported by Jābir b. Yazīd al-Juʿfī who claims to hold it from the fifth Imam, Muḥammad al-Bāqir. There, ʿAlī assimilates himself to Christ and declares himself the Messiah: 'I am him and he is me (. . .) Jesus son of Mary is from me and I am from him.'[226] This *ḥadīth* comes under the tradition of the mystical sermons attributed to ʿAlī which bring into play the question of the divinity of the Imam and in which 'the Imam is not only presented as the man of God par excellence but as participating fully in the Names, Attributes and Acts that theology usually reserves for God alone'.[227] In the *ḥadīth* reported by *Kitāb al-Kashf*, the allusion to Jesus must be understood by the exceptional status of the latter, which the Qur'an calls 'Spirit of God' and to which he attributes powers of healing, resurrection or even of

---

[223] Cited in M.A. Amir-Moezzi, "La Nuit du *Qadr*' (Coran, sourate 97)', p. 185.

[224] *Kashf* I, p. 12, § 25.

[225] *Kashf* I, pp. 7–8, § 13.

[226] *Kashf* I, p. 8, §§ 14 and 16.

[227] M.A. Amir-Moezzi, *La Religion discrète*, Ch. 3: 'Remarques sur la divinité de l'imâm', p. 89 (English trans.: *Spirituality of Shiʿi Islam*, Ch. 3: 'Some Remarks on the Divinity of the Imam', p. 103). This chapter is precisely dedicated to the literary genre of the 'mystical sermons' and their theological implications.

creation.[228] That ʿAlī ibn Abī Ṭālib claims these qualities for himself is characteristic of a tendency of ancient Shiʿism.

Surprisingly, the *Kashf* does not elaborate on this aspect and rather uses the *ḥadīth* to support the continuity of *amr*, 'from His first Prophets, Envoys and Imams of His religion, to the last'.[229] It is true that the notion of *amr* does not exclude a metaphysical conception of the Imam according to which a 'celestial' ʿAlī would be the source of the esoteric knowledge that the various prophets and Imams draw from. Inasmuch as the Imam preexists as a spiritual being created before Adam (as in the pentadist cosmogony at the end of treatise I, or as in several Twelver *ḥadīth*s), it is perfectly conceivable that the succession of prophets and Imams takes place by participation, almost in the Platonic sense of the term: each Prophet or Imam would thus derive his knowledge from its exemplary depository, the metaphysical Imam. But this argument, that links, on the one hand, the identification of ʿAlī with the Messiah (as the Word of God), and on the other hand, the continuity of divine revelation through a series of representatives of God, does not appear here; as a result, the comment seems slightly out of step with the explicit content of the *ḥadīth*. This discrepancy would seem to indicate an intervention to mitigate the potential *ghulāt* implications of the text. Indeed, the comment on ʿAlī's sermon moderates the affirmation of his quasi-divinity by interpreting it as an affirmation of the transmission through the ages of the Divine Trust

[228] Like in Q. 3:49 or 5:110, where the infant Jesus gives life to a bird made of clay by simply breathing in it. In early Shiʿism, such powers of healing and resurrection are attributed to the Imams; see e.g. A.J. Newman, *The Formative Period of Twelver Shīʿism. Ḥadīth as Discourse Between Qum and Baghdad* (Richmond, 2000), pp. 81–82; M.A. Amir-Moezzi, *La Religion discrète*, Ch. 6: 'Savoir c'est pouvoir', pp. 151–175 (English trans.: *Spirituality of Shiʿi Islam*, Ch. 6: 'Knowledge is power', pp. 193–229), where the divine knowledge of the Imams appears as the sources of their supernatural powers. The *Kitāb al-Kashf* also reports an account in which ʿAlī has the power to resurrect the dead; *Kashf* I, pp. 37–39, § 80. In Treatise V, Q. 3:49 is interpreted metaphorically, in reference to the spiritual life (i.e. the esoteric knowledge) which the Imam provides for his disciples; see *Kashf* V, p. 98, § 15; p. 100, § 22. It is worth noting that the 'birds' are a symbol for the Summoners in early Ismailism; see *Kashf* VI, p. 171, §30, and related footnote.

[229] *Kashf* I, p. 8, § 17.

— a trust of which ʿAlī is the archetypical representative. Thereby, the editor of the treatise can introduce the crucial idea of the 'continuity of God's Order', stating that: 'whoever obeys the last of [the Messengers and the Imams], it is as if he obeyed the first of them',[230] and that 'whoever obeys the first, his obedience will guide and lead him to the last.'[231] This is evidently in keeping with the idea that no time lacks a depositary of God's Order. There is therefore an unbroken line of transmission of sacred knowledge, from Adam to the current Imam. This option characterises the Ismaili *daʿwa* — both pre-Fatimid and Fatimid — and its campaign in favour of a living Imam. Indeed, the 'continuity' implies the actual, physical, and living presence of an Imam — and his representatives.

The second passage of the treatise dedicated to the concept of *amr* also follows a sermon attributed to ʿAlī. The tone of the latter is this time less 'mystical' (ʿAlī does not take on Christic or divine attributes), and more compatible with the doctrine of 'continuity of the Order'. To a partisan who asks him his judgement on the Islamic community, he replies: 'By Him who splits the seed and blows the breeze, I have found more in the ancient communities than I have in this one!'[232] It seems astonishing, at first glance, that this declaration is glossed as follows: 'It is necessary, according to his words, that he be the first and the last.' The content of the first sermon, where ʿAlī compared himself to Christ, was attenuated by a doctrine of the transmission of the deposit and the continuity of *amr*; here, the moderate content of the subject is, on the contrary, interpreted in a sense corresponding to the literal meaning of the first sermon, since 'the first and the last' are divine and Christic ('I am the alpha and the omega') attributes. This must necessarily be explained by the hypothesis proposed above, namely that ʿAlī is conceived as a spiritual principle and the true content of *amr*, the continuity of this Order resulting from the continuity of participation in this unique principle. In short, the conception involved here is quite close to the conception of Christ as the divine Word in the Gospel of John (except the incarnation). ʿAlī is the Word of God, the primary

---

[230] *Kashf* I, p. 8, § 17.

[231] Ibid., pp. 8–9, § 17.

[232] Ibid., p. 11, § 23.

principle of being and knowledge, therefore both the source of the knowledge of Prophets and Imams, and the depositary par excellence of the knowledge bestowed by God on mankind.

This must also be linked to the doctrines which make each Prophet and each Imam successive appearances of ʿAlī — just as their enemies are successive appearances of Abū Bakr and ʿUmar. They are therefore successive manifestations of a unique principle, according to an interpretation of *tanāsukh*, metempsychosis, close to that which would be adopted by the Twelver Shiʿa. Prophets are neither incarnations of God, nor of a divine principle identified with Muḥammad or ʿAlī, but are the receptacles of a light transmitted from Prophet to Imam since Adam. M.A. Amir-Moezzi proposed translating this sense of *tanāsukh* by 'metemphotosis': rather than an individual, it is a luminous principle that transmigrates from one envelope to another, the light here representing esoteric knowledge, that is, the divine trust. This explains ʿAlī's statement that 'the Legatees are from me, and I am from them'.[233] But due to the *ghulāt* roots of the treatise, this remains ambiguous; initially, this statement probably involved a doctrine of metempsychosis according to which the Legatees are successive manifestations of a metaphysical ʿAlī.

It is therefore as if the doctrine of the continuity of *amr*, which appears as a gloss, is used to replace that of metempsychosis, thus refining and moderating an 'exaggerating' belief, in a way comparable to the treatment of *musūkhiyya*, as will be seen below. From this perspective, the two passages on *amr*[234] appear closely connected to the rejection of divine incarnation in § 13 (which immediately precedes the first sermon of ʿAlī). In an enigmatic *ḥadīth*, Jaʿfar al-Ṣādiq relates a vision he had of 'ten domes (*qubāb*) of light', which are respectively identified with the seven Speaking-Prophets, and with three ranks whose exact nature is not specified: the *kālī*, the Guardian (*raqīb*) and the Gate (*bāb*).

The very presence of the term *kālī*, exclusively found in Nuṣayri texts, demonstrates the ancient *ghulāt* origins of this *ḥadīth*.The term *qubba* (pl. *qubāb*) is also found in Nuṣayri texts where it is roughly

---

[233] Ibid., p. 11, § 24.

[234] *Kashf* I, pp. 8–9, § 17; p. 12, § 25.

synonymous with *kawr* or *dawr*, 'historical cycle'. Y. Friedmann points out that the earliest occurrence of the term seems to be a work by Muḥammad b. Sinān, where it designates 'the period of the Imams beginning with ʿAlī'.[235] Its meaning has, however, been broadened among Nuṣayri authors proper, since it has come to designate the great historical periods of humanity to which the main Speaking-Prophets lend their names.[236] Such is the meaning of the 'domes' in this passage of the *Kashf*, since seven out of ten persons who lend their names to the 'domes' are the Speaking-Prophets.[237] The role of the last three remains obscure, however. In any case, it seems clear that the doctrine of the domes was associated with a doctrine of metempsychosis and incarnation, given the commentary that follows the *ḥadīth*. Otherwise, it would be difficult to explain why the mention of the domes becomes the pretext for a refutation of divine incarnation. This doctrine of the domes can also be compared to what is found in some *ghulāt* sources where the historical cycles (*adwār*) are each inaugurated by an Adam (there are therefore several Adams, who presumably correspond to the Speaking-Prophets).[238] This can be interpreted in the sense of a metempsychosis of Adam, who would appear successively in the different Speaking-Prophets.[239]

[235] Y. Friedman, *The Nuṣayrīs-ʿAlawīs*, pp. 112–113.

[236] Ibid., pp. 112–115; M.M. Bar-Asher and A. Kofsky, *The Nuṣayrī-ʿAlawī Religion*, pp. 28–30.

[237] In this regard, I do not agree with Asatryan's contention that the *qubba* in *ghulāt* texts 'bears no similarity' to its usage in the *Kashf*; see M. Asatryan, 'Early Ismailis and other Muslims', p. 279, n. 23.

[238] See e.g. Jaʿfar b. Manṣūr al-Yaman, *Sarā'ir wa-asrār al-nutaqā'*, p. 31: 'Adam is a nickname (*laqab*) applied to each Speaking-Prophet in his age, and each Imam in his era.' See also ibid., p. 52, the expression 'one Adam after the other', and this statement: 'Each Speaking-Prophet who is the master of a [new] Law (*sharīʿa*) is the Adam of his era.'

[239] See e.g. M. Asatryan, 'An Early Shīʿi Cosmology', esp. pp. 26–35, 65–70; Mufaḍḍal al-Juʿfī, *Kitāb al-Haft wa'l-aẓilla*, Ch. 60–61, pp. 116–118. On the latter two chapters, see M. Asatryan, *Controversies in Formative Shiʿi Islam*, pp. 37–38. See also the belief in the seven Adams attributed to ʿAbd Allāh b. Ḥarb, a leader of the Kaysāniyya, by al-Nāshi' in his *Kitāb Uṣūl al-niḥal*, § 58, in J. Van Ess, *Frühe muʿtazilitische Häresiographie: Zwei Werke des Nāšiʾ al-Akbar (gest. 293 H.)* (Beirut, 1971), Arabic text, p. 39.

This type of doctrine is also found in Nuṣayri thought. We can thus cite, as an example, a passage from al-Ṭabarānī's *Kitāb al-Maʿārif*, where this idea is developed about ʿAlī. In a *ḥadīth* reported after Salmān al-Fārisī, someone asks ʿAlī: 'Were you present at the time of Noah?', to which he answers:

> 'And where was I not? I took Adam as a veil in his cycle (*fī kawri-hi wa dawri-hi*), and bore the name of Abel; I took Noah as a veil in his cycle, and bore the name of Seth [sic]; I took Jacob as a veil in his cycle, and bore the name of Joseph; I took Moses as a veil in his cycle, and bore the name of Joshua; I took Jesus as a veil in his cycle, and bore the name of Simon; I took Muḥammad as a veil in his cycle, and bore the name of ʿAlī. I am the origin of cycles (*mukawwir al-akwār wa-mudawwir al-adwār*) (. . .) I am eternally new (*jadīd abadan*), I do not fade away (*lam afni*).'[240]

Many other examples could be provided of such a belief in both the divinity of ʿAlī and his cyclical appearances in different persons. It is thus understandable why the gloss of Treatise I eagerly refutes the doctrines of the *ghulāt* and the Christians just after the *ḥadīth* of the domes.[241] Fatimid literature contains several similar refutations,[242]

240 Al-Ṭabarānī, *Kitāb al-Maʿārif*, p. 166. See also M.M. Bar-Asher and A. Kofsky, *The ʿAlawī Religion: An Anthology*, pp. 90–91. A comparable conception is expressed in several Ismaili sources; see e.g. the Nizārī Ismaili work by Maḥmūd-i Kātib, *Haft Bād*, in S.J. Badakhshani, *Spiritual Resurrection in Shiʿi Islam: An Early Ismaili Treatise on the Doctrine of Qiyāmat* (London and New York, 2017), Ch. 2, pp. 51–59, §§ 8–26.

241 *Kashf* I, pp. 7–8, § 13.

242 See e.g. Jaʿfar b. Manṣūr al-Yaman, *Sarāʾir wa Asrār al-nutaqāʾ*, p. 241, where the *ghulāt* are similarly likened to the Christians. See also al-Muʾayyad, *Al-Majālis al-Muʾayyadiyya*, ed. M. Ghālib (Beirut, 1974), vol. 1, pp. 172–173: a commentary of a passage of the *khuṭbat al-bayān*, where ʿAlī claims divine attributes, reads as follows: 'The *ghulāt* imitate the Christians and are similar to them. For the Christians, God (. . .), out of benevolence and mercy towards His servants, and reckoning that they were not able to take into consideration the speech on the salvation of their souls if it did not come from a human form like theirs, took on a body and appeared to them wearing the robe of humanity (*nāsūt*), to free them (. . .) The *ghulāt* say just as much about the Prince of the Believers.' The author goes on to explain that if God is indeed as omnipotent as the *ghulāt* would have Him, then it would better suit His nature to appear in whatever form He wants, instead of departing from His noble form to take on the vile form of humanity. Indeed, 'if one of us was omnipotent and wanted to

which leads to the conclusion that we are dealing here with a Fatimid gloss.

Other distinctly Ismaili passages include the one dealing with the 'Completer Imams'.[243] The term appears again in Treatise V and more briefly in Treatise VI. The passage from Treatise I which deals with them is a commentary of Q. 7:142: *'We appointed for Moses thirty nights, and We completed them with ten; thus was completed the time appointed by his Lord of forty nights.'* The thirty nights are interpreted as the five Speaking-prophets from Adam to Jesus (Adam, Noah, Abraham, Moses and Jesus; Muḥammad is not counted among them), and the six 'Completer Imams' who follow each of them. The last ten nights refer to the Prophet Muḥammad, to Muḥammad 'the Speaking-Prophet of Speaking-Prophets', and the Completer Imams who mark the transition from one to the other. We also note that the Speaking-Prophet is called the 'diurnal Proof' (*ḥujjat al-nahār*), while the completer Imam is called the 'nocturnal Proof', due to their respective roles: the Speaking-Prophets bring an exoteric revelation, while the Imams deliver its esoteric exegesis. These two roles correspond to successive historical cycles of manifestation and concealment, although these terms do not appear.

It is interesting to note, moreover, that the exegesis according to which the fast of Ramadan is a symbol of *taqiyya* takes place within a system of prophetic cycles with political implications related to the expectation of the Mahdī's return.[244] Indeed, the equivalence between

---

do good to a riding beast or a donkey, it would be foul for him to take on the form of a beast in order to be useful to it. And if this is foul for us (. . .) it is even more for the Creator'. It is therefore foul to say, as the *ghulāt* do, that a man who 'is born and grew, who eats and drinks, who has parents, a partner and children', is a god. On al-Mu'ayyad's refutation of the *ghulāt* in this section of the Majālis, see E. Alexandrin, 'Al-Mu'ayyad's Concept of the Qā'im: a Commentary on the *Khutbat al-Bayān*', *Ishraq. Islamic Philosophy Yearbook*, 4 (2013), pp. 294–303.

[243] *Kashf* I, pp. 15–16, §§ 32–35.

[244] The *ta'wīl* which equates fasting and the silence that surrounds the esoteric knowledge, and breaking fast with the exoteric revelation and the manifestation of the spiritual authority, is quite classical in early Ismailism; see D. De Smet, 'La *taqiyya* et le jeûne du Ramadan'; idem, 'Jeûner par le silence. L'interprétation ésotérique du ramadan selon l'auteur nuṣayri Maymūn b. Qāsim al-Ṭabarānī (m. 426/1034)', in S.H. de Franceschi et al, eds, *Affamés volontaires. Les monothéismes et le jeûne* (Limoges, 2020), pp. 315–334.

fasting and *taqiyya* is also found in al-Ṭabarānī's works,[245] which suggests that he himself draws from an older tradition that he shares with the *Kitāb al-Kashf*. Al-Ṭabarānī thus identifies each of the days and nights of Ramadan with historical individuals (*ashkhāṣ*) from the beginnings of Islam.[246] This falls within a tendency of certain *ghulāt* groups to interpret the recommendations and prohibitions of the Qur'an as referring to people, which led either to an antinomian doctrine such as the one upheld by the Khaṭṭābiyya, or simply to an esoteric interpretation of religious prescriptions which did not exclude their actual, exoteric, fulfilment.

Ismailism, as it appears in the *Kashf*, obviously drew from these sources and adapted them to its needs. As in al-Ṭabarānī's work, the days are identified with persons, but this general principle is used in support of a fully Ismaili conception of the prophetic cycles, and oriented towards the messianic expectation. This exegesis therefore states not only the continuity of *amr*, but also its culmination in the person of the Mahdī, 'the Speaking-Prophet of Speaking-Prophets', who symbolises the breaking of the fast, that is, the manifestation of 'the Order' (*amr*).[247] This shows that there is indeed a consistency throughout the latest passages of the treatise, since they all affirm a prophetic Order going from Adam to the Mahdī, or, in other words, an Order which has the Mahdī as the culmination of the transmission of the sacred trust since Adam.

Before concluding this matter of the continuity of the Order, a final point must be considered which is clearly related to it: the allusions to

---

[245] Al-Ṭabarānī, *Majmūʿ al-aʿyād*, pp. 16–17; idem, *Kitāb al-maʿārif*, pp. 65, 67–68. On *taqiyya* in Nuṣayrism, see Y. Friedman, *The Nuṣayrīs-ʿAlawīs*, pp. 143–144; M.M. Bar-Asher and A. Kofsky, in al-Ṭabarānī, *Kitāb al-maʿārif*, pp. 19–22; and the recent article by D. De Smet, 'Jeûner par le silence'.

[246] Al-Ṭabarānī, *Kitāb al-maʿārif*, pp. 67–69.

[247] On the connection between fasting as a symbol of *taqiyya* and prophetic cycles, see the report, based on texts by al-Sijistānī and al-Qāḍī al-Nuʿmān, by D. De Smet, 'La *taqiyya* et le jeûne du Ramadan', pp. 363–375, esp. p. 370: 'Le jour de la rupture du jeûne symbolise l'avènement du Mahdī et l'abrogation partielle de la *taqiyya*.'

'communities which preceded'. From the beginning of the treatise, we find paradoxical statements in this regard:

- in the *ḥadīth* on *kitmān*, where the Imams recommend silence regarding their teaching, one reads: 'There have been people from past communities who held to their trust and concealed our secret and did what they were ordered, and so God made them Messengers to His trustworthy ones, and Gates for His Friends.'[248]
- a few lines further on, another *ḥadīth*, attributed this time to the 'Greatest Master', that is, the Prophet Muḥammad,[249] states: 'The communities who have perished suffered this fate, because they did not consider this, did not reflect and divulged the secret.'[250]
- in the previously mentioned *ḥadīth*, where a Shiʿi asks ʿAlī what he thinks of the Islamic community, he replies: 'I found more in the ancient communities than I have in this one!'[251]
- in the commentary to this *ḥadīth*, the author writes that ʿAlī is the one whom 'the ancient communities had denied when the Legatees established [God's Order] after their prophets. This is an allusion to what the people of Moses did to Aaron, and what the people of Jesus did to Simon: they all denied God's Order that [the Legatees] had established, which is one'.[252]

In the Qur'an, 'former communities' are often presented as having betrayed or rejected their prophets. In a Shiʿi context, this is generally seen as an illustration of the steadfast opposition met by the prophets, as seen in the enumerations of enemies of Treatise I[253] or in the second development on *amr*.[254] How then should we understand the fact that the 'ancient communities' are apparently better than the Islamic community? Although this is not explicated here, all the previous communities were tested and divided, like the Islamic community

---

248 *Kashf* I, p. 3, § 3.

249 On this denomination of the Prophet Muḥammad, see above, p. 76, n. 9.

250 *Kashf* I, pp. 3–4, § 5.

251 *Kashf* I, p. 11, § 23.

252 *Kashf* I, p. 12, § 25.

253 *Kashf* I, pp. 10–11, §§ 21–22.

254 *Kashf* I, p. 12, § 25.

which, according to the Shiʿa, underwent a split between supporters and opponents of ʿAlī, that is, between those who followed the Prophet's exoteric revelation to its necessary consequence — the recognition of the esoteric key held by ʿAlī — and those who stuck with the exoteric, therefore, ultimately, to a religion cut off from the essential. This is how 'ancient communities' can be either faithful or unfaithful, depending on the part of these communities that is being considered. On the one hand, there is an ancient community which is that of the transmission of the trust; this is how Q. 22:78, which mentions 'the community of your father, Abraham', is understood.[255] But on the other hand, each prophet was confronted with the hostility of the people to whom he had the mission to preach.

As an illustration of this reference to past communities, a corpus of *ḥadīth*s found in both Sunni and Shiʿi collections, is frequently used in Shiʿi and Ismaili literature to support the notion that the Muslim community is imitating previous communities, for better and for worse.[256] One of these ('. . . in the exactly same manner', lit.: 'following them to the footstep', *ḥadhwa al-naʿl biʾl-naʿl*) is quoted in Treatise V of the *Kashf*, where it is explicitly connected with the idea that everything the Qurʾan says about Moses and Aaron applies to Muḥammad and ʿAlī.[257] The expression *ḥadhwa al-naʿl biʾl-naʿl* seems to have become a topos of Fatimid Ismaili literature when dealing with the opposition every prophet and his legatee are met with. Indeed, it also appears in other works attributed to Jaʿfar b. Manṣūr al-Yaman, to compare ʿAlī's fate with that of Joshua,[258] or ʿAlī's with that of Abel,[259] or even to compare the 'exaggerations' of Ḥusayn's status by the *ghulāt*

---

[255] *Kashf* I p. 12, § 25; pp. 17–18, § 38.

[256] See the *ḥadīth*s quoted by P. Walker, 'Ismaili Polemics against Opponents in the Early Fatimid Period', in O. Mir-Kasimov, ed, *Intellectual Interactions in the Islamic World. The Ismaili Thread* (London, 2020), pp. 29–30.

[257] *Kashf* V, p. 127, § 63.

[258] Jaʿfar b. Manṣūr al-Yaman, *Taʾwīl al-zakāt*, p. 138: 'What is meant by all the stories narrated by God about Moses, Pharaoh and the Israelites, is our prophet Muḥammad, his Pharaoh, his Legatee and his enemies; they put their footsteps in theirs.'

[259] Jaʿfar b. Manṣūr al-Yaman, *Sarāʾir wa-asrār al-nuṭaqāʾ*, p. 52.

with those of Jesus's status by the Christians.[260] It also appears in al-Qāḍī al-Nuʿmān's *Asās al-taʾwīl*, where an analogy is made between Noah's fate among his people and Muḥammad's,[261] and, more importantly, in the very first page of al-Nuʿmān's masterpiece, the *Daʿāʾim al-islām* — which is an indication of the place this *ḥadīth* had taken on in Fatimid rhetoric. Al-Muʾayyad fī'l-dīn al-Shīrāzī also quotes it several times.[262] Furthermore, this *ḥadīth* is repeated over and over in the seemingly 'Fatimid Propaganda Work' recently discovered by M. Pregill,[263] and then edited and translated by W. Madelung and P. Walker.[264] While this work does not contain any specifically Ismaili vocabulary, the above-mentioned scholars have considered as an Ismaili feature its emphasis on the analogy between the events surrounding the revelation brought by Muḥammad and his succession, on the one hand, and events met with previous prophets and their respective Legatees, on the other hand. This constant comparison between previous revelations and the Islamic revelation draws from the Qur'an itself, of course, and was systematized in Shiʿi literature. In this regard, al-Sijistānī states that 'knowing the reports

[260] Ibid., p. 241.

[261] Al-Qāḍī al-Nuʿmān, *Asās al-taʾwīl*, ed. ʿĀ. Tāmir (Beirut, 1960) p. 91. Al-Qāḍī al-Nuʿmān refers there to his quotation of the *ḥadīth* in his *Daʿāʾim al-islām*.

[262] See e.g. al-Muʾayyad fī'l-dīn, *Al-Majālis al-muʾayyadiyya*, ed. M. Ghālib, vol. 1, pp. 102, 127, 204.

[263] M. Pregill, 'Measure for measure: Prophetic History Qur'anic Exegesis and Anti-Sunnī Polemic in a Fatimid Propaganda Work (BL Or. 8419)', *JQS*, 16/1 (2014), pp. 20–57.

[264] W. Madelung and P. Walker, *Affirming the Imamate*, pp. 15–77 (Arabic: pp. 1–71). I do not share the editors' opinion regarding the attribution of this text to Abū ʿAbd Allāh al-Shīʿī — in fact, the evidence to support this claim is weak, at best. Hassan Ansari has criticised this attribution in a blog post, and proposed to identify this untitled and anonymous text with the *K. Ḥadhwa al-naʿl bi'l-naʿl* by al-Faḍl Ibn Shādhān al-Nīshābūrī, thus inscribing the work in the Imamī Shiʿi tradition, rather than the Ismaili tradition; see https://ansari.kateban.com/post/4835 (consulted on 4/10/2021). Whatever the origin of the work may be, it is very plausible that the Fatimids had taken special interest in it, given the importance of the *ḥadīth ḥadhwa al-naʿl bi'l-naʿl* in their literature, as I have just shown. The content, although not specifically Ismaili, does not contradict Ismaili beliefs.

regarding [people from the] past would be of no benefit to the creatures if they did not have analogues among the contemporaries'.[265] This general principle held special significance in the Fatimid context, since it was in fact the premise of another analogy, the one between Muḥammad and ʿAlī, on the one hand, and the Fatimid Imams, on the other hand. As a result, all mentions of Muḥammad and ʿAlī — especially when their enemies are discussed — in the *Kitāb al-Kashf* must be understood as references to the Fatimids themselves.

Indeed, the essential feature of this eternal repetition of a similar dramaturgy is the presence of what might be referred to as a 'counter-Order', or 'counter-initiation'; to the continuity of the divine Order is opposed a continuity of the opposition it meets. The authentic Imams designated by God are opposed, during the very lifetime of each Speaking-Prophet and after his death, by 'Imams of misguidance'.[266] The historical corollary of the transmission of the Divine Trust since Adam is the permanent adversity of the enemies of the truth, typified, according to the Shiʿa, by the figures of Abū Bakr and ʿUmar.

4. The continuity of antagonism: the enemies of the Imam

Shiʿism does not only consist of adhering to the *walāya* of ʿAlī, but also consists of 'dissociating' from his enemies or 'disavowing' them. This is the doctrine of *barāʾa*, 'dissociating oneself from someone', in this case the enemies of the Imams. *Walāya* and *barāʾa* are the two sides of the allegiance owed by the Shiʿa to their Imams. The term *barīʾ* appeared at the beginning of the treatise, in the sentence: 'If (. . .) you divulge [what follows], God, His Messenger and the latter's Legatee will be quit (*barīʾ*) of you.'[267] The doctrine of *barāʾa* may seem tautological, since it goes without saying that if one becomes the 'friend' of ʿAlī, one must necessarily become the enemy of his enemies. But that the corollary of the *walāya*, or its negative counterpart, has to be *barāʾa* can be understood as a necessary consequence of the dualistic Shiʿi idea that creation is the theatre of a war between the 'Armies of

265 Al-Sijistānī, *Kitāb al-Iftikhār*, p. 227.

266 *Kashf* I, p. 21, § 45.

267 *Kashf* I, p. 3, § 2.

Intelligence' and the 'Armies of Ignorance'.[268] *Barā'a* implies a dualistic conception in which it is not enough to join the ranks of Good — it is also necessary to reject Evil.

In the *Kitāb al-Kashf*, however, we find no trace of such a dualistic struggle on a cosmic plane. On the other hand, it clearly takes place on a historical level, in accordance with a Shiʿi reading of the succession of the Prophet Muḥammad. Several passages of the *Kitāb al-Kashf* resort to the exegetical technique that M.A. Amir-Moezzi has labelled a 'personalized Qur'anic commentary'. Verses that bear favourable connotations generally refer to ʿAlī b. Abī Ṭālib or his family, while unfavourable appreciations and condemnations refer to his historical adversaries. From this perspective, the Qur'an becomes a sort of encrypted historical account.

Treatise I offers several illustrations of such exegeses: the interlocutors of the Prophet who, in Q. 2:13, refuse to believe are thus identified with 'the First of the iniquitous, the Second and those who believe in them and follow them',[269] that is, Abū Bakr, 'Umar and their supporters. But while retaining the principle that the Qur'anic verses refer to persons, the author of the *Kashf* refines the process and broadens its scope in several respects. For example, each of the elements listed at the beginning of sūra 52 is identified with a different rank of the *daʿwa*, while other Shiʿi texts identify them all with ʿAlī.[270] This process is more fully found in Treatises III, V and VI; it is no longer just a question, as in al-Ḥibarī's *Tafsīr*, of identifying elements of the Qur'an with historical figures from the beginnings of Islam.

In the rather confused passage of §§ 21–22, different people mentioned in the Qur'an are identified with several characters whom the Shiʿa consider as enemies of ʿAlī b. Abī Ṭālib — an equivalence on which Treatise III builds. As with the 'ancient communities' discussed above, the reason for this is that these people are presented in the Qur'an as having been deaf to the warnings and revelations of the prophets who had been sent to them. The passage in question seems

---

[268] For traditions staging this cosmogony, see M.A. Amir-Moezzi, *Guide divin*, pp. 19–20 (English trans.: *Divine Guide*, pp. 7–8); idem, *La Religion discrète*, pp. 304–305 (English trans.: *Spirituality of Shiʿi Islam*, pp. 413–414).

[269] *Kashf* I, p. 6, § 9.

[270] *Kashf* I, p. 10, § 20.

corrupted, because 'the Pharaoh of Moses' and his companions are first identified with Muʿāwiya and the Umayyads, but then Pharaoh, Hāmān and Korah are respectively identified with Abū Bakr, ʿUmar and ʿUthmān. Two distinct exegeses seem to have been juxtaposed to one another, the second beginning with the words 'the second cycle' (*al-kawr al-thānī*).[271] The first part simply establishes equivalences between such ancient people mentioned in the Qur'an and such characters from the beginnings of Islam.

The second part, however, by introducing the concept of *kawr*, as well as the sentence: 'So it is in each century', seems to give the subject a whole new dimension. It is no longer a question of decoding the Qur'an and the history of Muḥammad's succession, but of proposing a doctrine of the cyclical reappearance of opponents to prophets. The history of humanity is that of the struggle between allies and enemies of God: it is the Shiʿi doctrine of *ḍiddiyya*, the 'theory of opponents'.[272] Does this mean that Abū Bakr, ʿUmar and ʿUthmān are the archetypes of the enemies of Abraham, Noah, Moses and Jesus? If ʿAlī is the archetypical figure manifested in prophets and Imams since the beginning of humanity, by metempsychosis or by participation, or if, at least, he is the archetype of Legatees, we can consider, in coherence with Shiʿi dualism, that the historical enemies of ʿAlī are also elevated to the rank of archetypes. The *Kashf* remains ambiguous on this point. On the other hand, another work attributed to Jaʿfar b. Manṣūr al-Yaman, the *Ta'wīl al-Zakāt*, is much more explicit:

> God named them the Jibt and the Ṭāghūt in His Book. The First of iniquity is the Jibt and the Second is the Ṭāghūt, and he is Satan. They are present in the [historical] cycle of each Speaking-Prophet, in the era of each Foundation (*asās*), in the age of each Imam. No era and no age is free from these two; they take on different repulsive bodies and forms, just as the Imams take on different excellent and subtle bodies.[273]

---

[271] *Kashf* I, p. 11, § 22.

[272] See M.A. Amir-Moezzi, *La Religion discrète*, p. 301, n. 24 (English trans.: *Spirituality of Shiʿi Islam*, pp. 409–410, n. 24).

[273] Jaʿfar b. Manṣūr al-Yaman, *Ta'wīl al-zakāt*, p. 206. This passage was also quoted from a manuscript of the *Ta'wīl al-zakāt* by I. Goldziher, 'Spottnamen der ersten Chalifen', p. 323, n. 4.

The issue of attribution arises as much for the *Ta'wīl al-Zakāt* as it does for the *Kashf*. Furthermore, the doctrine expressed here does not appear anywhere in the *Kitāb al-Kashf* — nor does the term *asās*, which designates the Legatee (*waṣī*) of the Speaking-Prophet in Ismaili doctrine. Yet it remains instructive because it provides the theoretical background for many passages of the *Kashf*. It is not, however, to say that the *Kashf* refrains from developing this thesis by *taqiyya*. Its absence seems rather due to a desire to articulate a 'moderate' doctrine, away from the old transmigrationist theories of the *ghulāt*. In Fatimid Ismailism, the idea of a cyclical succession of Speaking-Prophets in the course of history would thus be kept on, but the reappearance under different 'bodies', 'forms', 'envelopes' or bodily 'simulacra' of a unique principle would be downplayed. If there is a single principle, it is that of *amr*, that of the Divine Trust, transmitted through initiation, not through a form of metempsychosis. The *Kitāb al-Kashf* thus seems to want to preserve the elements of the doctrine of reincarnation (*tanāsukh*) which imply a cyclical history of revelation, without preserving this doctrine itself — the important aspect in this doctrine being that of continuity, which the Fatimid Imams claim to embody. Likewise, the cyclical historicity of enmity towards the Prophets and Imams, as confusedly expressed in the abovementioned passage which mentions *kawr*, had to make sense in the system evoked by the extract from *Ta'wīl al-Zakāt*, according to which it is always the same thing which manifests itself in the diversity of bodies in which the Opponents appear. It is true that the nuance between these two conceptions is quite subtle, and that it is all the more difficult to distinguish them since, as D. De Smet noted, several Ismaili authors, while openly rejecting *tanāsukh*, nevertheless propose a 'soteriology which presupposes, in one way or another, the transmigration of souls'.[274]

The fact remains that, while the *Kitāb al-Kashf* clearly takes up elements drawn from doctrines where *tanāsukh* was admitted — as

[274] D. De Smet, 'Eléments chrétiens dans l'ismaélisme ṭayyibīte', p. 48. On this matter, see also idem, 'Les racines docétistes de l'imâmologie shi'ite'; idem, 'La transmigration des âmes. Une notion problématique dans l'ismaélisme d'époque fatimide', in O. Mir-Kasimov, ed, *Unity in Diversity. Mysticism, Messianism and the Construction of Religious Authority in Islam* (Leiden and Boston, 2014), pp. 77–110.

confirmed by the use of the term *musūkhiyya*, which is discussed next — it seems to stick to a historical approach, founding the unity of the Prophets and Imams, not on metempsychosis, but on *amr*. The second paragraph on *amr* in Treatise I develops the corollary of the idea expressed in the first paragraph on *amr*: if 'whoever obeys the last of them, it is as if he obeyed the first of them',[275] then 'every enemy to a prophet is also an enemy to the prophets before and after him'.[276] Basically, the treatise sticks here to Qur'anic data, which it only systematises: not only do the prophets bring a message which is fundamentally the same, but according to verse 25:31,[277] each prophet is confronted with *'an enemy among the sinners'*. All it took then was to adapt these ideas to the Shiʿi historiography of the early days of Islam, and to identify the earlier enemies of the prophets. Treatise III gives the key to such identifications: 'They are named using the names of the past communities, because they acted and deviated as they did, and transgressed as they did.'[278] Their deviation consisted of their refusal to recognise ʿAlī's Imamate after the death of the Prophet: just as 'the people of Moses were thus tested through Aaron, but rebelled against him and obeyed the Sāmirī, and the people of Jesus were tested with Simon, but rebelled against him and obeyed Pilate', 'this community was tested with the Prince of the Believers, but they rebelled against him and obeyed Abū Bakr and 'Umar'.[279]

Remarkably, the famous *ḥadīth manzilat Hārūn*: "Alī is in relation to me as Aaron was to Moses', [280] is interpreted in the perspective of the opposition met by the Imam. ʿAlī is not only analogous to Aaron because he held the esoteric knowledge of the exoteric revelation brought by Muḥammad, as is commonly related in Shiʿi texts, but also because he was betrayed just like Aaron was by the Israelites — according to the Qur'anic narrative of the Golden Calf episode. Indeed, the author quotes the *ḥadīth* just after mentioning 'what the people of

[275] *Kashf* I p. 8, § 17.

[276] *Kashf* I p. 12, § 25.

[277] Quoted in *Kashf* I p. 12, § 25.

[278] *Kashf* III, p. 59, § 15.

[279] *Kashf* I, p. 31, § 65.

[280] Cited in *Kashf* I, p. 12, § 25; VI, p. 159, § 6; p. 161, § 9. See commentary of *Kashf* VI, pp. 458–463.

Moses did to Aaron, and the people of Jesus to Simon'.[281] ʿAlī's role vis-à-vis Muḥammad is thus defined both positively (he is the master of *ta'wīl*, which is the indispensable complement of the *tanzīl*) and negatively (he is the locus where true believers are separated from hypocrites and enemies). The 'dual vision' of Shiʿism which distinguishes the esoteric and the exoteric aspects of religion, is coupled with the 'dualistic vision' based on the struggle between good and evil.[282] As noted above, the *walāya* must be completed by the *barā'a*, the dissociation from the Imam's enemies. Thus, the criterion of betrayal of the revelation of Muḥammad is the attitude towards ʿAlī. The fact that he is 'taken as a thing to be shunned'[283] is an indication of his divine election. In the historical struggle between good and evil, the very fact that he arouses opposition from the forces of evil is a sufficient indication of his status as the representative of the divine 'cause'. As a matter of fact, Ibn al-Haytham, a Shiʿi converted to Ismailism and a contemporary of the advent of the Fatimids in North Africa, thus interprets the *ḥadīth manzilat Hārūn*: 'He meant by this that his community would break its covenant with him just as the community of Moses broke with Hārūn.'[284]

This *ḥadīth* was thus used in Shiʿi literature to establish a systematic analogy between Moses and Muḥammad, Aaron and ʿAlī. The enemies of Moses and Aaron became the obvious models of the enemies of ʿAlī. The worship of the idol of the Golden Calf was assimilated to following the first caliphs in place of ʿAlī; indeed, in some sources, Abū Bakr and ʿUmar are named 'the two idols (*ṣanamān*) of Quraysh' or identified with Pharaoh and Hāmān.[285] In the *Kitāb al-Kashf*, Abū Bakr, ʿUmar and ʿUthmān are respectively identified with Pharaoh, Hāmān and Qārūn.[286] In other sources, they are presented respectively as 'the Calf of this community' (*ʿijl hādhihi al-umma*), the 'Pharaoh of this

---

[281] *Kashf* I, p. 12, § 25.

[282] On the 'dual' (*ẓāhir/bāṭin*) and 'dualistic' (good/evil) conceptions at the heart of Shiʿism, see M.A. Amir-Moezzi and C. Jambet, *Qu'est-ce que le shīʿisme?*, pp. 31–40.

[283] *Kashf* I, p. 30, § 63.

[284] W. Madelung and P.E. Walker, *The Advent of the Fatimids* (London, 2000), p. 72 (Arabic: p. 12). See also Ibrāhīm b. al-Ḥusayn al-Ḥāmidī, *Kanz al-walad*, p. 224.

[285] E. Kohlberg, 'Some Imamī Shīʿī views on the *Ṣaḥāba*', p. 164.

[286] *Kashf* I, p. 11, § 22; V, p. 134, § 72.

community' and the 'Sāmirī of this community'; in some cases, the Calf and the Sāmirī are respectively identified with Abū Bakr and 'Umar[287] — the Sāmirī being the one responsible for the cult of the Golden Calf in the Qur'anic narrative. The latter identification is indeed to be found in another work attributed to Jaʿfar b. Manṣūr al-Yaman, the *Shawāhid wa'l-bayān*:

> These two iniquitous [men] from the community of Muḥammad — may God bless him and his family — are like the Calf and the Sāmirī among the people of Moses — peace be upon him — because, the Sāmirī summoned the people of Moses to the Calf and diverted them from Aaron, the successor (*khalīfa*) of Moses, [just as] the Sāmirī of this community summoned the community of Muḥammad to follow the First iniquitous, who is the Calf of this community, and diverted them from ʿAlī, the successor of Muḥammad.[288]

The numerous references in the *Kashf* to the figure of Pharaoh, especially in Treatise V, are part of this Shiʿi tradition which seeks the model of its own history in the story of Moses.[289] Other passages are devoted to Moses and Aaron, particularly in Treatise VI, which develops this theme through several pages.

It is unlikely that the Shiʿi reference to Moses and Aaron as precursors of the fate of Muḥammad and ʿAlī was directly connected to some kind of belief in the transmigration of the souls (specifically those of ʿAlī and his enemies). Yet, the connection is quite easy to make, and it is possible that this analogy provided the model for systematic analogies with all past Speaking-Prophets. Be that as it may, the *Kashf* is clearly dependent on both traditions, which are here brought together but also attenuated and geared towards new objectives. Indeed, in Fatimid context, parallels drawn between ancient

[287] See M.M. Bar-Asher, *Scripture and Exegesis*, pp. 115–117 and p. 115, n. 109.

[288] Jaʿfar b. Manṣūr al-Yaman, *Al-Shawāhid wa'l-bayān*, IIS MS. 734, ff. 138–139.

[289] In this regard, E. Kohlberg, 'The Term "Rāfiḍa" in Imamī Shīʿī Usage', *JAOS*, 99/4 (1979), pp. 677–679, explains how this term which was initially a pejorative one, came to be accepted by the Shiʿa, through a reference to the attitude of Pharaoh's magicians who 'refused' (*rafaḍa*) his authority and acknowledged Moses instead.

and Islamic histories serve another parallel, the one between the early Islamic and the Fatimid histories. Thus, whatever the Qur'an says about Aaron applies to 'Alī, and whatever applies to 'Alī applies to whomsoever claims to be his heir, both genealogically and spiritually, that is, the Fatimid Imam.

5. *Musūkhiyya*: from literal to metaphoric metamorphosis

The theme of metamorphosis (*maskh*) originates in the Qur'an, where several verses refer to the transformation of humans into swine or monkeys, as divine punishment.[290] However, the verb *masakha* itself appears only once, and the context does not explicitly point to metamorphosis, but rather to something like petrification: '*And had We willed, we would transform them (masakhnāhum) in their place; they could neither leave nor return*' (Q. 36:67). The possibility of such transformations being asserted by the Qur'an, the exegetes were forced to study the question and the status of people transformed into animals. It is not necessary to enter here into the details of the theological discussions that this question has entailed.[291] Since they could hardly contradict the Qur'an, 'orthodox' theologians generally considered that metamorphosis was possible, but did not dwell on this possibility, nor did they make it a central point of their theology: according to D. De Smet, 'the notion of metamorphosis plays only a marginal role in Sunni Islam. On the other hand, it is at the very heart of the so-called "extremist" Shi'ism (*ghuluww*)'.[292]

Metamorphosis into lower forms such as animals indeed held a particular doctrinal importance among the *ghulāt*, but is also found in Twelver Shi'i literature, because, as M.A. Amir-Moezzi's research has

---

[290] See Q. 2:65, 5:60, 7:166.

[291] For an overview of these discussions, see C. Pellat, 'Maskh', *EI2*; D. De Smet, 'Métamorphose', in M.A. Amir-Moezzi, ed, *Dictionnaire du Coran* (Paris, 2007), pp. 552–554. See also U. Rubin, 'Apes, Pigs and the Islamic Identity', *Israel Oriental Studies*, 17 (1997), pp. 98–105; P. Walker, 'The doctrine of metempsychosis in Islam', in W.B. Hallaq and D.P. Little, eds, *Islamic Studies presented to Charles J. Adams* (Leiden, 1991), pp. 219–238. See also the monograph dedicated to this doctrine in 'heterodox' milieus: R. Freitag, *Seelenwanderung in der islamischen Häresie* (Berlin, 1985).

[292] D. De Smet, 'Métamorphose', p. 553. The translation is mine.

shown, the Twelver corpus of *ḥadīths* echoes many doctrines attributed to the *ghulāt*, although attenuated and reduced to remnants. Amir-Moezzi thus notes that 'in the early corpus of Twelver traditions', namely in the works of al-Ṣaffār al-Qummī, al-Kulaynī, Ibn Bābawayh and al-Nuʿmānī, 'there are numerous attestations of *maskh*, namely a degrading reincarnation in animal form', and that the transformed beings are generally 'the historical adversaries of the Shiʿis'.[293] Thus, in Shiʿi context, the Quʾrānic datum of punishment by the transformation into monkeys or swine is used against the adversaries of the Imams, who are the enemies of God par excellence.[294]

Amir-Moezzi points to a tradition reported by al-Ṣaffār al-Qummī in which the Imam Jaʿfar al-Ṣādiq, having touched the eyes of his disciple Abū Baṣīr, 'enables him to see the true nature of the great majority (i.e. the non-Shiʿis) among the pilgrims to Mecca: they are monkeys (*qirada*) and swine (*khanāzīr*)'.[295] A very similar account is found in chapter 22 of the *Kitāb al-Haft wa'l-aẓilla*: Imam al-Ṣādiq promises one of his disciples to show him the progeny of Iblīs: 'You do not recognize it, but we recognize it.' One day, they both pass by a cemetery where 'people came and went'. The disciple tells the Imam: 'You promised to show me the *musūkhiyya*.' The Imam then passes his hand over the eyes of the disciple (*masaḥa bi-yadihi ʿalā ʿaynayya*): 'I

---

[293] M.A. Amir-Moezzi, *Spirituality of Shiʿi Islam*, pp. 296–297. Note the lexical proximity between *maskh* and *naskh*, the latter being the positive couterpart of the former and referring to the doctrine of the metempsychosis of the Imams — or, according to Amir-Moezzi's proposition, 'metemphotosis', that is, the transmigration of the light of the Imams. The latter doctrine would correspond to a 'moderate' Shiʿism, and therefore to an attenuated form of the doctrine of *naskh* or *tanāsukh*; see e.g. M.A. Amir-Moezzi, *Guide divin*, p. 109 (English trans.: *Divine Guide*, p. 42); idem, *La Religion discrète*, pp. 131, 166 (English trans.: *Spirituality of Shiʿi Islam*, pp. 165, 216–217).

[294] See e.g. *Tafsīr al-ʿAskarī*, where animal metamorphosis is a punishment for the refusal to acknowledge the Imams; cited in M.M. Bar-Asher, 'The Qurʾanic Commentary Ascribed to Imam Ḥasan al-ʿAskarī', *JSAI*, 24 (2000), p. 369. In the *Tafsīr al-ʿAyyāshī*, a fish who was formerly a man tells ʿAlī he has taken on this form because he did not acknowledge ʿAlī's *walāya*. Others are transformed into lizards or mice; cited in M.M. Bar-Asher, *Scripture and Exegesis*, pp. 200–201.

[295] M.A. Amir-Moezzi, *Spirituality of Shiʿi Islam*, p. 297. See also idem, *Guide divin*, p. 235 (English trans.: *Divine Guide*, p. 94).

looked at the people I had seen coming and going and behold, most of them were dogs, monkeys, swine, foxes, etc. So I asked: "Master, who are these?" He replied: "They are the descendants of Iblīs, they mingle with people and they are in the *musūkhiyya*.'" Further in the text, beings are divided into three categories: humans, jinns and demons (*shayāṭīn*). Humans are defined as 'those who know God, testify to His unicity and know His Friends (*awliyā'*) and His Gates (*abwāb*)', while demons are 'those who are metamorphosed (*masakhū*) in the bodies of *musūkhiyya*'.[296]

While this definition of humanity and the tripartition of beings corresponds to conceptions found in Twelver Shiʿi texts,[297] the latter do not seem systematically to consider the adversaries of the Imams as animals. And, unlike the *Kitāb al-Haft wa'l-aẓilla* which proposes an elaborate doctrine of what it calls *musūkhiyya* (rather than *maskh*),[298] the Twelver corpus does not situate this identification of the enemies of the Imams with lower beings within the framework of a precise and consistent doctrine of creation, reincarnation and salvation. It is as if the Twelver corpus has kept merely traces of more complex theories found in the literature of the *ghulāt*.

The presence of the concept of *musūkhiyya* in the *Kitāb al-Kashf* is an additional indication of its anchorage in *ghulāt* origins. Yet, the meaning of the term is modified, in line with a clear trend throughout the collection consisting of attenuating or refining elements that are manifestly connected to *ghuluww*. Among these data, we note that the *musūkhiyya* has received special attention, since it is found not only in

---

[296] Mufaḍḍal al-Juʿfī, *Kitāb al-Haft wa'l-aẓilla*, Ch. 22, pp. 56–57.

[297] See the tripartite division of humanity between Imams, initiated followers and 'monsters in human form' in M.A. Amir-Moezzi, *La Religion discrète*, Ch. 8: 'Seul l'homme de Dieu est humain: Théologie et anthropologie mystique à travers l'exégèse imamite ancienne', pp. 214–218, 222–223 (English trans.: *Spirituality of Shiʿi Islam*, Ch. 8: 'Only the Man of God is Human: Theology and Mystical Anthropology according th Early Imami Exegesis', pp. 284–291, 296–298).

[298] On the *musūkhiyya* in the literature of the *ghulāt*, see M. Asatryan, *Controversies in Formative Shiʿi Islam*, pp. 149–154; idem, 'Early Ismailis and Other Muslims', esp. p. 276, note 12. The latter article also examines the occurrences of *musūkhiyya* in the *Kitāb al-Kashf*. While I share Asatryan's general approach in this regard, my interpretation partly differs from his. In addition, the article overlooks some passages of the *Kashf* relevant to this question.

Treatise I, but also in Treatises III and V. In the latter two, the passages on *musūkhiyya* are accompanied by references to the previous occurrences of the term within the volume, which seems to demonstrate that the *Kashf* as a whole is a coherent work — or that it bears the marks of an attempt to unify its various components.

Musūkhiyya is usually metamorphosis into an animal form in punishment for disbelief. In the *Kitāb al-Kashf*, the notion of punishment is preserved in some occurrences, but that of metamorphosis is systematically discarded — inasmuch as, by 'metamorphosis', an actual transformation into a lower physical form is meant. However, the *musūkhiyya* as defined by the *Kashf* is still a process or a change of nature with eschatological consequences, even though this change is not physical. As we will see, the *musūkhiyya*, here, is the result of a fall into the lower ranks of disbelief — rather than into lower animal forms.

The first mention of this notion appears at the beginning of Treatise I, in a passage setting out the consequences of the breach of the pact which had just been concluded with the reader. This is to warn the neophyte against a volte-face: either a betrayal of the *daʿwa* to join the ranks of the 'Opponents' or an unauthorized disclosure of the esoteric teachings. Q. 2:7 is applied to them: '*God has set a seal on their hearts and on their hearing, and on their eyes is a covering, and they will have a painful torment.*' Whoever enters the *daʿwa* and then abandons it is deprived of 'the benefits of science' and is assimilated to 'beasts who profess no religion'.[299] These 'beasts' (*bahāʾim*) evoke the 'cattle' (*anʿām*) of Q. 7:179: '*We have created for Gehenna many jinn and men: they have hearts wherewith they understand not, eyes wherewith they see not, ears wherewith they hear not. They are like cattle.*' Just like in Q. 2:7, the verse mentions the absence of vision and hearing, as well as the defectiveness of the heart. The *Kitāb al-Kashf*'s interpretation of the *musūkhiyya* is therefore fairly faithful to the Qurʾanic text: unbelievers are likened to beasts because they are deprived of the Truth, and not because their unbelief would result in a literal metamorphosis or reincarnation in animal form, as seems to be the case in the doctrines of the *ghulāt*.

The rest of the passage confirms that the metaphorical 'beasts' are traitors, that is, former members of the *daʿwa* who had started their

---

[299] *Kashf* I, p. 4, § 6.

initiation and received instructions before turning away from it: 'The one who does not know is more forgivable than the one who knows and yet does not retain what he knows and does not profit from it.'[300] According to the *Kashf*, such is the true meaning of the *musūkhiyya*: it is a change of state, a transition from faith to disbelief, from adherence to Truth to adherence to Falsehood. The result of such a transfer is to become a *metaphorical* beast. The passage ends with the statement that 'this is the correct meaning of the allusion to metamorphosis',[301] implicitly referring to an incorrect meaning of the term, that is, *literal* metamorphosis. This passage is therefore polemical on two levels: on the one hand, it is an attack against enemies of the *da'wa* who initially came from within its ranks. On the other hand, it is a refutation of the *ghulāts*' understanding of the *musūkhiyya*. The latter aspect is further confirmed, but only implicitly, by citing Q. 95:4–5: '*We created man in the fairest stature, and then We reduced him to the lowest of the low.*'[302] Indeed, as Heinz Halm had already noted in his short summary of the *ghulāt* themes of Treatise I,[303] these two verses were used in *ghulāt* circles (Ibn Ḥarb[304] and the *Kitāb al-Haft wa'l-aẓilla*[305]) in support of transmigrationist doctrines. Therefore, it can be contended here that the *Kashf* is alluding to such doctrines and proposing an alternative reading of Q. 95:4–5 by reinterpreting the term *musūkhiyya*, rather than renouncing it altogether.

In Treatise III, there is another example of such an implicit refutation of the transmigrationist exegesis of a Qur'anic verse. Indeed, the *Kashf*'s exegesis of Q. 17:50: '*Say: Be of stone or iron, or any other creation that grows in your hearts*', seems to allude to yet other 'incorrect interpretations' of metamorphosis. It begins by attributing to al-Ḥakīm[306] the idea that these words are addressed to Abū Bakr and

---

[300] *Kashf* I, p. 5, § 7.

[301] Ibid.

[302] Ibid.

[303] H. Halm, 'Das 'Buch der Schatten'', II, pp. 83–84.

[304] According to 'Abd Allāh b. Muḥammad al-Nāshi' in his *K. Uṣūl al-niḥal*, this verse was among those used by 'Abd Allāh b. Ḥarb to support his transmigrationist doctrine; see J. Van Ess, *Frühe mu'tazilitische Häresiographie*, Arabic p. 39. See also German trans. of the relevant passage in H. Halm, 'Das 'Buch der Schatten'', II, p. 24.

[305] Mufaḍḍal al-Ju'fī, *Kitāb al-Haft wa'l-aẓilla*, Ch. 11, p. 43.

[306] See commentary of *Kashf* III, pp. 252–256.

'Umar, because those who refuse to follow 'Alī and receive true knowledge from him are similar to 'inert matters that do not hear any knowledge and do not do anything, because they have no life such as the one found in animals'.[307] 'Stone' and 'iron' are thus not understood in a literal sense, but are defined according to their inert quality: the absence of life — life itself symbolising spiritual life, and therefore esoteric knowledge. In fact, this argument is explicitly made in the passage of Treatise V dedicated to the distinction between 'subtle essence' and 'dense body': 'Inert and dense objects are all made of dust, stones, [dead] wood and similar things. The same goes for the exoteric without the esoteric, etc.'[308] This confirms that *musūkhiyya* concerns the 'people of exotericism'.

Here, the Ismaili interpretation of Q. 17:50 does not explicitly mention the *musūkhiyya*, but it clearly echoes transmigrationist exegeses of this verse among certain circles. Indeed, according to the heresiologist al-Qummī, the *ghulāt* sect of the *mukhammisa* (the 'pentadists'),[309] apparently linked to the Khaṭṭābiyya, used this verse to support their theory of *tanāsukh* and affirmed that the souls of their adversaries would take on various forms, human and non-human, 'until there are, neither in the heavens, nor on the earth, any more beasts, or immobile or mobile beings, where the souls would not have passed, including stars and planets'. As an eschatological punishment, this cycle of successive reincarnations would end in *inert matter*: rock, earth or iron.[310] Similar interpretations of Q. 17:50 in support of metamorphosis are attested in *ghulāt*[311] and Nuṣayrī[312] sources. Like in

---

[307] *Kashf* III, pp. 65–66, § 27.

[308] *Kashf* V, p. 112, § 39.

[309] See al-Qummī, *Maqālāt*, pp. 56–59; H. Halm, *Die islamische Gnosis*, pp. 218–225; W. Madelung, 'Mukhammisa', *EI2*; M. Asatryan, 'Mokammesa', *EIr*.

[310] Al-Qummī, *Maqālāt*, p. 59.

[311] As noted by M. Asatryan, *Controversies in Formative Shi'i Islam*, p. 14, this verse is used in support of *maskh*, or *raskh*, 'transformation into mineral form', in the *Kitāb al-Haft wa'l-aẓilla* and the *Kitāb al-Ṣirāṭ*; see Mufaḍḍal al-Ju'fī, *Kitāb al-Haft wa'l-aẓilla*, Ch. 61, p. 118; L. Capezzone, 'Il *Kitāb al-Ṣirāṭ*', pp. 372, 400. In the *Kitāb al-Haft*, ascending mineral reincarnations (*naskh*) into precious gems such as ruby or peridot, are opposed to descending mineral reincarnations (*maskh*) into iron, copper or lead.

[312] See al-Khaṣībī, *al-Risāla al-rastbāshiyya*, cited in M.M. Bar-Asher and A. Kofsky, *The 'Alawī Religion: An Anthology*, p. 104.

the interpretation of this verse in Treatise III, the hermeneutics rests on the notion that 'stone and iron' are eschatological punishments, an eschatology which the *Kashf* interprets as exposure of the true nature of the enemies of the Imam, while the *mukhammisa* insert them into a cycle of successive transformations. Again, we are dealing with an Ismaili reinterpretation of an earlier exegetical tradition in favour of metamorphosis, now understood metaphorically. The unbelievers do not literally become 'stone' and 'iron', but merely *similar* to those matters inasmuch as they are deprived of spiritual life.

The other passages of the *Kashf* explicitly dealing with metamorphosis similarly reject the *ghulāt* connotations and literal interpretations of the *musūkhiyya*. The final section of Treatise III interprets several eschatological verses from Q. 22 in relation to Abū Bakr's torment upon the return of the *qā'im*. The sentence: *'For him in this world is ignominy'* (Q. 22:9), is remarkably glossed as follows: 'He means by this [Abū Bakr's] metamorphosis into a variety of figures and forms' (*mā yumsakh fī-hī min ikhtilāf al-ṣuwar wa'l-hayākil*).[313] There can hardly be a more explicit transmigrationist statement. Yet, it is immediately neutralized by a 'moderate' definition of *maskh* as 'a transfer from a class to another', and passing from the ranks of Muslims and 'companions of the Messenger of God' to those of the ignorant, deniers and polytheists.[314] This may allude to the Shiʿi distinction between *muslim* and *mu'min*, that is, between those who refused to follow ʿAlī and those who did.[315] The *musūkhiyya* would thus designate the status of those Muslims who, according to the Shiʿi narrative, renounced the true faith after the Prophet Muḥammad's death. But again, in mentioning the companions who rejected ʿAlī's Imamate, the author's intention is to target former members of the *daʿwa* who turned away

[313] *Kashf* III, p. 88, § 81.

[314] Ibid.

[315] According to M.A. Amir-Moezzi, the technical meaning of the term *mu'min* in early Shiʿi texts is 'initiate', and it defines the Shiʿites as opposed to the rest of the Muslim community; see M.A. Amir-Moezzi, *Guide divin*, index s.v. *mu'min*; idem, *La Religion discrète*, index s.v. *mu'min*; idem, *La Preuve de Dieu*, pp. 157, 167–168. On this distinction, see now M. Massi Dakake, *The Charismatic community*, pp. 177–211. In Ismaili context, this technical Shiʿi term came to designate the members of the *daʿwa*, as illustrated by *Kashf* V, p. 134, § 71; p. 142, § 87; VI, pp. 165–166, § 21, etc.

from it. It is interesting, and perhaps revealing, that once again the affirmation of the 'correct' meaning of *maskh* or *musūkhiyya* is so closely connected to an allusion to dissensions within the *daʿwa*. This could indicate that the 'dissidents' hinted to here adhered precisely to the 'incorrect', that is, literal, conception of metamorphosis.

The passage from Treatise V dealing with *musūkhiyya* emphasizes more the connection to animality that the term originally implies. This is where the metaphorical nature of *musūkhiyya* is most explicitly expressed. Abū Bakr — apparently the privileged victim of metamorphosis — is thus likened to a dog and a swine for having left 'the ranks of the people of truth to join those of falsehood'.[316] This is because a human, in the full sense of the term, is 'favoured with the knowledge that allows them to distinguish truth from falsehood, and impure from pure'.[317] He who shows himself incapable of such discernment, who 'turns away from the truth to falsehood (. . .) metaphorically left humanity to join the dogs and the swine. This is the meaning of metamorphosis.'[318] Further in the same treatise, another passage sheds light on this, although it is not directly a question of metamorphosis: 'Inert and dense objects are all made of dust, stones, [dead] wood and similar things. The same goes for the exoteric without the esoteric.'[319] The analogy between beings who do not benefit from life and intellects who do not benefit from esoteric knowledge thus clarifies the Ismaili conception of metamorphosis — as it appears in the *Kashf* — as metaphorical. That the disbelievers are unconscious beasts or lifeless stones requires a *taʾwīl* that takes these statements in a symbolic sense. The enemies of the *daʿwa* are beasts or inanimate objects in the sense that they are not enlightened and enlivened by the esoteric knowledge imparted by the Imam.

One might be tempted to consider that this attenuation of the original meaning of metamorphosis is a matter of *taqiyya*, but it seems that we are rather dealing with a sincere reinterpretation — as sincere as the one that motivated the rejection of divine incarnation in the

---

[316] *Kashf* V, p. 95, § 9.

[317] Ibid.

[318] *Kashf* V, p. 96, § 9.

[319] *Kashf* V, p. 112, § 39.

commentary of Ja'far al-Ṣādiq's vision.[320] The softening of the doctrines of the *ghulāt* is not to be understood as a form of compromise. Indeed, the orientation of *Kashf* on this point agrees with that of other Ismaili authors, such as al-Sijistānī or al-Kirmānī, who both reject the possibility for sinful human souls to transmigrate into an animal, vegetable or mineral form.[321] The difference, perhaps, resides in the proximity of the *Kashf* to *ghulāt* doctrines to the point of preserving their concepts by means of reshaping them. In any case, the *Kashf* definitely adopts a symbolic approach of *musūkhiyya*, which results in a greater subtlety of its doctrine.

6. The Mahdī and his Return

The first mention of the Mahdī in Treatise I comes immediately after the passage on *musūkhiyya*,[322] which suggests a connection between the two ideas, although not explicitly made in Treatise I. The discussion of the Mahdī is in line with the previously mentioned themes. *Musūkhiyya* has been defined as the change of state of one who is on the path of truth and then turns away from it. The recognition of this truth extends to the recognition, and therefore the expectation, of the Mahdī. Thus, the affirmation of the hypocrites in Q. 2:8: '*We believe in God and in the Last Day*' is attributed to the 'Shi'is who fall short' (*al-shī'a al-muqaṣṣira*)[323] whose faith does not include recognition of the Mahdī, the 'Master of the age' (*ṣāḥib al-zamān*).[324] The use of the

320 *Kashf* I, p. 7, § 12.

321 See D. De Smet, 'La transmigration des âmes', esp. pp. 82–93. However, De Smet shows that the refutation of transmigration by al-Kirmānī also extends to human souls taking on other human bodies, whereas al-Sijistānī's refutation focuses on *maskh* proper, that is, reincarnation into animal form. On the problem of metempsychosis in Ismailism, see also idem, *La philosophie ismaélienne: Un ésotérisme chiite entre néoplatonisme et gnose* (Paris, 2012), pp. 113–149; W. Madelung, 'Abū Ya'qūb al-Sijistānī and metempsychosis', in J. Duschesne-Guillemin, ed, *Iranica varia: Papers in honor of Professor Ehsan Yarshater* (Leiden, 1990), pp. 131–143. For another Ismaili metaphorical understanding of metamorphosis, see also al-Rāzī, *Kitāb al-Iṣlāḥ*, pp. 173–174.

322 *Kashf* I, p. 4–5, §§ 6–7.

323 Ibid.

324 *Kashf* I, p. 6, § 8.

term *muqaṣṣira* is noteworthy insofar as it is the counterpart of the accusation of *ghuluww*: if the *ghulāt* are those who attribute too much power to the Imams, or who, in one way or another , 'go too far' or 'exaggerate', the *muqaṣṣira*, on the other hand, are those who 'do not go far enough' or 'lessen' the doctrine. The *muqaṣṣira* are such in the eyes of those whom they call the *ghulāt*, and vice versa. It is unclear whether the coexistence in the same text of these two terms must be seen as an inconsistency (e.g. due to the juxtaposition of distinct layers), or if it indicates the editor of the *Kashf*'s position, on a ridge line between *ghuluww* and *taqṣīr*[325] — a position which would, again, correspond to the Fatimid option in this regard.

It is clear, in any case, that, in Treatise I, *ghuluww* only includes the notions of divine incarnation and metamorphosis in the literal sense: of what is usually considered as falling under *ghuluww* with the *Kashf* rejecting only the idea that God can take a human form or that the infidels are literally swine and monkeys, etc. On the other hand, it retains the extreme anti-Sunni tendency (Treatise III is the most vindictive in this respect, but it also appears in Treatise I),[326] and especially the doctrine of *raj'a*, which is undoubtedly the initially 'exaggerating' doctrine which has best survived in the so-called 'moderate' currents. In the Treatise V, another doctrine characteristic of *ghuluww* will be refuted in turn: that of antinomianism.

In the second mention of the Mahdī in Treatise I, the '*heaven rent asunder*' from Q. 55:37 is interpreted as follows: 'The Order of the Speaking-Prophets will be rent asunder.'[327] Evidently, the Mahdī is part of 'the continuity of the Order', as its last, final, point. 'The Speaking-Prophet of Speaking-Prophets' (*nāṭiq al-nuṭaqā'*)[328] is thus

---

[325] *Taqṣīr* is the verbal noun from the same root as *muqaṣṣira*.

[326] This anti-Sunni tendency, a classic feature of early pre-Buyid Shi'ism, may in the context of the *Kashf* be used for polemical purposes, not so much against Sunnis as such, as against rival Shi'i trends or internal dissidents. As mentioned earlier, the vilification of Abū Bakr and 'Umar takes place within a larger analogy likening the Ismaili Imam to 'Alī, and his enemies to those of 'Alī'. Therefore, it is not so much about the historical events that followed the Prophet's death as it is about legitimizing the Fatimid rule.

[327] *Kashf* I, p. 10, § 19.

[328] *Kashf* I, p. 16, § 35.

the culmination of the Order, towards which the latter has tended since Adam, and especially since the last Speaking-Prophet, Muḥammad.

The Mahdī is interpreted as the real meaning of the Qur'anic verses referring to the afterlife or the Day of Resurrection.[329] This is what the concept of *raj'a* entails. People will then receive retribution on the basis of their attitude towards the *walāya*:[330] 'The Prince of the Believers (. . .) will do justice to every man among them on the Day of Resurrection. Even if he has [accomplished] works as [lofty as] the firm mountains (*al-jibāl al-rawāsī*), if he does not meet God in 'Alī's Friendship (*walāya*), his work will profit him nothing.'[331] The emphasis is therefore on a historical interpretation of Qur'anic eschatology: all the verses evoking the 'mustering' (*al-ḥashr*), the 'return' and so on are interpreted in this sense.

At the end of the treatise, a relatively long *ḥadīth*, which can be considered a kind of 'Shi'i apocalypse', enumerates the facts and gestures of the Mahdī upon his return.[332] In an important article, Colin Turner has studied a Shi'i apocalyptic narrative known as 'the tradition of Mufaḍḍal' and narrated in al-Majlisī's *Biḥār al-anwār*. The original text is very long, and C. Turner only translates part of it.[333] It presents several similarities with the account of the *Kashf* — the latter thus appears to transmit the short version of a longer account, even if the order of events is not exactly the same.

In the Apocalypse reported by al-Majlisī, long developments are dedicated to the fate of Abū Bakr and 'Umar during the Resurrection, whilst the *Kitāb al-Kashf* only briefly alludes to them: 'He will order them both to be crucified' — even so, this sentence is coded using the secret alphabet. Given the importance of the treatment of the 'two' in

---

[329] See e.g. *Kashf* I, p. 19, § 42, where the 'hereafter' is identified with the 'Return' (*al-karra*), that is, the physical return of the Mahdī.

[330] The '*ḥadīth* of retribution' attributed to Ja'far al-Ṣādiq also seems to allude to an earthly retribution at the hands of the Mahdī; see *Kashf* I, pp. 13–14, § 27.

[331] *Kashf* I, p. 20, § 43.

[332] *Kashf* I, pp. 32–35, §§ 68–73.

[333] C. Turner, 'The 'Tradition of Mufaḍḍal' and the Doctrine of the Raj'a: Evidence of 'Ghuluww' in the Eschatology of Twelver Shi'ism?', *Iran: Journal of the British Institute of Persian Studies*, 44 (2006), pp. 177–180.

the *Biḥār*, it seems necessary to resort to the latter in order to clarify the *Kashf* and reveal what is hidden behind this very elusive mention. This elusiveness may mean that the text has been censored here, perhaps according to the method of 'scattering of knowledge' (*tabdīd al-ʿilm*). It thus comes down to the reader to complete the account according to the other mentions of the fate of Abū Bakr and ʿUmar during the Return, in particular in Treatise III. Indeed, one finds there the idea that Abū Bakr will undergo the 'chastisement of the burning' — the latter being identified with the appearance of the Resurrector — and that he 'will be killed seventy thousand deaths and burnt as many times'.[334] It is after this passage, moreover, that the text deals with metamorphosis in this treatise, which clearly shows that it must be linked to the Resurrector insofar as it is a punishment.

In the *Biḥār*'s Apocalypse, Abū Bakr and ʿUmar are exhumed and their bodies are discovered perfectly preserved. The Mahdī then asks if anyone has doubts about them. On a negative response from the audience, he re-buries them. When exhumed again, three days later, their bodies are still preserved, which their supporters will take as a sign of their election. Supporters of the Mahdī will call those who love these two to stand on one side, so that the assembly will be split into two groups. This illustrates the role of the Mahdī as a judge and executor of the divine justice that separates the elect from the damned. The devotees of Abū Bakr and ʿUmar will then be annihilated, and Abū Bakr and ʿUmar themselves will be resurrected to stand trial. Significantly, they will be reproached not only for refusing to follow ʿAlī and for the misdeeds they committed against him and Fāṭima, but also for all the crimes since the dawn of humanity: the murder of Abel by Cain, Abraham having been thrown Abraham into the furnace, Joseph having been thrown into the pit, the punishment of Jonah locked in the belly of the whale, the murder of John the Baptist, the crucifixion of Jesus, the wounds of Salmān, the murder of all the Imams, and more generally all the crimes of blood committed since the dawn of time, all the vices, all the acts of treason, iniquity and oppression. They will then confess their crimes, be hanged on a tree and burned. Their ashes will be scattered in the sea. On the Day of

---

[334] *Kashf* III, p. 87, § 79.

Resurrection (which is therefore distinguished here from the Return of the Mahdī), the Fourteen Impeccables of Twelver Shiʿism will be assembled to fulfil the revenge against the first two Caliphs. The latter will then be killed and resurrected a thousand times a day and their tortures will never stop.[335]

In addition to the sadism and revengeful obsession manifested in this text, it should be noted that Abū Bakr and ʿUmar are accused of all crimes of humanity since its inception. They are the personifications of the principle of evil, and will be judged as such. The role of the Mahdī is therefore to play the historical part of the cosmic rebalancing which must take place at the end of time.

Conclusion

Treatise I includes at least two editorial layers: an ancient core, with typical concepts and technical terms of the *ghulāt*, which was then reworked to fit Ismaili orientations. Whether this Ismailism is Fatimid or pre-Fatimid is unclear and this matter can hardly be decided based on what has often been the criterion to determine the provenance of early Ismaili texts, that is, the mention of a Mahdī that is yet to come; indeed, the messianic expectation was always a tenet of Ismaili faith, even after the reform of the first Fatimid caliph. Whatever the case may be, the important feature of Treatise I is that it represents a stage of Ismaili doctrine prior to its full formalization during the Fatimid period (especially during and after the reign of al-Muʿizz). Ismailism is here clearly rooted in Shiʿi and *ghulāt* speculations. A list of the features of Treatise I with *ghulāt* and Nuṣayrī parallels was established by H. Halm: it includes the mentions of Jābir b. Yazīd al-Juʿfī and Mufaḍḍal b. ʿUmar al-Juʿfī, the pentadist cosmology at the end of the treatise with Fāṭima being named 'Fāṭir', the domes of light contemplated by Jaʿfar al-Ṣādiq, the *kālī*, the Orphans, the mentions of Abū'l-Khaṭṭāb and other sacred figures of the Nuṣayrī tradition, and the *musūkhiyya*.[336]

[335] See al-Majlisī, *Biḥār al-anwār*, cited by C. Turner, 'The 'Tradition of Mufaḍḍal' and the Doctrine of the Rajʿa', p. 179.

[336] H. Halm, 'Das 'Buch der Schatten'', II, pp. 83–84.

To these, one can add Muḥammad being named *al-sayyid al-akbar*, the *ḥadīth* on the vision of God, as well as the mentions of Muḥammad b. Abī Bakr.

Beside its *ghulāt* accents, this treatise is fundamental in approaching the origins of Ismailism: we thus discern not only its genealogy (rooted in the *ghulāt* groups), but also the first Ismaili intuitions, by which the movement distinguished itself from rival Shiʿi trends. Among these specifically Ismaili features is notably the 'continuity of the Order' which leads to an elaborate conception of the prophetic cycles and seems to correspond perfectly to the early Fatimid conception of the Imamate: the continuity of the Order is a legitimist argument, not a messianic one. On this point and on transmigration, Ismailism as it appears in the treatise breaks with its *ghulāt* origins and elaborates its own 'moderate' doctrine — while still using connotated vocabulary (in particular the *musūkhiyya*) and drawing its contents from a pool of Shiʿi beliefs, representations and exegeses. The *Kashf* also retains two aspects which will be considered specific to *ghuluww*: the hostility to Abū Bakr and ʿUmar, and the doctrine of *rajʿa*, intended to justify its political organization.

TREATISE II

Treatise II stands out in the collection since it is the only one entirely dedicated to ontological and cosmological speculations. It deals indeed with the nature of God, the Throne and the Footstool, understood as two hierarchized ontological hypostases, and it ends with a rather confusing, yet remarkable, alphabetical cosmogony. These three main themes correspond to the three parts of the treatise, the first two of which are in fact *ḥadīth*s that are also attested in Twelver Shiʿi *ḥadīth* collections. These two *ḥadīth*s both represent the Twelver promotion of *tawḥīd* in the face of anthropomorphism, and this polemicising dimension is particularly patent in the second *ḥadīth*.

Thus, the original (i.e. Ismaili) parts of the treatise are the third one, which presents how the letters of the Arabic alphabet emanate from each other, as well as a few transitional paragraphs inserted by the author of the treatise to articulate the three parts of the text. The structure of the treatise can be broken down as follows:

1) The Divine Transcendence: first *ḥadīth*.

   - [§§ **1–3**] First part of the first *ḥadīth*
   - [§§ **4–5**] Inserted passage: discussion of names of God
   - [§ **6**] Second part of the first *ḥadīth*
   - [§ 7] Transition with the second *ḥadīth*

2) [§§ **8–17**] The Throne, the Footstool and the rejection of anthropomorphism: second *ḥadīth*.

[§§ **18–20**] Transition with the third part: how the Throne and the Footstool are connected, and the possibility of knowing them

3) [§§ **21–25**] The alphabetical cosmogony: the emanation of the letters from the Throne and the Footstool

Treatise II Translation

In the name of God, the Merciful, the Compassionate
[First *ḥadīth*: the Divine transcendence][1]

1. Praise be to God, Unique in His Unicity, Alone (*mutafarrid*) in His Lordship. There is no god but Him, Alive without <'how'> (*bi-lā kayf*);[2] He did not come to being (*lam yakun lahu kāna*), and there was no 'how' (*kayf*) to His <being> (*li-kawnihi*).[3] He did not have a place; He was not in anything nor on anything, and He did not create (*ibtadaʿa*) a space for His being. He did not become stronger after there was something, nor was He weak before creating (*kawwana*) something. He was not bound by necessity (*mustawjiban*)[4] before creating something. There is nothing similar to Him. <He was not lacking of a kingdom before He created it, and will not be lacking of it after it fades away. He is a living god without [the existence of] life, a possessor of a kingdom before He created anything *and* after He

---

[1] As I have shown elsewhere, four versions of this *ḥadīth* appear in Twelver Shiʿi sources, two short versions and two long ones; see F. Gillon, 'Une version ismaélienne', pp. 484–509, esp. pp. 487–498. This article contains discussions of some variants as well as detailed comparative tables between the various versions of this *ḥadīth*. Here, I will only refer to the Twelver variants when I have used them to modify the text of the *Kashf*.

[2] Mss. A, B: *bi-lā ḥayāt* ('without life'). Corrected after the Twelver Shiʿi versions; see F. Gillon, 'Une version ismaélienne', p. 490, tab. 1.1, l. 4.

[3] Mss. A, B: *li kāfihi* ('to His condition, or: modality'). Corrected after the Twelver Shiʿi versions; see F. Gillon, 'Une version ismaélienne', p. 490, tab. 1.1, l. 6.

[4] Three out of the four Twelver Shiʿi versions read: *mustawḥishan*, 'deserted', 'isolated', meaning that God did not lack anything 'before' He created something, while the *Kashf* emphasizes the notion that God was not bound by the necessity to create. The fourth Twelver Shiʿi version does not contain this sentence; see F. Gillon, 'Une version ismaélienne', p. 491, tab. 1.1, l. 13.

created being> (*wa-lā kāna khalwan ʿan al-mulk qabl inshāʾihi wa-lā yakūn khalwan minhu baʿda dhahābihi kāna ilāhan ḥayyan bi-lā ḥayāt wa-mālikan qabl an yanshaʾa shayʾan wa-mālikan baʿda inshāʾihi liʾl-kawn*).[5]

2. Therefore, there is no 'how' to God's being, and He does not have a 'where', nor any limitation (*ḥadd*). He is not known through a form (*shabaḥ*).[6] He is neither worn by His permanence (*baqāʾ*), nor subject to annihilation (*fanāʾ*).[7] He does not harken to any summons (*daʿwa*), but on the contrary, it is to His summons that all things harken.[8] He was alive without created life (*bi-lā ḥayāt ḥāditha*), <without a describable being, without a defined 'how', without a determined 'where'> (*bi-lā kawn mawṣūf bi-lā kayf maḥdūd wa-lā ayn mawqūf*),[9] without occupying a space (*bi-lā makān sākin fī-hi*); nay, he is Alive and Powerful (*muqtadir*), a King who always retains His **[40]** Power (*qudra*) <and Kingship. He created what He wanted> (*waʾl-mulk anshaʾa mā shāʾa*)[10] where He <wanted>,[11] without [referring to] an archetypal model (*bi-lā ḥadd mithāl*), [and this creation entailed]

[5] Mss. A, B: *wa-lā kāna khalqan qabl inshāʾihi shayʾan malik anshaʾa al-kawn* ('there was not creature before He created something; He is a King who created being'). Here, I translate the version found in al-Kulaynī, *al-Rawḍa min al-kāfī, khuṭbat al-ṭālūtiyya*, ed. ʿA.A. al-Ghaffārī (Tehran, 1377 [1957]), p. 31. The *Kashf*'s version seems to be a simplification of the original *ḥadīth*, since it omits two sentences found in the Twelver versions, and does not include the idea that God remains king whether there is a kingdom or not; see F. Gillon, 'Une version ismaélienne', p. 491, tab. 1.1, l. 15–18.

[6] Here, all four Twelver versions provide various versions of the root *sh-b-h*, meaning that nothing is similar to God or that God cannot be known by the mediation of something similar to Him; see F. Gillon, 'Une version ismaélienne', p. 491, tab. 1.1, l. 22.

[7] Here, all four Twelver versions omit the second part of the sentence on extinction; see F. Gillon, 'Une version ismaélienne', p. 491, tab. 1.1, l. 24.

[8] The five versions of the *ḥadīth* all diverge on this sentence; see F. Gillon, 'Une version ismaélienne', p. 491, tab. 1.1, l. 25–26, and p. 496 for a short discussion of these variants.

[9] This does not appear in the *Kashf*. Added after the Twelver Shiʿi versions; see F. Gillon, 'Une version ismaélienne', p. 492, tab. 1.1, l. 28–31.

[10] Mss. A, B: *wa-mālik anshaʾa al-qudra mā arāda*. Corrected after the Twelver Shiʿi versions; see F. Gillon, 'Une version ismaélienne', p. 492, tab. 1.1, l. 35.

[11] Mss. A, B: *haythu anshaʾa*. Corrected to: *haythu shāʾa*, which makes more sense. The Twelver Shiʿi versions vary but all contain the verb *shāʾa* (except one); F. Gillon, 'Une version ismaélienne', p. 492, tab. 1.1, l. 36.

no dissolution or consolidation [of God]; it is only a favour from Him [returning] to him (*minhu wa-ilayhi*).

3. There is no god but Him. Glory be to He who is the first without 'how', and who is the last without 'where'! *'And all things perish, except His Face'* [Q. 28:88], *'His are the Creation and Order'* [Q. 7:54], *'His is the Judgment, and unto Him you will return'* [Q. 28:88].

[Passage inserted in the *ḥadīth*]

4. He was King before He created anything with [His] Power. He created the whole Creation through a Power from His Knowledge (*ibtadaʿa al-badʿ kullahu bi-qudra min ʿilmihi*). Thus did God's Knowledge appear through Power.

5. *'Praise be to God'* (*al-ḥamdu li-Llāh*) is the laudation (*al-thanā'*); *'Glory be to God'* (*subḥānahu*) [refers to His] sublimity (*ʿaẓama*); *'May He be blessed'* (*tabāraka*) is to affirm [His] might (*taʿazzuz*). Before (*min qabl*)[12] *'Praise be to God'* is God's Name by which is called the One whose knowledge cannot be accessed by the creatures, [which name] is neither Arabic, Persian (*aʿjamī*) or Syriac, and [which name] is only pronounced by the tongues of the creatures when uttering [the phrase]: *'In the Name of God'* (*bi-ism Allāh*). By this [expression], God opened (*fataḥa*)[13] everything. After that comes *'the Merciful'* (*al-Raḥmān*), an attribute describing highness (*ʿuluww*). Then [comes the epithet]: *'the Compassionate'* (*al-Raḥīm*), which is the attribute of the Lenient (*al-ḥalīm*). Then the praise (*al-ḥamd*), which is the laudation. Then: *'Glory'* (*subḥān*), which is the exhaltation (*taʿẓīm*). Then: *'May He be blessed'* (*tabāraka*), which is the affirmation of [His] might (*taʿzīz*). And *'the Sanctified'* (*al-quddūs*) is close to both (*jāruhumā*).[14] Sanctity (*al-quds*) is the loftiest of all these attributes: Praise, Merciful, **[41]** Compassionate and Glory. As for [the epithet] *'the Absolute'* (*al-ṣamad*), its pronunciation stands apart from these attributes. The absolute

[12] Mss. A, B: *man qīla*, which is probably a mistake. The text here seems to refer to the basmala, which, in the first chapter of the Qur'an, precedes the expression *al-ḥamdu li-Llāh*. From this textual precedence, the author seems to infer an ontological hierarchy, but this paragraph is quite obscure and clearly corrupted.

[13] An allusion to the first chapter of the Qur'an, *al-Fātiḥa*.

[14] It is unclear what is meant by this proximity and why *al-quddūs* is close to *subḥān* and *tabāraka*.

realities are the affirmation of God's oneness (*al-ṣamadiyyāt al-tawḥīd*). The Absolute (*al-ṣamad*) is the one whom . . .

[End of the first *ḥadīth*]

6. . . . the imaginations cannot liken [to anything]; He exhausts comparisons (*shubuhāt*). He is not created from anything, and nothing exceeds Him. He does not lose anything from determining something (*lā yazūl minhu shay' min amr ḥatamahu*). He is not affected by events, He is not seized by slumbers (*sināt*).[15] He is not questioned for anything [He did], and He does not regret anything. '*Slumber seizes Him not, nor sleep*' [Q. 2:255]; '*To Him belong all that is in the heavens and the earth, and all that is between them, and all that is underneath the soil*' [Q. 20:6].

[Gloss and transition to the second *ḥadīth*]

7. Such are the Gates (*abwāb*) of the attributes (*ṣifāt*). They are the Gates of his Knowledge that no one comprehends; nothing can reach the limits (*ḥudūd*) of its extension: '*His Footstool extends over the heavens and the earth*' [Q. 2:255]. The Footstool (*al-kursī*) is the Gate of the knowledge of the manifest part of the Mysteries (*bāb 'ilm ghayb ẓāhir min al-ghuyūb*); it is the Gate of the Marked Tablet (*al-raqīm*).[16] <And the Marked Tablet is the Prince of the Believers. And His words:

---

[15] It is unclear whether this is an allusion to Q. 2:255, quoted below — and in this case, why the plural *sināt* instead of the Qur'anic *sina*? — or if it is an error for *sanawāt*, 'years', meaning that God is not affected by the passage of time. The latter possibility would make sense inasmuch as the text just denied that God is subject to (temporal) events.

[16] Mss. A, B: *al-raqam*. Strothmann also reads *al-raqam*, while Ghālib corrects it into *al-raqīm* although he claims that his ms. reads *al-raqam* (p. 56, n. 2). The term reappears at the end of the treatise, p. 50, § 24. In the table of errors of his edition, Strothmann notes that this second occurrence of *al-raqam* is to be corrected to *al-raqīm*, but omits to make the same correction for the present occurrence. In his quotation of large extracts of Treatise II in his *Zahr al-ma'ānī*, pp. 127–131, Idrīs 'Imād al-Dīn also reads *al-raqīm* here; see Idrīs 'Imād al-Dīn, *Zahr al-ma'ānī*, p. 128. The term *al-raqīm* is Qur'anic (Q. 18:9) and has prompted numerous interpretations; among these, *al-raqīm* is identified with a book or a 'tablet' (*lawḥ*), and put in relation with the '*Marked Book*' (*kitāb marqūm*) from Q. 83:9 and 20 — as is also the case in the two occurrences of the term in *Kashf* II. See e.g. al-Ṭabarī, *Tafsīr al-Ṭabarī: Jāmi' al-bayān fī tafsīr āy al-qur'ān*, ed. 'A. al-Turkī (Gizeh, 2001), vol. 15, pp. 157–161. Inasmuch as the *bāb al-raqīm* is identified here to the Footstool, it is likely identical with the '*Preserved Tablet*' (*al-lawḥ al-maḥfūẓ*) from Q. 85:22, which traditionally forms a couple with the Qalam and receives its 'marking' from this superior ontological level.

'A Marked (marqūm) Book contemplated by those brought nigh (al-muqarrabūn)' [Q. 83:20–21] refer to the supports (*al-ḥamla*) [of the Footstool].>[17] His words: *'The Footstool extends . . .'* are about this Gate, the Knowledge of the heavens and the earth.

[Second *ḥadīth*: the Throne and the Footstool][18]

8. The Throne (*al-'arsh*) has many different attributes, but <the Qur'an has associated it with one attribute in particular>,[19] saying: *'Lord of the Sublime ('aẓīm) Throne'* [Q. 9:129], [meaning] Lord of the Sublime Kingdom. He [also] says: *'The Merciful sat Himself upon the Throne'* [Q. 20:5], meaning **[42]** that He encompasses the Kingdom. This is the modality (*kayfūfiyya*) in the beginning. The Throne is in conjunction (*fi'l-waṣl*) [with God], and it is in His proximity, to [His] side and vicinity.

9. If somebody were to ask: 'Why is the conjunction (*waṣl*)[20] isolated (*mufrad*) from the Footstool?', the answer would be: 'Do you not know that [the Throne and the Footstool] are two of the greatest Gates in the heart of the Qur'an? They are both wellsprings, and they are counted as part of the Mystery (*ghayb*) — <by the conjunction (*waṣl*), what is meant is Muḥammad — may blessings and peace be upon him>[21] — because the Footstool is the Exoteric Gate of the Mystery (*al-bāb al-ẓāhir min al-ghayb*), from which the created beings (*mubda'āt*) stem, and it is the principle (*mabda'*) of all things. It is <the attribute of the Will>,[22] the knowledge of words and vowel<s>[23] and its explanation, the knowledge of the Return and the Origin

[17] Added after Idrīs 'Imād al-Dīn, *Zahr al-ma'ānī*, p. 128.

[18] As I have shown elsewhere, another version of this *ḥadīth* appears in Ibn Bābawayh's *Kitāb al-Tawḥīd*; see F. Gillon, 'Une version ismaélienne', pp. 498–507. Again, I will only refer to the Ibn Bābawayh's version when I have used it to modify the text of the *Kashf*.

[19] Mss. A, B: *waḍa'a fīhi al-Qur'ān 'alā ṣifa wāḥida*. Corrected to: *wuḍi'a fī al-Qur'ān ṣifa 'alā ḥidda*, after Ibn Bābawayh, *Kitāb al-Tawḥīd*, p. 321. See F. Gillon, 'Une version ismaélienne', p. 499, tab. 2.1, l. 3, and pp. 504 -505.

[20] That is, the Throne (*al-'arsh*).

[21] Added after Idrīs 'Imād al-Dīn, *Zahr al-ma'ānī*, p. 128.

[22] Mss. A, B: *ṣifat al-adawāt*. Corrected to: *ṣifat al-irāda*, after Ibn Bābawayh, *Kitāb al-Tawḥīd*, p. 322. In the latter version, however, this is attributed to the Throne, and not to the Footstool; see footnote 24 below.

[23] Mss. A, B: *al-ḥaraka*. Corrected to: *al-ḥarakāt*, after Ibn Bābawayh, *Kitāb al-Tawḥīd*, p. 322. Given that the *alfāẓ* are mentioned just before, it is likely that the text is referring to the 'vowels' rather than to motion.

(*al-ʿawd wa'l-bad'*).[24] As for the Throne, it is the Esoteric Gate (*al-bāb al-bāṭin*) in which is the knowledge of Being (*kawn*), of totality (*mala'*), of the limit (*ḥadd*), of the 'where' (*ayn*), of the will (*mashī'a*), and of the form (*shabaḥ*). To the one who knows, they are two Gates, because the Kingdom of the Throne has formed (*sawwā*) the Kingdom of the Footstool, and its knowledge is greater (*aʿẓam*) than the knowledge of the Footstool. This is why He says: '*Lord of the Sublime (ʿazīm) Throne*' [Q. 9:129]; it is because its attribute is greater (*aʿẓam*) than the attribute of the Footstool. They are, in this regard, bound to each other (*maqrūnān*), representing the general and particular of knowledge (*yaʿimmān wa yakhiṣṣān bi'l-ʿilm*).

10. And if it is stated: 'It is necessary to know what becomes of the Throne when becoming in conjunction and proximity (*jār*) to the Footstool', the answer is: 'It came into its proximity because the modality [of its presence] in the exoteric aspect [of being] belongs to the Gates of permanence (*li'anna kayfūfiyyatahu fī'l-ẓāhir min abwāb al-baqā'*). **[43]** <And the spatiality (*aynūniyya*) [of these Gates] and the degree of their union and separation>[25] are found in the Gate of the Throne. They are both in proximity with each other, in the vicinity of each other by their side.[26]

11. It is in a similar way that the scholars (*al-ʿulamā'*) are known and that one learns about the veracity of their prayers (*daʿawāt*).[27]

---

[24] In Ibn Bābawayh's version, this sentence appears in the enumeration of the attributes of the Throne, rather than those of the Footstool; see Ibn Bābawayh, *Kitāb al-Tawḥīd*, p. 322; F. Gillon, 'Une version ismaélienne', p. 500, tab. 2.1, l. 18–19 and 22. See also the translation of this paragraph of the *Kitāb al-Tawḥīd* by M.A. Amir-Moezzi, *Guide divin*, p. 80, and the comments in n. 165 (English trans.: *Divine Guide*, p. 31 and p. 161, n. 165).

[25] Ms. A: Missing; ms. B: *aynūniyyatuhā wa-ḥadd ratqihā wa-wasʿihā*. Corrected to: *aynūniyyatuhā wa-ḥadd ratqihā wa-fatqihā*, after Ibn Bābawayh, *Kitāb al-Tawḥīd*, p. 322; Idrīs ʿImād al-Dīn, *Zahr al-maʿānī*, p. 129. This is an allusion to Q. 21:30: '*Do the unbelievers not see that the heavens and the earth were united (kānatā ratqan), and We separated them (fataqnāhā)?*

[26] The technical details of the doctrine conveyed by the *ḥadīth* are unclear in both the *Kashf* and the *Kitāb al-Tawḥīd* — particularly in this paragraph. The text is heavily corrupted. The apparent aim of this paragraph is to explain how the Footstool takes its qualities from the Throne, and how the latter manifests itself through the former.

[27] This sentence is particularly cryptic. Is it a tentative analogy between the relation of the scholars and those who learn from them, on the one hand, and the relation of the Throne and the Footstool, on the other hand?

'God bestows His Mercy upon whom He wills' [Q. 2:105]; *'He is the Strong, the Mighty'* [Q. 11:66]; *'Praise be to God, Lord of the Universes'* [Q. 1:2].

12. <Among the various attributes of the Throne, He said — may He be blessed:>[28] *'Exalted be God, Lord of the Throne, above what they describe'* [Q. 21:22]. This is the attribute of the Throne, and the attribute of Oneness (*waḥdāniyya*). Indeed, a people has associated with God that of which they had no knowledge, [but] God said: *'Lord of the Sublime Throne'* [Q. 9:129], meaning the Lord of Unity — *'exalted be He above what they describe'*.

13. Another group (*qawm*) described God — He is Mighty and Sublime — as having two hands, and they said: *'God's hand is fettered. May their hands be fettered and may they be cursed for what they have said!'* [Q. 5:64].[29] Others described Him <as having two feet>,[30] claiming that he placed His foot on the Rock of the Sacred House (*ṣakhrat bayt al-maqdis*)[31] and then rose therefrom to the sky. Others described Him as having fingertips (*anāmil*), saying that Muḥammad — may God bless him and his family — said: 'I felt the freshness of His fingertips on my heart.'[32]

14. May God — He is Mighty and Sublime — be exalted above such attributes (*ṣifāt*)! There is no god but Him, Lord of the Sublime Throne. May He be blessed; may the Lord of the *'highest likeness'* (*al-mathal al-aʿlā*) [Q. 16:60] be exalted above what they have likened Him to (*mā maththalūhu bi-hi*). He cannot be assimilated [to anything],

[28] Added after Ibn Bābawayh, *Kitāb al-Tawḥīd*, p. 323.

[29] It should be noted that the Qur'an does not curse the Jews for saying that God has hands, but for saying that His hand is fettered. Indeed, the following sentence states: *'Nay, but His hand are outspread.'*

[30] Mss. A, B: *waṣafūhu bi'l-tashbīh*. Corrected to: *waṣafūhu bi'l-rijlayn*, after Ibn Bābawayh, *Kitāb al-Tawḥīd*, p. 323; see F. Gillon, 'Une version ismaélienne', p. 501, tab. 2.1, l. 45. The *Kashf*'s version is however of importance as it provides the key concept of *tashbīh*, 'anthropomorphism', that the *ḥadīth* intends to refute.

[31] This refers to the rock of the Dome of the Rock in Jerusalem.

[32] For a discussion of this famous *ḥadīth*, see commentary of *Kashf* II, pp. 192–194. In a footnote (p. 44, n. 4), Strothmann provides a reference to a version of the '*ḥadīth* of the dream' or '*ḥadīth* of the best form' that does not contain the term *anāmil*. Since Ghālib provides the exact same reference instead of referring to a more relevant version, it is likely that he merely copied Strothmann on this occasion; see *Kashf*, ed. Ghālib, p. 57, n. 2.

nor described through any representation (*wahm*), '*the eyes attain Him not*' [Q. 6:103]. [**44**] It is [only] someone who did not rise to this knowledge that describes him as having hands. They describe their Lord with these likenesses and assimilate Him to these things out of their ignorance of Him. God — may He be exalted — said: '*You have been given of knowledge nothing except a little*' [Q. 17:85]. There is nothing similar to God, nothing alike, nothing equal.

15. To Him belong the most beautiful names by which none other is named. It is these names that are described when He says: '*To God belong the most beautiful names, so call Him by them and leave those who profane His names*' [Q. 7:180] and '*meddle with*' His '*signs*' [Q. 6:68] without knowledge. And elsewhere: they associate [something] to Him '*whence they know not*' [Q. 7:182], and they disbelieve (*yakfirūn*) in Him thinking '*that they are working good deeds*' [Q. 18:104]. He also said: '*And the most part of them believe not in God but they associate [other gods to Him]*' [Q. 12:106]. '*They meddle with*' His names and '*His signs*' [Q. 6:68] without knowledge, considering them inadequately and deviating from them, in spite of the fact that God ordered them to take as kin (*aqwām*), friends (*awliyā'*) and Imams those to whom He has granted His favour and to whom He entrusted a knowledge He entrusted to no one else.

16. Whoever follows other than them goes astray from the Path (*sabīl*). '*Those who disbelieve, their Friends are the Ṭāghūt*' [Q. 2:257] because they envy God's Friends (*awliyā'*) to whom is reserved the pursuit of the Path. The *Ṭāghūt* '*bring*' their Friends '*out from light to darkness*' [Q. 2:257], because when God — He is Mighty [**45**] and Sublime —established the proof (*al-burhān*), and made it a Friend (*walī*) to God and to the believers, thereby brought the servants '*out from darkness to light. And those who disbelieve, their Friends are the Ṭāghūt who bring them out from light to darkness. Those are the inhabitants of the Fire, therein dwelling forever*' [Q. 2:257]. They associate [something] with God, yet claiming to be believers; He said: '*They think they are guided*' [Q. 7:30].[33] Whoever is appointed (*nuṣiba*) without God is a *Ṭāghūt*.[34]

[33] This verse states: '*They have taken Satans (shayāṭīn) for Friends (awliyā') instead of God and think that they are guided.*'

[34] This paragraph is missing from both Ibn Bābawayh's *Kitāb al-Tawḥīd* and Idrīs 'Imād al-Dīn's *Zahr al-ma'ānī*.

17. God sent Muḥammad — may God bless him and his family — and he was a guide (*dalīl*) towards this light and this proof (*burhān*), with God's permission — may He be exalted. The favour that he brought to us was sublime. Then, he died (*qubiḍa*) — may God bless him — having established for the community after [his death] a guiding and guided proof (*dalīlan hādiyan muhtadiyan*). He was the one who was indicated from among [the Prophet's] close ones, both during [the Prophet's] lifetime and after his death;[35] his knowledge was manifested, yet they did not acknowledge that the authority (*al-amr*) belonged to the Proof (*al-ḥujja*) after [Muḥammad's death], and they went astray.

[The Throne and the Footstool]

18. The origin of the Gate of the Footstool rests in the fact that when God — He is Sublime and High — wanted to create (*yabtadiʿ*) a Kingdom, He wanted it to be knowledge (*ʿilm*).[36] Yet, God cannot be spatially described [in relation] to this knowledge (*laysa yūṣaf Allāh minhu bi-ayn*), nor can the modality of this knowledge['s relation] to God be described (*wa-lā yūṣaf al-ʿilm min Allāh bi-kayf*). This knowledge is not separate (*tafarrada*) from God, for there is no ontological degree (*ḥadd*) between God and His knowledge. He created (*ansha'a*) what He wanted to create through this knowledge, and this creation (*inshā'*) became a source (*ʿayn*) establishing (*ʿarasha*) all things <in their definition>.[37] It contained the definitions (*ḥudūd*) [of all beings]: their locations (*amkina*), their modality (*kayfūfiyya*), their spatiality (*aynūniyya*); **[46]** the disjunction and conjunction (*al-faṣl wa'l-waṣl*), the union and separation (*al-fatq wa'l-ratq*); the resemblance [of things] (*tashābuhuhā*) and their [particular]

[35] The Arabic is particularly convoluted here: *lammā kāna mā kāna mimman yadull ʿalyahi min qurābātihi fī ḥayātihi wa-min baʿd wafātihi*. My translation attempts to convey the apparent general meaning.

[36] Both Halm and Marquet read *ʿalam*, 'sign' or 'symbol', instead of *ʿilm*; see H. Halm, *Kosmologie*, p. 39; Y. Marquet, 'Quelques remarques à propos de *Kosmologie und Heilslehre der frühen Ismāʿīlīya* de Heinz Halm', *Studia Islamica*, 55 (1982), p. 117, and below, p. 195, n. 82. 182 ff.

[37] Mss. A, B: *waḥdahu*. Corrected to: *bi-ḥaddihi*, after Idrīs ʿImād al-Dīn's *Zahr al-maʿānī*, p. 129.

luminosities (*nayyirātuhā*), their signs (*aʿlāmuhā*), their decrees (*aḥkāmuhā*), their determination (*ithbātuhā*), their fixation (*maḍrūbuhā*), their manifestation and concealment (*ẓūhūruhā wa-buṭūnuhā*); all this is designed and established (*marsūm maʿrūsh*). <He built>[38] *'His Throne upon the water'* [Q. 11:7], and He established (*ʿarasha*) there the terms (*ajal*), definitions (*ḥadd*) and modalities (*kayfiyya*) of all things. This is [the meaning of] His words: *'Lord of the Sublime Throne'* [Q. 9:129].

19. And from one perspective (*fī makān*), the Sublime Throne is so, and from [another] perspective, it is the mysterious attribute (*al-ṣifa al-ghāʾiba*) that the describers (*al-wāṣifūn*)[39] cannot describe, although they are the most deserving (*al-mustaḥiqqūn*) and are specially assigned to this Throne. For this reason, [the Throne] is named the unknowable Mystery (*al-ghayb al-ghāʾib*), because each thing that has been created before another is an unknowable Mystery to this thing that was created after it. And God is the most knowledgeable about all this.

20. We know indeed that the human being is not able to describe the modality (*kayfūfiyya*) of [the presence of] his soul in the body (*al-jirm*). Similarly, no Mystery that God brings about (*aṭlaʿahu*) from His Mystery can describe the Mysteries that precede it.[40] Similarly, the

---

[38] Mss. A, B: *fī-nā* ('in us'). Corrected to: *fa-banā*, after Strothmann's suggestion in note 3. Halm follows this reading; H. Halm, *Kosmologie*, p. 39. See also Idrīs ʿImād al-Dīn's *Zahr al-maʿānī*, p. 130.

[39] The use of this term is confusing. Given the polemical stance against anthropomorphism in the previous pages, one might be tempted to understand *wāṣifūn* as a synonym for 'assimilationists' (*mushabbihūn*). Yet, what follows states that it designates the *mustaḥiqqūn*, the 'deserving' specially assigned to the Throne, without further explanation. It is likely that these 'deserving' are the eight angels specially assigned to carry the Throne according to Q. 69:17, but the use of *wāṣifūn* to designate them remains obscure and rather unusual. For an Ismaili interpretation of this verse and the symbolism of number eight, see al-Sijistānī, *Al-Maqālīd al-malakūtiyya*, 62nd *iqlīd*, pp. 290–294.

[40] Mss. A, B: *qablahā*. Corrected to *qablahu* (i.e. *al-ghayb*), after Idrīs ʿImād al-Dīn's *Zahr al-maʿānī*, p. 130. Marquet translates quite differently, reading *iṭṭalaʿahu* instead of *aṭlaʿahu*: 'Tout inconnaissable auquel Dieu a fait connaître [un peu] de son inconnaissable ne peut décrire les inconnaissables qui l'ont précédé'; Y. Marquet, 'Quelques remarques . . .', p. 118. See Idrīs ʿImād al-Dīn's *Zahr al-maʿānī*, p. 130, which reads *khalaqahu* instead of *aṭlaʿahu*.

Mysteries cannot describe their Mothers (*ummahāt*) that precede them. Similarly, the Mothers of the Mysteries cannot describe <their Lord, because>[41] they were not, and He then brought them into being (*lam takun fa-kawwanahā*). He knew [these realities] before their creation (*insha'ihā*); [otherwise], how could He[42] describe something that was not before He brought [the Mysteries] preceding it into being (*kawwana*)? The anthropomorphists (*mushabbihūn*) have therefore associated [something to God] by attributing (*nasabū*) to God that of which they have no knowledge. **[47]** And God has not sent down a power (*sulṭān*) upon them without saying: '*There is no God but Me, so worship Me*' [Q. 21:25].

[The alphabetic cosmogony]

21. When God established (*'arasha*) His Throne with His power (*qudra*), and separated these pillars at the basis of His Throne (*fataqa hadhihi al-arkān fī asās 'arshihi*) — [pillars] which are preceded [by the Throne] in [God's] ontological knowledge that precedes the [creation of a] being (*alladhī sabaqahā bi'l-'ilm al-kā'in alladhī fī-hi sabaqa al-kā'in*) — there were two Gates to this Throne. The first Gate is His Throne [itself], and He established (*'arasha*) these degrees (*ḥudūd*) in it, naming it 'Throne', and 'unknowable Mystery' (*ghayb ghā'ib*). And the second Gate is the one that God established (*aqāma*)[43] — may He be exalted — for this Throne, and in which He hid (*asarra*) the knowledge of the exoteric (*'ilm al-ẓāhir*), naming it 'Footstool'.

22. The Exalted said: '*His Footstool encompasses the heavens and earth and maintaining them does not fatigue him, and he is the High, the Glorious*' [Q. 2:255]. God appointed His flowing ontological degree (*ḥaddahu al-jārī*)[44] in the Gate of the Throne as an axis (*quṭb*), and He

[41] Mss. A, B: *bi-hā annahā*. Corrected to: *rabbahā li'annahā*, after Idrīs 'Imād al-Dīn's *Zahr al-ma'ānī*, p. 130.

[42] Strothmann believes this refers to the human being (note 5), but for Y. Marquet, 'Quelques remarques . . .', p. 118, it is God. I incline towards the latter's understanding.

[43] Mss. A, B: *wa-huwa al-bāb al-thānī alladhī aqāmahu Allāh*. Corrected to: *wa'l-bāb al-thānī huwa alladhī aqāmahu Allāh*, following Halm's suggestion in H. Halm, *Kosmologie*, p. 40, n. 20.

[44] On this technical term, see commentary of *Kashf* II, p. 198.

charged it with (*aqāma ʿalayhi*) everything He had created (*ansha'a*) in the Throne. He then gave it permission and the flowing axis (*al-quṭb al-jarī*) flowed unto the second Gate which is named the Footstool, and which contains the knowledge of every manifest being (*kull shay' kā'in lam yaghib*).[45] He placed in it the preservation of everything. When the axis had flowed unto the Gate of the Footstool, God made it into twenty-eight letters, through seven degrees (*ḥudūd*). God then named these twenty-eight letters by their names. He thus named the first degree [of the letters] (*awwal ḥadd minhā*): *alif*, then *bā'*, then *tā'*, then *thā'*, then *jīm*, then *ḥā'*, then *khā'*.

ا ب ت ث ج ح خ

He thus named these letters by these names. Out of these twenty-eight, He appointed seven Gates and named them 'signs' (*simāt*), gathering therein sixteen letters. These seven <became>[46] **[48]** Mothers (*ummahāt*) because the [other] degrees [came out] of them (*fa-minhā al-ḥudūd*). 'Signs' (*simāt*) mean the diacritics (*ʿajamiyyāt*). When these seven — *alif, bā', tā', thā', jīm, ḥā', khā'* — are spelled (*hujiyat*), one obtains sixteen letters.[47] As for the *sīn*, it the name of the Footstool, and the *shīn* is the name of the Throne.[48] He also made seven [other] letters containing the remaining letters — that is, the letters apart from the *sīn* and the *shīn*, and apart from those included in the previous

---

[45] The Footstool contains the principles of the beings below it, in contrast with the Throne, which contains the 'mysterious' principles, that is, spiritual and not accessible to human perception.

[46] Ms. A: *faṭarat*; ms. B: *fa-ṭaraba*. Corrected to: *fa-ṣārat*, following Strothmann in his table of errors.

[47] The technique here consists in drawing new letters from other letters by spelling the latter. For example, we obtain two new letters from the name of the first letter, the ا, called *alif* (ألف, ALF), namely the *lām* (ل, L) and the *fā'* (ف, F). Here, however, the calculation according to which sixteen letters are obtained by spelling the first seven letters of the alphabet is incorrect. To reach this number, one is to add the letters *sīn, shīn, nūn, wāw, hā'* — which are discussed independently in the following lines — to the first seven letters, and the four that we obtain when spelling these seven: *fā', lām, mīm, yā'*.

[48] The likely reason for this is that the name of the Footstool (*kursī*) contains the letter *sīn*, while the name of the Throne (*ʿarsh*) contains the letter *shīn*.

sixteen letters.[49] These remaining letters are twelve: *dāl*, *ḏāl*, *rā'*, *zāy*, *ṣād*, *ḍād*, *ṭā'*, *ẓā'*, *'ayn*, *ghayn*, *fā'*, *qāf*, *kāf*.[50]

د ر ص ط ع ف

ذ ز ض ظ غ ق ك

These letters are marked with seven signs (*simāt*),[51] that is, the diacritic points (*'ajamiyyāt*) on the letters with diacritics (*mu'jamāt*). These [seven signs] are an indication of the seven that gather the letters remaining after the first seven and [the letters] they gather. There is no additional letter in these twelve [letters] because [the letters] added when they are spelled had already been obtained by the spelling of the previous seven, and they are thus included within the [group of] sixteen.

23. As for the *nūn* and the *wāw*, they are obtained by spelling the *sīn* and the *shīn*, as well as by the spelling **[49]** of <the letters of both (*ḥurūfihimā*)>.[52] All that remains is the *hā'* alone, which is in the name of God — He is Mighty and Sublime. When someone utters the name of God — He is Mighty and Sublime, it is not apparent that he means God until he pronounces the *hā'*. If he does not, it is not apparent that he means the name of God.[53] Indeed, [the *hā'*] is the terminus (*ghāya*) of the letters forming God's name, just as God — He is Mighty and Sublime — is the terminus of what His creation can know from all that

---

[49] The formulation is confusing since it can lead the reader to think that the *sīn* and the *shīn* are not part of the group of sixteen letters — but they necessarily are; see above, p. 181, n. 47 and commentary of *Kashf* II, p. 199.

[50] As we can see, this is, again, erroneous: thirteen letters have been enumerated.

[51] There are in fact only eight diacritic points — unless the *fā'* is removed?

[52] The *nūn* (نون, *n-w-n*) is obtained by spelling the *sīn* (سين, *s-y-n*) and the *shīn* (شين, *sh-y-n*), and the *wāw* is obtained by spelling the *nūn*. Spelling the *wāw* therefore does not provide any new letter, and *ḥurūfihimā* is therefore incorrect.

[53] Before the *hā'* is pronounced, the name Allāh (*a-l-l-h*) could form the beginning of a word starting with the letter *lām* and preceded by the definite article *al-*. The idea that the *hā'* determines the name of God is also found in al-Sijistānī, *Kitāb al-Yanābī'*, in *Trilogie ismaélienne*, ed. H. Corbin (Tehran, 1961), p. 10: 'The word 'Allāh' assumes its definitive form (*istaqarra*) with the letter *hā*"; English trans.: P. Walker, *The Wellsprings of Wisdom. A Study of Abū Ya'qūb al-Sijistānī's Kitāb al-Yanābī'* (Salt Lake City, 1994), p. 46.

He created. The *hā'* is therefore an indication of Him — may His name be blessed and exalted be His glory.

24. The first seven letters indicate the seven Speaking-Prophets, and the last seven indicate the seven Imams, because they contain all the letters (*tamām al-ḥurūf*), just as the Imams contain all of the affairs (*tamām umūr*) of the Messengers and the Speaking Prophets — may God's blessings be upon them all. Thus do the sixteen and the twelve complete the twenty-eight letters, including the indication of the Throne, the Footstool, and God, who created all things.

25. When these letters were gathered together — and they are degrees within the seven degrees (*hiya ḥudūd fi'l-ḥudūd al-sab'a*) — He named them the Gate of the Marked Table (*al-raqīm*),[54] which is **[50]** *'the Marked (marqūm) Book contemplated by those brought nigh (al-muqarrabūn)'* [Q. 83:20–21], to whom God has reserved the inheritance (*al-wirātha*). These are the chosen ones (*al-muntajabūn*) from amongst the inhabitants of the heavens and the earth. The inheritance is the Sublime Kingdom, of which God — He is Mighty and Sublime — said: *'We gave the people of Abraham the Book and the Wisdom, and We gave them a Sublime Kingdom'* [Q. 4:54]. The Sublime Kingdom is the inheritance by which God has elected them — as He said: *'Solomon inherited from David'* [Q. 27:16]. And God has transferred the inheritance from Abraham and the family of Abraham, to Muḥammad and the family of Muḥammad — peace be upon them; [and] that included *'the Marked (marqūm) Book contemplated by those brought nigh'*. It is a favour by which God has favoured them over the universes, and this is the Sublime Kingdom. **[51]**

[54] Mss. A, B: *al-raqam*. Corrected following Strothmann's correction in the table of errors to his edition; see above *Kashf* II p. 42, § 7, and relevant footnote.

Treatise II Commentary

Treatise II shares with the first the characteristic of being a compilation of several texts gathered by an editor whose intervention is manifest, although it is not always quite legible, partly due to the corruption of the transmitted text. However, it is much shorter than the first treatise, and it is therefore composed of fewer textual units. Two of these, which make up the first two parts of the treatise, are relatively long *ḥadīths* that have also been transmitted in the Twelver Shiʿi tradition, since almost identical versions of them are found in works by al-Kulaynī and Ibn Bābawayh, as I have shown elsewhere.[55] However, it is unlikely that the *Kashf* drew from these works, as I argue that, for the most part, the *Kashf* is to be dated slightly earlier. As for the third part of Treatise II, it is mainly composed of an alphabetical cosmogony. This part of the treatise was studied by Heinz Halm in his *Kosmologie und Heilslehre der frühen Ismāʿīlīya.*

The author of Treatise II did not confine himself to reproducing these two *ḥadīths* which form about two thirds of the treatise. It is not implausible that he only reproduced the third part, rather than composing it himself. Yet, even if this were the case, his contribution remains visible in his effort to articulate these three textual units (the two *ḥadīths* and the alphabetical speculations) by adding comments in between. Furthermore, the very composition of the treatise reveals an intention to provide a doctrinal presentation on ontology and cosmology. Indeed, the treatise reads very straightforwardly as a progression down the ladder of being, from the unknowable Essence of God, through the two intermediary hypostases that are the Throne and the Footstool, to the alphabet which symbolically rules the cosmos and corresponds to the Speaking-Prophets and the Imams.

[55] See F. Gillon, 'Une version ismaélienne'.

The tone and the vocabulary of this treatise thus totally differ from those found in Treatise I. Indeed, while the latter was at odds with the *ghulāt* tendencies of its contents and tried to attenuate them, Treatise II is completely free of anything reminiscent of the *ghulāt*. In fact, it seems in line with the opposite tradition, since the quoted *ḥadīth*s clearly insist on God's absolute transcendence and harshly condemn anthropomorphism. While these orientations are to be understood as the expression of the 'moderate' Shiʿi leanings towards Muʿtazili positions in the face of the 'Sunni' anthropomorphists (*mushabbiha*), one may wonder whether they could have also been used for polemical purposes against *ghulāt* doctrines divinizing the Imam — precisely those doctrines that Treatise I echoed while moderating them at the same time.

1. Divine transcendence

The first part of the treatise, which corresponds to the first quoted *ḥadīth*, consists of a series of negations, aiming to establish the divine transcendence through an apophatic approach. It is a question of rejecting any subordination of God to creation: creation is an act of God's absolute freedom, it involves no necessity. God is not linked to creation, but rather, everything in existence must be referred to God for its existence. This idea is particularly apparent in the statement according to which God is king even before establishing a kingdom, or in the affirmation that the act of creation does not add anything to or take away anything from God.

As found in the *Kitāb al-Kashf*, there is no indication that this text is a *ḥadīth*: it does not include a chain of transmission (*isnād*), nor does it contain any evidence suggesting a dialogue between an Imam and his disciple. Yet, it is transmitted as such by al-Kulaynī and Ibn Bābawayh, each of these compilers transmitting two versions of it of differing lengths.

The two long versions, which correspond to the entire first part of the treatise (besides the inserted passage on the divine names and attributes), are both attributed to Imam Muḥammad al-Bāqir, and they both appear, among other *ḥadīth*s, in chapters devoted to the incompatibility of spatiality with divine transcendence. Thus, al-Kulaynī's version is found in a chapter of the *Uṣūl al-Kafī* dealing with 'being and space' (*al-kawn wa'l-makān*),[56] while Ibn Bābawayh's version appears in the chapter of his *Kitāb al-Tawḥīd* entitled: 'On the negation of God's spatiality, temporality, stillness, motion, descent, ascent and change of position' (*nafī al-makān wa'l-zamān wa'l-sukūn wa'l-ḥaraka wa'l-nuzūl wa'l-ṣuʿūd wa'l-intiqāl ʿan Allāh*).[57] Both of these chapters open with a similar short *hadīth* in which a man asks Muḥammad al-Bāqir: 'Tell me, when did God come to be?' (*akhbirnī ʿan Allāh matā kāna*), and is met with the reply: 'When was He not, so that I may tell you when He came to be?' (*matā lam yakun ḥattā ukhbiraka matā kāna*).[58]

The other *hadīths* in these chapters are generally based on this kind of rhetoric by which erroneous — i.e. anthropomorphic or assimilationist — representations of God are answered with proclamations of God's absolute transcendence. There is no referent, model or superior instance from which God would derive all or part of His being, since He is the origin of all things: God is not subject to time, space, movement, etc., since He is the one who created time, space, movement, etc. It is the meaning of the first lines of the *ḥadīth* that interests us here, which are omitted in the *Kashf* and in the two short versions, but are found almost identically in the two long versions:

> 'A man came to Abū Jaʿfar and asked him: "Tell me, when did your Lord come to be?" He replied: "Beware! It is only of a thing that was not [then came to be] that one can ask when it came to be, but my Lord — blessed and exalted be He — was and remains alive without a 'how', etc."'[59]

As for the two short versions, they are attributed to different Imams and appear in very different contexts. In al-Kulaynī's version, it appears

[56] Al-Kulaynī, *Uṣūl al-Kāfī, kitāb al-tawḥīd, bāb al-kawn wa'l-makān*, vol. 1, pp. 88–90. The *ḥadīth* under discussion is pp. 88–89, no. 3.

[57] Ibn Bābawayh, *Kitāb al-Tawḥīd, bāb* 28, pp. 173–184; the *ḥadīth* that compares with the *Kashf* is pp. 173–174, no. 2.

[58] Al-Kulaynī, *Uṣūl al-Kāfī*, vol. 1, p. 88, no. 1; Ibn Bābawayh, *Kitāb al-Tawḥīd, bāb* 28, p. 173, no.1.

[59] Al-Kulaynī, *Uṣūl al-Kāfī*, vol. 1, p. 88; Ibn Bābawayh, *Kitāb al-Tawḥīd*, p. 173. The section between brackets appears only in Ibn Bābawayh's version.

at the beginning of a mystical sermon attributed to ʿAlī b. Abī Ṭālib, the *khuṭba al-ṭālūtiyya.*[60] The version transmitted by Ibn Bābawayh appears once again in his *Kitāb al-Tawḥīd*, in a chapter dedicated to the 'attributes of the [divine] Essence and the attributes of the [divine] acts' (*ṣifāt al-dhāt wa-ṣifāt al-afʿāl*). It forms the content of a *ḥadīth* attributed to Mūsā al-Kāẓim.[61] The fact that al-Kulaynī and Ibn Bābawayh attribute the shorter version to different Imams may indicate that the shorter versions are simply incomplete versions of an original *ḥadīth* — corresponding to the longer versions, or to their source.

The version found in the *Kashf* is closer to these longer versions, if only by its length. It should be noted, however, that it contains at least two elements that are specific to the short versions. In the *Kashf*, the first lines of the text are thus closer to the short versions than to the long versions, since the latter do not contain the sentence: 'There is no god but Him' — nor the eulogy 'Praise be to God', found only in al-Kulaynī's short version.

Further on, the *Kashf* states: 'He does not harken to any summons (*daʿwa*), but on the contrary, it is all things that harken to His summons.'[62] Here, all five versions of the *ḥadīth* diverge, and it is only the short version reported by Ibn Bābawayh that contains the key term *daʿwa*.[63] In the absence of other versions of the *ḥadīth*, however, these elements are quite meagre. It appears nonetheless that the *Kashf* is an important piece in the perspective of a study of this *ḥadīth* and its transmission.

In the *Kitāb al-Kashf*, the *ḥadīth* is cut in two, precisely where the short version of Ibn Bābawayh ends — al-Kulaynī's ends several lines before — with a passage[64] that seems inserted ad hoc by the author-editor of the treatise, since it is not found in the Twelver Shiʿi versions of the text. This passage can be divided into two thematic parts. In the

---

[60] Al-Kulaynī, *al-Rawḍa min al-Kāfī, khuṭbat al-ṭālūtiyya*, p. 31.

[61] Ibn Bābawayh, *Kitāb al-Tawḥīd*, *bāb* 11, pp. 141–142, no. 6. The *isnād* of this *ḥadīth* only has one name in common with the *isnād* Ibn Bābawayh provides for the longer version.

[62] *Kashf* II, p. 40, § 2.

[63] See F. Gillon, 'Une version ismaélienne', p. 496.

[64] *Kashf* II, p. 41, §§ 4–5.

first, the author articulates the Qur'anic notions of divine knowledge (*'ilm*) and power (*qudra*), the latter expressing the former. This short paragraph echoes another passage found further in the third part of the treatise, where the divine knowledge is actualized by the divine omnipotence in order to create beings.[65]

That knowledge precedes power is a way to preserve the transcendence of God, and to free Him from all dependence on creatures: God does not know beings *a posteriori*, His knowledge embraces the 'fait accompli', so to say, but it is on the contrary according to the knowledge that He had of them *a priori* that they are created. The creation of beings unfolds according to a pre-existing model.

The second part of the passage inserted in the *ḥadīth* is very convoluted. The author seems to establish a hierarchy amongst different expressions of worship and divine names. Unfortunately, the text is corrupted, and the doctrinal content assigned to each of the attributes is not explained. As a result, the theological implications of this paragraph are unclear. The intention behind the insertion of this short development remains arcane — but it should be noted that it was inserted precisely where the short version of Ibn Bābawayh ends. Insofar as the Qur'anic notion of *ṣamad* (Q. 112:2) is discussed there, it is perhaps necessary to compare this passage with the *ḥadīth* quoted in Treatise IV of the *Kashf*. In fact, there seems to be more than one link between Treatises II and IV: in addition to this notion of *ṣamad*, Treatise IV contains a brief quotation from the first *ḥadīth* of Treatise II, and it is the only other treatise of the collection to mention an 'alphabetical' creation.

At the end of the first *ḥadīth*, a paragraph is used as a transition to the second *ḥadīth*. The editor conveniently uses a fragment of the famous Throne Verse (Q.2:255) which concludes the first *ḥadīth* ('*Slumber seizes Him not, nor sleep*') to introduce the second one which deals precisely with the Throne and the Footstool. Anticipating this second *ḥadīth*, the author declares that the Footstool corresponds to 'the manifest part of the Mysteries'.

---

[65] Ibid., p. 47, § 17.

In his quotation of *Kashf* II, Idrīs ʿImād al-Dīn adds that the Footstool, identified with *al-raqīm*, corresponds to ʿAlī, and a few lines further he identifies the Throne with Muḥammad.[66] This is missing completely in the *Kashf*, but provides an additional reading key to interpret the roles of the Throne and the Footstool as spiritual entities corresponding to the Messenger and the Legatee, respectively.

2. The Throne, the Footstool and the problem of anthropomorphism

The second *ḥadīth* of Treatise II is slightly longer than the first. Here, too, the *Kashf* does not present it as a *ḥadīth*, although it contains elements of a dialogue between a master and a disciple. It is via an external source that I was able to identify it as a *ḥadīth*, since it is transmitted by Ibn Bābawayh in his *Kitāb al-Tawḥīd* — and nowhere else to the best of my knowledge. Chapter 50 of this source corresponds in its entirety to the second part of Treatise II[67] — although the converse is not true, since the *Kashf* adds a paragraph that Ibn Bābawayh does not transmit.

The text is slightly unusual for a *ḥadīth* from a formal point of view. It is relatively long and the argument is more reminiscent of a brief treatise or speech, rather than a *ḥadīth* devoted to a particular theme in response to a question. Although the version reported by Ibn Bābawayh contains a question (absent from the *Kashf*), it remains quite vague: 'I interrogated Abū ʿAbdallāh [Jaʿfar al-Ṣādiq] about the Throne and the Footstool.'[68] It would seem that this question is in fact an addition aimed at introducing the following text and giving it the formal appearance of a *ḥadīth*.

The text itself, although it deals indeed with the notions of Throne and Footstool, suddenly takes a turn when it engages in a condemnation of anthropomorphic representations of God, before weaving a link between these cognitive errors and the refusal to follow the Imams. It then concludes with the mission of Muḥammad and the explicit

---

[66] Idrīs ʿImād al-Dīn, *Zahr al-maʿānī*, p. 128.

[67] *Kashf* II, pp. 42–46, §§ 8–17.

[68] Ibn Bābawayh, *Kitāb al-Tawḥīd*, *bāb* 50, p. 323.

designation of his successor. It is therefore not only about the 'Throne and its attributes', contrary to what the title of the chapter indicates in the *Kitāb al-Tawḥīd*, this theme being the subject of only the first half of the *ḥadīth*. There is of course a direct link between the first and second half of the text, since the discussions on the Throne and the Footstool were at the heart of Islamic debates on the nature of God and His attributes, partly prompted by apparently anthropomorphic verses such as Q. 20:5: '*The Merciful sat Himself upon the Throne*' — quoted in the *ḥadīth*.[69] This text is therefore a concise contribution on an ongoing Islamic debate from a Shiʿi perspective. The Shiʿi take on the matter of anthropomorphism thus tends towards a symbolic and cosmological understanding of the Throne and the Footstool. The text also implies that these debates would not take place if the community were to follow the Imams — rather than their passions and personal opinions.

In the first part of the *ḥadīth*, the Throne and the Footstool are conceived of as two celestial entities through which God governs 'the Kingdom', that is to say, all beings. Their spiritual nature is expressed through the Qur'anic notion of *ghayb*, or 'mystery', which designates the invisible and spiritual worlds, as opposed to the material and physical world. The Throne is described as the 'esoteric gate' of the *ghayb*, while the Footstool is the 'exoteric gate'. Unfortunately, the characteristics of neither hypostasis are clearly defined; they are only listed, without being commented on. Moreover, these characters differ in the *Kitāb al-Kashf* and in the *Kitāb al-Tawḥīd*, since 'the attribute of the Will, the knowledge of words and vowels and its explanation, the knowledge of the Return and the Origin', are attributed to the Footstool by the former, and to the Throne by the latter. While one cannot deduce from these contradictory statements a coherent theological doctrine, one nevertheless understands that it is a question of distinguishing two spiritual hypostatic levels, as in the ancient Ismaili

[69] *Kashf* II, p. 42, § 8; Ibn Bābawayh, *Kitāb al-Tawḥīd*, p. 323. There are several studies on the Islamic debates on anthropomorphism; see e.g. J. Van Ess, 'Tashbīh wa-tanzīh', *EI2*; idem, *Theology and Society*, vol. 4, pp. 403–514; D. Gimaret, *Dieu à l'image de l'homme Les anthropomorphismes de la* sunna *et leur interprétation par les théologiens* (Paris, 1997); L. Holtzman, 'Anthropomorphism', *EI3*.

speculations on Kūnī and Qadar,[70] or the 'Precedent' (*al-sābiq*) and the 'Follower' (*al-tālī*), which in turn are respectively identified with the Universal Intellect and Universal Soul in the Neoplatonic system as adapted and integrated into Ismailism by authors such as Abū Ya'qūb al-Sijistānī. The latter gives the Intellect and the Soul several other names, among which we find the Throne and the Footstool, but according to an order opposite to that of Treatise II: in his *Kitāb al-Iftikhār*, al-Sijistānī thus names the Intellect *kursī*, while the Soul corresponds to the *'arsh*.[71] In another text, he names the Intellect *'arsh*, but the Soul is then called *mulk*, 'kingdom'.[72]

Q. 21:22: *'Exalted be He, Lord of the Throne, above what they attribute to Him'*, then serves a pivotal function between the two parts of the *ḥadīth*, since it combines a mention of the Throne and a scriptural basis for the refutation of anthropomorphism, the latter theme forming the topic of the second part of the *ḥadīth*.

The rest of this section tackles the rejection of anthropomorphism by commenting on two scriptural quotations. The first of these is

---

[70] On Kūnī and Qadar, see Abū 'Īsā al-Murshid, *Risāla*, in S.M. Stern, 'The earliest cosmological doctrines of Ismā'īlism'; al-Sijistānī, *Kitāb al-Iftikhār*, Ch. 5, pp. 123–137. See also H. Halm, *Kosmologie*, pp. 53–66; idem, 'The Cosmology of the Pre-Fatimid Ismā'īliyya'; D. De Smet, *La philosophie ismaélienne*, pp. 65–70; M. De Cillis, *Salvation and Destiny in Islam, The Shi'i Ismaili Perspective of Ḥamīd al-Dīn al-Kirmānī* (London and New York, 2018), pp. 112–120. The latter study is dedicated to the notions of *qaḍā'* and *qadar*, respectively identified with the Intellect and the Soul, in al-Kirmānī's *Kitāb al-Riyāḍ*.

[71] Al-Sijistānī, *Kitāb al-Iftikhār*, Ch. 3, pp. 108–115. Note that in his abovementioned *Risāla*, Abū 'Īsā al-Murshid does not consider the Throne and the Footstool as equivalents of the 'First' and the 'Second', or the 'Precedent' and the 'Follower'. Instead, they are identified, respectively, with 'air' and 'water' and both emanate from the 'Follower'; see Abū 'Īsā al-Murshid, *Risāla*, in S.M. Stern, 'The earliest cosmological doctrines of Ismā'īlism', pp. 9, 22–23. Al-Kirmānī also seems to place the Throne and the Footstool in the 'world of nature' (*'ālam al-ṭabī'a*), where they govern the celestial spheres (*aflāk*); see Ḥamīd al-Dīn al-Kirmānī, *Rāḥat al-'aql*, ed. M. Kāmil Ḥusayn and M. Muṣṭafā Ḥilmī, pp. 163–181; ed. M. Ghālib, pp. 295–305.

[72] Al-Sijistānī, *Tuḥfat al-mustajībīn*, pp. 13–14. This divergence in the use of technical terms is one possible reason for questioning the *Tuḥfat*'s authenticity. Paul Walker suggests it might be a later Nizārī composition; see P. Walker, *Early Philosophical Shiism*, p. 165, n. 79. Notwithstanding the discrepancies with the Sijistānian doctrine noted by Walker, the text remains useful as a summary of al-Sijistānī's cosmology.

Q. 5:64, which rejects an assertion by the Jews who allegedly claim that God's hands are 'fettered', and affirms, on the contrary, that they are wide open. Therefore, the Qur'an does not reject the idea that God has hands, although this must probably be understood in a metaphorical sense, but the idea that they would be 'fettered', that is, either that they are powerless, or that they lack generosity as the continuation of the verse seems to indicate: *'He lavishes (yunfiqu) on His Will.'* Yet, the *ḥadīth* makes the verse about the attribution of hands to God and about the question of anthropomorphism, which is clearly a twist of the Qur'anic text, made possible by the fact that the quotation from the verse is truncated and that the statement: *'On the contrary, His hands are wide open'*, does not appear there.

A brief passage from the epistle of Abū ʿĪsā al-Murshid, a Fatimid author writing under the authority of al-Muʿizz (r. 341–365/953–975), cites this same verse in full in a context of rejection of anthropomorphism ('assimilation (*tashbīh*) of creatures to the Creator'). The text is not quite explicit, Abū ʿĪsā merely indicating that the two hands in question are an allusion 'to the First and the Second',[73] that is, Kūnī and Qadar, which, in the *Kashf* and in the *Kitāb al-Tawḥīd*, correspond to the Throne and the Footstool. Abū ʿĪsā's interpretation of the verse represents a slight shift in its understanding, since anthropomorphism no longer consists in assigning hands to God per se, but in not giving these 'hands' a metaphoric meaning.[74]

The second scriptural source discussed in the context of the refutation of anthropomorphism is a very famous *ḥadīth*, in which the Prophet Muḥammad reported his vision of God 'in the most beautiful form' and felt 'the freshness of the fingers *(anāmil)*' of God — or His 'palm' in alternative versions.[75] This *ḥadīth* is a topos of the discussions

---

[73] S.M. Stern, 'The Earliest Cosmological Doctrines of Ismāʿīlism', p. 10.

[74] A similar approach to that of this verse can be found in another chapter of Ibn Bābawayh, *Kitāb al-Tawḥīd, bāb* 25, pp. 167–168. For another Ismaili interpretation of Q. 5:64, yet unrelated to the matter of anthropomorphism, see Idrīs ʿImād al-Dīn, *Zahr al-maʿānī*, p. 132.

[75] See Ibn Ḥanbal, *Musnad al-imām* (Cairo, 1313 [1895]), vol. 1, p. 368; vol. 4, p. 66; vol. 5, p. 243. The *Kashf* and the *Tawḥīd* only allude to the part mentioning the 'fingertips'; see *Kashf* II, p. 44, § 13; Ibn Bābawayh, *Kitāb al-Tawḥīd*, p. 323.

on anthropomorphism.[76] Al-Shahrastānī quotes it among the expressions that 'anthropomorphists' (*mushabbiha*) understand literally in the chapter of his *al-Milal wa'l-niḥal* dedicated to the *ṣifātiyya* ('attributionists').[77] The latter, he says, 'did not distinguish between the attributes of the essence and the attributes of the act' and 'affirmed attributes from the scripture (*ṣifāt khabariyya*) such as the Hands, the Face, without interpreting them metaphorically (*lā yu'awwilūn dhālik*)'[78] — as opposed to the Muʿtazilites. Thus, the Shiʿi and Ismaili affirmation of God's absolute transcendence, and the refutation of the literalism and anthropomorphism it entails, both lean towards the Muʿtazili side of the debate. Although according to al-Shahrastānī, the great representative of the *ṣifātiyya* is al-Ashʿarī, it seems that there was another target to the refutations of anthropomorphism. Indeed, al-Shahrastānī indicates that the promoters of *tashbīh* were not only what he calls the *ḥashwiyya*, that is the Sunni traditionists, but also 'a group of exaggerating Shiʿis' (*jamāʿa min al-shīʿa al-ghāliya*).[79] The Ismailis seem to have opted for the symbolic approach on this point, thus setting themselves equidistantly from the rationalistic, metaphorical, approach of the muʿtazilites and the anthropomorphist approach of both the *ghulāt* and the Sunni traditionists. Indeed, the relevance of the *ḥadīth* found in the *Kashf* may not have been the same for the author of the *Kashf* and for Ibn Bābawayh. While the latter is in line with the adoption of rationalism by 'moderate' Shiʿism, thus understanding the anthropomorphic attributes of God as metaphors, the Ismailis seem to have taken the metaphorical approach further: the names and attributes do not stand

[76] For different versions of this *ḥadīth* and its relation to the debate on anthropomorphism, see D. Gimaret, *Dieu à l'image de l'homme*, pp. 143–153.

[77] Shahrastānī, *Kitāb al-Milal wa'l-niḥal, Book of Religious and Philosophical Sects*, ed. William Cureton (London, 1846), vol. 1, pp. 77–78.

[78] Shahrastānī, *Kitāb al-Milal wa'l-niḥal*, vol. 1, p. 64; idem, Le *Livre des Religions et des Sectes*, intro. and French trans. annotated by Daniel Gimaret and Guy Monnot (Louvain, 1986), vol. 1, pp. 308–309.

[79] Shahrastānī, Kitāb al-Milal wa'l-niḥal, vol. 1, p. 76; cited in B. Abrahamov, *Anthropomorphism and Interpretation of the Qur'ān in the Theology of al-Qāsim ibn Ibrāhīm. Kitāb al-Mustarshid*, edited with Translation, Introduction and Notes (Leiden, 1996), p. 3. See also ibid., pp. 1–8 for an overview of the Islamic debates on anthropomorphism.

for God's powers, but they are symbols of ontological realities or ranks of the *da'wa*.

This approach is illustrated by a Ṭayyibī Ismaili text edited by R. Strothmann, where the *ḥadīth* of the fingers *(anāmil)*' is briefly interpreted. The version provided here is slightly different from Ibn Ḥanbal's: 'The Almighty (*jabbār*) put His fingers (*anāmil*) on my back, and I felt their freshness in my body.' Contrary to the *ḥadīth* quoted in the *Kashf* and the *Kitāb al-Tawḥīd*, the anonymous author of this work does not reject the *ḥadīth* altogether, but rather gives it a symbolic scope allowing it to be removed from its apparent anthropomorphism. Thus, the *jabbār*, which is usually one of the names of God, is here interpreted as an allusion to Gabriel (*Jibrā'īl*), using a pun based on the root *j-b-r*. As for the *anāmil*, they actually refer to the 'intermediary ranks (*ḥudūd*)' between Gabriel and Muḥammad. The 'back' (*ẓahr*) is an allusion to the 'exoteric knowledge' (*'ilm al-ẓāhir*) to which Muḥammad was raised and by means of which he accessed the 'esoteric truths', thus finding the 'freshness of certainty in his heart'.[80]

At the end of the second *ḥadīth*, a correlation is established between the theological error of anthropomorphism and the fact of ignoring the Imams' guidance:

> '*They meddle with*' His names and '*His signs*' [Q. 6:68] without knowledge, considering them inadequately and deviating from them, in spite of the fact that God ordered them to take as kin (*aqwām*), friends (*awliyā'*) and Imams those whom He favoured and to whom He entrusted a knowledge He entrusted to no one else.'[81]

Inasmuch as the Imams are the custodians of a knowledge revealed by God, and even knowledge par excellence, any cognitive error must be linked to the refusal to take them as guides. Hence the last paragraph of the *ḥadīth* which evokes the succession of Muḥammad: the latter having expressly designated 'Alī as his successor, as the depositary of knowledge and of the 'Order', the refusal to follow him amounts to deviating from the truth, and to becoming entwined in erroneous

---

[80] *Sab' masā'il wa-ajwibatuhā*, in R. Strothmann, *Gnosis-Texte der Ismailiten*, p. 70.

[81] *Kashf* II, p. 45, § 15. This passage does not appear in the version of the *Kitāb al-Tawḥīd*.

theological opinions. Thus the magisterium of the Imams and their authority to intervene in the theological controversies which agitated the Islamic community in the 8th and 9th centuries are justified. Implicitly, the text seems to affirm that the knowledge given to ʿAlī gives Jaʿfar al-Ṣādiq (the alleged author of the second *ḥadīth*) a pre-eminence as regards the technical speculations of theology.

It is noteworthy that the penultimate paragraph of the *ḥadīth*, as reported by the *Kashf*, is found neither in the *Kitāb al-Tawḥīd*, nor, more surprisingly, in the *Zahr al-maʿānī* by Idrīs ʿImād al-Dīn, although the latter quotes in full a long passage from Treatise II. This means either that there existed another version of the *Kitāb al-Kashf*, or that the missing paragraph is a gloss of a later copyist. It is also possible that Idrīs ʿImād al-Dīn simply did not find it useful to copy this passage, but its absence from the *Kitāb al-Tawḥīd* as well remains a remarkable coincidence. The paragraph in question is unfortunately not very original, apart perhaps from a certain vehemence of its tone, since it identifies the enemies of the Imams and those who do not follow them with the Ṭāghūt.

3. The alphabetic cosmogony

Before the passage dealing with the alphabetical cosmogony proper, there is a short development supplementing the purpose of the above *ḥadīth*: it again evokes the Throne and the Footstool, and ends with a brief allusion to assimilationists. In the middle of the passage, it contains traces of an argument advocating the impossibility for a being to fully know and access the realities that precede it ontologically. As is the case throughout Treatise II, the corruption of the text and its allusiveness make it difficult to grasp the precise doctrine that is at play.

The first sentence of this passage states its intention, which is to go back to the origin of the Footstool: 'When God wanted to create a Kingdom, He wanted for it to be knowledge.'[82] The following sentences

---

[82] *Kashf* II, p. 46, § 18. The elusiveness of this sentence is probably what prompted the previous translators to read *ʿalam*, 'sign', instead of *ʿilm*, 'knowledge'; see H. Halm, *Kosmologie*, p. 39: 'Zeichen'; Y. Marquet, 'Quelques remarques . . .', p. 117: 'symbole'. However, this 'sign', or 'knowledge', is eventually identified with the Throne at the end of the paragraph (*Kashf* II, p. 47, § 17), the Throne itself having been identified with divine knowledge. Therefore, I see no reason to read *ʿalam* in this specific occurrence while all the other occurrences of the term are read *ʿilm*.

hint at two philosophical issues: on the one hand, the text emphasizes the fact that God's knowledge contain all beings, and that the latter's determinations are all established by virtue of this knowledge. On the other hand, the passage briefly deals with the relationship between God and the said knowledge: 'This knowledge is not isolated from God, and there is no ontological degree (*ḥadd*) between God and His knowledge.'[83] If the term 'knowledge' indeed refers to the Throne, that is, the first being, then this sentence is about the nature of the connection between God and the first being. Although the text does not elaborate further, this resonates with the philosophical speculations of the Persian *dāʿīs* and their debate on the status of God's command (*amr*) that brought the Intellect into existence. The problem was to preserve God's absolute transcendence, without considering him as the cause of beings, since a cause is necessarily coordinated to its effects.[84] Yet, God had to be the origin of being; so how was one to conceive of the relation between the Creator and the creation? Al-Sijistānī theorized the notion of God's command (*amr*) as an intermediary between the divine Essence and the first being.[85] In doing so, he only displaced the problem, since the same questions rose about the *amr*: was it part of God or part of the Intellect? It is because of these difficulties that al-Kirmānī later criticized al-Sijistānī's approach, particularly in his *Kitāb al-Riyāḍ*.[86]

The 'resonance' with the sentence of the *Kashf* cannot be considered more than just that at this point. The text is far too ellusive to draw any final conclusions. Yet, one might wonder whether in this case too, the author of Treatise II which offers several indirect parallels with the

[83] *Kashf* II, p. 46, § 18.

[84] See e.g. the chapter of al-Sijistānī's *Maqālīd* dedicated to the demonstration of this point, which is in line with Neoplatonic speculations: al-Sijistānī, *al-Maqālīd al-malakūtiyya*, 8th iqlīd, pp. 68–71.

[85] See e.g. al-Sijistānī, *Kitāb al-Yanābīʿ*, in *Trilogie ismaélienne*, pp. 16–17; idem, *Kitāb al-Iftikhār*, Ch. 2, pp. 100–107; idem, *al-Maqālīd al-malakūtiyya*, 19th *iqlīd*, pp. 111–114; 25th *iqlīd*, pp. 131–133; 28th *iqlīd*, pp. 140–143.

[86] See al-Kirmānī, *Kitāb al-Riyāḍ*, ed. ʿĀ. Tāmir (Beirut, 1960), *Ch.* 10, pp. 213–230. On this debate, see D. De Smet, 'Le verbe-impératif dans le système cosmologique de l'Ismaélisme'. See also P. Walker, *Early philosphical Shiism*, Ch. 6: 'Creation as command', pp. 81–86; idem, *Ḥamīd al-Dīn al-Kirmānī. Ismaili Thought in the Age of al-Ḥākim* (London and New York, 1999), pp. 83–94.

Sijistānian cosmology, is not trying to take a stand in this debate. The rejection of the idea that there is an intermediary between God and His 'knowledge', the first being, would thus be a subtle way to advocate a cosmological rival doctrine to that of al-Sijistānī.

The Sijistānian resonances do not stop here, since the following paragraphs deal with the notion that each ontological degree is a 'mystery' for the degree which follows it. Thus an ontology made of successive ruptures emerges, which is undoubtedly intended to break the assimilationist claims: if one is by nature ignorant of the ontological levels preceding one's own existence in this world, any attempt to describe them by analogy is doomed to failure. It is therefore not possible to rely on what we know to access what we do not know: the unknowable remains unknowable, out of all proportion to the knowable. Again, this echoes some considerations in a chapter of al-Sijistānī's *Wellsprings of Wisdom.*[87]

The treatise then returns to the Throne and the Footstool: the first lines summarize what is acquired from the second *ḥadīth*, namely the existence of the two 'thresholds' or 'gates'. There are, however, some new nuances. First, the term *'arsh*, 'Throne', is used in two different senses, one general and the other particular, respectively corresponding to the Throne proper and the Footstool. Second, the text mentions the divine knowledge and power, as well as that of the pillars of the Throne. Power had already been briefly mentioned and linked to knowledge in the passage inserted in the first *ḥadīth.*[88] However, all these passages are obscure and one can hardly draw any precise theological doctrine from them. They refer in any case to several Qur'anic verses in which God is named *'alīm* and *qadīr*, and it is obviously an attempt to theorise the relationship of these two attributes, God's knowledge being somehow actualized by His power, the latter manifesting the former.

One can hardly draw more from the text, except for the idea, already mentioned, of the independence of the divine knowledge vis-à-vis created beings: God knows them even before they are created, His knowledge of them is not dependent on their existence. As for the

---

[87] Al-Sijistānī, *Kitāb al-Yanābī'*, Ch. 15, pp. 40–41; English trans.: P. Walker, *The Wellsprings of Wisdom*, pp. 67–68.

[88] *Kashf* II, p. 41, § 4.

pillars (*arkān*), this is their first and only appearance in the *Kitāb al-Kashf*, but their exact role is not clearly defined. The verb *fataqa*, used to express the separation of the pillars, is used in Q. 21:30 for the separation of Heaven and Earth, as noted by Heinz Halm, who deduces an analogy between Heaven and the Throne, on the one hand, and the Earth and the Footstool, on the other hand.[89] The pillars would thus correspond to the Footstool.

The text then approaches the processional movement which leads to the alphabetical cosmogony: through 'His *jārī*', God successively establishes the Throne and the Footstool, the alphabet being derived from the latter.[90] The use of these two expressions: *ḥaddahu al-jārī*, 'His flowing ontological degree', and *al-quṭb al-jarī*, 'the flowing axis', is remarkable. The term *jārī* appears in several other works attributed to Jaʿfar b. Manṣūr al-Yaman, in the *Asās al-taʾwīl* by al-Qāḍī al-Nuʿmān, the *Risāla al-mudhhiba*, as well as in the works of representatives of the 'Persian school' of Ismailism.[91] The *jarī* designates the 'flow' that comes down from the spiritual entities unto the earthly *daʿwa* hierarchy. It is synonymous to *taʾyīd* inasmuch as it does indeed apply to the spiritual influence received by the Prophets and the Imams, but it also extends to the emanative force that travels through all the spiritual entities, that is, through the Intellect and the Soul — and in certain texts, the triad *al-jadd / al-fatḥ / al-khayāl*.[92] The term *jārī* thus fits in a certain typically Ismaili ontological system, which is only hinted at in Treatise II.

---

[89] H. Halm, *Kosmologie*, p. 43.

[90] *Kashf* II, p. 48, § 22.

[91] See references provided by D. Hollenberg, *Beyond the Qurʾan*, p. 144, n. 107. In addition, see e.g. Jaʿfar b. Manṣūr al-Yaman, *Sarāʾir wa-asrār al-nuṭaqāʾ*, pp. 22, 24, 61–62; idem *Taʾwīl al-zakāt*, pp. 54, 64, 66, 68, 72, 83, 84, 101, 103 107, 115; al-Rāzī, *Kitāb al-Iṣlāḥ*, pp. 108, 187, 268–269; al-Sijistānī, *al-Maqālīd al-malakūtiyya*, p. 314.

[92] On this triad, see P.E. Walker, 'Cosmic Hierarchies in Early Ismāʿīlī Thought: the view of Abū Yaʿqūb al-Sijistānī', *The Muslim World*, 66/1 (1976), pp. 14–28; H. Halm, *Kosmologie*, pp. 67–74; idem, 'The Cosmology of the Pre-Fatimid Ismāʿīliyya'; D. De Smet, 'La fonction noétique de la triade *al-Jadd, al-Fatḥ, al-Khayāl*: Les fondements de la connaissance prophétique dans l'ismaélisme', *Differenz und Dynamik im Islam* (2012), pp. 319–336; A. Straface, 'The representations of *al-Jadd, al-Fatḥ* and *al-Khayāl* in the Ismaili literature. Some examples and further remarks', in M.A. Amir-Moezzi et al, eds, *L'ésotérisme shiʿite, ses racines et ses prolongements* (Turnhout, 2016), pp. 423–440.

The *jārī* establishes a first heptad of letters which are the 'Mothers' of all the other letters.[93] But the text then becomes more confused. After listing the first seven letters, the *Kashf* goes on: 'He thus named these letters by these names. Out of these twenty-eight, He appointed seven Gates and named them 'signs' (*simāt*), gathering therein sixteen letters.'[94] The author repeats himself, since the 'seven gates' are the first seven letters that have just been listed. But the rest of the sentence poses a problem: these seven gates are called *simāt*, while the rest of the text states that 'signs (*simāt*) mean the diacritics (*'ajamiyyāt*)'.[95] The text is obviously corrupted here, since the observation on the diacritics in fact only concerns the twelve letters remaining once the group of sixteen has been drawn from the first heptad.

As for the number sixteen, it is obtained by spelling the first seven letters, the text tells us. However, this is not exactly the case. What follows is a reconstruction of the probable meaning of an extremely confused text, since the detail of the calculation to reach the number of sixteen is not provided. First, we have the first heptad: *alif*, *bā'*, *tā'*, *thā'*, *jīm*, *ḥā'*, *khā'*. By the spelling of these letters, we further obtain: *fā'* and *lām* out of the *alif* (*a-l-f*), and *mīm* and *yā'* out of the *jīm* (*j-y-m*), which makes a total of eleven. To reach sixteen, it is therefore necessary to add two letters which do not come from the first heptad, but from the Footstool and the Throne to which correspond the letters *sīn* and *shīn* (*s-y-n*, *sh-y-n*), respectively. Spelling the latter two provides us with one more letter: the *nūn* (*n-w-n*). And when spelling the *nūn*, we obtain the *wāw*. That makes a total of fifteen, to which we must add the *hā'*, which symbolises God.

The passage dealing with the twelve remaining letters of the alphabet is just as obstruse. It is thus stated that: 'He also made seven other letters gathering the remaining and letters (. . .) in the number of twelve.'[96] The play on the numbers seven and twelve is quite universal, and it is also found in Ismaili cosmological texts where a heptad is governing a dodecade. For instance, in the *Risāla* by Abū 'Īsā

[93] *Kashf* II, p. 49, § 22.
[94] *Kashf* II, p. 48, § 22.
[95] *Kashf* II, p. 49, § 22.
[96] *Kashf* II, p. 49, § 22.

al-Murshid, the heptad of angels called *karrūbiyya* emanated from Kūnī's light is followed in existence by a group of twelve 'spiritual beings' (*rūḥāniyya*) who come from Qadar's light. These beings serve as intermediaries between Qadar and the Speaking-Prophets.[97] The 'Precedent' (*sābiq*) then creates the air (*hawā'*), which he names 'Throne' (*'arsh*), and water, which he names 'Footstool' (*kursī*).[98] He then separates the air into seven waves, corresponding to the seven heavens, and divides the spheres into twelve (probably the twelve signs of the zodiac), as a symbol of the twelve 'spiritual beings'.

Other early Ismaili examples of a connection between a heptad and a dodecade can be provided. In the *Kitāb al-Rushd wa'l-hidāya*, attributed to Ibn Ḥawshab, the author notes that the first verse of the Qur'an, the basmala, is formed of nineteen letters, which he divides into a group of seven and a group of twelve. The seven correspond to the seven Speaking-Prophets and the seven Imams, while the twelve correspond to their twelve 'chiefs' (*nuqabā'*) or 'proofs' (*ḥujaj*).[99]

In the *Kitāb al-'Ālim wa'l-ghulām*, the first teaching the disciple receives, after taking the oath, concerns the creation of beings. From God thus successively proceed a triad, a heptad and a dodecade: the triad is formed by God's will (*irāda*), order (*amr*) and speech (*qawl*). In the Qur'an, when God wants to create a thing, He only has to say to it: 'Be!', and it is: *kun fa-yakūn*. This formula has seven letters in Arabic, which corresponds to the seven heavens, as is also the case in as in Abū 'Īsā al-Murshid's *Risāla*. Finally, the letters composing the terms *irāda*, *amr* and *qawl*, are twelve, corresponding to the twelve signs of the zodiac.[100] These examples illustrate to what extent lettrist speculations

---

[97] See S.M. Stern, 'The Earliest Cosmological Doctrines of Ismā'īlism', p. 9. Note that although Abū 'Īsā announces twelve beings, he only names eleven.

[98] As we can see, the terms 'Throne' and 'Footstool' do not bear the same meaning as in the *Kashf*.

[99] Ibn Ḥawshab, *Kitāb al-Rushd wa'l-hidāya*, ed. M. Kāmil Ḥusayn, in W. Ivanow, ed, *Collectanea: vol. 1* (Leiden, 1948), p. 189 (English trans., W. Ivanow, 'The Book of Righteousness and True Guidance', in W. Ivanow, *Studies in Early Persian Ismailism*, (Leiden, 1948), p. 55).

[100] J.W. Morris, *The Master and the Disciple*, pp. 79–80 (Arabic: pp. 14–15). For a discussion of the numbers 7 and 12 in the *Risālat Abū 'Īsā al-Murshid*, the *Risāla al-Mudhhiba* by al-Qāḍī al-Nu'mān and the *Kitāb al-Fatarāt* by Ja'far b. Manṣūr al-Yaman, see H. Halm, *Kosmologie*, pp. 91–100.

in early Ismaili literature are linked to both the cosmogony and to the members of the Ismaili hierarchy, that is to say to both the spiritual and terrestrial *ḥudūd*. This does not appear so explicitly in the *Kitāb al-Kashf*, and it is therefore useful to clarify it with parallel sources.

These parallels allow us to understand why the author of Treatise II is trying to subordinate the 'twelve remaining letters' to a heptad. The problem is that his attempt to do so is very approximate — although, once more, the confusion of the text may be partly due to a flawed transmission. Indeed, while he announces twelve letters, he actually lists thirteen. The system in which one series of letter is emanated from another would work well if the twelve letters were divided into two groups of six, the second group being only the diacritical version of the first: the *dāl* emanates the *dhāl* by adding a diacritic point, and so on for the *rā'* and the *zāy*, the *ṣād* and the *ḍād*, the *ṭā'* and the *ẓā'*, the *'ayn* and the *ghayn*, the *fā'* and the *qāf*.

د ر ص ط ع ف

ذ ز ض ظ غ ق

But in such a configuration, we lose the heptad, which is key. Furthermore, the *kāf* is left out, unless it is given the place of the *fā'*, which already appeared in the first group of sixteen letters.

If we recapitulate the data of the text, we obtain the following diagram (the arrows refer to the letters obtained by spelling other letters):[101]

Group of sixteen letters:

هـ (God)

ش (Throne)

س (Footstool) → ن → و

ا ب ت ث ج ح خ (First heptad: the Speaking-Prophets) → ل ف م ي

[101] See also the diagram of the 'gnostic' cosmology of early Ismailism provided in H. Halm, *Kosmologie*, p. 116.

Group of twelve letters:

د ر ص ط ع (ف) ك (Second 'heptad': the Imams)

ذ ز ض ظ غ ق

It should however be noted that the two heptads that respectively stand for the seven Speaking-Prophets and the seven Imams, according to the penultimate paragraph of Treatise II,[102] may be the two groups of letters forming the group of twelve.

Whatever may be the case, the confusion of the presentation seems due to the mixing by the author of two divergent and hardly reconcilable systems: a first system dividing the twenty-eight letters of the Arabic alphabet into four heptads, and another one which divides them into a group of sixteen and a group of twelve.

At this point, the text leaves several questions unanswered: to what does the distribution of letters in sixteen and twelve correspond? To what realities do the letters obtained through spelling correspond? The same question goes for the second pseudo-heptad (in the group of twelve) of letters with diacritics.

In the chapter of *Kosmologie und Heilslehre der frühen Ismāʿīlīya* where he analyses the alphabetical cosmogony Treatise II, Heinz Halm briefly recalls Fragment II of an Ismaili manuscript edited and translated by Stanislas Guyard.[103] In this text, the twenty-eight letters of the alphabet are divided into four 'weeks', or heptads.[104] Just as in the *Kashf*, the first heptad is formed by the first letters of the alphabet: *alif*, *bāʾ*, *tāʾ*, *thāʾ*, *jīm*, *ḥāʾ*, *khāʾ*, which correspond to the 'spiritual degrees' (*al-ḥudūd al-rūḥāniyya*) governing the seven planets. Then comes the second 'week', which is 'corporeal' (*jismānī*): *dāl*, *rāʾ*, *sīn*, *ṣād*, *ṭāʾ*, *ʿayn*, *qāf*, and which symbolises the Speaking-Prophets: 'None of these [letters] has diacritics (*munaqqaṭ*), except for the *qāf*.'[105] This 'week' emanates the third week, simply by adding diacritic points, each one corresponds to the 'Foundation' (*asās*) of the corresponding

[102] *Kashf* II, p. 50, § 24.

[103] H. Halm, *Kosmologie*, pp. 44–45.

[104] S. Guyard, *Fragments relatifs à la doctrine des Ismaélîs* (Paris, 1874), fragment no. 2, pp. 19–26 (French trans: pp. 108–122).

[105] Ibid., p. 24 (French trans: p. 113).

Speaking-Prophet. The letters are thus: *dhāl*, *zayn*, *shīn*, *ḍād*, *ẓāy*, *ghayn*, *fā'*. As we can see, the couple *qāf* / *fā'* is an exception to the general rule: this is because the *qāf* represents the Qā'im. The Qā'im 'will judge the corporeals (*al-jismāniyyīn*) in his era and age, and this has been given to none other than him'.[106] The exceptional role of the Qā'im, which is referred to as the *raj'a*, thus explains why the rule of the emanation of letters is different here. Finally, the last heptad corresponds to the hidden (*mastūrīn*) Imams.

H. Halm considers this text to be the result of a 'secondary' stage in the evolution of the doctrine in comparison to the *Kitāb al-Kashf*, as if the doctrine of the latter had been arranged and systematized so as to produce a more coherent presentation.[107] Rather, it seems that the inconsistency and confusion of the *Kashf* is due, as we have said, to the merging of two distinct systems into one, either intentionally, to mislead the uninitiated reader, or unintentionally, by a copyist or an author who did not understand his subject well.

In the same chapter, Halm discusses a series of other examples of lettrist speculations which can be compared to the *Kitāb al-Kashf* in one aspect or another. He begins with an extract from a work of al-Daylamī, a 14th-century Zaydi author, who quotes Ismaili texts. He continues with the pre-cabbalistic speculations of the Sefer Yeṣīrāh, the speculations of Mark the Gnostic, and the reflection on the letters and the language in the *Kitāb al-Zīna* by the Ismaili philosopher Abū Ḥātim al-Rāzī. I refer the reader to Halm's book. As Halm acknowledges, not all the texts he mentions contribute to clarify the *Kashf*, but they are useful inasmuch as they show that several characteristics of the latter's lettrism are found elsewhere, the *Kashf* being apparently the only text to gather them all. These essential features are the following:

— the cosmological role of the alphabet;
— a cosmology in three stages: the Throne, the Footstool and the alphabet;
— the spiritual flow that goes through all these hypostases and creates them (the *jārī*);

[106] Ibid., p. 25 (French trans., p. 114).
[107] H. Halm, *Kosmologie*, p. 45.

— the division of the alphabet into heptads;
— the notion of a heptad governing a dodecade;
— the technique of spelling out the names of letters;
— the method of emanating letters with diacritics from those without diacritics;
— the correspondence between letters and ranks of the *daʿwa*.

Regarding the latter point, Idrīs ʿImād al-Dīn provides additional elements. We have seen that in his quotation from Treatise II, he identified the Throne with Muḥammad and the Footstool with ʿAlī. No doubt deeming the alphabetical cosmogony of the *Kashf* too confused, he interrupts his quotation with the sentence: 'When the axis had flowed unto the Gate of the Footstool, God made it into twenty-eight letters',[108] without entering into the detail of these; therefore, he neither refers to the heptads, nor to the diacritic points and the spelling of the names of the letters. Instead, he recalls that Muḥammad and ʿAlī correspond respectively to the esoteric and exoteric thresholds of the Throne, and continues:

> When His axis proceeded to (from?) the Law (*sharīʿa*) up to the threshold of the Footstool, that is to say to ʿAlī, He made twenty-eight letters, that is to say that he established twenty-eight ranks (*ḥadd*). Twelve of them are exoteric (*ẓāhira*) — six emigrants and six auxiliaries, who committed no mistake and were not misled with the misled — and sixteen are hidden (*maktūmīn*) ranks, like Fāṭima, Ḥasan, Ḥusain, and like Muḥammad b. Abī Bakr, of whom the Prince of the Believers ʿAlī, said: 'As for Muḥammad, he was a son to me.'[109]

This constitutes another possible interpretation of the symbolism of the letters of the alphabet, and in any case confirms that they were put in correspondence with the members of the terrestrial hierarchy, that is to say of the *daʿwa*. Another noteworthy point is the division of the twenty-eight *ḥudūd* into a group of twelve, and a group of sixteen, just like in Treatise II.

---

[108] *Kashf* II, p. 48, § 22.

[109] Idrīs ʿImād al-Dīn, *Zahr al-maʿānī*, p. 131.

While, because of its confusion, it is not possible to fully analyse the alphabetical cosmogony of Treatise II, it is however possible to identify here some essential features which make the *Kashf* a unique example of an otherwise widespread practice of lettrism in the Islamic world.

Conclusion

This treatise, despite its brevity, is extremely dense. Although the text clearly suffers from a flawed transmission, contributing to the confusion of several passages, it has an overall coherence. This latter is, however, slightly scrambled by a multiplicity of layers. Indeed, as the treatise is composed for a large part from *ḥadīth*s also found in Twelver Shiʿi compilations, it appears to be dedicated to the affirmation of the divine transcendence (*tawḥīd*) as well as the refutation of anthropomorphism — since, as we have seen, the speculations on the Throne and the Footstool are directly connected to the debates on anthropomorphism. Yet, the reason why these two *ḥadīth*s were included in Treatise II goes beyond the intentions which led al-Kulaynī and Ibn Bābawayh to preserve and transmit them. It is in fact the third part of Treatise II, the one that is original, which provides the true intentions of the text. The objective of the treatise is to sketch a cosmology which clearly echoes the Ismaili speculations on the Intellect and the Soul or the 'Precedent' (*sābiq*) and the 'Follower' (*al-tālī*). It is therefore all the more interesting that the author of Treatise II mobilized the two abovementioned *ḥadīth*s to support an Ismaili cosmology.

Yet, while the similarities with, for instance, al-Sijistānī's cosmological system are striking, the differences are not negligeable. How are we to understand this proximity of the two systems? Should it be interpreted as a dialogue between the cosmological systems of the Western and the Eastern *daʿwa*s? In other words, is the difference between the cosmology of the *Kashf* and that of al-Sijistānī just an insignificant variation due to the independence that the Ismaili missionaries had so long as they conformed to a general model? Or is it an attempt to produce a rival system, overall similar but free from Neoplatonic vocabulary and exclusively based on Shiʿi sources? In the absence of better manuscripts which might help elucidating these questions by providing a less confused text, we can only note the clear resonances between Treatise II and what is known from the Ismaili cosmology based on other sources.

Treatise III Commentary

Following the general pattern of the *Kashf*, the argument of Treatise III does not unfold straightforwardly. As in Treatise I, the various textual units of which it is composed are not formally connected to each other. It is only in examining the themes of the text that a certain unity of discourse emerges. These themes are distinctly Fatimid, once we go beyond broadly Shiʿi appearances. The text thus mainly deals with the *daʿwa* and its enemies (hence the strong presence of ʿAlī's enemies, implicit archetypes of the enemies of the *daʿwa*) and the return of the Resurrector. Approximately in the middle of the treatise, a key passage on Salmān seems to justify a religious reform that is probably the one carried out by ʿAbd Allāh al-Mahdī. The structure of the text is quite easily legible, although it contains neither an introduction, nor a conclusion. It can roughly be analysed as follows:

1) The *daʿwa*.

   [§ **1–2**] Exegesis of verses dealing with the theme of God's 'houses'
   [§§ **3–9**] Exegesis of Q. 107
   [§§ **10–26**] Exegesis of Q. 89
   [§§ **27–32**] Exegesis of Q. 17:50–52; 17:71

2) The Imam and his Proofs: ʿAlī, al-Miqdād, Abū Dharr and Salmān.

   [§ **33**] The Praise is to obey both Muḥammad and ʿAlī: exegesis of Q. 10:10
   [§ **34**] The Imam as a shade shelter: exegesis of Q. 25:45–46
   [§§ **35–39**] The three-branched shade: al-Miqdād, Abū Dharr and Salmān.
   [§§ **40–41**] Salmān
   [§ **42**] Exegesis of Q. 25:45–46 continued

3) *Raj'a* and retribution

    [§ **43**] Exegesis of Q. 19:96–97

4) [§ **44**] Inserted passage: Moses and Aaron: exegesis of Q. 20:25–31
5) *Raj'a* and retribution (continued)

    [§§ **45–53**] The Summoners and the *raj'a*: exegesis of Q. 20:108–112
    [§§ **54–64**] Exegesis of Q. 20:124–131; 20:135
    [§§ **65–68**] Abū Bakr: exegesis of verses from Q. 21
    [§§ **69–73**] Exegesis of verses from Q. 22

6) [§§ **74–75**] Additional paragraphs on the *raj'a* and the enemies of 'Alī
7) [§ **75**] Conclusion

Treatise III Translation

In the name of God, the Merciful, the Compassionate
[God's mosques and houses]

1. God — He is Mighty and Sublime — says in the firmness of His Book: *'The mosques belong to God, so do not call (lā tadʿū), along with God, upon anyone'* [Q. 72:18]. The mosques are the Imams and the Speaking-Prophets — may God's blessings be upon them all. It is not permissible for anyone to claim (*yaddaʿī*) their sacred station. God has ordered that their Summons be answered and their Order received; [He has ordered] to hold fast to their obedience, and that no rivals or equals are invoked (*yudʿā*) along with God, because God does not accept this, nor does He order it. Rather, the Summons of the Speaking-Prophets — may God's blessings be upon them — is toward God — He is Sublime and High — and this is the meaning of His word: *'Only those who believe in God and the Last Day shall inhabit God's mosques'* [Q. 9:18], that is, the Speaking-Resurrector (*al-nāṭiq al-qāʾim*) — may God's blessings be upon him. He means that only those who accept and hear [the Resurrector] in regard to this Summons, and who respond by hastening to his mosque (*labbā masjidahu*), shall be illuminated by the light of wisdom <and be guided>[1]. He is the Speaking-Prophet of the Age, who summons to God, and is known as the Last Day — may his peace be upon us.

2. *'In houses God has permitted* **[52]** *to be erected, and His Name to be remembered therein; therein is He praised in the mornings and the evenings by men whom neither commerce nor trafficking diverts from the*

1 Missing from ms. A.

remembrance of God' [Q. 24:36–37].[2] The 'Houses' are those who manifest God's judgment and firmly stand by His Laws, and they are the Proofs — peace be upon them. They are the 'permitted Houses' which have been ordered to be raised above filth and impurities (*al-arjās wa'l-anjās*). It is a duty for the believers to know them, to glorify what God has glorified — may He be exalted — to comply with their orders and prohibitions, to approach them with love, to accept what they say and hear what they order. It is through these Houses that God is known — may He be praised. His most glorious Name, if one asks [for something using] it, he will receive, if one invokes it, he will be answered. '*He is praised in the mornings and the evenings by men*' [Q. 24:36–37] refers to the night and the day, two realities (*bābān*) indicating these Houses. 'Praise', in the esoteric order, is the knowledge of the Truth in every era and every age through the Imam — peace be upon him.

[Exegesis of Q. 107]

3. God — He is Mighty and Sublime — says: '*Have you seen the one who denies religion?*' [Q. 107:1]. God gives him as an example to the people who know. Al-Ḥakīm — peace be upon him — said: 'The decree and the esoteric knowledge belong to the Master of the source (*ma'din*).'[3] '*Have you seen the one who* **[53]** *denies religion? That is who repels the orphan*' [Q. 107–74]. This means that the one who denies religion is the one who repels the Imam from his sacred station, because the Imam is the pillar (*qawām*) of religion and of the believers' worship. There is no Imam but the one chosen by God for His religion and as a guidance to His Order. The apparent (*fī'l-ẓāhir*) meaning of

---

[2] Cf. the exegesis of Q. 24:36 in *Kashf* V, pp. 104–107, §§ 27–29. See also occurrences of this verse in Ja'far b. Manṣūr al-Yaman, *Al-Shawāhid wa'l-bayān*, IIS MS. 734, ff. 89–90; idem, *Ta'wīl al-zakāt*, p. 200.

[3] Qualifying the Imams as 'mines' or 'sources' of knowledge is a classical feature of the Shi'i lexicon. See e.g. al-Ṣaffār al-Qummī, *Baṣā'ir al-darajāt*, pp. 123–126; al-Kulaynī, *Uṣūl al-Kāfī*, *k. al-ḥujja*, *bāb anna al-a'imma ma'din al-'ilm wa-shajarat al-nubuwwa . . .*, vol. 1, p. 221, no.1–3. For other occurrences of *ma'din*, see index s.v.

'to repel' *(yadu''u)* is 'to push away' the orphan, as in God's saying — He is Mighty and Sublime: *'The day they shall be repelled (yuda''ūn) into the Fire of Gehenna'* [Q. 52:13].

4. The Imam is named 'the orphan' (*yatīm*) because his father has disappeared (*ghāba*), as has the father of the Imam who established him (*aqāmahu*). The Imam does not become an Imam and is not named after the Imamate until the Imam who transmitted the Imamate to him (*afḍā ilayhi bi'l-imāma*) has disappeared and he becomes the Imam in his era. Whichever one of them is [the Imam] in his era is the one who receives the name 'orphan'.

5. When the people of the exoteric [religion] speak about 'the orphan pearl' (*al-durra al-yatīma*), they mean that it is peerless, that there is no better pearl than it. So is the Imam: he is peerless and there is no one in his era better than him.

6. *'The one who denies religion'* [Q. 107:1] of which God — may He be exalted — has perfected both exoteric and esoteric aspects, is the one who pushes the orphan away; namely the sacred station of the Imam through whom God establishes the esoteric aspect of religion, the exoteric aspect of which was established by the Messenger. The one who denies the Imam and the esoteric aspect of religion is 'the one who denies religion'. This applies to the iniquitous who, after the Messenger['s death] — may God bless him and his family — **[54]** pushed ʿAlī — when he was the Imam — away from the sacred station of the Imamate in which the Messenger had established him. They then claimed the Imamate for themselves, by iniquity and enmity — God *'loves not the aggressors (al-muʿtadīn)'* [Q. 2:190].

7. He then says: *'And urges not the feeding of the poor* [Q. 107:3]. The 'poor' (*miskīn*) is one of the names of the Proof, because, from one viewpoint, the believers take refuge (*yaskun*) with him in search of the esoteric knowledge. From another viewpoint, [the Proof] is poor and needs (*miskīn faqīr*) the Imam to provide (*yamuddahu*) him the esoteric knowledge the latter established within the former. The food is the knowledge he acquires from him. This means that the one who denies religion does not urge the seeking of the esoteric knowledge possessed by the Proof. ʿAlī b. Abī Ṭālib — peace be upon him — was Muḥammad's Proof, and an Imam to his community after [Muḥammad's death]. With ʿAlī is the esoteric aspect of Muḥammad's religion (*bāṭin dīn muḥammad*), just as with every Proof is the esoteric aspect of the knowledge of the Imam of his age. Such is God's tradition and the organization of His religion.

8. God — may He be exalted — then says: '*Woe to those who pray, and are heedless of their prayers*' [Q. 107:4–5]. He means the iniquitous. He says 'Woe to them' because they pray the exoteric prayer, and yet are heedless of the esoteric prayer, of the guardian who has it in charge (*walī al-amr fīhā*), as well as the whole of religion. They are the ones of whom God — He is Mighty and Sublime — says: '*Their deeds have failed, and on the Day of Resurrection We shall not assign to them any weight*' [Q. 18:105]. As for prayer itself, it is similar to the wellspring of pure drinking water (*al-ʿayn al-maʿīn mashrabihā*)[4] that is not altered by the ages. It is the Summons to the Master of Truth in every era and every age — may God bless him **[55]** and his family.

9. He then says — He is Mighty and Sublime: '*Those who make display, and yet refuse charity*' [Q. 107:6–7]. This refers to the iniquitous and their followers who display in front of the people their apparent worshipping, abandon their [impious] speech in public and come to bowing and prostration.[5] And yet they refuse charity, which God made a duty: [and they refuse] obedience to the Master of Truth, who is the Imam of the community, acknowledgment of his right, following the tradition God and His Messenger have traced [by following him]. He is the Prince of the Believers, ʿAlī b. Abī Ṭālib — peace be upon him — and every Imam of his progeny in every era and every age. Whoever follows the iniquitous, does not give the right to whom it belongs, and does not grab God's '*handhold*' [Q. 2:256] and His '*cable*' [Q. 3:103],[6] is among those '*who make display, and yet refuse charity*'. This is the explanation of '*Have you seen the one who denies religion? etc.*' [Q. 107:1].

[Exegesis of Q. 89]

10. God says: '*By the dawn*' [Q. 89:1]. Al-Ḥakīm — peace be upon him — says the dawn is Muḥammad — may God's blessing and peace

---

[4] See *Kashf* I, p. 24, § 53, where the 'pure water' (*maʿīn*) of Q. 67:30 is identified with ʿAlī.

[5] That is: they pray in public thereby hypocritically displaying their faith.

[6] Same expression in *Kashf* I, p. 9, § 17; V, p. 99, §18; p. 122, § 55.

be upon him. '*And ten nights*' [Q. 89:2] means the Prince of the Believers — peace be upon him. '*And the even and the odd*' [Q. 89:3] means Ḥasan and Ḥusayn. '*And the night when it passes away*' [Q. 89:4] means Fāṭima al-Zahrā' — peace be upon her. '*Is there in that an oath for a mindful one?*' [Q. 89:5]: He means: 'There is no oath more noble than the one I have just sworn.' '*Is there in that an oath for a mindful one?*' means 'Is the exoteric aspect of these words an oath for someone of intellect and reason who understands what I have sworn?'

11. Do not examine whatever you consider without the Truth, do not follow the path of [other] sects (*madhāhib*), **[56]** so that you may abandon falsehoods and not follow any other path or way than that of rectitude. Otherwise, you will perish with those who perish, your deeds will be frustrated, and you will be among the losers. Whoever knows what God has sworn upon will be guided: it is on the Five Eminences (*al-khamsa al-aʿlām*) that a *qā'im* points and indicates in every era and every age.

12. '*Have you not seen how your Lord did with ʿĀd, Iram of the pillars?*' [Q. 89:6–7]. ʿĀd refers here to Abū Bakr the accursed[7] because he returned (*ʿāda*) to the lying and the iniquity he had begun with [before converting to Islam]. He then claimed (*iddaʿā*) what he had no right to claim. God — He is Mighty and Sublime — said: '*Even if they were brought back, they would return unto that which they are forbidden. They are truly liars*' [Q. 6:28]. Such is the one who returns (*al-ʿā'id*) to denial and rejection [of the truth], to ignorance after knowledge, to rebellion after obedience. '*Iram of the pillars*': the meaning of this is in what precedes: '*with ʿĀd*'. [On the one hand], whoever says 'he returned' (*ʿāda*) means 'he came back' (*rajaʿa*), and ["*ʿĀd*"] is thus the one who returns (*al-ʿā'id*). [But on the other hand], the *dāl* in "*ʿĀd*" is lowered [i.e. vocalized in the indirect case]: the meaning is therefore

[7] See above *Kashf* I, pp. 10–11, § 21, where the same Qur'anic people and characters mentioned here and in the following pages are identified with the same protagonists of the beginnings of Islam.

'enemy' (*mu'ādin*).[8] The enemy (*mu'ādī*) is the iniquitous, and the transgressor (*al-'ādī*) is the one who crosses (*'adā*) something and bypasses it towards something else. *'Iram of the pillars, the like of which was never created among the lands (bilād)'* [Q. 89:7–8], that is, among the Proofs. He is the pillar (*'imād*) of religion. His words **[57]** — He is Mighty and Sublime: "*'Ād, Iram of the pillars, the like of which was never created among the lands*' [Q. 89:6–8] designates 'Alī b. Abī Ṭalib — peace upon him; he is the one the like of whom was never created among the Proofs, and he is the pillar of religion. His words — He is Mighty and Sublime: "*'Ād Iram of the pillars*' mean the one who crossed (*'adā*) 'Alī, bypassed him, was overweening toward him and refused to obey him. He did not place him where God had placed him, [that is,] as an intermediary (*wāsiṭa*) between His worshippers and Him. This iniquitous, the First of iniquity, transgressed his limits (*'adā ṭūrahu*),[9] rebelled against the holder of authority (*walī al-amr*), and transgressed his sacred station (*'adā 'alā maqāmihi*).

13. *'And Thamūd, who hewed (jābū) the rocks in the valley'* [Q. 89:9]. By Thamūd, he means 'Umar — may God curse him.[10] And God's words: *'They hewed the rocks in the valley'* mean that they cut them, because 'to hew' (*al-jawb*), in the language of the Arabs, is 'to cut' (*al-qat'*). It is said: 'he hewed something' when he cut it. So, this Second iniquitous and those who followed him have cut off the Proofs from

---

[8] Instead of reading 'Ād as a proper noun, in accordance with the usual understanding of this verse, the author refers it to two different roots: the root *'-w-d*, which implies the notion of return, that the root *'-d-w*, from which stems the word *'aduww*, 'enemy'. The latter interpretation is made possible by the vocalization of the *dāl* in *'ād* with an indirect case *'-in'*; the author thus reads *'ādin* as if it were the active participle of the verb *'adā*, 'to oppose', 'to transgress' or 'to bypass'. In fact, this vocalization in the Qur'an is merely due to the fact that *'ād* is preceded by the preposition *bi-*, which is followed by an indirect case. For the present interpretation to be grammatically correct, the *dāl* should have been vocalized with a simple *kasra*, rather that a *tanwīn*.

[9] This idiomatic expression is usually thus translated, but this might also be a pun with the word *ṭūr*, 'mount' or 'mountain', a Qur'anic term (Q. 52:1) identified with the Speaking-Prophet; see *Kashf* I, p. 10, § 20. This would mean that Abū Bakr 'opposed', or 'transgressed', his Speaking-Prophet, that is, Muḥammad, by refusing to acknowledge 'Alī's position.

[10] See *Kashf* I, p. 10, § 21.

establishing God's Order (*min iqāmat amr Allāh*). For the rocks, on the earth are analogous to the Proofs.[11] The valleys are the water course (*majrā al-mā'*), and the Proofs are the courses of God's Order. So He says that they cut the Proofs from [God's Order] by cutting off the sacred station of the Master of the Truth (*ṣāḥib al-ḥaqq*); it is from his hands that streams the stream of God's Order, as well as the knowledge of His religion and His wisdom — may God bless him — and he is ʿAlī b. Abī Ṭālib. [God] designated him by mentioning the valley — such is his sacred station.

14. The meaning of His words — He is Mighty and Sublime: *'And Pharaoh, lord of stakes'* [Q. 89:10], here, is ʿUthmān — may God curse him — because he behaved with pride (*tafarʿana*) toward **[58]** God's Friends (*awliyā'*), acted like a king, and claimed the veil (*ḥijāb*) for himself, thus likening himself to his brethren Hāmān, Pharaoh and Corah.

15. *'Those who were insolent in the lands, and worked much corruption therein, your Lord unloosed on them the scourge of chastisement'* [Q. 89:11–13]. He means by this Muʿāwiya, his companion ʿAmr b. al-ʿĀṣ,[12] those who follow them and those [who fought at the Battle] of the Camel. He named them with the names of the past communities, because they acted and deviated as they did, and transgressed as they did.[13] The 'scourge of chastisement' is the sword

---

[11] See *Kashf* I, p. 25, § 54; VI, pp. 169–171, §§ 27–30, and related footnotes, where the mountains are identified with the Summoners or the Proofs. See also Ibn Ḥawshab, *Kitāb al-Rushd wa'l-hidāya*, p. 209 (English trans., p. 78), where, within a similar interpretation of Q. 89:6–12, we find the following hermeneutical key: 'Rocks, in the esoteric [sense], are the Proofs, because rocks come from mountains, and the mountains are the Proofs'.

[12] A companion of the Prophet, he conquered Egypt where he founded the city of Fusṭāṭ. Among the important traits that made him an enemy of the Shiʿa is his siding with Muʿāwiya in the conflict that set him against ʿAlī. He is also credited with the ruse of placing Qur'an leaves on the spears of his troops' spears at the battle of Ṣiffīn. He also governed Egypt on behalf of Muʿāwiya after removing ʿAlī's governor, Muḥammad b. Abī Bakr, and torturing him to death; see A.J. Wensinck, "Amr b. al-ʿĀṣ', *EI2*; K.M.G. Keshk, "Amr b. al-ʿĀṣ', *EI3*.

[13] On this reference to past communities, see *Kashf* I, p. 10, § 23, and commentary of *Kashf* I, pp. 144–147, and 147–154.

that the Prince of the Believers unsheathed (*aẓhara*) — peace be upon him — and with which he killed the people of [the battle of] the Camel, annihilated their might and killed their tyrants. *'Surely your Lord is ever on the watch'* [Q. 89:14]: this means that He watches the actions of the worshippers, punishing the iniquitous of the later [people] like He punished the iniquitous of the earlier [people].

16. *'As for man, when his Lord tries him by honouring him and is gracious onto him, then he says: "My Lord has honoured me."'* [Q. 89:15]. These are the words of Muḥammad — may God bless him — acknowledging the blessings of his Creator who honoured him with his revelation (*waḥī*) and his message. *'But when he tries him by straitening his provision, then he says: "My Lord has despised me"'* [Q. 89:16]. This refers to Abū Bakr — may God curse him — because he is the man specifically blamed with the words: 'by straitening his provision', that is, for desiring the sacred station of the Prince of the Believers ʿAlī — may God's blessings be upon him. He had been ordered to listen to the wisdom of God from him and to make himself closer to God by obeying him, but he was too proud **[59]** and said: *'My Lord (rabb) has despised me'*, that is that the Messenger of God — may God bless him — scorned him by preferring his cousin. The Messenger is the master of the affair (*ṣāḥib amr*) of the Muslims, and so he is their lord (*rabb*) in the language of the Arabs. He is the lord of every Muslim, that is, his master (*sayyid*), the Master of his affair (*ṣāḥib amrihi*) and the Master of the grace (*al-niʿma*) he receives.

17. *'Nay! But you honour not the orphan'* [Q. 89:17]: this phrase is directed to Abū Bakr and ʿUmar — that is, Zufar —, as well as <. . .>[14], Khālid b. al-Walīd,[15] Sālim, the slave of Abū Ḥudhayfa,[16] ʿUthmān,

---

[14] The mss. read 'Nufayl b. Shuʿba', otherwise unknown. The text is corrupted here; there is probably a confusion between two characters in the list, since it mentions al-Mughīra, who must be al-Mughīra b. Shuʿba.

[15] A general from the early Islamic conquests, he fought against the Prophet before converting to Islam. He was one of Abū Bakr's trusted men, which explains the hostility of the Shiʿa towards him; see P. Crone, 'Khālid b. al-Walīd', *EI2*.

[16] A Companion of the Prophet who he fought the *ridda* wars. He seems to have been close to Abū Bakr and ʿUmar.

Muʿāwiya, ʿAmr b. al-ʿĀṣ and al-Mughīra [b. Shuʿba].[17] Those are the ones who denied the orphan's right, that is, the Imam's — may God bless him and his family. They did not obey God regarding the honour He bestowed upon him, that is, the sacred station of the Imamate, as well as the Legacy and the succession (*khilāfa*) of the Messenger: they did not honour the one that God — may He be exalted — had honoured. The Imam is ʿAlī b. Abī Ṭālib, the Legatee of God's Messenger — may God bless him and his family.

18. The meaning of His words — He is Mighty and Sublime: '*And you urge not on the feeding of the poor (ṭaʿām al-miskīn)*' [Q. 89:18]. They are those who were previously mentioned by name and their notables. They do not urge the people on the feeding of the poor. 'Poor' is a name for the Proof, while 'feeding' is the knowledge of the esoteric, and the Proof is the Master of the esoteric (*ṣāḥib al-bāṭin*); therefore, they do not urge to feed the Proof, which is exegesis (*ta'wīl*).[18] By this Muḥammad — may God bless him — indicated ʿAlī, who was his Proof in his era. And the Proof of a given Imam is the Master of exegesis (*ṣāḥib al-ta'wīl*) in his era.[19] The Proof is named **[60]** the 'poor' (*miskīn*) because the souls find peace (*taskun*) in his knowledge. This is also because his sacred station is the refuge of the believers, and 'refuge' (*ma'wā*) is the abode (*maskan*). Also, [the Proof] has tranquillity (*al-sakīna*), eminence and graciousness. [In addition, the Proof] relies upon the Imam (*miskīn ilā al-Imam*) for the principles (*qawāʿid*) of his knowledge that [the Imam] provides him (*yamudduhu*) with God's divine assistance (*ta'yīd*) — He is Mighty and Sublime.

---

[17] A Companion of the Prophet, he stayed close to the circles of power after his death. Muʿāwiya appointed him governor of Kūfa, 'a region disturbed by the intrigues of the Shīʿa and the continual risings of the Khāridjīs'; see H. Lammens, 'al-Mughīra b. Shuʿba', *EI2*.

[18] While the Qur'anic verse means that the poor is not fed, the interpretation provided here understands the genitive in the opposite way: the feeding (*ṭaʿām*) is not what is given to the *miskīn*, but what the latter provides.

[19] This is an attempt to establish an analogy between the Proof of the Speaking-Prophet (*nāṭiq*) Muḥammad and the Proof of the Imam — that is, in early Fatimid times, the appointed successor of the Imam. On this meaning of 'Proof', see discussion in commentary of *Kashf* V, pp. 395–408.

19. And God — may He be exalted — said: *'And you devour the inheritance entirely, and love wealth with an ardent love'* [Q. 89:19–20]. This refers to the notables of a certain people — may God curse them — because they devoured the Lady's (*al-sayyida*) inheritance — peace be upon her — and deprived her of Fadak.[20] In the exoteric realm, they regarded it as permissible to severe the ties of kinship (*qaṭīʿat al-raḥm*).[21] In the esoteric realm, they dashed to the position (*makān*) she was assigned by God, and they usurped it by force. '*Entirely*' means that their devouring encompasses and comprises everything, because the iniquitous deprived Fāṭima — may God's blessings be upon her — of her entire inheritance, both religious and worldly (*fi'l-dīn wa'l-dunyā*). They said: 'The Prophets do not leave an inheritance',[22] even though God — He is Mighty and Sublime — has said: *'Solomon inherited from David'* [Q. 27:16], and, reporting Zachariah's words: *'Give me from Thee a heir (walī) who will inherit from me and from the family of Jacob'* [Q. 19:5–6]. These iniquitous [people] thus opposed the words of God — He is Mighty and Sublime — and His tradition (*sunna*) regarding His prophets. *'Is not God's curse is upon the iniquitous'* [Q. 11:18] from the first generations to the last. They also deprived her of her religious inheritance of the Imamate, which God allocated to her and her progeny until the Hour comes. Because of this, this description and these words are applied to them.

[20] This is an allusion to Fāṭima, the daughter of the Prophet and wife of ʿAlī. Fadak was an oasis pacifically conquered by the Muslims which belonged to the Prophet. Upon the Prophet's death, Fāṭima claimed it as part of her inheritance but Abū Bakr refused to grant her request, attributing to the Prophet the statement that 'prophets do not leave inheritance' (see below, p. 308, where this *ḥadīth* is quoted). After that, Fāṭima did not speak with Abū Bakr until her death. See e.g. Bukhārī, *Ṣaḥīḥ*, *k. farḍ al-khums*, *bāb* 1, no. 3092, 3093, vol. 2, p. 386; *k. al-maghāzī*, *bāb* 14, no. 4035–4036, vol. 3, p. 99; *k. al-maghāzī*, *bāb* 38, no. 4240–4241, vol. 3, pp. 142–143. See also L. Veccia Vaglieri, 'Fadak', *EI2*; H. Munt, 'Fadak', *EI3*; W. Madelung, *The Succession to Muḥammad*, index *s.v.* Fadak. This episode is also mentioned in *Kashf* V, p. 125, § 59.

[21] Allusion to Q. 47:22: *'Would you then, if you were given the command, work corruption in the land and sever your ties of kinship (tuqaṭṭiʿū arḥāmakum)?'*

[22] This is the *ḥadīth* Abū Bakr claimed to have heard from the Prophet Muḥammad to motivate his refusal to grant Fadak to Fāṭima; see L. Veccia Vaglieri, 'Fadak', *EI2*; W. Madelung, *The Succession to Muḥammad*, pp. 50 ff. On the highly symbolic matter of Muḥammad's inheritance, see also ibid., pp. 360–363.

20. Then, God — He is Mighty and Sublime — said: '*Nay! When the earth is ground to powder,* **[61]** *and your Lord comes, and the angels rank on rank*' [Q. 89:21–22]. By 'earth', he means the Proof[23] — may God's blessings be upon him —, as well as his manifestation (*ẓuhūr*), his rising (*qiyām*) and his spreading (*inbisāṭ*) back from his withdrawal (*munqabaḍ*). '*When your Lord comes*': by this, He means the Resurrector (*qā'im*) — may God's blessings be upon him — the Master of the age. The 'angels' are his friends, his auxiliaries and the people of his Summons.[24] [In this case, however],[25] this speech applies to a specific angel, that is, the one who will hold up the sword (*yaqūm bi'l-sayf*) before the Master of the age, because His words — He is Mighty and Sublime: '*the angels rank on rank*' mean that the Imam will send before him someone who will hold up the sword and warn people about his power and the scourge of his chastisement. He will then come in person, after the earth has been prepared and arranged for him — may God bless him and his family. This means that God will send the Imam who bears the sword (*al-qā'im bi'l-sayf*), and that he will warn the peoples, one after the another, with his tongue and sword. '*Upon that day, Gehenna is brought out*' [Q. 89:23]: 'Gehenna', here, means the Speaking-Prophet who will appear with the sword (*yaẓhar bi'l-sayf*) and their sentencing to death, which means [their doom in] Gehenna.

21. '*Upon that day, man will remember, but how will remembrance profit him?*' [Q. 89:23]. By this blamed man, He refers to Abū Bakr — may

---

[23] On this hermeneutical equivalence, see also *Kashf* III, p. 85, § 76; V, p. 101, § 22; p. 155, § 106.

[24] Members of the *da'wa* are sometimes referred to as angels; see also *Kashf* V, p. 154, § 104, where the Summoners are designated as 'venerable Angels'. In other sources, the angels are identified with the Proofs or various other ranks of the *da'wa*; see e.g. Ja'far b. Manṣūr al-Yaman, *Sarā'ir wa-asrār al-nutaqā'*, pp. 34, 38, 40; idem, *Ta'wīl al-zakāt*, pp. 91, 103; Ibn Ḥawshab, *Kitāb al-Rushd wa'l-hidāya*, p. 206 (English trans., p. 74), where the reason for this identification is that the Imams have 'given' or 'entrusted' (*mallaka*) the 'knowledge of religion and guidance' to the Proofs.

[25] The text seems to present two meanings for the word 'angel'. The first one, which identifies the angels with members of the *da'wa*, would be the 'classical' Ismaili interpretation; see previous footnote. The second meaning seems to be a reinterpretation of the term in order for it to fit the requirements of the context of composition of *Kashf* III.

God curse him —, who, on that day, will remember how he opposed the Prince of the Believers — peace be upon him. It thus means Abū Bakr and those whose station and state are similar to his and who believe in his lie. He and the people of his era will remember on the day of Resurrection **[62]** and Return. Whoever is similar to him will remember on the manifestation of the Resurrector (*ẓuhūr al-qā'im*) — peace be upon him. He will blame his followers, and they will blame him, and he will tell them: *'I had no power over you save that I summoned you and you listened to me. So do not blame me, but blame yourselves. I cannot listen to your cries, and you cannot listen to mine. I reject what you have associated me with [i.e. God]'* [Q. 14:22].[26]

22. After the words: *'Upon that day, man will remember, but how will remembrance profit him?'* [Q. 89:23], [God] — He is Mighty and Sublime — adds: *'He will say: "O would that I have forwarded for my life!"'* [Q. 89:24]. He means that his life and the life of all creation lies in the knowledge of the Prince of the Believers — peace be upon him. Then He says: *'Upon that day, non shall punish as He punishes, none shall bind as He binds'* [Q. 89:25–26]. This description and this speech apply to him,[27] as well as his accomplice[28] because the latter misled him and drove him astray. This also applies to Naʿthal[29] who assisted them, accepted what they claimed and turned away from the Order as they did. Each of them is a Satan.

23. Then, God — He is Mighty and Sublime — said: *'O soul at peace, return unto your Lord, well-pleased, well-pleasing'* [Q. 89:27–28]. This is the soul (*nafs*) of the Prophet — may God bless him — because it is from the Spirit of God and will return to the source (*maʿdin*) from whence it came. It has another meaning on the esoteric level: *'O soul at peace, return'* refers to the soul of the believer which comes from the

[26] In the Qur'an, this speech is attributed to Satan who thus puts the blame on those who listened to him.

[27] See al-Qummī, *Tafsīr*, ed. Ṭ. al-Mūsawī al-Jazā'irī, vol. 2, p. 421; ed. Mu'assasat al-Mahdī vol. 3, p. 1156, where Q. 89:25–26 is interpreted as referring to *fulān* or to 'the Second'.

[28] ʿUmar.

[29] Derogatory nickname of ʿUthmān in Shiʿi literature. On the meaning of the term (either 'old fool' or 'long-bearded'), see M.M. Bar-Asher, *Scripture and Exegesis*, p. 117 and p. 117, n. 115.

soul [**63**] of God. It is 'at peace' through the knowledge of God in every era. 'Return unto your Lord, well-pleased, well-pleasing': this refers to the soul of the Prophet — may God bless him — because upon the return (*al-rujūʿ*), that is, the Recurrence (*al-karra*), it will be with the Resurrector of the age (*qāʾim al-zamān*) — may God bless him.

24. *'Enter among my worshippers, enter My Paradise'* [Q. 89:29–30]. The worshippers are the Imams and the Speaking-Prophets — may God's blessings be upon them. Whoever does not enter into their obedience is not a believer. Whoever does enter into their obedience and knows them in their age, necessarily obtains satisfaction and contentment (*al-riḍā wa'l-riḍwān*) from God. 'Paradise', in this context, is the Proof — peace be upon him — because every Imam is reached only through his Proof, and the Proofs are the Gates of the Imams.

25. According a certain explanation, in this context, the 'Lord' is, esoterically, the Prince of the Believers, [because] he is the Lord and Master of the covenant of faith (*ʿuqdat al-īmān*) — peace be upon him. It is therefore necessary for every believing man and woman from the community of Muḥammad — may God bless him — among those who believe in the esoteric and act upon what they know, to acknowledge the sacred station of the Prince of the Believers, in accordance with the testament (*waṣiyya*) of Muḥammad the Messenger of God — may God bless them both and their family. [It is necessary that] they [the believers] make use of their knowledge that ʿAlī is the Master of exegesis (*ṣāḥib al-taʾwīl*) and its key, and that, had he not opened [the door of exegesis] for the believers, they would not know it.

26. *'On the day when all men'* shall be summoned *'by their Imam'* [Q. 17:71],[30] every Imam will make it known to the people of his age and his Friendship (*walāya*) that he is the sacred station, and that the knowledge of faith emanates [**64**] towards them exclusively from the Prince of the Believers, ʿAlī b. Abī Ṭālib, through what he indicates and establishes. It is through this that they connect to the Messenger of God — may God bless him — then, through the latter, to God — He is Mighty and Sublime.

[30] This verse is quoted and commented on below, *Kashf* III, p. 67, § 32.

[Exegesis of Q. 17:50–52]

27. About God's words — He is Mighty and Sublime: '*Say: "Be stones or iron, or some other creation that is yet greater in your hearts."*[31] *They will say: "Who will bring us back?" Say: "He who created you the first time." They will shake their heads at you and say: "When will that be?" Say: "It will perhaps be soon."*' [Q. 17:50–51], al-Ḥakīm says that this is about Abū al-Faṣīl and Zufar.[32] Indeed, <the community has associated these two>[33] to the Prince of the Believers <— may God bless him — regarding the sacred station of the Legacy, of the diffusion of the exegesis and the completion of the Messengers's Order. The Messenger>[34] — may God bless him and his family — had said indeed: 'I am the Master of revelation, and 'Alī is the Master of exegesis.' Their pride prevented them from being drawn toward him and listening to the exegesis from him, and jealousy overcame them. So God told His Messenger about them: '*Say: "Be stones or iron*"', meaning: 'If you do not obey God's order to have faith in the Master of exegesis and to acquire the knowledge of the exegesis from him, then be inert (*jamād*) stones or iron. You will not hear any knowledge, and none of your efforts and deeds will be accepted.' This is because stones and iron are inert matter that can neither hear knowledge nor do nothing, because there is no life in them **[65]** as there is in animals.

---

[31] That is, 'any other creation that you deem harder to revive'. In the Qur'an, these verses are a response to those who doubt the resurrection: '*They say: "What, when we are bones and remains, shall we really be raised up again in a new creation?"*' [Q. 17:49].

[32] Nicknames of Abū Bakr and 'Umar. According to Bar-Asher, *faṣīl* means 'young camel' and was 'substituted for its synonym, *bakr*'; see M.M. Bar-Asher, *Scripture and Exegesis*, p. 119.

[33] Ms. A: *ishrākahum*; ms. B: *ushrikū* crossed out and replaced by: *ashrakahum*. In a footnote, Strothmann suggests that the meaning is as translated (*la'alla al-murād ashrakat al-umma al-ithnayn al-madhkūrayn ilā amīr al-mu'minīn*). In his edition, p. 73, Ghālib reproduces this suggestion word for word, but replaces *ashrakat* by *ashrakū*. In this instance, Ghālib seems to have plagiarised Strothmann's edition.

[34] Missing in Ghālib's edition, p. 73. This could also indicate that Ghālib has plagiarised Strothmann's because this sentence fits exactly in one line of Strothmann's edition, which would mean that Ghālib overlooked it when copying Strothmann. However, there is also the possibility that we are dealing here with an homeoteleuton in Ghālib's manuscript, since the missing sentence is between two occurrences of *ṣallā Allāh 'alayhi*.

28. Then He says: *'Or some other creation that is yet greater in your hearts'* [Q. 17:51], meaning: 'Or be associating and disbelieving creatures whose destiny is Fire, since it is *'greater in your hearts'* to be considered among these.' *'God will gather hypocrites and disbelievers, all together, into hell'* [Q. 4:140]. *'They will say: "Who will bring us back?"'* [Q. 17:51], meaning that they will say: 'Who will bring us back among the disbelievers and the associators after we left them and converted to Islam?' *'Say: "He who created you the first time."'* [Q. 17:51]. He summoned you to faith and to the exegesis, but since you rejected the summons to faith and exegesis and rebelled, he will bring you back among the rebels, the unbelievers and the associators, and will gather you, all together, in hell, as God said — He is Mighty and Sublime.

29. *'They will shake their heads at you'* [Q. 17:51]. 'They shake', in the language of the Arabs, means 'they raise'. This means that they will raise their heads towards you and will say: 'Let us hear the Summons of the exegesis from you, just like you let us hear the Summons of the revelation.' They thus raise their heads with pride towards the one that God has raised above their heads and placed at their head, that is, the Legatee ʿAlī b. Abī Ṭālib — may God's blessings be upon him. God chose him and the Messenger — may God bless him — indicated him for the diffusion of the exegesis. The meaning of: *'They will shake their heads at you'* is therefore that they will raise themselves above ʿAlī, your Legatee, to listen to you and not to him.

30. Then, God — He is Mighty and Sublime — said: *'They will say: "When will that be?"'* [Q. 17:51], meaning: 'When is the time when we will be brought back with the associators **[66]** and the disbelievers even though we are Muslims?' So, God told His Messenger: *'Say: "It will perhaps be soon."'*, thus showing to you the consequence of your pride — your destiny among the people of the Fire.

31. *'On the day when He will summon you, and you will answer with His praise (ḥamd), and you will think that you have tarried but a little'* [Q. 17:52]. On the esoteric level, the 'praise' names the Legatee. God — He is Mighty and Sublime — said: *'On the day when He will summon you, and you will answer'* — on the Day of Resurrection (*al-baʿth*) — *'with His praise'* — the Legatee that God has chosen for His Messenger; you will answer him. *'And you will think that you have tarried but a little'* before the Day of Resurrection, because you will find the Order of God as you heard it soft and tender. No one repels

His Order, no one delays His Judgement, no one replaces His tradition (*sunna*).

32. Such is the meaning of His words: *'On the day when We will summon all men by their Imam'* [Q. 17:71]. 'Alī — may God's blessings be upon him — is the Imam of the companions of Muḥammad — may God bless him — and it is by 'Alī that they are summoned to Muḥammad, because he is his Gate. This is why it is said: "Alī will bear the Standard of Praise (*liwā' al-ḥamd*) in his hand on the Day of Resurrection.'[35] This means that he bears in his hand the sacred station of the Legatee which the Lord of the universes has bestowed upon him.

[Meaning of the Praise: exegesis of Q. 10:10]

33. Indeed, in the esoteric sense, it is said: *'Praise be to God, Lord of the universes'* [Q. 1:2], [meaning] praise be to God on the Day of Resurrection (*yawm al-qiyāma*), to emphasize that the Order and the sacred station of the Legatee belong to God, just like the Messenger belongs to God. He says: *'The close of their prayer (da'wāhum) will be: "Praise be to God, Lord of the Universes"'* [Q. 10:10]. The esoteric meaning of this verse: *'Their prayer (da'wāhum) therein* **[67]** *will be: "Glory to you, O God"'* [Q. 10:10], is that they are summoned to exalt God and acknowledge His sovereignty, until they pronounce it with their tongues and believe it in their hearts. *'And their greeting: "Peace"'* [Q. 10:10]: by

[35] The 'Standard of Praise' appears in several Sunni collections of *ḥadīths*, except that it is attributed to Muḥammad rather than 'Alī. The eschatological context yet remains the same; see e.g. Ibn Ḥanbal, *Musnad*, vol. 1, pp. 281, 295; vol. 3, p. 144. For other occurrences of the 'Standard of Praise' in the main Sunni collections, see A.J. Wensick and J.P. Mensing, *Concordance et indices de la tradition musulmane* (Leiden, 1943), s.v. *ḥamd* (*liwā' al-ḥamd*). Strothmann also provides other references to Sunni sources; see *Kashf*, p. 67, n. 3. The 'Standard of Praise' is also found in numerous Shi'i *ḥadīths*, and is attributed to either Muḥammad, 'Alī or the angel Gabriel. In some versions, Gabriel transmits the standard to Muḥammad, who in turn gives it to 'Alī, which obviously symbolizes the latter's appointment as Legatee; see e.g. al-Majlisī, *Biḥār al-anwār*, *juz'* 7, *abwāb al-ma'ād*, *bāb* 17: *al-wasīla wa-mā yaẓhar min manzilat al-nabī wa ahl baytihi fī'l-qiyāma*, no. 21, vol. 3, p. 523; *juz'* 8, *abwāb al-ma'ād*, *bāb* 18: *al-liwā'*, no. 1–12, vol. 3, pp. 526–529. In Ismaili sources, the standard is sometimes attributed to 'Alī and sometimes to Muḥammad; for the former, see e.g. Ja'far b. Manṣūr al-Yaman, *Sarā'ir wa-asrār al-nuṭaqā'*, p. 18; idem, *Ta'wīl al-zakāt*, p. 44; for the latter, see e.g. al-Mu'ayyad fī'l-dīn, *Al-Majālis al-mu'ayyadiyya*, ed. Ḥ. Khaḍḍūr (Salamiyya, 2019), vol. 2, p. 147.

this, what is meant is their acknowledgement of the Messenger, their surrender (*taslīm*) to him in their pursuit [of knowledge], and their conversion to Islam. Indeed, when they are summoned to God, they are summoned to the Messenger until they believe in him and acknowledge [that] his Message (*risāla*) is from God. Then, *'the close of their prayer (daʿwāhum) will be: "Praise be to God, Lord of the Universes"'* [Q. 10:10]: the meaning of the close of their prayer — that praise be to God — is that they acknowledge that the Legatee belongs to God, that he rose on His order, that the esoteric [aspect] of his knowledge belongs to God, that to obey him is to obey God. He is the Lord of the universes, and His Judgement applies to all of them together. He put the revelation in the charge of the Messenger, and the exegesis in the charge of the Legatee — and they are the knowledge and the deeds (*al-ʿilm wa'l-ʿamal*). God made it a duty to obey the Messenger and the Legatee, and to follow their knowledge and their deeds. And whoever acknowledges the Legatee and obeys him, it is as if this summons him to obey every Imam after him. And if the believer consents to the creed (*shahāda*) that there is no god but God and that Muḥammad is the Messenger of God — may the blessings and peace of God be upon him — it is a duty for him, after that, to acknowledge the Legatee of the Messenger of God, to acknowledge that his sacred station is to God — since he is the Praise — and that it is from God that he rose with the exegesis. He is to be acknowledged by his esoteric name, the Praise, as an indication to the acknowledgement of what he rose with and of the fact that he is the Master of the esoteric part of God's Order — He is Mighty and Sublime. Such is the meaning of His words in the first verse: *'On the day when He will summon you, and you will answer'* [Q. 17:52] **[68]** *'willingly or unwillingly'* [Q. 3 :83].[36] <. . .>[37] The Messenger is Muḥammad and the

[36] Also Q. 13:15.

[37] 'They are not summoned unless he is the fourth': the meaning of this sentence is unclear. As a matter of fact, the whole passage on the Praise, although understandable, is written in poor syntax and is apparently corrupted. As for this specific sentence, Strothmann suggests it might be an allusion to Q. 58:7: *'Three men do not have a confidential speech, but He is the fourth of them.'* In Strothmann's edition, there is a misprint here: *lā yadʿūn li'annahu al-rābiʿ*, instead of what ms. A reads: *lā yadʿūn illa annahu al-rābiʿ*. Ghālib reproduces the same error (p. 75) and suggests that the 'fourth' refers to the 'califate' of ʿAlī b. Abī Ṭālib, who is the fourth 'from the exoteric perspective' (p. 75, n. 3) — but this explanation is very implausible.

Legatee is ʿAlī — may God's blessings be upon them both. There is no excuse for the community of Muḥammad not to obey them both.

[The Imam as shadow: exegesis of Q. 25:45–46]

34. Concerning God's words: *'Have you not seen how your Lord has stretched out the shadow? If He willed, He could have made it still. Then We made the sun its guide, thereafter We seize it to Ourselves with ease'* [Q. 25:45–46], al-Ḥakīm — peace be upon him — says: 'The 'stretched shadow' here refers to the Prince of the Believers — peace be upon him. The 'Lord' is the 'Follower' (*al-tālī*)[38] who guides towards the stretched shadow. The stretching of the shadow is the unfolding of his knowledge for the elite of the people of his Friendship (*khawāṣ ahl walāyatihi*). *'If He willed, He could have made it still (sākin)'*: if God willed, He could have made this knowledge still (*askana-hu*), so that people would not know what it is, or what his sacred station and his esoteric knowledge are.[39] However, it is necessary that Truth becomes manifest, because if it remained still, the entire world would perish and all would topple, and be vanquished.

[The three-branched shade: al-Miqdād, Abū Dharr and Salmān. Exegesis of Q. 77:30–31]

35. The speech now returns to the Speaker of each age (*nāṭiq kull zamān*)[40] — may God's blessings be upon him — who is the glorified

---

[38] In Ismaili terminology, the 'Follower' (*al-tālī*) is usually paired with the 'Preceder' (*al-ṣābiq*). These terms designate the first two ontological hypostases (i.e, Universal Intellect/Universal Soul; Kūnī/Qadar), which, in the material realm, correspond to the couple Muḥammad/ʿAlī. However, the *Kashf* does not generally engage in such ontological speculations — except in Treatise II, as we have seen — and therefore, it is peculiar to find a term relating to ontology here, in a passage which deals with something quite different. In addition, one would expect the *tālī* to correspond to ʿAlī, as is usually the case in Ismaili texts, but here the *tālī* guides towards ʿAlī. It is therefore likely that the *tālī* is the Proof, as hinted to by the following paragraphs which are dedicated to this rank. Yet, it remains unclear why the Proof would be named the 'Follower'.

[39] Apart from the interpretation of 'Lord', a similar interpretation of Q. 25:45–46 is found in Jaʿfar b. Manṣūr al-Yaman, *Al-Shawāhid wa'l-bayān*, IIS MS. 734, ff. 91–92.

[40] Here, the term *nāṭiq* does not seem to refer to the Speaking-Prophet, but to the Imam present in each time. This is in line with the characteristically early Fatimid analogy between *nāṭiq* and *imām*.

Imam, the veil of the Resurrector, the illuminating sun who points toward the radiant moon,[41] the One who speaks marvels and is the locus of epiphany for beings (*al-nāṭiq bi'l-ʿajā'ib wa'l-maẓhar li'l-badā'iʿ fīhi*),[42] who is guided by the shade-giving shadow of which God said: '*Rush to a shadow split in three branches, which yet yields no shade and nor any relief from the flame*' [Q. 77:30–31].

36. The shadow refers to the Prince of the Believers — peace be upon him. It is necessary to know him in his esoteric truths (*ḥaqā'iq*) and his sacred stations. The explanation **[69]** of this is that God — may He be exalted — tells the Speaking-Prophet: 'Tell your people: "Rush to the Legatee"', who will address his community on this. '*Split in three branches*' refers to his Gates that he establishes to summon towards him and whom he appointed for those who seek him. They are the Proofs of the Legatee, and the Legatee is the Proof of the Messenger, and the Messenger is the Proof of God; all these Proofs are for the worshippers, in this world and in the hereafter. By 'rush', He means that it is necessary for you to meet him, to stand before him, to seek him and to present [yourselves] to him. Whoever belongs to the Summons of one of these three branches — peace be upon them — who speak with wisdom and sword (*nuṭaqā' bi'l-ḥikma wa'l-sayf*) <. . .>[43]

37. Among them is al-Miqdād, named so because he cut off (*qadda*) falsehood and eliminated it; he illuminated the Truth and summoned to it. He is one of the wellsprings; whoever drinks from him will never be thirsty again.[44]

38. The second wellspring is Abū Dharr because he inseminated (*dhara'a*)[45] the people, taught them and they drank from him. His

---

[41] In line with our previous footnote, this would mean that the Imam, here identified with the 'sun', indicates his successor, the *ḥujja*, 'Proof', identified with the 'moon'.

[42] Ms. A: *bi'l-ḥijāb*; ms. B: *bi'l-ḥijāb* and *bi'l-ʿijāb* in the margin, instead of *bi'l-ʿajā'ib*. I correct into the latter reading, following Ghālib, p. 76, because his suggestion presents the advantage of creating an effect of rhymed prose with *badā'iʿ*. It is however unclear to me what and who is meant by this.

[43] The sentence is incomplete here, the text seems corrupted. Yet, neither Strothmann nor Ghālib seemed to take notice.

[44] This is reminiscent of John 4:13.

[45] Same etymology in *Kashf* V, pp. 100–101, § 22.

name is Jundub. On the day when Satan rose and people swore allegiance to him after the summons of Iblīs, following [the death of the Prophet], they came to Abū Dharr — peace be upon him — and told him: 'Swear allegiance, Abū Dharr.' 'To whom?', he asked. [They replied] 'To the Satan of the community.' [He stated] 'No, by God, I will absolutely not swear allegiance to the brother of Taym.[46] I will not repel the Prince of the Believers — may God's blessings be upon him. **[70]** You have disobeyed,[47] you have exchanged [truth for falsehood],[48] and you have disbelieved when he was a rebel! [Abū Bakr] will say: *"Woe to me! Would that I had not taken So-and-so (fulān)*[49] *for a friend (khalīl)! He indeed led me astray from the remembrance"* — that is, from knowing the Prince of the Believers —[50] *"after it had come to me. Satan leads man astray"* [Q. 25:28–29].' Then Abū Dharr <. . .>[51]

---

[46] This refers to Abū Bakr. Taym was the clan of Quraysh he belonged to; it is also mentioned in *Kashf* I, p. 21, § 46. See E. Kohlberg, 'Some Imamī Shīʿī views on the *Ṣaḥāba*', p. 166, n. 139, where the expression 'brother of Taym' is commented on with reference to the present passage of the *Kashf*. The expressions 'brother of Taym', for Abū Bakr, and 'brother of ʿAdī', for ʿUmar, are found elsewere; see e.g. the declaration attributed to Muʿāwiya by Ibn Abī al-Ḥadīd, cited by W. Madelung, *The Succession to Muḥammad*, p. 335.

[47] Ms. A: *ḥalaftum*; ms. B: *khalaftum*. Strothmann suggests correcting into: *khālaftum*, which I translate.

[48] The verb *baddala*, 'to exchange' recalls Q. 14:28: *'Have you not seen those who exchange the grace of God for disbelief?*', quoted in *Kashf* I, p. 21, § 46.

[49] With regard to the present passage of the *Kashf*, Kohlberg, 'Some Imamī Shīʿī views on the *Ṣaḥāba*', p. 166, suggests that *fulān* here refers to Abū Bakr. It is generally true that the term appearing alone mean Abū Bakr, while the expression *fulān wa-fulān* means both Abū Bakr and ʿUmar; see M.M. Bar-Asher, *Scripture and Exegesis*, p. 118. However, this does not seem to apply to the other interpretation of Q. 25:28–29 in *Kashf* I, p. 30, § 63, where *fulān* is identified with Satan, that is, ʿUmar, while the lament: '*Woe to me! etc.*' is put in Abū Bakr's mouth, the 'man' forsaken by Satan in the verse.

[50] On the 'remembrance', see *Kashf* I, p. 30, § 63; III, p. 79, § 62; VI, p. 158, § 3.

[51] Ms. A: *thumma khalafa Abū Dharr lammā quri'a (sic) hādhihi al-āya lammā nazalat*; ms. B: *wa-qāla thumma khalaqa Abū Dharr (yaqūm qiyāmahu bi'l-sayf idh qama ʿalā al-kafara al-fujjār fa-lā ẓill lahum yastiẓillūn bi-hi min al-qatl wa-la yaljaʾūn ilayhi wa'l-ẓill alladhī yughnī ʿan al-lahab) huwa qarra hādhihi al-āya lahā li-dhā (sic) nazalat.* The passage is obviously corrupted, particularly in B. The part of the sentence that I put between brackets in the B variant is misplaced; it appears a few lines further in ms. A.

39. The third wellspring, which is the end of all ends and the wellspring of all wellsprings, is Salsabīl or Salmān, as in God's words — He is Mighty and Sublime: '*There is a spring [in Paradise] named Salsabīl*' [Q. 76:18]. [Salmān] is the Great Ark (*al-safīna al-kabīra*). His very name is an indication of its meaning, because it is the name of salvation (*ism salāma*) <. . .>[52] He saves whoever is in peace with him (*sallama li-man sālamahu*).[53] The Gate of ʿAlī, whoever **[71]** knows him knows [ʿAlī]. Whoever does not know the wellspeing, that is, the Prince of the Believers — peace be upon him — in his esoteric truths (*ḥaqā'iq*), though his three faces, will not be saved from destruction and from the sword, because he will have '*no shade and nor any relief from the flame*' [Q. 77:31]. Al-Ḥakīm — peace be upon him — says that the meaning of this verse is that he will rise with the sword (*qiyāmuhu bi'l-sayf*) against the dissolute disbelievers. They will then have no shade to shelter from being killed. The shadow that offers relief from the flame is one of the three Gates — peace be upon them.

[Salmān, the origin of Islam]

40. He then returned to the topic of Salmān and to why he was named Salmān and said that it is because he is the origin of Islam, and it is through him that [Islam] is known. Among those who were questioning him, someone asked al-Ḥakīm for a proof (*dalīl*) from the Book of God. 'Such is the meaning of God's words — He is Mighty and Sublime: '*The true religion with God is Islam*' [Q. 3:19]. By 'religion', He means that the true *ḥanīfī*[54] religion that you are in is with God. Salmān was a ladder (*sullam*) towards his master, and he gave himself (*aslama nafsahu*) to him based on the knowledge he had of the truth of religion within the Law (*sharīʿa*) of Jesus — may the blessing of God be upon him. He thus went from one truth (*ḥaqīqa*) to another truth.

---

[52] *Jamʿ karāma*: there is a literary effect of rhymed prose with *ism salāma*, but the meaning escapes me.

[53] The author is playing on the root letters *s-l-m*, from which the words 'Islam' and 'salvation' (*salāma*) are derived.

[54] Ms. A: *ḥanafī*; ms. B: *ḥaqīqī*. Strothmann follows A, Ghālib reads the same as B. Corrected to *ḥanīfī*, as the text obviously refers to the authentic monotheism of Abraham as mentioned in the Qur'an, not to the juridical Sunnī school.

God — He is Mighty and Sublime — said: '*The true religion with God is Islam*', which means that perfection in religion is to surrender (*taslīm*) [to God], to have purity of intention and certainty about God's Order with all those who **[72]** were appointed (*aqāma*) by God, Speaking-Prophet after Speaking-Prophet, Legatee after Legatee, Imam after Imam. When Salmān surrendered (*aslama*) to Muḥammad after [he had surrendered to] Jesus — may God's blessings be upon them both — he perfected his religion, first with Jesus, and he completed it by following Muḥammad — may God bless him.

41. This is the meaning of the prayer of Muḥammad, the Mesenger of God — may God bless him. In the beginning of Islam, he prayed towards the Sacred House;[55] his prayer in this direction, and the prayer of those who prayed with him, were approved (*yataqabbal*) by God. And God did not make them lose the reward of the first direction in which they prayed. It is thus said that a Muslim was leading the prayer of an assembly of Muslims, when someone informed him, just as he was praying, that the Messenger — may God bless him — was [now] praying in the direction of Mecca by an order from God. So [the Imam] turned to Mecca and completed his prayer. When this reached the Messenger of God — may God bless him — he lauded and praised him for it, and he said: 'God has accepted both the beginning and the end of his prayer, and has doubled his reward.' This is a sign from God validating what Salmān did and indicating that he should be imitated in this, because the religion of God is not broken off by the death of the Messengers and the Imams; rather, it is perpetuated by successive representatives (*qā'im ba'da qā'im*) in accordance with God's order and election. The perfection of religion and the completion of Islam thus reside in the succession of God's chosen ones, one after another — may God's blessings be upon them all.

[Exegesis of Q. 25:45–46 continued][56]

42. On God's words — He is Mighty and Sublime: '*Then We made the sun its guide, thereafter We seize it to Ourselves with ease*'

---

[55] Jerusalem.

[56] The interpretation of these two verses started a few pages above on § 34 and was suddenly interrupted by the passage on the three Proofs, only to resume here.

[Q. 25:45–46], al-Ḥakīm — peace be upon him — said **[73]** that by the sun, He means the Speaking-Prophet in every age — may the blessings of God be upon him. It is he [the Speaking-Prophet] who guides towards the eternally still shadow — peace be upon it. '*Thereafter We seize it (qabaḍnāhā)*[57] *to Ourselves with ease*': by this, He means the occultation (*ghayba*) that takes place in every age.[58] The 'ease' is the interval (*fatra*) that extends between two Speaking-Prophets — may the blessings of God be upon them all.[59]

[Exegesis of Q. 19:96–97]

43. '*Those who believe and do good deeds (al-ṣāliḥāt), the All-merciful shall assign love (wuddan) unto them*' [Q. 19:96]. About these words of God — He is Mighty and Sublime — he said — peace be upon him — that by 'those who believe', He means those who believe in the secret of the family of Muḥammad. '*Those who do good deeds*': they know the Imam of their era and they are righteous to him and by him (*ṣalaḥū lahu wa-bihi*); they are the good deed. The deed has several meanings: one of its meanings is what a man conveys from his righteous earnings as goodness to himself (?).[60] The second [type of] deed, which is the ultimate purpose (*al-ghāya*), is to know (*ma'rifa*) the Master of the age — peace be upon him. '*The All-merciful shall assign love (wuddan) unto them*' means: 'I have assigned love in the hearts of the created beings.' [The name] 'the All-merciful' (*al-raḥmān*) [derives] from 'the Compassionate' (*al-raḥīm*), and it is one of the

[57] See *Kashf* III, p. 62, §20, where the verb *inqabaḍa*, from the same root *q-b-ḍ*, designated the occultation of the Proof before its manifestation.

[58] Similar interpretation of Q. 25:45–46 in Ja'far b. Manṣūr al-Yaman, *Al-Shawāhid wa'l-bayān*, IIS MS. 734, ff. 91–92.

[59] Ms. A: *al-quwwa*; ms. B: *al-quwwa* and *al-fatra* in the margin. On the notion of *fatra*, see C. Pellat, 'Fatra', *EI2*; W. Madelung, 'Das Imamat', pp. 104–105; H. Halm, 'Zur Datierung . . .', pp. 97–98.

[60] Ms. A: *wa-aḥad ma'ānīhi mā arāda bi-hi al-rajul min ṣāliḥ kasbihi ṭayyibatun bi-dhālika nafsahu*; ms. B: *wa-aḥad ma'ānīhi mā arāda bi-hi al-rajul min ṣāliḥ yanqasim 'alā ma'ānin wa-aḥad ma'ānīhi mā arāda bi-hi al-rajul min ṣāliḥ kasbihi ṭayyibatun bi-dhālika nafsahu*. As we can see, ms. B repeats itself, but even ms. A is unclear. Also, Strothmann replaces *arāda bi-hi* with *yu'addīhi* without noting this correction. At the end of the paragraph, we find the same confusion between *arāda* and *addā*, which probably explains Strothmann's correction

names of God — He is Mighty and Sublime. And love, in the esoteric sense, is the Prince of the Believers — peace be upon him. He therefore said that he will assign the Legatee as an intercessor for them on the Day of Resurrection. '*We have made it easy in your tongue that you may bear good tidings unto the godfearing, and warn a people stubborn*' [Q. 19:97]. The godfearing (*al-muttaqūn*) are the believers who fear sedition (*fitna*) and enmity — they are the party of the Imam and his auxiliaries (*anṣār*), they are the people who protect him and know his reality.[61] The 'people stubborn' are **[74]** Abū al-Faṣīl, Zufar and Naʿthal, and their followers. They stubbornly opposed the Master of Truth (*aladdū ʿalā ṣāḥib al-ḥaqq*), they usurped his name and did not convey their deeds (*addū aʿmālahum*) through his gate. They behaved with stubborn opposition with regard to what they had been ordered — may God curse them.

[Moses and Aaron: exegesis of Q. 20:25–31]

44. And God — He is Sublime and High — said: '*[Moses] said: Lord, expand my breast, ease my affair (amr) for me, and unloose the knot upon my tongue, that they may understand my words. And give me a minister from my folk, Aaron my brother, and by him add to my strength*' [Q. 20:25–31]. This was a request from Moses concerning his brother and Proof, Aaron — may God's blessings be upon them both. In the esoteric sense, this is a request from Muḥammad — may God bless him — to his Lord — He is Sublime and High — concerning his brother the Prince of the Believers — peace be upon him — to add to his force by him. And God — He is Mighty and Sublime — did this for them both so that they conveyed God's messages, advised His worshippers and guided the community to the Imamate and the Imams — may God's blessings be upon them. God — He is Mighty and Sublime — thus said: 'I approved this one for you as a brother, minister, companion and assistant.' The meaning of the 'knot' upon his tongue is that he asked Him to lift the [seal of] dissimulation (*taqiyya*), which He did through his minister and companion.

---

[61] *Ahl ḥimyat al-ʿārifūn bi-ḥaqīqatihi*: the text is grammatically incorrect. We should either have *al-ʿārifīn*, instead of *al-ʿārifūn* (this would translate as follows: 'the people who protect those who know his reality'), or: *ahl ḥimyatihi al-ʿārifūn bi-ḥaqīqatihi*, which I have translated.

[The role of the Summoners in preparing the *raj‘a*:
exegesis of Q. 20:108–112][62]

45. About God's words — He is Mighty and Sublime: '*That day they will follow the Summoner (dā‘ī) in whom is no crookedness*' [Q. 20:108], al-Ḥakīm said that the Summoner, in this context, is the Bearer of the sword (*al-qā'im bi'l-sayf*); there is no lie in his coming, and no pushing back his Summons. '*Voices will be hushed for the Merciful, and you will hear but a murmuring*' [Q. 20:108]. [Al-Ḥakīm] — peace be upon him — said: 'The murmuring is [the sound] **[75]** of steps [that will be heard] until the Prince of the Believers is done disputing (*munāẓara*) with his enemies about the Return (*raj‘a*) after which there will be no return.'

46. This is the meaning of God's words — He is Mighty and Sublime: '*He against whom the word of chastisement is realised — shall you deliver him out of the Fire?*' [Q. 39:19]. He means by this that he who is defeated on that day and who makes friendship (*walāya*) with the iniquitous, will be taken by the sword of the Resurrector — may God's blessings be upon him — and will not be delivered out of '*the Fire whose fuel (wuqūd) is people and stone, prepared for the unbelievers*' [Q. 2 :24]. 'People', from this perspective, are the believers who are enlightened by the Light of Truth; they showed the path to people and guided them towards their guides. The 'stones' are the Summoners; He means that they are those who take charge of the chastisement of those who disbelieved in them and their wisdom, and who summoned towards Imams other than the Imams of Truth, to whom [the Summoners] summon. The explanation for this is that the Summoners and the believers cause (*asbāb*) the combustion (*wuqūd*) of the Fire for the deniers, because God — He is Mighty and Sublime — only chastises after sending forth the proof (*ḥujja*) to His worshippers along with the excuse and the warning (*al-i‘dhār wa'l-indhār*). The Summoners and those among the believers who respond to them are this proof against the deniers and the misguided, because the Summoners excuse from

[62] The interpretation of Q. 20:110, however, is missing. Is this voluntary or was the passage lost? The former possibility should not be ruled out as the missing verse does not deal with the events of the Resurrection, which is the focus of the following paragraphs.

the Order of the Imams (*aʿdharū ʿan amr al-aʾimma*),[63] and they warn, and the believers respond. The Summoners are thus proof of excuses and warnings, and the believers are proof of the response and the necessity to accomplish the deeds that God has ordered. The unbelievers and the misguided will see the deeds of the believers <who fulfil their duty>[64] out of fear of **[76]** and desire for God. When the [acknowledgment of the] proof became a duty for them,[65] [the believers] became the means of the Fire, because they are those who fuel it for the misguided deniers by order of God.

47. About God's words — He is Mighty and Sublime: *'Surely We shall inherit the earth, and all that are upon it, and unto us they shall be returned'* [Q. 19:40]. He means by this the final Return (*rajʿa*) to God's Friends (*awliyāʾ*). They are the inheritors of the earth, and they are God's Proof for His servants. [The Proof] emanated from them and returned to them. It is by them that the world knows their guidance, it is to them that all creation returns, and their reckoning is with them. He means by this that they return to them, that the truth emanated from them and that all creation will return to them.[66]

---

[63] The meaning is apparently that the Summoners excuse those who acknowledge the 'Order of the Imams'. This is probably an allusion to the Qur'anic verses which reject the excuses and pretexts of the hypocrites who refuse to go to battle (Q. 9:90–94), and, more generally, the excuses of the damned on the Day of Judgment (Q. 30:75; 66:7; 75:15; 77:36). The text seems to imply that, inasmuch as, according to the Qur'an, the unbelievers will not be excused, the believers, on the contrary, will be. Note that Q. 66:6 also mentions *'the Fire whose fuel is men and stone'*, just like Q. 2:24 which is commented on here, while the following verse states precisely: *'O you unbelievers, make no excuses for yourselves this day. You are only being paid for what you were doing.'* This might be a key to understand this passage of Treatise III. However, the argument of the text is not very clear, partly because of a flawed transmission.

[64] This does not appear in the mss. and is a suggestion by Strothmann, p. 76, n. 2. The text is again corrupted, and the link between the two parts of the sentence is not clear: *al-kāfirūn wa'l-ḍāllūn yarūn aʿmāl al-muʾminīn wa-yaʿmalūn* (here, Strothmann adds: *wājibahum*). I translate as suggested by Strothmann and delete the *wa-* before *yaʿmalūn*.

[65] Does this refer to the duty of responding to the 'excuse and warning' of the Summoners?

[66] This paragraph is particularly corrupted, as can be seen from the repetition of the last sentence. This only obscures a passage which, due to the multiplicity of unidentified pronouns, was already unclear.

48. About God's words — He is Mighty and Sublime: *'On that day, shall no intercession avail except for those for whom the Merciful has given permission (adhina) and whose word He accepted'* [Q. 20:109]. Al-Ḥakīm said: 'On the day the Resurrector — may God's blessings be upon him — will rise with the sword (*qiyāmihi bi'l-sayf*), no one will obtain his intercession *'except for those for whom the Merciful has given permission'*, that is: except for those who will come to him with God's permission (*idhn*) and the permission of the followers of the Silent Imam who was hidden (*al-imām al-ṣāmit al-mastūr*) before the manifestation of the Resurrector (*ẓuhūr al-qā'im*) — may God's blessings be upon him. For, God's permission — He is Mighty and Sublime — is in the hands of the Imams and the Messengers, as stated in the story of Jesus — peace be upon him.[67] So whoever follows the Imam of his era, [this Imam][68] will guide him to and indicate the One who rises with the edge of the sword[69] with God's permission (*al-qā'im bi-ḥadd al-sayf min idhn Allāh*). He said that intercession [77] is from him, and that it is destined for whoever is among the people of Friendship (*walāya*) unless he has fallen short of [performing] the obligatory deeds (*qaṣṣara 'an wājib al-'amāl*); yet, if [the Bearer of the sword] approves of one of the deeds he did in obedience to [the Imams], and if he dies fearing for their Friendship (*muwālāt*), their love and their affection, then God will approve his deed.

49. About His words — He is Mighty and Sublime: *'And faces shall be humbled unto the Living, the Self-Subsisting. And he who bears iniquity shall fail'* [Q. 20:111], he said: 'the iniquity towards the family of

---

[67] Strothmann sees here an allusion to 'Alī's sermon in Kūfā as reported in *Kashf* I, pp. 8–9, §§ 14–16, but that passage does not mention God's 'permission' or 'licence'. The notion, as well as the term *idhn*, do appear in the *ḥadīth* at the end of *Kashf* I in which 'Alī resurrects the dead; see *Kashf* I, pp. 37–38, § 80. Strothmann was probably referring to this latter *ḥadīth* rather than to 'Alī's sermon. However, the present reference to 'the story of Jesus' is probably not to another passage of the *Kashf*, but rather to the passages of the Qur'an where Jesus performs miracles *'with God's permission'*; see Q. 3:49; 5:110. See also the interpretation of Q. 3:49 in *Kashf* V, p. 98, § 15.

[68] Mss. A, B, Strothmann and Ghālib all read: *wa-huwa*, which renders the sentence incorrect. I translate by deleting the *wa*.

[69] Mss. A, B: *bi-hādhā al-bayt*. I translate the version provided by the two editors who both correct into: *bi-ḥadd al-sayf*, without comment.

Muḥammad' (*ẓulm āl-Muḥammad*). The verse was thus revealed (*hākadhā unzilat hādhihi al-āya*).[70] God — He is Mighty and Sublime — said: '*Whoever does good deeds being a believer . . .*' [Q. 20:112], which means whoever does good deeds and knows the truth of faith as well as the two [types of] deeds; we explained this in its due place.[71] As for the 'believer', he is the one who believes in God's secret and knows its truths (*ḥaqā'iq*).

50. In God's words — He is Sublime and High: '*[O mankind! We have created you] male and female*' [Q. 49:13], by 'male', He means the one who disdains penetration (*kabura 'an al-nikāḥ*) and becomes a male who is not penetrated (*lā yunkaḥ*).[72] As for the female, she needs penetration (*taḥtāj ilā al-nikāḥ*).

51. So whoever does a deed receives retribution, and '*he shall fear neither inquity nor injustice*' [Q. 20:112] regarding what has already taken place, but he will receive retribution for all of it and will reach the degree of the one who is known from [his] deed.

52. The explanation of this in the esoteric sense is that the male is like the one whose degree in religion has been elevated and who has joined the ranks (*ḥudūd*) of the Summoners. He then does not need any Summons — this is because coitus (*al-nikāḥ*) is analogous to the Summons and the Prophets.[73] The one whose degree is not elevated cannot dispense with the Summons, with harkening to knowledge and with being reared in wisdom, as long as he belongs to this rank (*ḥadd*); it is so until his rank is elevated and he reaches the rank in which he is not summoned — which is analogous to **[78]** the male who is not penetrated, as previously said.

---

[70] The anonymous person quoted by the author of *Kashf* III is here referring to a variant reading, allegedly omitted from the 'official' Qur'an, in line with an early Shi'i tradition of Qur'anic commentaries.

[71] Cf. *Kashf* III, p. 74, § 51.

[72] The term *nikāḥ* can translate as 'marriage' or refer to coitus or penetration. In this instance, I have chosen the latter possibility since the argument of the text seems to be that the difference between male and female is that the former is active in the sexual relationship while the latter is passive — which symbolically corresponds respectively to the activity of the master passing on the initiatory teachings and the passivity of the disciple receiving this teaching.

[73] See *Kashf* I, pp. 26–27, §§ 57–59; V, p. 114, § 41; p. 123, § 57; VI, p. 166, § 23, and commentary of *Kashf* I, pp. 128–134.

53. He thus says that whoever accomplishes a deed, be he a Summoner or a believer,[74] his deed will not be lost, his endeavour will not be denied (*lā kufrān*) by God, and '*he shall fear neither iniquity nor injustice*' [Q. 20:112], as has previously been explained.[75]

[Exegesis of Q. 20:124–131, 135][76]

54. About God's words — He is Mighty and Sublime: '*And whosoever turns away from My Remembrance, his shall be a life of narrowness*' [Q. 20:124], [al-Ḥakīm] — peace be upon him — said that by this, He means the people who turned away from the Friendship (*walāya*) of the Prince of the Believers[77] — may God's blessings be upon him — and sat in his place.[78] On the exoteric level, this corresponds to the words of the Prophet, the Master of the Law — may God bless him: 'O people! Follow my guidance for it is God's guidance. And follow the guidance of ʿAlī b. Abī Ṭālib. Whoever follows his guidance in my life and after my death will not deviate from the Path and will not be wretched.'

55. '*And whosoever turns away from My Remembrance, his shall be a life of narrowness, and on the Day of Resurrection We shall gather him blind. He shall say: "My Lord, why have You gathered me blind when I was wont to see?" And [God] shall say: "Thus Our signs came unto you and you forgot them, and so today you are forgotten."*' [Q. 20:124–126]. This means: 'Thus My signs came unto you, 'Atīq[79], and you forgot them,

[74] *Mu'min* here refers to a member of the *daʿwa* hierarchy.

[75] The text is again corrupted, which makes it very cryptic. It seems that at some point in the history of the transmission, there was a mix-up between different passages. As a consequence, the interpretation of Q. 20:112 in §§57 and 59 is intertwined with the esoteric interpretation of male and female in §§58 and 60. The latter two paragraphs are apparently unrelated to the topic at hand — retribution within the *daʿwa*. The final paragraph of the passage, §61, could therefore be a later addition by a copyist trying to make sense of the whole passage by establishing a lose connection between the two themes — retribution and the symbolic male/female distinction.

[76] The discontinuity of the interpretation, which jumps from Q. 20:112 to Q. 20:124, then from Q. 20:131 to Q. 20:135, may indicate that the interpretation of the missing verses was lost in transmission — as may also be the case of Q. 20:110 above.

[77] On the 'remembrance', see *Kashf* I, p. 30, § 63; III, pp. 71, § 46; VI, p. 158, § 3.

[78] Mss. A, B, Strothmann: *jalasū fī majlisihi*, which I translate. Ghālib, p. 83: *jalasū fī ghayr majlisihi*.

[79] A non-derogatory nickname for Abū Bakr.

and so today you are forgotten, 'Umar.' *'And thus do We reward him who is prodigal'* [Q. 20:127] in hostility towards his Imam, sits in a seat that is not his[80] *'and does not believe in the signs (āyāt) of his Lord'* [Q. 20:127], that is, in 'Alī and the Imams among his progeny.[81] *'And verily the chastisement of the Hereafter'*, O 'Umar and 'Atīq, *'is more terrible and more lasting'* [Q. 20:127], [which means that they will be] permanently and perpetually in the narrowness and constraint of distorted bodies, and in all kinds **[79]** of chastisements and varieties of calamity.

56. His words: *'[Why have You brought me back] blind when I was wont to see?'* [Q. 20:125], mean that [God] brings back a blind person who has deviated from the Path of guidance, and is unguided by an Imam of truth, and [the blind person] says: *'I was wont to see'*, that is: 'I was wont to be guided by following the Messenger'. He will be answered: 'You stayed in this world after [the death of] the Messenger, [and] you received his order (which he had received from God) regarding the sacred station of the Legatee and the Imams among his progeny. They are the 'signs' of God, and yet you forgot them, that is: you renounced following them and emulating them, *'and so today you are forgotten'*, you are renounced and abandoned, with no guide to guide you since there is no guide but the one established by God and His Messenger as a guide.' This speech is addressed to the iniquitous after [the death of] the Messenger of God — may God bless him — and to all those who followed a Speaking-Prophet but did not follow his Legatee [as well], or followed an Imam but did not follow the one that this Imam appointed as his Legatee (*awṣā ilayhi*) and to whom he transmitted his authority (*afḍā ilayhi bi-amrihi*).[82]

57. Al-Ḥakīm said that God's words — He is Mighty and Sublime: *'Is it not a guidance to them, how many generations We destroyed before*

---

[80] Mss. A, B: *jalasa fī ghayr majlisihi*. Cf. § 54.

[81] The identification of the Qur'anic term *āya*, pl. *āyāt*, 'sign', with the Imams is a common feature in early Shi'i sources; see e.g. al-Kulaynī, *Uṣūl al-Kāfī, kitāb al-ḥujja, bāb anna al-āyāt allatī dhakarahā Allāh fī kitābihi hum al-a'imma*, vol. 1, p. 207, no. 1–3. See also *Kashf* V, pp. 130–133, §§ 68–70; VI, pp. 167–168, § 25; pp. 173–174, §§ 36–37. The *Kashf* illustrates, here too, the way exegeses and terms applied to the Imams in early Shi'ism are extended, in the Ismaili exegetical system, to various ranks of the *da'wa* hierarchy; see *Kashf* V, p. 151, § 102 ('signs' identified with the Proofs); VI, pp. 177–178, §§ 41–42 ('signs' identified with the Summoners, the Gates and the Proofs).

[82] Note the analogy between the two couples *nāṭiq/waṣī* and *imām/ḥujja*, 361 ff.

them in whose dwellings they walk? Surely in that are signs for men of thought [Q. 20:128], refer to the Imams — may God's blessings be upon them and upon those who follow them. And the meaning of His words: '*Is it not a guidance to them, how many generations We destroyed*', is that the downfall of those who opposed and resisted was unveiled to the people. They looked at the various exemplary [punishments], then at themselves, but their iniquity and disbelief only increased — may God curse them.

58. And the explanation His words: '*Surely in that are signs for men of thought*', is that the revenge and the exemplary [punishments] that came down from God unto the rebels are signs of the Imams and those **[80]** who follow them, for those who rebel against [the Imams] to consider [the signs], to be driven away [from rebellion] by them and to be admonished through them, and so that [the signs] may be proofs against those who are not driven away and do not consider [them]. Indeed, those whose iniquity and disbelief have increased do not consider what they are guided to through the examples of others. The delay God grants them and His longanimity misled them away from [the examples] — although He said — He is Mighty and Sublime: '*And let not those who disbelieve suppose that our respite to them is good for them. We grant them respite only that they may increase in sin; and there awaits them a shameful chastisement*' [Q. 3:178].

59. Al-Ḥakīm — peace be upon him — said about God's words — He is Mighty and Sublime: '*And but a word that preceded from your Lord, and a term already fixed, (the judgment) would have been inevitable*' [Q. 20:129] [that they mean]: 'Muḥammad, you see that the punishment is [deserved by] certain specific people. But, the 'word preceded' — [the word] is the duration of the lives in human form (*fī'l-nāsūt*). And it is a 'fixed term' because their lives in human form already took place in God's prescience and decree, as a known fixed term. It is not fitting for the wisdom of the Wise One <for Him to cut them off from their terms>,[83]

[83] Ms. A: *anna sharrahum aḥālahum*; ms. B: *anna sarrahum ājālahum*. Strothmann suggest that the meaning is: *an yabtarhum ājālahum*, which I translate. The text is slightly convoluted, but it is understood that the verse is thus interpreted: in spite of Muḥammad's longing for God's punishment of the disbelievers, it is necessary that those who deserve this punishment fully live the lives that were predetermined for them in God's prescience — thus actually deserving the punishment by the accomplishment of their lives. God then has a 'case' or a 'proof' (*ḥujja*) against them.

nor for Him to remove them from the lives He wanted for them — [He does not do this] in order for Him to have a case (*ḥujja*) against them. There is no part of the punishment He wants for someone that escapes Him. He is — may He be exalted — *'the First and the Last'* [Q. 57:3], and *'He encompasses all things'* [Q. 41:54] — glory be to His name.

60. He then said — may He be exalted: *'So be patient'*, O Muḥammad, and those who believe with you, *'with what they say'* [Q. 20:130] when they call you a magician, a madman or a liar, you and anyone who summons them to what you have summoned them, *'and proclaim the praise of your Lord before the rising (ṭulūʿ) of the sun and after its setting (ghurūb)'* [Q. 20:130]. **[81]** By this, He means the Resurrector's judgment (*ḥukm al-qāʾim*) — may God's blessings be upon him — upon his enemies — may God curse them — when what is rightfully his is returned to him and he rises with the sword — this is the rising of the sun. As for the sunset, it is the occultation (*ghayba*) that affects the Speaking-Prophet — may God's blessings be upon him — upon his death , in every era and every age, until another Speaking-Prophet appears by God's will and order at a time which God desires — He is Mighty and Sublime.

61. *'Do not turn your eyes to that We have given pairs of them to enjoy — the flower of the worldly life, that We may seduce (naftinahum)*[84] *them thereby'* [Q. 20:131]. Al-Ḥakīm — peace be upon him — said that He wants to dissuade the Speaking-Prophet of the age from turning his eyes to the pleasant life he sees in the people of misguidance, for this might distract him and he might be seduced by [their] enmity towards the Prince of the Believers — peace be upon him. Indeed, the enmity that the Speaking-Prophet — may God's blessings be upon him — saw from this wretched (*mankūs*) world towards the Prince of the Believers — peace be upon him — alarmed him and he almost doubted his position (*manzila*) with God — He is Sublime and High. This is the meaning of the verse: *'Had We not confirmed you, you would nearly have inclined to them a little'* [Q. 17:74]. He means that had he not received secret sciences and subtle [truths] (*al-ʿulūm al-maknūna*

---

[84] In the context of this verse, the verb *fatana* is usually understood as meaning 'to try' or 'to test'. But here, the interpreter of the verse understands it in the sense of 'to seduce', 'to tempt'.

wa'l-laṭā'if) regarding the Prince of the Believers — peace be upon him — had he not [reached] the highest degrees and the eminent position in every moment and in every glimpse, thus accessing unveilings and [divine] conversations (*yukāshaf mukāshafa wa-yukhāṭab mukhāṭaba*) — this is the 'confirmation'— he would have almost doubted the cause (*amr*) [of the Prince of the Believers], due to the great number of the people of deviation and corruption. And so a warning and a threat came to him from God — He is Mighty and Sublime. This happens with all the people of truthfulness (*ṣidq*) and knowledge (*ma'rifa*): **[82]** without God's confirmation to His Messengers, they would have turned on their heels (*irtaddū 'alā a'qābihim*) out of fear, not out of depravity (*khā'ifīn ghayr khāsirīn*).[85]

62. He then said: '*The provision of your Lord is better and more lasting*' [Q. 20:131]. This means the knowledge of the esoteric that God ordered him to bestow upon the Prince of the Believers — peace be upon him — and this is the 'provision' that comes out from this knowledge to the world. And it is 'better and more lasting' because the people of the world will have their world vanish from them, and '*they shall be returned to the most grievous chastisement*' [Q. 2:85] and the '*terrible abode*' [Q. 2:126].

63. About God's words — He is Mighty and Sublime: '*You shall know who are the owners of the even Way, and who is guided*' [Q. 20:135], he said — peace be upon him — that it is a threat to the people 'Atīq, Zufar and Na'thal and their supporters — may God curse them — because they are the enemies of the people of Truth. The 'owners of of the even Way' are the companions of the Imam — may God's blessings be upon him — and the 'guided' are those who are guided to obey him.

64. And similar to this in the Book of God — He is Mighty and Sublime — are His words: '*Verily, I am All-forgiving to him who repents, believes and does good, and at last is guided*' [Q. 20:82]. The repentant is the one who is from the people of Friendship (*walāya*), and the

---

[85] Prophets may be seized by doubt, not because they lose their way and are corrupt, but because they may fear the worldly consequences of the revelations they receive. The author's intention is to emphasize the fact that Prophets remain pure even though they may experience episodes of weakening faith.

believer is the one who knows this affair (*hādhā al-amr*) but does not act on it.[86] And the one who does [good] is the one whose goodness of action is accepted and whose endeavour is lauded. '*And at last is guided*' means that he is guided by his Friendship, his faith, his knowledge (*maʿrifa*) and his good deeds to the knowledge of his Imam — may God's blessings be upon him in all his eras.

[Exegesis of verses from Q. 21]

65. About God's words — He is Mighty and Sublime: '*This is a remembrance of those with me and those before me*' [Q. 21:24], he said — peace be upon him — that this means **[83]** that the '*remembrance of those with me*' is the same as the one '*those before me*' summoned to: it is the knowledge which the Prince of the Believers brought — may God's blessings be upon him. The Summons is to him in every era and every age.

66. '*But most of them do not know the Truth, and so turn away*' [Q. 21:24]. He means by this the people of ʿAqaba (*aṣḥāb al-ʿaqaba*),[87] because they turned away from the Truth and from its acknowledgment, that is, from the Imam — may God's blessings be upon him. He

[86] Ms. A: *wa-yaʿmal*; ms. B: *wa-lam yaʿmal*. I believe Ms. B and Strothmann are correct, since the text seems to establish a hierarchy between the members of the *daʿwa*, and to open the door the repenting members who had displeased the Imam. Treatise III generally seems to allude to dissensions within the *daʿwa* — particularly in the passages on retribution that preceded.

[87] This refers to an alleged plot to assassinate the Prophet Muḥammad in an ambush at the pass (*ʿaqaba*) of Harsha, the night following the proclamation of Ghadīr Khumm. According to Shiʿi sources, several major companions participated in the ambush, among them Abū Bakr, ʿUmar, ʿUthmān, Ṭalḥa, Muʿāwiya, ʿAmr b. al-ʿĀṣ, al-Mughīra b. Shuʿba, etc. — protagonists mentioned in several passages of the *Kashf*. On this episode, see E. Kohlberg, 'Some Imamī Shīʿī views on the *Ṣaḥāba*', pp. 152–156. In a footnote, p. 84, n. 4, Strothmann suggests 'the people of ʿAqaba' could allude to the expression met earlier in §69: *irtaddū ʿalā aʿqābihim*, 'they turned on their heels'. While this explanation is insufficient, since the text clearly refers to the abovementioned plot, it is nevertheless possible that the author did intend a pun between this expression and the ʿAqaba episode, since the plotters are indeed those who followed Muḥammad but then turned away when required to acknowledge ʿAlī's position as the Legatee. See also *Kashf* I, p. 32, § 69, where Gabriel is said to sit in ʿAqaba during the eschatological events.

possesses the knowledge of everything the people need — [knowledge of] calamities and fates, of instructions, of means, of destinies and terms — which the Messenger taught him from God's knowledge — He is Mighty and Sublime; indeed, [the Messenger] [only] knows what God has taught him — as God said — may He be exalted — to His Prophet Muḥammad — may God's blessing and peace be upon him: '*Say: I am not an innovation among the Messengers, and I know not what shall be done with me or with you. I only follow what is revealed to me*' [Q. 46:9]. And elsewhere: '*Say: I do not say to you that I possess the treasures of God, nor that I have knowledge of the Mystery (ghayb), nor do I tell you I am an angel*' [Q. 6:50]. These are also the words of Noah — peace be upon him — as reported of him by God in His Book.[88] All of this is an indication that the Imams **[84]** and the Messengers only know what God has made known to them, through His revelation (*waḥī*), His divine assistance (*ta'yīd*) and His light. The confirmation (*tathbīt*)[89] [of this knowledge] comes from God — glory be to His name.

67. '*[We have sent down unto you a Book wherein is] your remembrance*' [Q. 21:10] means that He knows [which of you is] a believer or an unbeliever. '*Will you not reflect*' [Q. 21:10] upon His commands and His prohibition and acknowledge His place?[90]

68. About God's words — He is Mighty and Sublime: '*We have written in the Psalms (al-zabūr), after the remembrance, that the earth will be inherited by My righteous worshippers*' [Q. 21:105], he said — peace be upon him — that the 'Psalms' are the Imam — may God's blessings be upon him. And the 'earth' is like the Proof — peace be upon him.[91] The 'righteous worshippers' are the Summoners to God — may He be

---

[88] Indeed, the same sentence as in Q. 6:50 is pronounced by Noah in Q. 11:31.

[89] Mss. A, B: *tathabbutihi*. Corrected to *tathbītihi*, following Strothmann's suggestion, p. 85, n. 1.

[90] This paragraph seems out of place, although it does mention the term *dhikr*, 'remembrance', which appears in both the previous and the following paragraph.

[91] On this hermeneutic equivalence, see also *Kashf* III, p. 62, § 20; V, p. 101, § 22; p. 155, § 106. It is noteworthy that the mention of the Proof is followed by the words 'peace be upon him', usually reserved for the Imam. This indicates that the Proof, here, is the successor of the Imam; see commentary of *Kashf* V, pp. 395–408.

exalted — <with their goods and possessions; they are the people of the military camps. He will give them authority over [their goods and possessions]>[92] upon the Return, that is, when the right is returned to its people, after the victory of the iniquitous and the veiling (*istitār*) of the Proofs and the Imams.

[Abū Bakr: exegesis of verses from Q. 22]

69. About God's words - He is Sublime and High: '*Among men is he who disputes concerning God, without knowledge, and follows every rebel Satan, against whom it is written that whoever takes him for friend (tawallāh), him he leads astray, and he guides him to to the chastisement of the burning*' [Q. 22:3–4], he said — peace be upon him — that is about 'Atīq — may God curse him — because he disputed concerning God — He is Sublime and High — over whether He ordered the Messenger — may God bless him — [to establish] the Imamate of the Prince of the Believers, [claiming] that his sacred station was not from God, and that the exegesis (*ta'wīl*) was not taught **[85]** by the Messenger of God to the Prince of the Believers on God's order. He disputed this out of denial, jealousy and pride, without knowledge, and '*followed every rebel Satan*'. Satan is 'Umar — may God curse him — because 'Atīq only acted on his opinion and his order.[93] 'Atīq believed himself to be knowledgeable, and disdained the search for knowledge, displaying his disdain toward all — and this was unbelief (*kufr*) on his part. He thought that he had knowledge and acted publicly accordingly, when he was really 'without knowledge'.

70. Have you not seen God's words — He is Mighty and Sublime: '*Turning away with pride to lead astray from God's path. For him in this world is ignominy, and on the Day of Resurrection the chastisement of the burning*' [Q. 22:9]? This verse came down concerning him — may God

---

[92] Ms. A: *bi-mulkihim wa-amwālihim ma'nā ahl al-amṣār wa yumlikuhum al-ḥukūma 'alayhi*; ms. B: *yumlikuhum wa-amwālihim ma'nā ahl al-amṣār wa yumlikuhum al-ḥukūma 'alayhimi*. The text is again corrupted, and Strothmann leaves a blank. The probable meaning of the sentence is that upon the Return, the Summoners will be confirmed, legitimized in their actions and functions. It is interesting that the expression *ahl al-amṣār* is apparently used for the members of the *da'wa* who have been preparing for the Return.

[93] See *Kashf* I, p. 30, § 63, and pp. 109–110, n. 134.

curse him. On the day of Juḥfa,[94] when the Master of the Law (*ṣāḥib al-sharīʿa*) appointed the Prince of the Believers — may God's blessings be upon him — saying: 'This is your Imam, so know him! This is your Gate to God, so glorify him!' ʿAtīq turned away so as not to hear these words, because of the hatred and the enmity to the Prince of the Believers — peace be upon him — his Satan and his partisans had charged him with. He speculated that God would not know everything he and his companions did — may God curse him.

71. It is about him that this verse was revealed: *'That is for what your hands have forwarded'*, ʿAtīq, *'for God is not* **[86]** *iniquitous to His worshippers'* [Q. 22:10]. This will be said to him after *'the chastisement of the burning'* [Q. 22:9], that is, after the rising of the Resurrector — may God's blessings be upon him — with the sword (*qiyām al-qā'im bi'l-sayf*). On that day, the iniquitous Abū Bakr will be killed seventy thousand deaths and burnt as many times. The meaning of the deaths endured by this iniquitous is to show his iniquity and his enmity to the universes, and [to show] that he lost his Islam when he disobeyed the Messenger after [his death]. Such is the esoteric meaning of the killing.[95] As for the seventy thousand deaths, it means that seventy among the elite of the Gates, the Proofs and the Hands (*ayādī*)[96] from among the believers, will appear along with the Resurrector — may God's blessings be upon him — when he appears with the sword

[94] This is also known as the day of the proclamation of Ghadīr Khumm, a place situated near Juḥfa, which is a locality on the outskirts of Medina in the direction of Mecca. Not long before his death and after the farewell pilgrimage, the Prophet Muḥammad is said to have declared to his community: 'Whoever's Lord (mawlā) I am, then ʿAlī is his Lord as well'. This famous *ḥadīth* is found both in Shiʿi and Sunni sources, although its interpretations obviously differ. On Ghadīr Khumm, see L. Veccia Vaglieri, 'Ghadīr Khumm', *EI2*; M.A. Amir-Moezzi, 'Ghadīr Khumm', *EI3*; M. Massi Dakake, *The Charismatic Community*, pp. 33–48. The *ḥadīth* is quoted in *Kashf* VI, p. 159, § 6.

[95] Death in the esoteric sense thus consists of the refusal to follow Muḥammad in the person of his Legatee. It is refraining from giving life to the letter of *tanzīl* by the spirit of *ta'wīl*.

[96] A rank of the hierarchy of the *daʿwa*; see e.g. F. Daftary, *The Ismāʿīlīs. Their History and Doctrines*, p. 218, where it is identified with the Proof. Here, however, it seems distinct from this rank. See *Kashf* V, p. 102, § 24, where the 'Hand' appears again in a passage dedicated to this elite formed of seventy members.

(*al-qā'im 'inda ẓuhūrihi bi'l-sayf*) — as God said — He is Mighty and Sublime: '*And Moses chose seventy of his people for Our appointed time*' [Q. 7:155]. These seventy are with every Speaking-Prophet when he appears and God perfects his sacred station; they will thus appear with the Resurrector — may God's blessings be upon him — when he appears with the sword.[97] Each one of these seventy is followed by a thousand [men], and more — but the latter are all related to the seventy. Then will the loss of this iniquitous [man] be manifest, as well as the fact that his rebellion against the Messenger of God Lord of the Universes, and his iniquity toward the Prince of the Believers, have driven him out of the assembly of believers. Seventy thousand words (*kalima*) will gather against him testifying of the calamity of his station.[98] His hypocrisy will be manifest.

72. And [the fact that] he will be burnt as many times, reminds [one] that he deserves **[87]** the Fire, in the exoteric sense of the term, and shows what [actions] deserve this [punishment]. In the esoteric sense, he will be reminded of his faults and his crimes will be enumerated by the seventy thousand tongues of the people of truthfulness and faith (*ahl al-ṣidq wa'l-īmān*), who are the elite [among the companions] of the Resurrector and his auxiliaries (*ansār*) — peace be upon him. Such is the explanation of this symbolic image (*ishāra*).

73. '*For him in this world is ignominy*' [Q. 22:9]: He means by this his metamorphosis into a variety of figures and forms (*mā yumsakh fīhī min ikhtilāf al-ṣuwar wa'l-hayākil*) — may God curse him. The meaning of this metamorphosis (*maskh*) is his transfer from one class to another. Indeed, he was counted among the Muslims and the companions of the Messenger of God — may God bless him and his family — but he left this class for the class of the ignorant — and they set him out of the ranks of knowledge (*ḥudūd al-'ilm*) into the class of the unbelievers, out of the ranks of obedience and faith into the class of the associators, because he associated to God's order the choice of his own soul and the personal opinion of his Satan who misguided

---

[97] The repetition of this sentence may result from a copyist's error.

[98] Ms. A: *tumīt maqāmahu*; ms. B: *baliya maqāmahu*. Both editors (Ghālib p. 89) read as A, but B is more intelligible here.

him and misguided himself. Such is the meaning of the reference to metamorphosis (*maskh*): it is the change from a praiseworthy state to these blameworthy states. And this has partly been explained previously.[99]

74. About God's words — He is Mighty and Sublime: '*I do not know whether that which you are promised is nigh, or whether my Lord has set a distant term for it*' [Q. 72:25], al-Ḥakīm — peace be upon him - said **[88]** that they are about the rising of the Bearer of the sword (*al-qāʾim biʾl-sayf*) — may God's blessings be upon him.

75. '*Indeed, He knows what is spoken aloud and He knows what you conceal*' [Q. 21:110]. This verse concerns those who opposed the Prince of the Believers — may God's blessings be upon him —, those who betrayed him and conspired against him out of enmity towards him and the one who appointed him in his sacred station by [order of] God.

76. This is the end of the exegesis (*taʾwīl*) we have received from the treasury of grace (*khizānat al-faḍl*) — may God be praised as He should be! **[89]**

---

[99] See *Kashf* I, pp. 4–5, §§ 6–7, and commentary of *Kashf* I, pp. 154–162.

Commentary

Although Treatise III seems, at first glance, to contain few identifiable Ismaili doctrines and themes — such as the prophetic cycles, the succession of Completer Imams,[100] the initiation, etc. — it is in fact a key treatise in the collection. In Treatise I, the few clearly Ismaili elements were intertwined with others originating in pre-Nuṣayrī and *ghulāt* circles. In Treatise III, the *ghulāt* origins are more questionable. In his article on the 'Mufaḍḍal tradition', Heinz Halm stated that Treatises I and III preserved '*ghulāt* opuscules' or 'tracts' ('*gulāt*-Traktate') which had been reworked by an Ismaili hand.[101] Yet, while he gave numerous examples of *ghuluww*-related doctrines in Treatise I, he noted but three such features in Treatise III: Abū Dharr's refusal to pledge allegiance to Satan,[102] the statement that 'Salmān is the origin of Islam',[103] and the identification of the 'Orphan' (*yatīm*) with the Imam.[104] A few others can be added: another mention of *maskh*,[105] the use of puns and debatable etymologies in relation to Abū Bakr,[106] 'Umar,[107] and the names of al-Miqdād, Abū Dharr and Salmān.[108] The very presence of this latter triad in the treatise is suggestive: these

---

[100] They briefly appear in *Kashf* I, pp. 15–16, §§ 32–34, in a passage I identified as Ismaili. They are found more extensively in *Kashf* V, p. 110, § 36; p. 113, § 40; p. 132, §§ 69–70; p. 134, § 71; p. 151, § 101.

[101] H. Halm, 'Das 'Buch der Schatten'', II, pp. 83–84.

[102] *Kashf* III, pp. 70–71, § 38.

[103] *Kashf* III, p. 72, § 40.

[104] *Kashf* III, p. 54, §§ 3–5; p. 60, § 17.

[105] *Kashf* III, p. 88, § 73. See commentary of *Kashf* I, pp. 154–162.

[106] *Kashf* III, pp. 57–58, § 12.

[107] *Kashf* III, p. 58, § 13.

[108] *Kashf* III, pp. 70–72, §§ 37–39.

three characters are only discussed in the *Kashf* in Treatise I, and there only en passant;[109] in Treatise V, Abū Dharr is mentioned alone,[110] using the same pun for his name as in Treatise III.[111]

Another aspect of Treatise III could possibly have roots in *ghuluww*, although it is a general feature of pre-Buwayhid exegesis: the 'vilification of the Companions' (*sabb al-ṣaḥāba*), as well as 'negative personalized commentaries' consisting of identifying negative figures or entities from the Qur'an with ʿAlī's opponents in the early days of Islam. Of course, this also appears in Treatises I and V, but still holds a considerable place in Treatise III, the 'anti-Sunni' stance of which is very pronounced; this treatise is indeed the only one in the collection to mention the nicknames given to Abū Bakr and ʿUthmān in early Shiʿism.[112] One of ʿUmar's nicknames appears in Treatise I,[113] but in Treatise V, all these nicknames no longer feature.

The elements of *ghuluww* in Treatise III are therefore quite scant, all the more so since they are reinterpreted in a new sense and detached from the meaning they had in the 'exaggerating' sects: such is the case of the 'Orphan', which we will deal with in the present chapter, and the

---

[109] *Kashf* I, pp. 14–15, §§ 30–31.

[110] *Kashf* V, pp. 100–101, § 22.

[111] *Kashf* III, p. 70, § 38.

[112] For Abū Bakr: ʿAtīq (§§ 55, 63, 69–71) and Abū al-Faṣīl (§§ 27, 43); for ʿUthmān: Naʿthal (§§ 22, 43, 63). On ʿAtīq, see e.g. M.M. Bar-Asher, *Scripture and Exegesis*, p. 84 (where it is noted that this nickname has no pejorative connotation, but is on the contrary an honorific title); E. Kohlberg, 'Some Imamī Shīʿī views on the *Ṣaḥāba*', p. 147. See also M.A. Amir-Moezzi, "Alī et le Coran', p. 699, n. 109, who reports that the expression 'the religion of ʿAtīq' (*dīn al-ʿAtīq*) was forged in Sunni circles in reaction to the Shiʿi expression 'the religion of ʿAlī'; on *dīn ʿAlī*, see idem, *La Religion discrète*, Ch. 1: 'Considérations sur l'expression *dīn ʿAlī*: Aux origines de la foi shiite', pp. 19–47 (English trans.: *Spirituality of Shiʿi Islam*, Ch. 1: 'Reflections on the Expression *dīn ʿAlī*: the origins of the Shiʿi Faith', pp. 3–44). On Abū al-Faṣīl, see e.g. M.M. Bar-Asher, *Scripture and Exegesis*, p. 119; W. Madelung, 'Introduction', in F. Daftary and G. Miskinzoda, *The Study of Shiʿi Islam* (London and New York, 2014), p. 9. On Naʿthal, see e.g. I. Goldziher, 'Spottnamen der ersten Chalifen', pp. 327, 334; E. Kohlberg, 'Some Imamī Shīʿī views on the *Ṣaḥāba*', p. 164; W. Madelung, *The Succession to Muḥammad*, p. 138; M.M. Bar-Asher, *Scripture and Exegesis*, p. 117.

[113] Zufar: *Kashf* I, p. 19, § 41; p. 31, § 66. See E. Kohlberg, 'Some Imamī Shīʿī Views on the *Ṣaḥāba*', p. 162 and p. 163, n. 107; M.M. Bar-Asher, *Scripture and Exegesis*, p. 118.

musūkhiyya, discussed above. Even the 'negative personalized commentaries' of Treatise III are just as much reminiscences of ancient Shiʿi exegeses as they are updates of these old exegetical processes geared towards a new end, that is, the legitimation of the Ismaili *daʿwa*. Rather than a '*ghulāt* opuscule', Treatise III is an Ismaili text playing with some of the codes and concepts of the *ghulāt*, reformulating them to serve the Ismaili Fatimid ideology.

Indeed, there is evidence that this treatise is in fact a polemical one, which, under the cover of Qur'anic exegesis and references to the early days of Islam, has a very concrete, i.e. political, aim. While it is clear that older exegetical resources were mobilized for the composition of the treatise, the composition itself seems to be linked to a particular historical context, a pivotal moment in the *daʿwa* during which a reform occurred. In the absence of explicit historical evidence, such as references to specific historical events or protagonists, one can only formulate hypotheses as to the events to which the treatise implicitly responds: they may correspond either to the investiture of the one who would become the first Fatimid caliph and who declared himself the Mahdī, to the end of his reign, or to the beginning of the reign of his successor, al-Qāʾim.

Among the reasons for the difficulty in distinguishing the pre-Fatimid and the Fatimid phases is their chronological proximity: between the period immediately preceding the proclamation of ʿAbd Allāh al-Mahdī and the period of his reign, or even that of his successor, there was no clear break. At the time, the Ismaili scholars were trying to adapt their doctrinal texts to new circumstances. The aim was to support Fatimid legitimacy unsurprisingly by the use of earlier material: it would be unthinkable to argue in favour of the already fragile legitimacy of the Fatimid Imam while refraining from using the very texts, doctrines and exegeses that were supposed to have announced his appearance. Therefore, it is only natural that an early Fatimid composition would quote so many exegeses of the 'Sage', who must be the predecessor of ʿAbd Allāh al-Mahdī at the head of the *daʿwa*. Their occurrences do not necessarily mean that the treatise, in the form in which it came to us, is contemporary with this 'Sage'.

Treatise III poses the delicate question of the very definition of Ismailism, already problematic due to the diversity of Ismaili currents, and the lack of sources for the initial period of the movement: where does the passage from Shiʿism to Ismailism take place? Where are we dealing with a specifically Ismaili doctrine? I began to answer the last question in my study of Treatise I: the Ismaili contribution is revealed in the *reinterpretation* of certain ancient terms, *ḥadīth*s or doctrines, often originating from what was labelled as *ghuluww*. But Ismailism was indeed an underground revolutionary movement, a missionary organization aiming at taking power, and then it became the doctrine of a new ruling elite trying to consolidate itself and struggling with various opponents, revolts and rebellions. Therefore, here is another criterion that allows us to identify a number of elements of the *Kitāb al-Kashf* as Ismaili, particularly those referring more or less directly to a network of 'Summoners', to a *daʿwa*, and to those likely to be mobilized for apologetic and political purposes.

Treatise III is witness to a key moment in the formation of Ismailism, during which its concepts were gradually built, its doctrines, exegeses and technical terms drawn from the Shiʿi intellectual background, selected and reinterpreted. Apart from the *rajʿa*, characteristic doctrines of the Ismaili creed are not firmly asserted there, but the inflections that distinguish it from other Shiʿi currents can already be detected. First, the emphasis on the very concept of *daʿwa*, that is, of an organized political network of propaganda, must be understood as a criterion allowing the identification of Ismailism. What characterises positively the Ismaili novelty of *Kitāb al-Kashf*, relatively to Shiʿism in general and to *ghuluww* in particular, are indeed the more or less clear allusions to such an organization. Treatise III clarifies in this respect the few references to such a *daʿwa* that appeared in Treatise I, and introduces the clearer data of Treatises V and VI.

Other doctrines and concepts discussed in Treatise III must be interpreted as Ismaili inflections. This is the case with the term 'Orphan', which H. Halm considers to be a mark of *ghuluww*, while acknowledging that, as it appears in Treatise III, the term was indeed the result of an Ismaili reinterpretation.[114] Similarly, the concepts of *rajʿa* and Mahdī initially come from older currents, but are also reinterpreted and adapted to the needs of Ismailism. Thus, a new

[114] H. Halm, *Kosmologie*, pp. 165–166.

character appears here, that of the 'Bearer of the sword' (*al-qā'im bi'l-sayf*) who precedes the Resurrector[115] and 'prepares the earth'[116] for his coming. It is in such a reinterpretative perspective that one must understand the many mentions of the misdeeds and the fate of the 'three Satans' — i.e. Abū Bakr, ʿUmar and ʿUthmān — enemies of ʿAlī to which the enemies of Ismailism are assimilated, in terms suggesting that the latter are former Ismaili subjects who rebelled against the authority of the Imam. The allusive justification of a reform is one more element in favor of the approximate dating that we have proposed for the composition of this treatise.

The following pages will therefore be an attempt to show how this treatise, rather than a '*ghulāt* opuscule', was indeed initially composed by an Ismaili hand by reusing exegeses and other earlier material, in response to specific historical circumstances. While it does not seem possible to determine the nature of these circumstances beyond any dispute, I will nevertheless formulate the hypothesis that the treatise was composed in the aftermath of ʿAbd Allāh al-Mahdī's rise to power.

1. Identifying the 'Sage' (*al-ḥakīm*) and dating Treatise III

In Treatises III and V, several exegeses are attributed to a certain 'Sage' (*al-ḥakīm*). In his reference article on the Imamology of early Ismailism, Madelung briefly addresses al-Ḥakīm's identity. He first notes that the mentions of the Sage in *Kitāb al-Kashf* were, most of the time, followed by blessing formulas indicating that he was considered a successor to the Prophet.[117] He would therefore be an Imam. In addition, Madelung identifies in Treatise V the elements which led him to identify our Sage with Muḥammad b. Aḥmad, that is, the predecessor of ʿAbd Allāh al-Mahdī at the head of the *daʿwa* in Salamiyya. Indeed, Muḥammad b. Aḥmad is mentioned by name in this treatise, which is all the more remarkable since he is one of the only two Ismaili characters to be openly named in the *Kitāb al-Kashf*.[118]

---

[115] As in Treatise I, *qā'im* is preferred over *mahdī* in Treatise III.

[116] *Kashf* III, p. 62, § 20.

[117] W. Madelung, 'Das Imamat', p. 55.

[118] The other being al-Qā'im bi-Amr Allāh, the second Fatimid caliph; see *Kashf* V, p. 103, § 25.

About Muḥammad b. Aḥmad, Treatise V states that 'he started by concealing his identity in order to preserve his secret from the hypocrites. He presented himself as the Proof who guides towards the Imam, while, in fact, he was guiding towards himself, and no one knew this except a few among the elite of his Summoners'.[119] What is at stake here, is to justify ex post facto the continuity of the lineage of the Imams from Jaʿfar al-Ṣādiq to Muḥammad b. Aḥmad, then to his successor at the head of the *daʿwa*, namely the soon-to-become first Fatimid caliph. According to this passage, the Ismaili organization would have regarded its leader as an Imam from the start, even though in the propaganda intended to recruit partisans, this leader was only presented as the representative, the 'Proof', of an Imam whose return as the Mahdī was foretold and expected. However, the *Kashf* does not specify whether this Imam was presented under the name of Muḥammad b. Ismāʿīl.

Madelung's identification of al-Ḥakīm with Muḥammad b. Aḥmad is the most plausible, if we are to believe the Ṭayyibī author Idrīs ʿImād al-Dīn, who indeed calls Muḥammad b. Aḥmad, 'Abū ʿAlī al-Ḥakīm' in his *ʿUyūn al-akhbār*.[120]

Madelung considers the *Kashf*'s mention of Muḥammad b. Aḥmad a Fatimid gloss inserted into the original treatises at a later stage, yet earlier than the reign of the fourth Fatimid caliph al-Muʿizz. Indeed, starting from the latter's reign, Muḥammad b. Aḥmad was no longer considered one of the Imams in the official lineage: at that time, the Fatimid dynasty claimed direct ancestry, from father to son, from Jaʿfar al-Ṣādiq to ʿAbd Allāh al-Mahdī — that is, through Ismāʿīl b. Jaʿfar, Muḥammad b. Ismāʿīl, ʿAbd Allāh, Aḥmad and

[119] *Kashf* V, p. 99, § 16.

[120] As noted by W. Madelung, 'Das Imamat', p. 56, n. 78; see also H. Halm, *Kosmologie*, p. 18. See also A. Hamdani and F. De Blois, 'A Re-examination of al-Mahdī's Letter', p. 190, where it is noted that the passages from *ʿUyūn al-akhbār* which identify Abū ʿAlī al-Ḥakīm and Muḥammad b. Aḥmad seem partly based on sources dating back to a time when the Fatimid official lineage had not yet been established — in spite of the fact that Idrīs adheres to the post-al-Muʿizz lineage. See Idrīs ʿImād al-Dīn, *ʿUyūn al-akhbār*, vol. 5, pp. 153–154.

al-Ḥusayn.[121] Before al-Muʿizz's reform, ʿAbd Allāh al-Mahdī himself declared, in a rather confusing letter, that his ancestor was ʿAbdallāh al-Afṭaḥ, who was Jaʿfar al-Ṣādiq's eldest son when the latter died. Al-Mahdī also indicates that his predecessor at the head of the Ismaili organization was his uncle, Muḥammad b. Aḥmad, not his father al-Ḥusayn.[122]

The passage that Madelung considers a Fatimid gloss therefore clearly belongs to a period prior to the establishment of the orthodox line of succession under al-Muʿizz. But is it really a gloss? According to Madelung, if al-Ḥakīm is indeed Muḥammad b. Aḥmad, the omnipresence of the exegeses by al-Ḥakīm in Treatises III and V proves that the latter was written at the time of ʿAbd Allāh al-Mahdī's predecessor. Yet, several hints suggest that Treatise III could in fact have been composed at the very beginning of the Fatimid period, probably under the reign of ʿAbd Allāh al-Mahdī. As we will see below, the general orientation of the treatise points towards a period when the *daʿwa* was not clandestine anymore. The production of writings against enemies of Ismailism who 'returned' to their false beliefs after knowing the truth is not consistent with the clandestine period; it is rather an attempt to bring back dissident Ismailis in line after the proclamation of al-Mahdī's Imamate. And such passages cannot be considered as mere glosses added to an original core, since they form the essence of Treatise III, both quantitatively and qualitatively: this treatise was written to reassure the partisans of the *daʿwa*, to threaten those who were tempted to turn their backs on it and to justify the legitimacy of the Imam. Older exegetical material was mobilized for this aim — as attested by the various quotations of al-Ḥakīm — but the composition of the treatise itself is an answer to new circumstances: a particular event has taken place, a continuity has been broken, leading to a reaction that the central organization of the *daʿwa* had to counter.

---

[121] On al-Muʿizz's reform of the Fatimid genealogy, by which he claimed Muḥammad b. Ismāʿīl's ancestry, see W. Madelung, 'Das Imamat', pp. 86–118; A. Hamdani and F. De Blois, 'A Re-examination of al-Mahdī's Letter', pp. 186–195.

[122] H.F. Hamdani, *On the Genealogy of Fatimid Caliphs*, English text pp. 13–14, Arabic text p. 11; W. Madelung, 'Das Imamat', p. 55; A. Hamdani and F. De Blois, 'A Re-examination of al-Mahdī's Letter', p. 176.

Let us briefly examine the exegeses attributed to al-Ḥakīm in Treatise III: he is cited by name thirteen times.[123] While most of the *qāla* ('he said') of the treatise introduce Qur'anic verses and therefore have God as subject, several point to an exegete that must probably be identified with the 'Sage'.[124] If we only consider these passages, the exegetical comments that can be attributed to al-Ḥakīm fall into three main types:

— personalized commentaries identifying Qur'anic elements with the Imam or the Ahl al-Bayt, and therefore aiming to base the Imamate on the text of the Qur'an, according to a typically Shiʿi method;[125]
— the counterparts of the first type, that is, the negative personalized commentaries, by which certain Qur'anic elements are identified with the enemies of the Imams, mainly Abū Bakr and ʿUmar, but also ʿUthmān. These exegeses are more numerous than those of the first type, and their tone suggests that their actual aim is not so much to curse the enemies of ʿAlī b. Abī Ṭālib in his time, as it is to curse the enemies of the 'Imams of his descent', that is, the enemies of the *daʿwa* and its leaders;[126]
— exegeses that relate to the return of the Qāʾim and interpret Qur'anic verses on the Last Judgement as allusions to the *rajʿa*.[127]

These exegeses do not, per se, contradict Madelung's hypothesis that Treatise III was written at the time of al-Ḥakīm. But the general tone and other clues that will be examined lead one to believe that Treatise

---

[123] *Kashf* III, p. 53, § 3; p. 56, §10; p. 65, § 27; p. 72, §§ 39, 40; p. 73, § 42; p. 75, § 45; p. 77, § 48; p. 79, § 54; p. 80, § 57; p. 81, § 59; p. 82, § 61; p. 88, § 74.

[124] *Kashf* III, p. 74, § 43; p. 77, § 48; p. 78, § 49; p. 83, §§ 63, 65; p. 85, § 68, 69. It should be reminded that such *qāla*-s are very common in the *Kashf*. It is a delicate task to identify the verb's subject, especially when instances of this appear in treatises I or VI, where al-Ḥakīm is never mentioned.

[125] *Kashf* III, p. 53, § 3; p. 56, § 10; p. 69, § 34; pp. 73–74, § 42; p. 74, § 43; pp. 77–78, § 48–49; p. 80, § 57; pp. 82–83, § 61; pp. 83–84, § 65; p. 85, § 68.

[126] *Kashf* III, p. 65, § 27; p. 79, § 54; p. 83, § 63; p. 85–96, §§ 69–70.

[127] *Kashf* III, p. 72, § 38; pp. 75–76, § 45; pp. 77–78, § 48; p. 81, § 59; p. 85, § 68; pp. 88–89, § 74.

III, in its current form, is not a piece of writing contemporary to al-Ḥakīm, or a simple account of his teachings, but rather an aide-memoire of the latter: its purpose is to mobilize ancient exegeses and to place them in the service of a new doctrine. However, it will be conceded that the time of al-Ḥakīm was very close to the time Treatise III was composed, otherwise the authority of these exegeses would have been diminished. The composition of Treatise III took place after al-Ḥakīm's Imamate, but at a time when his prestige had not yet faded. The new policy of the *daʿwa* could thus be based on his authority. Evoking his words was supposed to win the support of the recalcitrant elements of the *daʿwa* and convince them. We can suppose that the latter were those who were called the 'Qarmatians', members of the *daʿwa* who had not accepted ʿAbd Allāh al-Mahdī's claim to the Imamate and the Mahdiship, or who rebelled against him.

2. The *daʿwa*: an organization and its enemies

The notion of *daʿwa* implicitly appears on the very first pages of the treatise. Although it is not dealt with directly, it is clearly in the background of the first fifteen pages at least, either through the exegesis of Qur'anic verses containing terms from the same root, or through terms from similar but distinct roots. The presentation unfolds through a subtle series of alliterations which suggests an opposition between the organization of the *daʿwa* and its adversaries, who reject it, oppose it, or abandon it. Such composition around the term *daʿwa* suggests that the treatise is indeed the product of a clearly political organization which wished to justify its legitimacy by attaching itself to Qur'anic notions and to the most classical Shiʿi historiography.

The term *daʿwa* is Qur'anic, and is found for instance in Q. 30:25, where it designates the summons of the dead on Judgment Day — a verse that lends itself well to an esoteric interpretation, since men are dead, symbolically, as long as they do not have access to the esoteric knowledge obtained from the Imam.[128] The *daʿwa* is a call, an invitation or a summons, either from man to God, or from God to man. In the Ismaili context, it is found in the latter sense, that is, as God's summons

[128] On this theme, see e.g. the interpretation of Q. 16:21 in *Kashf* V, p. 98, § 15.

to humanity[129] through the prophets, the Imams and the entire network of Ismaili propagandists. Indeed, the term also refers to ideological activism as it designates any form of propaganda or campaign summoning people to a given position or faith. It then acquired a definitely political-religious meaning: the *daʿwa* is thus a propaganda campaign during which missionaries or propagandists (*duʿāt*) try to recruit supporters in order to rally them behind a contender to power. The Abbasid revolution is a typical example of a successful *daʿwa*,[130] and it is on this model that the Ismaili *daʿwa* was formed, using the religious connotation of the term to support its political claims, just as the Abbasids had done.

Treatise III clarifies several passages from Treatise I — or, more precisely, those passages of Treatise I that are most obviously of Ismaili provenance, that is, those added to the *ghulāt* core. Therefore, it seems necessary to review the extracts from Treatise I which dealt with the *daʿwa*, as well as its representatives (*dāʿī*, pl. *duʿāt*), or with the act of calling to, 'summoning' to the Imam and to God.

The first mention of the 'Summoners' (*duʿāt*) appears in the unusual chain of transmission which precedes the 'keeping of the secret *ḥadīth*'.[131] This *isnād* sketches out an esoteric hierarchy, but we can hardly consider that there is more than a sketch here — a rather confused one moreover. The following hierarchy can be derived from the *isnād*:

- *awliyāʾ* (Friends)
- *awṣiyāʾ* (Legatees)
- *duʿāt* (Summoners)
- *nuqabāʾ* (Chiefs)
- *nujabāʾ* (Nobles)
- *abwāb* (Gates)
- *ḥujaj* (Proofs).

[129] This meaning had Qurʾanic roots, as in Q. 14:44: '*We will answer Your call and follow Your prophets*'.

[130] See M. Canard, 'Daʿwa', *EI2*.

[131] *Kashf* I, p. 3, § 3.

The problem is that the order in which these ranks are supposed to be organized is not quite clear: is the rank of the 'Friends' (*awliyā'*) the highest? Although it is possible that this term designates the prophets, it would be unusual. It is even less likely that the chain should be read in the opposite direction, as this would place the 'Legatees' (*awṣiyā'*) among the lowest ranks. I suggest that the text is corrupted here, and that the *awṣiyā'* should be placed after the Proofs (*ḥujaj*). The chain would thus read in ascending order.

What is interesting here is the way various religious groups use these ranks and adapt them for their respective agendas. Indeed, the chain of transmission contains several ranks (*abwāb*, *nuqabā'* and *nujabā'* in particular) also found in Nuṣayrī literature or in works such as the *Kitāb al-Haft wa'l-aẓilla*. Among the Nuṣayrīs, there is indeed a seven-rank hierarchy, in ascending order: *mumtaḥan* (Tested) / *mukhliṣ* (Loyal) / *mukhtaṣṣ* (Elect) / *najīb* (Noble) / *naqīb* (Chief) / *yatīm* (Orphan) / *bāb* (Gate).[132] The 'Summoners', however, do not appear in this literature, which means we are probably dealing here with an enumeration of older ranks, to which an Ismaili hand has added the Summoners. Thus, the very use of the term *duʿāt* should be read as a mark of 'Ismailization', so to speak.

This can also be deduced from the passage on metamorphosis (*musūkhiyya*) in Treatise I. I have shown above that this notion was given a new interpretation, which we identified as the Ismaili contribution to earlier doctrines.[133] The metaphorical metamorphosis, the text tells us, applies to those who are drawn out of 'the Summons of Truth' (*daʿwat al-ḥaqq*) 'in following the whispers of Satan'.[134] The presence of the notion of *daʿwa* in a passage which clearly belongs to the Ismaili layer of Treatise I is an additional indication in favour of the specifically Ismaili character of the use of the root *d-ʿ-w*. In another passage that is clearly Ismaili as it mentions the 'Completer Imams',[135] the verb *daʿā* appears once more, in relation to Muḥammad who 'summons' the people to the Revelation (*tanzīl*).

---

[132] See H. Halm, *Kosmologie*, p. 156, and references given there. See also M. Asatryan, *Controversies in Formative Shiʿi Islam*, pp. 145–149.

[133] See commentary of *Kashf* I, pp. 154–162.

[134] *Kashf* I, p. 4, § 6.

[135] *Kashf* I, pp. 15–16, §§ 32–35.

Even more decisive is a short passage interpreting Q. 16:68: ‘*Your Lord revealed to the bees, saying: Take unto yourselves houses of the mountains and of the trees*’.[136] The bees are the Imams, while the mountains and the trees are hierarchized and correspond to two types of Summoners: those who are called ‘Proofs’ and those who are simple Summoners of a lower level. This verse and its exegesis are probably connected to one of ʿAlī’s nicknames, found in Nuṣayrī[137] and Shiʿi texts: Prince of the bees (*amīr al-naḥl*) or Queen Bee (*yaʿsūb*).[138] In some Nuṣayrī texts, the ‘Prince of the bees’ is identified with the ‘Prince of the stars’, the stars being, as René Dussaud explains, ‘le lieu d’habitation des hommes justes, des croyants’.[139] In several Shiʿi *ḥadīths*, ʿAlī declares ‘I am the Queen Bee of the believers’ (*anā yaʿsūb al-muʾminīn*),[140] which is consistent with the Nuṣayrī interpretation in identifying the bees with the believers.[141] Yet, Goldziher points to Shiʿi texts in which the bees of Q. 16:68 are identified with the Ahl al-Bayt, while the ‘*drink of diverse hues wherein is healing for men*’ (Q. 16:69), that is, honey, corresponds to the Qurʾan.[142] In his *Tafsīr*, al-ʿAyyāshī

---

[136] *Kashf* I, p. 25, § 54.

[137] See e.g. al-Ṭabarānī, *Kitāb al-Maʿārif*, index s.v. *amīr al-naḥl*; M.M. Bar-Asher and A. Kofsky, *The Nusayrī-ʿAlawī Religion*, p. 168 (Arabic: p. 200).

[138] *Amīr al-naḥl* and *yaʿsūb* also appear in other Ismaili texts; see e.g. Jaʿfar b. Manṣūr al-Yaman, *Sarāʾir wa-asrār al-nuṭaqāʾ*, p. 115 (*yaʿsūb*); Ḥātim b. Ibrāhīm al-Ḥāmidī, *Zahr bidhr al-ḥaqāʾiq*, p. 171 (*amīr al-naḥl*). See also al-Naysābūrī, *Ithbāt al-Imama*, p.48, § 28 (Arabic text, p. 26), where Muḥammad calls ʿAlī the *yaʿsūb* of the believers. Note that al-Qāḍī al-Nuʿmān opposes bees to wasps, the former, which produce honey, being identified with the ‘people of Truth’ (*ahl al-ḥaqq*), while the latter are similar to the ‘people of misguidance’ (*ahl al-ḍālala*); see al-Qāḍī al-Nuʿmān, *Asās al-taʾwīl*, p. 91.

[139] R. Dussaud, *Histoire et religion des Noṣairîs*, p. 59, n. 3. On the connection between the ‘Prince of bees’ and the ‘Prince of stars’, based on the notion that the true believers become stars, see also H. Halm, ‘Das ‘Buch der Schatten’’, II, p. 60.

[140] See M.A. Amir-Moezzi, *La Religion discrète*, pp. 99, 108, 138, 190, 287, and references given there (Eng. trans.: *Spirituality of Shiʿi Islam*, pp. 118, 130–131, 174, 251, 390). On the *khuṭbat al-bayān*, the main source for this expression, see also above, pp. 141–142, n. 242.

[141] As noted by both M.A. Amir-Moezzi and Y. Friedman, al-Majlisī also identifies the bees with the believers (i.e. the Shiʿis); cited in M.A. Amir-Moezzi, *La Religion discrète*, p. 108, n. 92 (Eng. trans.: *Spirituality of Shiʿi Islam*, p. 130, n. 92); Y. Friedman, *The Nusayrī-ʿAlawīs*, p. 125. On this symbolism, see also E. Kohlberg, ‘Taqiyya in Shīʿī Theology’, p. 358 and pp. 358–359, n. 74.

[142] See I. Goldziher, ‘Schiʿitisches’, *ZDMG*, p. 532.

(d.320/932) provides a similar interpretation: the bees are the Imams, the mountains are the Arabs and the trees are their freed clientele (*mawālī*). As for the fruits of Q. 16:69 ('*Eat of all fruits* . . .'), they represent the knowledge taught by the Imams to their disciples.[143] The interpretation of these verses and the symbolism of bees in Shiʿi context could be the subject of an independent study; while Friedman has provided a useful summary of the question, it calls for further research.[144] Here, we must confine to note the proximity between al-ʿAyyāshī's exegesis and that of *Kitāb al-Kashf*: not only are the bees identified with the Imams in both cases, but the mountains and the trees, identified with their followers, are similarly hierarchized, corresponding to Arabs and non-Arabs respectively according to al-ʿAyyāshī, and to Proofs and Summoners according to the *Kashf*. Finally, in both texts, the 'fruits' symbolise knowledge. The exegesis of the *Kashf* is even more detailed as it also assimilates the 'paths' of Q. 16:69 ('. . . *and follow the paths of your Lord in humility*') to the deeds (*ʿamal*), thus forming a complementary couple with the knowledge (*ʿilm*) symbolized by the fruits. It also contributes an etymological novelty which, to my knowledge, does not appear elsewhere, when explaining that the Imams are called bees (*naḥl*) because they 'dispense' or 'donate' (verb *naḥala*) knowledge. The *Kitāb al-Kashf* therefore appears as an important document in the study of the expression 'Prince of the bees'; it obviously depends on a tradition close to that of

---

143 Al-ʿAyyāshī, *Tafsīr*, vol. 3, p. 15; see M.M. Bar-Asher, *Scripture and Exegesis*, pp. 111–112. For a similar but slightly less detailed interpretation, see also al-Qummī, *Tafsīr*, ed. Ṭ. Al-Mūsawī al-Jazā'irī, vol. 1, p. 387; ed. Mu'assasat al-Mahdī vol. 2, p. 553.

144 See Y. Friedman, *The Nusayrī-ʿAlawīs*, pp. 124–126. The author suggests that the Shiʿi and Nuṣayrī speculations on this symbolism might be inherited from religious conceptions of the Late Antiquity. See also D. De Smet, 'Abeille, Miel', in *Dictionnaire du Coran*, ed. M.A. Amir-Moezzi, pp. 6–7, where it is recalled that the Ikhwān al-Ṣafā' also stage a dialogue between a king and a bee in which the latter presents the virtues of its species. The presentation seems to subtly combine Shiʿi references with zoological considerations drawn from Greek sources; see Ikhwān al-Ṣafā', *Rasā'il* (Beirut, 2006), Epistle 22, vol. 2, pp. 301–305; L.E. Goodman and R. McGregor, ed. and trans., *Epistles of the Brethren of Purity, The Case of the Animals versus Man Before the King of the Jinn* (Oxford, 2009), Ch. 25, pp. 232–237 (Arabic text, pp. 172–178). See also Y. Marquet, *La philosophie des Iḫwān al-Ṣafā'* (Milan, 1999), pp. 195–198.

al-ʿAyyāshī, a tradition to which it nevertheless brings an Ismaili inflection by integrating the ranks of the Proofs and the Summoners. The identification of the mountains with the Summoners is particularly noteworthy; such equivalence forms the exegetical key of several passages in Treatise VI,[145] and it seems to characterize early Ismailism. This exegesis of Q. 16:69 appears as yet another example of the 'Ismailization' of earlier Shiʿi material.[146]

The symbolic equivalence between coitus and initiation should also be considered a specific feature of early Ismailism building on previous similar notions among Shiʿi groups. The passage of Treatise I dealing with this symbolism is the last of the treatise to mention the *daʿwa*, while portraying Joseph as a *dāʿī*.[147] We have already established that this symbolic interpretation of sexuality appeared in all treatises of the *Kashf*, except for Treatises II and IV.[148] It should be added here that every occurrence of this symbolism is connected to the *daʿwa*,[149] which provides another case of an older doctrine refashioned in Ismaili terms.

It appears that in Treatise I, the notion of *daʿwa* is still tied to the *ghulāt* background which forms the core of the treatise, as we have shown. It is difficult to say whether this notion was added, more or less artificially, to the original core during a Fatimid reworking of the text, or if the treatise presents a stage of Ismaili thought where it was just beginning to see its own concepts emerge from a *ghulāt* environment. In favour of this second possibility, we can mention the overlapping of the occurrences of terms from the root *d-ʿ-w* with an Ismailism still very much dependent on its Shiʿi and *ghulāt* sources. Such is the case of the passages which temper the doctrine of *musūkhiyya* while retaining the term, those interpreting lawful coitus as an authorized initiation, or even as the implicit allusion to the name 'Prince of the

---

145 See *Kashf* VI, pp. 169–171, §§ 27–30.

146 The interpretation of Q. 16:68–69 provided in the *Kashf* should be compared with that found in Jaʿfar b. Manṣūr al-Yaman, *Al-Shawāhid wa'l-bayān*, IIS MS. 734, ff. 321-322, which is a little different, mainly because the bees are the Summoners, not the Imams. Also, the 'mountains', 'trees' and 'houses' are not interpreted.

147 *Kashf* I, pp. 26–27, §§ 57–59.

148 See commentary of *Kashf* I, pp. 128–134.

149 See *Kashf* III, p. 78–79, § 60; V, p. 114, § 41; p. 123, § 57; VI, p. 166, § 23.

bees'. We will see that in Treatise III, we are dealing with a more independent Ismailism, despite the persistence of ancient concepts and the centrality of the traditional Shiʿi historiography of the beginnings of Islam.

The notion of *daʿwa* is the focal point of Treatise III: indeed, while the term only appears occasionally — albeit starting from the very first page — it is in reference to it that at least the first four textual units of the treatise have been gathered. The treatise opens with two verses referring to the 'mosques' that belong to God (Q. 72:18) and to 'the houses that God has permitted to be raised up' (Q. 24:36–37), where mosques and houses represent the Imams. The verse on the houses intervenes only as an explanation of the 'mosques' of Q. 72:18; the emphasis here is on the *daʿwa.* A term from the same root (*d-ʿ-w*) indeed appears in Q. 72:18: *'The mosques belong to God, so do not call (lā tadʿū), along with God, upon anyone.'* Having identified the 'mosques' with the Imams, the two following explanatory sentences also use terms from the root *d-ʿ-w*: *'Do not call (lā tadʿū), along with God, upon anyone'*, means that one must be mindful not to claim (*iddaʿa*) a function that God has reserved for his Imams. 'God has ordered that their Summons (*daʿwa*) be answered.' It is a question of identifying the Summons that, from Adam and through all His prophets, God sends to humankind, on the one hand, and the Ismaili *daʿwa*, on the other hand. The first two paragraphs of the treatise are therefore devoted to the need to follow the Speaking-Prophet and the Imams, and to present the *daʿwa* as the means to do so.

The three following textual units consist of: i) an integral exegesis of sūra 107;[150] ii) a complete exegesis of sūra 89;[151] iii) an exegesis of Q. 17:50–52.[152] Let us note the presence of two integral, verse by verse, exegeses of sūras, in an Ismaili text, which is remarkable. While these units address several themes, their succession seems to be justified by a set of alliterations based on the word *daʿwa*, or, in the case of Q. 17:52, with the verb *daʿā*, derived from the same root.

---

[150] *Kashf* III, pp. 53–56, §§ 3–9.

[151] *Kashf* III, pp. 56–65, §§ 10–26.

[152] *Kashf* III, pp. 65–67, §§ 27–32.

i. Sūra 107

This sūra contains the verb *daʿʿa*, 'to repel', 'to repulse', from the root *d-ʿ-ʿ*: *'Have you seen the one who denies religion? That is he who repels (yaduʿʿu) the orphan'* (Q. 107:1–2). The orphan is the Imam; to 'repel' the Imam, that is, to usurp his 'sacred station' can only lead to 'being repelled' (*yuddaʿʿūn*) to the Fire of Gehenna:[153] the *Kitāb al-Kashf* here underlines the Qurʾanic use of the active and passive voices of the verb *daʿʿa*, the latter appearing in verse 52:13. The choice of sūra 107 seems to be partly guided — the notion of orphan being another important reason — by the alliteration of *daʿʿa* with *daʿwa*. Whoever rejects the Imam is also considered an 'aggressor' (*muʿtadī*),[154] a term from the root *ʿ-d-w*, the author thus spinning out the alliteration which continues in the exegesis of Q. 89.

The exegesis of Q. 107 addresses the main themes that will be the subject of the treatise. It thus talks about the 'orphan', to which we will return. Here, the rejection of the Qurʾanic orphan, assimilated to the rejection of the Imam, becomes the symbol of the rejection of the esoteric aspect of religion. Therefore, esotericism consists above all of the recognition of the Imam, while exotericism consists, on the contrary, of taking a false Imam, not elected by God, in place of the legitimate Imam, and therefore in breaking the continuity of the 'Order', 'the handle and the cable of God'.[155] These are *topoi* of Shiʿism. The Ismaili touch lies in the subversive application of this reading of the beginnings of Islam to a situation contemporary to the redaction of the treatise. To all appearances, the text speaks of Muḥammad's succession, of the division of the community between the true Muslims who followed ʿAlī, and the false ones who accepted Abū Bakr's authority. Yet, there are signs that encourage us to broaden the point and apply to others what the text says about ʿAlī, his supporters and his opponents. Indeed, the expression 'in every era and every age',[156] hints at the fact that the drama of the Prophet's succession is replayed at all times, and therefore at the time when the treatise was composed.

---

[153] *Kashf* III, p. 54, § 3.

[154] *Kashf* III, p. 55, § 6.

[155] *Kashf* III, p. 56, § 9.

[156] *Kashf* III, pp. 55, 56, §§ 8–9.

Besides the theme of the orphan, and the analogy between the couple esotericism / exotericism and the couple continuity / rupture of the 'Order', the exegesis of Q. 107 briefly alludes[157] to another of the main themes of Treatise III, that of retribution on the Day of Resurrection — given that this Day is none other than that of the appearance of the Mahdī, who will then judge those who have taken the exoteric path and rejected the Imam.

ii. Sūra 89

This sūra contains the name ʿĀd, a mysterious ancient people, whom we have already met in Treatise I:[158] *'Have you not seen how your Lord did with ʿĀd, Iram of the pillars?* (Q. 89:6–7). The exegesis of the *Kitāb al-Kashf* consists of reading the verb *ʿāda*, 'to return', from the root *ʿwd*, in place of the proper noun "Ād'. It is therefore about 'the one who returns', this return consisting of 'rejecting the Truth after acknowledging it', to put it in the terms of Treatise I.[159] Secondly, ʿĀd is read as the active participle of the verb *ʿadā*, 'to be the enemy of' or 'to oppose' (root *ʿdw*). The verse, as the author of the exegesis reads it, would therefore be translated as follows: 'Have you not seen how your Lord did with the *enemy of* (or: *whoever opposed*) Iram etc.', where Iram represents ʿAlī. Based on an alliteration, the paragraph devoted to these two short verses opposes the *daʿwa*, on the one hand, and its enemies, on the other hand, the latter being characterized in the first place by their 'return' to their pre-Islamic customs and doctrines.

The archetype of this 'return' is obviously Abū Bakr, who, according to Shiʿi historiography, admittedly embraced Islam during the Prophet's lifetime, but renounced it upon the death of the Prophet by refusing to follow ʿAlī b. Abī Ṭālib and by usurping the latter's rightful position. This applies more broadly to the 'reversion' of the companions of the Prophet who, upon his death, renounced their adherence to Islam by opposing ʿAlī b. Abī Ṭālib's Imamate. This is the primary form of 'shortcoming' (*taqṣīr*), mentioned twice in the *Kitāb al-Kashf*. The latter defines it either as the refusal to recognise the Mahdī,[160] or

[157] *Kashf* III, p. 55, § 8.

[158] *Kashf* I, p. 10, § 21.

[159] *Kashf* I, p. 4, § 6.

[160] *Kashf* I, pp. 5–6, § 8.

as the fact of adhering to the exoteric religion, that is to say, the refusal to follow 'the Legatee after the Messenger, and the exegesis (*ta'wīl*) after the revelation (*tanzīl*)'.[161] Ancient Shiʿism thus distinguishes the *muslim* from the *mu'min*, the one who sticks with the exoteric aspects of Islam from the true believer, or initiate, who has access to its esoteric aspect through the Imam's teaching.[162]

The *Kitāb al-Kashf*'s particularity, here, consists first of all of identifying the prophetic teaching with the *daʿwa*: the head of the latter is the last depositary to date of an 'Order' transmitted from Prophet to Prophet, and Imam to Imam, since Adam. Secondly, the text opposes to the *daʿwa* (root *dʿw*) the notion of return (root *ʿ-wd*) which it ties closely to that of enmity: to retrace one's steps after knowing the truth is to become an enemy (*ʿaduww*, root *ʿdw*) of the truth, to oppose it (*ʿādā*, root *ʿdw*) and to transgress (*ʿadā*, root *ʿdw*) divine instructions. Conversely, to be an enemy of the Imam is defined mainly as a return 'to ignorance after knowledge, to rebellion after obedience'.[163] The emphasis on this notion of a 'return to ignorance' seems to be an indication that the text is less aimed at Sunnis in general, and more at worried and sceptical Ismailis who are about to abandon the cause, if not to betray it. The 'enemies' would thus be those who originally came from within the Ismaili organization, and who behaved towards the Imam as the Companions behaved towards ʿAlī. The mention of the figure of Abū Bakr has exemplary value; it is a way of issuing an ultimatum to the Ismailis who have reservations about the *daʿwa*'s leadership and orientations. The assimilation of the actions of Ismailis imbued with Shiʿi *topoi* to Abū Bakr's betrayal is intended to strike a blow.

The exegesis of Q. 89 is certainly based on earlier traditions. First, the identification of the Qur'anic peoples of ʿĀd and Thāmūd with Abū Bakr and ʿUmar already appeared briefly in Treatise I.[164] While I have not been able to find other Shiʿi sources with a similar interpretation,

---

[161] *Kashf* V, p. 122, § 55. Note that in this passage, *taqṣīr* seem to designate both the people who do not follow the esoteric aspect of Islam and adhere to its exoteric dimension, on the one hand, and those who do not abide by the exoteric laws of the *sharīʿa*; on this other meaning of *taqṣīr*, see commentary of *Kashf* V, pp. 387, 414–416.

[162] See above, p. 160, n. 315.

[163] *Kashf* III, p. 57, § 12.

[164] *Kashf* I, p. 10, § 21.

it nevertheless falls under the genre of the personalized commentary, and its general content is compatible with Shiʿi orientations. On the other hand, the *Kitāb al-Rushd wa'l-hidāya*, a pre-Fatimid Ismaili work attributed to Ibn Ḥawshab, contains an exegesis of Q. 89 very close to that of the *Kitāb al-Kashf*. The latter version, however, is more complete: the sūra is entirely commented on, verse by verse, while the exegesis in the *Rushd wa'l-hidāya* is limited to verses 6 to 12.[165] In addition, the exegeses of the *Kitāb al-Kashf* are elaborated to a greater extent. The comparison of the two texts reveals striking similarities, not only with regard to the content of the interpretation of the verses and the identifications of ʿĀd with Abū Bakr, Iram with ʿAlī, Thāmūd with ʿUmar, etc., but also in its identical use of certain expressions or sentences: the two texts clearly draw from the same source. But their differences are as interesting to us as their similarities: indeed, while the *Kitāb al-Rushd wa'l-hidāya* identifies ʿĀd with 'the first who was iniquitous towards ʿAlī' — without being more specific — and very briefly inserts a pun on the name ʿĀd by bringing it closer to *ʿādī*, 'enemy', and the expression *ʿadā ṭūrahu*, 'to transgress the limit',[166] it does not further indulge in dubious etymologies. In particular, the entire development of the *Kitāb al-Kashf* I have just spoken of, which links ʿĀd to the notion of enmity, and above all, to the return, is missing. On occasions, the version of the *Rushd wa'l-hidāya* brings elements that are absent from the *Kashf*. For instance, the latter does not say why ʿAlī is 'the column of religion', while the *Rushd* connects this to Q. 13:2: '*God is He who raised up the heavens without columns you can see*', the invisible columns being those of the science of *ta'wīl*.[167] Furthermore, the rock of Q. 89:9 is said to symbolise the Proofs, but only the *Rushd* explains the reason for this comparison when recalling that the rock originates from the mountains, and that the mountains are the Proofs,[168] according to an Ismaili exegetical convention, several illustrations of which are found in the *Kitāb al-Kashf*.[169]

---

[165] Ibn Ḥawshab, *Kitāb al-Rushd wa'l-hidāya*, pp. 208–210 (English trans., pp. 77–79).

[166] Ibid., p. 209.

[167] Ibid.

[168] Ibid.

[169] *Kashf* I, p. 25, § 54; VI, pp. 169–171, §§ 27–30.

It is unlikely that the author of Treatise III was inspired here by the *Kitāb al-Rushd wa'l-hidāya*, since the version in the *Kitāb al-Kashf* covers all of Q. 89. Rather, it must be assumed that both texts restate, each in its own way and according to its specific doctrinal and practical needs, an exegesis that was prevalent in Ismaili circles. If, as we believe, the composition of Treatise III must be dated to the early Fatimid period, its arguments and goals must differ from those of the *Rushd*, which is apparently oriented towards eschatological events that are yet to come. The insistence of Treatise III on the notion of a return to false opinion — which is absent from the *Kitāb al-Rushd* — thus seems to corroborate the interpretation according to which the treatise is not so much a didactic presentation of the doctrine as it is an attempt to convince recalcitrant Ismailis. Their scepticism may have brought them to the point of 'returning' to a faith that did not imply acknowledging the Imam-Mahdī, and the author warns them they are rejecting the continuity between the Imams and the Mahdī, in the same way that Abū Bakr and his people rejected the continuity between Muḥammad and ʿAlī.

iii. Exegesis of Q. 17:50–52

This exegesis does not fall within the series of alliterations around the word *daʿwa* as clearly as the previous passages. However, it is a continuation of the previous themes, on the one hand, and it quotes verses containing terms derived from the root *dʿw*, on the other hand. Thus, the verb *daʿā* appears in Q. 17:52, as well as Q. 17:71, and the passage ends with an exegesis of Q. 10:10, which contains the word *daʿwāhum*, 'their prayers' or 'their invocations', twice. The passage is built on the opposition between esotericism and exotericism, between exegesis and revelation, and therefore between those who have access to the knowledge delivered by the Imam and those who are deprived of it. Again, the text defines unbelief as a refusal to follow ʿAlī after Muḥammad: 'They will raise themselves above ʿAlī, your Legatee, to hear from you and not hear from him.'[170] Abū Bakr and ʿUmar, by their rejection of ʿAlī b. Abī Ṭālib and their usurpation of his right, became deniers again: they abandoned Islam and returned to their

[170] *Kashf* III, p. 66, § 29.

pre-Islamic ignorance.[171] The theme of the return to false beliefs is however more discrete this time, as the emphasis here is on the corollary: it is not only that the rejection of esotericism represented by ʿAlī is an abandonment of Islam, but also that the acceptance of this esotericism is Islam in the true sense. It is impossible to be a true Muslim without obeying ʿAlī, without considering his *ta'wīl* as the absolutely essential complement to the revelation received by Muḥammad: 'He put the revelation in charge of the Messenger, and the exegesis in charge of the Legatee — and they are the knowledge and the deeds.'[172] Again, this is about establishing an analogy between the status of ʿAlī and that of the Ismaili Imam, on the one hand, and between the enemies of ʿAlī, therefore of the Islam wanted by God, and those of the Imam, on the other hand: 'Whoever acknowledges the Legatee and obeys him, it is as if this summons him to obey every Imam after him.'[173]

To this, we must add the eschatological tone: Q. 17:50–52 indeed mention the incredulity of those who do not believe in the Day of Resurrection. Now, this Day is of course identified with the Mahdī himself, as we have seen before, according to the doctrine of the *rajʿa*. The Mahdī thus appears as the *locus* distinguishing those who remained faithful to Muḥammad by following ʿAlī b. Abī Ṭālib and the Imams from his descent from those who betrayed them at one point or another of the 'cable of God'. The previously discussed 'continuity of the Order' finds its conclusion in the person of the Mahdī, who fulfils and completes it. Therefore, 'since you disbelieved in faith and exegesis and rebelled, he will bring you back among the rebels, the disbelievers and the associators, and will gather you, all together, in hell.'[174]

The hypothesis that the treatise is aimed against Ismailis who were sceptical of new policies of the *daʿwa* is based on the evident intention in it to establish analogies between the beginnings of Islam and a more recent historical situation. The developments sketched out in Treatise I on the 'continuity of the Order' were meant not only to support the claim of the Ismaili leader to be ʿAlī b. Abī Ṭālib's successor, but also

---

[171] Ibid.

[172] *Kashf* III, p. 68, § 33.

[173] Ibid.

[174] *Kashf* III, p. 66, § 28.

to identify all of his opponents with ʿAlī's. Insofar as: 1) Treatise III is one of the most eloquent in the collection when it comes to the Shiʿi vilification of the Companions of the Prophet (it is thus the only one to give the nicknames of Abū Bakr and ʿUthmān); 2) the tone of the reproaches addressed to the Companions emphasizes the notion of a return to a previous belief and the usurpation of authority by false Imams, and we can deduce that, in this treatise in particular, the use of personalized commentary is not merely meant as a summary of Shiʿi historiography. This historiography provides positive and negative archetypes, to which various actors correspond 'in every era and every age'. In this case, they seem intended as edifying arguments towards former Ismailis who began to show reservations, or even to betray the Imams and disobey their orders, and reverted to local authorities instead. The text does not give any indication as to the exact circumstances that governed the composition of the treatise, nor to the reasons which might have prompted Ismaili dignitaries to rise up against their hierarchy. It is likely that the upheaval which caused Ismailis to 'return' to 'falsehood' is ʿAbd Allāh's claim to be the Mahdī, but unfortunately, we cannot be sure of this argument.

The negative personalized commentaries found in Treatise I therefore take on a different hue. The use of this exegetical method remained quite anecdotal there, and could be simply understood as a rehearsal of Shiʿi themes. But if one is to admit that the omnipresence and refinement of personalized negative commentaries in Treatise III must lead to reading the names of Abū Bakr, ʿUmar and ʿUthmān as allusions to Ismailis sceptical about the reform of ʿAbd Allāh al-Mahdī, then it should be noted that some of the first pages of Treatise I can also be interpreted in the same sense. The text is too elusive to suggest such an interpretation at first sight. But one can legitimately wonder, given what can be drawn from Treatise III, whether the developments of Treatise I on the *musūkhiyya* also allude to dissident Ismailis. Indeed, the *musūkhiyya* concerns those who 'rejected the Truth after knowing it, even though they knew it was the Truth. This shows that he refers to those who entered the Summons of Truth, then were driven out of it by one of the Gates of faithlessness and hypocrisy in following the whispers of Satan'.[175]

[175] *Kashf* I, p. 4, § 6.

Let us recall that Treatise III also contains a short paragraph on *musūkhiyya*, where it is defined as moving from faith to disbelief,[176] which, in the context of this treatise, can easily be understood as an allusion to the Ismailis who refused ʿAbd Allāh al-Mahdī's reform or split up from the *daʿwa* in one way or another.

The subsequent pages of Treatise I can be understood in the same way, as they deal with the 'Shiʿis who fall short' (*muqaṣṣira*), as well as the people who follow 'the First of iniquity', 'the Second' and the 'Pharaohs' and turn away from the Prince of the Believers. All these enemies of truth who refuse to believe in the Last Day, identified with the Mahdī, seem to correspond perfectly to members of the *daʿwa* who parted from it following the reform. Identifying the *muqaṣṣira* as those who refuse to follow the Mahdī, 'the Master of the age' (*ṣāḥib al-zaman*) is particularly explicit . . . provided that the reader is put on the right track by the general tone of Treatise III, and in particular by a key passage, which we will examine below, advocating the legitimacy of a reform in religious matters. Yet, taken alone, each of these elements remains very elusive and could fully apply to a situation prior to the appearance of the Mahdī. Such is the difficulty of the *Kitāb al-Kashf*: it is a constant challenge to determine whether a particular passage was written before or after the *rajʿa*.

Another difficulty stems from the fact that the collection claims to 'unveil' hidden meanings from the Qur'an; in reality, the unveiling itself requires further unveiling. In the case of the historical enemies of ʿAlī b. Abī Ṭālib with whom we are dealing here, everything happens as if there were two levels of reading, as the exegesis itself calls for an exegesis. When, using the technique of personalized commentary, the text explains that such a Qur'anic verse alludes to Abū Bakr, for example, one must understand that behind the very name 'Abū Bakr' are other unnamed characters who are thus referred to an archetype. Abū Bakr, ʿUmar, ʿUthmān, Muʿāwiya, etc. are but figureheads of the historical enemies of the *daʿwa* at the time of composition of the treatises. The typical Shiʿi historiography of early Islam, to which Qur'anic verses are referred throughout Treatise III, is here a simple instrument in the service of the Ismaili propaganda.

---

[176] *Kashf* III, p. 88, § 73.

Drawing parallels between the *daʿwa* and the Prophet's *sīra* (biography) is not unique to the *Kitāb al-Kashf.* We know, for example, that the strongholds that the *duʿāt* were responsible for organising were called *duyūr al-hijra*, in reference to the Prophet's emigration from Mecca to Medina; the members of the *daʿwa* were thus 'summoned', called to leave their regions of origin to join the perfect community which was preparing the return of the Mahdī — the *Kitāb al-Kashf* illustrates this when declaring that the esoteric meaning of pilgrimage consists in 'the migration (*hijra*) from one's nation to that of the Messenger or the Imam in his era'.[177] Moreover, according to an article by James E. Lindsay the traditional narration of Abū ʿAbd Allāh al-Shīʿī's *daʿwa* in North Africa in preparation for the advent of the Mahdī rests on implicit parallels with episodes from Muḥammad's life.[178] Lindsay thus reminds his reader that, during the Abbasid revolution, the restoration of the ideal community of Medina was already the objective of the *daʿwa* of Abū Muslim in Khurasān.[179] This constant analogy between the founding period of Islam and its protagonists, on the one hand, and the Fatimid period, on the other hand, would eventually become a *topos* of the Fatimid rhetoric. Therefore, it is not surprising that, in Treatise III, the theme of the Ismaili *daʿwa* is largely based on a Shiʿi historiography of the beginnings of Islam, leaving to the reader the responsibility of identifying the contemporary equivalents of the protagonists of that time.

A distinction must be made, however, between an exegesis and the use made of it in the treatise. It can hardly be argued that the negative personalized commentaries of Treatise III were originally designed to fit the propagandist perspective of the treatise; it is very likely that several of them, if not most, actually originate from traditions prior to the composition of the treatise, traditions that were either Shiʿi in the

---

[177] *Kashf* V, p. 118, § 47.

[178] J.E. Lindsay, 'Prophetic Parallels in ʿAbd Allah al-Shiʿi's mission among the Kutama Berbers, 893–910', *International Journal of the Middle East Studies*, 24 (1992), p. 43: 'Al-Qadi al-Nuʿman does not draw direct parallels between Muḥammad and Abu ʿAbd Allah in the *Iftitāḥ*, but his presentation certainly enables his readers to come to the conclusion that Abu ʿAbd Allah was symbolically reenacting parts of the Prophet's career.'

[179] Ibid., pp. 43–44.

broad sense, or specific to the pre-Fatimid Ismaili tradition of Salamiyya (and particularly to al-Ḥakīm, who is designated as the author of several personalized commentaries of the treatise). Yet, the composition of these exegeses, the arrangement of the treatise, do indeed serve an Ismaili political-historical objective, the most constant and most identifiable argument of which is that of the 'continuity of the Order', which portrays the leaders of the Ismaili community as the last representatives of a line of guardians of the Alliance going back to Adam — through Muḥammad and ʿAlī, here archetypes of the continuity between, probably, al-Ḥakīm and his successor, ʿAbd Allāh al-Mahdī.

3. The Orphan: evolution of a concept, from *ghuluww* to Fatimid Ismailism

It is in the light of this context that the use of the term 'orphan' (*yatīm*), which appears with significant comments in Treatise III (in the exegesis of sūras 107 and 89), must be considered. The word 'orphan' has important implications, as it echoes the Shiʿi speculative profusion of the 2nd–3rd/8th–9th centuries, and is a marker of *ghuluww*. Its use in the *Kitāb al-Kashf* is to be interpreted as the expression of the Fatimid take on earlier Shiʿi debates.

Obviously, its importance in the speculations of certain Shiʿi groups is due to its presence in the Qur'an, which repeatedly recommends the protection of orphans and warns against the usurpation of their property.[180] The Qur'anic sensitivity to this theme is likely to be related to the status of the Prophet Muḥammad himself, an orphan placed under the protection of his uncle Abū Ṭālib, ʿAlī's father. The method of drawing parallels between the *daʿwa* and the prophetic *sīra* may have led the author of Treatise III to identify the Imam with the Qur'anic orphan, the latter being connected to the orphan Muḥammad. Yet, it cannot be ruled out that the insistence of the text on the notion of *yatīm* is an indirect response to the *ghulāt*, amongst whom this term had a particular fortune. Indeed, although its use in Treatise III does not appear to be directly related to *ghulāt* influences, the same is not

[180] Apart from the verses quoted in Treatise III, see e.g. Q. 4:10; 6:125; 93:6–9, etc.

true of Treatise I which is clearly dependent on *ghulāt* traditions promoting the concept of the Orphan.

i. The Orphan and the struggle for spiritual legitimacy

Treatise I contains the only other occurrences of the term 'orphan' in the collection. It thus contains an enumeration of twelve Orphans, followed by six other names presented as the 'fathers' of the Orphans.[181] To each 'father' corresponds a couple of Orphans:

— Salmān: Abū Dharr and al-Miqdād
— [?]: ʿAmmār b. Yāsir and a certain Dāwud
— Ibn Abī Zaynab (i.e. the heresiarch Abū'l-Khaṭṭāb): Muḥammad b. Abī Bakr (?) and ʿAbd Allāh b. Rawāḥa (?)
— Safīna: al-ʿAbbās and Jaʿfar b. al-Ḥārith
— Rushayd al-Hajarī: Ḥamza b. ʿAbd al-Muṭṭalib and Ḥanẓala b. Asaʿd al-Shibāmī
— Abū Khālid: Aswad and Shuʿayb.

H. Halm has previously examined this list and noted its oddities, namely its anachronisms and its disorderly nature, but he has also contributed to clarifying this confusing passage by detecting coherent elements, particularly links with the Nuṣayri doctrine.[182] The Nuṣayri system is indeed organized around a divine triad: *maʿnā / ism / bāb* ('meaning'/ 'name' / 'gate'),[183] which is followed by a pentad of Orphans in charge of creating the luminous and material worlds.[184] The triad and the pentad, which are ontological and cosmological entities, are personified par excellence by ʿAlī b. Abī Ṭālib, Muḥammad and Salmān, as regards the triad, and by companions of ʿAlī who are particularly revered in the Shiʿi milieu, as regards the pentad:

— al-Miqdād b. al-Aswad al-Kindī ('the Supreme Orphan', *al-yatīm al-akbar*)

[181] *Kashf* I, pp. 14–15, §§ 30–31.
[182] H. Halm, *Kosmologie*, pp. 153–155.
[183] See Y. Friedman, *The Nuṣayrī-ʿAlawīs*, pp. 73–81.
[184] Ibid., pp. 85–88.

— Abū Dharr Jundab b. Junāda al-Ghifārī
— ʿAbd Allāh b. Rawāḥa al-Anṣārī
— ʿUthmān b. Maẓʿūn al-Najashī
— Qanbar b. Kādān al-Dawsī.

Although these personifications are the most emblematic, they in fact vary from one era to another, that is, from one Imam to the other. Each Imam thus has his own *bāb*, and each of these *abwāb* supervises five 'Orphans'.[185] Now, all the 'fathers' mentioned in Treatise I of the *Kashf* correspond to the *abwāb* of the Nuṣayri system, although they are cited out of order and the list has clearly been transmitted with errors. Thus, in place of the second 'father', who should be Safīna (since, in Nuṣayrism, ʿAmmār b. Yāsir, is one of his Orphans), the *bāb* of the second Imam, the text of the *Kashf* is incomplete;[186] Safīna is not mentioned until further on. We should then have successively Rushayd al-Hajarī and Abū Khālid, who are the *bāb*s of the third and fourth Imams, respectively. Yaḥyā b. Maʿmar al-Thumālī,the *bāb* of Muḥammad al-Bāqir according to Nuṣayrism, does not appear. As for Ibn Abī Zaynab, who is none other than the heresiarch Abū'l-Khaṭṭāb mentioned in the introduction to the present study, he should appear in the last position, not in the third, as he was considered the *bāb* of Imam Mūsā al-Kāẓim.[187] Of course, the Ismailis do not recognise the Imamate of Mūsā al-Kāẓim, which explains — but only partially — the discrepancies between the *Kashf* and Nuṣayri data here.

The case of the Orphans cited in the *Kitāb al-Kashf* is more complex. Several indeed appear as Orphans in the Nuṣayri system: al-Miqdād,

[185] Ibid., pp. 88–91, esp. p. 90: 'Although the appearances of these eight persons, the triad and the pentad, are seen as the most prominent personifications of the deity, they are not the only ones. The Nuṣayrī tradition mentions additional appearances of all the eight beings in the form of other figures from Shīʿī culture.'

[186] This is one of the elements in favour of the fact that the two available manuscripts of the *Kashf* belong to the same manuscript tradition and have a common source.

[187] See Y. Friedman, *The Nuṣayrī-ʿAlawīs*, p. 287; see also the list of *abwāb* and *aytām* by al-Ḥasan b. Shuʿba, *Ḥaqā'iq asrār al-dīn*, in *Silsilat al-turāth al-ʿalawī*, ed. Abū Mūsā and Shaykh Mūsā (Diyār ʿAql, 2006), vol. 4, pp. 58–60, and p. 59 for Abū'l-Khaṭṭāb.

Abū Dharr and ʿAmmār b. Yāsir (if the text is amended by placing Safīna where the *Kashf* is incomplete) are correctly assigned to their *bāb*/'father'. Regarding the couple of Orphans subordinated to the 'father' Ibn Abī Zaynab, 'Muḥammad and ʿAbd Allāh', I have assumed that they were Muḥammad b. Abī Bakr and ʿAbd Allāh b. Rawāḥa, respectively Orphans of Safīna and Salmān in Nuṣayrism. But it is obvious that it would be anachronistic for their father to be Ibn Abī Zaynab, and this is probably what kept Halm from proposing to complete the text in this way. Finally, Jaʿfar b. al-Ḥārith, as already noted by H. Halm, usually appears among the Orphans of the Prophet Muḥammad.[188]

As for the other characters, they do not appear in the Nuṣayri lists of Orphan. Dāwud is unknown, as is Aswad, whom we could not identify. The others are identifiable, but their role and the reason for their presence in this list remains unclear. Shuʿayb's subordination to Abū Khālid nevertheless has a certain coherence, since both belong to the entourage of the Imam ʿAlī b. al-Ḥusayn, as Halm noted.[189] As for Ḥanẓala, he is not considered an Orphan in Nuṣayrism, but Halm signals a passage from a Nuṣayri text edited by R. Strothmann which may explain his presence in our list: Ḥanẓala was a companion of Imam Ḥusayn, which is consistent with his subordination to Rushayd al-Hajarī, the *bāb* of Ḥusayn according to Nuṣayrism.

The list from the *Kitāb al-Kashf* therefore presents several points that make it closer to Nuṣayri lists, and first of all, the very use of a list, a method particularly favoured by Nuṣayri authors. Several of the characters cited in Treatise I appear in Nuṣayri lists, and the 'fathers' are all *abwāb* in the Nuṣayri system, as we have seen. Yet, the differences are not negligeable and seem to point to another system.

From a formal point of view, we also note the distribution into two Orphans for one 'father', instead of five for a *bāb* as in late Nuṣayri doctrine. Y. Friedman and H. Halm provide different but convergent explanations in this regard. Halm notes that in some Nuṣayri texts, only two Orphans are mentioned: Abū Dharr and al-Miqdād. From this, he concludes that this form must represent an older layer of tradition, upon which both the *Umm al-kitāb* and the *Kitāb al-Kashf* are dependent.[190]

---

[188] See H. Halm, *Kosmologie*, p. 155; M.M. Bar-Asher and A. Kofsky, *The Nuṣayrī -ʿAlawī Religion*, p. 190 (Arabic: p. 215).

[189] Ibid., p. 155 and note 72.

This older layer can be identified in part with the doctrine of the 'pentadist' (*mukhammisa*) *ghulāt*, several teachings of which are found in the *Umm al-kitāb*, among other sources; the *mukhammisa* doctrine indeed included the 'Great Orphan', al- Miqdād, and the 'Small Orphan', Abū Dharr.[191] It should be noted that this current owes its name to its deification of the five *ahl al-kisā'*, the 'People of the Mantle': Muḥammad, 'Alī, Fāṭima, Ḥasan and Ḥusayn. The *ḥadīth* of the creation of these Five, at the end of Treatise I in the *Kashf*,[192] probably originates in this 'pentadist' tradition of which we also find traces in Twelver Shi'i literature.[193] Now, according to Y. Friedman — who follows in this the intuitions of Samuel Lyde, the 19th-century English missionary and pioneer of Nuṣayri studies — it might be a wish to subordinate the pentad to the triad, which was more essential to their system, that led the Nuṣayris to replace the five 'People of the Mantle' with the five Orphans.[194] Thus, the number of the Orphans evolved from two (the 'Great' and the 'Small') to five Orphans, and then to five Orphans per *bāb*. It should be noted that the 'taste' for pentads, so to speak, has also passed into Ismailism and Imamism through various forms.[195]

---

[190] See H. Halm, *Kosmologie*, p. 154, n. 56, and references given there. The *Umm al-kitāb* mentions twice two orphans whose identity and role are not indicated; see W. Ivanow, 'Notes sur l'Ummu'l-kitâb des ismaéliens de l'Asie centrale', *Revue des études islamiques*, 6 (1932), pp. 442, 463.

[191] See al-Qummī, *Maqālāt*, p. 57; H. Halm, *Kosmologie*, p. 158; idem, *Die islamische Gnosis*, p. 220; W. Madelung, 'Mukhammisa', *EI2*.

[192] *Kashf* I, pp. 35–36, §§ 76–78. See also *Kashf* III, p. 57, § 11, where there is a mention of the 'Five Eminences' (*al-khamsa al-a'lām*) towards whom a representative leads 'in every era and every age'.

[193] See e.g. M.A. Amir-Moezzi, *Guide divin*, p. 78 (English trans.: *Divine Guide*, p. 30), where a text close to the one found in the *Kashf* is quoted.

[194] See Y. Friedman, *The Nuṣayrī-'Alawīs*, p. 87. However, R. Dussaud asserts that the two pentads, that of the *ahl al-kisā'*, which he calls 'the chosen' ('les Elus'), and that of the Orphans (or 'Incomparables'), coexist in the Nuṣayri system; see R. Dussaud, *Histoire et religion des Noṣairis*, p. 68.

[195] In Ismailism, it is the cosmologic and noetic pentad formed by the following entities: *al-'aql, al-nafs, al-jadd, al-fatḥ, al-khayāl*; see above p. 211, n. 92. Amir-Moezzi notes that these five hypostases are identified with the Orphans in the *Umm al-kitāb*; see M.A. Amir-Moezzi, 'Les cinq esprits de l'homme divin (Aspects de l'imamologie duodécimaine XIII)', *Der Islam*, 92/2 (2015), pp. 297–320, esp. pp. 313–314. This article also deals with the pentads in Twelver Shi'ism, in the form of the 'five spirits' of the Imam; the author examines several parallels to this doctrine in other Islamic and pre-Islamic traditions.

In any case, the two Orphans tradition is very old, clearly pre-Nuṣayri, and Treatise I is dependent on it: it does not borrow from Nuṣayrism, rather it draws from the same sources. The latter are probably based themselves on the Qur'an, which, in Q. 18:82, within one of the stories most valued by esotericists, evokes *two* orphans whose heritage is saved by the intervention of the mysterious 'worshipper' of God and initiator of Moses.

The question remains, however, whether the list of Treatise I which subordinates *twelve* Orphans to *six* fathers is a trace of a system distinct from both the 'pentadist' and Nuṣayri developments, or if it is the result of an early Ismaili adaptation. We can simply note that the *Kitāb al-Kashf* here retains an ancient term of esoteric Shiʿism, to which it attributes a new meaning in Treatise III, in order to neutralise its 'exaggerating' connotation.

Before tackling the concept of Orphan as reflected in *Kashf* III and in the Fatimid context, other historical and doctrinal implications of this concept should be mentioned. Indeed, the term *yatīm* does not only appear in the literature of the *ghulāt* and the Nuṣayris, but also in the alchemical corpus of Jābir b. Ḥayyān, along with other concepts reminiscent of Shiʿi esotericism.[196] Indeed, it appears in the *Kitāb al-Khamsīn* (*Book of the Fifty*), which lists fifty-five 'ranks' of an esoteric hierarchy.[197] In his article on this work, Paul Kraus notes that: 'la plupart des appellations qu'on rencontre dans cette liste offrent des affinités indéniables avec les doctrines de la gnose šīʿite, en particulier dans le système ismaélien'.[198] He concludes that: 'l'auteur des écrits

[196] On the relation between the Jābirian corpus and the Shiʿa, see P. Lory, 'Esotérisme shiʿite et alchimie. Quelques remarques sur la doctrine de l'initiation dans le Corpus Jābirien', in M.A. Amir-Moezzi et al, eds, *L'ésotérisme shiʿite, ses racines et ses prolongements* (Turnhout, 2016), pp. 411–422; L. Capezzone, 'The Solitude of the Orphan: Ǧābir Ibn Ḥayyān and the Shiite heterodox milieu of the third/ninth-fourth/tenth centuries', *BSOAS*, 83/1 (2020), pp. 51–73.

[197] Enumerated in P. Kraus, 'Les dignitaires de la hiérarchie religieuse selon Ǧābir Ibn Ḥayyān', *Bulletin de l'Institut français d'archéologie orientale*, 41 (1942), p. 84; P. Lory, *Alchimie et mystique en terre d'islam* (Paris, 1989), p. 71.

[198] P. Kraus, 'Les dignitaires de la hiérarchie religieuse', p. 85. Among these 'degrees' or 'ranks', we find the Veil (*ḥijāb*), the Star (*kawkab*) (cf. *Kashf* I, p. 17, § 37, about Fāṭima), the Gate (*bāb*), the Orphan (*yatīm*), the Speaking-One (*nāṭiq*), the Silent One (*ṣāmit*), the Noble (*najīb*), the Chief (*naqīb*), the Angel (*malak*), the Sacred Station (*maqām*), the Proof (*ḥujja*), etc.

ǧābiriens (...) *puise dans l'arsenal des doctrines de la Šīʿa extrémiste*, avec le seul but de les dépasser et de construire, avec les matériaux ismaéliens et autres, un système original'.[199] This process of 'drawing from the arsenal of the doctrines of the extremist Shiʿa' is essential to understand the permanence of 'exaggerating' themes in institutionalized Shiʿi currents such as Fatimid Ismailism or Buwayhid Twelver Shiʿism.

In the *Kitāb al-Khamsīn*, the Orphan is defined thus: 'The Orphan is educated by the Imam (*tarbiyat al-imām*), and is always bound to him. He is veiled, and only the Imam can see him.'[200] The Orphan thus accessed the knowledge bestowed upon the Imam, yet without being genealogically tied to him. Moreover, he does not have a public and political role as do the Prophet or the Imam.[201]

While Kraus noted that the notion of *yatīm*, 'connu de l'*Umm al-kitâb*, des écrits nusairis, ainsi que de quelques anciens textes ismaéliens de l'époque Fatimide, semble avoir joué un rôle considérable dans les spéculations šīʿites du IIIe siècle',[202] he did not formulate any hypothesis as to the reasons and stakes of the role it played in such a large variety of groups. It is only in a recent article that Leonardo Capezzone has convincingly argued that the term *yatīm* appeared in those parts of the Jābirian corpus that were probably composed between the two Occultations and were thus a contribution to the Shiʿi

[199] Ibid., pp. 96–97. Italics added.

[200] English translation in L. Capezzone, 'The Solitude of the Orphan', pp. 68–69. See also French translations in P. Kraus, 'Les dignitaires de la hiérarchie religieuse', p. 88; P. Lory, *Alchimie et mystique*, p. 82.

[201] See P. Lory, *Alchimie et mystique*, pp. 81–83. According to Kraus and Lory, the 'Glorious' (*al-majīd*) from the alchemical Jābirian treatise, the *Kitāb al-Majīd*, must be identified with the 'Orphan'. See ibid., pp. 83–84; P. Kraus, 'Les dignitaires de la hiérarchie religieuse', p. 88, n. 5. Indeed, the *majīd* is presented as having attained gnosis, not through his genealogical ties to the *ahl al-bayt*, but because of 'des lumières qu'il emprunte [directement et personnellement] au 'AYN', that is, the Imam; see H. Corbin, *Alchimie comme art hiératique*, p. 188. As P. Lory summarizes it: 'Le Glorieux est l'étranger qui, par son propre effort et sa propre abnégation, atteint le niveau de connaissance le plus proche de l'Imâm'; see P. Lory, *Alchimie et mystique*, p. 83. On the *Kitāb al-Majīd*, see French translation and study by H. Corbin, *Alchimie comme art hiératique*, pp. 145–219; see also L. Capezzone, 'The Solitude of the Orphan', pp. 63, 70, 73.

[202] P. Kraus, Les dignitaires de la hiérarchie religieuse', p. 86.

debates on determining the legitimate spiritual authority in the absence of the Imam. In advocating this figure of the 'Orphan', what Capezzone labels the 'Jābirian community' was laying a claim to spiritual legitimacy that aimed to compete with the rival claims of other Shiʿi groups, namely the 'esotericist' and the 'rationalist' trends.[203]

Thus, building on Capezzone's demonstration, one is led to believe that the references to the *yatīm* in the *Kashf* and in other Fatimid sources are not only the result of an Ismaili drawing from a common pool of Shiʿi concepts, but, more importantly, the Fatimid Ismaili answer to rival Shiʿi groups. By including and reinterpreting a concept with such strong resonances, the early Fatimids were taking part in contemporary debates as to the identity and nature of the spiritual leadership — just as the reinterpretation of the *musūkhiyya* in the *Kashf* was a response to the doctrines of reincarnation held by rival groups.

ii. The Orphan in Fatimid context

In Treatise III, the 'triad' Salmān, al-Miqdād and Abū Dharr appears again,[204] but in terms very different from those of Treatise I: al-Miqdād and Abū Dharr are no longer presented as Orphans, nor Salmān as their father. Even the hierarchy that puts Salmān above al-Miqdād and Abū Dharr is not explicitly affirmed. The text is ambiguous in this regard: on the one hand, it states that Salmān is 'the end of all ends and the wellspring of all wellsprings', 'the Great Ark',[205] and 'the origin of Islam'.[206] The passage dedicated to Salmān is also much longer that those dealing with al-Miqdād and Abū Dharr. But, on the other hand, the passage where these three characters appear is an exegesis of Q. 77:30–31, which evokes a shadow with three branches, interpreted here as the Imam and his three representatives who are called 'Proofs' and 'Gates'.[207] They therefore seem to be placed on the same level: the 'three branches' 'refer to his Gates that he establishes to summon towards him and that he appointed for those who seek him. They are

[203] L. Capezzone, 'The Solitude of the Orphan'.

[204] *Kashf* III, pp. 70–73, §§ 36–40.

[205] *Kashf* III, p. 71, § 39.

[206] *Kashf* III, p. 72, § 40.

[207] *Kashf* III, pp. 69–72, §§ 35–39.

the Proofs of the Legatee'.[208] The text seems to 'Ismailize' *ghulāt* references, thus using the reverence inspired by these great Shiʿi figures, but isolating them from the systems where they were usually found and integrating them to a new doctrine. The choice of the term 'Proof' to designate the members of the triad is not incidental: the goal is to assimilate the Ismaili 'Proof' to these three characters. It is a matter of confirming, through their example, that the Proof is 'the Master of the esoteric' (*ṣāḥib al-bāṭin*),[209] and especially that 'every Imam is reached only through his Proof, and the Proofs are the Gates of the Imams'.[210] 'The Proof is the path to the Imam by which the people are summoned to God.'[211] Thus, the one who, in the organization of the *daʿwa*, bears the title of Proof is analogous, vis-à-vis the Imam, to what Salmān, al-Miqdād and Abū Dharr were vis-à-vis ʿAlī b. Abī Ṭālib. The use of the term 'Proof', present in Treatises I, III and VI, and one of the essential topics of Treatise V, is clearly Ismaili. The equalization of the respective statutes of Salmān, al-Miqdād and Abū Dharr through the exegesis of Q. 77:30, is also to be understood as an Ismaili reinterpretation that goes hand in hand with a new conception of the Orphan.

Just as the use of the figures of Salmān, al-Miqdād and Abū Dharr is obviously aimed at a Shiʿi public, particularly at the part of this public familiar with concepts and doctrines related to *ghuluww*, the use of the term *yatīm* in Treatise III is not neutral. It is true that *yatīm* appears about twenty times in the Qur'an, which could make the connection to *ghuluww* unnecessary; the identification of the Qur'anic orphan with the Imam could be an end in itself. However, the presence in the same treatise of the triad Salmān, al-Miqdād and Abū Dharr, and its use for Ismaili purposes (as will be shown in the next section), suggest that the text intentionally plays with the codes of the *ghulāt* and seeks to subvert them. It is significant that the Qur'anic orphan is identified with the Imam precisely in a treatise where the Orphans al-Miqdād and Abū Dharr are deprived of this title in favour of that of 'Proof', which is

208 *Kashf* III, p. 70, § 36.
209 *Kashf* III, p. 60, § 18.
210 *Kashf* III, p. 64, § 24.
211 *Kashf* V, p. 153, § 103.

manifestly used in an Ismaili sense. It can therefore be suspected that the *yatīm* of Treatise III is not a residual trace of a pre-existing *ghulāt* treatise, but is rather the result of a deliberate and tactical use of a notion that would find some resonance among the intended public of the treatise. This re-use of the vocabulary of the *ghulāt* is similar to that of the Jābirian corpus: the term is preserved, but the meaning changes completely. Treatise III therefore appears as an illustration of the Ismaili appropriation of the *yatīm*, of which several aspects can be noted.

The orphan is identified with the Imam twice: 1) in the exegesis of Q. 107; 2) in the exegesis of Q. 89. These sūras both mention the one '*who repels the orphan*' (Q. 107:2) or those who '*honour him not*' (Q. 89:17). In both sūras, the mentions of the orphan are followed by a mention of the 'poor' (*miskīn*): '*He urges not on feeding the poor*' (Q. 107:3); '*You urge not on the feeding of the poor*' (Q. 89:18). According to al-Nawbakhtī and al-Qummī, the *khurramdīniyya* sect already identified the orphan and the poor from Q. 89:17–18 with the Prophet and the Imam respectively.[212] It can therefore be considered that their respective identification with the Imam[213] and with the Proof[214] in Treatise III is the result of an Ismaili reinterpretation of these verses — just like the intention to confer to the Proof the prestige of ʿAlī's status vis-à-vis Muḥammad: 'With ʿAlī is the esoteric aspect of Muḥammad's religion, just as with every Proof is the esoteric aspect of the knowledge of the Imam of his age';[215] 'The Proof is the Master of the esoteric (. . .) Muḥammad — may God bless him — indicated ʿAlī, who was his Proof in his era. And the Proof of a given Imam is the Master of exegesis (*ṣāḥib al-taʾwīl*) in his era.'[216] The Ismaili identification of the orphan with the Imam goes hand in hand with an identification of the 'poor' with the Proof, since the Proof is the necessary mediation between the Imam and the believers. We shall return to the treatment of the Proof in the *Kashf*.[217]

---

212 Al-Nawbakhtī, *Firaq al-Shīʿa*, p. 34; al-Qummī, *Maqālāt*, p. 46.

213 *Kashf* III, pp. 54–55, §§ 3–6: p. 60, § 17.

214 *Kashf* III, pp. 55, § 7; pp. 60–61, § 18.

215 *Kashf* III, p. 55, § 7.

216 *Kashf* III, p. 60, § 18.

217 See commentary of *Kashf* V, pp. 396–408.

The conception of the orphan as it appears in Treatise III seems to represent an intermediary stage between earlier doctrines — that of the *ghulāt* in particular, but also of groups such as the *khurramdīniyya* who had an exegetical tradition on the question — and later Fatimid developments. Although it is closer to the latter, it nevertheless appears in a context bearing clear marks of *ghuluww* as we have seen. However, the *ghulāt* connotations of the term are neutralized, and its meaning undergoes a reorientation. *Yatīm* can also have the meaning of 'unique', or 'incomparable'. This is the meaning it bears in the well-known Arabic expression of 'the orphan pearl' or 'the incomparable pearl' (*al-durra al-yatīma*), which Treatise III attributes to the 'people of the exoteric': thus, when the latter 'speak about 'the incomparable pearl', they mean that it has no equivalent and that no pearl is better than it. So is the Imam: he has no equivalent and no one in his era is better than him'.[218] Similar explanations are found in other Fatimid sources.[219] The following passage by the Fatimid *dāʿī* al-Mu'ayyad fi'l-Dīn (d.1078) is illustrative of this tradition:

> 'They cut apart from the Path; according to the exegesis (*ta'wīl*), these are the imams of misguidance who cut people off from the way of the hereafter, by leading them astray from the knowledge of *tawḥīd*, by preventing them from following the intermediaries (*al-wasā'iṭ*) and the dignitaries (*al-ḥudūd*) (. . .) They are, par excellence, those who *'eat the properties of the orphans out of iniquity'* [Q. 4:10] (. . .) Orphans, in the theological (*ḥikma*) and exegetical (*ta'wīl*) meanings, are the Imams of the family of the Prophet. This comes from [the phrase] 'the incomparable pearl' that has no like. Indeed, none of them has a like in his time and age. God — may He be exalted — named their forefather Muḥammad 'the orphan', in His words: *'Did He not find you an orphan? So He sheltered you'* [Q. 93:6]. Eating the orphan's

[218] *Kashf* III, p. 54, § 5.

[219] See e.g. Jaʿfar b. Manṣūr al-Yaman, *Ta'wīl al-zakāt*, p. 65: 'The Imam is the orphan in his era, which means he has no equal nor like'; ibid., p. 225: 'The orphans are the Completer Imams, because each one of them in his era transcends all associates, all forms, all similitudes. He is unique in his era and age. He has no father nor mother. He is unique and has no chief, that is, there is no Completer above him, etc.'

> property, according to the exegesis (*ta'wīl*), is claiming their position in the Imamate.'[220]

Treatise III and al-Mu'ayyad agree on the fact that the orphan is the Imam of the time. Al-Mu'ayyad specifies that the term applies to 'Imams of the Prophet's family'. Thus, while the *Kitāb al-Kashf* applies it to ʿAlī b. Abī Ṭālib,[221] it is clear that this plea in favour of 'the sacred station of the Imamate' applies to a situation that goes far beyond ʿAlī's case. Consequently, the episodes of ʿAlī's 'passion', particularly the usurpation of his authority and the spoliation of the heritage of the Prophet symbolized by the oasis of Fadak,[222] are the models for the opposition met by the Imams of his progeny. As an archetype, the usurpation of ʿAlī's 'Order' is the key to the enmity encountered by the men of God both before his time *and after*. Shiʿi historiography and all the Shiʿi rhetoric exhorting the recognition of the true Imam are thus used in the context of a political *daʿwa* seeking to legitimize itself by recycling otherwise well-known Shiʿi themes.

The *Kitāb al-Kashf*, however, develops an aspect that does not appear in al-Mu'ayyad's *majlis*. The discussion of the orphan is thus bound to the question of the Imam's succession; the Imam is named 'orphan' because 'his father has disappeared': 'The Imam does not become an Imam and is not named after the Imamate, until the Imam who transmitted the Imamate to him (*afḍā ilayhi bi'l-Imama*) has disappeared.'[223] The Imam is therefore an orphan by definition, since he can only become an Imam upon his father's[224] death — or disappearance, as the verb *ghāba* is used, rather than *māta*. These few lines are enigmatic; they would not make much sense if they were applied to ʿAlī. It may be suspected that there is something more here than a general rule of succession, and that the text is alluding to a specific application of this rule. It seems to point to a situation where

---

[220] Al-Mu'ayyad fī'l-Dīn, *Al-Majālis al-mu'ayyadiyya*, vol. 1, *majlis* 54, pp. 266–267. I am grateful to the late Bassām al-Ṣafadī for drawing my attention to this passage.

[221] *Kashf* III, pp. 54–55, § 6; p. 60, § 17.

[222] *Kashf* III, p. 61, § 19.

[223] *Kashf* III, p. 54, § 4.

[224] It is not clear, however, if the Imam's 'father' should be understood in a biological or initiatory sense. On the spiritual fatherhood, see above, pp. 129–131.

the succeeding Imam had already been designated, without however being 'named after the Imamate'; he would thus be an Imam in potentiality, so to speak, and would not become Imam in actuality until the 'disappearance' of his predecessor and father.

It is likely that this passage on the succession of the Imams is an allusion to the succession of al-Qā'im bi-Amr Allāh to ʿAbd Allāh al-Mahdī. Indeed, W. Madelung recalls on the one hand that certain ruling prerogatives had been partially transferred to al-Qā'im during al-Mahdī's lifetime, and that propaganda was deployed in his favour. On the other hand, he points out several reports according to which the first Fatimid caliph, al-Mahdī, before his accession to power and after his arrival in the Maghrib, had presented a young man as the descendant of Muḥammad b. Ismāʿīl, this young man being none other than the future al-Qā'im bi-Amr Allāh, the second Fatimid caliph. According to Akhū Muḥsin, the latter was nicknamed 'the Master's Orphan' (*yatīm al-muʿallim*).[225] According to another source, the future al-Mahdī presented the future al-Qā'im as an orphan under his protection.[226] Such reports have nourished doubt regarding al-Qā'im's genealogical filiation to al-Mahdī. It is on such doubt that Bernard Lewis based his theory on the genealogy of the Fatimids.[227] Madelung rejected this thesis, considering that there was no decisive reason to doubt the filiation between the first two caliphs.[228] One may take this refutation further by formulating the following hypothesis: could it be that the doubt over the genealogy of al-Qā'im is the result of a misunderstanding of his designation as an 'orphan'? Instead of understanding *yatīm* in a symbolic sense, the adversaries of the *daʿwa* may have interpreted it in its literal, genealogical, sense, thus genuinely or intentionally ignoring the spiritual implications of the term in Shiʿi circles.

It seems in any case that the theme of the orphan is indeed connected to al-Qā'im, since it made its way into his official rhetoric — if we

---

[225] Al-Maqrīzī, *Ittiʿāẓ al-ḥunafā' bi-akhbār al-fāṭimiyyīn al-khulafā'*, cited in W. Madelung, 'Das Imamat', p. 68.

[226] Cited in W. Madelung, 'Das Imamat', p. 68.

[227] See B. Lewis, *The Origins of Ismāʿīlism: A study of the historical background Fatimid Caliphate* (Cambridge, 1940), pp. 44–75.

[228] W. Madelung, 'Das Imamat', pp. 73–80.

deem authentic a speech he delivered in 302/915 — that is, before he became caliph but after he was appointed to suppress the revolt of Abū ʿAbd Allāh al-Shīʿī's partisans. In this speech, he accuses his audience of following leaders who are hostile to the *daʿwa*, stating that: 'They spend the funds of orphans and the poor, wrongly on their part and unjustly.'[229]

One can at least draw from the mysterious passage of Treatise III the idea that the Imams succeed one another, which clearly corresponds much better to the Fatimid phase of Ismailism than to its pre-Fatimid phase, where there was no need to insist on matters of succession. In this sense, this passage seems to be close to one found in Treatise V:

> 'Thus, the Imam guides to the Imam after him; without his guidance, no sacred station of an Imam would be valid after another Imam, and no believer would receive guidance after the first guide. It is in this sense that the Imams guide on a *'straight Way'*; it means that each one of them guides [people] to an Imam he establishes; his sacred station and his affair are then established. Such is the path God [provides] to his worshippers in His religion and tradition.'[230]

The idea that 'the Imam guides to the Imam after him' is an allusion to the principle of *naṣṣ*, the explicit designation by an Imam of his successor.[231] This successional preoccupation is linked to the 'continuity of the Order', which we, as we have established, is a Fatimid marker. Indeed, the continuity of the Imamate is relevant in a context where it is a matter of inscribing an Imam in a lineage and justifying the very notion of a succession, which corresponds to an early Fatimid concern. We will return to this passage from Treatise V.

Treatise III testifies to the Ismaili reinterpretation of an important Shiʿi notion. On the one hand, the *Kashf* appropriates a term popular

---

[229] See P.E. Walker, *Orations of the Fatimid Caliphs*, p. 89 (Arabic: p. 3). This speech is reported by Idrīs ʿImād al-Dīn, *ʿUyūn al-akhbār*, ed. M. Ghālib, vol. 5, p. 216.

[230] *Kashf* V, p. 119, § 49.

[231] On *naṣṣ* in Shiʿi tradition, see M.G.S. Hodgson, 'How did the early Shīʿa become sectarian?', *JAOS*, 75 (1955), pp. 10–12; R. Adem, 'Classical *Naṣṣ* Doctrines in Imāmī Shīʿism', *SSR*, 1 (2017), pp. 42–71.

in the *ghulāt* circles where it is rooted (as indicated in the passage from Treatise I on the Orphans). On the other hand, more faithful to the letter of the Qur'an and to a more 'moderate' Shiʿism, it implicitly reconnects the notion of orphanhood with that of inheritance. The treatise does not really explain in what capacity the Imam is an orphan. Apart from the fact that the Imam is 'unique' and 'incomparable', the main explanation lies in what the Qur'an says about the orphan: the Imam, like the orphan, is repelled. Like the orphan, he is not honoured. The connection to the question of inheritance is here only implied by Q. 89:17–19: *'Nay! But you honour not the orphan. And you urge not on the feeding of the poor. And you devour the inheritance entirely.'* The inheritance in question is obviously that of the orphan/Imam, despoiled from his rights by 'the iniquitous'. It is here symbolized by the oasis of Fadak which Abū Bakr refused to grant to Fāṭima, claiming that 'the Prophets do not leave inheritance'.[232] For the Shiʿa, this episode is emblematic of the usurpation of the rights of the Prophet's descendants by the first three caliphs of Islam. The orphan of Treatise III is therefore the one whose inheritance is usurped, the inheritance being of course the *amr*, the Imamate, of which the Fatimids claim in turn to be the legitimate heirs.

4. Salmān, a Shiʿi figure in support of the Fatimid reform

In a passage which I believe is the key to the treatise, we find a decisive element to back the hypothesis according to which the treatise was composed *after* the Mahdī's appearance. While a quick reading of the treatise may lead us to believe that we are grappling with a relatively banal Shiʿi theological text, the short development on Salmān which I will now examine opens other perspective. Inasmuch as the exegeses of Treatise III are referring to a specific event or set of events, the significance of the negative personalized commentaries should be determined in relation to this context: the treatise is no longer dealing with events that happened in the early days of Islam, but with an immediate and very much present situation.

[232] Cited in *Kashf* III, p. 61, § 19.

In the passage dealing with al-Miqdād, Abū Dharr and Salmān,[233] these essential figures of Shiʿi Islam are given as examples and serve to edify the addressees of the treatise. Firstly, all three are 'Proofs of the Legatee', just as 'the Legatee is the Proof of the Messenger, and the Messenger is the Proof of God':[234] here there is a causal chain which, from faith in God, must lead to the successive acknowledgement of the Messenger, the Legatee, the Legatee's Proof and the following Imams' Proofs. The choice of the term 'Proof' (*ḥujja*) to designate these three characters is obviously a way for those who thus designate themselves at the time of the treatise to be acknowledged as the legitimate successors of ʿAlī's three Proofs. Thus, the description of the virtues and the role of the triad al-Miqdād, Abū Dharr and Salmān actually corresponds to the functions and virtues of the said Proof.

Al-Miqdād summons to the Truth and is 'one of the sources'[235] — of esoteric knowledge probably. He would therefore be one of the intermediate initiatory masters between the faithful and the Imam. The passage concerning Abū Dharr is slightly longer: he is also presented as a source, a holder and disseminator of esoteric knowledge who 'inseminates' (*dharaʾa*) the initiates, according to a pun on his name — a process which also benefited al-Miqdād who 'cuts off' (*qadda*) the False. By virtue of the analogy between these two saints and the Ismaili Proof, we can see how useful such a presentation can be. But there is more: Abū Dharr is described refusing to pledge allegiance to Abū Bakr, who is presented as the 'Satan of the community'.[236] Abū Dharr's refusal to submit to the false authorities is an example given to the members of the *daʿwa* in order to urge them to remain loyal to the one who claims the title of 'Prince of the Believers', and to dissuade them from following the Abū Bakr of their time — which probably corresponds to dissident dignitaries of the *daʿwa*, but may also refer to the Abbasid or even Umayyad rivals. Finally, Salmān is 'the wellspring of wellsprings',[237] identified with one of the sources of Paradise.

---

233 *Kashf* III, pp. 69–73, §§ 35–41.

234 *Kashf* III, p. 70, § 36.

235 Ibid.

236 Ibid.

237 *Kashf* III, p. 71, § 39.

The pretext for this development was the exegesis of the Qur'anic verses: '*Rush to a shadow split in three branches, which yet yields no shade and nor any relief from the flame*' (Q. 77:30–31). Previously, 'the shadow' of Q. 25:45 had been identified with the Prince of the Believers, that is to say ʿAlī b. Abī Ṭālib. Thus, 'the shadow split in three branches' is interpreted as the Imam and his three emanations, the Proofs or the Gates, while the 'flame' refers to the punishment inflicted on the infidels upon the *rajʿa* of the Qā'im. The passage ends with the following sentence: 'The shadow that offers relief from the flame is one of the three Gates',[238] which means that the only way to shield oneself from the Qā'im is to shelter under the shadow of the Gates or Proofs, that is to say, the highest members of the *daʿwa*. The evocation of the triad of ʿAlī's companions serves a concrete purpose.

The following lines confirm this and provide some explanation of the nature of this purpose, with a paragraph more specifically devoted to Salmān, 'the origin of Islam'.[239] While the text does not elaborate on this designation, it is possible that it is not solely due to his surrendering to or relying on God, the Prophet and the true religion, but also to the fact that his personal spiritual journey symbolises a change of religious paradigm. Indeed, Salmān became a Muslim 'based on the knowledge he had of the truth of religion within the Law of Jesus',[240] which must be analyzed through the notion of 'continuity of the Order'. Salmān recognized the truth of Islam on the basis of his Christian faith; by converting to Islam, he did not apostatise his former faith, but only updated and fulfilled it, in accordance with the principle that 'whoever obeys the last of [the Messengers and Imams], it is as if he obeyed the first of them, because of the continuity of God's Order from the first of them, to the ones after him, and up to the last of them. Whoever obeys the first, his obedience will guide him and lead to the last.'[241] As we have seen, the 'continuity of the Order' has a practical consequence which is to legitimize the claims of the Imam. Here, it is a matter of showing that Salmān did not renounce anything when becoming a

[238] *Kashf* III, p. 72, § 39.

[239] *Kashf* III, pp. 72–73, §§ 40–41.

[240] *Kashf* III, p. 72, § 40.

[241] *Kashf* I, pp. 8–9, § 17.

Muslim: 'When Salmān surrendered (*aslama*) to Muḥammad after [he had surrendered to] Jesus, he perfected his religion, which was first with Jesus, since he completed it by following Muḥammad.'[242]

However, the following paragraph shows that we must go further and that it is not only a question of continuity and unity of religion. What is at stake is not simply to use the aura of Muḥammad, ʿAlī or his companions for the benefit of the Imam of the Ismaili community, but to show that it is legitimately possible to pass from one religion to another without going from falsehood to truth, nor from truth to falsehood. In short, it is possible to be on the truthful path by successively adopting two apparently contradictory positions, precisely because this contradiction is only apparent. An apparent rupture can actually be rooted in real continuity.

Taken alone, Salmān's example could be just as useful in the pre-Fatimid Ismaili context, in order to justify the change of the religious paradigm that the faithful should expect. Just as Salmān, who came from the tradition established by the Speaking-prophet (*nāṭiq*) Jesus, is, in a way, a 'completer'[243] leading to the next Speaking-prophet, who is Muḥammad, so are the Ismailis, who, coming from the tradition established by the Speaking-prophet Muḥammad, should follow the Salmān of their time who will lead them to the seventh Speaking-prophet — the latter being either conceived as the bearer of a new Law, or as the one who will lift the Law. Of course, the information available to us is insufficient to determine whether the *daʿwa* of Salamiyya preached the coming of an antinomian Speaking-prophet or not. The fact remains that the model of Salmān passing from one religion to another, from the Law and Revelation of one Speaking-prophet to another, may have been used to justify the approach of the Ismailis of Salamiyya awaiting the arrival of a new Speaking-prophet. This passage has a certain pre-Fatimid tone, all the more so as it appears to be reported after the 'Sage'.[244]

However, as it stands in Treatise III, the passage must be interpreted differently. First, Salmān is presented as a Proof (*ḥujja*), on the one

---

[242] *Kashf* III, p. 73, § 48.

[243] The term *mutimm* is not mentioned here, but Salmān's conversion is indeed presented as a 'completion' (*tamām*) of his former religion; see *Kashf* III, p. 73, § 40.

[244] *Kashf* III, p. 72, § 40.

hand, and as one who somehow ensures the transition from one Speaking-Prophet to the next, on the other. But the passage mentioning him in Treatise III is immediately followed by another which not so much legitimizes the advent of a new religion as it does the mere possibility of a religious reform. The model invoked here is that of the modification of the direction of prayer during the Prophet's lifetime. Not only does the author recall that Muḥammad changed the direction of prayer from Jerusalem to Mecca without this affecting the validity of previous prayers,[245] he also reports the anecdote of a man who changed the direction of his prayer while performing it — which accentuates the rupture, the opposition of both directions, and therefore makes more spectacular the fact that they are both approved by God and His Messenger. If the Prophet was able to reconcile two exactly opposite directions, it is unsurprising that the *daʿwa* and its leader, successor of the Prophet, can do the same. What would such a passage allude to if it was pre-Fatimid? If the Mahdī was still to come, it would probably not be the smartest move to present his return as something apparently contrary to what had been taught until then. There is clearly an allusion to a far-reaching, ambitious reform, destabilising to the point of instilling doubt among the supporters of the earlier doctrine. And this reform has already taken place at the time these lines were written; they are precisely because the reform surprised those who awaited the Mahdī. While the passage remains discreet, it is nevertheless the one which indicates most clearly the purpose and intentions of the treatise when it was written (or composed, if we admit that the author has collated older exegetical material, that of al-Ḥakīm in particular, and put it at the service of the reform). And one might think that the reform in question is very probably that of ʿAbd Allāh al-Mahdī proclaiming himself as the Mahdī.

The conclusion of the passage confirms its Fatimid origin. After urging the reader to follow Salmān's example, the author continues:

> 'The religion of God is not broken off by the death of the Messengers and the Imams; rather, it is perpetuated by successive

[245] *Kashf* III, p. 73, § 41: 'God did not make them lose the reward of the first direction in which they prayed.'

> representatives (*qā'im ba'da qā'im*) in accordance with God's order and election. The perfection of religion and the completion of Islam thus resides in the succession of God's chosen one after the other.'[246]

To begin with, such a doctrine is particularly suitable for an organization whose leaders claim the legacy of the Messenger and the Imams. In this regard, the expression *qā'im ba'da qā'im*, 'one *qā'im* after another', which applies to the Imams a term usually reserved for the central protagonist of the *raj'a*, is of particular importance. Another passage from the treatise states that, 'in every age and every era', there is a *qā'im* to guide towards 'the Five eminences',[247] who are probably the 'Five of the mantle' (*ahl al-kisā'*) raised to the rank of spiritual entities as seen at the end of Treatise I.[248] Similarly, in Treatises I and V, other occurrences of the term *qā'im* seem no longer to link the term strictly to eschatology — except for initiatory eschatology — and make it a quasi-synonym of Imam or representative of the Imam. In Treatise I, *qā'im* generally refers to the main character of the eschatological events, namely the seventh Speaking-Prophet.[249] There are however two exceptions to this, both of which are embedded in distinctly Fatimid passages — as they deal with the theme of God's 'Order.[250] In Treatise V, the author states that: 'Each *qā'im* in his era is the name by which God is called in this era' (*kull qā'im fī 'aṣrihi huwa ism Allāh alladhī yud'ā bi-hi fī dhālika al-'aṣr*).[251]

Qā'im thus applies to any representative of God in a given time and is therefore a synonym of Imam, inasmuch as the latter term includes the notions of continuity and succession. Such a shift in the meaning of *qā'im*, which strips it from its classical messianic connotations (although the latter also appear in Treatise III, as will be seen in the following section),[252] is consistent with the need of the early Fatimid

---

[246] *Kashf* III, p. 73, § 41.

[247] *Kashf* III, p. 57, § 11.

[248] *Kashf* I, pp. 35–37, §§ 76–78.

[249] *Kashf* I, p. 8, § 16; p. 10, § 20; p. 11, § 24; p. 14, § 29; p. 22, § 46; pp. 25–26, §§ 55–56; p. 28, § 60; p. 29, § 62; pp. 32–35, §§ 68–73.

[250] *Kashf* I, p. 9, § 17; p. 12, § 25.

[251] *Kashf* V, p. 109, § 33.

[252] It thus appears several times in the form *qā'im bi'l-sayf*; see *Kashf* III, p. 62, § 20; p. 75, § 45; p. 77; § 48; p. 89, § 74, and commentary of *Kashf* III below, pp. 293–298.

rule to neutralize the eschatological expectations of its partisans and divert them towards a dynastic concept of the Imamate. Later Fatimid literature continues this use of the term *qāʾim*. Al-Naysābūrī, for instance, who was active under the reigns of al-ʿAzīz (r. 365–386/975–996) and al-Ḥākim bi-Amr Allāh (r. 386–411/996–1021) thus writes that 'the Imam is a *qāʾim*, he is the proclaimer (*nāṭiq*) in his age and time and he is the one who assumes the sacred station [of the *qāʾim*] (*yaqūm maqāmahu*)'.[253]

As for determining the time when this doctrine was adopted by the Fatimids, it is a difficult matter. In his article on the Ismaili Imamate, W. Madelung established that the reform of al-Muʿizz justified the status of the Fatimid Imams by considering them deputies (*khulafāʾ*) of the Qāʾim.[254] This seems close, although not identical, to the doctrine we are dealing with in the *Kashf*, since the term *qāʾim*, in this system, retains its eschatological connotation, and the Imams are apparently not named so themselves. A possible hypothesis would be to date the abovementioned shift of the meaning of *qāʾim* from the reign of the second Fatimid caliph, whose reign-name was eponymously al-Qāʾim bi-Amr Allāh.

It has been assumed that this name had been chosen for its eschatological connotations, but it might in fact be the result of the 'de-eschatologization' of the Fatimid Ismaili doctrine. Indeed, the problem the Fatimids were facing at the time was to justify the transfer of the Imamate from the first caliph to his successor, thus establishing a dynasty, that is, a continuous Imamate. The name al-Qāʾim bi-Amr Allāh would thus have been a way to tackle the messianic expectations of some *daʿwa* members by reorienting the very meaning of *qāʾim*, thus attaching the term to the Arabic expression *qāma bi-*, 'to accomplish', 'to take on', rather than to the *qiyāma*, the Resurrection. Instead of the Resurrector, the partisans of the Fatimids would thus

---

[253] Al-Naysābūrī, *Ithbāt al-Imama*, p. 42, § 16 (Arabic text, p. 17). I have modified the translation.

[254] See W. Madelung, 'Das Imamat', pp. 86–101. See also F. Daftary, *The Ismāʿīlīs. Their History and Doctrines*, pp. 163–167, esp. pp. 164–165. On the identification of the Fatimid Imam with the *qāʾim* and the evolution of this doctrine in al-Kirmānī's thought, see M. De Cillis, *Salvation and Destiny*, index s.v. '*qāʾim*', esp. pp. xv-xvi, 5–7, 11, 14–17, 100–101, 149–154.

have an 'upholder' of the truth (*qāʾim biʾl-ḥaqq*) and of God's (continuous) Order (*qāʾim bi-amr Allāh*).

In any case, this passage on Salmān and the reform must be Fatimid. Therefore, the question arises whether it was inserted there as a (long) Fatimid gloss within a pre-Fatimid core, as was the case in Treatise I, where the *ghulāt* core was amended by a Fatimid hand — with the difference here being that the core of Treatise III is not of *ghulāt* origin but pre-Fatimid Ismaili. I incline towards the alternate hypothesis: Treatise III indeed seems to have fewer interpolations than Treatise I, as it has a certain unity of style and themes. While it is obvious that pre-Fatimid material was used, giving the text the appearance of a heterogeneous compilation of exegeses, the treatise nevertheless presents itself as a composition dating to a time later than the proclamation of the Mahdī.

5. The 'Bearer of the Sword' and the *rajʿa*

The treatment of the *rajʿa* in Treatise III places us at the heart of the general problem one faces when trying to date the *Kashf*. On the one hand, it is clear that the collection contains many pre-Fatimid elements of various origins. Yet, it is equally clear that these elements were either recomposed, or simply amended and glossed, at the beginning of the Fatimid period. The problem resides in distinguishing the pre-Fatimid aspects from the Fatimid ones. Regarding the seventh Speaking-Prophet in particular, one often wonders whether, when the *Kitāb al-Kashf* was composed, he had already appeared or was yet to come. For instance, when, in Treatise III, the words of the Sage on the events of the *rajʿa* are quoted, or when the author mentions the retribution of those who joined the *daʿwa* and those who rejected it, must we understand that we are dealing with a pre-Fatimid text predicting events to happen upon the Mahdī's arrival? Or should we consider, on the contrary, that the Mahdī has indeed appeared and that these passages are meant to legitimize his claims by restating the pre-Fatimid traditions that circulated about him? Indeed, in the latter case, it is quite probable that, confronted with hesitation or open rebellion, the leaders of the *daʿwa* needed to remind the recalcitrant of the advantages of following God's chosen one, and the disadvantages of joining the ranks of his adversaries, heirs of ʿAlī's enemies. The *Kashf* is thus a collection straddling two periods, adapting the theoretical tools of the first, pre-Fatimid, period, to the circumstances of the second, early Fatimid.

The second part of Treatise III, after the development on Salmān, is mainly devoted to the *raj'a*, the eschatological return. While the Resurrector is also mentioned in the first part, eschatology is only one theme among others, mainly the opposition met by the Imams. As explained previously,[255] the *raj'a* implies a historical and political — material — understanding of eschatology. The 'Last Day' does not take place in the hereafter, but it is the Mahdī himself or the day of his coming. As seen in Treatise I, the Qur'anic verses on Judgment Day are thus interpreted as referring to the historical event of the return of Imam-Mahdī.

At the beginning of the treatise, a passage, while not directly dealing with the *raj'a*, nonetheless illustrates how the Qur'anic expressions concerning punishment are interpreted in a physical and literal sense. In the exegesis of Q. 89, where several verses are interpreted as referring to 'Alī b. Abī Ṭālib and his enemies, the '*scourge of chastisement*' from Q. 89:13 is thus identified with 'the sword that the Prince of the Believers drew out (*aẓhara*) — peace be upon him — and with which he killed the people of [the battle of] the Camel, annihilated their might and killed their tyrants'.[256] The Qur'anic punishment, which takes place in the hereafter, is considered as an immediate material event: it takes place in this worldly life. It is on this model that the punishment brought by the Resurrector is understood. According to al-Ḥakīm, the 'flame' of Q. 77:31 is the sword of the Resurrector.[257] There is an analogy between 'Alī and the Resurrector, on the one hand, and their respective enemies, on the other; as we have shown above, by virtue of the verse: '*We appointed to every prophet an enemy among the sinners*' (Q. 25:31), and of the 'continuity of the Order', the Resurrector, a descendant of 'Alī, is confronted with enemies who are the 'Abū Bakr', the ''Umar', etc., of his time. The Resurrector re-enacts the struggle between 'Alī and his enemies, except that this time, he will eventually be victorious.

---

[255] See above, pp. 10–11.

[256] *Kashf* III, p. 59, § 15.

[257] *Kashf* III, p. 72, § 39.

In another passage from the treatise, eternal, rather than earthly, punishment of the Opponents seems to be advocated. Q. 20:127: '*the chastisement of the Hereafter is more terrible and more lasting*', is thus intended for Abū Bakr and ʿUmar, and its interpretation mentions a permanent 'narrowness and constraint'.[258] However, this is also reminiscent of transmigrationist views, since this takes place 'in distorted bodies'.[259] At the end of the treatise, the author mentions the metamorphosis of Abū Bakr 'into a variety of figures and forms',[260] an ambiguous formulation immediately neutralized by a metaphorical interpretation of the *musūkhiyya*, according to the general orientation of the *Kashf* on that matter, as I have shown previously. In several texts of the *ghulāt*, divine punishment is indeed seen as a series of reincarnations into human and, worse, non-human bodies subjected to various vicissitudes. This is the original meaning of the *musūkhiyya* as it is found in the *Kitāb al-Haft wa'l-aẓilla*, for example, where the unbelievers (*kuffār*) are embodied into the bodies of animals intended for consumption and therefore subjected to slaughter.[261] But *musūkhiyya* does not appear in this sense in the *Kashf*, the latter visibly striving to dismiss this doctrine of reincarnation, even if traces of it remain.

Just as the doctrine of *musūkhiyya* is somehow rationalized, the *rajʿa* is not presented in the *Kashf* as a resurrection, as the reappearance of the Imam according to the principle of metempsychosis or as his return after an occultation of a miraculous duration. Rather, it is integrated within the dialectic between occultation and manifestation of the Order. When a Speaking-Prophet appears, as a 'diurnal Proof',[262] he manifests the Order. Upon his death, a period of occultation (*ghayba*) begins, which extends until the rising of the next Speaking-Prophet. It is in this sense that Q. 20:130 is interpreted: '*Proclaim the praise of your Lord before the rising of the sun and after its setting*': 'before the rising of the sun and after its setting' means the period between the disappearance of a Speaking-Prophet and the appearance of the

---

[258] *Kashf* III, p. 79, § 55.

[259] Ibid.

[260] *Kashf* III, p. 88, § 73.

[261] Mufaḍḍal al-Juʿfī, *Kitāb al-Haft wa'l-aẓilla*, Ch. 20, p. 54.

[262] *Kashf* I, p. 15, § 32.

following one.[263] During this period, the 'nocturnal Proofs'[264] are in charge of the Order. The *raj'a* of the Mahdī, the last of the Speaking-Prophets, is only made possible through the preparation of his return by the silent, 'nocturnal' Imams of the occultation period.

One of the attributes of the Speaking-Prophets is the sword, the symbol of temporal power, of a *da'wa* finally manifested, and no longer 'silent' and hidden. It was indeed attributed to the Resurrector in Treatise I,[265] and presented there as the attribute of the 'diurnal Proof', as opposed to the 'nocturnal Proof', who is the 'Master of the confidential speech and the Covenant'.[266] The sword is the attribute of the exoteric religion, it belongs to the Speaking-Prophets, *a fortiori* to 'the supreme Speaking-Prophet' (*nāṭiq al-nuṭaqā'*).[267] In the *ḥadīth* on the return of the Mahdī of Treatise I, the sword figured prominently, 'stained' with the blood of Quraysh, before being laid down once Abū Bakr and 'Umar have been crucified, that is, once it has restored order — or, rather, 'Order'.

The expression *al-qā'im bi'l-sayf*, the 'Bearer of the sword', does not appear until Treatise III. It appears again in Treatise V,[268] which also mentions the 'sword of the *qā'im*'.[269] One might think that this is simply the Resurrector, that is the last Speaking-Prophet. As noted by Heinz Halm, the expression *ṣāḥib al-sayf*, the 'Master of the sword', already designated Ja'far al-Ṣādiq according to the sect of *nāwūsiyya*, who believed that Ja'far was not dead and that he was the Qā'im-Mahdī.[270] H. Halm considers that this figure of the 'Bearer of the sword' was 'the prototype of the one who would put an end to the political powerlessness of the Imam'.[271] Several passages from Treatise III thus describe the *raj'a* as a time when the Resurrector will wield the sword.[272]

263 *Kashf* III, pp. 81–82, § 60.
264 *Kashf* I, p. 15, § 32.
265 *Kashf* I, p. 11, § 24.
266 *Kashf* I, p. 15, § 32.
267 *Kashf* I, p. 16, § 35.
268 *Kashf* V, p. 103, § 25.
269 *Kashf* V, p. 135, § 72.
270 Al-Nawbakhtī, *Firaq al-shī'a*, p. 57; al-Qummī, *Maqālāt*, p. 80.
271 H. Halm, *Kosmologie*, p. 26.
272 *Kashf* III, p. 72, § 39; pp. 75–76, § 45: p. 82, § 60.

The end of the treatise mentions 'the rising of the Resurrector with the sword' (*qiyām al-qā'im bi'l-sayf*) and 'the Resurrector when he appears with his sword' (*al-qā'im 'inda ẓuhūrihi bi'l-sayf*).[273] On the following page, in an exegesis attributed to the Sage, the Qur'anic promise of the Day of Judgment is interpreted as an allusion to the 'Bearer of the sword' (*al-qā'im bi'l-sayf*).

Yet, another passage presents the 'Bearer of the sword' as a *predecessor* of the Resurrector proper. This appears in the exegesis of Q. 89:21: '*When the earth is ground to powder, and your Lord comes, and the angels rank on rank*', understood as an allusion to a *preparation* for the coming of the Resurrector.[274] The 'earth' is the Proof, according to an exegetical equivalence found elsewhere in the *Kashf*.[275] The 'Lord' is the Resurrector, 'the Master of the age'. As for the angels, the text gives two interpretations. According to the first one, they are the 'Friends' (*awliyā'*) of the Resurrector, probably the Summoners and other members of the *da'wa*. In the second interpretation, it is actually 'a specific angel, that is, the one who will rise with the sword (*yaqūm bi'l-sayf*) before the Master of the age'[276] — as a type of pioneer-scout. The Imam-Resurrector 'will send before him someone who will rise with the sword and warn people about his power and the scourge of his chastisement. He will then come in person, after the earth has been prepared and arranged for him.'[277] So far, the text is clear, although unusual. It is indeed understandable that the coming of the Resurrector has to be prepared in advance — which was precisely the role of the clandestine *da'wa*: the leader of the community was in charge of this mission and responsible for 'warning' the people. What is more surprising is the distinction made between the Resurrector and 'the one who bears the sword'; insofar as the sword is associated with the Resurrector, or at least with the Speaking-Prophet, attributing it to an authority preceding him, that is to say, logically, a 'silent' Imam, appears contradictory. All the more so since another passage explicitly mentions 'the Silent Imam who was hidden before the manifestation

[273] *Kashf* III, p. 87, § 71.

[274] *Kashf* III, pp. 61–62, § 20.

[275] *Kashf* III, p. 85, § 68; V, p. 101, § 22; p. 155, § 106.

[276] *Kashf* III, p. 62, § 20.

[277] *Kashf* III, p. 62, § 20.

of the Resurrector' and who 'indicates the One who rises with the edge of the sword' (*al-qā'im bi-ḥadd al-sayf*).[278]

The end of the passage is rather confusing: 'God will send the Imam who bears the sword (*al-qā'im bi'l-sayf*), and he will warn the people by his tongue and by the sword. '*Upon that day, Gehenna is brought out*' [Q. 89:23]: 'Gehenna', here, means the Speaking-Prophet who appears with the sword.'[279] Here, 'the One who bears the sword' has the status of Imam, his role is twofold: he warns 'by tongue and by sword'. But then, one does not understand what makes the specificity of the Resurrector, 'who appears with the sword', if he is preceded by an Imam who holds the same warlike and public role — because the sword also symbolizes open action, as opposed to covert action.

The confusion would appear to arise from the coexistence of two distinct systems, one pre-Fatimid, the other Fatimid. According to the pre-Fatimid doctrine, the coming of the Resurrector is indeed prepared by a silent Imam and his adjutants: Proofs, Summoners, and believers. But with the appearance of ʿAbd Allāh al-Mahdī, the eschatology is modified, and the appearance of the Resurrector goes through two stages. A first 'bearer of the sword' Imam appears; he is not the Resurrector, but his role is to announce the latter. This 'sword-bearer' is probably ʿAbd Allāh al-Mahdī. Indeed, as Halm points out,[280] ʿAbd Allāh al-Mahdī's famous letter to the Ismaili community of Yemen holds that 'there should be an imam vested with authority who will appear with visible power and with the sword' (*mumallak yaẓhar bi'l-sulṭān al-ẓāhir wa'l-sayf*) between two Speaking-Prophets,[281] this Imam being ʿAbd Allāh al-Mahdī himself. We are therefore dealing with the first stage of an apologetic 'tinkering' aimed at transmuting eschatological promises into the legitimization of a dynastic power.

---

[278] *Kashf* III, p. 77, § 56.

[279] *Kashf* III, p. 62, § 20.

[280] H. Halm, *Kosmologie*, p. 36.

[281] See A. Hamdani and F. De Blois, 'A Re-examination of al-Mahdī's Letter', p. 178; H.F. Hamdani, *On the Genealogy of Fatimid Caliphs*, Arabic text, p. 13.

Conclusion

Treatise III is heavily imbued with pre-Fatimid Ismaili material, the Ismaili nature of which is unmistakable, given the importance of the *daʿwa* theme. It is quite distant from the tradition of the *ghulāt* as found in Treatise I. The main part of the text comes from exegeses which prevailed during the clandestine phase of the *daʿwa*, as indicated by the numerous interpretations attributed to the 'Sage', as well as the exegesis of Q. 89, attested in another early Ismaili source, namely the *Kitāb al-Rushd wa'l-hidāya*. The rare elements which echo the *ghulāt* tradition are reinterpreted in a new sense: such is the case of the *musūkhiyya*, of the role of Salmān, al-Miqdād and Abū Dharr, and of the orphan. It is however difficult to determine to what extent this Ismaili reinterpretation pre-dates the Fatimid period. Among the more clearly Fatimid elements, one can include a subtle justification of the reform of the *daʿwa*, the emphasis on the *rajʿa*, particularly on the role of the 'Bearer of the sword'. As for the frequent mentions of ʿAlī's enemies under various names, this is one of the characteristics of Treatise III. The treatise should not, however, be essentially understood as a composition directed against those who respected the first three caliphs and the Umayyads. It is rather a mobilization of Shiʿi 'anti-Sunni' material in favour of Fatimid claims, yet aimed at an 'internal' public; the insistence on the notion of 'returning to the truth after knowing it' is a strong indication of this. One cannot dismiss the possibility that the treatise was glossed here and there, from an older core. I hope to have shown here that the general orientation and tone of the text rather suggest a complete reworking of earlier material (pre-Fāṭimid, both Shiʿi or Ismaili), oriented towards the justification of the fledgling Fatimid rule.

TREATISE IV

Treatise IV is the shortest in the collection, but it is also the most puzzling, since it seems impossible, given the state of corruption of the text, to determine its meanings with exactitude. Several sentences, if not whole parts, are missing. This is confirmed by a comparison of the text with chapter 59 from the *Kitāb al-Haft wa'l-aẓilla*; as M. Asatryan has remarked, the second part of Treatise IV presents a version of the same text that constitutes chapter 59 of the *Haft wa'l-aẓilla.*[1] The latter's version is thus useful for correcting and completing the version found in the *Kashf*, but it is not enough to fully make sense of the treatise.

The general theme of the treatise seems to be human language, although its underlying doctrine is unclear. The first part of the treatise is formed of an assemblage of three *ḥadīth*s which have parallels in Twelver Shiʿi sources, one of which is very similar to the first *ḥadīth* of Treatise II, as it is devoted to the matter of *tawḥīd.*[2] The second part of Treatise IV is formed of speculations on language. The structure of this treatise can therefore be analysed as follows:

1) [§§ **1–2**] Two fragments of one *ḥadīth*: the creation of the letters by God
2) [§ **3**] *Ḥadīth* on the notion of *ṣamad*
3) [§ **4**] Fragment of *ḥadīth*
4) [§§ **5–10**] *Ḥadīth*: Jaʿfar al-Ṣādiq on language

[1] M. Asatryan, *Controversies of Formative Shiʿi Islam*, pp. 38–39; idem, 'Early Ismailis and other Muslims', pp. 285–298.

[2] This explains why the first part of Treatise IV has no parallel in the *Kitāb al-Haft wa'l-Aẓilla*: the two parts are unrelated and have only been gathered by the compiler of the *Kashf*. Disjoining the two parts of Treatise IV as two independent texts solves some of the questions raised by M. Asatryan in his study of Treatise IV; see. M. Asatryan, 'Early Ismailis and other Muslims', pp. 287, 290–291.

Treatise IV Translation

In the name of God, the Merciful, the Compassionate
[Fragments of *ḥadīth*]

1. Abū al Ḥasan narrated to us from Aḥmad b. Muḥammad, from Ḥamal b. Ṣabāh,[3] from Zurāra,[4] that Abū Jaʿfar[5] said: 'The first thing God created was the letters of the alphabet.'[6]

2. Muʿāwiya b. Ḥakīm[7] increased my knowledge in this regard, with the same chain of transmission (*isnād*). Muḥammad b. ʿAlī b.

[3] I have not been able to identify these three transmitters.

[4] Zurāra b. Aʿyan (d. 765 or 767) was a disciple and a *ḥadīth* transmitter of the Imams Muḥammad al-Bāqir and Jaʿfar al- Ṣādiq. Al-Kashshī provides contradictory accounts on him: he is at times praised by Jaʿfar al-Ṣādiq for transmitting *ḥadīth* faithfully and being one of his four favourite disciples. In other accounts, he is disavowed by the same Imām saying that 'he does not belong to our religion'; see al-Kashshī, *Rijāl*, in al-Ṭūsī, *Ikhtiyār maʿrifat al-rijāl al-maʿrūf bi-rijāl al-Kashshī*, ed. J. al-Qayyūmī al-Iṣfahānī (Qom, 2005), no. 63, pp. 123–144. According to certain reports, he supported the Imamate of ʿAbdallāh al-Afṭaḥ b. Jaʿfar, after Jaʿfar al-Ṣādiq's death, but then rallied around Mūsā al-Kāẓim because he found ʿAbdallāh too ignorant. On Zurāra, see J. Van Ess, *Theology and Society*, vol. 1, pp. 373–393; E. Kohlberg, 'Imam and Community in the Pre-*Ghayba* Period', in idem, *In Praise of the Few. Studies in Shiʿi Thought and History*, ed. A. Ehteshami (Leiden and Boston, 2020), pp. 187–212, esp. pp. 198–199, 201–203; Shahrastānī, *Livre des Religions et des Sectes*, vol. 1, p. 493, n. 100; pp. 537–538, and references provided there. On the supporters of ʿAbdallāh al-Afṭaḥ, the *faṭḥiyya* or *afṭaḥiyya*, see ibid., pp. 488–489 and related footnotes.

[5] Imam Muḥammad al-Bāqir.

[6] Ibn Bābawayh transmits a *ḥadīth* that begins approximately this way; see Ibn Bābawayh, *Kitāb al-Tawḥīd*, *bāb* 32, p. 232, no. 1.

[7] A transmitter of *ḥadīth* who apparently supported the Imamate of ʿAbdallah al-Afṭaḥ b. Jaʿfar. He is briefly mentioned in the section on the *faṭḥiyya* in al-Kashshī, *Rijāl*, no. 359, p. 465.

al-Ḥusayn used reflection and speculation [on this] (*istaʿmala al-fikr wa'l-naẓar fīhā*),[8] according to some who had informed him after Abū ʿAbdallāh (*ʿan baʿḍ man akhbarahu ʿan Abī ʿAbdallāh*) — peace be upon him and upon his noble and honourable family. He said: 'The first thing God created was the letters of the alphabet.'

[*Ḥadīth* on the notion of *ṣamad*][9]

3. God — may He be blessed and exalted — is One and Unique (*wāḥid aḥad*), Singular (*fard*), Absolute (*ṣamad*), First (*awwal*), Eternal (*ṣamadī*), and Everlasting (*daymūmī*). He is not held by any shadow (*ẓill*), but He is the One who holds <things>[10] by their shadows (*aẓilla*).[11] He knows the unknown (*al-majhūl*) and He is known [even] by the praise of every ignorant person (*jāhil*) as One and Unique (*wāḥid fard*). He does not contain anything created, nor is He perceived or tangible in His Creation. *'The eyes attain Him not, He is Subtle, Aware'* [Q. 6:103]. When He is on High, He determines; when He approaches, He is worshipped (*ʿalā fa-qaddara wa-danā fa-ʿubida*).[12] He is disobeyed and He forgives. He is obeyed and He rewards. <His earth does not encompass Him, and His heavens do not support Him.>[13] **[90]** He carries all things by His Power (*qudra*). <Everlasting, Eternal (*daymūmī azalī*),>[14] He never forgets, is never distracted,

---

[8] What is meant by this is unclear. This second paragraph seems corrupted.

[9] This *ḥadīth* is attested in Twelver Shiʿi sources; see al-Kulaynī, *Uṣūl al-Kāfī, k. al-tawḥīd, bāb al-nisba*, vol. 1, p. 91, no. 2; Ibn Bābawayh, *Kitāb al-Tawḥīd, bāb* 2, pp. 57–58, no. 15. I used these two other versions to correct and complete the *Kashf*'s version when needed.

[10] Mss. A, B: *al-samā'*, 'the sky'. Corrected to: *al-ashyā'*, after al-Kulaynī, *Uṣūl al-Kāfī*, vol. 1, p. 91; Ibn Bābawayh, *Kitāb al-Tawḥīd*, p. 58.

[11] This term is reminiscent of *ghulāt* speculations, as noted by M. Asatryan, 'Early Ismailis and other Muslims', p. 291, but it is also part of the Twelver Shiʿi cosmology; see above, p. 18, n. 43.

[12] Al-Kulaynī, *Uṣūl al-Kāfī*, vol. 1, p. 91; Ibn Bābawayh, *Kitāb al-Tawḥīd*, p. 58: *ʿalā fa-qaruba wa-danā fa-baʿuda*, 'When He is High, He is close, and when He approaches, He is distant.'

[13] Ms. A: *lā yuẓilluhu samā*; ms. B: *lā tuẓilluhu samā*. Corrected to: *lā taḥwīhi arḍuhu wa-lā taqulluhu samāwātuhu*, after al-Kulaynī, *Uṣūl al-Kāfī*, vol. 1, p. 91; Ibn Bābawayh, *Kitāb al-Tawḥīd*, p. 58.

[14] Mss. A, B: *wa-daymūmiyyatihi al-ūlā*. Corrected to: *daymūmī azalī*, after al-Kulaynī, *Uṣūl al-Kāfī*, vol. 1, p. 91; Ibn Bābawayh, *Kitāb al-Tawḥīd*, p. 58.

never errs, is never bored, never plays. He is eternal (*azalī*). There is no <interruption (*faṣl*)>[15] to His will, and His <decision (*faṣl*)>[16] is retribution. His Order is effective and executory (*wāqiʿ nāfidh*). He is *'Absolute, He has not begotten'* [Q. 112:2–3], <so that He would transmit inheritance>,[17] *'and has not been begotten'* [Q. 112:3], <so that He would have associates>,[18] *'and there is none equal to Him'* [Q. 112:4].

[Fragment of *ḥadīth*]

4. He was King before He brought forth Being, and [remained] King after His creation of Being. He has no definition (*ḥadd*) and no quality (*kayf*), *'and He is powerful over all things'* [Q. 5:120].

[A *ḥadīth* on language][19]

5. A certain companion of Abū ʿAbdallah narrated from al-Ḥasan that Abū ʿAbdallah said: 'God never created a name (*ism*) without giving it a meaning (*maʿnā*). He never gave it a meaning without giving it a form (*shabaḥ*). He never gave it a form without giving it a definition (*ḥadd*). He never gave it a definition without giving it a segmentation (*qutr*). He never gave it a segmentation without giving it separation (*faṣl*). He never gave it separation without giving it <a

[15] Mss. A, B: *faḍl*. Corrected after al-Kulaynī, *Uṣūl al-Kāfī*, vol. 1, p. 91; Ibn Bābawayh, *Kitāb al-Tawḥīd*, p. 58.

[16] Mss. A, B: *faḍl*. Corrected after al-Kulaynī, *Uṣūl al-Kāfī*, vol. 1, p. 91; Ibn Bābawayh, *Kitāb al-Tawḥīd*, p. 58. This is an allusion to the expression *yawm al-faṣl*, 'the Day of Judgment'.

[17] *Fa-yūrath*: Added after al-Kulaynī, *Uṣūl al-Kāfī*, vol. 1, p. 91; Ibn Bābawayh, *Kitāb al-Tawḥīd*, p. 58.

[18] *Fa-yushārak*: Added after al-Kulaynī, *Uṣūl al-Kāfī*, vol. 1, p. 91; Ibn Bābawayh, *Kitāb al-Tawḥīd*, p. 58.

[19] The last part of the treatise corresponds to chapter 59 of the *Kitāb al-Haft wa'l-aẓilla*. Based on the various editions of both the *Kitāb al-Kashf* and the *Kitāb al-Haft wa'l-aẓilla*, Mushegh Asatryan has proposed a critical edition of this *ḥadīth*; see M. Asatryan, 'Early Ismailis and other Muslims', pp. 296–298. However, my editorial choices differ from his a few times. Furthermore, since the focus is here on the *Kashf*, I have taken it as the basis of my translation, modifying or completing it based on the *Haft wa'l-aẓilla* only when necessary, that is, on the several occasions in which when the *Kashf* is illegible, inconsistent or lacks sentences. I have indicated in the footnotes all modifications to the text published by Strothmann.

connection (*waṣl*)>.[20] For <the separated (*al-mafṣūl*)>[21] can only be known through the connected (*al-mawṣūl*), [because] <when one talks to people with the separated (*bi'l-mafṣūl*), they do not comprehend him (*la-mā ʿaqalūh*)>[22] [but] when one talks to people with the connected (*bi'l-mawṣūl*), they comprehend him (*ʿaqalūh*).

6. <Mufaḍḍal said: 'O my master, how is that? And how do people know words and their meanings?' Al-Ṣādiq replied: 'The letters are divided into twenty-eight letters by which the connected [things] are comprehended (*ʿaqalū bihā al-mawṣūlāt*).'>[23] <'And how is that, o my master', Mufaḍḍal asked, 'may God make me your ransom!'>[24] He said: 'Do you not know that the Arabic language is made of twenty-eight letters, and four others? And the four others are contained in a single letter, and that is all!' 'How is that', I asked. He said: 'The letters were divided into twenty-eight letters, as a way of communication between creatures, and to make <them>[25] know what they have negated. <If we were to say to a man: '*alif*', we would not understand it at all. And if it were said to a man: '*lām*', he would not understand it at all. And if it were said to him: '*hā*'', we would not understand it at all.>[26] But if they are arranged, gathered, [91] united and attached [together], with knowledge, <and that it is said to him: 'Allāh', he knows that it is God (*Allāh*)>[27] [you are talking about]. Do you not see

[20] Mss. A, B: *faḍlan*. Corrected after Mufaḍḍal al-Juʿfī, *Kitāb al-Haft wa'l-aẓilla*, Ch. 59, p. 115.

[21] Mss. A, B: *mafḍūl*. Corrected after Mufaḍḍal al-Juʿfī, *Kitāb al-Haft wa'l-aẓilla*, Ch. 59, p. 115.

[22] Added after Mufaḍḍal al-Juʿfī, *Kitāb al-Haft wa'l-aẓilla*, Ch. 59, p. 115.

[23] Added after Mufaḍḍal al-Juʿfī, *Kitāb al-Haft wa'l-aẓilla*, Ch. 59, pp. 115–116, except for my correction of *ʿallaqū* into *ʿaqalū*.

[24] Mss. A, B: *qultu wa-kayfa dhalik*. Corrected to: *qāla al-Mufaḍḍal wa-kayf dhālik yā mawlāy jaʿalanī Allāh fidāk*, after Mufaḍḍal al-Juʿfī, *Kitāb al-Haft wa'l-aẓilla*, Ch. 59, p. 116.

[25] Added after Mufaḍḍal al-Juʿfī, *Kitāb al-Haft wa'l-aẓilla*, Ch. 59, p. 116.

[26] Mss. A, B: *fa-law qīla inna aḥadan allafa mā fihim bihā shay'*. Strothmann corrects *fihim* into *fuhima*. Corrected to: *fa-law qulnā li'l-rajul alif mā fahima minhā shay'an aw qīla li'l-rajul lām fa-mā fahima minhā shay'an aw qīla lahu hā' mā fahima minhā shay'an*, after Mufaḍḍal al-Juʿfī, *Kitāb al-Haft wa'l-aẓilla*, Ch. 59, p. 116.

[27] Mss. A, B: *qāla Allāh ʿalimū annahu lā ilāh illā huwa*. Corrected to: *fa-qīla lahu Allāh ʿalima annahu Allāh*, after Mufaḍḍal al-Juʿfī, *Kitāb al-Haft wa'l-aẓilla*, Ch. 59, p. 116, except for my correction of *ʿalīm* into *ʿalima*.

that the name (*ism*) is <different>[28] than its spelling (*hijā'*), <and that the separation (*al-tafsīl*) is different than the connected (*al-mawṣūl*)>?[29] Do you not know that speech is a copy of writing (*al-kalām nuskhat al-kitāb*), that writing is not possible without spelling, and that spelling is not possible without the letters — in Syriac or in any other [language]? <Do you not know that speech comes entirely from the twenty-eight letters of the alphabet?'

7. Mufaḍḍal said: 'O my master, is knowledge complete with this?' He said — from him comes salvation (*minhu al-salām*): 'Regarding Arabic, it is complete, but regarding other [languages], no.'>[30] I said: 'Why is that?' 'Because <the languages were divided (*tabalbalat*)>[31] at the time of Abraham — may God's blessings be upon him — into Hebrew, Syriac, Persian (*a'jamī*) and Arabic.'

8. <The pillars (*da'ā'im*) of speech are four.>[32] Whistling (*al-ṣafīr*), shouting (*al-zajr*), snapping (*al-naqr*) and cooing (*al-hatf*) developed speech. Whoever knows how to separate and connect them knows speech, and he knows <all the divided languages (*jamī' al-alsun al-mutabalbila*)>,[33] as well as the language of the birds (*manṭiq al-ṭayr*), of the cattle (*manṭiq al-bahā'im*), and of all quadrupeds. Do you not know that when you whistle to the birds, or snap to the cattle, <or coo to the pigeons>,[34] they flee? If you had made them understand something, they would not have fled. [In fact], you made them understand something that you did not understand yourself by shouting, cooing, snapping, whistling <barking, braying, or howling>[35] <. . .>[36]

---

[28] Mss. A, B: *'amma*. Corrected to: *ghayr*, after Mufaḍḍal al-Ju'fī, *Kitāb al-Haft wa'l-aẓilla*, Ch. 59, p. 116.

[29] Ms. A: *ghayr al-tafsīl*; ms. B: *ghayr al-tafḍīl*. Corrected to: *wa'l-tafṣīl ghayr al-mawṣūl*, after Mufaḍḍal al-Ju'fī, *Kitāb al-Haft wa'l-aẓilla*, Ch. 59, p. 116.

[30] Added after Mufaḍḍal al-Ju'fī, *Kitāb al-Haft wa'l-aẓilla*, Ch. 59, p. 116.

[31] Mss. A, B: *al-suryāniyya tuthbit*. Corrected to: *al-alsun tabalbalat*, after Mufaḍḍal al-Ju'fī, *Kitāb al-Haft wa'l-aẓilla*, Ch. 59, p. 116.

[32] Mss. A, B: *wa-kānat da'ā'im*. Corrected to: *wa-inna da'ā'im al-kalām arba'a*.

[33] Added after Mufaḍḍal al-Ju'fī, *Kitāb al-Haft wa'l-aẓilla*, Ch. 59, p. 116.

[34] Added after Mufaḍḍal al-Ju'fī, *Kitāb al-Haft wa'l-aẓilla*, Ch. 59, p. 116.

[35] Ms. A: blank followed by *al-hatf*; ms. B: *wa'l-masḥ qāla wa'l-hatf*; Ghālib, p. 92: *wa'l-nabḥ qāla wa'l-hatf*. Corrected to: *wa'l-nabḥ wa'l-nahīq wa'l-'awī*, after Mufaḍḍal al-Ju'fī, *Kitāb al-Haft wa'l-aẓilla*, Ch. 59, p. 116.

[36] Based on mss. A and B, which he slightly corrects, Strothmann proposes: *mimmā kharaja ḥattā tabalbalat alsun al-nās min al-thamāniya wa'l-'ishrīn ḥarfan*. I have deleted this sentence which repeats previous information and does not appear in the *Haft*.

9. Every [sound produced] by opening the mouth is shouting. [The sound produced] by tightening the mouth is the whistle. [The sound produced] by what you send back to the uvula is the snapping. <And [the sound] you make by opening the mouth and that comes out>[37] of the throat is the cooing.

10. Understand this — may God teach you goodness and make you good.**[92]**

[37] Mss. A, B: *wa-mā yuftaḥ bihi qāla fa-mā kharaja*. Corrected to: *wa-mā futiḥta bihi al-famm wa-yakhruj. . .*, Mufaḍḍal al-Juʿfī, *Kitāb al-Haft waʾl-aẓilla*, Ch. 59, p. 116.

Treatise IV Commentary

Like Treatise II, the very brief Treatise IV is a compilation of fragments of *ḥadīth*s gathered around a theme. It is less a treatise proper than a form of interlude intended to separate Treatises III and V. Yet, this interlude has several interesting features, some of which are reminiscent of Treatise II. While the latter was devoted to the themes of the Throne and the Footstool, and ended with an alphabetical cosmogony, Treatise IV pursues this alphabetical theme by quoting two *ḥadīth*s referring to the twenty-eight letters of the Arabic alphabet and their role. However, it also recalls the *tawḥīd* discussion of Treatise II, since it contains a sentence from the first *ḥadīth* quoted in Treatise II, as well as a full *ḥadīth* (found in Twelver Shiʿi sources) dedicated to the Qurʾanic notion of *ṣamad*, which was also dealt with in Treatise II. While the first part of Treatise IV is formed of an amalgamation of *ḥadīth*s related to *tawḥīd*, the second and longer part consists of a highly corrupted *ḥadīth* corresponding to the whole of Chapter 59 of the *Kitāb al-Haft waʾl-aẓilla*.

1. Several *ḥadīth* fragments

At first sight, the first part of the treatise appears as a single *ḥadīth* preceded by a detailed *isnād*, which is almost unique in the *Kitāb al-Kashf*.[38] In reality, a comparison of the text with Twelver Shiʿi sources reveals that the *matn* amalgamates three different *ḥadīth*s: the main one, relating to sūra 112 is almost complete, but it is preceded and followed by fragments of other *ḥadīth*s.

[38] With the exception of the minimalist *ḥadīth* by Muḥammad al-Bāqir reported by Jābir b. Yazīd al-Juʿfī in *Kashf* I, p. 8, § 14.

Furthermore, the chain of transmission, which apparently only concerns these three *ḥadīths*, is more problematic than it seems. Two of the transmitters' names are incomplete, which prevents their identification: they are Aḥmad b. Muḥammad and Abū al-Ḥasan. Likewise, I was unable to identify Ḥamal b. Ṣabbāḥ. The only intelligible part of the chain is the fact that it goes back to Muḥammad al-Bāqir, via Zurāra b. Aʿyan, a well-known transmitter of this Imam.

The *isnād* in the second part of this first fragment is no more satisfying: it is true that Muʿāwiya b. Ḥakīm, presented as an alternative source for the *ḥadīth* of letters, is indeed a known transmitter. This time, the chain of transmission goes back to Jaʿfar al-Ṣādiq, through one Muḥammad b. ʿAlī b. al-Ḥusayn. Is this Muḥammad al-Bāqir? Furthermore, it is unclear who has 'used reflection and speculation' on the *ḥadīth*, or what that expression may mean in this context.

The paragraph is clearly corrupted and incomplete. Yet, two names of transmitters provide some information as to the milieu in which the *ḥadīth* originated. Indeed, Zurāra b. Aʿyan and Muʿāwiya b. Ḥakīm both allegedly supported the Imamate of ʿAbdallāh al-Afṭaḥ after the death of Jaʿfar al-Ṣādiq. This could be an indication of the immediately post-Jaʿfar origin of the text, which would thus have been imported from this milieu to the proto-Ismaili milieu. Furthermore, when connecting this to the first Fatimid caliph's claim that his ancestor was ʿAbdallāh al-Afṭaḥ, one could formulate the hypothesis that there may have been some connections between the *faṭḥiyya*, i.e. the followers of ʿAbdallāh al-Afṭaḥ, the eldest living son of Jaʿfar al-Ṣādiq after the latter's demise, and the early Ismailis — although more evidence is required.

As for the *matn* of the *ḥadīth*, there is at least one attestation of a *ḥadīth* beginning with a similar sentence: it is reported by Ibn Bābawayh in his *Kitāb al-Tawḥīd.*[39] Yet the latter version is more restrictive: 'The first thing that God — praised and exalted be He — created to make known the writing to His creation (*li-yuʿrifa bihi al-kitāba li-khalqihi*) was the letters of the alphabet.' In the rest of the *ḥadīth*, each letter of the alphabet is related to a divine quality beginning with the corresponding letter. The perspective of this creation of

[39] Ibn Bābawayh, *Kitāb al-Tawḥīd, bāb* 32, pp. 232–233, no. 1.

letters is therefore not cosmological; letters are not created 'beings', as was the case in Treatise II, or as the version of Treatise IV suggests.

Furthermore, the *isnād* provided by Ibn Bābawayh goes back to the eighth imam, ʿAlī al-Riḍā, and he himself traces the *ḥadīth* back to ʿAlī b. Abī Ṭālib through his fathers. None of the transmitters named by Ibn Bābawayh corresponds to those found in Treatise IV — except possibly for Aḥmad b. Muḥammad al-Hamadānī, who could be the Aḥmad b. Muḥammad of Treatise IV.

The second *ḥadīth* of Treatise IV is more satisfying, since it is a complete *ḥadīth* on *tawḥīd*, unrelated to the previous one and attested in Ibn Bābawayh's *Kitāb al-Tawḥīd*, as well as in al-Kulaynī's *Uṣūl al-Kāfī*.[40] In both these versions, the *ḥadīth* is attributed to Jaʿfar al-Ṣādiq.

In al-Kulaynī's version, the *ḥadīth* is presented as a commentary on sūra 112 by the Imam: 'I asked Abū ʿAbdallāh about: *"Say that God is one"* [Q. 112:1].' The Imam answers with a number of sentences absent from both the *Kitāb al-Kashf* and the *Kitāb al-Tawḥīd*: 'In relation (*bi'l-nisba*) to His creation, God is one, absolute (*ṣamad*), etc.' In the *Kitāb al-Tawḥīd*, the text is introduced as follows: 'I asked Jaʿfar b. Muḥammad about *tawḥīd*.' Apart from slight variations in the chain of transmission and the introduction to the *ḥadīth*, there is almost no difference between the two Twelver versions. On the other hand, they differ from *Kitāb al-Kashf* in several respects, but these variations are mainly due to errors in the manuscript transmission of the latter. The Twelver sources therefore allow us to correct the text of the *Kashf*. This confirms that a large part of the difficulties met in the *Kashf* is due to scribal errors.

The *ḥadīth* deals with *tawḥīd*, the affirmation of God's transcendence and absolute independence vis-à-vis created beings. It is similar in spirit and style to the one which opened Treatise II. This is undoubtedly why the last fragment of the *ḥadīth* — in fact a quotation from the first *ḥadīth* of Treatise II — was attached to this elaboration on *ṣamad*.

There is therefore a play of resonances between Treatises II and IV, which both combine texts on *tawḥīd*, on the one hand, and

[40] Al-Kulaynī, *Uṣūl al-Kāfī, k. al-tawḥīd, bāb al-nisba*, vol. 1, p. 91, no. 2; Ibn Bābawayh, *Kitāb al-Tawḥīd, bāb* 2, pp. 57–58, no. 15.

considerations on the letters of the alphabet, on the other hand. The terms *ṣamad* as well as *ṣamadiyyāt* already appeared in Treatise II,[41] in a passage inserted between the two parts of the first *ḥadīth*. This play of resonances is probably intentional; in the architecture of the collection, Treatises II and IV have been used to separate the more important treatises. We should also note that in Treatises II and IV, a first part devoted to *tawḥīd* is followed by a second relating to another intellectual trend, pre-Fatimid Ismaili in the case of Treatise II, and *ghulāt* (or at least transmitted by the *ghulāt* tradition) in Treatise IV. In Treatise II, this second part was devoted to the alphabetical cosmogony, while in Treatise IV, it is devoted to language, two fairly close themes, although they are treated very differently.

2. A *ḥadīth* on language

As previously noted, the second part of Treatise IV corresponds to chapter 59 of the emblematic *ghulāt* work, the *Kitāb al-Haft wa'l-aẓilla*. Given the serious corruption of the text transmitted in the *Kashf*, the version found in the *Haft* is helpful in clarifying the argument; as it appears, the *Kashf* is missing entire sentences. Yet, while the *Haft* provides essential phrases highlighting the structure of the text, the *Kashf* also contains a few items that are absent from the *Haft*. As a result, both sources must be used to reconstruct an intelligible text. M. Asatryan has thus proposed a critical edition of this text, based on both the *Haft* and the *Kashf*.[42] Unfortunately, this endeavour, in my opinion, remains insufficient to reconstruct the text, which in its original version is probably lost. Indeed, even when combining the two sources, the result obtained, although much better than what each of these two sources transmits individually, is still highly problematic and fragmentary.

Among the challenges presented by this *ḥadīth* is the fact that in both the *Kashf* and the *Haft*, it stands in sharp contrast with the rest of their respective contents. Treatise IV is entirely free from any Ismaili features, but, as we have seen, the first part at least resonates with the

[41] *Kashf* II, p. 42, § 5.

[42] M. Asatryan, 'Early Ismailis and other Muslims', pp. 294–298.

tawḥīd speculations of Treatise II. The second part, however, bears no similarity with any of the other contents of the *Kashf*. M. Asatryan reaches the same conclusion regarding the relation of chapter 59 of the *Haft* to the rest of the book, thus noting that 'it seems to be inserted, as it has nothing to do with the rest of the text' and 'bears no stylistic or thematic similarity to the other parts of the book'.[43]

This raises two main questions related to the circulation of the text: 1) where did it originate, and what was its initial milieu of composition? 2) Through which channels, did it find its way into two books belonging to different traditions? In his brief study of the *ḥadīth*, Asatryan discusses these questions and proposes a series of hypotheses regarding the possibilities of mutual influence between Ismaili and Nuṣayrī circles, and the transmission of texts between the Syrian and Indian Ismaili communities.[44] However, because the text, to the best of our current knowledge, only appears in an Ismaili book and in a proto-Nuṣayrī one, Asatryan focuses his enquiry on the possibilities of textual transmission between these two traditions *after* they were well established. Yet, as Asatryan himself admits, there is 'not enough evidence to ascertain' that the text originated in a 'Ghulāt-Nuṣayrī' milieu, since he only identifies 'two elements reminiscent of Ghulāt-Nuṣayrī ideas', namely the use of the term *ẓill*, pl. *aẓilla*, in the first part of Treatise IV, and the use of the term *shabaḥ* in the part of Treatise IV that is common with the *Haft*.[45] As I have shown, however, the first part of Treatise IV is in fact a combination of *ḥadīth*s found in Twelver Shiʿi sources, and therefore, its mention of *aẓilla* cannot necessarily be understood as a 'Ghulāt-Nuṣayrī' feature. This leaves us with only one feature that can be identified as such: the mention of *shabaḥ*.

One could add the fact that the *ḥadīth* is presented as a dialogue between Jaʿfar al-Ṣādiq and his disciple Mufaḍḍal, an important figure for the *ghulāt*, but this only appears in the *Haft*, whereas the *Kashf* attributes the *ḥadīth* to Jaʿfar al-Ṣādiq without specifying who his interlocutor is. It may be hypothesized that the mention of Mufaḍḍal was added ad hoc by the compiler of the *Haft*, in order for the *ḥadīth*

---

[43] Ibid., pp. 286, 290.

[44] Ibid., pp. 290–294.

[45] Ibid., pp. 291–292.

to fit the usual framework of the other chapters of the work — which, for the major part, are dialogues between Jaʿfar and Mufaḍḍal.

At this point, one can question the very notion that the *ḥadīth* belongs to the *ghulāt* tradition, given the weakness of the evidence pointing in that direction. The only strong evidence would be its presence in the *Kitāb al-Haft wa'l-aẓilla*, but, as previously said, it seems to have been inserted there.

Another possibility would be to identify this text as a Shiʿi take on speculations on language from the time of the composition of the text. Just like in the second *ḥadīth* of Treatise II, we would be in presence of a Shiʿi endeavour to intervene in an Islamic debate over a specific theme; in Treatise II, the theme was *tawḥīd* and anthropomorphism, and the Shiʿi approach consisted of establishing a correlation between professing the correct doctrine in this regard, on the one hand, and the acknowledgement of the rightful Imam, on the other. Here, the general theme is the origin of language and the faculty of mastering all languages based on a certain knowledge of its elementary components, the letters of the alphabet. Evidently, such a faculty would be one of the sacred prerogatives of the Imam. The problem is that, if this is indeed the intention of the text, it is nowhere stated explicitly. As a result, the Shiʿi origin and aim of the *ḥadīth* remain hypothetical, and is only predicated on the sources in which the *ḥadīth* appears.

Let us examine the contents of the *ḥadīth* in more detail, in order to show how this interpretation can be reached. The problem one is immediately faced with is that the overall argument of the text is unclear, and that the parts that are clear seem quite trivial. The text also seems to be missing some key information or steps of the argument that would allow the reader to fully comprehend its intentions and goals. Although the version transmitted by the *Kashf* is clarified by the one found in the *Haft*, the text remains very elusive. It is possible that we are dealing with an extract from a longer text — but in this case, it is striking that the *Kashf* and the *Haft* transmit relatively similar versions with almost the same gaps (particularly between §§ 7 and 8).

In § 5, Jaʿfar al-Ṣādiq traces a certain number of principles back to the 'name' (*ism*), but the relationships between these principles and their very nature are not explained. In addition, the perspective is unclear: is it in ascending or descending order? In other words, is the 'name' the final result of a procession or, on the contrary, the first principle of a procession? Are we even dealing with a hierarchized enumeration? This passage could be interpreted as the enumeration of the principles that make the 'name' what it is: the essence of any name is to have a 'meaning', a 'form', a 'limit' or 'definition' (*ḥadd*), and a 'dimension'. But, again, the exact meaning assigned to these concepts is not specified.

The following lines, which include the last sentence of § 5 and most of § 6, are dedicated to the notions of *mafṣūl* and *mawṣūl*, that is, to the difference between the letters taken individually, 'separated' from each other, on the one hand, and the letters combined, 'connected', to form meaningful words. An example — half of which is missing in the *Kashf*, to the point that it is 'distorted beyond recognition' —[46] is provided to illustrate this: if the letters forming the word 'Allāh', namely *alif*, *lām*, *hā'*, were enumerated separately to someone, they would not be understood. But once connected to effectively form the word 'Allāh', then it is understood that what is meant is God.[47] The question remains, however, of the general conclusion one should draw from this fact which is altogether obvious, if not trivial.

The following sentence, although not entirely explicit, may provide an answer: 'Do you not know that speech is a copy of writing (*al-kalām nuskhat al-kitāb*), that writing is not possible without spelling, and that spelling is not possible without the letters?'[48] It seems that letters are conceived of as celestial archetypes — in accordance with the first *ḥadīth* quoted in Treatise IV where God creates the letters, and the alphabetic cosmogony of Treatise II. Contrary to what modern linguistics would have, letters are not just conventional and arbitrarily chosen signs. They are not a way to put in writing a pre-existing oral speech but are the source of all languages. Writing precedes speech, not the opposite.

The text then proceeds to a brief consideration of languages other than Arabic, apparently prompted by the sentence: 'Do you not know

---

[46] Ibid., p. 288. See ibid., pp. 287–288, for a discussion of the way the *Haft* dramatically improves our understanding of the example.

[47] The *Haft* and the *Kashf* provide very different readings in the conclusion of the example. The *Haft* inserts here a sentence on the notions of noun and adjective, as a commentary of the sentence: 'God is All-knowing'. I believe however this is out of place and does not sit well with the rest of the argument. See the translation of this passage in the *Haft*, in M. Asatryan, 'Early Ismailis and other Muslims', p. 288 and n. 49.

[48] *Kashf* IV, p. 92, § 6.

that speech comes entirely from the twenty-eight letters of the alphabet?' This applies to Arabic, the Imam says, but not to other languages. The disciple then asks why, and the Imam explains that, at the time of Abraham, the languages *tabalbalat*, which can be translated as 'were divided', or 'became confused'. Asatryan translates it as 'became intermixed'.[49] From this, one can infer that the multiplicity of languages proceeds from a unique source and that, before the time of Abraham, there was only one language. This is of course a reference to the incident of Babel, although in Genesis, this 'confusion' occurs after the Flood, and not at the time of Abraham. It is unclear how this fits in the previous speculations of the text; is the unique language before Abraham Arabic? Or is Arabic just one among several others? And what is the relation of the variety of languages to the archetypal letters?

The connection of paragraph 8 to what precedes is even looser. After mentioning the four languages (Hebrew, Syriac, Persian and Arabic), the discussion suddenly deals with four 'pillars' of language, namely 'whistling, shouting, snapping, cooing';[50] is there a relation between these *four* pillars and the *four* languages? And if not, what are we missing between these two stages of the argument?

The text goes on to explain that full knowledge of these 'pillars' allows for the mastery of all languages, both human and animal. This is the unique point of the *ḥadīth* that could be used in a Shiʿi perspective — that is, in an Imam-centred approach. The text, however, does not mention the concept of Imam at all. Yet, the idea that the Imam masters languages, including animal languages as Solomon did, is found in early Shiʿi sources, such as the *Baṣāʾir al-darajāt* for instance.[51]

---

[49] M. Asatryan, 'Early Ismailis and other Muslims', p. 289.

[50] More animal noises are mentioned at the end of § 8, in the version transmitted by the *Haft*. This is either a mistake, or the 'pillars' should be more than four.

[51] See al-Ṣaffār al-Qummī, *Baṣāʾir al-darajāt, juzʾ* 7, *bāb* 11: *fī al-aʾimma annahum yatakallamūn biʾl-alsun kullahā* ('On the fact that the Imams speak all languages'), pp. 587–600; *bāb* 12: *fīʾl-aʾimma annahum yaʿrifūn al-alsun kullahā* ('On the fact that the Imams know all languages'), pp. 600–604; *bāb* 14: *fī al-aʾimma annahum yaʿrifūn manṭiq al-ṭayr* ('On the fact that the Imams know the language of birds'), pp. 606–618; *bāb* 15: *fī al-aʾimma annahum yaʿrifūn manṭiq al-bahāʾim wa-yaʿrifūnahum wa-yujībūnahum idhā daʿūhum* ('On the fact that the Imams know the language of beasts and know them, and that they answer [the Imams] when they call them'), pp. 618–631.

Apart from this very subtle allusion to 'someone' who could master human and animal languages, the text is entirely free of Shiʿi features, and in fact, looks like an extract of a theoretical treatise on language that may be compared with linguistic speculations of grammarians or theologians. Again, the question arises as to, not only how, but *why* such a text would find its way in works that have such a strong Shiʿi identity. Apart from the allusion to the supernatural ability of mastering all languages, there is none.

To conclude, it appears that: 1) this *ḥadīth* almost certainly forms part of a larger text, a treatise on language, now lost; 2) while the *ḥadīth* in its extant form does not contain any indication of a Shiʿi origin, its presence in Shiʿi works may indicate that it was deemed to represent the Shiʿi take on linguistic debates, notably by theoretically establishing the possibility that 'someone' could effectively master all the languages — although this ability could also be attributed to certain sacred individuals who are not necessarily the Shiʿi Imams. Furthermore, the text displays a certain inclination to explain rationally, particularly in the passage on the meaningless separated letters or the one on the four 'pillars' as the origins of language. This may be the result of an attempt to support rationally 'non-rational' Shiʿi miraculous beliefs about the magical and supernatural abilities of the Imams, in this case, the ability to speak all languages, both human and non-human.

Conclusion

The *Kitāb al-Haft wa'l-aẓilla* is extremely valuable to our understanding of Treatise IV. Unfortunately, even so, the text remains very obscure, as its version in the *Haft*, although not as deteriorated as that of the *Kashf*, is nevertheless corrupt. In the absence of additional sources that would help to reconstruct the original text, it is difficult to interpret it further and to ascertain the hypotheses I have proposed, and many questions must remain unanswered for now.

Among these is the question of the historicity of the presence of Treatise IV in the *Kitāb al-Kashf*. I have already mentioned its structural and thematic similarity to Treatise II, as both texts dedicate a first part to *tawḥīd*, and a second part to matters related to the letters of the alphabet and/or language. These two treatises are connected in this regard, and also inasmuch as they both differ radically from the other treatises of the collection. Furthermore, both treatises are loosely connected to Ismaili doctrine — in fact, there is no trace of Ismailism whatsoever in Treatise IV. It seems quite clear that these treatises were inserted where they are in the collection as interludes, and that, in this respect, they manifest an editorial intent: the editor of the *Kashf* did not simply randomly gather the treatises, but carefully arranged them.

TREATISE V

At first sight, Treatise V appears to be an 'Epistle on pilgrimage' (*ḥajj*). The argument unfolds around several verses dedicated to this topic, as well as other elements related to it, such as the figure of Abraham as builder of the Kaʿba, the Kaʿba itself, the 'proclamation' (*adhān*) of pilgrimage which is identified with the *daʿwa* in favour of the Imam, and the essential theme of the 'Houses', places of manifestation of the Divine Order, a theme which appears briefly in the opening pages of Treatise III. The general aim of the treatise is to support the spiritual prestige of the Imam as the 'House of God', while extending it to the whole hierarchy of the *daʿwa*, the organization of which is hinted at in several important passages. The special emphasis on the notion of 'Proof' (*ḥujja*) seems to reflect the redefinition of the term in the beginning of Fatimid rule — as indicated by the explicit mention of the second Fatimid caliph, al-Qāʾim bi-Amr Allāh.[1]

The overall structure of the treatise is rather confusing as it is bears the marks of the technique of 'scattering the knowledge' (*tabdīd al-ʿilm*). Indeed, exegeses of verses are often interrupted by various digressions, only to be resumed a few paragraphs further. This particular method appears in previous passages of the *Kashf*,[2] but it is much more systematic in Treatise V, to the point that it determines its entire structure. In the following plan of the treatise, one is to pay particular attention to the distribution of the main Qurʾanic verses:

1) [**§§ 1–3**] Introduction: a response to a question on the meaning of Q. 5:97

---

[1] *Kashf* V, p. 103, § 25.

[2] See introduction, pp. 67–68.

2) Biological and spiritual fatherhood

   — [§§ **4–6**] Abraham and his father
   — [§§ **7–8**] Muḥammad b. Abī Bakr and his father
   — [§§ **9–10**] A gloss on metamorphosis

3) The Kaʿba, the Proof and his spiritual role

   — [§ **11**] Return to the topic of pilgrimage
   — [§§ **12–15**] The Kaʿba as Proof, the *ʿAyn* and the *Fāʾ*
   — [§ **16**] Muḥammad b. Aḥmad as Proof
   — [§§ **17–21**] The Speaking-Prophet and the Proof (*Fāʾ*): exegesis of Q. 3:97 (*'The first House. . .'*), mention of Q. 5:97
   — [§ **22**] The Proof and the 'new creation'

4) The Call to the 'Great Pilgrimage'

   — [§ **23**] The 'person' of the *ʿAyn*: exegesis of Q. 9:3
   — [§ **24**] Interruption: the 70 dignitaries
   — [§§ **25–26**] Return to exegesis of Q. 9:3

5) The Houses of God

   — [§§ **27–35**] Exegesis of Q. 24:36 and 26:193–197

6) The Call and Abraham's sacred station

   — [§§ **36–38**] Exegesis of Q. 22:27
   — [§ **39**] Interruption: Subtle essence and dense body
   — [§ **40**] A lettrist exegesis of Abraham's name
   — [§§ **41–42**] Return to exegesis of Q. 22:27
   — [§§ **43–44**] Interruption: digression on *mathal* and Veil
   — [§§ **45–46**] Return to exegesis of Q. 22:27

7) Exegesis of Q. 2:197

   — [§§ **47–53**] The meaning of pilgrimage and the Proof
   — [§ **54**] Exegesis of 'obscenity'
   — [§§ **55–57**] Exegesis of 'immorality'
   — [§ **58**] Exegesis of 'dispute'
   — [§ **59**] Conclusion of the exegesis of Q. 2:197

8) Pharaoh and Egypt: the false Mahdī

- [§§ **60–63**] Pharaoh's pride: exegesis of Q. 43:51–54
- [§§ **64–66**] The esoteric meaning of Egypt, mention of Joseph 'the Truthful'
- [§ **67**] The Pharaoh of this age

9) Speaking-Prophets and Imams

- [§§ **68–70**] Exegesis of Q. 3:7
- [§ **71**] *Ḥadīth*: Jaʿfar al-Ṣādiq on the seven ranks of the 'Order'
- [§ **72**] Return to the exegesis of Q. 3:7

10) [§ **73**] Return to the exegesis of Q. 2:197
11) [§§ **75–79**] House and Veil: return to the exegesis of Q. 3:96–97
12) Three sacred ranks: exegesis of Q. 4:69

- [§§ **80–86**] The 'Truthful ones': Joseph and Idrīs
- [§§ **87–92**] The 'Witnesses' as 'Masters of Laws', the Prophets and the 'intermediaries'
- [§§ **93–96**] Betrayal of the *daʿwa*
- [§§ **97–99**] The 'Virtuous ones' as Imams

13) [§§ **100–104**] Return to the exegesis of Q. 3:96–97
14) [§§ **105–107**] Conclusion: initiation of the members of the *daʿwa*

Treatise V Translation

In the name of God, the Merciful, the Compassionate

1. [Here are] questions we have elucidated, arranged and explained; they provide healing for souls, life for hearts, and proximity for the spirit. Through them, the people of remembrance (*ahl al-dhikr*) will remember, the people of intellect (*ahl al-ʿaql*) will gain benefit, and the people of good manners (*ahl al-adab*) will find rest in the knowledge of these — in accordance with what our master (*sayyidnā*) Muḥammad said: 'Adopt the good manners (*ādāb*) [taught] by God, for they are the best of manners.'

2. The most eloquent exhortation is the Book of God — He is Sublime and High— which '*no falsehood comes to, from before it nor from behind; a revelation from the Wise and Praiseworthy*' [Q. 41:42]. It came down from Him and returns to Him. And we place our trust in God, and to Him we surrender (*muslimūn*).[3] There is no power or strength except through God.

3. You have asked —[4] may God guide you and fully satisfy your hope — about the meaning of the words of God — He is Mighty and Sublime: '*God has appointed the Kaʿba, the Sacred House, a standard (qiyāman) for the people*' [Q. 5:97].

---

[3] This may also read *musallimūn*. On *musallim*, *taslīm*, and the *islām/taslīm*, *muslim/musallim* distinctions, see M.A. Amir-Moezzi, *Guide divin*, pp. 38–39, n. 64; p. 192, n. 387 (English trans.: *Divine Guide*, p. 149, n. 64, p. 196 n. 387); idem, *La Religion discrète*, pp. 202–203, n. 122 (English trans.: *Spirituality of Shii Islam*, p. 269, n. 122).

[4] W. Madelung, 'Das Imamat', p. 55, n. 71, reads *sa'altu*, 'I asked', and considered the following *ḥadīth* by al-Ḥakīm as the answer. However, it can be argued that *sa'alta*, 'you asked' is the correct reading, and that Treatise V as a whole is the answer. Further in the text, the author addresses an 'asker' (*sā'il*), which seems to confirm my reading; see *Kashf* V, p. 107, § 31.

[Abraham and his father: exegesis of Qur'an 19:42–44 and 46–47]

4. Al-Ḥakīm — peace be upon him — said**:** 'The Ka'ba is that from the knowledge of which people of dissension (*ahl al-khilāf*) have turned away (*kā'a*)[5]. They distanced themselves from its Friendship (*walāya*) and its acknowledgement, worshipping that which neither hears nor sees, nor suffices them one whit in place of God.'

5. Have you not **[93]** seen the words of the pure Creator when [Abraham] said: *'Father, why do you worship that which neither hears, nor sees, nor avails you anything? Father, there has come to me knowledge such as came not to you. Follow me and I will guide you to an even Way'* [Q. 19:42–43]. In the exoteric sense (*fi'l-ẓāhir*), he accuses him of worshipping stones, but in the esoteric sense (*fi'l-bāṭin*), these are the idols (*awthān*) that are worshipped in place of God— He is Sublime and High —, that is, the three accursed ones,[6] because they are the idols of this community who were followed in spite of God's decrees and the Messenger's order — may God's blessing and peace be upon him. Regarding God's words: *'Follow me and I will guide you to a even Way'*, he states that the 'even Way' refers to the Prince of the Believers — peace be upon him. Have you not seen God's words — He is Mighty and Sublime: *'You will know who the owners (aṣḥāb) of the even Way are'* [Q. 20:135]? It is a way wherein is no crookedness; no doubt on its rectitude.

6. Yet the accursed heretic (*mulḥid*) rejected it: *'Are you rejecting my gods, Abraham? If you cease not, I shall stone you. Depart from me a long while!'* [Q. 19:46]. The Intimate (*khalīl*) [of God] said to his father: *'Peace be upon you, I will ask forgiveness of my Lord for you, for He is ever gracious to me'* [Q. 19:47]. When he spoke intimately (*nājā*) with his Lord about this — may God's blessings be upon him — he told Him: 'I have met him and proposed to hear and obey You. I told him: "Do not worship an idol", but he rejected this, and I disavowed him (*anā barī' minhu*).' God — may He be exalted — also said this regarding the story of Abraham — may God bless him: *'Abraham prayed for his father only because of a promise he had made to him, but when it became clear to him that he was an enemy to God, he disavowed (tabarra'a) him'* [Q. 9:114].

---

[5] A pun on the word Ka'ba.

[6] Abū Bakr, 'Umar and 'Uthmān.

[Muḥammad b. Abī Bakr and his father: exegesis of Qur'an 19:44]

7. The equivalent (*mithāl*) of Abraham's story— may God bless him — in this community is the story of Muḥammad b. Abī Bakr— may God be pleased with him. Indeed, he was exhorting (*waʿaẓa*) his father and ordering him to follow ʿAlī, the Prince of the Believers — may God's [**94**] blessings be upon him —, telling him that ʿAlī is the Legatee, the Gate of Salvation, the Master of Truth, the Interpreter (*mutarjim*) of the Qur'an, and the Conveyer (*muballigh*) of the Exegesis.[7] But the Second started forbidding him from following his son Muḥammad, and, with all his iniquity, his pride, his tyranny (*ṭughyān*), his sorcery (*siḥr*) and his whispering (*wiswās*), he diverted him from following the Prince of the Believers — may God's blessings be upon him — and from acknowledging his sacred station. Muḥammad b. Abī Bakr told his father what Abraham said: *'O father, do not worship Satan (al-shayṭān), indeed Satan is disobedient to the Merciful'* [Q. 19:44].[8] Satan is ʿUmar. Muḥammad b. Abī Bakr [also] told his father not to follow Satan's words, because that would be tantamount to a rebellion against God and His Messenger; indeed, the Messenger of God had [clearly] indicated [ʿAlī], and he only did so on the Order of God.

8. When his father failed to obey him and obeyed his Satan instead, he disavowed him (*tabarra'a min-hu*) in favour of the Prince of the Believers — peace be upon him — and saved himself; and so God saved him from the Fire. The Prince of the Believers made the Truth of truths and the landmarks (*maʿālim*) of religion known to him. He claimed him entirely for himself (*istakhlaṣahu li-nafsihi*) and [Muḥammad] was [made] a Proof (*ḥujja*) among the Proofs of the Prince of the Believers, for the latter praised his desire, his certainty (*yaqīn*)[9] and his loyalty. When he discerned the path and knew the argument (*dalīl*), he saw that his father was in a station and position (*maḥall*) similar (*mithl*) to those of a dog or a swine.

---

[7] This is of course unlikely since Abū Bakr died when his son Muḥammad was two or three years old.

[8] On ʿUmar as *shayṭān*, and his influence on Abū Bakr, see *Kashf* I, p. 30, § 63, and pp. 109–110, n. 134.

[9] Ms. B reads *taqiyya*, 'his discretion'.

[A gloss on metamorphosis]

9. Only those who have left the people of Truth to join the people of falsehood[10] can be compared to these two [animals]. Indeed, humans are like the people of truth who know guidance (*rushd*), love it, and follow it, and [and who also] know error (*ghayy*),[11] hate it, and avoid it. They are graced with knowledge that allows them to distinguish truth from falsehood, and bad (*khabīth*) from good (*ṭayyib*). **[95]** When *'they are guided aright'*, God *'adds to their guidance, and gives them their protection (taqwā)'* [Q. 47:17]. But the people of falsehood are like dogs and swine which cannot distinguish between truth and falsehood, nor between bad and good. They are not guided aright, and do not follow guidance. Their food is vile, and their actions are worthless. Whoever turns away (*irtadda*) from truth to falsehood, tumbles and becomes a loser, because he turned on his heals (*irtadda ʿalā aʿqābihi*) and metaphorically (*fi'l-mathal*) left humanity to join the dogs and swine. This is the meaning of metamorphosis (*musūkhiyya*), as has also previously been explained.[12]

10. The torment that is meant by the state of metamorphosis (*maskh*) is this deprivation endured by this apostatizing (*murtadd*) loser. Whoever follows him is akin to him: they are deprived of the benefits of guidance (*hidāya*) and knowledge, of the pointers to guidance, of the blessings of victory, and of the reminder (*dhikhrā*) — as God has said — He is Sublime and High: *'A vision and a reminder, for every penitent worshipper'* [Q. 50:8]. The penitent (*munīb*) heart is the one which turns (*anāba*) to God by following the truth and its Master, who was appointed by the Messenger, by an order of God, to complete His Order (*amr*) and [deliver] the exegesis of His Book. That one is the Prince of the Believers, the Legatee (*waṣī*) of the Messenger of God — may God bless them both.

---

[10] Strothmann mistakenly reads: *ahl al-bāṭin*, instead of: *ahl al-bāṭil*, which appears in the mss.

[11] An allusion to Q. 2:256: *'Guidance is henceforth distinct from error.'*

[12] See *Kashf* I, pp. 4–5, §§ 6–7; III, p. 88, § 73; see also below, V, p. 135, § 72. On metamorphosis, see commentary of *Kashf* I, pp. 154–162.

[On pilgrimage (*ḥajj*)]

11. Let us return to the initial explanation (*tafsīr*) of pilgrimage. We ask God to accept our pilgrimage, to reward our effort, to make us reach the goal of our hope; may He give us a direction (*qibla*) through which we may turn to Him, and a life we may give to others through our hands, and may He make us a blessing (*baraka*)**[96]** wherever we may go. *'He is Hearing, Nigh'* [Q. 34:50].

[The Kaʿba, analogue realities and spiritual rebirth][13]

12. The Kaʿba is analogous to the Proof — peace be upon him. It corresponds to the Ark in the age of Noah — peace be upon him. Have you not seen God's words — He is Mighty and Sublime: *'We said: "Load in [the Ark] two of every kind'* [Q. 11:40]? [In this verse,] it is to [the Kaʿba or the Proof] that [Noah] is called (*hiya al-mandūb ilayhā*). In every era and every age, whoever embarks in it is safe and is saved; whoever knows it is victorious and rightly guided. [The Kaʿba] was Eve (*Ḥawwāʾ*) in the era of the first Adam[14] — peace be upon him — because she contained (*ḥawat*) all hidden and secret things, and the concealed sciences (*al-ʿulūm al-maṣūna*).[15] Knowledge of the truth (*ʿilm al-ḥaqīqa*) is only obtained from her. [The Kaʿba] is [also] analogous to Joshua (*Shuʿayb*) — peace be upon him — in the era of Moses — peace be upon him; all things ramified (*inshaʿabat*) from him,[16] and the knowledge of the Staff to which Moses resorted was from him.

---

[13] A short paraphrase of the following paragraphs can be found in H. Corbin, 'De la gnose antique à la gnose ismaélienne', pp. 198–199.

[14] See below *Kashf* V, p. 98, § 14, where the Prophet Muḥammad is named the 'sixth Adam'. Adam therefore appears as a designation of the Speaking-Prophets.

[15] Cf. Jaʿfar b. Manṣūr al-Yaman, *Sarāʾir wa-asrār al-nutaqāʾ*, p. 41: '[Adam] then looked at the place the light came from and made the Kaʿba out of it. He placed the black stone within it as a symbol of his Proof, that is Eve (*Ḥawwāʾ*), who contains (*ḥawā*) his knowledge and wisdom.'

[16] A pun based on the root *sh-ʿ-b*. The 'things' here are likely to be the knowledge of which Shuʿayb, as Proof of Moses, is the guardian and the source. This is reminiscent of the explanation for Ibn Nuṣayr's *kunya*, 'Abū Shuʿayb': 'The meanings of the *ism* and the *bāb* were split in him' (*tashaʿʿabat fihī maʿānī al-ism wa al-bāb*); see al-Khaṣībī, *Fiqh al-risāla al-rāstbāshiyya*, cited by Y. Friedman, *The Nuṣayrī-ʿAlawīs*, p. 15.

13. Through the Proof, you are connected to the sublime *ʿAyn* (*al-ʿayn al-ʿaẓīma*),[17] who is the Imam— peace be upon him. [The Proof][18] is the Greater Mary— may her peace be upon us –[19] who desired (*rāmat*)[20] all things and produced them, appeared through them and thus created them. The explanation for this is that she opened up the gates of knowledge after they had been closed; the attribute of faith and the faithful were perfected through her. She distinguished herself (*infaradat*) by guiding whoever followed her towards the Master of Truth, that is, Jesus — peace be upon him –, thus pointing toward him before anyone else. On God's order, she turned the people towards God's religion's new Law — may He be exalted; [Jesus was] the Speaker of His Order, and his sacred station was new from God. Such is the 'new creation' (*al-khalq al-jadīd*) in the esoteric sense.

14. [The Proof] is [also] the Greater Fāṭima **[97]** in the time of the sixth Adam, who is Muḥammad — may God bless him. [Fāṭima] is the sublime *Fāʾ* (*al-fāʾ al-ʿaẓīma*), and the veil that is established for the people who know him intimately and are familiar with his spirit

---

[17] The letter *ʿayn* is the first letter of ʿAlī's name. The use of this term reflects the Shiʿi speculations on the triad *mīm-ʿayn-sīn*, corresponding to Muḥammad, ʿAlī and Salmān. While the *mīm* briefly appears a few pages later, in *Kashf* V, p. 113, § 40, the *sīn* is totally absent from the *Kashf* — at least in this form, since Salmān is mentioned in *Kashf* I p. 17; III, pp. 71–73. The discussions on this triad were at the centre of the Shiʿi debates on spiritual authority between the two Occultations; see H. Corbin, *Alchimie comme art hiératique*, esp. pp. 159–173, 186–195; H. Halm, *Die islamische Gnosis*, index s.v. "Ain-Mīm-Sīn'; M. Brett, 'The Mīm, the ʿAyn and the making of Ismāʿīlism', *BSOAS*, 57/1 (1994), pp. 25–39; L. Capezzone, 'The Solitude of the Orphan', pp. 60–64, 69–70; R. Adem, 'Early Ismailism and the Gates of Religious Authority', pp. 37–38, 64.

[18] The text is ambiguous here, and one might understand that the Imam is the 'Greater Mary', but this is not the case: Mary is the *Fāʾ* here, rather than the *ʿAyn* who is the Imam.

[19] Mss. A, B: *ʿalaynā salāmuhu*, masculine instead of feminine. R. Strothmann proposes the hypothesis that the pronoun refers to the Imam and does not correct the text. Yet, it seems that the mss. are erroneous here, and I have amended it to the feminine. This kind of eulogy, unusual in Fatimid literature but more frequent in Ṭayyibī sources, appears again in *Kashf* V, p. 99, § 16.

[20] A pun based on the root *r-y-m*, from which the author seems to derive the name Miryam (Mary).

(*rūḥ*). Indeed, he into whom [the *Fā'*] breathes his spirit is renewed, refreshed and unchanged.

15. God's words confirm yours (*sic*): *'I will breathe into it, and it will be a bird by the permission of God'* [Q. 3:49]. This is in the story of Jesus— peace be upon him. Analogous to this in the community of Muḥammad — peace be upon him — is that the Proof of Muḥammad is the Master of exegesis (*ṣāḥib al-ta'wīl*), ʿAlī — peace be upon him— who breathes the spirit into bodies.[21] The esoteric meaning of this is that he projects the esoteric knowledge onto the exoteric knowledge, thus affirming the right religion and perfecting it, with the permission of God. Through this knowledge he gives life to those who are dead from ignorance. The spirit is indeed like knowledge, while the works are like the body; any body without spirit is dead, [just as] any work that is not accompanied by knowledge is a body without spirit. The ignorant is thus dead until the Master of Truth revives him through knowledge of the truth. God's words are about this: *'Dead, not alive, and they are not aware'* [Q. 16:21]. [God] is telling the people of the exoteric life (*ahl al-ḥayāt al-ẓāhira*) that they have died the death of ignorance, [but] are not aware that they are dead. On the contrary, they consider themselves alive by this exoteric life of theirs. As for the bird,[22] it is the one whose heart flies towards the knowledge of His Creator — He is Mighty and Sublime. The breath [that is breathed into it] is the divine hidden and veiled knowledge that reaches the believer.

[On Muḥammad ibn Aḥmad, pre-Fatimid Imam]

16. The Proof, in our era, is our master (*sayyid*) and our shaykh, and the master of every believer, man **[98]** and woman. We find an illustration of this in the time of Imam Muḥammad b. Aḥmad — may his peace be upon us — since he started by concealing his identity in order to preserve his secret from hypocrites (*li'l-taqiyya min al-munāfiqīn*). He presented himself as the Proof who guides towards the Imam, while, in fact, he was guiding towards himself. No one knew this, except a small number among the elite of his Summoners.

---

[21] See the *ḥadīth* on ʿAlī resurrecting the dead in *Kashf* I, pp. 37–39, § 80.

[22] The bird of clay in which Jesus breathes, from Q. 3:49 cited above. The birds are a symbol of the Summoners in several Ismaili texts; see *Kashf* VI, p. 171, § 30, and p. 83, n. 33; p. 442, n. 352.

[The Speaking-Prophet and the *Fā'*: exegesis of Q. 5:97 and 3:97]

17. God's words— He is Mighty and Sublime: *'A standard (qiyāman) for the people'* [Q. 5:97], refer to the Ka'ba which He made a standard for the people. It means that He made the Proof an Imam who applies the Law (*qā'im bi'l-sharī'a*) and indicates the Speaking-Prophet — may God's blessings be upon him. He said: *'The Sacred House'* (*al-bayt al-ḥarām*) [Q. 5:97], that is, the silent one,[23] for the Speaking-Prophet is a Silent Imam before becoming a Speaking Imam.

18. *'Whoever enters [the House] is safe'* [Q. 3:97], means that whoever connects with the Imam, Master of the Esoteric, will be safe from the Speaking-Prophet's sword and vengeance when he appears. Indeed, the Silent Imam is the House of houses and the culmination of all explanation. *'Whoever enters it is safe'*, and whoever is taken under his covenant and embraced by his pact is safe from dissension (*fitna*). He is the Prince of the Believers, as well as his Veil (*ḥijāb*) and his Proof —[24] peace be upon him. Whoever is delivered something from this knowledge [by the Imam] is favoured and safe; he is attached to the *'cable of God'*[25] [Q. 3:103] and to the cable of the Imams of His religion, and he has not been cut off from them. **[99]**

19. The Silent Imam is [thus called because he is] the Master of the esoteric. He does not speak an exoteric Law himself, but he is the guide towards the Law of the Speaking-Prophet who preceded him (*imām li-sharī'at al-nāṭiq qablahu*). He does not speak a [new] Law, and hence he is called 'silent': in order to distinguish him from the One who speaks the Law (*al-nāṭiq bi'l-sharī'a*), for silence is different from speaking.

20. Such is the meaning of the sublime *Fā'* which was mentioned before along with the mention of Fāṭima, daughter of the Messenger — may God bless them both. This is because the *Fā'* is the One who

---

[23] The connection between the root *ḥ-r-m* and silence may be due to the fact that whatever is *ḥarām* is a taboo about which silence must be kept. The Imām is *ḥarām* because he represents the secret doctrine, unlike the 'Speaking-Imām' whose teachings are public. See also *Kashf* VI, p. 166, § 22, for a mention of the *muḥarram* believer, who is not allowed to disclose the teachings he has received.

[24] *ḥijābuhu wa-ḥujjatuhu*: The text is difficult to follow here, but it is probable that the possessive pronoun refers to the Speaking-Prophet, the Silent Imām being his Veil and Proof.

[25] See *Kashf* I, p. 9, § 17; III, p. 56, § 9; V, p. 122, § 55.

manifests the Truth of God (*qā'im bi-ḥaqq Allāh)* after having been ordered to do so. And he is the Lord of the [conjunction] 'and so' (*fa*) in language. [The *Fā'*] says: 'God commands me (*ya'murunī*), *and so* I shall do' (*ya'murunī Allāh fa-af'al*), just as when He says: '*And so I breathe into it*' [Q. 3:49]. This is an indication through the meanings of language that no one is glorified in [the eyes of] God, nor obeyed and followed in the religion of God, except the one who was raised up by God and rose (*aqāmahu Allāh fa-qāma*), who was commanded [by God] and obeyed (*fa-aṭā'a*), and who was sent and summoned (*fa-da'ā*) to Him.

21. Such is the *Fā'*, and his characteristic (*āya*) is this reference of the one who is commanded to the one who commands. In this, there is evidence showing that, when it comes to the religion of God, it is not a matter of choice (*ikhtiyār*) and that the only order is that given by God. The one He chooses is to be obeyed with His permission, as God — He is Mighty and Sublime — said: '*We sent no Messenger save that he should be obeyed, by God's permission*' [Q. 4:64]. Indeed, no obedience is due save to the one who was sent by God to be obeyed and whom He has established (*aqāmahu*).

[The 'new creation' and the Proof]

22. Thus rose (*qāma*) Abū Dharr in our own era. He is the Proof — peace be upon him — who inseminated (*dhara'a*)[26] the world, created it in a new creation (*bara'ahum wa-khalaqahum al-khalq al-jadīd*) by the Summons of the esoteric **[100]** Truth (*bi-da'wat al-ḥaqq al-bāṭin*). Have you not seen God's words — He is Sublime and High: '*Shall He not know what He created? He is Subtle, Aware*' [Q. 67:14]? This means that He — He is Mighty and Sublime — knows who created His worshipper in a new creation by the Summons of Truth, by His permission. He said: '*Say: He is the one who seeded you (dhara'akhum) in the earth, and to Him you will be gathered*' [Q. 67:24]. By the 'earth', he means the Summons of Truth; it means <that He is also pleased (*arḍā ayḍan*)>[27] by the Proof, the Master of the Summons (*ṣāḥib*

[26] Same etymology in *Kashf* III, pp. 70–71, § 38.

[27] Both manuscripts seem to transmit a corrupted version here, but we gather that they echo a pun on *arḍ*, 'earth', et *arḍā*, 'more agreeable [to God]' — although these two words have different roots (respectively *a-r-ḍ* and *r-ḍ-y*). The two words are put in relation a few lines further: 'the earth pleased with God'.

al-daʿwa).[28] He thus says: 'He inseminated you with the Summons of the esoteric Truth under the authority of the Proof.' *'And to Him you will be gathered'*, that is, to God — He is Mighty and Sublime — on the Day of the Gathering (*yawm al-ḥashr*). To Him you will return with your Summons, complying with your religion and your faith. And the Proof, Proof of God — He is Sublime and High — is named 'the earth pleased with God' (*al-arḍ al-rāḍiya bi'llāh*), pleased with the actions of His creation.[29] The Proof is the one who inseminated the world and created them in a new creation, and with this creation of his is the creation of religion completed and accomplished.[30] He is also knowledgeable about them, 'subtle, aware' of their actions, and it is to him that they return concerning their religion; it is him that they interrogate [on religious matters]. In this is an explanation for who has a heart or listens carefully as a witness (*shahīd*).

[The Call to the Great Pilgrimage: exegesis of Q. 9:3]

23. You asked about the words of God— He is Mighty and Sublime: *'A Call (adhān), from God and his Messenger, unto mankind, on the day of the Great Pilgrimage: God is quit (barī'), and His Messenger, from the associators'* [Q. 9:3]. The answer is the following: the Call (*adhān*) is what indicates God — He is Mighty and Sublime — **[101]**, and he is a talking Speaker (*nāṭiq mutakallim*), a person (*shakhṣ*) who, on the day of the Great Pilgrimage, makes the knowledge of the goal clear to people, in every era and every age. This is the meaning of God's words— He is Mighty and Sublime: *'The Day when shall avail not. . .'*.[31] The 'Day' means the person (*shakhṣ*) in whom the Great Pilgrimage is manifested, and it has yet another meaning in the esoteric doctrine. Al-Ḥakīm — peace be upon him — said: 'The Day is the manifestation

[28] On this hermeneutical equivalence, see also *Kashf* III, p. 62, § 20; p. 85, § 76; V, p. 155, § 106.

[29] The text is unclear here and might be corrupted — which may explain the repetitions in this paragraph.

[30] The 'new creation' is the initiation to the esoteric knowledge, which complements and accomplishes the exoteric religious teachings.

[31] Either Q. 44:41: *'The Day a friend (mawlā) shall avail nothing a friend, and they shall not be helped'*, or Q. 52:46: *'The Day when their guile shall avail them not, and they shall not be helped'*. The former is quoted in *Kashf* I, p. 23, § 51.

of the Great Pilgrimage, the sublime *'Ayn*.' The *'Ayn* is the sublime end, the End of all ends. This is an indication about the Creator— He is Sublime and High — who created all things by His Order; He originated all things, and to His Order all things return, as He said — He is Mighty and Sublime: *'As He originated you so you will return'* [Q. 7:29]; *'We originated the first creation, so We shall make it'* [Q. 21:104]. It is He who originates, and He who returns — glorified and may He be exalted highly above what the slanderers and the heretics say.

[The Seventy Forms]

24. He manifests Himself to His Friends in seventy sacred forms (*haykal*).[32] This is the meaning of His words — He is Mighty and Sublime: *'What do they look for, but that God shall come to them in the shadows of the clouds with the angels? The matter (al-amr) is settled and to God all matters are returned'* [Q. 2:210]. This is about the manifestation, by His Order, of the Truth in His Houses[33] and His most glorious forms (*hayākil*). The Houses and the forms (*hayākil*) are the sources (*ma'ādin*) of God's Order and revelation (*waḥī*); they are the Messengers and the Imams through whom the blessing of God and His divine assistance (*ta'yīd*) descend (*tatanazzal*). He chooses them in every era and in every age in order to establish a Proof over His creation and for them to guide His worshippers towards Him, by His Order. As for the seventy sacred forms, the meaning of a form (*haykal*) is a person (*shakhṣ*), and the seventy are the best among the Imams, Proofs, Hands, Gates, and Summoners,[34] who accomplish God's Order (*al-qawwām bi-amr Allāh*), the Summoners of Truth through eras[**102**] and ages, alongside the Messenger of that age or the Imam of that age. He is the best of the forms (*hayākil*) of the one mentioned earlier,[35] because he is the greatest of His agents (*asbāb*), through whom His Order and prohibition are completed, and through whom the revelation (*tanzīl*) and inspiration (*waḥī*) are completed.

---

[32] This term also means 'temple', which is why it is mentioned alongside the 'Houses' hereafter. Cf. *Kashf* I, p. 7, § 13, where the term was rejected as belonging to the *ghulāt*.

[33] On the 'Houses', see *Kashf* III, pp. 52–53, §§ 1–2; V, pp. 104–109, §§ 27–34.

[34] See *Kashf* III, p. 87, § 71, where the same hierarchy also forms a group of seventy 'persons'. See also *Kashf* V, pp. 119–120, § 51; p. 128, § 65; VI, p. 177–178, § 41, where the same hierarchy appears but without the 'Hands'.

[35] This probably refers to the *'Ayn*.

[Return to exegesis of Q. 9:3]

25. The Call (*adhān*)[36] [from Q. 9:3] is an indication of the one who makes people know their term (*mīqāt)* and their direction (*qibla*); he is the glorified Imam in his era, and he is Muḥammad, our lord and master (*mawlānā wa-sayyidnā*), the Bearer of the sword (*al-qā'im bi'l-sayf*) — peace be upon him —, and the Speaker (*nāṭiq*), for his era and his age, of the exoteric Summons to the Truth; he is the Bearer of the sword (*al-qā'im bi'l-sayf*) of the Summons. This attribute corresponds to the Imam al-Qā'im bi-Amr Allāh Muḥammad Abū al-Qāsim —[37] may God's blessings be upon him.

26. The Great Pilgrimage [from Q. 9:3], today, is the Silent One (*al-ṣāmit*). This means he did not appear speaking God's Order (*yanṭiq bi-amr Allāh*), as if he were the seventh Speaking-prophet. [The latter's] age is the Seal of ages; he is the most sublime of [God's] agents (*asbāb*) and His mightiest, the sublime *ʿAyn*. The *ʿAyn* is mentioned here because it is the End of all ends. [The *ʿAyn*] refers to the Creator of glorious might — the attributes of creation do not reach Him, nor is He touched by any stain or temporal alteration, for He is the cause of time itself (*muzmin al-zamān*), and the meaning (*maʿnā*)[38] of every era and <the truth of every epoch (*dahr*)>.[39] Glory be to the cause of all epochs (*mudahhir al-duhūr*) who achieved the <esoteric>[40] sublimities of things, [yet] remains known <on this earth>,[41] and described (*mawṣūf*) in all His Houses; He is apparent in all His forms (*ashkāl*), [yet] alone in the perfection of His permanence (*baqā'*). <He is Unique to him who knows Him, and present to him who describes Him>.[42]

---

[36] The *adhān* — which is also the call to prayer in Islam — is a synonym of *daʿwa*.

[37] The second Fatimid caliph who reigned from 322/934 to 334/946.

[38] Notice the use of the term *maʿnā* in a sense close to the one it has in the Nuṣayri context. Even closer to this sense are its uses in *Kashf* V, p. 112, § 40; p. 137, § 77.

[39] Mss. A, B: *ḥaqīqa wa-dahr*. Corrected to: *ḥaqīqat kull dahr*, after Idrīs ʿImād al-Dīn, *Zahr al-maʿānī*, p. 217.

[40] Mss. A, B: *mawāṭin*. Corrected to: *bawāṭin*, after Idrīs ʿImād al-Dīn, *Zahr al-maʿānī*, p. 217.

[41] Mss. A, B: *fi'l-azal*. Corrected to: *fi'l-arḍ*, after Idrīs ʿImād al-Dīn, *Zahr al-maʿānī*, p. 217.

[42] Mss. A, B: *muwaḥḥadan ʿinda man waṣafahu*. Corrected to: *wāḥidan ʿinda man ʿarafahu mawjūdan ʿinda man waṣafahu*, after Idrīs ʿImād al-Dīn, *Zahr al-maʿānī*, p. 217.

Exalted and glorified may He be, there is no god except Him. Whoever knows the veil (*ḥijāb*) is clothed with splendour and perfection, and has reached the Goal of all hopes and the End of all <causes>.[43] **[103]**[44]

[The Houses of God and the Books of the Ancients:

exegesis of Q. 24:36 and 26:193–197]

27. God— He is Mighty and Sublime — disavows (*barī'*) anyone who associates another to Him, who takes a god alongside Him, or worships a person (*shakhṣ*) whom He has not established, or takes a House He has not erected, because He has made things clear, by showing His Laws and manifesting His Judgment. God — He is Sublime and High— said: *'In houses which God has allowed to be erected, and His Name to be commemorated therein in the mornings and in the evenings by men'* [Q. 24:36–37]. Whoever claims that God has Houses other than those who announced the Laws (*al-sharā'i'*), manifested the deposits (*wadā'i'*), appeared with miracles (*mu'jizāt*), and were praised for their attributes; whoever declares that He is subject to change and extinction, then this person belongs to those who have apostatized (*alḥada*) God's signs — He is Sublime and High —, who have summoned to laws other than His, and who have despaired of His mercy (*ablasa min raḥmatihi*).[45] The Houses are those who have been calling to the Laws (*al-mu'adhdhinūn bi'l-sharā'i'*) in every era and every age; they are those whom God — He is Sublime and High— has erected, and ordered to be followed: *'So follow their guidance'* [Q. 6:90].

---

[43] Ms A: *al-athīl*; ms. B: *al-aṣl*. Strothmann leaves a blank. Corrected to: *al-asbāb*, after Idrīs 'Imād al-Dīn, *Zahr al-ma'ānī*, p. 217.

[44] The aim of this paragraph is apparently to explain the *'ayn* as a twofold concept which has both a spiritual 'essence' (*ma'nā*) and a terrestrial manifestation (hence the reference to the fact that he is known 'on this earth' 'in all His forms'). The paragraph thus contrasts the inaccessibility of the essence of the *'ayn* with its appearances in the 'Houses', that is, the Prophets, Imams, and, to a certain extent, the higher ranks of the *da'wa*. Just before his quotation of this passage from the *Kashf*, Idrīs 'Imād al-Dīn discusses the appearances of a unique spiritual principle in various 'forms' (*ṣūra*) and 'shirts' (sing. *qamīṣ*): 'The shirts change, but I do not (*tatabaddal al-qumuṣ wa-lā atabaddal*). The Prophets and the Imams are the receptacles (*hayākil*) of the Light'; Idrīs 'Imād al-Dīn, *Zahr al-ma'ānī*, pp. 216–217.

[45] Same expression in *Kashf* V, p. 121, § 55.

He made models (*qudwa*) out of them and ordered their model to be followed and their guidance to be sought. The explanation for this is that these 'Houses' are the Speaking-Prophets who speak the revelation (*tanzīl*) and the Laws, and they are Adam, Noah, Abraham, Moses, Jesus, Muḥammad (who is Aḥmad) and Muḥammad al-Mahdī, the seventh Speaking Messenger — may God's blessings be upon them all. They are the Houses of God's revelation (*waḥī*) — may He be blessed and exalted — to each of them in his era, in accordance with God's decree and order, as He said to the Speaking-Prophet Muḥammad — may God bless him and his family: '*[A revelation] brought down by the Faithful Spirit upon your heart, that you may be one of the warners, in a clear,* **[104]** *Arabic tongue. Truly, it is in the scriptures of the ancients. Was it not a sign for them, that it is known to the learned of the Children of Israel?*' [Q. 26:193–197]. This means that His Book and His revelation (*waḥī*) descended on the heart of Muḥammad — may God bless him. Whatever is in the heart is contained (*ḥawā*) and veiled (*satara*) by the body, just as a house contains and conceals what is in it. Just as it is not possible to access the house except through its door (*bāb*), it is not possible to access the heart of the Messenger except through his tongue as he speaks and indicates with it, when it is listened to, his Legatee, as our Master (*sayyidnā*) Muḥammad said — may God bless him: 'I am the city of knowledge and ʿAlī is its gate. Whoever aims for the city must go through the gate.'[46] God has thus taken the houses as a metaphor (*ḍaraba al-buyūt mithālan*) for His Messenger and the Imams of His religion who accomplish His Order (*al-quwwām bi-amirihi*), because they are the dwelling (*mustaqarr*) of His revelation (*waḥī*), and the sources (*maʿādin*) of His order and prohibition. Similarly, the Messenger of God — may God bless him — has taken the city as a metaphor for himself, and its gate as a metaphor for his Legatee and Veil (*ḥijāb*) in whom he veiled (*satara*) the esoteric aspect of his knowledge — just as God veiled His revelation (*waḥī*) with His Veils (*ḥujub*), that is, His Messengers in whom His revelation (*waḥī*) dwells until He makes them speak it to His creation in order to either guide them or have proof against them.

---

[46] Famous *ḥadīth* widely spread in both Sunni and Shiʿi sources. It is quoted again in *Kashf* V, p. 129, § 66.

28. God — He is Mighty and Sublime— then said: *'That you may be one of the warners'* [Q. 26:194], that is, that he might be one of the many Messengers (*mursalīn*) [sent] *'in a clear, Arabic tongue'* [Q. 26:195]. Then He said: *'Truly, it is in the scriptures of the ancients'* [Q. 26:196]. This means that the religion of God, the succession (*tartīb*) of His Messenger and His Imams who accomplish (*al-mutimmīn*) His Order and are the agents (*asbāb*) of His tradition (*sunna*) and of the prescriptions of His religion — the knowledge of this is in the '*scriptures of the ancients*', even though their tongue was different from this *'clear, Arabic tongue'*. But God's Order is one in **[105]** every era and every age. He then said: *'Was it not a sign for them, that it is known to the learned of the Children of Israel?'* [Q. 26:197]. This refers to the fact that the Messenger — may God bless him — spoke the affair (*amr*) of God's religion in the Arabic tongue, and that the knowledge of this was with the learned of the Children of Israel, although neither did they know the Arabic tongue that the Muḥammad — may God bless him — spoke, nor did the Arabs know the language of the Children of Israel who knew that it was the knowledge of God's religion. And so this is a sign and an indication for the people of Muḥammad that the Order of God descended upon the prophets of the ancients, and that He made them speak it, before He brought it down upon Muḥammad and made him speak. And each of them spoke in the tongue of his people, as He said — may He be exalted: *'And We have sent no Messenger save with the tongue of his people, that he might make clear to them'* [Q. 14:4]. It is in this sense that the Houses are given as a metaphor (*mathal*) for the Messengers and Imams, and they are referred to by this name as the Houses of God's Order. His revelation (*waḥī*) descends from one House to another House, and it is only in *'Houses which God has allowed to be erected, and His Name to be commemorated therein in the mornings and in the evenings'* [Q. 24:36].

29. If someone were to say that for every one of them that is manifest (*ẓāhir*), there is an esoteric veil (*ḥijāb bāṭin*), we would approve. Indeed, none of them — peace be upon them — has said: 'I am a god in place of God — He is Sublime and High', but they would bring orders and prohibitions saying: 'Gabriel — peace be upon him — came to me', without taking for themselves a name they were not named with — [if they had done so] they would have apostatized (*alḥada*) God's signs. It is God — He is Sublime and High— who erected them and made them Houses for His wisdom; He chose them to [fill] His sacred stations and made them mediators (*wasā'iṭ*) between Him and His worshippers. It is through them that He ordered to obey Him and prohibited from rebelling against Him, in His words:[**106**] '*In houses which God has allowed to be erected, and His Name to be commemorated therein* [Q. 24:36]. It is God — He is Sublime and High — who ordered to erect them up and to glorify them in all their eras for the duration of their existence. These are the Houses who made clear the Laws, manifested the deposits (*wadā'iʿ*) and established the indications. They glorified the Creator God — He is Sublime and High — for them, they summoned them to Him and purified (*bari'at*) them from associating anything to God — He is Mighty and Sublime.

30. There are those among them who know God and became Houses, that is, He established them with His Order (*aqāmahum bi-amrihi*) and they became a dwelling (*mustaqarr*) for His revelation (*waḥī*). Given how they are described, one must submit to them (*taslīm*) and accept [what comes] from them. Have you not seen God's words— He is Mighty and Sublime: '*Indeed, God elected Adam and Noah and the family of Abraham and the family of ʿImrān above all beings, descendants one of another. God is Hearing, All-knowing*' [Q. 3:33–34]? How clear is this speech for who has received a gift (*qarīḥa*) and an assistance (*tawfīq*) from God — He is Mighty and Sublime.

31. O you who ask, examine under the light of truth, repel away the ignorance of those who swerved from the truth, and know what is being said; is it not a duty and an obligation for you to know the meaning of 'divine election' (*iṣṭifā'*)? It is a veil that the Creator — may He be exalted— has veiled Himself with and chosen as the repository (*qarār*) of His revelation, and the source of His order and prohibition. It is the Purity [**107**] of purity, the End of ends. It is a House of exalted power, and of glorious position (*manzila*) with God — He is Mighty and Sublime — because the Creator — may His names be exalted — requested that none should be elected except the one He approves, whose Meaning (*maʿnā*) has appeared, whose branches were completed, whose affairs (*umūr*) were elevated, and who established for himself indications of a knowledge He summons to. And this is clear among the people of acumen and discernment (*ahl al-naẓar wa'l-taḥṣīl*). No one should erect a House, and then urge or order [others] to follow it, compelling people to acknowledge it and ordering them to prostrate before it, saying: 'This is my House and my direction (*qibla*), prostrate before me through it', — [all this] in spite of what preceded [his claim] in terms of election [of the rightful Imam by God], of separation from [one who was not elected] (*al-infiṣāl ʿanhu*) and of attachment to [one who was] (*al-ittiṣāl bihi*). [This one] is attached to one who deserves the name of error after rightness, and repudiation [of truth] (*juḥūd*) after acknowledgment.[47]

32. <Whoever says such a thing about his Creator utters a detestable lie and provides an abominable description. If anyone were described in such a way, he would deserve to be called ignorant and erroneous. So how could the Creator [be described in such a way], the Originator (*mubdiʿ*), the Inventor of all things, who knows what they are before they are created and after they are created? His knowledge is of what comes first just as He knows what will come last - He is Mighty and High.>[48]

33. Sanctified be His Names who call to Him and by Him.[49] It is through them that one accesses and approaches Him. The explanation of his words on the Names is that they are the Speaking-Prophets and the Imams — peace be upon them — who guide and point toward Him. **[108]** Each *qāʾim* in his era is the name by which God is called in this era, as God has said: '*To God belong the most beautiful names, so call Him by them*' [Q. 7:180], that is: 'To God are the guided Imams and the Messengers He has chosen and who approached Him with their obedience, sought His approval and what belongs to Him within them (*mā ʿindahu bi-him*). They are His Gates and the means for His creatures to [access] Him.'

---

[47] The text is very allusive and probably corrupted, but it seems to refer to the emergence of a rightful man of God which was followed by a rival claim to spiritual leadership. The false imam referred to here lays his claim in spite of the designation of the rightful Imam by God, and the obligation to befriend him and to disavow any other.

[48] The meaning and relevance of this paragraph escape me. It is likely that the text is once more corrupted in this place.

[49] It is worth noting that 'sanctified' is in the feminine form (*taqaddasat*), in accordance with the rules of Arabic grammar for inanimate objects (the Names), while the verb 'to call' and the relative pronoun are in masculine plural, which indicates that they are considered as persons.

34. The first House that God — He is Mighty and High— erected, honoured and elected was Adam, whose laws and lineage were established for the worshippers of God on the exoteric level, and for the worship of God, on the esoteric level.[50] His proofs (*barāhīn*) manifested in a House, a mosque, a direction (*qibla*), a way (*ṣirāṭ*), a face (*wajh*) and a dignitary (*ḥadd*). God — He is Mighty and Sublime— has provided the explanation of all of these things, and He — He is Mighty and Sublime— guided His worshippers to them — the House and the mosque. He named them so that His worshippers would know that He will not accept their worship except through a unique face chosen to the exclusion of all others, a rank (*ḥadd*) chosen to the exclusion of all others, a place (*mawḍiʿ*) chosen to the exclusion of all others, a path chosen to the exclusion of all others. He compelled them to [resort to] a guide to guide them. He summons them to Him through a Messenger, and He makes it known to them that the one who guides them is only one that He has chosen to the exclusion of all others. He does not accept their worship except through him, nor does He accept that they choose for themselves by excluding God's choice of the one He has chosen and elected for them.

35. The religion of God — He is Mighty and Sublime— is continuous (*muttaṣil*) since Adam — may God bless him — at the hands of the Speaking-Prophets and the Imams — may God's blessings be upon them — until God accomplishes His religion and His Order by the seventh Speaking-Prophet, the Mahdī — may God's blessings be upon him. It is to him [i.e. the Mahdī] that the Summoners have summoned, and to his knowledge (*maʿrifa*) that the Messengers invited **[109]** — peace be upon them. By his Law all Laws are completed, and he is the Master of the Manifestation of the Order (*ṣāḥib iẓhār al-amr*) in its entirety. It is by his hands that [the Order] is sealed (*yakhtatim*), and by him that God — He is Mighty and Sublime — is worshipped. It is by his Call (*adhān*) that God invites the worshippers, meaning by the fact that he is a Proof of God and by his Summons to God, he is the Call (*adhān*) to [God] — because of God's words — He is Mighty and Sublime: *'A Call (adhān), from God and his Messenger, unto mankind, on the day of the Great Pilgrimage'* [Q. 9:3]. He calls it 'great' because

[50] The lineage and laws are established to the benefit of mankind, but their meaning and purpose is to worship God.

there is nothing greater than it, and nothing is similar or close to it. It is the greatest and most glorious of the Houses, the most sublime Veil and its terminus: it is the manifestation of God's supreme Veil.

[The Call: exegesis of Q. 22:27]

36. The Call (*adhān*) is the Master of the Summons, and he deserves (*yastaḥiqq*) Abraham's sacred station. Have you not heard the words of God— He is Mighty and Sublime: '*And proclaim (adhdhin) the pilgrimage unto mankind. They will come unto you on foot and upon every lean beast, they will come from every deep ravine*' [Q. 22:27]. The meaning of this is that there must always be a <Completer>[51] Imam who summons to and indicates the Imam and the Speaking-Prophet. Indeed, the Call (*adhān*) is like the Completer Imam, and the second call to prayer (*iqāma*)[52] is like the Speaking-Prophet. Thus, in the call to pilgrimage, pilgrimage is analogous to the Speaking-Prophet, while the call to prayer on the pilgrimage is like the Imam who calls to the Speaking-Prophet. His words: '*And proclaim (adhdhin) unto mankind* **[110]** *the pilgrimage. They will come unto you on foot*' [Q. 22:27], therefore mean: 'Establish an Imam amongst the people so that he summons to the Speaking-Prophet.'

37. Thus, it is in the station of Abraham[53] in the mosque of Mecca that the one who leads (*ya'ummu*)[54] the people in prayer, stands facing the house. Here, Abraham's sacred station is analogous to the Imam from whom the Summons emanates, due to his obedience and his allegiance to the Speaking-Prophet — peace be upon him. The meaning of this is therefore that the Call is the Master of the Summons and that he deserves (*yastaḥiqq*) Abraham's sacred station. How clear is this speech to someone who has a heart!

[51] Missing from ms. A; ms. B: *fa-tamma*. Strothmann suggests in a footnote to correct *fa-tamma* into *mutimm*. The following page confirms that this is the correct reading.

[52] The *adhān* is the call to prayer that precedes the supererogatory prayer. It is followed by the *iqāma* which precedes the obligatory prayer.

[53] An allusion to Q. 2:125: '*Take as your place of worship the maqām of Abraham.*' The majority of Muslim scholars consider that this Qur'anic expression designates the stone bearing this name in the sanctuary of Mecca; see M.J. Kister, 'Maḳām Ibrāhīm', *EI2*.

[54] Same root as the word 'Imām'.

38. Understand, O you who ask, and comprehend (*iʿqil*) the design of God — may He be exalted — in this speech, so you will know that God has balanced in all things their exoteric and esoteric [aspects]. People only seek the existent (*mawjūd*), not the non-existent (*maʿdūm*).[55] This is why He established a muezzin (*muʾadhdhin*) for them, to call (*yuʾadhdhin*) them to the knowledge (*maʿrifa*) of God — may He be exalted — and to show them His hidden secret (*maknūn sirrihi*). Whoever responds to this muezzin and to the Speaking-Prophet will find happiness. Therefore, the muezzin is necessary, because it is through his call (*adhān*) that the worshippers are invited, that the people can see, and it is to his Summons that they come from all lands, both near and far.

[Subtle essence and dense body]

39. This is a subtle and hidden esoteric meaning, for him who has a subtle essence (*jawhar laṭīf*) and does not have a dense body (*jism kathīf*) without a subtle essence. The subtle essence is the pure and piercing intellect (*ʿaql*). It is the sheer and unsoiled spirit (*rūḥ*), and it is the esoteric knowledge. All these things attest to each other and are images (*mathal*) of each other. If the spirit is removed from the composite (*murakkab*) dense body, the latter becomes part of those inert objects (*al-jamādāt*). It is impossible to imagine (*yataṣawwar*) anything without a spirit; one only reasons and hears through it. It is only **[111]** through subtle essence that subtle sensation (*al-maḥsūs al-laṭīf*) is possible. Inert and dense objects are all made of dust, stones, [dead] wood and similar things. The same goes for the exoteric without the esoteric, these things are similar to each other and are images of each other. All this indicates that the exoteric aspects (*ẓawāhir*) of God's religion and its esoteric aspects (*bawāṭin*) are [related] to knowledge and action (*ʿilm wa-ʿamal*). Action is indeed analogous to the body, and spirit is analogous to knowledge; both knowledge and action remain obligations as long as the spirit and the body coexist.

---

[55] This is a declaration of the necessity of a physically present Imam, and therefore an allusion to the absent Imam of the Twelver Shiʿa. Note the use of the term *mawjūd* to speak of a present Imam, which recalls al-Ṭabarānī's point that God is 'present' (*mawjūd*) in His creation through the presence of the Imam; see below, pp. 393–394. Another statement to the same effect can be found further, when the Veil is described as the only way to worship God; see *Kashf* V, p. 115, § 44.

[A lettrist exegesis of Abraham's name by al-Ḥakīm]

40. Al-Ḥakīm— peace be upon him — asked: 'Do you know why Abraham was called Abraham — may God's blessings be upon him?' His children answered: 'Teach us, o teacher of the good, benefactor of wisdom, life of our hearts, light of our sights, for we have no knowledge except what you teach us.' He said: 'Its meaning is derived from his name (*maʿnāhu mushtaqq min ismihi*): the first *alif* is the first Meaning (*maʿnā*) from the sublime Creator, and the name of the 'Veil' was fixed upon it. Then the sublime *bā'* was added, and it became the Gate (*bāb*) to the Creator— He is Mighty and Sublime. Then followed God's providence — He is Mighty and Sublime— which He dressed with the mantle of the sublime *rā'*, and he became benevolent (*ra'ūf*) and merciful (*raḥīm*), compassionate, endowed with insight, and a noble Messenger (*rasūl*). He was then linked to the pre-eternal Light and He established within him some divinity (*askana fīhi shay'an min al-lāhūtiyya*) — it is the split *hā'* (*al-hā' al-mashqūqa*).[56] The Proof then came from him; it fixed his meanings, perfected his being, opened (*shaqqat*) his hearing, and lifted all the veils (*kashafat jamīʿ al-ghashāwāt*) from his sight. He was then able to see, to view, to contemplate, and he became His intimate (*khalīl*) through his friendship and his position **[112]** with God — He is Mighty and Sublime. Then the *yā'* of high dignity and elevated degree (*ṭawīlat al-khaṭr jalīlat al-rutba*) was added, and it was bonded to the sublime *mīm*, by which [Abraham] reached the point where he became the Master of a Law, a direction (*qibla*), a face and a truth. Indeed, the *yā'* is universal bliss (*ḥaẓẓ kullī*) and a protection from his Nimrod and his Pharaoh. Through the *mīm*, his affair (*amr*) was completed, his power manifested, his name was known, his sacred person (*shakhṣ*) appeared; he reached a sublime degree (*rutba*) and an eminent position. This means that his pursuit and his desire of knowledge, as well as his holding fast on to the knowledge he had to reach a higher knowledge, allowed him to elevate himself. And God elevated him, degree by degree through the divine

[56] That is, the *hā'* in the form it takes at the beginning of a word — as opposed to its form in the middle or at the end of a word. Note the omission of the second *alif* in Abraham's name in Arabic, even though the 'first *alif*' is mentioned at the beginning of the paragraph.

assistance (*ta'yīd*) of God, His guidance, His blessing and His Inspiration (*ilhām*), until he became deserving of the sacred station of Speaking-Prophet and became connected to God's Order (*ittiṣāl amr Allāh ilayhi*), and His revelation and His book were sent down unto him. The Imams after him then became the completers (*mutimmīn*) of his Order, just as he and those who preceded him were the completers of the Order of another, namely Noah — may God bless him. God has said: '*Indeed, Abraham was from his partisans (shīʿa)*' [Q. 37:83], thus indicating that Abraham believed in Noah and was from his partisans, until God — He is Mighty and Sublime— established Abraham with his Law and made him a Speaking-Prophet to whom those who followed him would refer to (*yantahī ilayhi man baʿdahu*). When the time of Abraham's Speaking (*nuṭq*) came, he was ordered to call (*al-adhān*) upon the people, that is, to tell them to become close to him and to desert any other, to refuse to associate (*al-shirk*) anything with God, to adequately affirm God's unicity (*tawḥīd*), and to die as Muslims. So when he called them to the pilgrimage, they responded to him based on what they knew from before. **[113]** They acknowledged his Summons and recognized the rank (*al-ḥadd*) of all eras, that is, the seventh Speaking-Prophet, the Master of manifestation, the unveiling of the veil (*kashf al-mastūr*), the seal of all eras, ages and aeons (*duhūr*).[57] Whoever knows him, fulfils his pilgrimage and completes his Command — may God's blessings be upon him.

[Return to exegesis of Q. 22:27]

41. '*They will come unto you on foot (rijālan)*'[58] [Q. 22:27]: by *rijāl*, he means the Summoners to God (*al-duʿāt ilā Allāh*), because God favoured them, in that they sexually penetrate and are not penetrated (*yankaḥūn wa-lā yunkaḥūn*), which in the esoteric [sense] means that they summon and are not summoned.[59] Their names were lauded;

---

[57] The seventh Speaking-Prophet appears in all the previous *nuṭaqā'* and is their common principle.

[58] The following interpretation is based on the understanding that *rijāl* is here a plural of *rajul*, 'man'. Hence, the quotation of Q. 4:34. According to the author, the Qur'anic text here reads: 'Men will come to you' — a reading that is grammatically incorrect. Further, the term is interpreted in its usual sense; see *Kashf* V, p. 115, § 45.

[59] See *Kashf* I, pp. 26–27, §§ 57–59; III, p. 78–79, § 60; V, p. 123, § 57; VI, p. 166, § 23, and commentary of *Kashf* I, pp. 128–134.

God — He is Mighty and Sublime - said: *'Men (al-rijāl) are given preeminence over women because God has preferred one of them over the another, and because of what they spend of their property'* [Q. 4:34].[60] They are the people of response (*ahl al-ijāba*) in every era and every age. It is through them that the people reach the pilgrimage, under their authority that their rituals (*manāsik*) are completed, and through them that the hidden things become known.

42. *'[They will come] upon every lean beast (ḍāmir), they will come from every deep ravine'* [Q. 22:37]: this is because the best and the fastest horse is the lean one (*al-ḍāmr*). Have you not seen how the kings of our era do? When they want to race, they slim down (*ḍammarū*) the horse to reinforce its limbs by many walks, and to become more resistant by the length and rapidity of the runs.

[Digression on *mathal* and *ḥijāb*]

43. This is an image (*mathal*) given by al-Ḥakīm— peace be upon him— to awaken the people of intellect (*ʿaql*), of knowledge (*maʿrifa*) and sagacity (*fiṭna*). Indeed, God — He is Mighty and Sublime— said: *'God strikes images (yaḍribu al-amthāl) for men in order that they may reflect'* [Q. 14:25] or[**114**] take heed and say: *'Our Lord! You have not created this in vain'* [Q. 3:191]. *'Yet, most men refuse all but unbelief'* [Q. 17:89],[61] and rejection of truth, and *'behaving arrogantly in the land and plotting evil; but evil plotting encompasses only those who do it'* [Q. 35:43]. God — He is Mighty and Sublime— is the striker of images (*ḍārib al-amthāl*) for men; to Him belongs *'the most elevated Image (al-mathal al-aʿlā)'* [Q. 16:60]. By this, he only means the sublime thing and the lofty power that the people of truth say. They thus say that God is the Lord of the universes inasmuch as He is close in His elevation, and elevated in His proximity; He is the Governor (*al-sāsī*) [of all things, and yet] He is close to the hearts of those who know Him (*ʿārifīhi*). We return to Him with humility and submission.

[60] See Jaʿfar b. Manṣūr al-Yaman, *Ta'wīl al-zakāt*, pp. 153–154, where this verse is used in support of the idea that 'masculine leads over feminine' (*al-dhakar yufḍī ilā al-unthā*), and that 'every conveyer [of knowledge] (*mufīd*) is in the position of the masculine (*ḥadd al-dhukūr*), and every beneficiary [of knowledge] (*mustafīd*) in the position of the feminine (*ḥadd al-ināth*)'; on this 'gendered' symbolic of initiation, see commentary of *Kashf* I, pp. 128–134.

[61] Or Q. 25:50.

44. He said — peace be upon him: 'His most elevated Image is something that nothing surpasses; nothing is similar to it and nothing can reach it. He grants us connection to His most elevated Image, which is His Greater Veil (*ḥijāb*), His most sublime House, His sacred form (*haykal*) from where His wisdom manifested. He does not cut us off from his proximity; He is the master of this and has power over it. The Veil of God is added to Him because He is the one who established him and made His power clear through him, manifesting it in [the Veil]. Nothing is more elevated than him, and without him, God — He is Mighty and Sublime — would not be worshipped. [The Veil] is the most sublime of God's Proofs for His creation — peace be upon him.

[Return to exegesis of Q. 22:27]

45. God's words— He is Mighty and Sublime: '*Proclaim the pilgrimage unto mankind. They will come unto you on foot* (*rijālan*)' [Q. 22:27] are a demonstration of this: this is about those who walk to the pilgrimage on foot, rather than riding. His words: '. . .*upon every lean beast*' refer to those who ride to the pilgrimage on a camel or any other four-legged animal whose bodies have become lean. This is similar to God's words[**115**] — He is Mighty and Sublime: '*And if you are afraid, then on foot (rijālan) or riding*' [Q. 2:239]. 'Lean beasts' (*al-ḍawāmir*) become by dint of walking and fatigue. The one who goes on pilgrimage on foot is like the believer who has responded to the Summons and entered the covenant with the Imam, but whose degree has not been elevated to the dignities (*ḥudūd*) of a Summoner or of more advanced believers (*al-bālighīn min al-mu'minīn*). '*Upon every lean beast*' [Q. 22:37] refers to those who are mounted. They are like the Summoners and the advanced believers who rose to eminent ranks (*ḥudūd*). They are called 'lean beasts' because of the ranks that they have reached. The lean beast (*al-ḍāmir*) is the one that became lean due to walking and to fatigue, until it quits the rank (*ḥadd*) of leanness that it has gained, by stopping calmly and abandoning the walk. It then returns to its original constitution (*aṣl bunyatihi*), to the creation in which it was first created, and becomes stronger by reason of the walk and fatigue that it suffered. On the esoteric level, this refers to one who has struggled (*ijtahada*) in his pursuit of and search for [knowledge], and who did not stop due to the exoteric aspect of what he thus perceived — [the exoteric aspect] does not suffice in place of the esoteric aspect. Through his pursuit and search, he reached the origin of what was created for him and to which he was invited, namely the knowledge upon which he acts, and the ranks (*ḥudūd*) to which his own degrees (*darajāt*) are attached. This means that the believer must not stop at the exoteric aspect of knowledge without seeking the knowledge (*maʿrifa*) of its esoteric aspect. Nor [must he stop] at the first rank (*ḥadd*) that he reaches. [He must not stop] until[**116**] he strives (*yajtahid*) in his search to elevate his degree, for he will not reach the esoteric aspect unless he pursues and strives for it through his actions and by seeking it. Similarly, in the exoteric realm, the pilgrim will only reach the goal of his pilgrimage by enduring the fatigue of his walk to the point of slimming down his mount (*rāḥila*). And the mount of the believer, in the esoteric sense, is his intention (*niyya*), his conviction (*iʿtiqād*) and his insight (*baṣīra*). If he reaches by his intention what he has struggled for (*al-majhūd*), he will know what he had been seeking from his religion, and God will facilitate it for him.

46. '*They will come from every deep* ravine': on the exoteric level (*fī'l-ẓawāhir*), this means that the mounts (*al-rawāḥil*) will come from every distant country. On the esoteric level (*fī'l-bāṭin*), it means the dignities (*ḥudūd*) to which the believer rises all come from the exalted sacred station of the Imam — peace be upon him — because he is the one who arranges the ranks and dignities of religion (*yurattib marātib al-dīn wa-ḥudūdahu*). The dignities (*ḥudūd*) ramify from his sacred station upon his order and choice, with the assistance (*tawfīq*) of God.

[On pilgrimage and the Proof: exegesis of Q. 2:197]

47. The meaning of God's words — He is Mighty and Sublime: '*The pilgrimage is in months well-known: whoever undertakes the duty of pilgrimage, let there be no obscenity (rafath), no immorality (fusūq) and no dispute (jidāl) on the pilgrimage. Whatever you do of good, God knows it. Take provision; but the best provision is piety (taqwā), so be pious to Me, men possessed of minds!*' [Q. 2:197]. The pilgrimage is of two types: exoteric and esoteric. The exoteric pilgrimage is what is commonly known as setting out toward Mecca and performing both the obligatory and supererogatory rituals of pilgrimage that must be performed there. As for the esoteric pilgrimage, it has two aspects. [**117**] The first is the migration (*hijra*) from one's homeland to that of the Messenger or the Imam in his era, knowing the one to whom you are migrating, and [knowing] the truthfulness of his grace and sacred station — this, so that your pilgrimage is accepted, your heart is grateful, your effort is virtuous, and that your doubt may be lifted. The second esoteric aspect is the knowledge of the Imam — may God's blessings be upon him — in every era and every age, who speaks the wisdom, who manifests in the glory of the Summons. [He is] the Master of Laws, their Seal and their Interpreter. He deserves every bountiful name and attribute and meaning. He is our lord (*mawlānā*) and the lord of every believing man and woman— may God's blessings be upon them.[62]

48. The 'months well-known' months are the Proofs in each of their eras— peace be upon them. They are the twelve months. They have all the Names and Meanings (*asmā' wa-maʿānī*) they wish in their eras and ages, because whatever they wish, God wishes it, since they only wish what God wishes. As for us, we are informed of His wish — He is Mighty and Sublime — through theirs, and [we are informed] of what He hates through what they hate. They are the Messengers and the Prophets who summon to God — He is Mighty and Sublime— [they are] the organizers (*muṣliḥ*) of the world, which they bring out from the darkness into the light[63] and guide, on the Order of their Lord,**[118]** to a *'straight Way (ṣirāṭ mustaqīm)'* [Q. 1:6].

49. *'Straight Way'*, in the esoteric [teaching] is how the Imam — peace be upon him — is named and designated. He is the Imam whose affairs have been established (*istaqāmat umūrahu*) and whose branches[64] rise. *'Perfect is the word of your Lord in truthfulness (ṣidq)'* from God *'and justice. None can change (lā mubaddil) his words; He is Hearing, the All-Knowing'* [Q. 6:115]. Thus, the Imam guides to the Imam after him; without his guidance, no sacred station of an Imam would have been be valid after another Imam,[65] and no believer would

[62] For another (partial) translation of this paragraph, see M.M. Bar-Asher, 'Outlines of Early Ismāʿīlī-Fātimid Qur'an Exegesis', p. 286.

[63] In reference to Q. 2:257.

[64] The 'branches' (*furūʿ*) might be the Imam's Proofs, or his representatives in general; see the passage on the 'three-branched shade' (*shuʿab*) in *Kashf* III, pp. 69–70, §§ 35–39.

[65] This refers to *naṣṣ*, the explicit designation of his successor by an Imam. This can be read as a justification for a particular succession, maybe in relation to al-Qā'im bi-Amr Allāh's access to the throne.

have received guidance after the first guide. It is in this sense that the Imams guide on a *'straight Way'*; it means that each one of them guides [people] to an Imam he appoints (*yuqīm*); his sacred station and his order (*amr*) are then established (*yastaqīm maqāmuhu wa-amruhu*). Such is the path God [provides] to his worshippers in His religion and tradition (*sunna*).

50. In addition, the words of God are the *'months well-known'* in their era and age. They are the twelve zodiac signs; they are the twelve chiefs (*naqīb*). As for the singular Word (*al-kalima al-mufrada*), it is the Supreme Proof (*al-ḥujja al-kubrā*) who is next to [hold] the sacred station of the Imamate, after the Imam of his era — peace be upon him. He is the one designated as the sublime *Fā'*, as has been explained before.

51. As for the Proof, the rivers flow from him and the Book invites to him. He is the Master of Laws (*sharā'i'*) and the Universal Gatherer (*al-jāmi' al-kāmil*). All the words are his veils that he establishes for people and who summon to his Order (*yad'ūn bi-amrihi*). The explanation of this is that the rivers are the esoteric sciences (*'ulūm al-bāṭin*) that flow under the authority of the Proof; the Book invites to him, which means that the Imam has designated [him][66] and invited the people to obey him and listen to the esoteric knowledge **[119]** from him. He is the Master of Laws, that is, in the esoteric sense, the Master of the ranks (*marātib*) of religion; it is he who arranges the Gates and the Summoners, and he is the gatherer of all the ranks (*al-jāmi' li-l-ḥudūd*). All [ranks] beneath him refer to him. He is the dignity (*ḥadd*) that indicates the rank of the Imam above him. One cannot access the rank of the Imam unless it is through that of the Proof. He is 'universal' because he is the highest among the ranks (*marātib*) of the Proofs; there is no dignity (*ḥudūd*) of the Proofs that is not below him, and he is elevated above all. There is no dignity (*ḥadd*) above his, because he is the Gate of the Imam, and so there is no rank (*martaba*) above his except for that of the Imam — peace be upon him.

[66] Because 'Book' is code for 'Imam'; see *Kashf* VI, pp. 167–169, §§ 25–26; pp. 171–173, §§ 31–35; pp. 175–177, § 39, and commentary of *Kashf* VI, pp. 458–463.

52. This is the meaning of the 'months well-known': whoever completes his pilgrimage during these months fully achieves it, because [the month] makes the pilgrimage known to him and [the pilgrim] completes it by him and by his order.[67] [The Proof] is the Supreme Father of the believer, the Precious of sublime dignity (*al-nafīs al-ʿaẓīm al-khaṭr*)[68] and of glorious might, the river Kawthar,[69] the elevated essence (*jawhar*), the noble vault (*al-samk al-karīm*),[70] the sweet water purified from all murk, preserved from all stain. He made pilgrimage a duty (*faraḍa al-ḥajj*), knowing the meaning of this duty of pilgrimage that was imposed on the worshippers. He established it for them, indicated it to them, ordered them to follow, listen and obey it. All these are the attributes of the Proof in every age, the attributes of the one who fixates the true religion where there is no ambiguity nor perplexity, no exaggeration[71] nor shortcoming (*lā ghuluww wa-lā taqṣīr*). It is from him that knowledge is drawn, and wisdom is poured; he is the one who makes reference to the good deed by following the Imam, of whom pilgrimage is a symbol (*ishāra*). **[120]**

53. It is an obligation that every believer knows his father, the one who breathed in him something spiritual (*nafakha fīhi shay'an min al-rūḥāniyya*). 'Spiritual' means esoteric knowledge and the exegesis of the revelation (*waḥī*) *'brought down by the Faithful Spirit'* [Q. 26:193] upon Muḥammad's heart, the Master of the revelation— may God bless him. Every believer must glorify that father, because he is related

---

[67] The esoteric pilgrim takes the 'months well-known', i.e, the Proofs, as guides to the Imam.

[68] See *Kashf* V, p. 113, § 40, for another expression with *khaṭr*.

[69] In reference to the eponymous sūra (Q. 108). Usually translated by 'abundance', the term has been interpreted as the name of one of the rivers in Paradise. In the Shiʿi context, this river is sometimes associated with ʿAlī: Mullā Ṣadrā (d.1640) thus names him the 'Cupbearer of Kawthar'; see M.A. Amir-Moezzi, *Spirituality of Shiʿi Islam*, p. 311. The Ismaili *dāʿī* al-Mu'ayyad considers it a symbol of ʿAlī; see al-Mu'ayyad fī l-Dīn, *Al-Majālis al-mu'ayyadiyya*, cited in D. De Smet, 'La prédication chiite ismaélienne', p. 149. In a *ḥadīth* reported by Ibn Bābawayh and al-Mufīd, the river Kawthar is dedicated to Muḥammad, while the source of Salsabīl is devoted to ʿAlī; cited by M.A. Amir-Moezzi, *La Religion discrète*, p. 142 (English trans.: *Spirituality of Shiʿi Islam*, p. 179).

[70] An allusion to Q. 79:28: *'He lifted up the [heavenly] vault (samk) and levelled it.'*

[71] Ms. A: *ghuluww*; ms. B: *ʿulūm*; Strothmann: *ghalaq*; Ghālib (p. 112): *ghuluww*.

to him, he is known through him, he is returned to him and summoned to him. Have you not seen His words — He is Mighty and Sublime: *'Summon them to their fathers (idʿūhum li-ābāʾihim);*[72] *that is more equitable in the sight of God'* [Q. 33:5].

[Obscenity: exegesis of Q. 2:197 continued]

54. The believer must not approach *'obscenity, immorality and dispute'* [Q. 2:197]. Obscenity, in the esoteric sense, is a blameworthy person (*shakhṣ*) cursed in every era and every age. It also has another meaning; al-Ḥakīm — peace be upon him — said: 'Obscenity is to disclose (*idhāʿa*) the secret of the family of Muḥammad — peace be upon him.' 'Obscene' is the one who disclosed [the secret] to someone who does not deserve it — may God make him taste the coldness of iron. You thus must remain silent (*kitmān*) until the deposit (*wadīʿa*) [you have been entrusted with] is claimed from you. We are its masters, and there is no doubt that we will ask it from you one day.

[Immorality: exegesis of Q. 2:197 continued]

55. 'Immorality' is fornication, and it is not allowed for a believer to indulge in immorality. Whoever does so becomes an Iblīs who despairs (*ablasa*) of [God's] Mercy[73] and is expelled from the gate of the wall (*sūr*) whose *'interior (bāṭin) is Mercy and whose exterior (ẓāhir) is punishment'* [Q. 57:13]. The punishment is deprivation of the benefits of the knowledge of religion **[121]** suffered by the people of exotericism (*ahl al-ẓāhir*), for they have relinquished the Truth and *'entered the Houses from behind (ẓuhūrihā)'* [Q. 2:189]; they have climbed up on the enmity towards God's Friends (*awliyāʾ*)— may God's blessings be upon them. They are condemned to be restrained by ties and chains and covered with them — we seek protection from God against these. Among the believers too, there might be one covered with ties for a sin he has committed,[74] because he has fallen short (*muqaṣṣir*) and

[72] The Qurʾanic text means adopted children should be named after their biological fathers, which is quite the opposite of the present interpretation, which states that initiatory children should be called *to* (rather than *after*) their initiatory fathers.

[73] Same etymology in al-ʿAyyāshī, *Tafsīr*, vol. 3, pp. 148–149 (interpretation of Q. 38:75); Mufaḍḍal al-Juʿfī, *Kitāb al-Haft waʾl-aẓilla*, Ch. 17, p. 49.

[74] Lit.: 'for something that stayed with him' (*li-shayʾ baqiya ʿalayhi*).

whoever [falls short] must [suffer] ties and chains. The believer must be pure, clean and graceful, and he must avoid fornication and not go near it, or his soul will perish. This means that the wall is the Book of God — He is Mighty and Sublime— while its gate is each Imam in his era. '*The interior is Mercy*' [Q. 57:13]: this is the esoteric knowledge that the Imam reveals (*yaftaḥ*), with God's permission, to the one who gained his Mercy through loyalty (*ikhlāṣ*) and sincerity of intention (*ṣidq al-niyya*); [the Imam] then opens his Mercy for [the believer] to strengthen his certainty and to purify (*yukhliṣ*) his spirit. '*The exterior is punishment*' [Q. 57:13]: whoever deserts the exoteric duties, punishment will reach him, and the esoteric knowledge will not serve him. And whoever sticks to the exoteric without the esoteric, punishment will [also] reach him because he has not connected what God has ordered to connect to the continuous cable and the 'firm handhold',[75] that is, [to connect] knowledge and deeds, spirit and body, to follow the Legatee after the Messenger and the knowledge of exegesis (*ta'wīl*) after the revelation (*tanzīl*). The truth of this esoteric knowledge is suitable for those who seek it, because whoever obeys the Messenger on the exoteric [aspects] but disobeys him on the esoteric [aspects] — by which [the Messenger] designated his Legatee — '*his work will be annihilated and he will be among the losers in the Hereafter*' [Q. 5:6]. Indeed, the Messenger is the Imam of his era, and when he leaves this world, it is necessary **[122]** that there is an Imam whom God has made it an obligation to obey, as He made it an obligation to obey the Messenger. God's words — He is Mighty and Sublime: '*Obey God, obey the Messenger and the holders of authority (ūlū al-amr) from amongst you*' [Q. 4:59][76] are an indication of this. There is no era at all where worshipping is possible without the Imam of that era. After the Messenger, the Imamate is not suitable except for the one appointed as

---

[75] Similar expression in *Kashf* I, p. 9, § 17; III, p. 56, § 9; V, p. 99, §18.

[76] In the Shiʿi context, this verse has been frequently used to legitimize the authority of the Imam. Of course, this verse and its Shiʿi interpretation holds a special significance in Fatimid Ismailism; see e.g. al-Qāḍī al-Nuʿmān, *Daʿāʾim al-islām*, vol. 1, pp. 20–21, 23–24 (English trans.: *The Pillars of Islam*, vol. 1, pp. 27–29, 31–33); al-Manṣūr bi'llāh, *Tathbīt al-imāma*, in S. Makarem, *The Shiʿi Imamate, A Fatimid interpretation* (London and New York, 2013), pp. 28, 45, 62–63 (Arabic: pp. 17, 36–37, 57); Ibrāhīm b. al-Ḥusayn al-Ḥāmidī, *Kanz al-walad*, pp. 28–29, 289.

an Imam by the Messenger — may God bless him — in the same way that God appointed the Messenger as a Messenger, and not as an Imam. Therefore, this connection and this hierarchy (*al-ittiṣāl wa'l-tartīb*) are not suitable without the truthful indications (*shawāhid*) from the esoteric knowledge.

56. It is about this that He said— He is Mighty and Sublime: '*The interior is Mercy*', because Mercy is in the esoteric knowledge. '*Its exterior is punishment*': to this corresponds the explanation given previously, that is, that whoever abandons the exoteric aspects of the Laws (*asqaṭa ẓāhir al-sharāʾiʿ*), or whoever holds on to the exoteric and abandons the esoteric (*tamassaka bi'l-ẓāhir wa-asqaṭa al-bāṭin*), must suffer punishment. This punishment of 'the exterior' suits both situations.

57. Fornication in the esoteric sense is falling short (*taqṣīr*);[77] it is the lifting of the veil (*kashf al-satr*)[78] for someone or summoning (*daʿwa*) without permission.[79] It is not allowed for you to do this. It also has another meaning; al-Ḥakīm— peace be upon him— said: 'The immorality of the believer is the slander of a believer like himself. Whoever slanders his believing brother indulges in immorality and eats the dead.'[80] Then he recited the verse: '*Would one of you like to eat the flesh of his dead brother? You would abhor it*' [Q. 49:12]. We seek protection from God against eating the flesh of the believer. The dead, here, is the one who is absent from the place[**123**] where he is defamed.

[Dispute: exegesis of Q. 2:197 continued]

58. Whoever knows the pilgrimage is not allowed to be obscene, to indulge in immorality or to dispute. You know what 'dispute' means: it

---

[77] Mss A, B: *muqaṣṣir*.

[78] This might be a scribal error for: *kashf al-sirr*, 'unveiling the secret'.

[79] See *Kashf* I, pp. 26–27, §§ 57–59; III, p. 78–79, § 60; V, p. 114, § 41; VI, p. 166, § 23, and commentary of *Kashf* I, pp. 128–134.

[80] It is worth noting that the accusation of eating 'dead things' (*mayta*) is a common one in various heresiographies; on this, see M. Asatryan, 'Early Muslims and Other Muslims', pp. 281–282; idem, 'Of Wine, Sex, and Other Abominations', pp. 4–5. Yet, in the Ismaili context, the prohibition on eating carrion is symbolically understood as a prohibition on following or initiating people of the *ẓāhir*; see above, p. 127, n. 191. The present passage could refer to either of these contexts — or both.

is what the believers do when they gather from various [Ismaili] communities (*daʿwāt*) and one of them says: 'My father is better than your father, and my community (*daʿwa*) is better than your community' — that is, the father in knowledge — and another replies: 'It is my father who is better than your father, and my community that is better than your community', in spite of the fact that the fathers — peace be upon them — all summon to God— He is Mighty and Sublime. Therefore, it is not permissible to anyone to discredit someone to whom the Imam has given a position (*rattabahu*) with the blessing of God — He is Mighty and Sublime — and whom he did not establish to dispute nor to indulge in immorality. God — He is Mighty and Sublime— said: '*And dispute not with the People of the Book save in the fairer manner*' [Q. 29:46]. You and those like you are among the People of the Book because you know the clear Book that has no crookedness; he is the Imam — may God's blessings be upon him — and his people are those who know him in his era. So, it is not permissible for you to dispute with the People of the Book, because you might be disputing with someone among them who is more knowledgeable than you. Save if you dispute with them '*in the fairer manner*' <when some benefit (*fā'ida*) is asked from you>.[81] Be very cautious not to unveil something that you know, [in case] <he is smaller than you, for he would then deny (*yakfur*)>[82] [the doctrine]. Do not be anything other than a humble asker, be cautious not to call a lie anything **[124]** from the [sacred] knowledge, and desire it always.

[Conclusion of the exegesis of '*obscenity, immorality and dispute*' from Q. 2:197]

59. We have thus explained obscenity, immorality and dispute. These are also blamed in the esoteric order— may God curse them — and

---

[81] Ms. A: *tuṭlab minka al-fā'ida*; ms. B: *taṭlub minhu al-fā'ida*. Strothmann leaves a blank space, while Ghālib, p. 115, reads the following, which I translated: *ʿindamā tuṭlab minka al-fā'ida*. The 'benefit' in question is most likely that of 'esoteric' teaching, whether it concerns the doctrine or practical information on the *daʿwa*.

[82] Ms. A: *fa-yakūn aẓfar minka fa-yakfur*; ms. B: *fa-yakūn aṣghar minka fa-yakfur fa-kawn anna mālahu* (?). I translate the version of ms. A, which gives the same text as Ghālib, p. 115, and corrected *aẓfar* into *aṣghar*. Strothmann stops at *minka*. The text is obviously corrupted here.

they are <Abū Bakr, ʿUmar and ʿUthmān>,[83] because they discredited the Proof — peace be upon him. They kept <his right>[84] from him on the exoteric [level], and <took away Fadak from him>[85] and from his wife Fāṭima, the daughter of the Messenger of God — may God bless her and them all. The Proof [here] is the Proof of the Messenger of God, ʿAlī b. Abī Ṭālib. [Abū Bakr] claimed his sacred station; he took his wife's inheritance on the exoteric [level], while, on the esoteric level, he was obscene (*rafatha*) by disobeying him, by denying (*kufr*) his sacred station, by following the order of ʿUmar,[86] the Satan <of his age >,[87] who disobeys (*al-fāsiq*)[88] the order of his Lord.[89]

[Pharaoh's pride: exegesis of Q. 43:51–54]

60. Have you not seen the words of God— He is Mighty and Sublime: *'Indeed, Iblīs was from the jinns and he disobeyed (fasaqa) the Order of his Lord'* [Q. 18:50]? <He belonged to a rank from among the ranks (*ḥadd min ḥudūd*) of Abū Ṭālib>.[90] He was among those who heard God's wisdom and had reached a high position (*rutba*); they are the jinns. They are called 'jinn' because they have buried (*ajannū*) the knowledge, and attributed [it] to themselves in the sense of the words of God — He is Mighty and Sublime: *'Do I not possess the kingdom of Egypt (miṣr), and these rivers flowing beneath me? What, do you not see?*

---

[83] Ms. B leaves a blank.

[84] Ms. B leaves a blank

[85] Ms. A: *akhadhahum minhu*; ms. B: *akhadhahum minhu*. The name 'Fadak' does not appear in either manuscript, but both editors thus correct the manuscripts: *akhadhū Fadak minhu*. What is more surprising is the fact that, for an unknown reason, 'Fadak' was added by both editors in the secret alphabet, although it does not appear in the manuscripts (which suggests that Ghālib is here plagiarizing Strothmann's edition).

[86] Ms. B: No secret alphabet.

[87] Ms. B: blank.

[88] The term from Q. 2:197 translated here as 'immorality' is *fusūq*, of the same root as *fāsiq* and *fasaqa*. 'Obscenity, immorality and dispute' must have been identified respectively with Abū Bakr, ʿUmar and ʿUthmān in the original version of this exegesis. Unfortunately, the last part on 'dispute' and ʿUthmān is missing.

[89] For another English translation of this paragraph, see M.M. Bar-Asher, 'Outlines of Early Ismāʿīlī-Fātimid Qurʾan Exegesis', pp. 288–289. The author presents it to illustrate the use of secret alphabet in Ismaili exegetical tradition. On the secret alphabet, see introduction, pp. 35–38.

[90] Ms. B: blank.

[Q. 43:51]. He means by this: 'I am among those who know the Imam— may God's blessings be upon him — who is the destination (*maṣīr*) of the entire world, and the City of all cities (*miṣr al-amṣār*).' What is meant **[125]** by this is the Mahdi, the seventh Speaking-Prophet. This means is that this Satan who has just been mentioned said to himself and to those who were seduced by his whispering: 'Have I not acknowledged the seventh Speaking-Prophet? I have knowledge that exempts me.' As God said — may He be exalted: '*And these rivers flowing beneath me*' [which means]: 'This suffices me and I have no need to obey anyone after the Messenger.' This means that his knowledge exempts him from obeying the Legatee ʿAlī b. Abī Ṭālib after the Messenger — may God's blessings be upon them both.

61. His words after this: '*Or am I better than this man, who is despicable and scarcely makes things clear?*' [Q. 43:52], mean: 'Am I not better that this Legatee?' — peace be upon him. He said that he is 'despicable', which means that his words are deficient and that he did not let you hear anything from his knowledge. He then said: '*He scarcely makes things clear*', which means that he does not even explain to you a small amount of his exegesis (*ta'wīl*). By this, he means that the Legatee does not unveil the exegesis and does not manifest it, except for the deserving, after taking the covenant and the pact (*al-ʿahd wa'l-mīthāq*), in accordance with God's tradition (*sunna*) [regarding] the esoteric of His religion. The iniquitous who had diverted the people from the Legatee thus said: 'Do you not see that he does not explain anything and does not make clear anything? He has no knowledge but what you already know.' He whispered this '*in the breasts of men*' [Q. 114:5], diverted them and led them astray from the truth and its Master, the Prince of the Believers. Yet, they did not harm him nor God, '*it is only themselves they destroy*' [Q. 6:26].

62. Among his words, which according to God he said, are also the following: '*If only bracelets of gold had been cast on him, or if angels had come with him conjoined*' [Q. 43:53]. Gold is like Messengers and Imams, **[126]** and silver is like Legatees and Proofs. And so this iniquitous [man] said: 'If only a revelation (*tanzīl*) had been sent down to [ʿAlī], like it was sent down to Muḥammad, the Messenger of God — may God bless him — and if [ʿAlī] had spoken in a manifest way like [Muḥammad] did (*yanṭuq kamā naṭaqa bi-ẓāhir amrihi*), and did not conceal his knowledge.' Then he said: '*Or if angels had come with* *him conjoined'*, that is: 'If Gabriel and Michael had come to him as they came to Muḥammad — may God bless him.' 'Conjoined' means that these two angels, as well as others, would be conjoined to his prophethood and the descent of revelation (*waḥī*) upon him, just as they were conjoined to Muḥammad. They are conjoined to him and to Muḥammad so that what was due to Muḥammad is also due to him.

63. God — He is Mighty and Sublime — said: *'And he persuaded his people to make light [of Moses], and they obeyed him: truly they were a dissolute (fāsiqīn) people'* [Q. 43:54]. This means that they strayed from the obedience [due] to the Messenger [by refusing to acknowledge] his Legatee, after they had manifested their obedience to the Messenger in everything he ordered them. In the Qur'an, these verses are about the story of Moses and Pharaoh, but the same thing happened in the community of Muḥammad: they rejected God's Order with regard to the Imam after the Messenger — that is, ʿAlī, his Legatee — may God bless them both. This one[91] is, for the community of Muḥammad, similar to what Pharaoh was in Moses' era for his people. Indeed, Muḥammad — may God bless him — said: 'Embark in the tradition (*sunna*) of the Children of Israel to the footstep (*ḥadhwa al-naʿl bi'l-naʿl wa'l-qudhdha bi'l-qudhdha*), such that if one of them entered a lizard hole, one of you would follow him.'[92] **[127]**

[The esoteric meaning of Egypt]

64. Among God's mentions of Egypt— He is Mighty and Sublime— there is this discourse He tells that Moses said: *'Get you down to Egypt (miṣr), you shall have there what you demanded'* [Q. 2:61]. This means that the Speaking-Prophet tells his people: 'Enter the obedience of the Imam— may God's blessings be upon him — '*you shall have there what you demanded*': the benefits of knowledge, the advantages of God's Mercy and His reward. These were the words of Moses to his people, and so was the word of Muḥammad to his — may God bless him. They both ordered that the Imam after them be obeyed.

---

[91] *Hādhā*: this refers to the abovementioned 'Satan'.

[92] A similar *ḥadīth* appears in Sunni sources; see e.g. Bukhārī, *Ṣaḥīḥ*, *kitāb al-manāqib*, *bāb* 50, no. 3456, vol. 2, p. 492; ibid., *kitāb al-iʿtiṣām bi'l-sunna*, *bāb* 14, no. 7320, vol. 4, p. 368; Ibn Ḥanbal, *Musnad*, vol. 4, p. 125. On this *ḥadīth* and its use in the Fatimid context, see commentary *of Kashf* I, pp. 144–147.

65. [The Imam] is this Egypt that Joseph the Truthful (*al-ṣiddīq*)[93]— may God bless him — mentioned, saying: '*Enter you into Egypt, if God will, in security. And he raised his two parents on the throne, and they fell before him in prostration*' [Q. 12:99–100]. The best exegesis of this verse is what al-Ḥakīm — peace be upon him — said: 'Joseph the Truthful himself — peace be upon him — was Egypt. He demanded that the people accept him, enter into his obedience and hold fast to his guidance. Whoever did so would be 'in security' and find happiness. The first who answered him were his parents in the exoteric sense, that is, with regard to [biological] ancestry. As a result, he made them reign over all the people. And when their vision (*baṣīra*) grew, they knew that they were but his worshippers, and they prostrated before him — out of obedience, not out of coercion. They knew that God was the Truth (*ḥaqq*) and that any god besides Him is false and vain. They knew and ascertained that he was the Master of Truth (*ṣāḥib al-ḥaqq*) whom God had entrusted with the choice, to the exclusion of any other. Prostration (*sujūd*) is surrendering (*taslīm*) to the Imam — peace be upon him. It is from [the Imam] that the sciences are transmitted to the Proofs, Gates and Summoners; whoever[**128**] believes them will enter the Egypt he is invited to. He is saved from chastisement and is among the victorious saved ones, who are without fear nor affliction.

66. In common parlance (*fī'l-lugha*), 'Egypt' (*al-miṣr*) is the city; it is an esoteric allusion to the Speaking-Prophet and the Imam. Indeed, the Messenger of God — may God bless him — said: 'I am the city of knowledge and ʿAlī is its gate. Whoever aims for the city must go through the gate.'[94] This confirms this esoteric meaning of 'Egypt'.

[Return to Pharaoh]

67. Let us return to the Pharaoh of this age— may God curse him. He symbolises those who oppose [all the hierarchy of the *daʿwa*] from the Summoners to the Imams, in this age — may God's blessings be upon them. The accounts and stories about them are well-known — may God curse them. Al-Ḥakīm — peace be upon him — said that Pharaoh was among those who had obeyed the Imam — may God's blessings

[93] Joseph is thus named in Q. 12:46. On Joseph, see *Kashf* I, pp. 26–27, §§ 57–59. On the category of the 'Truthful Ones' (*al-ṣiddīqīn*), see *Kashf* V, pp. 139–142, §§ 80–86.

[94] Also quoted in *Kashf* V, p. 105, § 27.

be upon him — and settled (*sakana*) in Egypt. But he wandered away from the Friends (*awliyā'*) of God — He is Sublime and High — and he denied the Imam — peace be upon him — access to what he had been contemplating (*ḥajara ʿalā al-imām li-mā naẓara*), while Summoners went out to summon, on his command.[95] *'He denied and turned away'* [Q. 20:48],[96] he rebelled (*ṭaghā*) and was pleased with himself. Have you not seen His words — He is Mighty and Sublime: *'Nay, but verily man is rebellious (yaṭghā), for he thinks himself self-sufficient'* [Q. 96:6–7]. This is the man who rebelled against his Lord because his vanities sufficed him, **[129]** and he speculated that no one had power over him. *'[Korah] said: "What I have been given is only because of a knowledge that is in me." Did he not know that God had destroyed before him generations of men superior to him in strength and greater in the amount of riches collected? The criminals are not questioned of their sins'* [Q. 28:78], because they follow <what harms them>[97] and does not benefit them — may God curse them. *'They were among those who laughed at those who believed, and winked at one another when they passed them'* [Q. 83:29–30]. They would say, these misguided: *'Are these the ones whom God favours among us?'* [Q. 6:53]. They lied — may God curse them — for they are the misguided, the denying and criminal ones who denied the Day of retribution (*yawm al-dīn*) and distanced themselves from the *'straight Way'* (*al-ṣirāṭ al-mustaqīm*) [Q. 1:6] to worship *'the Jibt and the Ṭāghūt'* [Q. 4:51]. They said: 'We are *"better guided on the Path than those who believe"* [Q. 4:51]'. *'Such are they whom God has cursed, and so made them deaf, and blinded their eyes'* [Q. 47:23], and made them perish in a variety of punishments without concerning Himself with them (*lam yaʿba' bihim*).[98]

[Exegesis of Q. 3:7]

68. The beginning (*al-ibtidā'*) belongs to God — He is Mighty and Sublime — and to Him is the end (*al-intihā'*). His is the ability to

---

[95] It is unclear whether these Summoners are those of the rightful Imam, or those sent out by 'Pharaoh' to preach against the Imam.

[96] Also: Q. 75:32; 92:16; 96:13.

[97] Mss. A, B: *mā yaḍurruka*, corrected to: *mā yaḍurruhum*.

[98] An allusion to Q. 25:77: *'My Lord would not concern Himself with you (lā yaʿba' bikum) but for your prayer.'*

manifest His signs (*yuẓhir āyātahu*) where He wants and desires. Have you not seen His words — He is Mighty and Sublime: *'It is He who sent down upon you the Book, wherein are clear signs (āyāt muḥkamāt) — they are the Mother of the Book (umm al-kitāb) — and others that are ambiguous (mutashābihāt). Those in whose hearts is perversity (zaygh), they follow the ambiguous part, desiring dissension (fitna), and desiring its interpretation (ta'wīl)'* [Q. 3:7]? God did not count us among those in whose hearts is perversity; because when they saw 'the people' (*al-qawm*), they followed them. 'The people' are those who **[130]** claimed the Imamate, saying falsely: 'We are Imams' — may God curse them. They are imams who will be summoned to the Fire: *'On the Day of Resurrection, they will be among the spurned'* [Q. 28:42]. God has ordered that they should be fought and cast out: *'Fight the imams of disbelief; they have no sacred oaths, haply they will give over'* [Q. 9:12]. [God] also said: *'And on the Day of Resurrection you will see those who lied about God, their faces blackened; is there not in Gehenna a lodging for those who are proud?'* [Q. 39:60]. They are the *'obscenity, immorality and dispute'* [Q. 2:197][99] that God — He is Mighty and Sublime— forbade His Friends in both their deeds and words. He ordered [His Friends] to disavow them (*al-barā'a minhum*) and to follow the *'clear signs which are the Mother of the Book'*. The 'Book' is the Resurrector — peace be upon him. What is meant by 'Mother of the Book' is that they[100] summon to the knowledge (*ma'rifa*) of the meaning (*ma'nā*) of the Mother of the Book, they do not rebel against His words, and, when it comes to His prohibitions and orders, they take as guides (*yatawallūn*) God's Prophets, His Messengers, the Imams and the Summoners in all eras — may God's blessings be upon them.

69. As for the explanation of God's words— He is Mighty and Sublime: '. . .*wherein are clear signs which are the Mother of the* Book', 'Book' is among the names of the Speaking-Prophet, while 'signs' (*āyāt*) is among the names of the Imams.[101] And so He says: *'He sent down upon you the Book, wherein are clear signs — they are the Mother*

[99] See the exegesis of this verse above, *Kashf* V, pp. 121–125, §§ 54–59. The present passage confirms the personalized interpretation of these terms, identified with Abū Bakr, 'Umar and 'Uthmān.

[100] It is not clear who this refers to, but it is probably the 'Friends' (*awliyā'*).

[101] On *āyāt* and Imams, see *Kashf* III, p. 79, § 55, and related footnote.

of the Book'. By 'Book', He means that He established him (*aqāmahu*) in the sacred station of the Speaking-Prophet. '. . .*Wherein are clear signs*' means than there are Imams set out from his progeny and his sacred station. 'Clear' (*muḥkamāt*) means that their sacred stations are in accordance with God and with God's wisdom (*ḥikma*). He placed (*tartīb*) the testaments (*waṣāyā*), in accordance with God's tradition (*sunna*), with the Imams who, after the Speaking-Prophet, complete his Order (*yutimmūn amrahu*). He then says: '*They are the Mother of the Book*', meaning that they are the root (*aṣl*) of the Speaking-Prophet **[131]** that follows, since the Completer Imams are the branches of the first Speaking-Prophet <and the root of the following Speaking-Prophet>.[102] The 'mother'[103] of a thing, in all domains, is its root, both lexically and semantically. Thus, after Adam — peace be upon him — there were no Speaking-Prophets who were not preceded by Imams indicating him by God's Order; the well-guided follow their indication, while the denying misguided ones distance themselves from them, until the Speaking-Prophet appears. Those who have followed the Imam will then be saved, while God will destroy <. . .>[104] by the sword of Truth at the hands of the Speaking-Prophet when he appears; He will then give them the Fire as their destiny. This is just like when God— He is Mighty and Sublime— indicated Adam— may God bless him — by ordering the angels to prostrate to him and '*they prostrated except for Iblīs, who refused and was arrogant and was one of the disbelievers*' [Q. 2:34]. He and all of his followers became subject to God's wrath and punishment, in this world and in the hereafter.

70. Also, the Completer Imam is like the mother, while the Speaking-Prophet is like the father in the ranks (*marātib*) of the Imamate. God— He is Mighty and Sublime— says: '*[The Book] wherein are clear signs — they are the Mother of the Book*', meaning there are Imams from the sacred station of the Speaking-Prophet established (*qā'imūn*) by the light of God's Wisdom. And His words: '*They are the Mother of the Book*'

[102] I follow the reading of Ms. A, which neither Strothmann nor Ghālib, p. 120, include.

[103] Strothmann: *amr*. Corrected to *umm* after the manuscripts.

[104] There must be a lacuna here, since the text does not specify who are those destroyed by God — although they must be the 'denying misguided ones' who were just mentioned.

mean they are the mother of the seventh Speaking-Prophet while Muḥammad the Speaking-Prophet is his father. The Imams are named by the unique name of 'mother', because 'father' designates the sacred station of all the Speaking-Prophets. The Imams between the sixth [Speaking-Prophet], Muḥammad — may God bless him — **[132]** and the seventh Speaking-Prophet, the Mahdī — may God's blessings be upon him — are those who are named the 'clear verses'. <And, in relation to Muḥammad, they are at the summit of kinship. . . The Imam attached to the cause. . .>[105] They are in the position (*maqām*) of the mother, and the Speaking-Prophets are in the position (*maqām*) of the father.

[A *ḥadīth* by Jaʿfar al-Ṣādiq]

71. Al-Ṣādiq Jaʿfar b. Muḥammad— may God's blessings be upon him — said: 'This Order is established upon seven: four from among us, and three other than us.'[106] By these seven, [the Imam] — peace be

---

[105] Ms. A: *wa-hum min Muḥammad fī dharwat al-nasab fi'l-imām al-muttaṣil bi'l-sabab*; ms. B: *wa-hum min Muḥammad fī dharwat al-nasab fi'l-imām al-muttaṣil wa'l-dīn*. The manuscripts are corrupted here and the sentence is unclear. My translation is only an attempt to render the text of ms. A.

[106] As W. Madelung pointed out, the present version of the *ḥadīth* reverses numbers three and four when compared to the versions of other sources; see W. Madelung, 'Das Imamat', p. 63, n. 116. Indeed, this *ḥadīth* appears elsewhere in Ismaili literature; for instance, al-Majdūʿ states that the *Mafātīḥ al-niʿma* by Ḥātim b. Ibrāhīm (d. 596/1199) contains an exegesis of this *ḥadīth* in the following version: 'The completion of our Order rests on three from among us and four other than us' (*tamām amrinā fī thalāthā minnā wa arbʿa min ghayrinā*); see al-Majdūʿ, *Fihrist*, p. 261. In the *Risāla al-Mudhhiba* attributed to al-Qāḍī al-Nuʿmān, the 'three from among us' are identified with Jaʿfar al-Ṣādiq, his son Ismāʿīl and his grandson Muḥammad b. Ismāʿīl. On this and the role of this *ḥadīth* in the discussions on the genealogy of the Fatimids, see W. Madelung, 'Das Imamat', pp. 111–112. See also the short and enigmatic interpretation of this *ḥadīth* in Jaʿfar b. Manṣūr al-Yaman, *Kitāb al-Fatarāt wa'l-qirānāt*, p. 87. It is interesting that the version of the *ḥadīth* as found in the *Kashf* is not a mistake, since the 'four' are detailed afterwards. The variety of versions of the *ḥadīth* may reflect the variations of the Fatimids' official stance on their genealogy. Furthermore, the *Kashf*'s version is consistent with the analogy *nāṭiq/waṣī, imām/ḥujja* which appears in several early Fatimid sources, and particularly in Jaʿfar b. Manṣūr al-Yaman's works, including the *Kashf*. My hypothesis is that this analogy was initially destined to legitimize al-Qāʾim bi-Amr Allāh's role as *ḥujja*, and that it has to do with the general reform of this concept in favour of the second caliph.

upon him — alludes to sacred stations and degrees (*rutab*). The Summons of Truth is established through the four among them;[107] they are Muḥammad and ʿAlī. It is necessary that the Summons be in favour of Muḥammad, due to his sacred station as a Speaking-Prophet, and of ʿAlī, due to his sacred station as the Legatee; these are two out of the four. The other two are an Imam and a Proof in every era. This sacred station is necessary. If they — may God bless them — are more than two, then it is the first two who are designated [here], and they are the Substitutes (*abdāl*), as God said— He is Mighty and Sublime: '*When we substitute one sign (āya) for another. . .*' [Q. 16:101] meaning one Imam for another.[108] As for as the Speaking-Messenger and the Legatee, their two sacred stations are firmly rooted (*thābitān*) in Muḥammad's Law (*sharīʿa*) without substitute (*bi-ghayr badal*) until the seventh Speaking-Prophet. This is the indication of the four that are from them; it is through them that the Summons of Truth (*daʿwat al-ḥaqq*) is established (*taqūm*). As for the three, he said that <'not from among them' means 'not from among the People of the House (*ahl bayt*) of the Messenger — may God bless him'; indeed, the sacred station of the Messenger of God is his 'house' in the esoteric [discourse].>[109] By the 'three [that are not from among them]', he means **[133]** [they are] among believers (*al-muʾminīn*). They are [organized] in three ranks (*marātib*). Indeed, there are many believers, but they are [of] only three [types] [divided] into these three ranks: the rank of the Gate (*martabat al-bāb*), who elevates the degrees of the believers upon the Imam's order; the rank of the Summoner (*martabat al-dāʿī*) who summons under the authority of the Gate, thus summoning the seekers (*al-ṭālibīn*) so that they become believers; the rank of the believer (*martabat al-muʾmin*) by which one enters the

[107] *Wa-yaqūm bihim daʿwat al-haqq*. I deleted the *wāw* and attempted to make sense of the Arabic which is incorrect here.

[108] See Ibn Ḥawshab, *Kitāb al-Rushd wa'l-hidāya*, p. 200 (English trans., p. 68), where this verse is similarly interpreted and where the term *abdāl* appears.

[109] Mss. A, B: *min ghayrihim yurīd min ghayr ahl bayt rasūl Allāh ṣallā Allāh ʿalayhi wa-huwa baytuhu fī'l-bāṭin*. Strothmann: *min ghayr li-Llāh yurīd min ghayr ahl bayt maqāmāt al-imāma fa-maqām rasūl Allāh ṣallā Allāh ʿalayhi huwa baytuhu fī'l-bāṭin*; Corrected to: *min ghayrihim yurīd min ghayr ahl bayt rasūl Allāh ṣallā Allāh ʿalayhi <fa-maqām rasūl Allāh> huwa baytuhu fī'l-bāṭin*.

community of the believers (*jumlat al-mu'minīn*), yet without reaching the ranks of the Summoner or the Gate. To this rank belong all the believers; the Summons of Truth is not established without [this rank]. This is an indication confirming what was previously mentioned concerning the sacred station of the Speaking-Prophets and the Completer Imams.

[Return to the exegesis of Q. 3:7]

72. The '*ambiguous [signs]*' [Q. 3:7] are those who have obscured (*labisū*) the Imams; they obscured for the people the fact that they are Imams who save their followers. [The ambiguous signs] indicate a way (*ṭarīq*) other than the Way (*ṭarīq*) of Truth, and they summon in a direction (*qibla*) that God — He is Mighty and Sublime — has not appointed and to which He has not ordered to turn. [In the verse, God,] says that the ambiguous signs are in the Book because these doubters (*al-mushtabihūn*) are from among the community of Muḥammad the Speaking-Prophet — may God bless him. It is him that is meant by the 'Book', in the sense of the Speaking-Prophet. All those who are from among the people who deviate from truth (*ahl al-zaygh 'an al-ḥaqq*) and whose hearts deviate (*zāghat*) from the knowledge of God — He is Sublime and High — they are the adversaries [of 'Alī] (*ahl al-naṣb*)[110] — may God curse them. They say that Pharaoh, Hāmān and Qārūn[111] are in the position (*manzila*) of the Prince of the Believers— peace be upon him — and are not only equal to him but are even **[134]** better than him in their opinion. Such are the 'ambiguous signs'— may God curse them — for whom the knowledge of the truth is dubious (*ishtabaha 'alayhim*): '*Satan has gained the mastery over them, and caused them to forget God's remembrance. They are Satan's party, surely they are the losers!*' [Q. 58:19]. '*They followed the order of Pharaoh, and the order of Pharaoh was not right. He will go before his people on the Day of Resurrection and will lead them to the Fire as watering-place*' [Q. 11:97–98] by the sword of the Resurrector — peace be upon him. '*Hapless is the watering-place to which they are led! A curse will follow them in this*' world '*and on the Day of Resurrection. Hapless is the gift offered (to them)*' [Q. 11:98–99].

---

[110] A common designation of 'Alī's enemies in a Shi'i context.

[111] They refer here to Abū Bakr, 'Umar and 'Uthmān; see *Kashf* I, p. 11, § 22.

This means they will be given the curse, that is, the metamorphosis (*musūkhiyya*) on the Day the Resurrector rises (*qiyām al-qā'im*), [on the Day] his Order manifests and his veil is lifted (*kashf qināʿihi*). This is the Day they have been promised and on which they hoped they would benefit from intercession and access to Paradise, [although] they had denied and ignored what they were ordered, desisting from it and following the Head of the curse (*ra's al-laʿna*) — may God curse them. They followed what was ambiguous to them [dismissing] the Friends of God — peace be upon them. *'They disputed falsely to refute the'* manifest and sublime *'truth'* [Q. 40:5] [in the eyes] of God — He is Mighty and Sublime — that is, God's Friend (*walī*), the Master of the Age (*ṣāḥib al-zamān*) — peace be upon him. And the meaning of: 'He will lead them to the Fire as a watering-place by the sword of the Resurrector' is that, when he manifests — may God bless him — God will kill all those who opposed Him by [the Resurrector's] sword. And all those killed by the sword of the Resurrector will end up in the Fire.

[Return to the exegesis of Q. 2:197]

73. *'Whatever you do of good, God knows it'* [Q. 2:197]: he means by the abundance of works and efforts, for no one should **[135]** fall short (*yuqaṣṣir*) in any of this. Whoever falls short opposes God's Order — He is Mighty and Sublime: *'Take provision; but the best provision is piety (taqwā)'* [Q. 2:197]. The provision is the abundance of knowledge and the excellence of action, which leads to piety and helps accessing it. No one is to spread the teaching of the knowledge of the hidden and safe-guarded secret (*lā yajib li-aḥad an yushīʿ taʿlīm ʿilm al-sirr al-maknūn al-maṣūn*); it contains the healing of the hearts and the life of the spirits. This is the 'best provision'. <Whoever acquires the knowledge of the secret must abide by dissimulation until the time when the Order is unveiled and manifested.>[112] *'Be pious to Me, men possessed of minds!'* [Q. 2:197], means: 'Affirm My Unicity truly, do not associate

[112] Ms. A: *man iqtabasahu li-waqt kashf al-amr wa-iẓhārihi*; ms. B: *wa-min al-taqiyya ilā waqt kashf al-amr wa-iẓhārihi*. I translate the corrected sentence as suggested by Strothmann: *man iqtabasa ʿilm al-sirr tajib ʿalayhi al-taqiyya ilā waqt kashf al-amr* (to which I added: *wa-iẓhārihi*). Ghālib's text (p. 123) provides the same sentence as Strothmann proposes, which suggests once more that the former plagiarized the latter.

anything to Me, and worship Me truly', that is: 'Obey My Veil (*aṭīʿū ḥijābī*), for your obedience to him is to worship Me, since he leads you to the affirmation of My Unicity (*tawḥīdī*).' '*Men possessed of minds!*': 'Men of intellect whom I have <clothed>[113] with My Light, the Subtle and Preserved Intellect' (*al-ʿaql al-laṭīf al-maḥfūẓ*). '*Haply will you prosper*' [Q. 2:189],[114] that is: 'Haply will you be saved if you do so.' If you do, you will have reached [the goal] and will be attached [to God's Order] (*waṣaltum wa-ittaṣaltum*).

74. As for me, I ask God the High, the Sublime, the Great, the Elevated in His Friend (*bi-waliyyihi*), the Manifest through His sacred form (*al-ẓāhir fī haykalihi*) who speaks (*nāṭiq*) His wisdom and expounds the Mystery of His secret, that He allows me to be attached (*muttaṣil*) to Him, not separated from Him; that my spirit flows (*jārī*) in the spirits of His Friends, and that my body is close to theirs. Vie for the degrees of the virtuous (*rutab al-ṣāliḥīn*) from His worshippers. '*He is Hearing, Nigh*' [Q. 34:50].**[136]**

[Exegesis of Q. 3:96–97]

75. Know— may God guide you (*arshadaka Allāh*) — the meaning of God's words— He is Mighty and Sublime: '*The first House laid down for the people was at Bakka, as a blessing and a guidance to the universes. Therein are clear signs: the sacred station of Abraham. Whosoever enters it is in security. Pilgrimage to the House is a duty unto God for the people, for him who can find a path thither. As for him who disbelieves, God is independent from the universes*' [Q. 3:96–97].

76. By this, He wanted to make known to His worshippers the first House He appointed as a Proof; it is the ancient House (*al-bayt al-ʿatīq*),[115] preceded by no other and to which no other measures up. This is why He — He is Sublime and High- singled it out, saying: '*The first House laid down for the people*', that is, appointed (*nuṣiba*) for the people. Whoever knows it, knows Him, and whoever rejects it, rejects Him. The first one is also the last, because the Creator (*al-bāriʾ*)

[113] Mss. A, B: *kasawtuhum* (same root as the 'cloak' of the expression *ahl al-kisāʾ*), which I translate. Strothmann and Ghālib both read: *hasawtuhum*, which does not make sense.

[114] Among other occurrences.

[115] The traditional name of the Kaʿba.

— glory be to His name — made it incumbent upon Himself not to change His first Veil (*ḥijābahu al-awwal*), nor the edifices (*abniya*) from which His wisdom manifested, and not to change any of its sacred stations (*maqāmāt*). 'He made it incumbent upon Himself' means that He executed His will by His judgment which '*nothing can repel*' [Q. 13:41].

77. He said: Your Lord '*has written Mercy upon Himself*' [Q. 6:12], meaning that He has decreed Mercy for you from Himself. And He said — He is Mighty and Sublime: '*Your Lord has decreed that you should worship none but Him*' [Q. 17:23]. All of this has one meaning (*maʿnā*). Indeed, the first sacred station of the Creator — He is Mighty and Sublime — is the last; just as He started with it, He returns (*ʿāda*) with it in all eras. The meaning (*maʿnā*) of this is one, and it is the Imam in his era and the Speaking-Prophet in his era — peace be upon them both. The demonstration of this is that the beginning of the Order sent by God with the first of His Messengers is the [same as the] one with which the last of them rises (*yaqūm bihi ākhiruhum*); it is the one about which they will be asked upon the Day of Resurrection (*yawm al-baʿth*) in the hereafter, after the worldly life. **[137]**

78. God — He is Mighty and Sublime— said: '*You will find no substitution (tabdīl) to God's tradition (sunna)*' [Q. 33:62], and He said: '*There is nothing that can change (mubaddil) His words*' [Q. 6:115].[116] This is an indication to His Order and His wisdom by which He establishes (*yuqīm*) the Messengers and the Imams as <Proofs>[117] for His creation, as bringers of glad tidings and of warnings (*mubashshirīn wa-munadhdhirīn*). The first of His Veils, and the first sacred station in which He veiled Himself, was Adam — may God bless him. He sent him with His religion, which [consists in] obeying Him, affirming His Unicity and worshipping Him, acknowledging that He is the one of which there is no god but Him and that He has no associates, and that He is obeyed by the obedience of those He has elected for the people by His Message and His Revelation. The last [of His Veils] is the seventh Speaking-Prophet; through this one — may God bless him — He rises and summons to Himself. All [the Veils] declare lawful (*yuḥillūn*) what

[116] Among other occurrences.

[117] The manuscripts seem to read: *ḥujajan*. Ghālib (p. 124) reads: *ḥujuban*, which is also plausible given the focus of the paragraph.

God has declared so, announce God's reward and warn against His punishment, and they summon [the people] to worshipping Him. Such are God's Order and religion; He is the beginning and the end (*al-awwal wa'l-ākhir*) [of the Order and religion], and everything in-between.

79. It is in this regard that al-Ḥakīm — peace be upon him — said that the first Veil in which the Creator — He is Sublime and High— veiled Himself is [also] the last one that manifests to His Friends. This is indeed the meaning of His words: '*He is First and the Last*' [Q. 57:3], [for] He is the First of all firsts that come after His order to the first of His creation, and He is the Last after all lasts. The Order returns to Him entirely (*ilayhi yarja' al-amr kulluhu*). He is '*the Manifest*' (*al-ẓāhir*) [Q. 57:3] for all His Prophets, Summoners and Messengers. He is the One who manifested them upon His Order. He is '*the Hidden*' (*al-bāṭin*) [Q. 57:3] who hid (*baṭana*) the things so that they are not known except through Him. '*He is Knower of all things*' [Q. 57:3] both the great and the small from His creation; [He is Knower] of what those who summon to Him do not know — may the blessings of God be upon them; they are the Messengers and the Imams who summon to Him with His permission and guide His worshippers at His Order. He is the last thing to appear to His Friends **[138]** and His worshippers at the end of His Order, through the action of the last of His Messengers and those who accomplish His religion (*al-qawwām bi-dīnihi*).

[The 'Truthful ones' (*al- siddīqūn*)]

80. While the attributes and the names (*al-ṣifāt wa'l-asmā'*) may differ, the meaning (*ma'nā*) upon which they rest (*qā'imūn*) is one. [This meaning is] the one sent in every age, used by God to call upon the people in whom He has perceived sound judgment.[118] They then know the Truth, they see with the Perfect Light, they read the Leaf (*al-ṣaḥīfa*) [i.e. the Qur'an] and they respond to the Truth (*ḥaqīqa*). *'They are with those whom God has blessed, the Prophets, the truthful (al-ṣiddīqīn), the witnesses (al-shuhadā')*[119] *and the virtuous (al-ṣāliḥīn). The best of*

[118] Allusion to Q. 4:6: *'Test well the orphans, until they reach the age of marrying; then, if you perceive in them sound judgment, deliver to them their property, etc.'*

[119] The usual translation of this term is 'martyr' (the Greek root of which means, in any case, 'witness'). I chose to translate it as 'witness' because of the discussion of the term below, in *Kashf* V, p. 142, § 87.

company are they (ḥasuna ulāʾika rafīqan)! [Q. 4:69], because they are the companions (*rufaqāʾ*) of God's Friends, each one in his age. [God's Friends] elevate themselves (*yartaqūn*) and find peace (*yaskunūn*) thanks to them. Have you not heard God's words — glory be to His name — describing the Paradise and its inhabitants, how the universally healing and life-giving knowledge (*al-ʿilm al-shāfī li'l-kull wa'l-muḥyī li'l-kull*) flows (*jarā*) [from Paradise]? He said it is '*the best of resting-places (ḥasunat murtafaqan)*' [Q. 18:31], because it accompanied them (*rāfaqat bihim*) et was gentle (*rafaqat*) until they responded to Him; it is the Proof — peace be upon him. '*Those whom God has blessed*' are the people of response, acceptance, submission and sincerity (*ahl al-ijāba wa'l-riḍā wa'l-taslīm wa'l-ikhlāṣ*). Every time [these people] reached a [certain] knowledge, <they referred their ranks to their Creator>,[120] they repented so that He knew the merit of their gratitude, and they stayed under God's approval. They then migrated from this degree (*rutba*) until they became Prophets and Truthful ones (*ṣiddīqīn*).

81. Among them are those in whom prophecy (*nubuwwa*) was combined with truthfulness (*taṣdīq*); and this is what He said — He is Sublime and High— about those who combine both meanings: '*Joseph, you truthful one*' [Q. 12:46]. In him are combined **[139]** prophecy (*nubuwwa*) and truthfulness (*taṣdīq*), and truthfulness is better (*afḍal*) than prophecy. [God] — He is Sublime and High— said about Idrīs: '*Idrīs was a truthful one, a prophet (siddīqan nabiyyan), and We raised him to a high place*' [Q. 19:56–57]. And He said — may He be blessed and exalted: '*And Ishmael, he was truthful (ṣādiq) to his promise. He was a Messenger and a Prophet, and he ordered his family to prayer and alms giving, and he was acceptable in the sight of his Lord*' [Q. 19:54–55]? How clear is this speech for one who has a heart! The truthful one (*ṣādiq*) is the Noble Messenger who spreads [the message] (*al-muballigh*) and underneath whom rivers flow.[121]

82. Have you not seen His words: '*So travel with your family in a part of the night*' [Q. 11:81]? And His words elsewhere: '*We saved him and his family from the great affliction*' [Q. 21:76]. The family of the

[120] Ms. A: *waḍaʿū ḥadīthahum li-bārīhim*; ms. B: *wa-ṣanaʿū ḥudūdahum li-bārīhim*; Strothmann and Ghālib: *waḍaʿū khudūdahum li-bārīhim*. Corrected to: *waḍaʿū ḥudūdahum li-bārīhim*.

[121] Cf. *Kashf* V, pp. 119–120, § 51; pp. 125–126, § 60.

Truthful ones (*al-ṣiddīqīn*) are the Summoners who, under the authority [of the Truthful ones], are disseminated (*mutafarriqūn*) in various cities and regions (*al-amṣār wa'l-jazā'ir*); they are the rivers flowing (*al-jāriya*) from the seas because they have taken [the Truthful ones] as family (*ta'ahhalū bihim*), prepared themselves to the Summons, and taken [as guides] those that they have given them.

83. Have you not seen the words of God — He is Mighty and Sublime: '*O John! Hold fast the Book. And We gave him wisdom when a child*' [Q. 19:12]? This John was a servant from among the servants of the first John — peace be upon him. This address falls upon both of them. And the meaning of: '*Hold fast of the Book*' is to know the Speaking Imam (*al-imām al-nāṭiq*) in every era and every age — peace be upon him, as God — He is Mighty and Sublime— said: '*This is Our Book, speaking (yanṭuq) to you the Truth*' [Q. 45:29]

84. He gave this account about the one who disbelieved the speech (*al-khiṭāb*): **[140]** '"*Woe to us! How is it with this Book, that it leaves out nothing, small or great but it has numbered it?" They will find all their works present, and your Lord is not iniquitous to anybody*' [Q. 18:49]. Blessed be the One who made things to indicate each other, and made them known through each other. How difficult is the way (*al-ṭarīq*) and how far without a guide (*dalīl*)! And how close and easy is it with the right halt (*al-mawqif al-rashīd*) and a merciful stopover (*al-mu'arrif al-shafīq*) the name of which is drawn from one of the Names! It was said to him: '*You are before our eyes*' [Q. 52:48]. Had he not been before their eyes, he would not have been a guide and a Proof to them — so peace be upon him!

85. The meaning of His words '*Hold fast the Book*' means: 'Strengthen the people of your community (*da'wa*) and, through it, give life to the souls of those who know you (*'ārifika*) and the people who responded to you (*ahl ijābatika*) because you are God's blessing (*baraka*) — He is Sublime and High— to them. '*And We gave him wisdom when a child*': 'We gave him the knowledge, and he was the youngest of his people, the most knowledgeable, the best, the wisest and the most intelligent. So We made him a Speaking-Prophet for them, We elevated (*nawwahnā*) his name and greatly favoured him.' Blessed be God, the best of creators.

86. This should have illustrated what we have said and intended with regard to our doctrine (*madhhab*). We wished to explain the meaning of the words 'Prophets' and 'the Truthful ones'. And [God]

— He is Sublime and High— has taught us that He made exceptions out of the Truthful ones, and we have found them to be above (*fawq*) the Prophets. Yet, it is possible for one to be both a Prophet and a Truthful one — the people of Friendship and Response (*ahl al-walāya wa'l-ijāba*) do not deny this. What [illustration] of this is more abundant than the story of Joseph — peace be upon him? [God] made him the Master of the sack and of the interpretations (*ṣāḥib al-wiʿāʾ wa'l-fatyā*),[122] **[141]** from whom the Summoners draw [their knowledge], because he is a Sublime Sea and the Imam of his era — peace be upon him — as [exemplified] by their words: *'Joseph, you truthful one (al-siddīq), expound to us (aftina) the seven fat kine'* [Q. 12:46]. God — He is Mighty and Sublime — wanted to make him the Master of the Summoners, so that they would deem his word true (*yuṣaddiqūn qawlahu*), <consult him>[123] regarding their affair (*amrihim*), and take refuge in him, because he is the Gate to their [access to] wisdom.

[Prophets, 'Witnesses' and intermediaries]

87. His words: *'They are those whom God have blessed'* [Q. 19:58],[124] mean the Speaking-Prophets in every era and every age. They are the Summoners towards God — He is Mighty and Sublime. They are from among those who love the Prophets and the Truthful ones. They are named 'Speaking-Prophets' because the Imams make them 'speak' the Summons (*anṭaqahum al-aʾimma bi'l-daʿwa*), unlike the other believers who are silent (*al-muʾminīn al-ṣāmitīn*). By this name, they are distinguished from the mass of Respondents (*al-mustajībīn*). Then, God — He is Mighty and Sublime — wanted to mention a degree (*daraja*) superior to the degrees of the Prophets and the Truthful ones, present during their ages, and He said: *'The witnesses (al-shuhadāʾ) are with their Lord'* [Q. 57:19]. They are the Messengers who are witnesses (*shuhadāʾ*) to God — He is Mighty and High — in all eras, and He

---

[122] The 'sack' is an allusion to Joseph's ruse when he placed a stolen object in his brother's sack to keep him from leaving, in Q. 12:76. Joseph is the master of interpretations because of his *taʾwīl* of dreams in Q. 12:41 and 12:46.

[123] Mss. A, B: *wa-yusammūnahu*. Corrected to: *yastaftūnahu*, after Strothmann's suggestion in n. 2.

[124] It is possible that the text is in fact an incorrect quotation of Q. 4:69, cited above: '*They are with those whom God has blessed*'.

made them witnesses to His creation (*shuhadā' ʿalā khalqihi*). They are the Masters of Laws (*aṣḥāb al-sharāʾiʿ*). Have you not seen His words — He is Sublime and High: *'How then shall it be, when We bring forward for every nation a witness (shahīd), and bring you a witness to these (ʿalā hāʾulāʾ shahīdan)?'* [Q. 4:41]? As for the Masters of Laws, they are God's witnesses to His creation. The Summoners are under their authority. And the Prophets, they are [divided into] Messengers (*al-mursalūn*) and Prophets **[142]** that are not Messengers, because among God's Prophets, some are better (*afḍal*) than others. Have you not seen God's words — He is Mighty and Sublime: *'We have preferred (faḍḍalnā) some Prophets over others'* [Q. 17:55]?

88. This is the rank (*martaba*) of the Prophets, because their Creator arranges (*yurattibuhum*) them according to the merit (*faḍl*) of their positions (*manāzil*) vis-à-vis Him. The choice in this regard belongs to the Master of the Law (*ṣāḥīb al-sharīʿa*), who honoured them, elevated (*nawwaha*) their names, ordered [people] to obey them and forbade [people] to rebel against them. Have you not seen God's words — He is Mighty and Sublime: *'He has laid down for you as religion that He charged Noah with, and that We have revealed to you, and that We charged Abraham, Moses and Jesus: Establish the religion, and be not divided therein'* [Q. 42:13]? The ones God talks to are *'the Messengers of inflexible purpose (ūlū al-ʿazm min al-rusul)'* [Q. 46:35][125], like when He — He is Mighty and Sublime — ordered some of the Prophets, saying: *'Be patient, just as the Messengers of inflexible purpose had patience'* [Q. 46:35]. Those who had the inflexible purpose (*ʿazamū*) of pleasing God, they do not fear anyone in the universes and inflexibility is bestowed upon them (*ʿazama bihim*). They devoted themselves entirely to their Creator (*inqaṭaʿū ilā bāriʾihim*), they were enlightened by His Light and became luminaries (*maṣābīḥ*) for others, and lamps (*suruj*) for whoever imitates them and is guided by their guidance, <. . .>[126] — peace be upon them.

---

[125] On the *ūlū al-ʿazm* in early Ismaili thought, see D. De Smet, 'Adam, premier prophète et législateur ? La doctrine chiite des *ulū al-ʿazm* et la controverse sur la pérennité de la *šarīʿa*', in *Le shīʿisme imāmite, quarante ans après. Hommage à Etan Kohlberg*, ed. Mohammad Ali Amir-Moezzi, Meir M. Bar-Asher, Simon Hopkins (Turnhout, 2009), pp. 187–202.

[126] Mss. A, B: *wa-jaʿalahum khaṣāʾiṣ*. It is unclear what is meant by this.

89. Those to whom God speaks without any human intermediary (*wāsiṭa min al-bashar*) nor impediment between Him and them have received a great favour and a high **[143]** rank; no one is to claim their sacred station, unless he is dead, not alive, as He has said— He is Mighty and Sublime: *'They have hearts wherewith they understand not, eyes wherewith they see not'* [Q. 7:179]. And He said: *'It is not the eyes that grow blind, but it is the hearts in the breasts that grow blind'* [Q. 22:46]. We take refuge in God from blindness and death of the heart, and we ask Him for the life of our hearts, for the light of our sights and the increase of our insights — *'He knows what is hidden in the breasts'* [Q. 3:119].[127] Among all mankind, God's worshippers — He is Mighty and Sublime— are intermediaries (*wāsiṭa*) to one another between His people and Himself, [each] according to the capacity of the ranks [arranged] in degrees[128] — thus, up to the Messenger, who is the intermediary between God the Exalted and mankind. No one has a rank above [mankind] — except the intermediary between God the Exalted and the mediations flowing unto [the Messenger] (*al-asbāb al-jāriya ilayhi*), namely the spiritual angels Gabriel and Michael, and those whom God has set as an intermediary between Him and His Messengers.

90. The evidence for this is God's words — He is Mighty and Sublime— to His Prophet Muḥammad, His Messenger to mankind — may God bless him: *'And ask those of Our Messengers We sent before you: Have We appointed, apart from the Merciful, gods to be worshipped?'* [Q. 43:45]. This means: 'Ask those of our angels (*malā'ika*) we sent before you, they are Our messengers to the Messengers (*rusulinā ilā'l-rusul*).' *'Have We appointed, apart from the Merciful, gods to be worshipped?'*: By this, He means that there is no god but Him, no god to be worshipped but Him, and that the angels are subjugated (*musta'badūn*) [to Him] just as mankind is subjugated to God, Lord of the universes. Thus, between you, Muḥammad, and God, there is nothing but the subjugated messengers from among the spiritual angels

[127] Among other occurrences.

[128] The sentence is convoluted, but the meaning is that the 'worshippers', i.e, the true believers, are organized in a hierarchy, each degree of which is an intermediary between the degree below it, and the one above it. At the top of this ladder stands the Messenger, who is the supreme intermediary for all mankind.

(*al-malā'ika al-rūḥāniyyīn*). God — He is Mighty and Sublime— has said indeed: *'God chooses* **[144]** *from the angels messengers, and from mankind'* [Q. 22:75]. His messengers that He has chosen from mankind are His messengers to mankind, whereas His messengers that He has chosen from the angels are His messengers to the Messengers. These are the ones [God] ordered Muḥammad — may God bless him and his family — to interrogate in His words: *'And ask those of Our Messengers We sent before you'* [Q. 43:45]. It is not His Messengers from the past whom God ordered His Prophet to interrogate.

91. God — He is Mighty and Sublime — said: *'It belongs not to any mortal that God should speak to him, except by revelation (waḥī), or from behind a veil (ḥijāb), or that He should send a Messenger to reveal what He will, with His permission'* [Q. 42:51]. The 'revelation' is the word (*kalām*) of God that the angels convey to the Messengers, and by which [God] speaks to mankind. Then He said: *'Or from behind a veil'*. This refers to God's word (*kalām Allāh*) and the esoteric knowledge (*'ilm al-bāṭin*) that the Messenger conveys to the Legatee, because the Messenger is a veil between God and the people. The revelation is God's word (*al-tanzīl kalām Allāh*), and so is the exegesis (*al-ta'wīl*), as God said — He is Mighty and Sublime: *'And if any of those who associate [something to God] seeks your protection, then grant him protection till he hears God's word (kalam Allāh), then bring him to his place of safety'* [Q. 9:6]. This is about the revelation (*tanzīl*), which is God's word, that is, the Qur'an. And the exegesis (*ta'wīl*) is also God's word. And His words: *'Or that He should send a Messenger to reveal what He will, with His permission'*, is the exegesis (*ta'wīl*) that the Legatee conveys to the people with God's permission — may He be exalted — and with His Messenger's permission. This is how [God] speaks to mankind when they hear His word with His permission.

92. And the esoteric meaning of God's words — He is Mighty and Sublime— in this verse: *'And if any of* **[145]** *those who associate [something to God] seeks your protection, then grant him protection'* [Q. 9:6], concerns those who associate [something with God] (*al-mushrikīn*) who associated with the Imam chosen by God and His Messenger another imam who is calling to the Fire and has not been chosen by God, nor by His Messenger. They associated their own choice with God's, and with the following of their passions. *'And if any of those who associate [something to God] seeks your protection, then* *grant him protection till he hears God's word'* [Q. 9:6]: '[if] one of those who associate [something to God] seeks your protection against the misguided (*al-ḍāllīn*), grant him the protection of the covenant and the alliance (*al-ʿahd wa'l-mīthāq*).' It is better to be guided on the ways of the truth. This is addressed to the Messenger in his era, and to every Imam in every era. He then said: '. . .*till he hears God's word'* regarding the exegesis (*ta'wīl*). *'Then bring him to his place of safety'*: he is to bring him to elevate his degree and to free himself from the yoke (*irtifāʿ darajatihi wa-fikāk ruqbatihi*),[129] until he is safe from misguidance by the increase of his certainty and his insight, and he is safe from the torment of the Day of Resurrection. Such is God's word, in both [its] exoteric and esoteric [meanings], one part attesting the other (*yashhad baʿḍuhu li-baʿḍ*) and one part confirming another (*wa-yu'akkid baʿḍuhu baʿḍan*).[130] Everything in [God's word] is timely and in its place. None contradicts the other (*lā yanquṣ baʿḍuhu baʿḍan*).[131]

[Betrayal concealed in the breasts]

93. Al-Ḥakīm — peace be upon him — said: 'The Prophets of God are [organized] in degrees (*darajāt*) — as God has said: "*We raise up in degrees who We will* [Q. 6:83]".' *'Not a leaf falls* **[146]** *but He knows it'* [Q. 6:59]. He arranges all that He created according to His wisdom. His Creation attests His Order, and His Order attests His Creation, *'and He has knowledge of everything'* [Q. 6:101]. He sees all things, and [particularly] what He established as a Proof to His creation.

---

[129] The expression *fikāk al-ruqba*, lit. 'liberation of the neck', comes from Q. 90:13: 'The freeing of a slave' (*fakku raqabatin*). In early Fatimid Ismaili literature, it apparently designates a certain stage in the initiation of the 'believer' (*mu'min*); see e.g. Jaʿfar b. Manṣūr al-Yaman, *al-Riḍāʿ fi'l-bātin*, pp. 47, 186.

[130] Almost identical sentence in Jaʿfar b. Manṣūr al-Yaman, *al-Riḍāʿ fi'l-bātin*, pp. 183–184, where it is the 'revelation' (*tanzīl*) and the 'exegesis' (*ta'wīl*) that 'attest and confirm each other' (*yashhad kull wāḥid minhumā ʿalā l-thānī wa-yu'akkiduhu*). The sentence of the *Kashf* is ambiguous, since it is possible to understand that it is 'God's word' that 'attest and confirm' itself, in the sense that it is consistent. The testimony of the *Riḍāʿ* however points towards the idea that it is the *ẓāhir* and the *bāṭin* that 'attest and confirm' each other.

[131] Same ambiguity as before: it could either be that no part of God's word does contradict another, or that the esoteric meaning and the exoteric meaning do not contradict each other.

94. He has knowledge because He *'knows what is hidden in the breasts'* [Q. 3:119], and He knows *'the treason of the eyes and what the breasts conceal'* [Q. 40:19]. The 'treason [against] the eyes' refers to those who betrayed God, His Messengers and His Friends with both their knowledge and their action (*bi-ʿilmihim wa-ʿamalihim*), and followed God's enemies. The 'eyes' of God, in His Creation, are the Prophets and the Imams — peace be upon them. Whoever betrays them has betrayed God, and God knows who has betrayed Him and has betrayed His Friends and Messengers. And His words: '. . .*and what the breasts conceal*', refer to the knowledge that the breasts of His Friends conceal; they do not manifest it to anyone who does not deserve it. If they manifest it to someone who deserves it, but then substitutes [something else] to it or violates it, and betrays them with regard to it, then God knows it.

95. It is about this that God — He is Mighty and Sublime— said: *'Do not betray God and the Prophet and do not betray your trusts (amānāt) when you know'* [Q. 8:27]. This is addressed to the believers who have become acquainted with (*iṭṭalaʿū*)[132] the secret knowledge (*maknūn al-ʿilm*). The betrayal of God is to be at variance with what pleases Him, both secretly and publicly. The betrayal of His Messenger is to disobey his Law and his tradition (*sunna*), and to abandon (*tark*) his order and his Legatee. And the betrayal of the trusts is the betrayal of the Imams concerning the secrets of their knowledge (*sarāʾir ʿulūmihim*). The betrayal of their knowledge is to show it to someone who does not deserve it and to **[147]** dignities (*ḥudūd*) to which it does not belong. *'When you know'*, means that you know the dignities of religion (*ḥudūd al-dīn*) and the rights of the trust (*ḥuqūq al-amāna*) in the hidden [Order] (*fi'l-mastūr*). This is because no one becomes acquainted (*yaṭṭaliʿ*) with the esoteric knowledge (*ʿilm al-bāṭin*) without knowing its rights and ranks (*ḥuqūqihi wa-ḥudūdihi*), and [knowing] that it is an obligation (*wājib*) to hide and conceal it (*satrihi wa-ṣiyānatihi*). The 'trusts' (*amānāt*) are the sacred stations of the Imams, and they are also the benefits [obtained] from their esoteric knowledge. And God's words — He is Mighty and Sublime: *'The*

[132] Mss. A, B: *ẓalamū*. Strothmann reads: *aṭlaʿū*, 'they have disclosed', and Ghālib (p. 131): *iṭṭalaʿū*. The latter reading seems more correct since the same verb is repeated a few lines below.

treason [against] the eyes' [Q. 40:19] mean the treason against the Imams and the Proofs, because they are God's eyes over His Creation <. . .>.[133] And the betrayal of '*what the breasts conceal*' [Q. 40:19] means the betrayal of the trusts of knowledge benefits that are concealed in the breasts of the Friends — as He said: '*Do not betray your trusts*' [Q. 8:27]. There is another meaning to this, namely that God knows the treachery concealed in the breasts, even though actions do not manifest it.

96. And there is yet another esoteric meaning to this: the 'breasts' (*ṣudūr*) are those who emanated (*ṣadarū*) from the Creator to the Creation on His order, so that [the Creation] is brought back (*li-yuṣdirū*) through them upon '*the straight Way (al-ṣirāṭ al-mustaqīm)*' [Q. 1:6] — that is, the obedience to the Imam — peace be upon him — in every era. They are the 'breasts' that 'conceal' God's knowledge. And God '*knows what you conceal and what you publish*' [Q. 27:25]. He knows them as well as others. They are the Imams — may God's blessings be upon them all. Among them is the one who keeps silent about esoteric wisdom, and who speaks with the exoteric sword (*al-ṣāmit ʿan al-ḥikma al-bāṭina al-nāṭiq bi'l-sayf al-ẓāhir*), as well as the one who keeps silent with the exoteric sword, and who speaks the esoteric wisdom — peace be upon them.

[The 'virtuous' (*al-ṣāliḥūn*)]

97. We return to the explanation and clarification of pilgrimage, which we had intended to give.[134] Since we started [our] explanation about the Imams, it is necessary that we take it to its conclusion, with God's assistance and force. We provided an explanation about the 'Witnesses' (*al-shuhadā'*), and we now want to clarify the meaning **[148]** of the 'Virtuous' (*al-ṣāliḥīn*). It is through their virtue (*ṣalāḥ*) that things and Laws are perfected (*tammat*) and become virtuous (*ṣalaḥat*). They are the Masters of the perfected Summons (*aṣḥāb al-daʿwāt al-tāmmā*), the Proofs of God to His Creation. They are firmly rooted in the Prophets and they return to them, they rely on them concerning the Order of God that they establish (*qāmū bihi*). The 'Witnesses' are those whom they made witnesses to their own

[133] *Fī asbāb ḥaqqihi*: The meaning is unclear.

[134] In fact, the theme of pilgrimage will not be directly resumed until a few pages further, with the lengthy exegesis of Q. 3:96–97.

creation in the new creation (*al-khalq al-jadīd*),[135] and they are the Masters of the Summons to the esoteric Truth (*al-ḥaqq al-bāṭin*). Have you not seen His words — He is Mighty and Sublime— about *'those who believe and do good deeds (al-ṣāliḥāt)'* [Q. 2:25]?[136] He means that it is by them that they established the 'good deeds' (*bihim aqāmū al-ṣāliḥāt*), as when He mentions *'the abiding good deeds (al-bāqiyāt al-ṣāliḥāt)'* [Q. 18:46]. He means the Proofs — peace be upon them. As for the 'Virtuous' (*al-ṣāliḥīn*), they were named 'remembrance' (*ism al-tadhkīr*),[137] and they became Imams. The 'good deeds' (*al-ṣāliḥāt*) are named 'Proofs' because their ranks (*marātib*) are lower than those of the Imams — peace be upon them.

98. He then said: *'The best of company are they!'* [Q. 4:69].[138] <. . .>[139] May His Glory be glorified and His Names sanctified, may His Veil (*ḥijāb*) be glorified, and His signs purified (*nuzzihat āyātuhu*), and may His Summoners translate the hidden part of His knowledge and the concealed part of His secret (*maknūn ʿilmihi wa-khafī sirrihi*). We ask God for approval and peace (*taslīm*); [We ask Him] access [to the goal] safe and sound (*fī khayr wa-ʿāfiya*), and [we ask Him] a total, perfect and favourable grace, an uncounted gift.

99. The noblest of His names — as He said: *'To God belong the most beautiful names, so call Him by them'* [Q. 7:180]— is the Speaking-Prophet with the sword (*al-nāṭiq bi'l-sayf*), the manifest through power (*al-ẓāhir bi'l-qudra*), the Master of the age, the dome (*qubba*) of the times, the source (*maʿdin*) of the Qur'an, the interpreter of the Mercy, the Gate of God in His Creation, and the intermediary (*wāsiṭa*) between Him and his noble worshippers; they do not precede him in speech, they act at his order, and **[149]** they refer themselves to his power

---

[135] The 'new creation' refers to the access to the initiatory and esoteric knowledge. The expression appears in several other early Fatimid works. Unfortunately, in this particular occurrence, the sentence is unclear, and it cannot be determined which, of the 'witnesses' or the 'virtuous', is responsible for the others' access to initiation.

[136] Among other occurrences.

[137] See index s.v. *dhikr*.

[138] This paragraph returns to Q. 4:69 as a conclusion to the long development on the 'Truthful ones', the 'Witnesses' and the 'Virtuous' — terms that appeared in this verse; see above *Kashf* V, p. 139, § 80.

[139] *Fa-abāna*. Something seems to be missing here.

(*qudra*). '*The best of company are they!*' [Q. 4:69]. He is the glorious, best name, by which the world is bettered, and the hereafter is illuminated. May God lead us to their destination, may He make us reach what they have reached. '*He knows what is hidden in the breasts*' [Q. 3:119].[140]

[Return to the exegesis of exegesis of Q. 3:96–97]

100. We return to the meaning of His words: '*The first House laid down for the people was at Bakka, as a blessing and a guidance to the universes*' [Q. 3:96]. The first House that God — may He be exalted — manifested is the Message (*al-risāla*) and the guide to worshipping by the chosen Messenger, that is, Adam — peace be upon him. As for the last House, he is the seal of His Message (*khātim al-risāla*) and His Proof. He is the last House that He has showed to the people, meaning the last Speaking-Prophet He sent to the people, the seventh Speaking-Prophet. The beginning of His Order is [like] the last, there is no change (*tabdīl*) to His Order, '*no repelling to His judgement*' [Q. 13:41]. And the 'people' [here,] are the believers who acknowledge the grace of the seventh, the Respondents (*al-mustajībūn*) to his Summons in every era and every age. 'Bakka' is the Proof who has reached the full capacity of his function (*al-bāligh iḥtijājahu*), whose word (*kalima*) is complete. He is the balance of justice (*mīzān al-ʿadl*) that the Creator ordered to follow, saying: '*Weigh with the straight balance (wa-zinū bi'l-qisṭās al-mustaqīm)*' [Q. 17:35], that is: 'Follow the order of the Proof and do what he says.' He is 'Bakka' who makes his enemies weep (*bakkat*), who humiliates and curses them. One says: 'He broke (*abakka*)[141] his enemies', meaning that he separated and expelled them. He is the blessing from whom comes the guidance, that is, the Summoners. **[150]**

101. The 'universes' [of Q. 3:96] are the Prophets and Messengers in every age and every era, to whom is unveiled the knowledge of the Truth (*ʿilm al-ḥaqīqa*). About them, God — He is Mighty and Sublime— said: '*Only those of His worshippers fear God who have*

[140] Inasmuch as the style of this paragraph, with its series of eulogies, is reminiscent of a conclusion (compare with the conclusion of the treatise itself), one may hypothesise that this whole passage (§ 80–100) was inserted by either a copyist, a later editor of the text, or the author himself. Indeed, the text was then interrupted precisely after a quotation of Q. 3:96, the interpretation of which will now be resumed.

[141] Ms. A: *abakka aʿdāh*; ms. B: *innaka aʿlāh*. B is clearly incorrect.

knowledge' [Q. 35:28]. They are the ones who were clothed with fear (*albasū al-khishya*). God is feared through them, which means that He is known through them and by them. Such is the meaning of: *'Only those of His worshippers fear God who have knowledge'*. God's Order and Assistance (*ta'yīd*) is within and with them, since He clothed them with the fear of Himself, and He made them worshippers who know His Mystery (*ghaybahu*), are illuminated by the Light of His guidance and are attached to the Light of His ipseity (*inniyya*). The noblest among those who know, in the eyes of God — He is Mighty and Sublime –, is the one who summons to Him with His permission, the source (*ma'din*) of His knowledge, the Completer of the revelation of His Messenger (*mutimm waḥī rasūlihi*), that is, his Legatee, who is meant here, the first of those who know, the Father of fathers, the Summoner of Summoners (*dā'ī al-du'āt*).

102. We return to the meaning of God's words — He is Mighty and Sublime: *'Therein are clear signs'* [Q. 3:97]. The clear signs are the Proofs — peace be upon them — who clarified for the people the knowledge of what seemed doubtful to them. They contemplate, indicate and summon to God's knowledge and the sacred station of the Master of Truth **[151]** — the symbol (*mathal*) of which is God's House. Such is the sacred station of Abraham (*maqām Ibrāhīm*). <One of his [i.e. 'Alī's] Proofs [i.e. Muḥammad b. Abī Bakr] did with his father the same as Abraham who disavowed his father in favour of his Creator (*tabarra'a ilā bāri'ihi*). So did Muḥammad [b. Abī Bakr] who disavowed>[142] his father in favour of God — He is Mighty and Sublime — and the Prince of the Believers — may God bless him — following what God — He is Mighty and Sublime — said about those who say: *'We disavow you and what you worship in place of God'* [Q. 60:4]. He is the one who disavowed the filth and impurity (*al-rijs wa'l-najas*)[143] [of]

---

[142] The text is corrupted here, and Strothmann leave two lines blank; see his footnote 1. In addition to the lack of clarity of the sentence, it seems the copyists have confused Muḥammad b. Abī Bakr and the Prophet Muḥammad. I have attempted to reconstruct an understandable sentence on the basis of the corrupted text of the manuscripts.

[143] Cf. *Kashf* III, p. 53, § 2, in the opening passage of the Treatise III which seems out of place since it deals with the theme of the 'Houses', the central one in Treatise V.

his father — may God curse him, the one who spoke to him and scolded him, saying: '*Will you take idols for gods? I see you and your folk in error manifest*' [Q. 6:74]. He scolded him and forbade him [to worship idols], but '*he refused and was arrogant and was one of the disbelievers*' [Q. 2:34]. The Creator — He is Sublime and High — rewarded [Muḥammad b. Abī Bakr] by the hand of the Legatee of His Messenger in this world, so that his reward in the hereafter would be double. He rewarded him by placing him in the sacred station of the Summoner. He ordered to follow his[144] Summons, to enter in his allegiance (*al-dukhūl fī bayʿatihi*), for whoever enters his Summons and responds is in security and finds happiness. Indeed, the Creator **[152]** — He is Mighty and Sublime — said: '*Whosoever enters it is in security*' [Q. 3:97]; [he is in security] in the Summons, by entering in his Friendship and being attached to it by his guidance.

103. We return to the meaning of the beginning of the words: '*Pilgrimage to the House is a duty unto God for the people, for him who can find a path thither*' [Q. 3:97]. He ordered — He is Sublime and High — to follow the Imam — may God's blessings be upon him; whoever chooses him is saved and victorious. The 'pilgrimage' is to acknowledge the Friend [supported by God] (*al-iqrār bi'l-walī al-maʿmūd*) — peace be upon him — '*for him who can find a path thither (man istaṭāʿa ilayhi sabīlan)*'. The worshippers all have the capacity to do so (*istiṭāʿa*), but they are deprived of the [divine] support (*tawfīq*). The path (*sabīl*) for them is clear; it is the Summoner to God's path — He is Sublime and High. This description applies to the Proof of the Imam, and the Legatee of the Messenger, for the Proof is the path to the Imam by which the people are summoned to God — He is Mighty and Sublime— as God — He is Mighty and Sublime — said: '*Say: This is my path. I summon to God (adʿū ilā Allāh) with insight (baṣīra), I and whoever follows me. Glory be to God, I am not among those who associate*' [Q. 12:108] to God someone to who He has not sent down a power (*sulṭān*). They have associated the passions of their souls and the choice of their chiefs (*kubarāʾ*) who led them astray from the path with God's order concerning the Imam — may God's blessings be upon him. In place of the Imam, they placed another who had not

[144] The text suggests that this refers to Muḥammad b. Abī Bakr, but in fact, it must be ʿAlī.

been placed there neither by God, nor by His Messenger, someone who had no right [to this position] and who does not guide to a *'straight Way (ṣirāṭ al-mustaqīm)'* [Q. 1:6]. God has not placed us among them, He is All-powerful over this. The path is obvious and clear, but He has laid *'veils (akinna) on their hearts so that they understand not, and in their ears a deafness. And though you call them to the guidance, yet they will not be guided ever'* [Q. 18:57]. How clear is this **[153]** speech for one who has a sharp vision! [It means:] do not consider anything that He has not ordered, o you who receive [knowledge] (*mustafid*).

104. He then said: *'As for him who disbelieves, God is independent from the universes'* [Q. 3:97]. Had God — He is Sublime and High — not known that they have the capacity (*yastaṭīʿūn*) — since He had established the path for them, and had showed them the guide (*dalīl*) — He would not have said to one who opposed His order: *'As for him who disbelieves'*. Had He not given them the capacity to make the effort and the sense of desire, He would not have called them 'unbelievers' (*kufr*). He — He is Sublime and High — does not deprive them of their guidance (*rushd*) in any way. He [only] hurled at them the name of 'disbelief' (*kufr*) when they opposed His order and abandoned their duty (*farḍ*) to Him. Then God — He is Mighty and Sublime — showed that He *'is independent from the universes'*, meaning by this His Summoners, from whom He is independent. For He is the one who assisted (*aʿānahum*) them and enriched them (*aghnāhum*). He entrusted them [with knowledge] (*mallakahum*)[145] and reigned through them (*malaka bihim*), He made them venerable angels (*malāʾika mukarramīn*)[146] and sincere Friends (*awliyāʾ mukhliṣīn*). May God place us among them and with them, and not cut us off from them. *'He is Seeing, Hearing'* [Q. 22:61].

[145] This translation is based on the explanation provided in the *Kitāb al-Rushd wa'l-hidāya*, where it is stated that the Proofs are identified with angels (*malāʾika*) because the Imams have 'given' them or 'entrusted' (*mallaka*) them with the 'knowledge of religion and guidance'; see Ibn Ḥawshab, *Kitāb al-Rushd wa'l-hidāya*, p. 206 (English trans., p. 74).

[146] On the designation of members of the *daʿwa* as angels, see *Kashf* III, p. 62, § 20 and above, p. 219, n. 24. See also commentary below pp. 413–414.

[Conclusion]

105. We have explained this verse and the explanation of other verses has followed. We ask God that He assists us and makes us reach the goal, [we ask Him] to be attached to Him, to be able to see Him (*muʿāyanatihi*) and speak to Him without a veil (*ḥijāb*); He is *'Hearing, All-knowing'* [Q. 2:181].[147] This means that, during a period of concealment (*istitār*) of the Imam, the Summoners pray (*yadʿūn*) God that He grants the believers the ability to see Him and to hear His word [directly] without the veil of the Summoners and the Proofs — for **[154]** they are the veils (*ḥujub*) of the Imam when he conceals himself from the sights of the iniquitous. *'God is Hearing, All-knowing'* [Q. 2:224],[148] He hears the prayer (*duʿā'*) of the believers, He knows their secrets and the virtue of their intentions. He encompasses every 'thing' by [His] knowledge: the 'thing' is [the succession of] the Imams, one after another — peace be upon them. God's knowledge encompassed them all, and so do His choice (*ikhtiyār*) and His Order. *'He knows all things'* [Q. 2:282],[149] because He knows what He sends out to a 'thing', that is, to the Imam, before He sends it out; indeed, He brought the Imam into existence (*awjada al-imām*) and gave him sight. He pointed toward him, and without His knowledge of him and His will, He would not be 'independent'. *'Blessed be God, the best of Creators'* [Q. 23:14] who *'created'* [Q. 87:2] the Imams as summoners to Him — peace be upon them — and *'disposed'* [Q. 87:2] them as guides (*a'imma*) for His worshippers, and a direction (*qibla*) to receive His guiding instruction (*li-rashādihi*). *'He determined and guided (qaddara wa-hadā)'* [Q. 87:3]: He determined them as He wished by placing in them the wisdom (*ḥikma*) by which they obey, as He said — He is Sublime and High: Your Lord *'very well knows you when He produced you from the earth, and when you were yet unborn in your mothers' wombs; therefore hold not yourselves purified; God knows very him who is godfearing'* [Q. 53:32]. From the earth, He gave rise to the Summoners; the earth is a symbol (*mathal*) of the Proof.[150] *'When you were yet*

---

[147] Among other occurrences.

[148] Among other occurrences.

[149] Among other occurrences.

[150] On this hermeneutical equivalence, see also *Kashf* III, p. 62, § 20; p. 85, § 76; V, p. 101, § 22.

unborn in your mothers' wombs' refers to when you were still suckling the esoteric' (*antum taḥt al-riḍāʿ fī'l-bāṭin*)[151] and being reared to the knowledge (*al-tarbiya bi'l-ʿilm*), and you had not yet reached the stage where you could eat and speak, that is, the degree (*rutba*) of the Summoners who are sent out to [disseminate] the Summons. When you reach the degree where you are created — the degree to which you were summoned — and where you are created anew (*khuliqtum al-khalq al-jadīd*) — which is the Summons to esoteric knowledge — this degree will bring you to the degree of uttering the Summons (*rutbat al-nuṭq bi'l-daʿwa*). '*Hold not yourselves purified*', because I am the one who will purify you and your work, who will approve your rearing. I **[155]** know best who is 'godfearing' among you, and I will bring him to the highest degree (*rutba*), I will make him a veil, I will bestow the power on him, and I will make him the Imam of his era— may God bless him and the Imams of His religion; the guidance of the worshippers is through them and under their authority. People reach their benefits through the Summoners of their Imam— may God's blessings be upon him.

106. May God let us reach our supreme hope and our ultimate quest, [may He give us] vision of the Beloved and closeness to the intended one, and not cut us from that; indeed, He is Benevolent and Generous.

107. The treatise is now complete, with all its explanations, its commentaries and its esoteric meanings. Praise be to God, Lord of the Universes. May God bless the best of His Creation, His Prophet Muḥammad, and his noble, pure and good family, and may His peace be upon them. '*God is sufficient for us, an excellent Guardian is He*' [Q. 3:173], an excellent Master (*mawlā*), and an excellent Helper. **[156]**

---

[151] Note the expression *riḍāʿ fī'l-bāṭin*, which is also the title of another work by Jaʿfar b. Manṣūr al-Yaman.

Treatise V Commentary

Treatise V is the longest of the six treatises. Like Treatises I and III, it has several editorial and doctrinal layers. In Treatise I, the two layers, the 'proto-Nuṣayri' layer and its Ismaili reinterpretation, could be distinguished with relative ease. Treatise III, on the other hand, is an inextricable tangle of pre-Fatimid and Fatimid material — all the more inextricable since the typically Fatimid features do not appear clearly and the text remains very elusive. Treatise V presents the same problems, to which are added the density of the text, as well as its complex structure. Indeed, if we admit, following W. Madelung,[152] that the *Kitāb al-Kashf* is the product of the Fatimid reworking of older data, it remains to define the nature and extent of this 'reworking': was there a pre-existing text that was subsequently glossed, with paragraphs added here and deleted there in order to 'smoothen' it? Or are we dealing with a re-composition of ancient texts to form a new unit, a new whole submitted to a coherent general idea? In short, did pre-Fatimid Ismailism already transmit an 'epistle on pilgrimage', or was it forged at the beginning of the Fatimid period by gathering pre-Fatimid exegeses relating to the theme of pilgrimage? The text appears to be made of a combination of traditions and various developments, which are ordered, however, with a clear concern for consistency. Yet, this is not enough to systematically distinguish the two editorial layers.

In any case, from a strictly formal point of view, we can note, as in Treatise III, the attribution of several exegeses to the 'Sage', which suffices to demonstrate that the treatise draws from pre-Fatimid sources. With regard to the Fatimid layer, Treatise V is the only one in the collection in which characters who are not protagonists of early

[152] W. Madelung, 'Das Imamat', pp. 52–53.

Islam are named. Indeed, the treatise evokes both the predecessor and the successor of ʿAbd Allāh al-Mahdī at the head of the *daʿwa*: respectively Muḥammad b. Aḥmad[153] and al-Qāʾim bi-Amr Allāh.[154] This makes it possible to date one of the layers of the treatise from the reign of al-Qāʾim, or that of al-Mahdī, since al-Qāʾim already played an important role in the Fatimid state shortly after its foundation, that is, two decades before succeeding his father in 322/934. This layer is in any case prior to the reform of the official genealogy of the Fatimids, since Muḥammad b. Aḥmad was then dismissed.[155]

Several other points of the treatise reveal a Fatimid origin. Among them, the refutation of antinomianism: just like the desire to keep a balance between *ghuluww* and *taqṣīr*,[156] the emphasis on the complementarity of *ẓāhir* and *bāṭin* undoubtedly represents the moderate and official Ismailism of the Fatimids, as illustrated by the works of al-Qāḍī al-Nuʿmān, Ḥamīd al-Dīn al-Kirmānī or al-Muʾayyad fīʾl-Dīn, for instance.

Also, the convoluted explanations of the notion of *ḥujja*, 'Proof', although they are difficult to untangle since they reflect several distinct historical phases and doctrines, nevertheless bear the marks of a Fatimid reworking. They are rooted in the pre-Fatimid period but have received a reinterpretation determined by new circumstances: most likely ʿAbd Allāh al-Mahdī's attempt to establish a dynastic succession following the repression of Abū ʿAbd Allāh al-Shīʿī's plot to overthrow the new caliph. The challenge, it seems, is to walk a fine line and maintain the eschatological horizon of the seventh Speaking-Prophet, while justifying a continuous Imamate at the same time. The appearance of ʿAbd Allāh al-Mahdī's had to be presented as a significant spiritual event, yet not an eschatological one. This nuanced doctrine may explain the vagaries and inaccuracies of the text, in particular for terms like that of *ḥujja*, which should be technical, but is at times inserted into a precise hierarchy, and defined elsewhere in a very general sense. However, there is a clear desire to alleviate the disappointment caused by a manifestation of the

---

[153] *Kashf* V, p. 99, § 16.

[154] *Kashf* V, p. 103, § 25.

[155] W. Madelung, 'Das Imamat', p. 100; A. Hamdani and F. De Blois, 'A Re-Examination of al-Mahdi's letter', pp. 186 ff.

[156] *Kashf* V, p. 120, § 52.

Imam that does not correspond to the eschatological expectations of the pre-Fatimid *daʿwa*. The passages rejecting antinomianism or those explaining that the 'Imam of the age' is not a Speaking-Prophet bringing a new Law,[157] thus seem to fit the context of the Kutāma messianic revolt following Abū ʿAbd Allāh al-Shīʿī's execution.

It is through this perspective that we should understand the developments on the continuity of 'God's Order', already encountered in Treatises I and III. As previously demonstrated, such doctrinal elaborations are designed to give the Fatimid Imamate a spiritual genealogy going back to Adam. This idea takes here the form of exegeses around the notion of 'House' or 'sacred station' (*maqām*), a place of divine manifestation of which the Kaʿba is the symbol.

Among the elements that seem to be related to a Fatimid context, one should also count the passages referring to the organization of the *daʿwa* and the dissensions within it. Thus, the cursed figures of Iblīs and Pharaoh are presented as former dignitaries of the *daʿwa* who then betrayed it.[158] We have seen before (in Treatises I and III) how the enemies of past Prophets and Imam are used by the Fatimids as archetypes of their own enemies. Complex prophetic narratives are produced to this effect, as attested in other works attributed to Jaʿfar b. Manṣūr al-Yaman's, particularly the *Sarāʾir al-nuṭaqāʾ*. In the latter book's chapter dedicated to Adam, for instance, this Prophet is presented as an initiate, while Iblīs is a high-ranking *daʿwa* member jealous of the favour bestowed on Adam by the Imam. According to D. Hollenberg, Adam is a veiled reference to the first Fatimid Imām ʿAbd Allāh al-Mahdī' and 'Iblīs is a *mathal* for Abū ʿAbd Allāh al-Shīʿī'.[159] The passages of Treatise V dealing with Pharaoh must likely be explained similarly as referring to a political context in which the *daʿwa* undergoes defections and betrayals. In fact, it is probable that they refer to the same crisis as the chapter on Adam in the *Sarāʾir*.

The long exegesis of 'obscenity, immorality and dispute' from which the 'believers', that is to say the 'Summoners', must refrain,[160] appears

157 *Kashf* V, p. 100, § 19; p. 103, § 26.

158 *Kashf* V, p. 125, § 60; p. 129, § 67.

159 See e.g. D. Hollenberg, *Beyond the Qurʾān*, p. 88, and pp. 85–91 for an overview of this chapter of the *Sarāʾir al-nuṭaqāʾ*.

160 *Kashf* V, pp. 121–125, §§ 54–59.

as a series of instructions to members of the *daʿwa*. These instructions could have been addressed to their recipients during the pre-Fatimid period of clandestinity, but several elements that can be identified as Fatimid are intertwined there: such is the case of the term *taqṣīr*, defined as the adherence to the exoteric without the esoteric, which is the usual 'esoteric' definition, as well as to the esoteric without the exoteric, which is more in line with the 'juridical' turn in Fatimid thought.[161] The insistence on the necessary coexistence of the esoteric and the exoteric is both a Fatimid mark and an element of anti-*ghulāt* polemics — maybe even anti-Qarmaṭian. This passage illustrates how various layers from different origins are superimposed on top of each other: it seems that, in the pre-Fatimid Ismaili tradition, there existed a particular exegesis of 'obscenity, immorality and dispute', as indicated by the attribution of interpretations of 'obscenity' and 'immorality' to the 'Sage'.[162] This pre-Fatimid exegesis would thus constitute an intermediate stage between, on the one hand, an earlier Shiʿi identification of these three elements with Abū Bakr, ʿUmar and ʿUthmān, in the vein of the pre-Buwayhid exegeses,[163] and, on the other hand, the interpretation found in Treatise V, which is the result of a Fatimid synthesis. While it is possible here to identify each of these layers, thanks to clues such as the explicit mention of 'Sage', the characteristic type of interpretations of the pre-Buwayhid 'school of exegesis', or the 'moderate' definition of *taqṣīr*, this is not always the case in the rest of the treatise: the developments on the respective roles of the Imam and the Proof are particularly difficult to make sense of.

Now, although the treatise in its final composition is Fatimid, it is also steeped in doctrines and concepts related to *ghuluww*. It indeed contains some elements of the technical vocabulary of the Nuṣayri or proto-Nuṣayri tradition, although they are not always the same as those found in Treatises I and III. Among the most notable terms, we must first mention the developments on the *ʿAyn*, which are part of ancient Shiʿi speculations on the *ʿAyn-Mīm-Sīn* triad. It seems that pre-Fatimid Ismailism held its own doctrines in this regard, since one of the

---

161 *Kashf* V, p. 122, § 55.

162 *Kashf* V, p. 121, § 54; p. 123, § 57.

163 See *Kashf* V, p. 125, § 59.

evocations of *ʿAyn* is attributed to the 'Sage'.[164] The *Fā'*, which here corresponds to Fāṭima and the *ḥujja*, is less common in Shiʿi literature, but it does appear in a work from the *ghulāt* tradition, the *Kitāb al-Ḥujub wa'l-anwār*, by Muḥammad b. Sinān.[165] The Treatise also mentions a 'veil' (*ḥijāb*) on numerous occasions, and thereby designates a person elected by God and endowed with a particular spiritual role;[166] this recalls the speculations of several currents linked to *ghuluww*. Twice, an exegesis evoking such a 'veil' is attributed to the 'Sage'.[167] Finally, the term *maʿnā* appears in a sense close to the one it assumes in Nuṣayrism; in one of these occurrences, the text mentions 'the one whose Meaning (*maʿnā*) has manifested'.[168] In another occurrence, the 'Meaning' is said to have a variety of attributes and names.[169] As for the 'names' themselves, they are the divine Names and they are identified with the dignitaries of the esoteric hierarchy, which recalls the speculations of the *ghulāt*, but also the Twelver Shiʿi *ḥadīth* collections.[170]

In summary, Treatise V presents a strange picture where the technical terms implying the most 'exaggerating' doctrines (in particular metempsychosis, which is the corollary of the speculations on the *maʿnā* and the plurality of names) stand alongside the firmest declarations of the complementarity of the *bāṭin* and the *ẓāhir*.

As mentioned before, the general theme of the treatise is apparently that of pilgrimage. Indeed, in spite of several digressions, the treatise is built around a series of verses in relation to pilgrimage. Yet, in addition to the digressions just mentioned, there are long passages that bear no connection to the theme of pilgrimage whatsoever. Among them, the passages dealing with Pharaoh and his people; the latter are identified

---

164 *Kashf* V, p. 102, § 23.

165 See M. Asatryan, *Controversies in Formative Shiʿi Islam*, p. 160, n. 113.

166 See esp, *Kashf* V, p. 98, § 14; p. 99, § 18; p. 103, § 26; p. 105, § 27; p. 106, § 29; p. 107, § 31; p. 110, § 34; p. 112, § 40; p. 115, § 44; p. 136, § 73; p. 137, § 76; p. 138, §§ 78–79; pp. 154–155, § 104.

167 *Kashf* V, p. 112, § 40; p. 138, § 79.

168 *Kashf* V, p. 108, § 31.

169 *Kashf* V, p. 139, § 80.

170 See e.g. M.A. Amir-Moezzi, *Guide divin*, pp. 115–116 (English trans.: *Divine Guide*, pp. 44–45); idem, *La Religion discrète*, p. 96 (English trans., *Spirituality of Shiʿi Islam*, p. 113), where 'the Names Most Beautiful' from Q. 7:180 are identified with the Imams (based on *Tafsīr al-ʿAyyāshī* and al-Kulaynī's *Rawḍat al-Kāfī*).

with the enemies of ʿAlī b. Abī Ṭālib, but, in fact, they refer to enemies of the *daʿwa* contemporary of the composition of the treatise.[171] Then follows an exegesis of Egypt as a symbol of the Imam and the esoteric knowledge,[172] the exegesis of Q. 3:7 on the clear and ambiguous verses.[173] The text then briefly returns to the 'Veils' and the 'Houses', before engaging in a quite long development which, again, has nothing to do with pilgrimage, but rather deals with the role and rank of the Prophets, the benefits for those who follow them, the necessity of their mediation, the necessity of the *bāṭin* as a fulfilment of the *ẓāhir*, and, finally, a warning against betraying the *amāna*. This passage also contains an explanation of three categories of sacred persons: the 'truthful ones', the 'witnesses' and the 'virtuous ones'.[174]

These long passages, which form nearly one third of the treatise, may seem off-topic at first sight, but they are in fact significant as they deliver the true intention of Treatise V. Indeed, the latter is not so much a simple exegesis of pilgrimage as such as it is a plea in favour of the representatives of the *daʿwa*, from the Summoners to the Speaking-Prophets, through the Completer Imams and the Gates. The whole treatise deals fundamentally with the question of *mediation*, which is moreover explicitly mentioned using the term *wasīṭa*, pl. *wasāʾiṭ* ('intermediary').[175] It is about the salvation one can hope to reach when embarking on Noah's Ark, in the Kaʿba, in the Imam and his representatives, who are the true 'houses' of God.

However, the theme of pilgrimage itself is not trivial, and it is no coincidence that this is where we find passages refuting antinomianism. Indeed, pilgrimage is one of the pillars of Islam, and its treatment in an Ismaili context falls within the debates on the esoteric meaning of the Islamic religious obligations; should these obligations be observed once one knows their secret meaning, the 'person' of which they are the symbols, or once the seventh Speaking-Prophet has appeared? The tendency of the *ghulāt* to interpret religious obligations as symbols of the Imam or other 'sacred stations' conceived of as intercessors, indeed paves the way to antinomian conceptions. Thus, the treatise rests on

---

171 *Kashf* V, pp. 125–127, §§ 60–63.
172 *Kashf* V, pp. 128–129, §§ 64–66.
173 *Kashf* V, pp. 130–133, §§ 68–70; pp. 134–135, § 72.
174 *Kashf* V, pp. 137–150, §§ 77–99.
175 *Kashf* V, pp. 106, § 29; pp. 143–144, § 89; p. 149, § 99.

an ambiguity insofar as it values the knowledge of the representatives of God (the Imam, the Proof and the subordinate ranks) as the true meaning of pilgrimage and the heart of the faith, and yet denies on several occasions the antinomian consequences that other groups have drawn from similar premises.

1. The Imam and his Proof, the *ʿAyn* and the *Fāʾ*

i. The Proof in Shiʿi Islam

All religious thought is confronted with the question of the divine presence in the human world. How is it possible to connect realities that are so radically and essentially different? Unless one is to renounce absolutely any kind of link between the two worlds, which would cut short the very possibility of religious experience, there must necessarily be some entity which plays the mediating role and thus connects what would otherwise be irreparably separated. It remains to define the nature of this mediation, the way in which God makes himself present to men. In a monotheistic context, and particularly in the case of Islam and its uncompromising monotheism, the problem is to preserve divine transcendence, while maintaining the possibility of a relationship between man and God. Indeed, if there is only transcendence, humanity is abandoned to its fate, and faith is but an abstraction. But on the other hand, if one conceives of the divine presence in an overly determined form, then divine transcendence is undermined.

A large part of the Shiʿi debates on the role and nature of the Imam are attempts to address this theological problem. As the mediation between God and humans, the Imam must have a touch of humanity, since the very concept of mediation is to provide the absolute transcendence of God with a 'face'. Yet, he must also be divine, for if he had absolutely nothing in common with divinity, he could in no way represent it in the eyes of men. The problem, therefore, is to define this divinity: in what capacity is the Imam divine? In what sense is he God? Several possibilities exist: a theology of incarnation, like in official Christianity, implies that God takes body. In Islam, however, the general tendency was to lean towards the notion of theophany:[176] the sacred

---

[176] On this concept in Islam, see S. Ayada, *L'Islam des théophanies, Une religion à l'épreuve de l'art* (Paris, 2010).

mediator between humans and God is a *manifestation* of the latter, rather than God Himself taking a physical form. As Henry Corbin states: 'If Imamology was confronted with the same problems as Christology, it always tended to find solutions which, although rejected by official Christianity, were nevertheless close to gnostic conceptions.'[177] The Imam is an epiphanic figure, which avoids both enclosing God in a incommunicable transcendence that does not *appear* (the Imam being a '*locus* of appearance', *maẓhar*), and identifying with God one who can only be a man, even if his humanity is sometimes endowed with supernatural characters or if it is considered only as a 'veil' (*ḥijāb*), a 'shirt' (*qamīs*) or an 'envelope' (*ghilāf*). The Islamic theological search for a balanced position between *tashbīh* and *taʿṭīl*, that is, between anthropomorphism and agnosticism, between attributing worldly qualities to God and preserving His absolute transcendence, thus has bearings on Imamology.

The problem of the divine and mediating nature of the Imam is related to the debates on the possibility or impossibility of seeing God, and on the meaning of such a 'vision'. In short, it is a question of knowing to what extent seeing the Imam is seeing God. The early Imami corpus, which echoes these debates, is full of ambiguous formulations identifying the vision of the Imam and that of God. This ambiguity was largely exploited by the *ghulāt*. Yet, in institutionalized Shiʿism, these formulations were generally attenuated by distinguishing the 'vision by the heart' from ocular vision.[178] Incidentally, one can wonder whether these attenuations were not added as a response to *ghulāt* claims.

---

[177] H. Corbin, *History of Islamic Philosophy* (London and New York, 2001), p. 48.

[178] On the 'vision by the heart' in Imami literature, see the chapter dedicated to this question in M.A. Amir-Moezzi, *Guide divin*, pp. 112–145 (English trans.: *Divine Guide*, pp. 44–55). See also idem, '*Al-Durr al-ṯamīn* attribué à Rağab al-Bursī', pp. 226–229; and for the modern period, idem, *La Religion discrète*, Ch. 10: 'Visions d'imâms en mystique duodécimaine moderne et contemporaine', pp. 253–276 (English trans.: *Spirituality of Shiʿi Islam*, Ch. 10: 'Visions of the Imams in Modern and Contemporary Twelver Mysticism', pp. 339–374). See also O. Ghaemmaghami, *Encounters with the Hidden Imam*, passim.

Whatever may be the case, there is a large literature on the vision of God and its nature, one of the most famous texts in this regard being ʿAlī's response to someone who asks him whether he has seen his Lord: 'Beware, I would not worship a God that I would not see', and specifies: 'Beware, eyes do not see Him, but it is the hearts which see Him, by the truths of faith.'[179] Elsewhere, a *ḥadīth* reported from Jaʿfar al-Ṣādiq poses the problem in a particularly clear manner: when asked about the possibility of seeing God on the Day of Resurrection, the Imam first answers that the believers had already seen Him before that, when He asked them, 'Am I not your Lord?', and they replied, 'Yes!'.[180] Then, after an hour of silence, the Imam declares: 'The believers already see Him in this world before the Day of Resurrection; don't you see Him right now?' 'May I serve you as a ransom, can I report this from you?' 'No, says the Imam, because if you do, a denier ignorant of the meaning of your words will deny them; he will take it for anthropomorphism (*tashbīh*) and will fall into unbelief (*kafara*). Vision with the heart is different from vision with the eye. Exalted be God beyond what the anthropomorphists and heretics attribute to him.'[181]

This *ḥadīth* is remarkable in several respects. It contains an ambiguous statement, namely that to see the Imam is to see God, which opens the way to anthropomorphic doctrines hardly compatible with 'orthodox' Islam. But, through an exegesis of this assertion, the shocking literal meaning is converted into a symbolic doctrine: the Imam is not physically God. It is therefore not the ocular vision which is vision of God, but the vision by the heart which is 'the vision of the Imam of Light of whom the ontological Imam is the archetype and the historical Imam is the manifestation available to the senses'.[182] Yet, despite this exegesis, which, in a way, saves the 'orthodoxy' of the literal formulation, *taqiyya* remains necessary, in case the letter was transmitted and

[179] Al-Kulaynī, *Uṣūl al-Kāfī, k. al-tawḥīd, bāb fī ibṭāl al-ru'ya*, pp. 97–98, no. 6; Ibn Bābawayh, *Kitāb al-Tawḥīd, bāb* 8, p. 109, no. 6. See also M.A. Amir-Moezzi, *Guide divin*, p. 123 (English trans.: *Divine Guide*, p. 47); idem, '*Al-Durr al-ṯamīn* attribué à Rağab al-Bursī', p. 228.

[180] With reference to Q. 7:172.

[181] Ibn Bābawayh, *Kitāb al-Tawḥīd, bāb* 8, p. 117, no. 20. See also M.A. Amir-Moezzi, *Guide divin*, p. 141, n. 277 (English trans.: *Divine Guide*, p. 180–181, n. 277).

[182] M.A. Amir-Moezzi, *Guide divin*, p. 143 (English trans.: *Divine Guide*, p. 55).

received without the spirit, the exoteric without the esoteric — or more exactly, the esoteric without the esoteric of the esoteric, since one can suppose that the statement 'to see the Imam is to see God' already constitutes an esoteric teaching. The danger mentioned in the *ḥadīth* is that of a misunderstanding leading to a rejection of Shiʿism and an accusation of infidelity. But there is another danger, which consists in accepting the literal meaning of the utterance and admitting the possibility of a vision of God with one's eyes, by identifying the latter and the Imam. It seems that certain *ghulāt* circles have adopted this view which was later rejected in Twelver Shiʿi teachings.

The *Kitāb al-Kashf* illustrates such a view in a discreet *ḥadīth* at the end of Treatise I which is also attributed to Jaʿfar al-Ṣādiq and yet states exactly the opposite of what is found in Twelver Shiʿi *ḥadīth* collections: there, the Imam declares indeed that the Prophet Muḥammad saw his Lord 'twice: with his heart (*bi-qalbihi*) and with his eyes (*bi-baṣarihi*)'.[183] This is reminiscent of texts like those of the Nuṣayri theologian al-Ṭabarānī who dedicates a chapter of his *Kitāb al-Maʿārif* to 'knowing God in [this] existence and through ocular vision' (*maʿrifat Allāh bi'l-wujūd wa'l-muʿāyana*). He reports several *ḥadīths* in which the Imam is expressly identified with God, without the theoretical precaution of the 'vision by the heart' found in the Twelver collections. Furthermore, the reference to the 'heart' is explicitly rejected in a *ḥadīth* attributed to Jaʿfar al-Ṣādiq: 'He who claims to know God by the imaginary representation of hearts (*tawahhum al-qulūb*) is a polytheist (*mushrik*).' In another *ḥadīth* attributed to the same Imam, we read: 'He who claims to have an invisible God has no Lord, and he who claims to have an unknowable God is from the party of the Satan of satans'; and further: 'He who seeks the God who is present in His creation (*man arāda Allāh al-mawjūd fī khalqi-hi*), and has neither opponent nor equal, I am Him'.[184] Another *hadīth* clearly links the need to know God by vision to the rejection of agnosticism: 'It is an attribute of the Sage to be worshiped as an apparent existing being (*mawjūd ẓāhir*), because the one who is absent is not seen, and it can then be doubted that he is anything at all.'[185] It is clear that, in al-Ṭabarānī's eyes, the

[183] *Kashf* I, p. 39, § 81.

[184] Al-Ṭabarānī, *Kitāb al-Maʿārif*, pp. 54–55.

[185] Ibid., p. 55.

matter is not so much to maintain a balance between presence and absence of God, between anthropomorphism and agnosticism, as it is to ensure the presence of God in this world — the term *wujūd* used several times refers to a earthly and manifested existence.

The *ḥadīth* in Treatise I thus relates to a tradition of *ghuluww* that it must have in common with Nuṣayrism. This deserves all the more attention as Q. 6:103: '*The eyes attain Him not*', appears twice in the collection, each time in *ḥadīths* affirming strict *tawḥīd* and found in Twelver Shiʿi *ḥadīth* collections.[186] The treatment of the problem of the vision of God in the *Kitāb al-Kashf*, that is, the fact that it contains contradictory data in this regard, is characteristic of the *Kashf*'s general oscillation between *ghulāt* doctrines (or traces of such doctrines) and more 'moderate' options.

It was necessary to provide an overview of these premises before approaching the meanings of the term *ḥujja*, 'Proof' or 'Argument', one of the titles of the Imam in early Shiʿism which expresses his mediating role. Indeed, this notion concentrates the problems which have just been mentioned since the *ḥujja* is the Proof of God, in the sense that he is a sign of God intended for men and by which God addresses them. But the *ḥujja* is also the one towards whom mankind turns to reach the inaccessible, the one who makes the invisible visible. The notion of *ḥujja* implies that of mediation. In the chapter entitled '*Kitāb al-ḥujja*' in his *Uṣūl al-Kāfī*, the traditionist al-Kulaynī reports a *ḥadīth* stating that 'the earth can never be empty of a *ḥujja*' and if there were only two people left on earth, one of them would be the *ḥujja*. The Imam is presented as a 'Pillar of the universe'.[187] In the previous chapter, dedicated to the oneness of God (*tawḥīd*), it appears that the corollary to the absolute transcendence of God is His accessibility through His Names and Attributes, which are manifested in the Imams. This is where the ontological necessity of the *ḥujja* in Shiʿi thought originates. The Proof is therefore always an intermediary who makes present an absent entity, who represents it, and who makes it knowable. According to a *ḥadīth* attributed to Ḥusayn, knowledge of God is 'for the people of every age, the knowledge of the imam to

---

[186] *Kashf* II, p. 44, § 14; IV, p. 90, § 3.

[187] On this chapter of the *Uṣūl al-Kāfī*, see the recent partial translation and commentary by M.A. Amir-Moezzi, *La Preuve de Dieu*.

whom they owe obedience';[188] the necessity of knowing the Imam is indeed predicated on his status as the Proof of God and his Messenger.

This general conception was shared by Ismailism throughout its history, and is actually at the core of the spiritual legitimacy of the *daʿwa* hierarchy. Indeed, devotion to the Imam is a consequence of pure *tawḥīd*: God is both hidden in essence and apparent through His Names, that is, the Imams. As we have seen here on numerous occasions, a great part of the Ismaili originality vis-à-vis other Shiʿi currents consists in the extension of the Imam's spiritual prestige to the members of the *daʿwa* — obviously, the higher the rank, the higher the prestige. Therefore, in Ismaili context, the corollary of *tawḥīd* is not only the representation of God by the Imam, but also the representation of the Imam by his representatives.[189]

ii. The Proof in Ismailism and in the *Kitāb al-Kashf*

While the term *ḥujja* in Twelver Shiʿi Islam is exclusively reserved for the Imam, it has been used with different meanings in other currents, like many other terms designating the Imam. When we briefly touched on Jābir b. Ḥayyān's *Kitāb al-Khamsīn*[190]and its list of dignitaries of the esoteric hierarchy, we found that there existed in ancient Shiʿism a common pool of doctrines and concepts from which different currents drew, each adapting a pre-existing vocabulary to its needs. This is the case for terms such as *ḥujja*, *bāb*, *naqīb*, *najīb*, etc. that we find at the beginning of Treatise I,[191] which, depending on the case, are either synonymous or designate different ranks. An example of the variety of meanings one term can convey was examined above when comparing the meaning of *yatīm* in different contexts. The term *ḥujja* as it appears in the *Kitāb al-Kashf* presents a similar polysemy, sometimes within the same treatise, or even within the same passage. While it may be applied to the Imam or the Legatee, it also designates at times the rank of the hierarchy immediately below that of the Imam.

---

188 Quoted in M.A. Amir-Moezz, *Guide divin*, p. 117 (English trans.: *Divine Guide*, p. 45).

189 See e.g. Ibrāhīm b. al-Ḥusayn al-Ḥāmidī, *Kanz al-walad*, Ch. 1, pp. 8–31, esp. p. 11: 'The affirmation of God's oneness is to know His ranks' (*tawḥīduhu maʿrifat ḥudūdihi*).

190 See commentary of *Kashf* III, pp. 277–279.

191 *Kashf* I, p. 3, § 3.

To provide an idea of the polysemy of this type of term within the *Kitāb al-Kashf*, one can consider the example of the word 'Gate' (*bāb*): it is sometimes cited as a degree of the esoteric hierarchy immediately below that of the Proof, and higher than that of the Summoners,[192] or at least as a hierarchical degree, even if its exact role and level are not clear.[193] But it also appears as a synonym for 'Proof', whether it applies to the Legatee,[194] or has a very general meaning based on the principle that 'it is not possible to access the house except through its door (*bāb*)';[195] in the latter sense, each level of the hierarchy is the Gate of a higher degree relative to a lower degree.[196] It can also be one of the names specifically given to the Proof of the Imam.[197]

M.G.S. Hodgson is therefore entirely justified in trying to unify the polysemy of the term *ḥujja* — comparable to that of *bāb*, except that its use has more decisive implications in the *Kashf* — in Ismailism, when explaining that it designates 'any figure in a religious hierarchy through whom an inaccessible higher figure became accessible to those below'.[198] This very broad definition makes it possible to account for the diversity of applications of the term in Ismaili texts. The author of Treatise III also seems to give it a definition of this type when, with regard to the Proofs, Salmān, al-Miqdād and Abū Dharr, he states:

> 'They are the Proofs of the Legatee, and the Legatee is the Proof of the Messenger, and the Messenger is the Proof of God; all these Proofs are for the worshippers, in this world and in the hereafter.'[199]

Thus, in the same sentence, the word 'Proof' appears in the technical sense which makes it a representative of the Imam, and in the general sense that the Proof is what makes an absent person present. In the

---

[192] *Kashf* I, p. 3, § 3; III, p. 87, § 71; V, p. 102, § 24; p. 120, § 51; p. 128, § 65; pp. 133–134, § 71; VI, p. 165, § 19; p. 167, § 23; p. 170, § 29; p. 178, § 41.

[193] *Kashf* I, p. 7, § 12; p. 9, § 18; p. 10, § 20; V, p. 112, § 40.

[194] *Kashf* I, p. 14, § 28; III, p. 67, § 32; p. 86, § 70; VI, p. 162, § 12.

[195] *Kashf* V, p. 105, § 27.

[196] *Kashf* I, p. 3, § 3; V, p. 109, § 33.

[197] *Kashf* III, p. 64, § 24; pp. 70–72, §§ 36–39; V, p. 120, § 52.

[198] M.G.S. Hodgson, 'Ḥu<u>dj</u>dja: in <u>Sh</u>ī'i terminology', *EI2*.

[199] *Kashf* III, p. 70, § 44.

'absence' of God, the Messenger is the Proof; in the absence of the Messenger, it is the Imam, and in the absence of the Imam, it is his representatives who are the Proofs in the technical sense of the term. As Hodgson says, the Proof is above all a sort of emanation from a higher authority; he is essentially an intermediary which draws his power and rank from a higher level from which he derives the knowledge and guidance with which he provides the lower levels. From there, several more precise meanings are possible.

W. Madelung points out three main meanings of *ḥujja* in Ismailism:[200] 1) the first is the one we discussed previously and corresponds to the classic Shiʿi conception: since the earth cannot be devoid of a Proof of God, this function is, in the absence of a Prophet, devolved to the Imam. Here, W. Madelung quotes the *Kitāb al-Kashf*: 'In every era, there is a Proof of God, whether it is a messenger Prophet or a chosen Imam.'[201] 2) According to the second meaning, *ḥujja* designates the degree of the esoteric hierarchy of the *daʿwa* that immediately follows that of the Imam; there are then several Proofs, each one in charge of a region — theoretically twelve *ḥujaj* for twelve provinces (sing. *jazīra*).[202] 3) Finally, according to the last sense, the *ḥujja* is the designated successor of the Speaking-Prophet or the Imam before the latter's death. 'Proof' thus refers to ʿAlī during the Prophet's lifetime, and upon the latter's death, ʿAlī becomes an Imam.

The *Kitāb al-Kashf* on several occasions mentions Proofs in the plural, within expressions such as 'the Proofs and the Summoners', 'the Proofs, the Gates and the Summoners',[203] or simply 'the Proofs' without situating them in relation to other hierarchical degrees.[204] In the singular, Proof refers either to the Legatee, that is to say to ʿAlī and

---

[200] W. Madelung, 'Das Imamat', pp. 61–63.

[201] *Kashf* I, p. 12, § 25.

[202] See esp. W. Madelung, 'Das Imamat', p. 63, n. 117. See also al-Nawbakhtī, *Firaq al-shīʿa*, p. 63; al-Qummī, *Maqālāt*, p. 84, where this division into twelve regions, each entrusted to a Proof, is attributed to the Qarmatians. This notion is widely found in Ismaili literature; see e.g. al-Sijistānī, *Tuḥfat al-mustajībīn*, p. 18.

[203] *Kashf* I, p. 25, § 54; p. 27, § 59; III, p. 87, § 71; V, p. 102, §24; pp. 119–120, § 51; p. 128, § 65; p. 154, § 106; VI, p. 171, §30; pp. 177–178, §§ 40–41.

[204] Esp. *Kashf* III, p. 53, § 2; p. 58, § 13; p. 70, § 36; V, p. 95, § 8; p. 118, § 48; p. 149, § 98; VI, p. 169, § 27; p. 170, § 29.

to his counterparts in previous cycles,[205] to any representative of God, without precise determination of his rank in the hierarchy,[206] or to the most important hierarchical degree after the Imam. If 'Proof' is understood in the technical sense, that is to say as the degree which immediately follows that of the Imam, there is apparently a distinction to be made according to whether the term is used in the plural or in the singular. In the latter case, we would be dealing with the person whom Treatise V calls the *Fā'*, that is, a Proof who is evidently superior to other Proofs.

The first mention of the Proof in Treatise V concerns Muḥammad b. Abī Bakr, 'Proof among the Proofs of the Prince of the Believers',[207] which corresponds to the idea that the Imam has several Proofs. A few pages further, a completely different vision is set out: the Proof is assimilated to Eve, Noah's Ark, the Kaʿba, Joshua, and Mary, Jesus's mother,[208] who, although this is not explicitly stated and these elements are not presented in this order, must respectively be the Proofs of Adam, Noah, Abraham, Moses and Jesus.

First, it should be noted that there is some discrepancy between some of the Proofs mentioned here and elsewhere in the collection: in Treatise I, it was Seth who was the Proof of Adam,[209] while Shem, Ishmael, Joshua and Simon were respectively the 'Gates' and the 'Proofs' of Noah, Abraham, Moses and Jesus. Yet, previously, Aaron had been identified as the Legatee of Moses.[210] Having noted this difference, H. Halm proposed a table in which he noted for each Speaking-prophet his enemy, his Legatee and his Proof, based on data from Treatise I.[211] However, such a table rests on the idea that Treatise I presents a coherent and unified doctrine, and that the passage where Aaron is the Legatee of Moses belongs to the same layer as the one

205 *Kashf* I, p. 14, § 29; II p. 46, § 17; III, p. 55, § 7; p. 60, § 18; p. 75, § 44; V, p. 125, § 59.

206 *Kashf* V, p. 137, § 76, and p. 150, § 100, where the seventh Speaking-Prophet is also a Proof.

207 *Kashf* V, p. 95, § 8.

208 *Kashf* V, pp. 97–98, §§ 12–14.

209 *Kashf* I, p. 14, § 28.

210 *Kashf* I, p. 12, § 25.

211 H. Halm, *Kosmologie*, pp. 27–28.

where Joshua is his Proof. Yet, if this were really the case, and if it were necessary to differentiate the Legatee from the Proof of the Speaking-Prophet in Treatise I, Ishmael or Simon would not appear there both as Proofs and as Legatees.[212] The distinction between Proof and Legatee therefore probably does not need to be in Treatise I; on the other hand, it does makes sense in Treatise V and in its strange enumeration of Proofs.

There, it is said in particular that 'the knowledge of the Staff to which Moses resorted' came to him from Joshua. Mary, for her part, was 'pointing toward [Jesus] before anyone else '.[213] Should we understand that the Proof precedes the Speaking-Prophet and that the latter takes part of his investiture from his Proof? This aspect seems present, but it is not the main one, because Eve does not precede Adam, nor the Ark, Noah. In addition, the text then adds that the Proof in question corresponds, at the time of the 'sixth Adam', Muḥammad, to his daughter Fāṭima, the latter being the 'veil' of her father;[214] obviously, Fāṭima does not precede her father either. It therefore seems that the role of the Proof is mainly a mediating one: 'Through the Proof, you are connected to the sublime *'Ayn*, who is the Imam.'[215]

However, the text reveals an inconsistency. Indeed, the 'sublime *Fā*'', which designates Fāṭima, has the role of 'breathing spirit' into people to 'renew' them.[216] As the rest of the text indicates, this breathed life is of course an allusion to the Christic power to give life, and it is here interpreted as 'projecting the esoteric knowledge onto the exoteric knowledge' and 'giving life to those who are dead from ignorance'. But these explanations come when the text is speaking of 'Alī, and no longer of Fāṭima. It is likely that this inconsistency is due to the interpenetration of two separate layers. It may be suspected that the entire passage on the Ka'ba and the analogous realities in different eras belongs to an ancient layer, perhaps stemming from the *ghulāt* — as suggested by the use of the first letter of Fāṭima's name, the *Fā*',

[212] *Kashf* I, pp. 12, 14, §§ 25, 28.

[213] *Kashf* V, p. 97, §§ 12–13.

[214] *Kashf* V, pp. 97–98, § 14.

[215] *Kashf* V, p. 97, § 13.

[216] *Kashf* V, p. 98, § 14.

to make it a kind of archetype.[217] On the other hand, the idea that 'any body without spirit is dead, [just as] any work that is not accompanied by knowledge is a body without spirit',[218] rests on well-attested Ismaili symbolism.[219]

The paragraph ends with the sentence: 'The Proof, in our era, is our master (*sayyid*) and our shaykh, and the master of every believer, man and woman.'[220] It is therefore a question of attributing to this Proof, visibly the head of the *daʿwa*, the ability to 'resurrect the dead of ignorance' by the esoteric knowledge of which he is the master. What follows, however, would seem to belong to a later layer of the text, as W. Madelung suggests.[221] This is the famous passage concerning the predecessor of ʿAbd Allāh al-Mahdī:

> 'We find an illustration of this in Imam Muḥammad b. Aḥmad's time — may his peace be upon us — since he started by concealing his identity in order to preserve his secret from hypocrites (*li'l-taqiyya min al-munāfiqīn*). He presented himself as the Proof who guides towards the Imam, while, in fact, he was guiding towards himself. No one knew this, except a small number among the elite of his Summoners.'[222]

We witness here an attempt to put an ancient doctrine at the service of the justification of the Imamate of Salamiyya, and therefore, at the service of the legitimacy of ʿAbd Allāh al-Mahdī. As Madelung states, and as we recalled earlier, this gloss must be dated to the beginnings of the Fatimid period, at a time when Muḥammad b. Aḥmad was still

---

[217] As noted above, p. 388, the *Fāʾ* appears in at least one text of the *ghulāt* tradition, the *Kitāb al-Ḥujub wa'l-anwār* by Muḥammad b. Sinān; see M. Asatryan, *Controversies in Formative Shiʿi Islam*, p. 160, n. 113. The *Fāʾ* corresponds there to one of the five prayers, just like the 'Veil' (Muḥammad), Ḥasan, Ḥusayn and Muḥassin. On Muḥassin, the child Fāṭima allegedly bore and lost after ʿUmar hit her, see L. Massignon, 'Al-Muḥassin b. ʿAlī', *EI2*; H. Halm, *Die islamische Gnosis*, p. 387, n. 689; M. Asatryan, 'Mok̲ammesa', *EIr*.

[218] *Kashf* V, p. 98, § 15.

[219] See e.g. Ibn Ḥawshab, *Kitāb al-Rushd wa'l-hidāya*, p. 205 (English trans., p. 73), where the 'death of ignorance' (*mawt al-juhl*) is also mentioned.

[220] *Kashf* V, pp. 98–99, § 16.

[221] W. Madelung, 'Das Imamat', p. 55.

[222] *Kashf* V, p. 99, § 16.

counted in the lineage of the hidden Imams of Salamiyya: it corresponds indeed to the statements of ʿAbd Allāh al-Mahdī in his letter to the Ismaili community of Yemen, where he explains that his predecessor at the head of the *daʿwa* was his uncle and that his name was Muḥammad b. Aḥmad.[223] The latter would then be removed from the list of the hidden Imams.

The inconsistencies which then arise are largely due to such untimely attempts to reconfigure older texts in favour of the Fatimid Imam. Thus, the doctrine of the *Fā'* and the *ʿAyn* — two distinct notions which, in the pre-Fatimid *daʿwa*, referred to the duality of the Proof and the one he represented, the expected hidden Imam — is used to justify the possibility that the Proof can become an Imam, that is to say to justify ʿAbd Allāh al-Mahdī's claim to be the Imam himself, and not only a Proof operating in the name of an Imam to come. As we will see, it may also have been used to justify the Imamate of ʿAbd Allāh al-Mahdī's successor, who was considered a Proof before his access to power (i.e. during his father's lifetime).

The following pages still seem to mix elements from different periods. Indeed, after the gloss on Muḥammad b. Aḥmad, the text returns to the Proof and to the Kaʿba. On the one hand, the Proof is apparently identified with the silent Imam, and therefore is not a degree distinct from that of the Imam. The silent Imam is presented as the 'Master of the esoteric' who prepares the coming of the Speaking-Prophet, and he is called the 'veil' and the 'Proof':[224] 'Whoever connects with the Imam, Master of the Esoteric, will be safe from the Speaking-Prophet's sword and vengeance when he appears.'[225] The silent Imam is thus turned towards the Speaking-Prophet to come, but he also leads 'towards the Law of the Speaking-Prophet who preceded him'.[226] This is what the concept of *Fā'* — which had previously been presented as a 'veil' — would refer to.

---

[223] H.F. Hamdani, *On the Genealogy of Fatimid Caliphs*, pp. 10–11 of the Arabic text; A. Hamdani and F. De Blois, 'A Re-examination of al-Mahdī's Letter', p. 176; W. Madelung, 'Das Imamat', pp. 55–56.

[224] *Kashf* V, p. 99, § 18.

[225] Ibid.

[226] *Kashf* V, p. 100, § 19.

On the other hand, the text explains that God 'made the Proof an Imam who applies the Law and indicates the Speaking-Prophet', then that 'the Speaking-Prophet is a silent Imam before becoming a Speaking Imam'.[227] How are we to understand that the Imam who applies the *sharī'a* 'indicates the Speaking-Prophet'? Does this mean that the role of the Proof, identified with the silent Imam, is to represent the Law of the previous Speaking-Prophet? The other question that arises when reading these two lines is due to their apparent contradiction: if the Imam indicates the Speaking-Prophet, then they must be two distinct characters. Yet, 'the Speaking-Prophet is a silent Imam before becoming a Speaking Imam' implies that the silent Imam and the Speaking-Prophet are the same person. Should we understand that the term 'Imam' in fact applies to two different persons? We would thus have on the one hand, 'the Imam who applies the Law and indicates the Speaking-Prophet', and, on the other hand, the 'silent Imam' who is to become the Speaking-Prophet. This is the most logical explanation, but the text does not clearly express this idea. In any case, it seems to justify two successive changes in rank: from Proof to Imam, and from Imam to Speaking-Prophet.

As for the *Fā'*, it is identified with the silent Imam who 'does not speak a new Law'.[228] With reference to the grammatical conjunction *fa-*, 'then' or 'so', in the sentence: 'God commands me (*ya'murunī*), *and so*, I act', the *Fā'* is presented as the dignitary who obeys the divine order, as well as the one to whom obedience is due.

There then follows a passage, inserted here and devoted to 'creation anew' (*al-khalq al-jadīd*) — a concept with eminently eschatological resonances, but defined here in the continuity of the previous developments on the resurrection of the 'dead of ignorance' through 'knowledge of the esoteric'. The figure of Abū Dharr reappears[229] and is presented as a Proof who 'inseminates' (*dhara'a*) the world, using the same pun on his name as in Treatise III.[230] The approach here seems to be the same as in the passage from Treatise III where Salmān, al-Miqdād and Abū Dharr were presented as Proofs; it is a question of

---

[227] *Kashf* V, p. 99, § 17.

[228] *Kashf* V, p. 100, § 19.

[229] *Kashf* V, p. 100, § 22.

[230] *Kashf* III, p. 70, § 38.

extending their prestige to whoever, at the time of the composition of the text, presented himself as a Proof. Here, it is no longer question of the Imam or the Speaking-Prophet. This passage should most probably be dated from the pre-Fatimid period, that is, when the management of the *daʿwa* was devolved to the Proof. But again, the probable pre-Fatimid origin of this passage does not prevent it from having been re-used in Fatimid context.

'The Call (aḏhān) to the Great Pilgrimage' is then interpreted as that of the Speaking-Prophet,[231] which must be understood as an allusion to the Imam and the *daʿwa*'s role as a 'muezzin', an announcer of the coming of the Speaking-Prophet, as is more fully explained a few pages later. The verse: *'Proclaim (adhdhin) the pilgrimage among mankind'*, means: 'Establish an Imam amongst the people so that he summons to the Speaking-Prophet.'[232] The entire passage thus deals with the role of the *daʿwa* in preparing the coming of the Speaking-Prophet.

The 'Great Pilgrimage', however, is also identified with the 'sublime *ʿAyn*': 'The *ʿAyn* is the sublime end, the End of all ends. This is an indication about the Creator who created all things by His Order; He originated all things, and to His Order all things return.'[233] While the *ʿAyn* had previously[234] been identified with the Imam, it seems that here it designates less a person than a principle. This principle is, moreover, the one who 'manifests Himself to His Friends in seventy sacred forms',[235] which correspond to the various Messengers, Imams and dignitaries of the Order of God, that is to say, to the 'Houses', a theme discussed at length afterwards.[236] Behind this meaning of *ʿAyn* looms the idea of the appearance of a single 'Meaning' (*maʿnā*) under a multiplicity of forms, as is explicitly affirmed further on in the treatise: 'While the attributes and the names may differ, the meaning (*al-maʿnā*) upon which they rest is one.'[237] And elsewhere, in a passage

---

[231] *Kashf* V, pp. 101–102, § 23.
[232] *Kashf* V, pp. 110–111, § 36.
[233] *Kashf* V, p. 102, § 23.
[234] *Kashf* V, p. 97, § 13.
[235] *Kashf* V, p. 102, § 24.
[236] *Kashf* V, pp. 104–110, §§ 27–35.
[237] *Kashf* V, p. 139, § 80.

that we have already pointed out: 'Each *qā'im* in his era is the name by which God is called in this era',[238] the Names of God being 'the guided Imams and the Messengers He has chosen'. The *Kitāb al-Kashf* here seems dependent on a conception of the *'Ayn* comparable to the one found in Nuṣayrism, at least insofar as the *'Ayn* is a *ma'nā* which manifests in several forms.

It may seem that, in attempting to identify the respective roles of the pre-Fatimid Imam, 'Abd Allāh al-Mahdī and his successor al-Qā'im bi-Amr Allāh, we are digressing here from what concerns the relationship between the Proof, the Imam and the Speaking-Prophet. In fact, it is the data relating to the beginnings of the history of the Fatimid dynasty which divert part of the elements composing the text from their original concerns and meanings. The author of the treatise thus grafted onto the theory of the *'Ayn* and the *Fā'* considerations aimed at legitimising the Fatimid Caliphate. Initially, the *Fā'* must therefore have been a Proof, a 'veil' — in the sense indicated above, which assimilates it to Noah's Ark, Joshua, Mary and Fāṭima — beckoning to the *'Ayn*, that is, towards the Resurrector and seventh Speaking-Prophet, as this passage indicates:

> '[The age of the seventh Speaking-Prophet] is the Seal of ages; he is the most sublime of [God's] agents (*asbāb*) and the mightiest, the sublime *'Ayn*. The *'Ayn* is mentioned here because it is the End of all ends. Through [the *'Ayn*] the Creator of glorious might is indicated — the attributes of creation do not reach Him.'[239]

Although the *'Ayn* appears through all the representatives of God, it appears to the highest degree in the last Speaking-Prophet, who is the end point of the succession of forms taken on by the *'Ayn*. The duality of the *Fā'* and the *'Ayn* as developed in pre-Fatimid Ismailism probably drew from the concepts which, in Nuṣayrism, would give birth to the tripartition *ḥijāb/ism/ma'nā*, Veil/Name/Meaning, except that pre-Fatimid Ismailism seems to have fused the *ḥijāb* and the *ism* into a single concept, that of the *Fā'*. After the advent of the Fatimids, the *'Ayn* and the *Fā'* were apparently identified with the Imam and the Proof, respectively, before seemingly being abandoned, since these

---

[238] *Kashf* V, p. 109, § 33.

[239] *Kashf* V, p. 103, § 26.

concepts are not to be found elsewhere in Fatimid literature, and reappear only in Ṭayyibī works.[240]

The identity of the historical persons to whom these terms have been applied remains to be determined. The commentaries on the 'Call to the Great Pilgrimage' from Q. 9:3, provide guidance in this regard. Insofar as the Great Pilgrimage had been identified with the *ʿAyn*,[241] we can consider that the Call corresponds to the *Fāʾ*. After the interlude on the seventy forms,[242] the text returns to Q. 9:3:

> 'The Call is an indication of the one who makes people know their term and their direction; he is the glorified Imam in his era, and he is Muḥammad, our lord and master, the Bearer of the sword (*al-qāʾim biʾl-sayf*) — peace be upon him –, and the Speaker (*nāṭiq*), for his era and his age, of the exoteric Summons to the Truth; he is the Bearer of the sword (*al-qāʾim biʾ l-sayf*) of the Summons. This attribute corresponds to the Imam al-Qāʾim bi-Amr Allāh Muḥammad Abū al-Qāsim — may God's blessings be upon him.'[243]

According to W. Madelung,[244] followed in this by H. Halm,[245] this passage was originally written with reference to Muḥammad b. Aḥmad (here: 'Muḥammad the Bearer of the Sword'), who had hoped to declare himself Imam but could not complete his project; it was therefore his nephew, ʿAbd Allāh al-Mahdī, who managed to do so. The part that mentions al-Qāʾim bi-Amr Allāh would thus be a late Fatimid gloss, seeking to update the identification of 'the Speaker of the exoteric Summons to the Truth'. It is noteworthy that the term *nāṭiq*, 'Speaking-Prophet', seems to have a here a meaning less strict than the one it usually bears in Ismaili prophetology; like the expression *al-qāʾim biʾl-sayf*,[246] it seems stripped of its eschatological meaning.

---

[240] See e.g. Ibrāhīm b. al-Ḥusayn al-Ḥāmidī, *Kanz al-walad*, pp. 179, 189, 195, 197; Idrīs ʿImād al-Dīn, *Zahr al-maʿānī*, p. 216, and esp. p. 217, where the passage of *Kashf* V, pp. 103–104, §§ 26–27, mentioning the sublime *ʿAyn* is quoted, and thus glossed: 'The sublime *ʿAyn* is the First Intellect.'

[241] *Kashf* V, p. 102, § 23.

[242] *Kashf* V, p. 102–103, § 24.

[243] *Kashf* V, p. 103, § 25.

[244] W. Madelung, 'Das Imamat', pp. 56–57.

[245] H. Halm, *Kosmologie*, pp. 26, 37.

[246] See commentary of *Kashf* III, pp. 293–298.

The Speaking-Prophet is no longer the one who brings a new *sharīʿa*, but simply the Imam who openly appears as such, and is therefore no longer 'silent'. He is the one who takes charge, not only of the dissemination of esoteric knowledge to initiates, but also of 'the exoteric Summons'. This less strict sense of *nāṭiq* could thus be in line with the passage discussed above according to which 'the Speaking-Prophet is a silent Imam before becoming a Speaking Imam'.[247]

It is only about fifteen pages further that a long passage[248] allows us to better understand the actual meaning of the *ʿAyn* and the *Fā'*, within an interpretation of Q. 2:197: '*The pilgrimage is in months well-known*'. The 'months well-known' are first identified with the Proofs, while the pilgrimage is 'the knowledge of the Imam in every era and every age'.[249] The use of the term 'Proof' in the plural is here in line with the notion that Proofs are representatives of the Imam in the provinces. On the following page, however, the 'months well-known (...) correspond to the twelve zodiac signs; they are the twelve chiefs (*naqīb*)',[250] while the term *ḥujja* is used in a completely different sense since the text speaks of 'the Supreme Proof (*al-ḥujja al-kubrā*) who is next to [hold] the sacred station of the Imamate, after the Imam of his era — peace be upon him. He is the one designated as the sublime *Fā*".[251] It is likely that there are two layers here, corresponding to the two definitions of 'months well-known', and therefore to the two definitions of *ḥujja*.

The second layer, which makes the *ḥujja* the successor of the Imam, was noted by W. Madelung who refers to this passage from the *Kashf*.[252] He also refers to two other passages, taken from Treatise III:

> "Alī b. Abī Ṭālib was Muḥammad's Proof, and an Imam to his community after [Muḥammad's death]. With ʿAlī is the esoteric aspect of Muḥammad's religion, just as with every Proof is the esoteric aspect of the knowledge of the Imam of his age.'[253]

[247] *Kashf* V, p. 99, § 17.
[248] *Kashf* V, pp. 117– 121, §§ 47–53.
[249] *Kashf* V, p. 118, § 47.
[250] *Kashf* V, p. 119, § 50.
[251] Ibid.
[252] W. Madelung, 'Das Imamat', p. 62.
[253] *Kashf* III, p. 55, § 7.

> 'The Proof is the Master of the esoteric (*ṣāḥib al-bāṭin*); therefore, they do not urge to feed the Proof, which is the exegesis (*ta'wīl*).[254] By this, Muḥammad – may God bless him – indicated ʿAlī, who was his Proof in his era. And the Proof of a given Imam is the Master of exegesis (*ṣāḥib al-ta'wīl*) in his era.'[255]

In supporting the idea that the *ḥujja* is the name of the Imam designated for succession before the death of his predecessor, the first passage is more convincing than the second. And both remain too allusive to positively ground this definition of the Proof. In fact, apart from the passage of Treatise V I just mentioned, the most convincing passage that W. Madelung points out in this regard is taken from the *Kitāb al-Rushd wa'l-hidāya*:

> 'The Proof becomes an Imam after his Imam, and before the Imam who succeeds him. The Imam who succeeds him is his Proof before becoming an Imam in turn.'[256]

Insofar as it is generally accepted that this work is from the pre-Fatimid period, the passages from the *Kitāb al-Kashf* with a similar orientation must be so as well. Another sentence from the same passage of Treatise V clearly implies that the Proof is the heir to the Imamate, when it is said that the Proof is the one whom 'the Book', i.e. the Imam, 'invites'.[257] The rest of the text puts the Proof in charge of the organization and command of the *daʿwa*: he is thus 'the one who arranges the Gates and the Summoners, and he is the gatherer of all the ranks. All [ranks] beneath him refer to him.'[258] He is also the necessary intermediary between the lower levels and the Imam: 'One cannot access the rank of the Imam unless it is through that of the Proof.'[259]

---

[254] While the Qur'anic verse means that the poor person is not fed, the interpretation provided here understands the genitive in the opposite way: the feeding (*ṭaʿām*) is not what is given to the *miskīn*, but what the latter provides.

[255] *Kashf* III, p. 60, § 18.

[256] Ibn Ḥawshab, *Kitāb al-Rushd wa'l-hidāya*, p. 201 (English trans., p. 69).

[257] *Kashf* V, p. 119, § 51.

[258] *Kashf* V, p. 120, § 51.

[259] Ibid.

The importance of the Proof in these lines is compatible with the pre-Fatimid conception of the *daʿwa*, where the Proof was the supreme authority. However, it can be suspected that, in the *Kashf*, these lines actually apply to al-Qāʾim bi-Amr Allāh. In our commentary on Treatise III, we noted the passage stating that 'the Imam guides to the Imam after him (. . .) It is in this sense that the Imams guide on a '*straight Way*'; this means that each one of them guides [people] to an Imam he establishes'.[260] Such emphasis put on the succession of Imams, rather than on the representation of the Imam by the Proof, better matches the situation of the Fatimid Imam during the reign of ʿAbd Allāh al-Mahdī, after the latter officially appointed the future al-Qāʾim bi-Amr Allāh as his successor and entrusted him with the highest responsibilities of the state. This would also explain why we move from the 'twelve Proofs' to the 'twelve Governors', the title of Proof then being mainly, if not exclusively, used to designate the new strongman of the Fatimid State.

The investiture of al-Qāʾim is said to have taken place during the year 912, in the wake of a revolt that he was charged to suppress. The investiture of a successor did not go without reservations; it was indeed a delicate matter for the Mahdī, an eschatological figure, to lay the foundations of a dynastic power. It is thus possible that these political events prompted the author of Treatise V to remobilise — to the benefit of another kind of Proof — the old pre-Fatimid texts that valued the notion of a Proof representing a hidden and awaited Imam, thus taking advantage of the homonymy of two very different realities. As we will see further, other elements of the treatise seem to indicate that the Fatimid composition of Treatise V is to be dated from this key moment of the early Fatimid caliphate

2. The rejection of antinomianism

The Ismaili application of the idea that 'religion is knowledge of men' (*al-dīn maʿrifat al-rijāl*),[261] which goes hand in hand with the 'personalized commentary', consists in extending this question of

[260] *Kashf* V, p. 119, § 49.

[261] See above, pp. 14 ff.

persons to the dignitaries of its esoteric hierarchy. While the classic Shiʿi personalized commentaries identify Qurʾanic elements with ʿAlī b. Abī Ṭālib and other protagonists from the early days of Islam, be they friends or enemies of ʿAlī, the *Kashf* provides several illustrations of the fact that these elements are understood as references to the Imam in general — and not only to ʿAlī — as well as to Proofs, Summoners, and other ranks of the *daʿwa* hierarchy. The Ismailism of the *Kitāb al-Kashf* is here dependent on the Shiʿi tradition in the broad sense, but also on the tradition of the *ghulāt* who claimed special status for certain disciples of the Imams as 'Gates' (*abwāb*). This 'knowledge of persons', which was at the heart of *ghulāt* doctrines, was closely connected to allegorical interpretations of religious prescriptions, and therefore to the question of antinomianism. Indeed, in Jaʿfar al-Ṣādiq's letter where we find the statement that 'religion is knowledge of men', Jaʿfar emphasizes that although religion is indeed such a personalized knowledge, this should not prompt the faithful to abandon the performance of the Islamic rituals. It is noteworthy that this very letter was partially reproduced by al-Qāḍī al-Nuʿmān in a chapter of his *Daʿāʾim al-Islām* dedicated to the refutation of the the *ghulāt* and their antinomianism.[262] This illustrates the fact that antinomianism was considered an immediate threat to Fatimid rule, especially since al-Qāḍī al-Nuʿmān mentions in this chapter the execution of several antinomian members of the *daʿwa* by the first Fatimid caliph.[263]

According to heresiological accounts, the Khaṭṭābiyya professed licentious teachings, substituting 'knowledge of the persons' for the actual observance of religious prescriptions that symbolise them. It could be argued that heresiological data should be taken with caution, but they are at least partially confirmed by several *ghulāt* texts. It is likely that heresiologists have exaggerated the antinomianism of certain sects, systematically deducing it from their allegorical interpretation of the works. Indeed, making compulsory prayer a symbol of the Imam must not necessarily lead one to abandon the

[262] Compare al-Ṣaffār al-Qummī, *Baṣāʾir al-darajāt*, pp. 939–941, 945–946, and al-Qāḍī al-Nuʿmān, *Daʿāʾim al-Islām*, vol. 1, pp. 51–53 (English trans.: *The Pillars of Islam*, vol. 1, pp. 67–70).

[263] Al-Qāḍī al-Nuʿmān, *Daʿāʾim al-Islām*, vol. 1, p. 54 (English trans.: *The Pillars of Islam*, vol. 1, pp. 71–72).

actual performance of prayer, or to consider that once the Imam is known, one could freely perform 'immoral' acts, as the heresiologists claim. It is true that the *Kitāb al-Haft wa'l-aẓilla*, for example, affirms that 'he who knows this esoteric is exempt from the accomplishment of the exoteric' (*saqaṭa ʿanhu ʿamal al-ẓāhir*).[264] But it is unclear how far this exemption could go, and to what extent it necessarily went hand in hand with allegorical interpretation.

In any case, it is clear that *ghulāt* sources are teeming with this type of esoteric interpretation of the religious prescriptions of Islam such as prayer, almsgiving, fasting and pilgrimage. The *Kitāb al-Haft wa'l-aẓilla* thus affirms that: 'Prayer is the Prince of the Believers, and almsgiving is knowing him' — statements that are also found in Treatise I of the *Kashf* where prayer corresponds to the Imam, and almsgiving is interpreted as the acknowledgement of the Imam, since to pay the *zakāt* to the legitimate Imam is to recognise him as such.[265] In other *ghulāt* texts, the five daily prayers correspond to Muḥammad, Fāṭir (= Fāṭima), Ḥasan, Ḥusayn and Muḥsin.[266] We previously recalled that the Nuṣayrī author al-Ṭabarānī identified each day of the month of Ramadan with a person (*shakhṣ*) in his *Kitāb al-maʿārif*,[267] but he also breaks down the other Islamic prescriptions to various parts or stages, identifying each one with a 'person'. As heir to the literature of the *ghulāt*, Nuṣayri literature presents many examples of this type of exegesis.[268]

Pilgrimage is no exception. While the matter is never openly tackled, it is nevertheless possible to argue that the treatment of this theme in Treatise V, centred on the Imam and the Houses, opens up the possibility of an exclusively 'personalized' interpretation of the

---

[264] Mufaḍḍal al-Juʿfī, *Kitāb al-Haft wa'l-aẓilla*, Ch. 13, p. 45.

[265] On prayer, see *Kashf* I p. 21, § 45: 'Prayer is Ḥusayn and the Imams from his progeny'; *Kashf* I p. 28, § 60: 'Prayer is obedience to the Prince of the Believers and the Imams God has chosen among his sons.' On almsgiving, (*zakāt*), see *Kashf* I p. 29, § 62, where the expression '*those who pay not the alms*' from Q. 41:6 is applied to whomever 'conveys the alms to the one appointed by his Satan and claims to be an Imam from God'.

[266] See M. Asatryan, *Controversies in Formative Shiʿi Islam*, pp. 95, 161.

[267] Al-Ṭabarānī, *Kitāb al-Maʿārif*, pp. 67–69.

[268] For an overview of Nuṣayri interpretations of Islamic religious duties, see Y. Friedman, *The Nuṣayrīs-ʿAlawīs*, pp. 130–152.

pilgrimage to Mecca. It is therefore probably not by chance that the typically Fatimid stance regarding the necessity of keeping esotericism and exotericism together is nowhere stressed as strongly as it is in this treatise. Here again, the *ghulāt* literature provides us with numerous examples of a strictly esoteric interpretation of the pilgrimage: in the chapter devoted to it by al-Ṭabarānī in his *Kitāb al-Maʿārif*, the various stages and elements of the pilgrimage are identified with several characters.[269] This method was already found in a fragment from a certain *Kitāb al-Ashkhāṣ* cited by Ḥasan al-Ḥarrānī, a Nuṣayri author of the 11th century.[270] Other Nuṣayri texts go so far as to take the plunge, clearly opposing esoteric interpretation to exoteric practice; the pilgrimage not only has an esoteric meaning and actually refers to persons, but the actual pilgrimage to Mecca is condemned as an idolatrous practice.[271]

There is no such thing in Treatise V of the *Kashf*. One paragraph states that pilgrimage has one exoteric and two esoteric meanings,[272] but these levels of interpretation are not opposed and nowhere is the exoteric fulfilment of pilgrimage rejected. Two passages in the treatise in fact address the issue of antinomianism, only to reject it.

---

[269] Al-Ṭabarānī, *Kitāb al-Maʿārif*, pp. 70–78. It is noteworthy that the *maqām Ibrāhīm* is identified with Muḥammad b. Abī Bakr; see ibid., p. 71. This seems to imply that within the *ghulāt* tradition from which stem both al-Ṭabarānī and *Kashf* V, Muḥammad b. Abī Bakr holds a special status in speculations on the Kaʿba and is portrayed as analogous to Abraham. On him, see index s.n., and pp. 90–91, n. 67.

[270] See. M. Asatryan, *Controversies in Formative Shiʿi Islam*, pp. 94, 161. On the *Kitāb al-Ashkhāṣ*, dedicated to the esoteric interpretation of religious duties and their identification with 'persons' (*ashkhāṣ*), see ibid., pp. 93–96.

[271] See Y. Friedman, *The Nuṣayrīs-ʿAlawīs*, pp. 140–141. See also D. De Smet, *Épîtres sacrées des Druzes*, epistle 6, pp. 174–177: the Druze doctrine rejects both the exoteric and the esoteric aspects of religions as taught in Ismaili circles. In this epistle Ḥamza reviews religious prescriptions, refuting both their exoteric and esoteric meanings, and asserts that 'whatever these people do while performing the rites of pilgrimage is a kind of madness'. 'The true meaning of pilgrimage, he adds, lies elsewhere and this prescription is of no use.' He then recalls the esoteric meaning given to it by the Ismailis, which consisted, for example, in identifying the Kaʿba with the Speaking-Prophet, and the seven circumambulations around the Kaʿba with the seven cycles of prophecy.

[272] *Kashf* V, pp. 117–118, § 47.

The first of these refutations of antinomianism appears in the 'philosophical' paragraph[273] that seems to be a later addition since its style is in line with the 'second Jaʿfar', so to speak, that is, the author of the *Taʾwīl al-zakāt* and the *Sarāʾir al-nuṭaqāʾ*.[274] The 'dense body' and the 'subtle essence' are here opposed, and assimilated to action and knowledge, respectively; however, the body without spirit, without its 'subtle essence' becomes an 'inanimate being' similar to dust, stones and wood. We have shown above that this can be used in favour of a symbolic interpretation of metamorphosis in animal or mineral form. But while it is stated that action without knowledge is like an inanimate body without an essence, it cannot be inferred from this that knowledge alone is sufficient to dispense from action. Indeed, the paragraph concludes with a statement of great importance: 'Both knowledge and action remain obligations as long as the spirit and the body coexist.'[275] If the spirit is the life of the body which prevents it from being an inanimate object, the fact remains that existence in the corporeal world requires that the body be taken into account. Insofar as man is spirit and body, and not a pure spirit, there can be no question of dispensing him from what corresponds to each, that is, knowledge and action, the esoteric and the exoteric.

Implicitly, this assertion is a refutation of the antinomian teachings of the *ghulāt*, but also of the docetist doctrines that theorise the idea of a subtle, luminous body, intermediate between the 'dense' body and the spirit. According to these doctrines, the luminous bodies of the Imams would not be subjected to the vicissitudes of the corruption undergone by dense bodies, and in particular they would escape death. This conception goes hand in hand with the tendency to deny the death of an Imam and to claim that this death was only an appearance, on the model provided by the crucifixion of Christ as described in the Qur'an: '*They did not slay him, neither crucified him, but it appeared so unto them (shubbiha lahum)*' (Q. 4:157). The *Kitāb al-Haft wa'l-aẓilla* indeed uses this verse to deny that God can subject His Friends to death. Jaʿfar al-Ṣādiq thus asks: 'Do you believe that God would make

---

[273] *Kashf* V, pp. 111–112, § 39.

[274] See introduction, pp. 52–60.

[275] *Kashf* V, p. 112, § 39.

them taste the heat of iron at the hands of their enemies?'[276] Another example of doceticism of the *ghulāt* is the episode of the massacre of Abū'l-Khaṭṭāb and his followers in the mosque of Kufa; the *khaṭṭabiyya* allegedly claimed that these deaths were illusory and that 'it only appeared so' (*shubbiha 'alayhim*) to the soldiers of the governor, using an expression close to the one the Qur'an uses to describe the illusory crucifixion of Jesus. The soldiers are said to have killed each other, believing they were killing Abū'l-Khaṭṭāb's supporters.[277]

In the same vein, the designation, in Ismaili texts, of the members of the *da'wa* as 'angels'[278] might be a reminiscence of a doctrine attributing subtle bodies, rather than dense bodies, to the elect and Friends of the Imam. As a result, they would be exempted from performing their religious duties externally. Indeed, taking the angels as an example, al-Sijistānī argues that it is possible 'to acquire the knowledge of *tawḥīd* and to worship God without going through an external Law'.[279] Al-Kirmānī, for his part, denied that they were exempt from the constraint of a *sharī'a*.[280] Now, if we view this debate on angels in relation to the exegeses of the *Kitāb al-Kashf* that identify the angels with the *du'āt*, it appears that the question of the religiosity of the angels is not as theoretical as it seems. It is possible that al-Sijistānī's doctrine on the relationship of the angels to the *sharī'a* derives from an older doctrine, related to the very concrete matter of the observance of the Law by the Friends of the Imam. In the *Kitāb al-Haft wa'l-aẓilla*, the Imam thus responds affirmatively to the following question from Mufaḍḍal: 'Do [believers] rise degree by degree until they become angels, so that they are then freed from the constraints of eating, drinking, and the like, and then rise to the sky and come back down to earth?' The text adds that the believers who thus become angels can take any form they like upon their descent to earth.[281] Other *ghulāt*

[276] Mufaḍḍal al-Ju'fī, *Kitāb al-Haft wa'l-aẓilla*, Ch. 38, pp. 78–79.

[277] Al-Nawbakhtī, *Firaq al-Shī'a*, p. 60; al-Qummī, *Maqālāt*, p. 82.

[278] See e.g. *Kashf* III, p. 62, § 20; V, p. 154, §105. More references above, p. 219, n. 24.

[279] D. De Smet, 'Loi rationnelle et loi imposée', p. 522; idem, 'Adam, premier prophète et législateur?', pp. 193–194.

[280] D. De Smet, 'Loi rationnelle et loi imposée', pp. 530–531; idem, 'Adam, premier prophète et législateur?', p. 196.

[281] Mufaḍḍal al-Ju'fī, *Kitāb al-Haft wa'l-aẓilla*, Ch. 19, pp. 51–52.

texts state the same idea: at the end of an initiatory progression, the believer becomes an angel and acquires miraculous powers.[282] It is against the backdrop of this doctrinal environment that the *Kitāb al-Kashf* elaborates its doctrines, if not its very texts. However, in a Fatimid context, such doctrines could only be preserved if they were counterbalanced by a tight solidarity of the esoteric and the exoteric 'as long as the spirit and the body coexist'.[283] It should be noted, however, that the latter formula remains ambiguous: it can mean that in this world, body and mind are necessarily linked, and this is how we interpret it in the context of *Kitāb al-Kashf*. But it could also imply that it is possible, as of this world, to reach a degree where the body and the spirit would no longer coexist; then, the deeds would no longer be necessary, but they remain so until this degree is reached.

However, this reading does not seem to correspond to the perspective of the editor of the *Kitāb al-Kashf*. In Treatise I, the explicit refutation of *ghuluww*[284] was preceded by a rejection of 'the Shiʿis who fall short' (*al-shīʿa al-muqaṣṣira*).[285] Treatise V also illustrates, even more directly, the Fatimid orientation to maintain a balance between *ghuluww* and *taqṣīr*, between those who go too far and those who do not go far enough. This 'third way' is undoubtedly that of the Fatimids. As we have seen, in Treatise I, *ghuluww* was defined as the affirmation that God took the forms of the Imams and the Messengers to descend to earth. As for *taqṣīr*, it was defined as the denial of the Last Day, that is, the refusal to follow the Mahdī. In Treatise V, on the other hand, *ghuluww* is not defined, and it is not clear what specific doctrines are aimed at in the passage mentioning 'the true religion where there is (. . .) no exaggeration nor shortcoming (*lā ghuluww wa-lā taqṣīr*)'.[286]

Nevertheless, some elements of *taqṣīr* are provided a little further, in the exegesis of Q. 2:197 which deals with 'obscenity, immorality and dispute', behaviours from which one must refrain during pilgrimage. In the discussion on immorality, the term is first understood in the literal sense: 'Immorality' is fornication, and it is not allowed for a

---

282 Cited in M. Asatryan, *Controversies in Formative Shiʿi Islam*, p. 147.

283 *Kashf* V, p. 112, § 39.

284 *Kashf* I, p. 7, § 13.

285 *Kashf* I, p. 5, § 8.

286 *Kashf* V, p. 120, § 52.

believer to indulge in immorality.'[287] This is followed by the quotation and exegesis of Q. 57:13 which mentions a wall whose *'interior (bāṭin) is Mercy and whose exterior (ẓāhir) is punishment'*. Unsurprisingly, the interior of the wall is identified with 'the esoteric knowledge dispensed by the Imam',[288] while the exterior of the wall, and therefore the punishment, corresponds 'the people of the exoteric',[289] as well as to those among the believers who are 'reductionists' (*muqaṣṣir*). The presentation is not very clear, but the text suggests, on the one hand, that the *muqaṣṣira* are members of the *da'wa*: they are indeed considered 'believers', unlike 'the people of the exoteric', which means that they are initiates. On the other hand, the *muqaṣṣira* are assimilated to the people of exotericism inasmuch as they engage in immorality; the literal interpretation of immorality seems to be confirmed by the sentence: 'The believer must be pure, clean and graceful, he must avoid fornication and not approach it, or his soul will perish.'[290] Does this mean that, according to the text, the people of exotericism are libertines and fornicators? In reality, the *muqaṣṣira* and the 'people of exotericism' are assimilated to each other because they commit reverse sins, so to speak. A few lines further, the sentence: *'Its exterior is punishment'*, is commented on as follows:

> 'Whoever deserts the exoteric duties, punishment will reach him, and the esoteric knowledge will not serve him. And whoever sticks to the exoteric without the esoteric, punishment will [also] reach him because he did not connect what God has ordered to connect to the continuous cable and the 'firm handhold'.'[291]

The rest of the text focuses on the refusal to follow the Legatee after the Speaking-Prophet, according to the classic Shi'i historiography of the Prophet's succession. The reader is now accustomed to the idea that the exotericism of the revelation must be completed by the esotericism of exegesis, otherwise obedience to the Messenger remains incomplete. On the other hand, the idea that esotericism is of no use

---

[287] *Kashf* V, p. 121, § 55.

[288] Ibid.

[289] *Kashf* V, pp. 121–122, § 55.

[290] *Kashf* V, p. 122, § 55.

[291] Ibid.

without exotericism does not constitute a *topos* of Shiʿi literature; it is rather a *topos* of an institutionalized Shiʿism such as Fatimid Ismailism, concerned with the excesses of esotericism. In the next page, the necessity of exotericism is again stressed:

> *'Its exterior is punishment*': to this corresponds the explanation given previously, that is, that whoever abandons the exoteric aspects of the Laws (*asqaṭa ẓāhir al-sharāʾiʿ*), or whoever holds on to the exoteric and abandons the esoteric (*tamassaka biʾl-ẓāhir wa-asqaṭa al-bāṭin*), must suffer punishment. This punishment of 'the exterior' suits both situations.' [292]

The 'third path' hinted at in these lines is typical of Fatimid doctrine. In this regard, the complete inversion of the definition of *taqṣīr* is enlightening: among the Shiʿi meanings of *taqṣīr* is the attitude of those who 'reduced' or 'limited' religion to the revelation (*tanzīl*) and did not embrace it fully by adhering to the Imam's rule and exegesis. In Treatise I, *taqṣīr* was disbelief in the Mahdī. But here, the term corresponds to the legal expression *al-taqṣīr ʿan al-ʿamal* in *fiqh* literature, that is, 'shortcoming in (religious) deeds'. Instead of being a name for those who doubt eschatology (and the potential antinomianism it entails), it becomes a name for antinomianism — a quasi-synonym of *ghuluww*.

This reading is confirmed further as we return to the exegesis of Q. 2:197 on 'obscenity, immorality and dispute'. The author defines the abandonment of 'works and efforts' as a form of *taqṣīr*: 'He means by this the abundance of works and efforts, for no one should be a shortcomer (*yuqaṣṣir*) in any of this.'[293] The text then refers to 'the abundance of knowledge and the excellence of action' (*kathrat al-ʿilm wa-khayr al-ʿamal*).[294] Although this passage remains imprecise, we can estimate that it contributes to subverting the notion of *taqṣīr*, by diverting it from the meaning it had in *ghulāt* circles, and by giving it a meaning which corresponds to a moderate Shiʿism: *taqṣīr* is thus 'reductionism' or 'shortcoming' with regard to exoteric works, and not a 'reduction' of the Imam's status or the importance of esoteric knowledge.

---

292 *Kashf* V, p. 123, § 56.

293 *Kashf* V, pp. 135–136, § 73.

294 *Kashf* V, p. 136, § 73.

Furthermore, it is interesting that the rejection of antinomianism seems to be prompted by the quotation of Q. 57:13. Indeed, this verse was used to support the distinction between *ẓāhir* and *bāṭin*, and was sometimes put in relation with the *ḥadīth* in which the Prophet Muḥammad declared: 'I am the city of knowledge, and ʿAlī is its gate.'[295] However, as Daniel De Smet points out, this verse 'easily lends itself to an antinomian reading which privileges the *bāṭin* over the *ẓāhir*: if the *bāṭin* is mercy, the *ẓāhir* — and therefore the Law — is punishment'.[296] In al-Sijistānī's philosophy, the notion that the exoteric Law is a punishment is bound up with the antinomian leanings that run through his work. He thus presents the religious Law as a burden, a necessary evil, a remedy that only exists because we live in a cycle of concealment and that we are suffering from ignorance. *Sharīʿa* is imposed upon mankind just as medicine and restrictions are imposed upon a medical patient. Once the latter has healed, the restrictions are no longer in order; once the Resurrector comes to restore a paradise state and make *tawḥīd* directly accessible, *sharīʿa* will no longer be useful. It is in this perspective that al-Sijistānī comes to consider the prescriptions of the *sharīʿa* as meaningless 'idolatrous cults'. Their value is reduced to their symbolic nature, as well as the practical utility of some (for example, the utility of ablutions with regard to hygiene).[297] It is therefore not by chance that the editor of Treatise V tackles the question of antinomianism, of esotericism without exotericism, in a commentary on Q. 57:13 which not only implies a superiority of the *bāṭin* over the *ẓāhir*, but can moreover support an antinomian conception which sees the *sharīʿa* as punishment.

Official Fatimid doctrine clearly rejects any exclusion of the *ẓāhir* in favour of the *bāṭin*, as we see for example in al-Qāḍī al-Nuʿmān's

---

[295] See e.g. Ibrāhīm b. al-Ḥusayn al-Ḥāmidī, *Kanz al-walad*, pp. 218–219; D. De Smet, *Épîtres sacrées des Druzes*, pp. 422–423, 445. On the 'city of knowledge', see D. De Smet, *La Quiétude de l'Intellect: néoplatonisme et gnose ismaélienne dans l'œuvre de Hamîd ad-Dîn al-Kirmânî (Xe-XIe s.)* (Leuven, 1995), pp. 16–18.

[296] D. De Smet, *Épîtres sacrées des Druzes*, p. 422, n. 1116.

[297] On al-Sijistānī's doctrine on *sharīʿa*, see D. De Smet, 'Loi rationnelle et loi imposée', pp. 521–529.

works,[298] or in al-Kirmānī's who 'emphasizes the balance between *ẓāhir* and *bāṭin*, between the Prophet and the Imam, as well as the complementarity between worship through knowledge and worship through religious practice' (*al-ʿibāda al-ʿilmiyya* and *al-ʿibāda al-ʿamaliyya*).[299] At the beginning of the Fatimid caliphate, an episode saw the caliph ʿAbd Allāh al-Mahdī suppress and execute several fanatical *duʿāt* who, it seems, professed antinomian doctrines,[300] although, as H. Halm remarks, his reaction to them was not immediate; Halm thus compares the attitude of ʿAbd Allāh al-Mahdī towards his antinomian partisans with that of the caliph al-Ḥākim vis-à-vis the Druze agitators.[301] According to Ibn ʿIdhārī, one of those arrested for having consumed pork and drunk wine publicly during Ramadan, was a certain al-Balawī, who used to pray in the direction where ʿAbd Allāh al-Mahdī was saying. Whether the repression of antinomianism by ʿAbd Allāh al-Mahdī was sincere or simply dictated by the political necessity of stability, it remains a notable fact. It illustrates how, almost from the outset, or at least as soon as the caliphate began to consolidate and a dynastic succession was considered, ʿAbd Allāh al-Mahdī reformed his eschatological status in order to establish a lasting political Imamate.

This is indeed the idea that Treatise V seems to express when it affirms that 'the Great Pilgrimage [from Q. 9:3], today, is the Silent One (*al-ṣāmit*). This means he did not appear speaking God's Order (*yanṭuq bi-amr Allāh*), as if he were the seventh Speaking-prophet'.[302] On this plane, as on the question of antinomianism, Treatise V is the theatre of the evolution of Fatimid Ismaili doctrine: building on the doctrinal ground of pre-Fatimid Ismailism, related to *ghuluww*, it slides gradually towards a more orthodox doctrine about the *ẓāhir* and

---

[298] Among many other references, including the abovementioned chapter of the *Daʿāʾim al-Islām*, see e.g. the references to his *Kitāb al-Majālis waʾl-musāyarāt* provided by H. Halm, *The Empire of the Mahdi*, p. 249, n. 382.

[299] D. De Smet, *La Quiétude de l'Intellect*, p. 393; see also ibid., pp. 311–312, 354, 357. On al-Kirmānī's conception of *sharīʿa*, see also idem, 'Loi rationnelle et loi imposée', pp. 529–534; idem, 'Adam, premier prophète et législateur ?', pp. 195–197.

[300] On this, see al-Qāḍī al-Nuʿmān, *Iftitāḥ al-daʿwa*, ed. Qāḍī, p. 276; ed. Dachraoui, pp. 328–329 (English trans., *Founding the Fatimid State*, p. 229); H. Halm, *The Empire of the Mahdi*, pp. 247–250.

[301] H. Halm, *The Empire of the Mahdi*, p. 249.

[302] *Kashf* V, p. 103, § 26.

pushes the coming of the Resurrector/Speaking-Prophet into the distance. In short, it subverts the eschatological prestige of the Resurrector to the benefit of the Imam.

Before concluding this discussion of antinomianism, it is worth noting that the mentions of Adam in Treatise V correspond to a conception opposite to the one implied by eschatological antinomianism — at least as presented by an author like al-Sijistānī. Adam is indeed a key figure in the Ismaili debate on the *sharīʿa*. Some authors, such as al-Nasafī and al-Sijistānī, consider that Adam was not a Speaking-Prophet, which means that mankind during his cycle was not subjected to a *sharīʿa*; the first Speaking-Prophet was Noah. In this perspective, the Resurrector had to abolish the Law and restore the Adamic state where men could worship God without the Law.[303] Therefore, it is significant that, unlike al-Sijistānī, Treatise V counts Adam and the Qāʾim among the Speaking-Prophets who 'speak' a Law.[304] Each Speaking-Prophets is an 'Adam':[305] 'Adam' is therefore apparently a name for the Speaking-Prophets inasmuch as each of them establishes a new *sharīʿa*.[306] Finally, Adam is explicitly described as the first House, which could be understood in an exclusively spiritual sense; but Treatise V specifies: 'Adam, whose laws and lineage were established *in the exoteric* for the worshippers of God, and in the esoteric for the worship of God.'[307]

3. Organizing the *daʿwa*: instruction to the missionaries and refutation of the false Mahdī

The exegesis of obscenity (*rafath*), immorality (*fusūq*) and dispute (*jidāl*), from which the pilgrim must abstain according to Q. 2:197, constitutes a long passage which deals directly with the organization of the *daʿwa*.[308] The instructions found there echo the incipit of Treatise I in which the initiate was pledged to remain silent on the teachings of the work, as well as the Ismaili passages of Treatise VI, in

---

303 On this debate, see D. De Smet, 'Adam, premier prophète et législateur ?'.

304 *Kashf* V, p. 104, § 27.

305 *Kashf* V, p. 97, § 12 ('first Adam'); p. 98, § 14 ('the sixth Adam, Muḥammad').

306 See commentary of *Kashf* I, pp. 134–147, esp. p. 140, n. 238, 239.

307 *Kashf* V, p. 109, § 34.

308 *Kashf* V, pp. 121–125, §§ 54–59.

which initiatory instructions are also given to Summoners.[309] However, it is in Treatise V that these instructions shed the most light on the practical aspects of the *da'wa*.

The passage in question clearly contains several editorial layers. We have studied above part of the section devoted to 'fornication'. Another layer, which must be the oldest, is found in the last paragraph of the passage:[310] obscenity, immorality and dispute are identified with Abū Bakr, 'Umar and 'Uthmān, but the section of the interpretation that concerns 'Uthmān is missing. The *Kitāb al-Kashf* is transmitting here a fragment of an ancient personalized commentary. The identification of these three Qur'anic terms with the first three caliphs of Islam recalls the identification by al-Ṭabarānī of the 'First', the 'Second' and 'Na'thal', with 'carrion', 'blood' and 'swineflesh'.[311] The personalized phase of Shi'i hermeneutics is preserved in Treatise V, but is pushed into the background, in favour of a specifically Ismaili exegesis of obscenity, immorality and dispute. There is an 'Ismailization' of ancient material, which, originally, was of the same type as the exegesis of 'carrion, blood and pork' preserved in Nuṣayri texts. This is an illustration of the Ismaili reworking of Shi'i exegeses on which the *du'āt* were dependent but which they adapted to their doctrines.[312]

It is neither in the layer of the personalized commentary, nor in the one that interprets immorality literally and attributes it to 'shortcoming' believers, that we find elements on the *da'wa*, but in a third layer composed of an exegesis of obscenity and immorality attributed to the 'Sage', as well as an exegesis of 'dispute', which remains anonymous but must belong to the same layer. According to the Sage, obscenity consists of 'disclosing the secret of the Family of Muḥammad'.[313] Whoever transgresses this instruction will taste the 'coldness of iron' — an expression reminiscent of 'the heat of iron' from which God spares His elect in the *Kitāb al-Haft wa'l-Aẓilla*.[314]

---

[309] *Kashf* VI, pp. 164–167, §§ 19–24.

[310] *Kashf* V, p. 125, § 59.

[311] Al-Ṭabarānī, *Kitāb al-Ma'ārif*, p. 116. See also my discussion of 'carrion, blood and swineflesh' above, p. 127, n. 191.

[312] On these Qur'anic trios in pre-Buyid Shi'i, Nuṣayri and Ismaili sources, see F. Gillon, 'Du *tafsīr* chiite au *ta'wīl* ismaélien'.

[313] *Kashf* V, p. 121, § 54.

[314] Mufaḍḍal al-Ju'fī, *Kitāb al-Haft wa'l-aẓilla*, Ch. 38, pp. 78–79.

At the end of the section on immorality, fornication — i.e. immorality — is compared to 'unveiling the secret for someone or summoning (*daʿwa*) without permission',[315] according to the sexual symbolism we already encountered. This exegesis is isolated here and does not give rise to any development. It is, however, immediately followed by al-Ḥakīm's exegesis: 'Immorality, for the believer (*muʾmin*), is to slander a believer like him.'[316] It is clearly a matter of disciplining some troublemakers within the *daʿwa*. The idea is illustrated in vivid terms, equating slander with a symbolic anthropophagy (in reference to Q. 49:12: '*Would any of you like to eat the flesh of your dead brother?*'). The dead, here, is 'the one who is absent from the place where he was slandered'.[317]

This brings to four the number of interpretations given to immorality: the first is literal and is used in support of the rejection of antinomianism. The second defines immorality as an unauthorized disclosure of the esoteric doctrine. The third identifies it with slandering, and the fourth identifies it with ʿUmar.

Finally, while the exegesis of the dispute[318] is not attributed to the Sage, its perspective is close to the exegeses of obscenity and immorality transmitted under his name; all three are practical instructions aimed at ranking members of the *daʿwa*. On the one hand, keeping the teachings and activities of the *daʿwa* secret (refraining from 'obscenity') is a matter of 'external' security. On the other hand, the prohibition of slander ('immorality') and unhealthy competition ('dispute') is meant to prevent dissension and ensure the internal cohesion of the organization. It is recalled here that the ultimate authority is that of the Imam, who appoints the various 'fathers', the members who are authorized to recruit.

It is worth noting here the use of the Qurʾanic expression 'People of the Book' to designate the members of the *daʿwa*; this, because they are faithful to the Imam, who is symbolically a Book.[319]

Other passages from Treatise V refer to difficulties encountered by the *daʿwa*, as they deal with anonymous adversaries from its own

[315] *Kashf* V, p. 123, § 57.

[316] Ibid.

[317] *Kashf* V, p. 123–124, § 57.

[318] *Kashf* V, p. 124, § 58.

[319] This hermeneutical equivalence is particularly present in *Kashf* VI.

ranks — hence, perhaps, the need to emphasize its cohesion. Again, we find the theme, already present in Treatises I and III, of the renegade 'who left the people of Truth to join the people of falsehood'.[320] But it is only after the exegesis of obscenity, immorality and dispute that the text makes a series of allusions to difficulties encountered by the *da'wa*, and particularly to its rivals. All the passage on 'the pride of Pharaoh'[321] — with the exception of the interlude on the esoteric meaning of Egypt[322], less directly related to this matter — visibly refers to specific historic episodes. What we suspected in Treatise III, that is, that the negative personalized commentaries referred to political opponents of the *da'wa*, appears here slightly more clearly.

The text also mentions an Iblīs who 'was among those who heard God's wisdom and had reached a high rank (*rutba*)' in the *da'wa*.[323] This character is likened to Pharaoh, and the Qur'anic verses in which the latter proclaims his royalty and his superiority over Moses (Q. 43:51–54) are applied to him. This anti-Ismaili Pharaoh would thus have claimed for himself the status of the seventh Speaking-Prophet: 'This Satan (. . .) said to himself and to those who were seduced by his whispering: 'Have I not acknowledged the seventh Speaking-Prophet?'[324] It is quite clear that the person alluded to was an adversary of the Fatimids who seemed to have turned their eschatology against them — a description that fits the young eschatological 'prophet' who led the Kutāma rebellion against 'Abd Allāh al-Mahdī after the execution of Abū 'Abd Allāh al-Shī'ī. Yet, the text maintains the fiction of an exegesis applicable to those who refused to recognise the Imamate of 'Alī b. Abī Ṭālib, a method which recalls the texts of Treatise III.

In Q. 43:52, Pharaoh declares himself superior to Moses whose 'words are deficient'. The *ta'wīl* interprets Moses' silence as *taqiyya*: 'The Legatee does not unveil the exegesis and does not manifest it, except for the deserving, after taking the covenant and the pact.'[325] The mysterious figure is accused of having conspired and fomented a

---

320 *Kashf* V, p. 95, § 9.

321 *Kashf* V, pp. 125–130, §§ 60–67.

322 *Kashf* V, pp. 128–129, §§ 64–66.

323 *Kashf* V, p. 125, § 60.

324 *Kashf* V, p. 126, § 60.

325 *Kashf* V, p. 126, § 61.

rebellion against the 'Prince of the Believers', an expression which here designates the Fatimid Imam, assimilated to ʿAlī b. Abī Ṭālib: 'He diverted [the people] and led them astray from the truth and its Master, the Prince of the Believers.'[326] In Q. 43:53, Pharaoh justifies his disobedience by the fact that no miraculous sign designates Moses as the prophet he claims to be: '*If only bracelets of gold had been cast on him, or if angels had come with him conjoined*'. According to the exegete of the *Kashf*, 'gold is like Messengers and Imams';[327] the Legatee ʿAlī b. Abī Ṭālib (and by extension, his descendant the Fatimid Imam) is disputed because he does not bring an exoteric revelation,[328] that is to say a new Law (*sharīʿa*).

After a digression on the symbolic meaning of Egypt as the city of knowledge, the text returns to Pharaoh with an exegesis by the 'Sage':

> 'Al-Ḥakīm — peace be upon him — said that Pharaoh was among those who entered into the obedience of the Imam — may God's blessings be upon him — and settled (*sakana*) in Egypt. But he wandered away from the Friends (*awliyāʾ*) of God and he denied the Imam access to what he was contemplating (*ḥajara al-Imam li-mā naẓara*), while Summoners went out to summon on his command.'[329]

The attribution of this interpretation to the Sage may raise doubts as to the fact that the adversaries of the *daʿwa* hinted to here are contemporaries of the Fatimids. Yet, it is entirely possible that the Sage did teach this type of interpretation, which was then taken up and applied to a new situation. In fact, the whole collection seems composed on this general premise, as we have shown. Furthermore, in this same passage, the adversaries are described as those 'who denied the Day of retribution',[330] which is the Day of Judgment, or the Last Day. Now, this expression is applied to the Mahdī elsewhere in the *Kashf*;[331] therefore, this must be about people who rejected ʿAbd Allāh

---

326 Ibid.

327 *Kashf* V, p. 126, § 62.

328 *Kashf* V, p. 127, § 62.

329 *Kashf* V, p. 129, § 67.

330 *Kashf* V, p. 130, § 67.

331 *Kashf* I, p. 6, § 8; III, p. 52, § 1.

al-Mahdī. The reproach that the Imam did not bring a new revelation and is not accompanied by angels expresses the disappointment of partisans who had been expecting the Imam to fulfil eschatological hopes and to perform miracles — it may therefore refer to the disillusionment of Abū ʿAbd Allāh al-Shīʿī and the Kutāma chiefs who were perplexed by the non-eschatological nature of ʿAbd Allāh al-Mahdī. The adversary described here by the *Kashf* is said to have claimed for himself the status of seventh Speaking-Prophet. It is likely that this description matches Kādū b. Muʿārik al-Māwaṭī, who not only rebelled against ʿAbd Allāh al-Mahdī in the aftermath of the execution of Abū ʿAbd Allāh al-Shīʿī, but also claimed to be the Mahdī and professed an antinomian doctrine. Indeed, it is on the occasion of this revolt that the future al-Qāʾim was officially appointed as the successor of ʿAbd Allāh al-Mahdī, and charged with suppressing the revolt, which he did successfully despite his lack of military experience.

Conclusion

Treatise V is the only treatise of the collection that contains explicit references to the historical context of the *Kitāb al-Kashf*, since it mentions Muḥammad b. Aḥmad and al-Qāʾim bi-Amr Allāh. It also bears clear marks of Fatimid Ismailism, particularly in its rejection of antinomian ideas and practices. But it is equally clear that it is largely based on pre-Fatimid sources, as the attribution of several interpretations to the 'Sage' certainly indicates. In addition, there are traces of doctrines and a vocabulary reminiscent of those of the *ghulāt*, such as the 'Veil' (*ḥijāb*) or the 'Meaning' (*maʿnā*), or the couple of the *ʿAyn* and the *Fāʾ*. Other examples are the theme of the Houses and its implications — namely the infusion of a unique divine principle appearing in various forms — and the mention of the 'seventy sacred forms' (sing. *haykal*), even as the term *haykal* was rejected as being specific to the *ghulāt* in Treatise I.

Apart from the explicit mentions of the two abovementioned persons, the treatise bears other marks hinting at early Fatimid history. Among these is the Fatimid reorientation of the pre-Fatimid meaning of the Proof in favour of the successor of ʿAbd Allāh al-Mahdī, al-Qāʾim bi-Amr Allāh. To this are added the anti-libertinist polemics and the refutation of antinomianism, which had immediate political implications at a time the caliphate was confronted with a revolt mimicking the messianic and revolutionary *daʿwa* of the Fatimids, and professing antinomian doctrines. ʿAbd Allāh al-Mahdī disappointed the eschatological expectations of those who had brought him to power; he was ultimately only a man and did not establish a divine reign or perform miracles. The last passages we examined must allude to Kādū b. Muʿārik al-Māwaṭī and his antinomian messianic rebellion. The rejection of antinomianism in this particular treatise must also have been motivated by the particular importance given to the Houses, which, in the old doctrine, had to correspond to places of epiphany of divinity. We have seen indeed that antinomianism often came with the idea that knowing certain sacred persons dispensed one from the performance of religious duties. Finally, among the evocations of the life of the *daʿwa* that we have been able to note, particular attention had to be paid to the fact that enemies of the *daʿwa* are described as former members. All these elements put together seem to point toward the specific historical context of the reign of ʿAbd Allāh al-Mahdī, and more precisely after 912, the date of the antinomian revolt of Kādū b. Muʿārik al-Māwaṭī and the official inauguration of al-Qāʾim bi-Amr Allāh.

Yet, some parts of the treatise seem to have been added later as they are in line with later evolutions of the Fatimid doctrine, namely the inclusion of philosophical vocabulary. In addition, the treatise echoes several of Jaʿfar b. Manṣūr al-Yaman's other works, notably the *Sarāʾir wa-asrār al-nuṭaqāʾ* which uses the same method of alluding to events of early Fatimid history through accounts on the prophets.

TREATISE VI

Treatise VI appears as a coherent whole, in a much more evident manner than some other chapters in the collection; it includes an introduction and a conclusion, as well as very identifiable themes and structure — even though the latter is not linear, as will be shown. This treatise is relatively short and is essentially devoted to three major themes. It is worth noting that the first two of these themes are typically Shiʿi in the broader sense, rather than specifically Ismaili: 1) the succession of Muḥammad and the usurpation of ʿAlī b. Abī Ṭālib's rights to the Imamate, built on the opposition between God's elect and men's elect, the latter being led by their 'passions'; 2) the analogy between Muḥammad and Moses, on the one hand, and ʿAlī and Aaron on the other hand; 3) the initiation and the hierarchy of the *daʿwa*, which is the theme that gives this treatise its Ismaili tone. Structurally, this treatise can be broken down into the following elements:

1) [§ **1**] Incipit
2) The Imamate of ʿAlī and its usurpation by his enemies

   — [§§ **2–7**] The rejection of ʿAlī by the community and choice of an Imam according to their passions
   — [§§ **8–10**] Exegesis of Q. 16:90
   — [§§ **11–15**] Exegesis of Q. 16:92

3) [§ **16**] The Imam as Book: exegesis of Q. 3:187
4) The Summoners and initiation

   — [§§ **17–18**] Exegesis of Q. 58:11
   — [§ **19**] Exegesis of Q. 2:233

- [§§ **20–24**] Exegesis of Q. 60:12

5) The succession of Muḥammad and the Imam as Book

   - [§ **25**] Exegesis of Q. 62:2
   - [§ **26**] Exegesis of Q. 46:12

6) The 'mountains' as Proofs

   - [§ **27**] Exegesis of Q. 20:105–107
   - [§§ **28–29**] Exegesis of Q. 78:12–20
   - [§ **30**] Exegesis of Q. 38:18–19

7) [§§ **31–35**] The Imam as Book
8) Following one's own choice of an Imam

   - [§§ **36–37**] Exegesis of Q. 10:17–18
   - [§ **38**] Exegesis of Q. 13:33

9) [§ **39**] The Imam as Book: exegesis of Q. 2:78–79
10) [§§ **40–43**] Conclusion: connection between 'Alī's Imamate and the necessity of following the Imam and his representatives (Summoners, Gates and Proofs)

Treatise VI Translation

In the name of God, the Merciful, the Compassionate,

1. Praise be to God who guided His servants and made His Proof manifest through His Book, which speaks His command and His interdiction through the tongue of his Truthful Prophet, through his message and the revelation (*waḥī*) he receives, through guidance and healing, through manifest signs, through the persuasive wisdom (*al-ḥikma al-bāligha*) that He perfected, through the evidence He brought into being (*awjada*) and placed — may He be exalted — in the Revelation (*tanzīl*) of the Book and in His Exegesis (*ta'wīl*). His Revelation is demonstration, and His Exegesis is proof (*burhān*).

[Exegesis of Q. 53:23 and 53:28–30]

2. Among the exegeses, which are the esotericism of the exotericism that is the revelation, is the meaning of the following verse of the Book of God — He is Mighty and Sublime, blessed and elevated be His Word: '*They follow nothing but speculation and what the souls desire, and yet guidance has come to them from their Lord*' [Q. 53:23]. This means that they followed none but the Imam they appointed for themselves based on their personal choice and the desire of their souls, without any choice from God or indication from His Messenger. They speculated that God would accept this from them but He will not. '*Yet guidance has come to them from their Lord*' means that the Messenger of God — may God bless him and his family — who is their lord on behalf of God, Lord of the Universes, has made the sacred station (*maqām*) of the Legatee clear to them, in order to guide them with God's guidance — and this is ʿAlī b. Abī Ṭālib — peace be upon him.

3. '*Indeed, speculation does not avail anything against the truth, so avoid* **[157]** *those who turn away from Our Remembrance and want but* *the worldly life. Such is the knowledge they have reached'* [Q. 53:28–30]. God's words here mean that their speculation that God will accept their action of following [someone other than][332] His Friend (*walī*) does not free them from their obligation to seek the actual Imam and his lawful position (*maqām*) according to the command of God's Messenger — may God bless him — and according to lawfulness as decreed by God. God — He is Mighty and Sublime — then tells His Prophet: *'Avoid those who turn away from Our Remembrance'*, which means: 'Reject those who turn away from ʿAlī', when he is the Legatee. He is the 'remembrance' intended by God in His Book.[333] *'He wants but the worldly life'* means that he wants but the exoteric and loathes the esoteric which is with ʿAlī. 'Wordly life' is the exoteric. Then God — He is Mighty and Sublime — said: *'Such is the knowledge they have reached.'* This means: such is what they have reached and what they were able [to grasp] regarding ʿAlī's matter (*amr*) as they envied him even though he was the [custodian of] Knowledge, and they rejected his sacred station. However, in so doing they caused no harm to him but only to themselves.

4. *'Everything (kull shay') we have enumerated in a clear Imam'* [Q. 36:12].[334] This means that every believer is known as such by the fact that he follows the Imam who provides the exegesis of the Book of God. This is because 'thing' (*shay'*) is a name for the believer.

5. *'Who is more iniquitous than the one who forges a lie against God when he is summoned unto Islam? God does not guide the iniquitous'* [Q. 61:7]. This means: 'Who is more iniquitous than the one who lies against God — may He be exalted?' The creatures show veneration to what they choose for themselves. *'Summoned unto Islam'* means that the Messenger of God — may God's blessing and peace be upon him— **[158]** summons him to follow ʿAlī. He was the first to convert to Islam, thus his name and the obedience [due to him] is 'Islam'. [The Messenger] also points to him the stations of the Prophets, Legatees

---

332 I have corrected the Arabic text by adding these words.

333 On the 'remembrance', see *Kashf* I, p. 30, § 63; III, pp. 71, § 38; p. 79, § 62.

334 The verse deals with the resurrection of the dead and the examination of their deeds. Therefore, the term 'Imam' has usually been understood as a synonym for 'register', 'record' or 'book'. This verse justifies the further developments of our treatise based on the notion that every Qur'anic mention of a book actually refers to the Imam.

and Imams that God has chosen — may He be exalted. *'God does not guide the iniquitous'*, meaning those who have been iniquitous to themselves and those who followed them in their lie against God concerning the establishment of His religion, as they impute it to [individuals] other than His Friends whom God has chosen for His Order (*amr*).

6. *'Whatever the Messenger gives you, take, and whatever he forbids you, give over'* [Q. 59:7]. Whatever the Messenger orders you to obey, follow it and act in obedience to it. This refers to the words of the Messenger of God — may God bless him — concerning ʿAlī — peace be upon him: 'Whoever's lord (*mawlā*) I am, then ʿAlī is his Lord as well'.[335] He also said: "ʿAlī is in relation to me as Aaron was to Moses',[336] acknowledging to them that every prophet points to his Legatee, and that ʿAlī was to [Muḥammad] as Aaron was to Moses. *'Whatever he forbids you, give over'* means: do not follow anyone he does not order you to obey and follow. That would entail going astray from God's path, and it is in this respect that He said: *'Do not follow the paths'* [Q. 6:153]. The variety of desires will lead you to forget God's Command, to the people's choice rather than the Messenger's Legacy (*waṣiyya*).[337] The Legacy is the Path of God, the tradition of His religion and His Prophets.

7. *'You have in the Messenger of God a good example* **[159]** *to those who hope for God and the Last Day'* [Q. 33:21]. This means that you have in the Messenger of God a good example insofar as he indicated ʿAlī, entrusted him with the Order and approved him for his Legacy. He established him in relation to Him as the Legatees to the Messengers, and yet they have not established ʿAlī in the position of the Imam as he was established by God and His Messenger — may God bless him. *'To those who hope for God and the Last Day'*, that is, to those who hope for

---

[335] Famous *ḥadīth* of Ghadīr Khumm, also alluded to above: see *Kashf* III, p. 86, § 70, and related footnote.

[336] Also quoted in *Kashf* I, p. 12, § 25. On Moses and Aaron, apart from the numerous mentions in *Kashf* VI, see also *Kashf* I, p. 31, § 65; III, p. 75, § 44.

[337] The term *waṣiyya*, from the same root as *waṣī*, 'Legatee', is thus translated throughout this volume. However, in this particular treatise, one should bear in mind that the notion of *waṣiyya* often has the connotation of 'testamentary disposition', 'recommendation', as we are dealing with the explicit designation of ʿAlī by Muḥammad — that is, the instruction rather than the content of the legacy.

God and the Mahdī[338] from ʿAlī's progeny whom the Messenger — may God bless him — indicated. He is 'the Last Day', the last of the Imams and the Speaking-Prophets — may God bless them all.

[Exegesis of Q. 16:90]

8. God — may He be exalted — says: *'God commands justice and good-doing and giving the kinsmen; and He forbids turpitude, abomination and outrage (al-faḥshāʾ wa'l-munkar wa'l-baghī), admonishing you so that you remember'* [Q. 16:90]. This means that God commands justice, that is, to follow His tradition through the Messengers, the Legatee and the Imams, tradition by which He does justice amongst the servants, from the first to the last. In every community and every nation, he put a Prophet, as well as an Imam He chooses for them, and He establishes the Imams for all, just as He made worship an obligation to all, as a justice from Him unto His worshippers; such is the justice He commands.

9. The 'good-doing' is to aim for this path and to act righteously in accordance with it. When He says: among them, *'some are good-doers, and some evidently are iniquitous to their own self'* [Q. 37:113], it is about this. One who is iniquitous to his own self is one who follows other than the Imams of Truth, and the good-doer is one who follows the Imams that God approved for His religion. **[160]** It is about this that He says: *'And those who follow them with good-doing, God approves them'* [Q. 9:100]. [About] His words: *'Give the kinsman their rights'* [Q. 17:26], 'the kinsman' is ʿAlī b. Abī Ṭālib; it is ordered that his rights, established by God, be given to him as the Legacy of God's Messenger — may God bless him. [It is also ordered to give him] the obedience and Friendship (*walāya*) God has made an obligation on all creation — just as He made them an obligation towards His Messenger. ʿAlī b. Abī Ṭālib is the kinsman of the Messenger — may God bless him — because he was the first to convert to Islam, and therefore he is the closest to him in all Creation in virtue of his Islam. And he is the kinsman in terms of blood-relation, and because of the position in which God's Messenger — may God bless him — placed him when he said: "ʿAlī is in relation to me as Aaron was to Moses'. There is no

338 On the equivalence of the Last Day and the Mahdī, see *Kashf* I, p. 6, § 8; III, p. 52, § 1.

closer proximity than that of Aaron to Moses, and so the Messenger — may God bless him — placed ʿAlī in his closeness, and this is what God ordered.

10. He then says: *'He forbids turpitude, abomination and outrage'* [Q. 16:90]. These three terms (*asmāʾ*) that He forbids refer to the three[339] who were iniquitous to themselves, to ʿAlī and who acted unjustly against his sacred station. Their action was 'turpitude, abomination and outrage', and so God forbade their action and forbade [people] to follow them. He then says: *'He admonishes you so that you remember'*, what He admonishes you about, and so that you avoid what He forbade you and so that you follow whom He ordered you to follow.

[Exegesis of Q. 16:92]

11. *'And be not as her who unravelled her thread after she made it strong, to thin filaments, taking your oaths as an object of disorder between you, to empower a community over another community. God only tests you thereby, and will make clear to you on the Day of Resurrection what you disagreed about'* [Q. 16:92]. This means: 'Do not

[339] Abū Bakr, ʿUmar and ʿUthmān. The same allusive interpretation appears in *Tafsīr al-Qummī* (*fulān wa-fulān wa-fulān*), and *Tafsīr al-ʿAyyāshī* (*al-awwal, al-thānī, al-thālith*); see al-Qummī, *Tafsīr*, ed. Ṭ. al-Mūsawī al-Jazāʾirī, vol. 1, p. 388; ed. Muʾassasat al-Imām al-Mahdī, Qom, vol. 2, p. 556; al-ʿAyyāshī, *Tafsīr*, vol. 3, p. 20. Al-Ṣaffār al-Qummī is less explicit but still interprets these three terms from Q. 16:90 as referring to 'the enemies of the Prophets and their Legatees whom it is forbidden to love and obey' (al-Ṣaffār al-Qummī, *Baṣāʾir al-Darajāt*, p. 942). On this verse in *Tafsīr al-ʿAyyāshī*, see M.M. Bar-Asher, *Scripture and Exegesis*, pp. 109–110. See also al-Daylamī, *Bayān madhhab al-bāṭiniyya*, p. 52, where the Zaydi author states that the Ismailis explicitly interpret *'al-faḥshāʾ wa'l-munkar wa'l-baghī'* from Q. 16:90 as referring to Abū Bakr, ʿUmar and ʿUthmān. The terms 'turpitude' (*faḥshāʾ*) and 'abomination' (*munkar*) also appear in Q. 29:45, without the third term, and are identified with Abū Bakr and ʿUmar in Ismaili, *ghulāt* and Nuṣayri sources; see e.g. Jaʿfar b. Manṣūr al-Yaman, *Taʾwīl al-zakāt*, p. 126 ('the *two* who inaugurated iniquity, brought turpitude into religion, denied the position of the Legatee, and violated the covenant took upon them on the day of al-Ghadīr'), 205 ('the First and the Second of iniquity'); idem, *Riḍāʿ fi'l-Bāṭin*, p. 104 ('the First and the Second who were iniquitous to ʿAlī'); al-Tabarānī, *Kitāb al-maʿārif*, p. 58 ('the First and the Second'). Compare the latter's explanation of Q. 29:45 to the one attributed to the heresiarch Isḥāq al-Aḥmar by al-Khaṭīb al-Baghdādī; cited by H. Halm, 'Das 'Buch des Schatten'', I, p. 246. On the Shiʿi 'personnalized' exegesis of these verses, see F. Gillon, 'Du *tafsīr* chiite au *taʾwīl* ismaélien'.

[**161**] be like her whose deeds were thwarted and whose endeavour was foiled, *'after she made it strong'*, that is, after a Proof by whom God strengthened them and after His Messenger. The strength is the Proof.[340] 'Filaments' (*ankāthan*) means they have breached (*nakathū*)[341] their covenant with the Messenger and rejected his tradition after it was arranged and connected with God's Path, just as a thread being unravelled after having been tied.

12. *'[We forbade the Jews certain good things that were lawful because of their wrongdoings] and their hindering from the Path'* [Q. 4:160]: By this, He means the community of Moses, their following the Sāmirī[342] in the absence of Moses and their separation from Aaron. And so God is saying to the community of Muḥammad: 'Do not be like that community in opposing ʿAlī, because he is the Proof and the Gate of Muḥammad, just as Aaron was the Proof and the Gate of Moses.'

13. *'Taking your oaths as an object of disorder between you'* means that you are taking the Pact which the Messenger of God made you contract with ʿAlī, the Pact that made his sacred station known to you, *'as an object of disorder between you'*, which means that [the Pact] is concealed amongst you, that you do not know it and do not obey God's command, and that you do not manifest it to the people so they can act accordingly.

14. *'To empower a community over another community'* means that they do this fearing that the community of Moses would be greater and higher in the worldly life — since they chose for themselves and became too arrogant to obey Aaron — [greater and higher] than the community of Muḥammad if they did not choose for themselves and become too arrogant to obey ʿAlī. That way, the Imamate becomes a matter of <negotiation>,[343] open to anyone, and anyone in the

---

[340] In this paragraph, the Proof refers to ʿAlī b. Abī Ṭālib.

[341] See al-Qāḍī al-Nuʿmān, *Daʿāʾim al-Islām*, vol. 1, pp. 388 (English trans.: *The Pillars of Islam*, vol I, p. 480), where the term *nākithūn* specifically refers to 'the people of Basra and others who fought [ʿAlī] at the Battle of the Camel'. For further references to this term in Shiʿi literature, see al-Qāḍī al-Nuʿmān, *The Pillars of Islam*, vol. 1, p. 62, n. 162.

[342] See *Kashf* I, p. 31, § 65, and commentary of *Kashf* I, pp. 147–154, esp. pp. 152–153.

[343] Mss. A, B: *mufāḍa*, corrected to *mufāwaḍa*, after Strothmann's suggestion in a footnote.

community can claim it, instead of organizing the community in accordance with the Messenger's Legacy and despite the fact that the Imams after him should be of his house (*min ahl baytihi*).

15. Then He says: '*God only tests you thereby.*' This means that God will try you **[162]** with the sacred stations of ʿAlī and the Imams after him, with the Legacy [transmitted to] his sons, and with the guide (*dalīl*) to the religion of God which God has approved and through which His Creation worships [Him]. '*He will make clear to you on the Day of Resurrection what you disagreed about*': this means that He will make clear to you that the choice you make for yourselves and your promulgation of the religion without the guide (*dalīl*) and in accordance your passions (*ahwāʾ*) are a deviation from divine guidance. [He will make clear] that the [true] guidance is God's: the Messenger of God — may God bless him— has guided (*dalla*) to it and has indicated his Legatee according to it. Thus is His religion organized, and His choice does not vary depending on the passions of the people nor on their choices.

[Exegesis of Q. 3:187]

16. It is in a similar way that one should understand God's words — He is Mighty and Sublime: '*When God made a pact with those who had received the Book [He said]: 'Make it clear unto mankind, and do not to conceal it.' But they cast it behind their backs and sold it for a small price — how evil was their selling!*' [Q. 3:187]. When God made a pact with those for whom He had appointed an Imam — who is the '*Book*' — [He said]: '*Make it clear unto mankind, and do not to conceal it*', so that they would manifest his sacred station and follow him. This means that they were iniquitous toward those to whom the Messenger of God — may God bless him — made ʿAlī's sacred station known, and with whom he contracted the Covenant of God and His Pact. But they concealed this among themselves and claimed his sacred station. Then He says: '*But they cast it behind their backs*' in their prayers and judgements, **[163]** '*and sold it for a small price*': they sold God's approbation to follow [ʿAlī] in favour of their leadership in iniquity for a small duration in this worldly life. '*How evil was their selling*' in favour of this iniquity they chose without approval from God, and without following the Imam of His religion whose right was approved, that is, ʿAlī b. Abī Ṭālib, the Legatee of the Messenger — may God's blessings be upon them both.

[The Summoners and the initiation: exegesis of Q. 58:11]

17. *'O you who believe! When it is said to you: 'Make room in the assemblies', then make room, and God will make room for you. And when it is said: 'Rise', then rise, and God will raise up those of you who believe and received knowledge in high degrees. And God is aware of what you do'* [Q. 58:11].

18. This means that when you are told: 'Spread out the explanation and the initiation (*al-sharḥ wa'l-tarbiya*)', then spread it out. And when it is said to you: 'Withhold it', then withhold it. This means that when the Imam tells you so, it is a guidance. '*God will raise up those of you who believe*' if they comply with what they have heard, '*and those who received knowledge*' if they withhold [the teaching] until they are ordered [otherwise]. They will be risen up '*in high degrees*' by their obedience and their submission.

[The Summoners and the initiation: exegesis of Q. 2:233]

19. *'The mothers shall suckle their children for two entire cycles, for those who wish to complete the suckling. It is for the father to provide their sustenance* **[164]** *and clothing in accordance with what is known (bi'l-ma'rūf)'* [Q. 2:233]. This means that the Summoners and the Gates make the believers whom they summon hear two Imams: an Imam who utters (*yanṭuq*) a Law and a Revelation, and an Imam who completes the Law with the Exegesis. '*For those who wish to complete the suckling*', that is, for those who wish to complete the rank of the believer and to rise up in degrees to the knowledge of the Completer Imam. '*It is for the father to feed and clothe them in accordance with what is known*': the 'father' is the Imam to whom people are summoned in his age. '*Their sustenance*' is the influx (*mādda*) of knowledge the believer receives from the Summoners. '*Their clothing*' is the covering of piety they wear, by which God raises to high degrees the believers and the Summoners and diffuses the wisdom and the knowledge of religion. '*In accordance with what is known (bi'l-ma'rūf)*' means that those whose merit (*istiḥqāq*) is known will receive this to the measure of their merit (*'alā qadar istiḥqāqihi*) at a time God deems appropriate for them. Then, the appropriateness of the initiation (*fatḥ*) of the believers will be known.

[The Summoners and the initiation: exegesis of Q. 60:12]

20. *'O Prophet! If believing women come to you, taking oath of allegiance that they will not associate with God anything, and will not steal, neither commit fornication, nor slay their children, nor forge a lie between their hands and feet, nor rebel against you in what is right, then accept their allegiance and ask God to forgive them. God is the Forgiving, the Compassionate'* [Q. 60:12].

21. What is meant by 'the Prophet' (*nabī*) here is the Proof, who communicates (*yunabbi'*) **[165]** esoteric knowledge to the believers, and what is meant by 'the believing women' are the believers who have been raised to high degrees, and whom the Proof wants to give permission to summon. So, God — may He be exalted — says to the Proof: If these believers come to you to take the covenant and the oath of allegiance to the Imam [swearing] *"that they will not associate with God anything"*, that is, that they will not summon in favour of anyone but the God-chosen Imam, because whoever does so associates something with God, since he associates someone who was not chosen by God for His creation to the Imamate of His religion. The Imam of Truth who is chosen by God — may He be exalted — is the one who is designated by an Imam before him. His designation comes to him, an Imam after another, from the Legatee of the Messenger designated by the Messenger, until the Imamate reaches him.

22. *'They will not steal'*: they will not divulge the esoteric knowledge of religion to someone who has not taken the covenant, for if the Summoner does this, then he is stealing. If the deprived believer (*mu'min muḥarram*)[344] learns what he is not permitted to be spoken to about or if he discloses what he has heard to the people of the exoteric, then he steals and enables others to steal.

23. *'They will not commit fornication'* means that they do not take the covenant with someone without permission or licence of the Imam.[345] *'They will not slay their children'*: they do not deprive a believer

[344] The term designates a low rank of the Ismaili hierarchy, and is usually opposed to the *ma'dhūn*, mentioned a few lines further in our text, who is 'the one who has permission' to hear and/or preach and disclose the esoteric knowledge.

[345] See *Kashf* I, pp. 26–27, §§ 57–59; III, p. 78–79, § 52; V, p. 114, § 41; p. 123, § 57, and commentary of *Kashf* I, pp. 128–134.

from the dignities of religion (*ḥudūd al-dīn*) he deserves, and do not invalidate him in the eyes of [**166**] the Imam by slandering him unjustly. '*They will not forge a lie between their hands and feet*': they do not summon toward any abomination in matters of religion, nor toward an Imam or a Proof they have chosen on their own initiative without an order from the Imam. The 'hands' are the Gates, the 'feet' are the summoning believers who have received permission (*al-mu'minūn al-du'āt al-ma'dhūn lahum*). '*They will not forge a lie*' concerning the Gates and the believers, [the latter] by attributing a lie to the Gates and [the former] by deceiving the believers. Otherwise, they would be iniquitous to themselves, that is, the Gates and the believers. '*They will not rebel against you in what is right* (*ma'rūf*)': they will not rebel against you concerning the Imam whose sacred station is known (*ma'rūf*). '*That they should not disobey you in what is right*' means they should not disobey you concerning the station of the known Imam, nor concerning any known (*ma'rūf*) matter of religion; the Truth is clear and evident.

24. '*Then accept their allegiance*': impose these conditions on them, release the Summons (*aṭliq lahum al-da'wa*) upon them and command them to give their oath of allegiance to the Prince of the Believers — peace be upon him.

[The succession of Muḥammad and the Imam as a Book:
exegeses of Q. 62:2 and 46:12]

25. '*It is He who has sent amongst the unlettered (al-ummiyyīn) a Messenger from among them, to recite His signs (āyāt), to purify them, and to teach them the Book and the Wisdom — though they had been, before, in manifest error*' [Q. 62:2]. The 'unlettered ones' <are those who did not have an Imam; he is the Book>[346] because the unlettered, in the exoteric, are <those who do not read>[347] books nor write. God sent Muḥammad — may God bless him — was sent to the two groups

---

[346] Mss. A, B: missing. Addition in the margin of B: *alladhīn lam yakun fīhim imām wa-ahl al-kitāb*. Corrected to: *alladhīn lam yakun fīhim imām wa-huwa al-kitāb*, after Ghālib, p. 145.

[347] Mss. A, B: *lā ya'rifūn al-kitāb*. Strothmann: *lā ya'rifūn wa-huwa al-kitāb* Corrected to: *lā yaqra'ūn al-kitāb*, after Ghālib, p. 145.

<. . .>[348] . . .the sons of Ismael who did not have an Imam, because the Imamate was in the hands of the sons of Isaac until Muḥammad — may God bless him — was sent. God sent him as *'a Messenger from among them, to recite His signs'*, that is, to inform them of the Imams of God's religion among **[167]** his progeny[349]. *'To purify them'*: by the Summons to the Truth of Islam, he cleanses them from the filth of the falsity of the state of ignorance (*jāhiliyya*). *'To teach them the Book and the Wisdom'*: he informs them of the Imam after him, who is His Legatee, so that his name and his place become known. The 'Book' is the Imam, and the 'Wisdom' is the Speaking-Messenger who comes after him from his progeny. He informs them of him; he is the Mahdī to whom the Messenger had pointed — may God bless him. *'Though they had been, before, in manifest error'*: before the Messenger of God, they did not have an Imam to guide them to the religion of God, and consequently their error was manifest because of their remoteness from the Imams of God's Truth.

26. *'Before him, there was the Book of Moses, an Imam and a Mercy, and this Book confirms the other ones in Arabic tongue, in order to warn the iniquitous and to give good tidings to those who do good'* [Q. 46:12]. Before the Book of Muḥammad, there was the Book of Moses. The Book of Muḥammad is the Imam he establishes after himself, that is, his Legatee ʿAlī b. Abī Ṭālib, just as the Book of Moses was the Imam he had indicated as the Imam after himself, namely Aaron. God says: *'This Book confirms the other ones in Arabic tongue.'* This refers to ʿAlī b. Abī Ṭālib who was the first to confirm Muḥammad as the Messenger of God. The 'tongue' (*lisān*) is Muḥammad, and ʿAlī is the Imam that Muḥammad pointed to — may God bless them both. *'In order to warn* **[168]** *the iniquitous'*, meaning those who deviated from the Imamate of the religion of God and took as friends [individuals] other than His Friends (*tawallū ghayr awliyāʾihi*). *'And to give good tidings to those who do good'*, that is, those who aim at the path of God and do good works on this path.

---

[348] The text is corrupted, maybe lacking some words. Should we understand that these two groups are the sons of Ismael on the one hand, and the sons of Isaac on the other hand?

[349] On the Imams as 'signs' (*āya*, pl. *āyāt*), see *Kashf* III, p. 79, § 55, and related footnote; V, pp. 130–133, §§ 68–70; VI, pp. 173–174, § 36–37.

[The mountains as Proofs: exegesis of Q. 20:105–107]

27. *'They ask you about the mountains, say: 'My Lord will scatter them into dust, leaving them as a level plain where you will see no crookedness nor relief* [Q. 20:105–107]. By the 'mountains' He means the Proofs. *'My Lord will scatter them into dust'* refers to the quivering (*ihtizāz*) of their hearts and to their joy in [obeying] the Command of God. '. . .*leaving them as a level plain*': the fear and glorification of God will humble and submit them. '*You will see no crookedness nor curvature*': you will see no 'crookedness' and no stubbornness among them as to the Truth, nor any doubt or disagreement. *'Nor relief*': on earth, there are low and high places. Thus, He says that there is no laziness, no unwillingness and no disagreement[350] among the Proofs.

[The mountains as Proofs in eschatological context: exegesis of Q. 78:12–20]

28. *'We have built above you seven unshakeable [heavens]'* [Q. 78:12]: 'We have established for your guidance seven Imams supported (*mu'ayyadīn*) by [divine] force as a means from God [to join Him]. *'Above you'*: between you and God. *'And We made a dazzling lamp'* [Q. 78:13]: this refers to the Gate who raises the degrees of the believers and gives life to the Summons under the Imam's command. *'Dazzling'*: **[169]** the word 'dazzling' means illuminating, luminescent, and this refers to knowledge and demonstration (*bayān*). *'And We have sent down from the rainy clouds abundant water'* [Q. 78:14]. The 'rainy clouds' represent the Summoners, 'water' represents knowledge. What is 'abundant' is what flows in great quantities. So this means: 'And we have sent down with the Summoners a greatly flowing knowledge by which the believers come to life.'

29. *'To bring forth grain and plants, and gardens luxuriant (alfāfan)'* [Q. 78:15–16], that is, 'rallied' (*multaffīn*) and regrouped around one Order (*amr*), which is the straight religion of God. *'Indeed a time is fixed for the Day of separation'* [Q. 78:17]. The 'Day of separation' is the Mahdī — may God bless him — through whom God separates Truth from falsehood, and a believer from an unbeliever. He is the fixed

---

[350] The term translated as 'relief', *amt*, may also bear the meaning of 'doubt', 'hesitation' or 'disagreement'.

term of God's Order (*amr*) and its end: he is the seventh of the seven Speaking-Prophets. '*The Day the Trumpet is blown, you will come in troops*' [Q. 78:18]: the Day when his Order becomes manifest and he announces the Summons toward him; '*you will come in troops*', one troop after another, willingly or not. '*And heaven is open, and become gates*' [Q. 78:19]: he will unveil the veiled, esoteric knowledge of the Imams, which will contain the sacred stations of Gates who teach everyone who asks and seeks. '*And the mountains are set in motion and become as a mirage*' [Q. 78:20]: the Proofs will be set in motion. When the Mahdī becomes manifest, they will be ordered to manifest and follow the path of Truth (*ṣirāṭ al-ḥaqq*). '*As a mirage*': on that day, the Proofs will be similar to a mirage, because their observance, their obedience and the manifestation of their Order will follow their refraining from [such manifestation] by staying veiled and silent (*al-satr wa'l-kitmān*).

[The mountains as Proofs: exegesis of Q. 38:18–19]

30. God says about David: '*We subjected the mountains with him to give glory at evening and sunrise, and the birds, mustered,* **[170]** *every one to Him reverting*' [Q. 38:18–19]. '*We subjected the mountains with him*' means: 'We established the Proofs with him'.[351] '*To give glory*' is to summon. '*At evening and sunrise*': sunrise is similar to the Messenger, because he is the starting point of the exoteric laws (*mubtada' al-sharā'iʿ al-ẓāhira*), just as the sunrise is the starting point of daylight — and the day is similar to the exoteric. The evening is similar to the Legatee, because he is the starting point of the knowledge of the esoteric, just as the evening is the starting point of the darkness of the night — and the night is similar to the esoteric. So this means: 'We established the Proofs with him, to summon to the exoteric and the esoteric by which God established the Legatee and the Messenger.'

[351] See the interpretation of Q. 21:79 and 34:10, both mentioning the subjection of the mountains to David, in al-Sijistānī, *Kitāb al-iftikhār*, pp. 224–225, where the mountains are identified with the Proofs as well. See also a similar interpretation of Q. 21:79 and 34:10 in al-Qāḍī al-Nuʿmān, *Asās al-ta'wīl*, p. 253, cited in I.K. Poonawala, 'Ismāʿīlī ta'wīl of the Qur'an', p. 216, n. 52; Jaʿfar b. Manṣūr al-Yaman, *Al-Shawāhid wa'l-bayān*, IIS MS. 734, ff. 154–156.

The 'birds' are like the Summoners.[352] He says: We have tasked him with establishing the Summons through the Summoners, 'mustered' with him, that is, assembled in obedience to him. *'Every one to Him reverting'* means they all summon toward him and refer to him as to their knowledge and Summons.

[The succession of Muḥammad and the Imam as a Book]

31. *'Those to whom We have sent the Book, who recite it as it should be recited, those believe in it. And those who disbelieve in it, they are the losers'* [Q. 2:121]. The 'Book' means the Imam. He then means: 'those to whom We gave the Imam and to whom we made him known' — and he is ʿAlī b. Abī Ṭālib. *'They recite (yatlūn) it as it should be recited'*: they follow him as he should be followed, because the one who recites (*al-tālī*) is the one who follows (*al-muttabiʿ*).[353] *'Those believe in it. And those who disbelieve in it, they are the losers'*: those are the ones who believe in the Imam, and those who disbelieve in him have lost themselves in this world and the hereafter, because they have not followed the Imam and God does not accept the deeds of anyone except those undertaken by following the Imam. **[171]**

32. *'And what of him who stands upon a clear sign from his Lord, and is followed (yatlūhu)[354] by a witness from Him, and before there was the Book of Moses as an Imam and a Mercy[355]? Those believe in it; but whoever disbelieves in it from the factions, the Fire is his appointed place. So be not in doubt concerning it; it is the Truth from your Lord'* [Q. 11:17].

---

[352] On the identification of the birds with the Summoners, see al-Qāḍī al-Nuʿmān, *Asās al-taʾwīl*, p. 253; Jaʿfar b. Manṣūr al-Yaman, *Sarāʾir wa-asrār al-nuṭaqāʾ*, pp. 23–24; idem, *Al-Shawāhid waʾl-bayān*, IIS MS. 734, f. 155. This is most probably related to the designation of the *duʿāt* as 'Wings' (*janāḥ* pl. *ajniḥa*); see *Kashf* I, p. 9, § 18, and above, p. 83, n. 33.

[353] The author uses the double meaning of the verb *talā*, which means 'to recite' as well as 'to follow'.

[354] Again, the author interprets the Qurʾanic occurrence of the verb *talā* as meaning 'to follow', instead of the usual understanding of the term as 'to recite'; see previous footnote. I have chosen to translate the verse accordingly in order for it to fit the interpretation that follows.

[355] See above *Kashf* VI, p. 168, §26 for an interpretation of Q. 46:12, which also mentions the 'Book of Moses which was an Imam and a Mercy'.

33. [The 'clear sign'] refers to Muḥammad — may God bless him. *'It is followed by a witness from Him'*: [the 'witness'] refers to ʿAlī b. Abī Ṭālib — peace be upon him — who followed (*ittabaʿa*) Muḥammad and whom God decreed to be Imam after him. *'And before there was the Book of* Moses': previously there was an Imam whom Moses indicated, who was Aaron. *'As an Imam and a Mercy'*: this means that *'it is followed by a witness from Him'* to be an Imam.[356] The 'Mercy' is the Messenger, and the 'Imam' is ʿAlī — peace be upon him — just as Moses and the Imam he had indicated, and who was his 'Book'. *'As an Imam and a Mercy'* means: as an Imam and a Messenger. *'Those believe in it'* refers to those who believe in ʿAlī and know his Imamate because of the Messenger's bequest (*waṣiyya*) to him. *'Whoever disbelieves in it from the factions'*: whoever disbelieves in ʿAlī among the people of division (*ahl al-iftirāq*) who separated (*faraqū*) from their religion and did not organize it according to the bequest (*waṣiyya*). The 'factions' are the separated groups (*al-firaq*). *'The Fire is his appointed place (mawʿid)'*: the punishment that is promised (*wuʿida*) is the 'appointed place' (*mawʿid*) for those who disbelieved in ʿAlī. God punishes them for their disbelief and their rebellion against God and His Messenger by [rebelling against] his sacred station. Then He says to His Prophet: *'So be not in doubt concerning it; it is the Truth from your Lord'*: be not in doubt concerning ʿAlī; he is the Imam of Truth, approved by your Lord for His Cause (*li-ḥaqqihi*). *'But most men do not believe'* [Q. 11:17], that is, they do not believe in ʿAlī's sacred station when he is the Truth from God. **[172]**

34. [God] says: *'We have not sent down upon you the Book except that you make clear to them that wherein they differ'* [Q. 16:64]: 'We have not sent down the sacred station of the Imamate, etc.'

35. *'We have sent down upon you the Book. Those to whom We have given the Book believe in it; and some of these believe in it. And none denies Our signs but the disbelievers'* [Q. 29:47]. This means: We inspired you to establish an Imam for your community, and a Legatee for you. Those who were before you, for whom We had appointed an Imam, believe in their Imam. *'And some of these believe in him'*, that is, some in your community believe in the Imam He established and know his

[356] The text adds '. . .and a Messenger', which makes no sense. The whole passage seems corrupted, possibly partly because of a homeoteleuton.

sacred station. *'And none denies Our signs but the disbelievers'*: And none denies the Imams of our religion but the disbelievers in religion.[357]

[Choosing one's own Imam: exegeses of Q. 10:17–18 and 13:33]

36. *'Who is more iniquitous than the one who forges a lie against God, and who denies His signs? Indeed, the criminals will not prosper. And they worship apart from God what hurts them not neither profits them, and they say: 'These are our intercessors with God'. Say: Will you inform God of what He knows not in the heavens or in the earth? Glory be to Him! High be He Exalted above whatever they associate [with Him]!'* [Q. 10:17–18].

37. This means: 'Who is more iniquitous than the one who forges a lie against God by establishing for His religion an Imam He did not establish?' *'And who denies* **[173]** *His signs'*: who denies the Imams of God's religion whom God has chosen. *'Indeed, the criminals will not prosper'*: they will not be saved from the punishment of God, nor will they gain any reward which is prosperity (*falāḥ*). And those who have committed a crime by forging [a lie] against God and denying the Imams of His religion, they will not prosper. *'They worship apart from God'*: they worship something apart from God and from His choice which *'hurts them not neither profits them'*; if they turned away from it and disobeyed it, it would not hurt them, while obeying and following it does not profit them. *'They say: 'These are our intercessors with God'*: God approves us and accepts our deeds in following these, obeying them and taking them as intercessors. *'Say: Will you inform God of what He knows not in the heavens or in the earth?'*: Will you inform God that you have established for yourselves Imams and chiefs and have followed them, when God does not know of them as Messengers, nor as Legatees, Imams or Proofs? *'Glory be to Him! High be He Exalted above whatever they associate!'* They have established associates to His choice by choosing for themselves. They follow their own choice and this choice has enslaved them. This is associating something with God, *'glory be to Him! High be He Exalted above whatever they associate!'*

---

[357] On the Imams as 'signs' (*āya*, pl. *āyāt*), see *Kashf* III, p. 79, § 55, and related footnote; V, pp. 130–133, §§ 68–70; VI, pp. 167–168, § 25; pp. 173–174, §§ 36–37.

38. Similar to this [verse is the one that states]: *'Will you inform Him of what He know not in the earth? Or is it in apparent words? Nay, but the stratagems of the disbelievers were decked out fair to them, and they deviated from the Path. Whoever God sends astray, no* **[174]** *guide has he'* [Q. 13:33]. This means: Will you inform Him that you have chosen for yourselves and you have followed one whom God does not acknowledge to be among the Legatees?' They have the audacity [to think] that God will accept this from them. *'Or is it in apparent words'*, namely the words in which you openly state that you obey God, while you have intentionally rebelled against Him [by not following] the Legatee of His Messenger. Again, they have the audacity to believe that He will accept their deeds. *'But the stratagems of the disbelievers were decked out fair to them'*: the stratagems of those who denied ʿAlī's sacred station were decked out fair to them when they rejected the Legacy and usurped the sacred station of the Imamate based on their passions, apart from the choice of God and His Messenger. It is Satan who decked this out fair to them. *'And they deviated from the Path'*, that is, from ʿAlī who is God's path; God accepts no worship but the one taken by following him and the Legacy of the Messenger. [The Legacy] is the Path of God and His tradition, but they have refused it. *'Whoever God sends astray, no guide has he'*: this means that God sent them astray when they deviated from His Path and followed their passions, and no guide have they, as God says: *'Have you seen the one who takes his passions (hawāhu) as his deity? God has left him astray purposely'* [Q. 45:23].

[The Imam as a Book: exegesis of Q. 2:78–79]

39. *'And some are unlettered (ummiyyūn) who know not the Book, but see only their fancy therein, and they do nothing but speculate.* **[175]** *So woe to those who write the book with their hands and then say: 'This is from God', to sell it for a small price. Woe to them for what their hands have written, and woe to them for their earnings'* [Q. 2:78–79]. Some do not have an Imam and do not believe. *'They know not the Book, but see only their fancy therein'*: they know no Imam but the one their fancy sees. God does not accept their deeds in obeying him whom they have chosen to lead them (*li-imāmatihim*). *'They do nothing but speculate'*: in following who they have chosen, they do nothing but speculate that God will accept this from them, but they have no certainty (*yaqīn*) of this, nor any insight, nor the approval of God concerning the Imams of His religion. *'So woe to those who write the book with their hands and then say: 'This is from God'*: Woe to those who appoint an Imam based on their passions, and then say: 'This is the Imam of the religion of God. God will approve whoever follows him and accept the deeds made by following and imitating him'. *'To sell it for a small price'*: to acquire with it what their souls desire (*mā tahwā anfusuhum*) and a little, evanescent stretch in this wordly life — such is the 'small price'. *'Woe to them for what their hands have written'*: Woe to them for whoever they established and followed based on their passions, because he will lead them down to the Fire, and to a *'terrible abode'* [Q. 2:126]. *'And woe to them for what they have earned*: Woe to them for the one they misguided with their own misguidance. They will earn his burden on top of theirs, as God — He is Mighty and Sublime- says: **[176]** *'They will bear their whole burden on the Day of Resurrection, as well as the burden of those they have misguided without knowledge. O terrible the burden they bear!'* [Q. 16:25].

[The Imams and their representatives:
Summoners, Gates and Proofs]

40. *'Say: 'Have you imagined if God took away your hearing and your sight and sealed your hearts, who is the deity who could restore it to you save God? See how We display the signs, and yet they turn away'* [Q. 6:46]: 'Have you imagined if God deprived you from the Summoners' from whom they hear the knowledge of religion — they are the ones meant by the 'hearing' — 'and deprived you from the knowledge' by which they see the Path of guidance — this is what is meant by the 'sight' — 'and hid from you the Imams who guide you to God's approbation through the Proofs and the Summoners' — they [the Imams] are the 'hearts', for the hearts are the seat (*mustaqarr*) of the physical (*ẓāhira*) life, just as the Imams are the seat of the <esoteric> life <which resurrects>[358] from the death of ignorance.

41. *'Who is the deity who could restore it to you'*: [who] could restore the religion He hid and deprived you from? *'See how We display the*

358 Mss. A, B: *wa'l-a'imma mustaqarr al-ḥayāt min al-ḥaqq*. Both manuscripts are corrupted here. The translation follows the suggested reconstitution of meaning in Strothmann's edition (p. 177, n. 4).

signs, and yet they turn away: see how the Imams appoint [**177**] the Summoners, the Gates and the Proofs for their guidance, and aid them by all means to guide toward God's religion (*yamuddūnahum bi-kull bāb ʿan al-hidāya ilā dīn Allāh*).[359] Yet, after the Imams and the guides (*hudāt*) are appointed, '*they turn away*' from them and from the Truth of God they bear.

42. Similar to this are His words: '*Who is more iniquitous than the one who denies*' the Imams of God's religion '*and turn away from them?*'[360] [Q. 6:157]. He also says: '*He followed and befriended other than them*'.[361] And similarly to what He says about hiding the guides and depriving [them] of them, if He wills, He says: '*We print upon their hearts so that they hear not*' [Q. 6:100]. This means that He hides the Imams of their age from them. As a result, [the Imams] do not appoint amongst them His Summoners from whom they would hear knowledge and guidance to God's religion.

43. The explanation of the meaning of these verses is complete. Praise be to God, may He bless Muḥammad the Prophet and the elect among his family, and may He grant them peace.

The *Book of Unveiling* is complete;
it was composed by our master Jaʿfar b. Manṣūr al-Yaman
based on knowledge transmitted by the guided
Imams — peace be upon them. [**178**]

---

[359] Corrected *ʿan* into *fī*.

[360] The text replaces 'God's signs' (*āyāt Allāh*) by 'the Imams of God's religion' (*aʾimmat dīn Allāh*). On the Imams as 'signs' (*āya*, pl. *āyāt*), see *Kashf* III, p. 79, § 55, and related footnote; V, pp. 130–133, §§ 68–70; VI, pp. 167–168, § 25; pp. 173–174, §§ 36–37.

[361] There is no such verse in the Qurʾan, even though there are several occurrences of the verbs *ittabaʿa* and *tawallā*.

Treatise VI Commentary

The style of Treatise VI is somewhat different from the rest of the collection. The doctrine elaborated here seems to fit the pre-Fatimid period, as Heinz Halm has noted in his short abstract of the treatise.[362] Indeed, the mention of the 'seven Imams'[363] is typical — and also rare in the *Kitāb al-Kashf*, as it appears only here and in the Treatise II.[364] Moreover, the mentions of the Mahdī, who is only named three times,[365] seem to imply he is still to come. A descendant of ʿAlī b. Abī Ṭālib, he is presented as 'the last of the Imams and the Speaking-Prophets',[366] 'the seventh of the seven Speaking-Prophets', who 'will unveil the veiled esoteric knowledge of the Imams'[367]. His coming will end the era of 'veiling and silence' during which it was the Proof who was in charge of the *amr*, i.e. the 'Affair' or the 'Cause'. Halm considers that this description of the role of the Proof, as well as its importance as head of the *daʿwa*, represents the 'the old Qarmaṭī doctrine of the Imamate',[368] prior to the Fatimid reform.

These assessments are however based on the Ismaili parts of the treatise, which are in fact intertwined with a series of passages that are Shiʿi in the broad sense, and bear no specifically Ismaili feature. These thus focus on the Imamate of ʿAlī's and the usurpation of his right to succeed the Prophet Muḥammad, emphasizing the notion that this usurpation was the result of men succumbing to their passions

[362] H. Halm, *Kosmologie*, p. 31.

[363] *Kashf* VI, p. 169, § 28.

[364] *Kashf* II, p. 50, § 24. As also noted by W. Madelung, 'Das Imamat', p. 54; see *Kashf* II, p. 50, § 24.

[365] *Kashf* VI, pp. 160, § 7; p. 168, § 25; p. 170, § 29.

[366] *Kashf* VI, p. 160, § 7.

[367] *Kashf* VI, p. 170, § 29.

[368] H. Halm, *Kosmologie*, p. 31.

instead of obeying and following the Prophet, who had explicitly appointed ʿAlī. Contrary to other treatises of the *Kashf*, particularly the first and the third, the enemies of ʿAlī are not named here. Several passages display another Shiʿi theme, also related to the Imamate of ʿAlī, namely the analogy between the latter and Aaron, on the basis of the famous *ḥadīth*: "Alī is to me in the position of Aaron to Moses.' This analogy includes quotations of several Qurʾanic verses mentioning the 'Book', which is identified with the Imam.

It is through the other type of passages that the reader knows that he/she is dealing with an Ismaili text. The Shiʿi and the Ismaili themes of the treatise, however, seem to run in parallel throughout the treatise. Indeed, the Shiʿi passages are almost completely free of Ismaili concepts, except for the mention of the Mahdī as 'the last of the Imams and Speaking-Prophets'.[369] The term 'Proof' as it appears in one of these passages[370] refers to the representative of the Speaking-Prophet, that is, the Legatee (*waṣī*), and does not bear the specific Ismaili meaning that will be discussed further as a rank below the Imam and above the Summoners.[371] It is only in the Ismaili passages, which are inserted between the 'Shiʿi' paragraphs, that we find Qurʾanic exegeses referring to the ranks of the *daʿwa*, particularly the Proofs and the Summoners. The text deals with their role and activities, mainly those related to initiation. It also discusses the necessity of observing certain rules before revealing the esoteric knowledge, the role of the Proof in preparing the Mahdī's return, and the intermediary role played by the Summoners between the Imam and his followers.

The two essential orientations of the treatise (ʿAlī b. Abī Ṭālib's right to succeed the Prophet Muḥammad and the Ismaili esoteric hierarchy) are not explicitly connected to each other up until the very last pages of the treatise. Throughout the treatise, they are intertwined in such a way we are led to suspect once more an intention to 'scatter knowledge',[372] by fragmenting the text into several units that are not

---

[369] *Kashf* VI, p. 160, § 7.

[370] *Kashf* VI, p. 162, § 12.

[371] On the Proof in Ismaili thought, see commentary of *Kashf* V, pp. 395–408.

[372] See introduction, pp. 63–68.

logically and formally connected. The fact that this is intentional seems plausible as it is frequent to see such exegeses suddenly interrupted by unrelated discussions and resumed a few pages later. What is specific to the Treatiise VI is that its parallel themes are reunited and linked together in the final pages of the text: from the necessity to obey God's command in following the Imam — here exemplified by ʿAlī — one must draw the necessity to follow the latter's representatives, that is, the missionaries of the *daʿwa*.

It seems fair to consider that this treatise is the one with the highest political potential, as its esoteric teachings can all be geared towards the justification of a political organization led by an Imam whose legitimacy directly derives from his ancestor, ʿAlī b. Abī Ṭālib. It is true that this is generally the case in the *Kitāb al-Kashf*, but the emphasis here is on ʿAlī b. Abī Ṭālib's right to rule, while his other classical Shiʿi attributes, such as his role as *ṣāḥib al-taʾwīl*, 'Master of the Exegesis', for example, seem to be left aside. This treatise particularly reminds us of the political nature of the Ismaili *daʿwa* in its early stages — though this statement does not diminish the spiritual aspects of the treatise. In the following pages, I will attempt to show how the text echoes, not only the historical context of its composition, but also larger political debates within Shiʿi Islam. It is also a testimony of the *daʿwa* as a strictly hierarchized and disciplined political organization.

1. God's choice challenged by human caprice

The treatise begins with Q. 53:23 which mentions 'what souls desire' (*mā tahwā al-anfus*). The verb *hawā* is derived from the common Qurʾanic root *h-w-y* from which also derives the noun *hawā*, pl. *ahwāʾ*, 'love, predilection, inclination, passion, desire, whim, caprice'. In the Qurʾan, the term generally has negative connotations and conveys the notion of irrational and subjective passions that drive people away from the certainty of faith. It is worth noting the Qurʾanic tendency to present faith, not as an epistemological jump beyond human rationality, but rather as in continuity with the natural state of humanity. Therefore, the denial of God's revelation can only result from an irrational deviation equated to a caprice or a whim. The *hawā* is a subjective and evil propensity away from the divine command as transmitted through the prophets.[373]

In the Islamic tradition, the term was often used in relation to so-called 'heretical' groups, as can be seen, for example, from the title of Ibn Ḥazm's heresiographical work, the *Fiṣal fi'l-milal wa'l-ahwā' wa'l-niḥal*. Hence the expression *ahl al-ahwā'*, 'people of passions', to designate groups considered deviant, such as the Qadariyya and others.[374] In a Shiʿi context, it is the non-Shiʿi groups who are accused of 'following their passions' when refusing to acknowledge ʿAlī's right to succeed the Prophet Muḥammad, and, more broadly, the Imams' religious status.

So far, while we have met several developments in the *Kitāb al-Kashf* dealing with ʿAlī's legitimacy, whether they be linked to his role as the Legatee, to the notion of inheritance and legacy, or to the necessity of an esoteric exegesis to complement the exoteric revelation, the question has only briefly been addressed in this particular way. As a matter of fact, the 'passions' only appear twice before Treatise VI, both times in Treatise V, in contexts dealing with the choice (*ikhtiyār*) of an Imam by the community without taking into account God's and Muḥammad's explicit designation of ʿAlī as the rightful Imam: 'They associated their own choice with God's, and with the following of their *passions*';[375] 'They have associated the *passions* of their souls and the choice of their chiefs (*kubarā'*) who led them astray from the path with God's order concerning the Imam'.[376] In Treatise VI, ʿAlī's legitimacy is essentially grounded on this opposition between the human passions and the profane choice of a leader, on one hand, and the sacred

373 For a better grasp of this notion, here are a few examples of its use in the Qur'an, among many others: *'Is it not that every time a Messenger came unto you with what your souls had no desire for (*bi-mā lā tahwā anfusukum*), you grew arrogant, etc.'* (Q. 2:87). *'Do not follow the passions (*ahwā'*) of those who deny Our signs, etc.'* (Q. 6:150). *'Do not follow the passions (*ahwā'*) of those who know not'* (Q. 45:18). *'Have you seen him who takes his caprice (*hawāhu*) as his deity? God has left him astray purposely. . .'* (Q. 45:23). *'Know that they only follow* their *passions (*ahwā'ahum*), and who goes further astray than one who follows his own passion without guidance from God'* (Q. 28:50).

374 See I. Goldziher, '*Ahl al-ahwā'*', *EI2*.

375 *Kashf* V, p. 146, § 92.

376 *Kashf* V, p. 153, § 103.

investiture of the divinely chosen Imam, on the other hand — ʿAlī's role as holder of the esoteric knowledge thus seems secondary.

However, as mentioned before, this motif of the 'passions' is far from an original contribution by the *Kitāb al-Kashf*. It is indeed a typical feature of Shiʿi literature which usually understands every Qur'anic occurrence of the term as an allusion to the usurpation of ʿAlī's authority after the death of the Prophet. In a *ḥadīth* reporting a *khuṭba* pronounced in Medina by ʿAlī, he reproaches the community for 'following its passions' and going astray from the Truth while knowing it was the Truth. Yet, if people had 'taken knowledge from its mine (*maʿdin*) and drunk the water from its source', they would have joined the Path. Instead, 'you took the path of iniquity' and 'the doors of knowledge have shut off before you'; 'you advocated your passions, you disagreed upon your religion, you delivered your opinion on God's religion without knowledge; you followed the misguided and they misguided you, you renounced the Imams and they renounced you, and you started to decide according to your passions'. A few lines further, the text is more explicit as to the truth the community has renounced: 'You knew I was your master (*ṣāḥibukum*) and the one you were ordered [to obey], that I am your savant (*ʿālimukum*) whose knowledge is your salvation, the Legatee of your Prophet, the choice (*khayra*) of your Lord, etc.'[377] There are countless other texts in which the usurping of ʿAlī's 'authority' or 'affair' (*amr*) is similarly attributed to the community succumbing to its passions, instead of obeying the explicit designation of ʿAlī by God, his Prophet and/or his Book.

Such interpretations typically concern the succession of the Prophet, and therefore the alleged coup d'état which deprived ʿAlī of power. Yet, they are also extended to his successors, often with political connotations, as we shall now see in another example that will shed some light on the political implications of Treatise VI. Al-Kulaynī, in the chapter dedicated to 'the criterion to discern the truthful and false claims to the Imamate' of his *Uṣūl al-Kāfī*, transmits a lengthy *ḥadīth* setting out a dialogue between Imam Muḥammad al-Bāqir (d.115/732) and his half-brother Zayd b. ʿAlī (d.122/740) who led a revolt against

---

[377] Al-Kulaynī, *al-Rawḍa min al-kāfī, khuṭbat al-ṭālūtiyya*, p. 32.

the Umayyads in Kūfa, only to die after being wounded in combat.[378] Given the political quietism adopted by the Imams after the martyrdom of Ḥusayn in Karbala in 61/680,[379] we can guess that the discussion will revolve around the religious legitimacy of political uprisings.

Zayd goes to his brother Muḥammad al-Bāqir with letters from the Shiʿi community of Kūfa, urging him to join them in their uprising against Umayyad power. Muḥammad al-Bāqir asks whether these letters are their initiative or a response to a call from Zayd — a question with important implications as will be seen. As the letters turn out to come from the free initiative of the believers, Muḥammad al-Bāqir gives a lengthy answer aimed at cooling Zayd's ardour: 'Do not be hasty, he says, God does not hasten according to the servants' hastiness.' In anger, Zayd declares: 'One who sits (*qaʿada*) in his home, draws the curtain and turns away from *jihād*, is no Imam to us. Our Imam is one who stands for his own and fights fully for the cause of God' (*jāhada fī sabīl Allāh ḥaqq jihādihi*). Again, Muḥammad al-Bāqir's response is quite long and this time grounded in Qur'anic evidence, as he asks Zayd whether his endeavour is supported by any kind of proof from God. All in all, he reproaches his brother for engaging in 'a doubtful and questionable issue' (*amran anta minhu fī shakkin wa shubhatin*), without any certainty (*yaqīn*), and concludes with these severe sentences:

> I take refuge in God from an Imam so misguided that those who follow him know better than the one they follow. Do you want, O brother, to revive the ways of the people who denied God's signs, disobeyed His Messenger, *followed their passions* without

---

[378] See W. Madelung, 'Zayd b. ʿAlī b. al-Ḥusayn', *EI2*; idem, 'Zaydiyya', *EI2*.

[379] On the quietism of the Imams, see M.A. Amir-Moezzi, *Guide divin*, pp. 155–173, esp. pp. 170–171 (English trans., *Divine Guide*, pp. 61–69, esp. p. 68), where several *ḥadīth*s are quoted, warning against the temptation to command and the claims for political power. On the problematic of political quietism in classical Shiʿism, see R. Gleave, 'Quietism and Political Legitimacy in Imami Shiʿi Jurisprudence: al-Sharīf al-Murtaḍa's Treatise on the Legality of Working for the Government Reconsidered', in S. al-Sarhan, ed, *Political Quietism in Islam. Sunni and Shiʿi Practice and Thought* (London, 2020), pp. 99–128.

> guidance from God,[380] and claimed the succession without any proof from God nor covenant from His Messenger?[381]

This *ḥadīth* opposes the quietist (*quʿūd*) tendencies of early Shiʿi Islam to its revolutionary (*qiyām, khurūj*) temptations. It falls within an Imami literature designed to justify the Imams' political quietism after the martyrdom of Ḥusayn in Karbala. This renunciation of power and refraining from political activities was bound to cause great disarray among some of their disciples. Indeed, holding that no power was legitimate but the Imam's, and yet refusing any attempt to seize power by force and to oppose directly an unjust rule, might have been an all too subtle argument in the eyes of the faithful thirsty for justice. This explains the fact that some Imami believers turned to the Ismaili *daʿwa*, in the hope that it would eventually restore the Ahl al-Bayt to their rights — as the archetypal example of Ibn Ḥawshab Manṣūr al-Yaman demonstrates.

Clearly, the Ismaili *daʿwa* was not quietist as it is characterized, from its very origins, by its leaning to the activist tendencies of Shiʿism. Indeed, some Ismaili texts elaborate on the necessity of *qiyām*,[382] that is, military action, a feature that would eventually lead al-Qāḍī al-Nuʿmān to include *jihād* as a pillar of Islam. Even *zakāt*, another pillar of Islam, may have the political implication of financial support (*ikhrāj al-amwāl*) for the *daʿwa*'s earthly endeavours.[383]

Nevertheless, it is by drawing on the very principles held by the quietist tendency of Shiʿi Islam that Ismailism legitimates its *daʿwa*: the sacredness of the Imam, the religious duty to obey him, and the idea that he is the 'summoner', not to be summoned by anyone. It is

---

380 A direct allusion to the abovementioned Qur'anic verse 28:50.

381 Al-Kulaynī, *Uṣūl al-Kāfī, kitāb al-ḥujja, bāb mā yufṣal bi-hi bayna daʿwā al-muḥiqq wa al-mubṭil fī amr al-imāma*, vol. 1, pp. 356–358, no. 16.

382 See e.g. Jaʿfar b. Manṣūr al-Yaman, *Taʾwīl al-zakāt*, p. 73: '[God] made [*jihād* against the deniers] a clear obligation, such that their faith would not be fulfilled without complying with it (*al-qiyām bi-hā*). There is no excuse for anyone to step back from *jihād* and no pretext to account for sitting (*quʿūd*) instead.'

383 The anonymous work recently published under the title *Mafātīḥ al-Niʿma*, and dated from the North African period of the Fatimid rule, is essentially a letter to a *daʿwa* member exhorting him to pay his dues to the organization; see W. Madelung and P. Walker, *Affirming the Imamate*, pp. 79–105 (Arabic: pp. 73–110).

indeed an interesting paradox that some of the same arguments were used to support the Ismaili propaganda in favour of political activism (whether in the name of the Mahdī or the Fatimid Imam), as well as political quietism. In the *ḥadīth* above, we notice that the Kufan revolt is implicitly discredited from the very beginning of the text because it was not called upon by the Ahl al-Bayt; it is not the believers' place to call upon their Imam, nor is it for them to put him in charge. The Imam, indeed, is no secular sovereign who holds his position and legitimacy from the people. He is not appointed by his partisans, nor is he accountable to them. He does not depend on them for his status, but it is they who depend on him for their salvation. At the core of the text is the rejection of an authority based on *contingent* circumstances, on the desires, whims and passions of the people. If Muḥammad al-Bāqir had responded to the invitation of his Kufan partisans, he would have placed himself in a situation of inferiority as this would have implied that he drew his power from the people, and would therefore reverse the hierarchical order; this is the meaning of the allusion to the 'Imam so misguided that those who follow him know better than the one they follow'.

The last sentence I have translated from the *ḥadīth* is a direct allusion to the succession of the Prophet Muḥammad. Muḥammad al-Bāqir is accusing his brother of following the path of the Sunnis, inasmuch as he accepts the idea that the Imam can be appointed by the people — even though the latter's choices are arbitrary, conjectural and based on irrational desires and passions — and respond to their call, whereas it should be the people who answer the divinely appointed Imam's call.

There are other examples of Imamī *ḥadīth*s supporting the political passivity of the Imams and their followers that can just as well be used to promote political activism. For instance, the following *ḥadīth*: 'Any banner raised before the uprising of the Qā'im belongs to a rebel against God (*ṭāghūt*)',[384] does not contradict the pre-Fatimid and early Fatimid Ismaili activities since the Ismailis specifically wished to raise their banner in the name of the Qā'im. Again, such a *ḥadīth* implies

[384] Cited in M.A. Amir-Moezzi, *Spirituality of Shi'i Islam*, p. 427 (*La Religion discrète*, p. 314).

the same political theology that opposes a 'democratic', earthly investiture, where the sovereign takes his legitimacy from his supporters, to a sacred investiture, where the Imam holds his legitimacy from God. Whereas — in the Shiʿi view — the Sunnis accept the first option and consider that the end of the prophetic era marks the end of sacred temporal authority, the Shiʿis hold that there must be a kind of continuity to the prophetic mission, not only on a hermeneutical and esoteric level, but also on an exoteric and political one.

This political theology is common in its principle to Imami and Ismaili sources: political power can, no more than any religious matter, be left to human arbitrariness.[385] It is only the conclusions drawn from this common axiom that vary from one tradition to the other.

It is not necessary to go through the details of the argumentation regarding ʿAlī's Imamate in Treatise VI, as we have met similar ones in the previous treatises of the *Kitāb al-Kashf.* It is sufficient to give some keys to appreciate the political theology implied by the idea, essential to this treatise, that the usurpation of authority in the aftermath of the Prophet's death falls within the submission to passions and the supremacy of personal choice over divine election. The consequence of such an argument, in the Ismaili perspective, is to base the Imamate, not on favourable military circumstances, but on irrevocable necessity: the Imamate is no matter of choice, it does not depend on temporal contingencies, on political manoeuvres and calculations, but is a divine decree one must abide by.

One easily perceives the use that can be made of such a view by the Ismailis vis-à-vis their adversaries: it allows them to present the Abbasids, their local governors, as well as the dissident Ismaili missionaries, the Qarmaṭis, as factions whose power was solely based on contingency. Their authority, therefore, was of a purely profane nature.

---

[385] This is indeed the idea developed in the *Tathbīt al-Imāma*, attributed to the third Fatimid caliph, al-Manṣūr bi'llāh. As a commentary on Qur'anic verse 4:59 (also quoted in *Kashf* V, p. 123, § 55): *'Obey God, obey His Messenger and those in authority among you'*, he makes the point that if it was acceptable for men to choose 'those in authority' relying on their personal conjecture and appreciation, then they would also be entitled to choose their own Messenger; see S. Makarem, *The Shiʿi Imamate*, esp. pp. 63–64 (Arabic: pp. 57–58).

Also, despite the absolute lack of historical hints in Treatise VI, there is at least one crucial episode of early Fatimid times with which the political reasoning we find here fits perfectly: the failed plot of Abū ʿAbd Allāh al-Shīʿī against the Imam-Caliph ʿAbd Allāh al-Mahdī. Thus, this would be about suggesting that despite appearances, ʿAbd Allāh al-Mahdī did not hold his authority from Abū ʿAbd Allāh al-Shīʿī. Positing that authority is God-given would enable the first Fatimid caliph to turn the perspective around, and present the concrete conditions of his access to power as the result of God's will, rather than Abū ʿAbd Allāh al-Shīʿī's patient activism. This way, the execution of the latter would not appear so ungrateful. Al-Mahdī's authority was not based on men's 'desires' and 'passions', because, if that were the case, they would have been entitled to overthrow him, as Abū ʿAbd Allāh al-Shīʿī indeed planned. Such an overthrow happened in another messianic context, that of the Qarmaṭī state, when the Qarmaṭī leader Abū Ṭāhir al-Jannābī (d. 332/943–4) ended up executing 'Abū al-Faḍl the Zoroastrian', whom he had previously presented as the Mahdī about three years before the death (934) of the first Fatimid caliph, ʿAbd Allāh al-Mahdī.[386] It is true that there are many other historical occasions when the political theology developed in Treatise VI might have been of use to the Fatimids. However, given the probability of several other texts of the collection — especially Treatise V — having been composed under the reign of the first two Fatimid caliphs, the hypothesis that Treatise VI is somehow related to Abū ʿAbd Allāh al-Shīʿī's plot is to be considered.

In any case, Treatise VI is an illustration of the general endeavour of Fatimid Ismailism to institute a sacred power. This is of course obvious for the pre-Fatimid period, oriented towards the arriving of the Mahdī and the establishment of his rule. This orientation, however, was maintained during the Fatimid period: accession to power did not lead to a form of secularization of the conception of power. Of course, it was necessary at first to temper, sometimes harshly, the eschatological hopes of over-enthusiastic supporters, to fight antinomianism, and to reform the doctrine in order to postpone the apparition of the seventh Speaking-Prophet. The Fatimid caliphate was nevertheless based on the sacrality of the Imam and a fully Shiʿi conception, that is, political *and* spiritual, of the Imamate. The messianic reign of al-Ḥākim bi-Amr

---

[386] On this episode, see H. Halm, *The Empire of the Mahdi*, pp. 257–264.

Allāh[387] would be the extreme consequence of such a profound belief in the sacredness of the Imam's rule.

2. ʿAlī and Aaron as Books of God

Another particularity of Treatise VI is the way it combines two classical Shiʿi themes. The first is the famous *hadīth al-manzila*: "Alī is in relation to me as was Aaron was to Moses.'[388] The second is the equivalence between the Imam and the Qur'anic occurrences of the word *kitāb*, 'book'. Both these themes already appeared in the previous treatises, but separately. Here, they are closely interlinked, this interlinking being based on the Qur'an itself.

In Treatise I, the analogy between ʿAlī and Aaron was addressed through the prism of the disobedience of the communities of which they were in charge. As we have shown in the commentary on Treatise I, the emphasis was on the 'negative' aspect of the analogy: ʿAlī and Aaron are compared inasmuch as their very existence reveals the unfaithfulness of the community towards its prophet.[389] In addition, Aaron appeared in the second development on the 'continuity of the Order' along with

---

[387] While historiography has generally depicted the 'madness' of this caliph, this so-called madness may have been the result of al-Ḥākim's eschatological conception of his role. It is not by accident that the Druze 'heresy' appeared under his reign, apparently shielded by his indulgence, to the great displeasure of al-Kirmānī. On this, see D. De Smet, 'Les interdictions alimentaires du calife Fatimide al-Ḥākim: marques de folie ou annonce d'un règne messianique?', in U. Vermeulen and Daniel De Smet, eds, *Egypt and Syria in the Fatimid, Ayyubid and Mamluk Eras* (Leuven, 1995), pp. 53–69; idem, *La Quiétude de l'intellect*, esp. pp. 6–8; idem, *Épîtres sacrées des Druzes*, esp. pp. 19–21, 29–30.

[388] For references to this *ḥadīth* in Shiʿi sources, see e.g. M.M. Bar-Asher, *Scripture and Exegesis*, p. 156, n. 122; M.A. Amir-Moezzi, *La Religion discrète*, p. 242, n. 42 (English trans., *Spirituality of Shiʿi Islam*, p. 324, n. 42). The *ḥadīth* is also found in several Sunni sources, although it is of course interpreted differently than in the Shiʿi context. In some versions, the sentence is completed as follows: '. . . except there are no prophets after me' (whereas there were prophets after Moses, Aaron being one of them). The Sunnis, as well as some Shiʿi authors, refer to this *ḥadīth* to support the Islamic dogma of *khatm al-nubuwwa* (sealing of prophethood); on this, see G. Miskinzoda, 'The significance of the *ḥadīth* of the position of Aaron for the doctrine of the formulation of the Shīʿī doctrine of authority', *BSOAS*, 78/1 (2015), pp. 67–82, esp. p. 69, n. 6, for references to this *ḥadīth* in Sunni sources.

[389] See commentary of *Kashf* I, pp. 147–154, esp. pp. 151–152, 147 ff.

Ishmael, Abraham's Legatee,[390] and he was then likened to Simon, Jesus's Legatee.[391] He was therefore just an illustrative adjunct to the role of the Legatee, or Proof of the Messenger. This approach comes within the idea, found in other Shiʿi texts,[392] of an uninterrupted initiatory chain of Prophets and Imams since Adam. Stemming from this is the Ismaili conception of history, with its Speaking-Prophets accompanied and followed by Legatees, themselves succeeded by a series of Imams connecting a Speaking-Prophet to the next.

In Treatise III, however, the short passage dedicated to the ʿAlī/Aaron analogy is not linked to such a sacred history, but rather to the larger parallelism between Aaron and ʿAlī. The esoteric interpretation of a verse where Moses asks God to appoint Aaron as his auxiliary puts the same words in Muḥammad's mouth concerning ʿAlī.[393]

We are here in presence of a form of 'personalized commentary', as the *bāṭin* of the Qurʾanic text actually refers to events of the beginnings of Islam. This is also the case of such passages likening Pharaoh and his men to ʿAlī's enemies, or applying various verses concerning Moses to the succession of Muḥammad, particularly in Treatises I and V as we have seen. Based on the *ḥadīth al-manzila* which establishes the analogy between ʿAlī and Aaron, and based on the Qurʾan itself, which presents Moses as a predecessor of Muḥammad and likens their missions, the Shiʿi interpreters established systematic parallels between the two periods, using the 'personalized commentary'. The objective was to point out the fact that ʿAlī was to inherit every prerogative of the Prophet Muḥammad, just as Aaron would have inherited Moses's prerogatives had he outlived him, the difference being that there would be no more prophets after Muḥammad.[394] In Treatise VI, this interpretation is reinforced by its immediate proximity to the *ḥadīth* of Ghadīr

---

[390] *Kashf* I p. 12, § 25.

[391] *Kashf* I, p. 31, § 65.

[392] See e.g. M.A. Amir-Moezzi, *Guide divin*, pp. 106–108 (English trans., *Divine Guide*, pp. 41–42).

[393] *Kashf* III, p. 75, § 44. This passage that has virtually nothing to do with what precedes or follows is likely to be a case of *tabdīd al-ʿilm* (scattering of knowledge), and it should probably be linked with the developments of Treatise VI on Moses and Aaron.

[394] See e.g. G. Miskinzoda, 'The significance of the ḥadīth of the position of Aaron', pp. 71–72, 76–77.

Khumm,[395] the masterproof in Shiʿi historiography, of the designation of ʿAlī b. Abī Ṭālib as the succssor to the Prophet Muḥammad.

In Treatise VI, the ʿAlī/Aaron analogy is closely connected to a hermeneutic key which translates to term 'Book' as 'Imam'. Such an interpretation of the term *kitāb* is to be found on several occasions in the *Kitāb al-Kashf*: in Treatise I, the '*Book wherein is no doubt*' (Q. 2:2) is identified with the 'Prince of the Believers',[396] while ʿAlī is clearly likened to the Qur'an a few pages further.[397] In Treatise II — at least in Idrīs ʿImād al-Dīn's quotation of it — the Prince of the Believers is the '*Marked Book*' of Q. 83:20.[398] The equivalence Book/Imam appears again in Treatise V.[399] There are also some variations on this theme: it is sometimes the Speaking Prophet who is the Book,[400] or the *daʿwa* itself.[401]

Again, the *Kitāb al Kashf* is merely reproducing old Shiʿi exegetical techniques, sometimes adapting them. In the genre of 'personalized commentaries', identifying ʿAlī b. Abī Ṭālib to the Qur'anic occurrences of *kitāb* is quite frequent.[402] Such identification must be linked to the doctrine according to which the revelation (*tanzīl*) of Muḥammad remains incomplete and impenetrable without ʿAlī's interpretation (*ta'wīl*). The Qur'an is therefore a Silent (*ṣāmit*) Imam, or Silent Book, while the Imam is a Speaking (*nāṭiq*) Qur'an.[403] This vocabulary is reversed in Ismaili literature, as we can see in Treatises III and V,[404] where it is the Prophet with a new revelation and religious Law who is the 'Speaking-Prophet', while the Imams intermediary between two Speaking-Prophets are 'Silent' — since they observe the *taqiyya* surrounding the teaching of esoteric doctrines and they have not come

[395] *Kashf* VI, p. 159, § 6.

[396] *Kashf* I, pp. 20–21, § 45.

[397] *Kashf* I, p. 30, § 63.

[398] *Kashf* II, p. 42, § 7.

[399] See e.g. *Kashf* V, p. 119, § 51; p. 140, § 83; see also p. 124, § 58, where the 'People of the Book' are the Ismailis themselves since they know the Book, that is, the Imam.

[400] *Kashf* V, p. 122, § 55; pp. 130–133, §§ 68–70; p. 134, § 72.

[401] *Kashf* V, p. 141, § 85.

[402] See e.g. M.A. Amir-Moezzi, 'Al-*Durr al-ṯamīn* attribué à Rağab al-Bursī', pp. 221, 222, 224, and p. 222, n. 74.

[403] See M. Ayoub, 'The Speaking Qur'an and the Silent Qur'an'; M.A. Amir-Moezzi, *Guide divin*, p. 200 (English trans., *Divine Guide*, p. 79); idem, *Le Coran silencieux et le Coran parlant*, p. 103.

[404] *Kashf* III, p. 77, § 48; V, pp. 99–100, §§ 17–19; p. 103, §§ 25–26.

bearing a *sharīʿa*. It is worth noting that Treatise V proposes a combination of the Shiʿi and the Ismaili approaches: 'Among [the Imams], there is the one who is silent as for the esoteric wisdom, but speaking with the exoteric sword, and there is the one who is silent as for the exoteric sword, but who speaks the esoteric wisdom.'[405]

Returning now to Treatise VI, the first part of the text, dedicated to ʿAlī b. Abī Ṭālib's Imamate, is built on the distinction between *bāṭin* and *ẓāhir*, God's and the adversaries' choices, truth and certitude from God and conjecture, guidance in following the Imam appointed by the Messenger and straying from the path by following another Imam based on one's passions. It is in this context that the *ḥadīth al-manzila* is first quoted, alongside the *ḥadīth* of Ghadīr Khumm.[406] Further, the *ḥadīth al-manzila* is quoted again, and the analogy between ʿAlī and Aaron is justified by the fact that 'there is no closer proximity than that of Aaron to Moses'.[407] In the case of ʿAlī, this proximity is both religious, as he was the first convert to Islam, and familial; just as Aaron was a blood relative of Moses so was ʿAlī related to Muḥammad.

The exegesis of Q. 16:92 approaches the analogy between the two Legatees from a 'negative' point of view, in a perspective quite similar to the one met in Treatise I: just as Moses's community, which was entrusted to Aaron, betrayed him at the instigation of the 'Sāmirī' (Q. 20:85, 87, 95), Muḥammad's community, entrusted to ʿAlī, turned away from him. The reason for such a repetition of history is the Islamic community's desire to measure up to the Jews by choosing its own guide and 'arrogantly'[408] betraying the Legatee. Again, we find the 'communities who preceded', a theme previously met in Treatise I.

After a first Ismaili interlude, devoted to the Summoners, the equivalence between the Imam and the Book is based on Q. 62:2. In this verse, the term *ummiyyīn*, which is usually understood as meaning the 'unlettered', is interpreted as a designation of those who do not have a Book, that is, a rightful Imam.[409] These 'unlettered' are mentioned again at the end of the text.

---

[405] *Kashf* V, p. 148, § 96.
[406] *Kashf* VI, p. 159, § 6.
[407] *Kashf* VI, p. 161, § 9.
[408] *Kashf* VI, p. 162, § 14.
[409] *Kashf* VI, p. 167, § 25.

Then, it is the verse Q. 46:12: 'Before him, the Book of Moses was an Imam and a Mercy', which is used to connect the *ḥadīth al-manzila* to the idea that the Imam is a Book: 'The Book of Muḥammad is the Imam he establishes after himself. . . just as the Book of Moses was the Imam he had indicated as the Imam after himself, that is, Aaron'.[410] The reasoning goes as follows: the 'Book of Moses' is an Imam, this Imam is Aaron. ʿAlī is analogous to Aaron. Therefore, ʿAlī is the 'Book' of Muḥammad. It should be observed that this hermeneutical syllogism is given at the very heart of the structure of the treatise, and is framed by two long passages that have a clear Ismaili tone (the one on the Summoners and initiation, and the one on the mountains and the Proofs); it is unlikely that this disposition is a coincidence. Treatise VI is the one where the Ismaili art of composition is the most patent. Such care in the construction of the text confirms our suspicion that the other treatises, as well as the whole collection, are probably not as disorganized as they may seem.

The following exegeses are based on this hermeneutical key (Book = Imam). Thus, all the hostility against the revelation of Muḥammad as mentioned in the Qur'an is interpreted as hostility against ʿAlī, just as the benefits of the Revelation are in fact the benefits of following ʿAlī. Muḥammad and ʿAlī, *tanzīl* and *ta'wīl*, are inseparable. After the second distinctly Ismaili passage of the treatise, dedicated to the interpretation of the mountains as Proofs, the Book-Imam reappears in the exegesis of two verses dealing with the recitation of the Book:[411] the verb *talā*, which usually means 'to recite' or 'to read' in the Qur'an is understood here in its primary meaning, 'to follow'. Thus, 'to recite the Book' means 'to follow the Imam'. Again, the Book-Imam exegesis is interrupted, and reappears at the end of the treatise,[412] in the exegesis of Q. 2:78–79, which summarises the views of the text. Indeed, these verses mention the 'unlettered' who do not know the Book, who prefer their own conjecture and 'write the Book with their own hands' (i.e. choose their own Imam). Their relation to the Book introduces 'passions', 'impulse' and speculation, where there should be nothing but apodictic certainty from God.

Except for minor details, this whole argumentation could be found in any Shiʿi text. One must therefore question the use Ismailis could

---

[410] *Kashf* VI, p. 168, § 26.

[411] *Kashf* VI, pp. 171–172, §§ 31–33.

[412] *Kashf* VI, pp. 175–176, § 39.

have had for such a doctrine. It is not enough to consider that, Ismailism being a Shiʿi trend, it is only natural to find Shiʿi themes in an Ismaili text: this text is not a mere exposé of Shiʿi doctrine but has wider and more practical implications. It is true the text never establishes a direct link between this Shiʿi legitimation of ʿAlī b. Abī Ṭālib's Imamate and Ismaili preoccupations, but it seems quite clear that the goal of the text is to consolidate the legitimacy of the Ismaili Imamate, whether pre-Fatimid or Fatimid, by anchoring it in Alid tradition. Again, we must unveil the unveiling: the occurrences of the term 'Book' in the Qur'an are allusions to ʿAlī, the *Kashf* tells us, but the mentions of ʿAlī in the *Kashf* are allusions to the Ismaili Imam claiming his succession and his prestige, both spiritual and political.

3. Proofs and Summoners

Inserted between the demonstrations of ʿAlī's Imamate, several passages are of clear Ismaili provenance. Out of these passages, we can find here and there brief and subtle allusions that can show the Ismaili origin of the treatise, such as the identification of the 'Last Day' with the Mahdī.[413] However, it is mainly in three specific passages that we recognise the marker of Ismailism.

The first passage consists of an initiatory interpretation of a series of Qur'anic verses.[414] We seem to be dealing with instructions to the Ismaili missionaries, the Summoners, during their recruiting missions. First, they are reminded that the decision to maintain *taqiyya* or to reveal the secret teachings is ultimately the prerogative of the Imam and entirely depends on him. Depending on each case, the Summoners may be encouraged to pursue the initiation of new recruits or to refrain from doing so. The initiation is therefore submitted to authorization by the higher degrees of the *daʿwa*, all under the supervision of the Imam. This ability to hide the secret doctrines is highly valued.[415]

In the exegesis of a verse dealing with suckling (Q. 2:233), the latter is likened to the initiatory process. Such symbolism is quite common, particularly, but not exclusively, in Nuṣayri initiation, as we have seen

---

413 *Kashf* VI, p. 160, § 7.

414 *Kashf* VI, pp. 164–167, §§ 17–24.

415 *Kashf* VI, p. 164, § 18.

previously in our commentaries of Treatises I.[416] It reminds us of the title of another of Jaʿfar b. Manṣūr al-Yaman's works, the *Riḍāʿ fī'l-bāṭin* (*Suckling the Esoteric*). At the end of Treatise V, the training of the Summoners was also described as suckling.[417] Here, the 'two entire cycles' of Q. 2:233 correspond to the 'Imam speaking a Law and a Revelation' and to the 'Imam accomplishing the Law through exegesis'.[418] The initiation is thus in line with the Law brought by the last Speaking-Prophet, and unfolds under the supervision of the Imam of the time, through his representatives, the Summoners and the Gates.

Then, the pact of allegiance of the 'believing women' (*mu'mināt*) of Q. 60:12 gives the author the opportunity to present the contents of the Ismaili pact. Although not explicitly stated, the *mu'mināt* here are members of the *daʿwa*. In Shiʿi esoteric texts, the term *mu'min* has a technical meaning and designates, not only the believers, but the initiates as distinct from the ignorant masses.[419] In the Ismaili context, the term has come to refer to members of the sect — as we can see on several occasions in the *Kitāb al-Kashf*, as well as in other Ismaili works.[420] Furthermore, it should also be noted that in some Nuṣayri texts dealing with initiation, feminine terms are systematically referred to the disciples, according to the symbolism we met before which considers that, within the initiatory relationship, the master is male and the disciple female.[421]

The members of the *daʿwa* to whom the text refers are about to be authorized to 'summon', that is, to preach and recruit. They are

---

[416] See commentary of *Kashf* I, pp. 128–134.

[417] *Kashf* V, p. 155, § 105.

[418] *Kashf* VI, p. 165, § 19.

[419] See above, p. 160, n. 315.

[420] See e.g. Ibn Ḥawshab, *Kitāb al-Rushd wa'l-hidāya*, p. 212 (English trans., pp. 82–83); Jaʿfar b. Manṣūr al-Yaman, *Riḍāʿ fī'l-bāṭin*, p. 133; al-Sijistānī, *Tuḥfat al-mustajībīn*, pp. 19–20.

[421] See e.g. al-Ṭabarānī, *Kitāb al-Ḥāwī fī ʿilm al-fatāwī*, pp. 66, 94, 111, and esp. p. 115, where the author provides a list of feminine names by which the Qur'an designates the disciples. See also commentary of *Kashf* I, pp. 128–134. For another Ismaili interpretation of *mu'mināt*, in Q. 60:10, a verse close to the one involved here, see W. Madelung and P. Walker, *Affirming the Imamate*, p. 85 (Arabic text, p. 84): 'The women who believe (*al-mu'mināt*) in the religion of God are the students (*mutaʿallimūn*), since the male is like the teacher (*mufīd*) and the student (*mustafīd*) is like the female.'

subjected to the authority of the Proof, and not directly of the Imam himself, even though the Proof receives the oaths of the 'believers' on his behalf.[422] The Proof here seems to be in charge of the practical matters of the *daʿwa* as well as the hierarchical organization, particularly the 'authorizations to summon', with the Imam remaining in the background. We notice that the text only mentions one Proof with a preponderant role. This seems to contradict the conception of the second Ismaili passage of Treatise VI that we shall analyse below, as the latter mentions several Proofs. The reason for such discrepancy is not clear, but it might be that two Qur'anic interpretations from different periods have been collected into the same treatise. The role of the Proof here could match the 'Salamiyya' period during which the head of the community presented himself as a representative of the Imam, that is, as his Proof. This approach is also present in Treatise V, however corrected by a Fatimid hand asserting that this Proof was in fact the Imam himself.

From the instructions to the initiates, we can deduce the following hierarchy:

— Imam
— Proof
— Gates
— Summoners, or believers 'with permission' (*al-ma'dhūn lahum*) to preach and recruit
— 'believers without permission' (*muḥarram*)[423]
— People of the exoteric

As for the instructions themselves, they are addressed to the Gates and the Summoners:[424] they must not associate with God, that is, acknowledge an illegitimate Imam, nor steal, that is, reveal 'the esoteric knowledge of religion to someone who has not taken the covenant'.[425] They must not fornicate, that is, initiate without permission, according to a symbolism we are now familiar with — in Treatise V, fornication

422 *Kashf* VI, pp. 165–166, § 21.
423 This confirms the technical meaning of the term *mu'min* as a *daʿwa* member.
424 *Kashf* VI, p. 167, § 23.
425 *Kashf* VI, p. 166, §§ 21–22.

was also described as 'lifting the veil for someone or summoning without permission'.[426] Also, the 'believers' will not 'kill their own children', which means that they will not unjustly prevent an aspirant from initiation if he deserves it. The notion of the neophytes as children puts us within the symbolism of initiatory paternity that we have already analysed. Finally, the members of the *daʿwa* will be loyal to each other and will not rebel against the Imam.

This passage gives us a valuable insight on the *daʿwa* as an organization. These instructions, indeed, must have been sent to the Ismaili missionaries. They are reminiscent of the instructions found in Treatise V.[427] Such passages lead us to consider the theme of initiation within a hierarchized organization as one of the key features of Ismailism. Of course, initiatory themes already played a role in Shiʿi Islam in general, but the Ismaili *daʿwa* somehow systematises this pre-existing data and uses it to build an actual secret organization, strictly hierarchized, closely disciplined, aimed at restoring the Imam to his rights, including the political ones.

The second distinctly Ismaili passage of Treatise VI is the one where several verses mentioning mountains are interpreted based on the hermeneutical equivalence between the mountains and the Proofs. Although none of the exegeses of this part is centred on the symbolism of the mountains, they all have this element in common. The general orientation of this passage is eschatological, except perhaps for the last part which focuses on the *daʿwa*.

Such a hermeneutical code already appeared in Treatises I and III. In Treatise I, it appeared in the interpretation of Q. 16:68, where the bees were identified with the Imam, while their houses, i.e. the mountains and the trees, were respectively the 'Summoners who belong to the position of Proofs' and the 'Summoners who are below the Proofs'.[428] In Treatise III, the 'rock' was identified with the Proofs.[429] As we saw then, the *Kitāb al-Rushd waʾl-hidāya*, where we find an interpretation similar to that of Treatise III, is however more precise and gives the intermediary term that allows to connect the

---

[426] *Kashf* V, p. 123, § 57.

[427] *Kashf* V, pp. 121–125, §§ 54–58.

[428] *Kashf* I, p. 25, § 54, and commentary of *Kashf* III, pp. 259–261.

[429] *Kashf* III, p. 58, § 13.

rock and the Proofs: 'The rock, in the esoteric, is the Proofs, because the rock stems from the mountains, and the mountains are the Proofs'.[430] We should also note another passage of Treatise III interpreting the 'Fire whose fuel is men and stones' (Q. 2:24): the Fire is the divine punishment of the *raj'a*, while the auxiliaries of the Resurrector, 'men and stones' respectively correspond to the believers and the Summoners.[431] This symbolism, identifying mountains, stones or rocks with the Proofs or Summoners must be considered as a pre-Fatimid Ismaili feature.[432] However, it is possible that its origin goes further back, as the *Kitāb al-Haft wa'l-aẓilla*, interpreting Q. 16:15: *'He cast on the earth firm [mountains] (rawāsī)'*, identifies the mountains with the Imams and the earth with the believers.[433]

Other elements of this part of Treatise VI have a pre-Fatimid origin, particularly in the exegesis of Q. 78:12–20.[434] The most important among them is of course the mention of seven Imams[435] who are identified with the Seven Heavens of the Qur'an. The text does not say much about them, apart from them seeming to be represented by 'a Gate who elevates the degrees of the believers and gives the *da'wa*

---

[430] Ibn Ḥawshab, *Kitāb al-Rushd wa'l-hidāya*, p. 209. See commentary of *Kashf* III, pp. 266–267.

[431] *Kashf* III, p. 76, § 46.

[432] The exegesis of Q. 33:72 in *Kashf* I, pp. 28–29, § 61, might have to do with this symbolism of the mountains: *'We offered the trust unto the heavens, the earth and the mountains, but they refused to carry it and were afraid of it. And man assumed it.'* The author interprets this refusal as an acknowledgement of the 'trust', identified with 'Alī b. Abī Ṭālib, while the 'man' who accepts the trust and therefore usurps it is Abū Bakr. There, the earth and the mountains are identified with the 'the people in heavens and on earth, as well as the *Angels of the mountains*'. This unusual expression is probably an allusion to ranks of the *da'wa*, since members of the *da'wa* are sometimes symbolically designated as angels: see *Kashf* III, p. 62, § 20, and related footnote. In fact, an interpretation of 'heavens, earth and mountains' in Q. 33:72 as referring to ranks of the *da'wa* is found in Ja'far b. Manṣūr al-Yaman, *Al-Shawāhid wa'l-bayān*, IIS MS. 734, ff. 228–229. 'Mountains' are in fact 'Chiefs' (*nuqabā'*), here and in ibid., ff. 155, 166.

[433] Mufaḍḍal al-Ju'fī, *Kitāb al-Haft wa'l-aẓilla*, Ch. 32, p. 72. Note that the *Kitāb al-Kashf* identifies the earth with the Proof; see *Kashf* III, pp. 62, § 20; p. 85, § 68; V, p. 101, § 22; p. 155, § 106.

[434] *Kashf* VI, pp. 169–170, §§ 28–29.

[435] *Kashf* VI, p. 169, § 28.

life';[436] this may be the Proof, but it is not clear whether one should understand the term *bāb* in its strict, technical sense, or in the general sense.

While the treatise remains quite discrete regarding the notion of *raj'a*, it is in this part of the text that we find most of what it says on the subject: the Mahdī, who is the seventh Speaking-Prophet, will openly summon the people to join the *da'wa*, separate the truth from falseness, and unveil 'the veiled, esoteric knowledge of the Imams'.[437] 'The mountains are set in motion and become a mirage' (Q. 78:20) means that the Proofs will act openly. The text is not clear as to what is meant by 'mirage', but a possible explanation is that the Proofs, who until then had acted secretly, will appear in plain sight when the Mahdī comes, just as mirages suddenly appear in places where they were not seconds before.[438]

Several other symbols of this part are typical of Shi'i and Ismaili esotericism. The 'abundant water' (Q. 78:14) is the esoteric knowledge transmitted by the Summoners 'by which the believers come to life'.[439] Water as a symbol of salvific knowledge has ancient origins and is a common feature of various spiritual traditions. It is also present in Treatise I, where 'Alī is compared to water because 'just as the living is brought to life by water, the world comes to life with the knowledge coming from the Savant'.[440] This is obviously connected to the idea found at the end of the treatise[441] that ignorance of the esoteric teachings is similar to death, while initiation is a form of rebirth, or resurrection.[442]

The last part of the 'exegesis of the mountains' rests on yet another symbol, that of day and night, respectively identified with exotericism and esotericism — again a typical feature of early Ismailism, one that was already found in Treatise I: 'The nocturnal Proof is the Master of

---

[436] Ibid.

[437] *Kashf* VI, p. 170, § 29.

[438] See also Ja'far b. Manṣūr al-Yaman, *Riḍā' fi'l-Bāṭin*, p. 147, where the 'mountains' of Q. 73:14 are also identified with the 'Chiefs' (*nuqabā'*) and the 'Proofs' in an eschatological context; they will 'manifest God's Order with the seventh Speaking-prophet' after a period of 'secrecy and silence' (*al-sirr wa'l-kitmān*).

[439] *Kashf* VI, p. 170, § 28.

[440] *Kashf* I, p. 24, § 53.

[441] *Kashf* VI, p. 177, § 40.

[442] See commentary of *Kashf* I, pp. 128–134.

the confidential speech and the covenant, while the diurnal Proof is the Master of the sword and the evident proof'.[443]

Lastly, the third Ismaili passage is the one concluding the treatise.[444] This page links together more clearly the themes of the text, which seemed, until then, totally parallel. Indeed, the text argues that the Imams would remain inaccessible if it was not for the Proofs and the Summoners. If a community is deprived of the Summoner, the Imam will be hidden from it, and it will therefore be deprived of divine guidance. Thus, the Ismaili organization of the *daʿwa* presents itself as the unique way of accessing the Imam who is ʿAlī's heir. The authority of the Imam is not due to the choices and 'passions' of the Proofs and Summoners: he is not the Imam because they placed him at their head. On the contrary, it is he who is the source of the knowledge diffused by them, and this knowledge is the consequence of his having been divinely elected.

This hierarchized organization is mainly grounded on the ranks of the Proofs and the Summoners, who are the most common *ḥudūd* in the *Kitāb al-Kashf*. In Treatise VI, the first Ismaili passage mainly focuses on the Summoners who are in the frontline of the recruiting efforts, while a unique Proof oversees their activities. However, in the exegesis of the mountains, these two ranks appear as simple auxiliaries of the Imam. They are still hierarchized, but by passing from singular to plural, the Proof does not seem to have the same importance in the *daʿwa* anymore. By contrast, this reinforces the role of the Imam himself. The last page of the treatise first mentions the Proofs and the Summoners,[445] then the Summoners, the Gates and the Proofs, in ascending order.[446]

It is worth noting that the exegesis of Q. 38:18–19, where mountains and birds are identified with Proofs and Summoners,[447] uses a method similar to the one we find in the exegesis of the 'bee verse' in Treatise I, where mountains and trees are also identified with Proofs and

---

[443] *Kashf* I, p. 15, § 32.
[444] *Kashf* VI, pp. 177–178, §§ 40–42.
[445] *Kashf* VI, p. 177, § 40.
[446] *Kashf* VI, p. 178, § 41.
[447] *Kashf* VI, pp. 170–171, § 30.

Summoners.[448] The similarity is not only due to the identity of the secret meaning of the mountains, but also to this way of identifying two terms of a Qur'anic enumeration with these two degrees of the *daʿwa*. It is very likely that these two passages belong to the same textual layer. More broadly, all the passages of the *Kitāb al-Kashf* mentioning the Proofs and the Summoners together should be considered as dating from the same period. We can mention here, as an example, the passage of Treatise I dedicated to Joseph: 'Yet, the covenant can only [be taken] by the Imam who takes it in person or has his Proofs and Summoners take it on his behalf.'[449] However, there can sometimes be variations. Several passages thus mention the Proofs, *the Gates* and the Summoners.[450] Occasionally, the rank of the 'Hands' is inserted in between the Proofs and the Gates,[451] which must correspond to an earlier stage of the hierarchy. Indeed, the 'Hands' are found in al-Nawbakhtī's and al-Qummī's reports on the doctrine of the Qarmaṭis,[452] as well as in al-Sijistānī's *Tuḥfat al-mustajībīn*.[453] In the *Kitāb al-Kashf*, the two occurrences of the Hands appear in passages dealing with the sacred elite formed of seventy members, which seem to be of *ghulāt* origin.

---

[448] *Kashf* I, p. 25, § 54.

[449] *Kashf* I, p. 27, § 59.

[450] See *Kashf* V, pp. 119–120, § 51; p. 128, § 65; VI, p. 178, § 41.

[451] See *Kashf* III, p. 87, § 79; V, p. 102, § 24.

[452] According to these two heresiologists, the Qarmaṭis professed that the world was divided into twelve regions, each under the responsibility of a Proof. Each Proof was assisted by a Summoner, and each Summoner by a Hand. They called the Proof 'father', the Summoner 'mother', and the Hand was the son; see al-Nawbakhtī, *Firaq al-shīʿa*, p. 63; al-Qummī, *Maqālāt*, pp. 84–85.

[453] Al-Sijistānī, *Tuḥfat al-mustajībīn*, p. 153–154. The Hand appears in the following hierarchy: Speaking-Prophet / Legatee or Foundation (*asās*) / Imam or Accomplisher / Proof or Attaché (*lāḥiq*) / Hand (deputy of the *lāḥiq*) / Summoner or Wing (*janāḥ*) / the One with full permission (*ma'dhūn muṭlaq*) / the One with limited permission (*ma'dhūn maḥdūd*) / Believer (*mu'min*) / Respondent (*mustajīb*). According to F. Daftary, *The Ismāʿīlīs. Their History and Doctrines*, p. 218, the Hands are one of the denominations of the Proofs, also called Chiefs (sing. *naqīb*) or Attaché (*lāḥiq*).

Conclusion

Treatise VI is probably the easier one to analyse. Its structure is more easily identifiable, and its contents are clear and focused on two or three themes. Furthermore, it does not seem to contain several layers, even if it is possible that its author relied on various sources for his Qur'anic interpretations. The dating of the text, however, remains unclear: it is true that the text bears no marks of Fatimid tampering. There are, on the contrary, what seem to be clear indications that the text is pre-Fatimid (the mention of the seven Imams, the Mahdī who is yet to come, the 'Proofs and Summoners'). However, as mentioned before, one must remain cautious: even though it can be speculated that a text has a pre-Fatimid origin, this does not mean it was not reused in early Fatimid times for new purposes. In this case, it should be noted that the political statement in Treatise VI (the Imam is not elected by men) perfectly fits the needs of the first Fatimid caliph when confronted to the revolt of his *dāʿī*, Abū ʿAbd Allāh al-Shīʿī. Also, the notion of a unique Proof acting on behalf of the Imam is quite mysterious and could indicate two opposing possibilities: it is either a reference to ʿAbd Allāh al-Mahdī's son and successor, the future al-Qāʾim bi-Amr Allāh, or a reflection of the 'Salamiyyan' doctrine in this regard. If the latter were the case, it would imply that there were two distinct pre-Fatimid hierarchical systems, one with a unique Proof, and another with several.

GENERAL CONCLUSION

A rehearsal of the main results reached in this study is now in order. While some points remain unsolved, or only partially solved, it is hoped that future collaborative efforts around the corpus attributed to Jaʿfar b. Manṣūr al-Yaman will contribute to clarifying some of them. In the following pages, I shall start by recalling some of the points I established and hypotheses I have formulated regarding the authorship of the *Kashf* and the figure of Jaʿfar, as well as the transmission of the *Kashf*. I will then move on to more general perspectives that have been either opened or confirmed by this study regarding early Ismailism and its origins, Fatimid ideology and the relation of Ismailism to earlier Shiʿi trends.

1. Authorship of the *Kashf* and the Jaʿfar b. Manṣūr al-Yaman corpus.

On the matter of the *Kashf*'s authorship, I have not reached any final conclusion. As previously stated, as long as the corpus transmitted under the name 'Jaʿfar b. Manṣūr al-Yaman' remains understudied, and unedited for the most part, attempting to solve the issue of the authorship of the *Kashf* can yield no results. I have provided here a few samples demonstrating connections and echoes between certain works attributed to Jaʿfar and the *Kashf*. This line of enquiry will have to be pursued in future research, in order to determine whether such connections result from these works belonging to the same tradition and dating from a similar period, or if they prove that we are dealing with a single author. The preliminary results reached here would seem to suggest that there are some similarities between Treatise I of the *Kashf* and the *Shawāhid waʾl-bayān*, (e.g. exegeses of Q. 16:68–69, 24:35, 25:27–31, 33:72–73) and that Treatise V is sometimes reminiscent of the style and doctrines of the author of the *Sarāʾir al-nuṭaqāʾ* and the *Taʾwīl al-zakāt* (particularly the 'philosophical' passage, and the part on the 'Truthful ones', the 'Witnesses' and the 'Virtuous'). But for now, 'Jaʿfar b. Manṣūr al-Yaman' should be considered a name designating a corpus belonging to what D. Hollenberg has called '*daʿwa* literature',[454] rather than an individual author — in a similar manner, the name of the famous alchemist Jābir b. Ḥayyān became a label for a corpus and a certain type of literature. A closer look at the whole corpus and a comparison with other (more or less) contemporary Fatimid sources (particularly the *Asās al-taʾwīl* and the *Taʾwīl al-daʿāʾim*, by al-Qāḍī al-Nuʿmān, as well as the *Mafātīḥ al-niʿma*) will probably result in a more precise dating of each work, and, possibly in the identification of one or several authors. At any rate, it is clear that the Jaʿfar corpus is essential to our knowledge of early Fatimid thought, while also providing some insights on pre-Fatimid Ismailism. In the perspective of outlining a history of Ismaili thought in general, and Fatimid Ismaili thought in particular, the study of this corpus should therefore be a priority for future scholarship.

2. Jaʿfar and al-Qāʾim bi-Amr Allāh.

While there can be no certainty when attempting to connect the corpus to the very little we know about the historical Jaʿfar, the study of the *Kashf* has nevertheless led me to a hypothesis regarding Jaʿfar's role as an intellectual of the Fatimid court. I thus suggested in the introduction that Jaʿfar may have joined al-Qāʾim bi-Amr Allāh *before* the latter became caliph, but *after* he was appointed as the official successor of ʿAbd Allāh al-Mahdī, and charged with the repression of the Kutāma messianic revolt, in the aftermath of Abū ʿAbd Allāh al-Shīʿī's execution. Several aspects of Treatise V seem to sit well within this context: the emphasis on the notion of 'Proof' (also in Treatise III) as the higher representative of the Imam must probably be read as an attempt the legitimize al-Qāʾim before he took office as Imam. The discussion of one 'Pharaoh' who was part of the *daʿwa* and then betrayed it, might allude to the conflict with Abū ʿAbd Allāh al-Shīʿī

[454] D. Hollenberg, *Beyond the Qurʾān*, pp. 36–52.

and his partisans. Not to mention that al-Qāʾim bi-Amr Allāh is explicitly named in this treatise. As we have seen, the political orientations of Treatise VI may also be explained by the same context. These elements lead me to suggest that the historical Jaʿfar was indeed the author of Treatise V — even though it might have been reworked at a later stage — and that he was charged with the elaboration of a new concept of the 'Proof' in order to justify the authority of his master — not the Imam himself, ʿAbd Allāh al-Mahdī, but his appointed successor. This sheds some light on Jaʿfar's career, which probably culminated under al-Qāʾim (before and after he became Imam) and al-Manṣūr, and started to wane under al-Muʿizz, who had new ideological plans and turned his attention to other scholars. The latter include al-Qāḍī al-Nuʿmān in particular, but may also concern the author of the *Sarāʾir al-nuṭaqāʾ* and the *Taʾwīl al-zakāt*, if I am correct in hypothesizing that he is distinct from the actual Jaʿfar b. Manṣūr al-Yaman. He was indeed active under the reign of al-Muʿizz and his works display a distinctive writing style, setting them apart from the rest of the corpus.[455]

3. The Ṭayyibī transmission.

This transmission may have resulted in interventions, additions, or even the composition of the collection itself. But this can only be a matter of conjecture, since we lack information from Ṭayyibī sources. Thanks to the testimony of Idrīs ʿImād al-Dīn (d. 872/1468), we know that the *Kashf* was known as a work by Jaʿfar, and that Idrīs probably had a version of it close to the one that reached the present day. But the composition of the collection may have occurred anytime between the beginning of the 10th and the 15th centuries! Yet, I do not believe this undermines the authenticity of the *Kashf* altogether. All the treatises indeed seem to date from the Fatimid period; there is no decisive reason to question this point. The issue is rather whether the *Kashf* was composed *as a collection of six treatises* during the Fatimid period, or if this was done at a later stage. One possibility, for instance,

[455] To complete the elements provided in the introduction on this matter, I am currently preparing an article dedicated to this 'other' Jaʿfar.

would be that a Ṭayyibī copyist brought together ancient Fatimid texts dating more or less from the same period — hence the relative consistency of the collection. This would concern in particular the insertion of Treatises II and IV, but also the mere act of gathering all the treatises together in a single volume, and, perhaps, the "scattering" across the treatises of fragments dealing with identical or similar themes (for instance, the passage on the Houses in Treatise III). But again, this is pure speculation. In the absence of other manuscripts and other witnesses of the *Kashf*, the issue of its final composition remains unsolved.

4. Aspects of Fatimid ideology and the *Kashf*.

While its title suggests the reader is dealing with an actual 'unveiling' of esoteric truths, a close study of the *Kashf* shows that this so-called 'unveiling' constantly requires further unveiling. Indeed, the numerous Qur'anic interpretations and doctrinal elements in the *Kashf* are almost never connected to specific events occurring in the early Fatimid period — yet, it is only in relation to these events that many parts of the *Kashf*, particularly in Treatises III, V, possibly VI (for its political stance), and some parts of Treatise I (those dealing with *amr*), become intelligible. The elusiveness of the text explains why the *Kashf* has not been considered a major Fatimid source until now. Michael Brett thus labels it the 'textbook of the revolution that brought the dynasty to power'.[456] Most commentators, while admitting a Fatimid reworking, tend to consider the *Kashf* as more informative on the pre-Fatimid Ismaili *daʿwa* than it is on the Fatimid period. In fact, as I believe I have shown, the *Kashf* is rather the 'textbook' of the first doctrinal reforms and polemics *after* the dynasty had come to power, at a time when Ismailism was still heavily dependent on its pre-Fatimid corpus of doctrines (messianism included) and Qur'anic interpretations, and was only starting to adapt them to the new situation.

Approaching the *Kashf* while emphasizing its Fatimid identity has yielded a series of important data on early Fatimid doctrinal

---

[456] M. Brett, *The Rise of the Fatimids*, p. 124.

orientations. I have thus highlighted how the early Fatimid rhetoric heavily relied on classical features of Shiʿi doctrine. This applies to historiography and historical analogies above all. As a result, all mentions of, or allusions to, the disputed succession of the Prophet Muhammad are to be understood as Fatimid attempts at self-legitimization: every Prophet has a Legatee and is followed by Imams, and each of them is confronted by the hostility of the majority of their respective communities. The Fatimids, as successors of both the Speaking-Prophet and his Legatee, have to deal with the same enmity; their enemies are portrayed as avatars of archetypal enemies from the past, be they Pharaoh, or Abū Bakr and ʿUmar. The Fatimid Ismaili reuse of the traditional Shiʿi historiography of the succession is not meant to be a dwelling on the past. It rather comes in support of the idea of a sempiternal re-enactment of the Shiʿi myth of origins. The events of the past are only relevant inasmuch as they have strict analogues 'in every era and every age' — and thus, in the Fatimid present. This interest in systematic historical analogies is a key point of Fatimid official rhetoric — whether this analogy is elaborated within a transmigrationist framework or downplayed as a theory of the 'continuity of the Order'. The Fatimids caliphs are representatives or successors of ʿAlī, and their enemies are the same as those of ʿAlī.

The *Kashf* illustrates the interest in such a cyclical history on quite a few occasions, but a major source in this regard is the *Sarāʾir al-nuṭaqāʾ*, also attributed to Jaʿfar b. Manṣūr al-Yaman. On the one hand, this work reads the narratives of the lives of past Prophets as analogues to each other. It is always more or less the same story following the same patterns: analogue figures endeavour to spread the true faith, and have to deal with enemies from their own communities, in addition to those on the outside. On the other hand, and this is another key point of early Ismailism (which probably pre-dated the Fatimid reforms), these narratives are read as episodes in the general history of the *daʿwa*. In other words, it is not only the Fatimid *daʿwa* that should be understood as a re-enactment of past events, but it is also, in reverse, these events themselves that symbolically represent, or prefigure, the adventures of the Ismaili *daʿwa*. The 'heroes' are not just the Prophet and his successors anymore; rather, sacred history now includes all ranks of the *daʿwa*. One could say that the 'hero' is the *daʿwa* itself. This extension of the Imam's spiritual prestige to the various *ḥudūd* of the *da'wa* is illustrated in several pages in the *Kashf*. It is a central aspect in the parting of ways between Shi'ism and Ismailism. The sense of the sacredness of history is a Shi'i feature that the early Ismaili *da'wa* adapted to its own needs.

However, sacred history is oriented towards eschatological events. History is in fact the transmission of *amr*, or *amāna*, from Adam to the Qā'im, who will fully restore it after the many vicissitudes and betrayals endured by the Prophets and Imams between these two poles. When the Fatimids gained power, they had to delay the messianic events in order to establish their dynastic rule. Initially, the opposition met by past Prophets and Imams, according to Shi'i historiography, had to find its resolution in the final appearance of the Mahdī. But, with the reform, the Fatimids had to walk a fine line, toning down the messianic features of their doctrine, without undermining the significance of 'Abd Allāh al-Mahdī's appearance. As we have seen, the term *qā'im* gradually lost its purely eschatological connotations (as illustrated by the expression *qā'im ba'd qā'im*), and came to be synonymous with 'Imam' — which is a direct response to the concerns raised among the Ismaili partisans by the early Fatimid non-messianic orientations. Instead of discarding eschatology altogether, Fatimid Ismailism designed a new form of eschatology, one that could be labelled 'continuous', or an 'eschatology in the present'. Eschatology, in this new sense, is a permanent process, rather than just an ultimate point. It is in the present, thanks to the presence of the Imam, rather than in an unknown future. While the prospect of the future messianic events is preserved, as Ismailism kept the figure of the Mahdī as a horizon, the emphasis is on the present Imam, 'Master of the Age', the 'Resurrector' of his time.

This sits well with the initiatory features of Ismailism, due to the philosophical and symbolic connexions between initiation and eschatology. Insofar as initiation, that is, access to esoteric knowledge, is a 'new birth' or a 'new creation', it can be expressed in eschatological terms as a 'resurrection'. The 'Master of the Age', as a representative in some way of the Resurrector, shares the latter's prerogative of granting spiritual life through his guidance; he is the Gateway to eternal life, just like the Resurrector. We have seen how, in the *Kashf* and other Ismaili sources, some Qur'anic eschatological concepts were diverted from their initial meaning and interpreted in initiatory terms. This allows for the Fatimid Imam-Caliph to be the locus where two spiritual roles are brought together: that of Resurrector (or representative thereof), and that of Chief Initiator. As a result, the idea, expressed by Michael Brett, according to which, in early Fatimid doctrine, 'Muḥammadan messianism was subordinated to ʿAlid legitimism',[457] remains largely true, but should be nuanced: in fact, 'Muḥammadan messianism' was never completely abandoned. Gradually, the Fatimid Imams came to conceive of their role in such 'Muḥammadan', that is, eschatological, terms.

Paradoxically, this eschatological conception of their role, as descendants of both Muḥammad *and* ʿAlī, seems to have been connected to the Fatimid stance against antinomianism. As we have seen, antinomianism is usually associated with messianic beliefs. The Fatimids managed to preserve this messianism to a certain extent, while strongly affirming the inseparability of the *ẓāhir* and the *bāṭin*. It is possible that the practical necessity of presenting themselves as guardians of the *ẓāhir*, as well as their rejection of *ghuluww*, led the Fatimids back to a 'Muḥammadan' approach. While the connexion between the eschatological dimension of the Imam and his guardianship of both the *ẓāhir* and the *bāṭin* is not quite explicit in the *Kashf*, it appears much more clearly in another work attributed to Jaʿfar b. Manṣūr al-Yaman, namely the *Riḍāʿ fī'l-bāṭin*. There, the Mahdī is presented as 'intermediate' between the *ẓāhir* and the *bāṭin*, and between Muhammad and ʿAlī, a description corresponding strictly to the Fatimid Imam.[458] The Fatimids thus elaborated a new form of 'continuous eschatology', free from antinomianism.

The emphasis of the notion of 'continuity' of the divine presence would eventually lead to two main problems: firstly, the Imam does not merely hold his legitimacy from his genealogy ("Alid legitimism'), but also from his spiritual charisma ('Muḥammadan messianism'). This eschatological conception of the Imam, even reformed as a 'continuous' eschatology, leaves the door open to potential antinomian resurgences. This would explain the emergence of Druzism and the Fatimid struggle against antinomian *dāʿī*s. Secondly, the 'continuity'

---

[457] M. Brett, *The Fatimid Empire* (Edinburgh, 2017), p. 47.

[458] See F. Gillon, 'Ismaili Taʾwīl of Religious Rites', esp. pp. 250–251.

raises the problem of metempsychosis, since the latter is one of the theoretical ways to ensure such continuity. On this issue, Fatimid sources display some ambiguity. The *Kashf* rejects literal metempsychosis and metamorphosis, but, as we have seen, still uses concepts (*musūkhiyya*, *haykal*, *ma'nā*...) that originated in transmigrationist theories. In the *Ta'wīl al-zakāt*, which is also attributed to Ja'far b. Manṣūr al-Yaman but must be in fact later, from the reign of al-Mu'izz, there are explicit statements in favour of metempsychosis; the latter is clearly conceived of in literal terms, using the concept of *intiqāl*, 'transmigration', and likening the 'apparent bodies' of the Imams to clothes worn by a single person.[459]

5. Ismailism and 'personalized commentaries' in pre-Buyid Shi'ism.

A striking feature of the *Kashf* is its liberal use and adaptation of the 'personalized commentary' technique, which identifies Qur'anic terms with the Imams or their enemies, with a special focus on the succession of the Prophet and the alleged betrayal of his legacy by the first three caliphs of Islam. In its negative form, this corresponds to what Bar-Asher listed as a characteristic of the 'pre-Buwayhid school of exegesis' under the expression 'extreme anti-Sunni tendency'.[460] I have identified several exegeses, either 'positive' or 'negative', in the *Kashf* that have parallels with, or are identical to, Qur'anic interpretations found in the pre-Buyid Imami exegetical 'school' studied by Bar-Asher. I have also found similar Qur'anic interpretations in *ghulāt* and Nuṣayri sources, as well as in other Ismaili sources. The variety of sources in resonance with the *Kashf* shows that these trends of Shi'ism shared a common pool of Qur'anic exegeses, from which the Ismailis also drew their own. Establishing the proximity of early Ismailism to the earlier Shi'i exegetical tradition is an important contribution of this study. It appears that a full picture of this tradition thus requires the consideration of sources beyond Imami literature, namely Ismaili and Nuṣayri ones. It should be noted, however, that early Ismailism, while

[459] See Ja'far b. Manṣūr al-Yaman, *Ta'wīl al-zakāt*, pp. 200–201.

[460] See M.M. Bar-Asher, *Scripture and Exegesis*, pp. 82–86.

indeed preserving and transmitting some data from this tradition, also sought to distinguish itself from rival Shiʿi groups, and adopted a whole new conception of the 'personalized' approach to religion. In keeping with the 'personalized' approach to religion, it redefined the 'persons'; instead of being companions and enemies of Muḥammad and ʿAlī, as they are in Imami and Nuṣayri sources, the 'persons' were identified with ranks of the *daʿwa*, understood as *maqāms*, places of epiphany.[461]

The 'personalized commentary' is but one application of the principle according to which 'religion is knowledge of men'. After the Minor Occultation, the Shiʿis sought to fill the void left by the Imam with representatives of the latter, whether these representatives shared some or most of the Imams' prerogatives. The various responses to the problem of the Imam's absence delineate the variety of Shiʿi trends. The Ismaili response was to transfer (when the Imam was hidden) or extend (after the Imam manifested as caliph) the Imam's charisma to the hierarchy of the ranks of the *daʿwa*. This Ismaili esoteric hierarchy must be understood in the backdrop of the more general problem of 'Gatehood' and the struggle for spiritual legitimacy between the two Occultations.[462]

6. Ismailism and the *ghulāt*: the origins.

The example of the 'personalized commentary' attests to the fact that the *Kashf* is an essential witness to the connection of Ismailism to earlier Shiʿi debates, doctrines and exegetical methods. However, the *Kashf* illustrates this connexion in other capacities, namely through its many resonances with *ghulāt* and Nuṣayri sources. The presence of concepts, vocabulary and doctrines that are typical of, or close to, those of *ghuluww* in an early Ismaili text sheds new light on the intellectual *origins* of Ismailism. It appears that early, pre-Fatimid, Ismailism indeed shared much with what came to be known as

---

[461] On this, see F. Gillon, 'Ismaili Ta'wīl of Religious Rites'; idem, 'Du *tafsīr* chiite au *ta'wīl* ismaélien', forthcoming.

[462] On the anchorage of Ismailism in the Shiʿi debates on 'Gatehood', that is, the role of representing the Imam, see R. Adem, 'Early Ismailism and the Gates of Religious Authority'.

ghuluww.[463] During the Fatimid period, these doctrines were progressively set aside, as emblematically illustrated by the condemnation of Abū al-Khaṭṭāb by al-Qāḍī al-Nuʿmān. Another symptom is the disappearance from subsequent Fatimid literature of Muḥammad b. Abī Bakr, a figure appreciated by the *ghulāt* and mentioned several times in the *Kashf*. As a result of this Fatimid reform of the Ismaili doctrine and a lack of access to early sources, and in spite of the partial information provided by Imami heresiographers, modern scholarship was at pains to establish a filiation between what was known of the *ghulāt*, on the one hand, and what appeared in Fatimid literature, on the other hand. The *Kashf* is the *missing link* between these two moments in the history of Ismailism. Its analysis provides a relatively precise evaluation of what Ismailism holds from its Shiʿi and *ghulāt* roots, which, by contrast, allows for a more accurate identification of its specificities. In fact, these two aspects are closely intertwined: the distinct doctrines elaborated in early Ismailism are to be understood as a reshaping of earlier *ghulāt* themes and debates, particularly those pertaining to metempsychosis, to the esoteric interpretation of religious duties, as well as to the 'intermediaries' (*wasāʾiṭ*) between God — or the Imam — and the faithful — all themes closely related to the matter of sacred 'persons'.

---

[463] In this regard, R. Adem's analysis of the *Kashf* and other sources is consistent with the conclusions reached in this study; see R. Adem, 'Early Ismailism and the Gates of Religious Authority'.

Bibliography

Primary Sources

al-ʿAyyāshī, Abū al-Naḍr Muḥammad b. Masʿūd. *Tafsīr*, ed. Muʾassasat al-Biʿtha. Qom, 2000, 3 vols.

Brethren of Purity. *Epistles of the Brethren of Purity, The Case of Animals versus Man Before the King of the Jinn*, ed. and trans. Lenn E. Goodman and Richard McGregor. Oxford, 2009.

al-Bukhārī, Abū ʿAbdallāh Muḥammad b. Ismāʿīl. *Al-Jāmiʿ al-ṣaḥīḥ al-musnad min ḥadīth rasūl Allāh wa-sunanihi wa-ayyāmihi*, ed. Muḥibb al-Dīn al-Khaṭīb. Cairo, 1400/1979, 4 vols.

al-Daylamī, Muḥammad b. al-Ḥasan. *Bayān madhhab al-bāṭiniyya wa-buṭlānihi, manqūl min Kitāb Qawāʿid ʿaqāʾid āl Muḥammad (Die Geheimlehre der Bāṭiniten nach der Apologie "Dogmatik des Hauses Muḥammed")*, ed. Rudolf Strothmann. Istanbul: Staatsdruckerei, Kommissionsverlag F.A. Brockhaus, 1939.

Furāt al-Kūfī, Abū al-Qāsim. *Tafsīr*, ed. Muḥammad al-Kādhim. Tehran, 1990.

al-Ḥāmidī, Ibrāhīm b. al-Ḥusayn. *Kanz al-walad*, ed. Muṣṭafā Ghālib. Beirut, 1970.

al-Ḥasan b. Shuʿba, *Ḥaqāʾiq asrār al-dīn*, in *Silsilat al-turāth al-ʿalawī*, ed. Abū Mūsā and Shaykh Mūsā. Diyār ʿAql: Dār li-ajl al-maʿrifa, 2006, vol. 4, pp. 9–179.

Ḥātim b. Ibrāhīm al-Ḥāmidī, *Zahr bidhr al ḥaqāʾiq*, in *Muntakhabāt ismāʿīliyya*, ed. ʿĀdil al-ʿAwwā. Damascus: Maṭbaʿat al-jāmiʿa al-sūriyya, 1958, pp. 157–180.

Ibn Bābawayh, 'Shaykh Ṣadūq', Abū Jaʿfar Muḥammad. *Kitāb al-Tawḥīd*, ed. Hāshim al-Ḥusaynī al-Tīhrānī. Tehran, 1398/1978.

Ibn Ḥanbal, Aḥmad. *Musnad al-imām*. Cairo, 1313/1895, 6 vols.

Ibn Ḥawshab Manṣūr al-Yaman. *Kitāb al-Rushd wa'l-hidāya*, ed. Muḥammad Kāmil Ḥusayn, in W. Ivanow, ed. *Collectanea: vol. 1*, Leiden, 1948, pp. 186–213.

Ibn ʿIdhārī al-Marrākkushī, Abū l-ʿAbbās Aḥmad b. Muḥammad. *Kitāb al-Bayān al-mughrib fī akhbār al-Maghrib*, ed. G.S. Colin and É. Lévi-Provençal. Leiden, 1948.

Ibn Māja. *Sunan*, ed. Muḥammad Fuʾād ʿAbd al-Bāqī. Cairo, 1952.

Ibn Mālik. *Kashf asrār al-bāṭiniyya wa-akhbār al-qarāmiṭa*, ed. Muḥammad Zāhid al-Kawtharī. Cairo, 1939.

Idrīs ʿImād al-Dīn. *Zahr al-Maʿānī*, ed. Muṣṭafā Ghālib. Beirut, 1991.

——. *ʿUyūn al-akhbār*, ed. Ahmad Chleilat, Mahmoud Fakhoury, Yousef S. Fattoum, Maʾmūn Sagherji, Ayman Fuʾad Sayyid. London: The Institute of Ismaili Studies, Beirut, Damascus and Amman: Institut Français du Proche-Orient, 2007–2010, 7 vol.

Ikhwān al-Ṣafāʾ. *Rasāʾil Ikhwān al-ṣafāʾ wa-khillān al-wafāʾ*. Beirut: Dār Ṣādir, 2006, 4 vol.

Isḥāq al-Aḥmar, *Ādāb ʿAbd al-Muṭṭalib*, in *Silsilat al-turāth al-ʿalawī*, ed. Abū Mūsā and Shaykh Mūsā. Diyār ʿAql: Dār li-ajl al-maʿrifa, 2006, vol. 6, pp. 261–287.

Jaʿfar b. Manṣūr al-Yaman. *Kitāb al-Kashf*, ed. Rudolf Strothmann. London, New York, Bombay, Calcutta, Madras: Geoffrey Cumberlege, Oxford University Press, 1952.

——. *Kitāb al-Kashf*, ed. Muṣṭafā Ghālib. Beirut: Dār al-Andalus, 1984.

——. *Sarāʾir wa asrār al-nutaqāʾ*, ed. Muṣṭafā Ghālib. Beirut: Dār al-Andalus, 1984.

———. *Kitāb al-ʿĀlim waʾl-ghulām*, in James W. Morris, ed. and trans., *The Master and the Disciple: An Early Islamic Spiritual Dialogue. Arabic Edition and English translation of Jaʿfar b. Manṣūr al-Yaman's* Kitāb al-ʿĀlim waʾl-ghulām. London and New York: I.B. Tauris, 2001.
———. *Kitāb al-Riḍāʿ fi-l-bāṭin*, ed. Ḥusām Khaḍḍūr. Salamiyya: Dār al-Ghadīr, 13th ed., 2018.
———. *Kitāb Taʾwīl al-zakāt*, ed. Ḥusām Khaḍḍūr. Salamiyya: Dār al-Ghadīr, 5th ed., 2018.
———. *Kitāb al-Fatarāt waʾl-qirānāt*, ed. Ḥusām Khaḍḍūr. Salamiyya: Dār al-Ghadīr, 2021.
———. *Al-Shawāhid waʾl-bayān*, Ms. 734, Library of the Institute of Ismaili Studies.
———. *Kitāb al-Farāʾiḍ wa-ḥudūd al-dīn*, Ms. 1406, Library of the Institute of Ismaili Studies.
al-Kashshī. *Rijāl*, in al-Ṭūsī, Muḥammad b. al-Ḥasan, *Ikhtiyār maʿrifat al-rijāl al-maʿrūf bi-rijāl al-Kashshī*, ed. Jawād al-Qayyūmī al-Iṣfahānī. Qom: Muʾassasat al-nashr al-islāmī, 2005.
al-Kirmānī, Ḥamīd al-Dīn. *Rāḥat al-ʿaql*, ed. Muḥammad Kāmil Ḥusayn and Muḥammad Muṣṭafā Ḥilmī. Cairo: Dār al-fikr al-ʿarabī, 1953.
———. *Kitāb Rāḥat al-ʿaql*, ed. Musṭafā Ghālib. Beirut: Dār al-Andalus, 1983.
———. *Kitāb al-*Riyāḍ, ed. ʿĀrif Tāmir. Beirut, 1960.
al-Kulaynī, Abū Jaʿfar Muḥammad b. Yaʿqūb. *al-Uṣūl min al-Kāfī*, ed. ʿAlī Akbar al-Ghaffārī. Tehran: Dār al-Kutub al-Islāmiyya, 2 vol., 1377 [1957].
———. *al-Rawḍa min al-Kāfī*, ed. ʿAlī Akbar al-Ghaffārī. Tehran: Dār al-Kutub al-Islāmiyya, 1377 [1957].
al-Majdūʿ, Ismāʿīl ʿAbd al-Rasūl al-Ujaynī. *Fihrist al-Kutub wa al-rasʿāʾil wa li-man hiya min al-ʿulamā wa al-aʾimma wa al-ḥudūd wa al-afāḍil*, ed. ʿAlīnaqī Manzavī. Tehran: Chāpkhānah Dānishgāh, 1345 Sh./1966.
al-Majlisī, Muḥammad Bāqir. *Biḥār al-anwār al-jāmiʿa li-durar akhbār al-aʾimma al-aṭhār.* Qom, 2008, 25 vol.
al-Manṣūr biʾllāh. *Tathbīt al-imāma*, in Sami Makarem, ed. and trans., *The Shiʿi Imamate, A Fatimid interpretation.* London and New York: I.B. Tauris, 2013.
Maḥmūd-i Kātib. *Haft Bāb*, in S.J. Badakhshani, ed. and trans., *Spiritual Resurrection in Shiʿi Islam: An Early Ismaili Treatise on the Doctrine of Qiyāmat.* London and New York: I.B. Tauris, 2017.
Mufaḍḍal al-Juʿfī. *Kitāb al-Haft waʾl-aẓilla*, ed. ʿĀrif Tāmir and Ignace-A. Khalifé. Beirut: Imprimerie catholique, 1960.
Mufaḍḍal b. ʿUmar al-Juʿfī. *Al-Haft al-sharīf*, ed. Musṭafā Ghālib. Beirut: Dār al-Andalus, 1977.
al-Muʾayyad fīʾl-Dīn Hibat Allāh al-Shīrāzī. *Al-Majālis al-muʾayyadiyya*, ed. Musṭafā Ghālib, vols. 1 and 3. Beirut: Dār al-Andalus, 1974.
al-Nawbakhtī, al-Ḥasan b. Mūsā. *Kitāb Firaq al-shīʿa*, ed. Helmut Ritter. Istanbul: Maṭbaʿat al-Dawla, 1931.
al-Naysābūrī, Aḥmad b. Ibrāhīm, *Ithbāt al-imāma*, in A. Lalani, ed. and trans., *Degrees of Excellence: A Fatimid Treatise on Leadership in Islam.* London and New York: I.B. Tauris, 2010.
al-Nuʿmān, al-Qāḍī Abū Ḥanīfa al-Tamīmī al-Maghribī. *Asās al-taʾwīl*, ed. ʿĀrif Tāmir. Beirut: Manshūrāt Dār al-Thaqāfa, 1960.
———. *Daʿāʾim al-islām*, ed. Asif Ali Asghar Fyzee. Cairo: Dār al-maʿārif, 1963, 2 vol.
———. *Kitāb al-Majālis waʾl-musāyarāt*, ed. Ḥabīb al-Faqī, Ibrāhīm Mashbūḥ and Muḥammad al-Yaʿlāwī. Tunis: al-Jāmiʿa al-tūnisiyya, 1978.
———. *The Pillars of Islam: "Daʿaʾim al-Islam" of Qadi al-Nuʿman*, English trans., A.A.A. Fyzee, revised and annotated by I.K. Poonawala. New Delhi: Oxford University Press, 2002, 2 vol.
al-Qummī, Saʿd al-Dīn b. ʿAbd Allāh. *Kitāb al-Maqālāt waʾl-firaq*, ed. Mohammad Javād Mashkūr. Tehran: Markaz Intishārāt ʿIlmī va Farhangī, 1963.

al-Qummī, Abū al-Ḥasan ʿAlī b. Ibrāhīm. *Tafsīr al-Qummī*, ed. Ṭayyib al-Mūsawī al-Jazāʾirī. Najaf, 1386–7 [1966–7], 2 vol.
———. *Tafsīr al-Qummī*. Qom: Muʾassasat al-Imām al-Mahdī, 1435 [2014], 3 vol.
al-Rāzī, Abū Ḥātim Aḥmad b. Ḥamdān. *Kitāb al-Iṣlāḥ*, ed. Ḥasan Mīnūchehr and Mahdī Moḥaqqeq. Tehran: Institute of Islamic Studies, 2004.
al-Ṣaffār al-Qummī. *Baṣāʾir al-darajāt fī faḍāʾil āl Muḥammad*, ed. Muʾassasat al-Imam al-Mahdī. Qom, n.d.
al-Shahrastānī, Abū al-Fatḥ Muḥammad b. ʿAbd al-Karīm. *Kitāb al-Milal waʾl-niḥal, Book of Religious and Philosophical Sects*, ed. William Cureton. London: Society for the Publication of Oriental Texts, 1842–1846, 2 vol.
———. *Le Livre des Religions et des Sectes*, introduction, French translation and annotations by Daniel Gimaret and Guy Monnot. Louvain: Peeters, 1986, 2 vol.
al-Sijistānī, Abū Yaʿqūb Isḥāq. *Tuḥfat al-mustajībīn*, in *Khams rasāʾil ismāʿīliyya*, ed. ʿArif Tāmir. Salamiyya: Dār al-anṣāf liʾl-taʾlīf waʾl-ṭibāʿa waʾl-nashr, 1956, pp. 145–155.
———. *Kitāb al-Yanābīʿ*, ed. and partial French translation by Henry Corbin, in Henry Corbin, *Trilogie ismaélienne*. Tehran: Institut franco-iranien; Paris: Adrien Maisonneuve, 1961, French pp. 5–127, Arabic pp. 1–97.
———. *The Wellsprings of Wisdom. A Study of Abū Yaʿqūb al-Sijistānī's Kitāb al-Yanābīʿ*, introduction, English translation and annotations by Paul E. Walker. Salt Lake City: University of Utah Press, 1994.
———. *Kitāb al-Iftikhār*, ed. Ismail K. Poonawala, Tunis: Dār al-Gharb al-islāmī, 2000.
———. *Kitāb al-Maqālīd al-Malakūtiyya*, ed. Ismail K. Poonawala. Tunis: Dār al-Gharb al-islāmī, 2011.
al-Ṭabarānī, Abū Saʿīd Maymūn b. Qāsim. *Majmūʿ al-aʿyād*, ed. R. Strothmann. *Der Islam*, 27 (1946), pp. 1–273.
———. *Kitāb al-ḥāwī fī ʿilm al-fatāwī*, in *Silsilat al-turāth al-ʿalawī*, ed. Abū Mūsā and Shaykh Mūsā. Diyār ʿAql: Dār li-ajl al-maʿrifa, 2006, vol. 3, pp. 45–116.
———. *Kitāb al-maʿārif*, ed. Meir M. Bar-Asher and Aryeh Kofsky. Leuven, Paris and Walpole: Peeters, 2012.
al-Ṭabarī, Abū Jaʿfar Muḥammad b. Jarīr. *Tafsīr al-Ṭabarī: Jāmiʿ al-bayān fī tafsīr āy al-qurʾān*, ed. ʿAbd Allāh b. ʿAbd al-Muḥsin al-Turkī. Giza: Markaz al-buḥūth waʾl-dirāsāt al-ʿarabiyya waʾl-islāmiyya bi-dār Hajar, 2001, 26 vol.

Studies

Abrahamov, Binyamin. *Anthropomorphism and Interpretation of the Qurʾān in the Theology of al-Qāsim ibn Ibrāhīm. Kitāb al-Mustarshid. Edited with Translation, Introduction and Notes*. Leiden, New York and Cologne: Brill, 1996.
Adem, Rodrigo. 'Early Ismailism and the Gates of Religious Authority: Genealogizing the Theophanic Secret of Early Esoteric Shiʿism', in *Reason, Esotericism and Authority in Shiʿi Islam*, ed. Rodrigo Adem and Edmund Hayes. Leiden: Brill, 2021, pp. 24–72.
Adem, R. 'Classical *Naṣṣ* Doctrines in Imāmī Shīʿism'. *Shii Studies Review*, 1 (2017), pp. 42–71.
Alexandrin, Elizabeth R. 'Al-Muʾayyad's Concept of the Qāʾim: a Commentary on the *Khuṭbat al-Bayān*'. *Ishraq. Islamic Philosophy Yearbook*, 4 (2013), pp. 294–303.
———. *Walāyah in the Fāṭimid Ismāʿīlī Tradition*. Albany: State University of New York Press, 2017.
Amir-Moezzi, Mohammad Ali. *Le Guide Divin dans le Shīʿisme Originel. Aux Sources de l'Ésotérisme en Islam*. Paris: Verdier, 1992. English translation by David Streight: *The Divine Guide in Early Shiʿism. The Sources of Esotericism in Islam*. Albany: State University of New York Press, 1994.

———. 'Note sur deux traditions "hétérodoxes" Imamites'. *Arabica*, 41/1 (1994), pp. 127–133.
———. 'Remarques sur les critères d'authenticité du hadîth et l'autorité du juriste dans le shi'isme imâmite'. *Studia Islamica*, 82 (1997), pp. 5–39.
———. 'Review of *Scripture and Exegesis in Early Imâmî Shiism* by Meir M. Bar-Asher'. *Studia Islamica*, 92 (2001), pp. 206–209.
———. *La Religion Discrète. Croyances et Pratiques Spirituelles dans l'Islam Shi'ite*, Paris: Vrin, 2006. English translation: *The Spirituality of Shiʿi Islam. Beliefs and Practices*. London and New York: I.B. Tauris, 2011.
———. *Le Coran silencieux et le Coran parlant*. Paris: CNRS Editions, 2011.
———. 'Dissimulation tactique (*taqiyya*) et scellement de la prophétie (*khatm al-nubuwwa*) (Aspects de l'imamologie duodécimaine XII)'. *Journal Asiatique*, 302/2 (2014), pp. 411–438.
———. "Alī et le Coran (Aspects de l'imamologie duodécimaine XIV)'. *Revue des Sciences Philosophiques et Théologiques*, 98 (2014), pp. 669–704.
———. 'Les cinq esprits de l'homme divin (Aspects de l'imamologie duodécimaine XIII)'. *Der Islam*, 92/2 (2015), pp. 297–320.
———. 'La Nuit du Qadr' (Coran, sourate 97) dans le Shi'isme ancien (Aspects de l'imamologie duodécimaine XV)'. *Mélanges de l'Institut dominicain d'études orientales* (*MIDEO*), 31 (2016), pp. 181–204.
———. '*Al-Durr al-ṯamīn* attribué à Rağab al-Bursī. Un exemple des "commentaires coraniques personnalisés" šī'ites (Aspects de l'imamologie duodécimaine XVI)'. *Le Muséon*, 130/1–2 (2017), pp. 207–240.
———. *La Preuve de Dieu. La mystique shi'ite à travers l'œuvre de Kulaynī IXe-Xe siècle*. Paris: Les Editions du Cerf, 2018: English translation by Maria De Cillis and Orkhan Mir-Kasimov, *The Proof of God. Shiʿi Mysticism in the work of Kulaynī (9th-10th centuries)*. London and New York: I.B. Tauris, 2023.
———. 'Les Imams et les Ghulāt. Nouvelles réflexions sur les relations entre imamisme "modéré" et shiʿisme "extrémiste"'. *Shii Studies Review*, 4 (2020), pp. 5–38.
———. 'Kaṭṭābiya'. *EIr*.
———. 'Ghadīr Khumm'. *EI3*.
———, and Christian Jambet. *Qu'est-ce que le shî'isme?* Paris: Fayard, 2004.
Anthony, Sean. *The Caliph and the Heretic: Ibn Saba' and the Origins of Shīʿism*. Leiden: Brill, 2011.
Asatryan, Mushegh, 'Heresy and Rationalism in Early Islam: The Origins and Evolution of the Mufaḍḍal-Tradition'. Ph.D. thesis, Yale University, 2012.
———. 'Shiite Underground Literature Between Iraq and Syria: "The Book of Shadows" and the History of the Early Ghulat', in *Texts in Transit in the Medieval Mediterranean*, ed. T. Langermann and R. Morrison. University Park, PA: Pennsylvania State University Press, 2016, pp. 128–161.
———. 'An Early Shīʿi Cosmology, *Kitāb al-ashbāḥ wa l-aẓilla* and its Milieu'. *Studia Islamica*, 110 (2015), pp. 1–80.
———. *Controversies in Formative Shiʿi Islam. The Ghulat Muslims and their Beliefs*. London and New York: I.B. Tauris, 2017.
———. 'An Agenda for the Study of early Shiʿi cosmologies', in *The Gnostic World*, ed. G.W. Trompf, G.B. Mikkelsen, J. Johnson. London and New York: Routledge, 2020, pp. 321–327.
———. 'Early Ismailis and Other Muslims: Polemics and Borrowing in Kitāb al-Kashf', in *Intellectual Interactions in the Islamic World. The Ismaili Thread*, ed. Orkhan Mir-Kasimov. London and New York: I.B. Tauris, 2020, pp. 273–298.
———. 'The Heretic Talks Back: Feigning Orthodoxy in al-Ṣaffār al-Qummī's *Baṣā'ir al-darajāt* (d. 902–3)'. *History of Religions*, 61/4 (2022), pp. 362–388.
———. 'Of Wine, Sex, and Other Abominations: The Meanings of Antinomianism in Early Islamic Iraq'. *Global Intellectual History*, forthcoming.

——. 'Esḥāq Aḥmar al-Naḵaʿī', *EIr.*
——. 'Mofażżal al-Joʿfī', *EIr.*
Asfaruddin, Asma. 'Abū Dharr al-Ghifārī'. *EI3.*
Ayada, Souad. *L'Islam des théophanies, Une religion à l'épreuve de l'art.* Paris: CNRS Editions, 2010.
Baffioni, Carmela. '*Ibdāʿ*, Divine Imperative and Prophecy in the *Rasā'il Ikhwān al-ṣafā*", in *Fortresses of the Intellect. Ismaili and Other Islamic Studies in Honour of Farhad Daftary*, ed. Omar Ali-de-Unzaga. London-New York: I.B. Tauris, 2011, pp. 213–226.
Bar-Asher, Meir M. *Scripture and Exegesis in Early Imamī Shiism.* Leiden and Boston: Brill; Jerusalem: Magnes Press, 1999.
——. 'The Qurʾanic Commentary ascribed to Imam Ḥasan al-ʿAskarī'. *Jerusalem Studies in Arabic and Islam*, 24 (2000), pp. 358–379.
——. '*Jibt* et *Ṭâghût*', in *Dictionnaire du Coran*, ed. M.A. Amir-Moezzi. Paris: Robert Laffont, 2007, pp. 444–445.
——. 'Outlines of Early Ismāʿīlī-Fātimid Qurʾan Exegesis'. *Journal Asiatique*, 296/2 (2008), pp. 257–295; repr. in *The Spirit and the Letter. Approaches to the Esoteric Interpretation of the Qurʾan*, ed. Annabel Keeler and Sajjad Rizvi. New York: Oxford University Press, 2016, pp. 179–216.
——, and Aryeh Kofsky. *The Nuṣayrī -ʿAlawī Religion. An Enquiry into its Theology and Liturgy.* Leiden: Brill, 2002.
——. *The ʿAlawī Religion: An Anthology.* Turnhout: Brepols, 2021.
Bayhom-Daou, Tamima. 'The Second-Century Šīʿite *Ġulāt*, were they really Gnostic?' *Journal of Arabic and Islamic Studies*, 5 (2003), pp. 13–61.
Bauer, Karen. 'Spiritual Hierarchy and Gender Hierarchy in Fatimid Ismāʿīlī Interpretations of the Qurʾan'. *Journal of Qurʾanic Studies*, 14/2 (2012), pp. 29–46.
Brett, Michael. 'The Mīm, the ʿAyn and the making of Ismāʿīlism'. *BSOAS*, 57/1 (1994), pp. 25–39.
——. *The Rise of the Fatimids; the World of the Mediterranean and the Middle East in the Fourth Century of Hijra, Tenth Century CE.* Leiden: Brill, 2001.
——. *The Fatimid Empire.* Edinburgh: Edinburgh University Press, 2017.
Buckley, Ron P. 'The Imam Jaʿfar al-Ṣādiq, Abū'l-Khaṭṭāb and the Abbassids'. *Der Islam*, 79 (2002), pp. 118–140.
Buhl, Frants P.W.F. "Ād', *EI2.*
——, and Clifford E. Bosworth. 'Madyan Shuʿayb'. *EI2.*
Cameron, Alan J. *Abû Dharr al-Ghifârî: an Examination of his Image in the Hagiography of Islam.* London: Royal Asiatic Society, 1973.
Canard, Marius. 'al-Ḥākim bi-Amr Allāh', *EI2.*
Capezzone, Leonardo. 'Il Kitāb al-Ṣirāṭ attribuito a Mufaḍḍal b. ʿUmar al-Ǧuʿfī. Edizione del ms. unico (Paris, Bibliothèque nationale) e studio introduttivo'. *Rivista degli Studi Orientali*, 69 (1995), pp. 295–416.
——. 'La questione dell'eterodossia di Mufaḍḍal b. ʿUmar al-Juʿfī nel *Tanqīḥ al-maqāl* di al-Māmqānī', in *Ḥadīth in Modern Islam*, ed. R. Tottoli. Special issue of *Oriente Moderno*, 21 n.s. 82/1 (2002), pp. 147–157.
——. 'The solitude of the Orphan: Ǧābir b. Ḥayyān and the Shiite heterodox milieu of the third/ninth-fourth/tenth centuries'. *BSOAS*, 83/1 (2020), pp. 51–73.
Chodkiewicz, Michel. *Le Sceau des saints: prophétie et sainteté dans la doctrine d'Ibn Arabî.* Paris: Gallimard, 1986.
Corbin, Henry. 'De la gnose antique à la gnose ismaélienne', dans *Oriente ed Occidente nel Medio Evo. Convegno di Scienze Morali, Storiche e Filologiche*, Rome, 1957, pp. 105–150; repr. in idem, *Temps cyclique et gnose ismaélienne.* Paris: Berg International, 1982, pp. 167–208.
——. 'Epiphanie divine et naissance spirituelle dans la gnose ismaélienne', in idem, *Temps cyclique et gnose ismaélienne* (Paris, 1982), pp. 70–166.

——. 'L'initiation ismaélienne ou l'ésotérisme et le Verbe'. *Eranos Jahrbuch*, 39 (1970), pp. 41–142; repr. in idem, *L'Homme et son Ange. Initiation et chevalerie spirituelle*. Paris: Fayard, 1983, pp. 81–205.

——. 'Un roman initiatique ismaélien', *Cahiers de civilisation médiévale*, 15/57 (1972), pp. 1–25; 15/58 (1972), pp. 121–142.

——. *Alchimie comme art hiératique*. Paris: L'Herne, 1986.

——. *History of Islamic Philosophy*, English translation by Liadain Sherrard, with Philip Sherrard. London and New York: Kegan Paul International, 1993.

Cortese, Delia. *Ismaili and other Arabic Manuscripts. A Descriptive Catalogue of Manuscripts in the Library of the Institute of Ismaili Studies*. London and New York: I.B. Tauris, 2000.

——. *Arabic Ismaili Manuscripts. The Zāhid 'Alī Collection*. London and New York: I.B. Tauris, 2003.

Crone, Patricia. 'Khālid b. al-Walīd'. *EI2*.

Dachraoui, Farhat. *Le califat fâtimide au Maghreb. Histoire politique et institutions. 296–362/909–973*, Tunis, 1981.

Daftary, Farhad. 'The Earliest Ismāʿīlīs'. *Arabica*, 38/2 (1991), pp. 214–245.

——. 'A Major Schism in the Early Ismāʿīlī Movement'. *Studia Islamica*, 77 (1993), pp. 123–139.

——. *The Ismāʿīlis: Their History and Doctrines*. Second edition, Cambridge: Cambridge University Press, 2007.

——. Review of M. Brett, *The Rise of the Fatimids* (2001). *BSOAS*, 65/1 (2002), pp. 152–153.

——. *'Ahl al-Kisā''*. *EI3*.

De Blois, François. *Arabic, Persian and Gujarati Manuscripts. The Hamdani Collection*. London and New York: I.B. Tauris, 2011.

De Cillis, Maria. *Salvation and Destiny in Islam, The Shiʿi Ismaili Perspective of Ḥamīd al-Dīn al-Kirmānī*. London and New York: I.B. Tauris, 2018.

De Smet, Daniel. 'Le verbe-impératif dans le système cosmologique de l'Ismaélisme'. *Revue des Sciences Philosophiques et Théologiques*, 73 (1989), pp. 397–412.

——. 'Les interdictions alimentaires du calife fatimide al-Ḥākim: marques de folie ou annonce d'un règne messianique?', in *Egypt and Syria in the Fatimid, Ayyubid and Mamluk Eras*, ed. U. Vermeulen and Daniel De Smet. Leuven: Peeters, 1995, pp. 53–69.

——. *La Quiétude de l'Intellect: néoplatonisme et gnose ismaélienne dans l'œuvre de Hamîd ad-Dîn al-Kirmânî (Xe-XIe s.)*. Leuven: Peeters, 1995.

——. 'Eléments chrétiens dans l'ismaélisme yéménite sous les derniers Fatimides. Le problème de la gnose ṭayyibite', in *L'Égypte fatimide, son art et son histoire. Actes du colloque organisé à Paris les 28, 29 et 30 mai 1998*, ed. Marianne Barrucand. Paris: Presses de l'Université de Paris Sorbonne, 1999, pp. 45–53.

——. 'Une femme musulmane ministre de Dieu sur terre? La réponse du *dāʿī* ismaélien al-Ḫaṭṭāb'. *Acta Orientalia Belgica*, 15 (2001), pp. 155–164.

——. 'L'alphabet secret des Ismaéliens ou la force magique de l'écriture', in *Charmes et sortilèges. Magie et magiciens* (Res Orientales 14), ed. Rika Gyselen. Bures-sur-Yvette, 2002, pp. 51–60.

——. 'La valorisation du féminin dans l'ismaélisme ṭayyibite. Le cas de la reine yéménite al-Sayyida Arwā (1048–1138)'. *Mélanges de l'Université Saint-Joseph*, 58 (2005), pp. 107–122.

——. *Les Épîtres sacrées des Druzes*. Rasāʾil al-Ḥikma. *Volumes 1 et 2. Introduction, édition critique et traduction annotée des traités attribués à Ḥamza b. 'Alī et à Ismāʿīl at-Tamīmī*. Leuven: Peeters, 2007.

——. 'Abeille, Miel', in *Dictionnaire du Coran*, ed. M.A. Amir-Moezzi. Paris: Robert Laffont, 2007, pp. 5–7.

——. 'Crucifixion', in *Dictionnaire du Coran*, ed. M.A. Amir-Moezzi. Paris: Robert Laffont, 2007, pp. 197–199.

———. 'Exagération', in *Dictionnaire du Coran*, ed. M.A. Amir-Moezzi. Paris: Robert Laffont, 2007, pp. 292–295.

———. 'Métamorphose', in *Dictionnaire du Coran*, ed. M.A. Amir-Moezzi. Paris: Robert Laffont, 2007, pp. 552–554

———. 'Les bibliothèques ismaéliennes et la question du néoplatonisme ismaélien', in *The Libraries of the Neoplatonists*, ed. Cristina d'Ancona. Leiden and Boston: Brill, 2007, pp. 481–492.

———. 'Loi rationnelle et loi imposée. Les deux aspects de la *šarī'a* dans le chiisme ismaélien des Xe et XIe siècles'. *Mélanges de l'Université Saint-Joseph*, 61 (2008), pp. 515–544.

———. 'La pratique de *taqiyya* et *kitmān* en islam chiite: compromis ou hypocrisie?', in *Actualité du compromis: La construction politique de la différence*, ed. M. Nachi. Paris: Armand Colin, 2011, pp. 148–161.

———. 'The *Risāla al-Muḏhiba* attributed to al-Qāḍī al-Nu'mān', in *Fortress of the Intellect, Ismaili and Other Islamic Studies in Honour of Farhad Daftary*, ed. Omar Ali-de-Unzaga. London and New York: I.B. Tauris, 2011, pp. 309–341.

———. *La philosophie ismaélienne : Un ésotérisme chiite entre néoplatonisme et gnose*. Paris: Editions du Cerf, 2012.

———. 'La fonction noétique de la triade *al-Jadd, al-Fatḥ, al-Khayāl*. Les fondements de la connaissance prophétique dans l'ismaélisme', in *Differenz und Dynamik im Islam. Festschrift für Heinz Halm zum 70. Geburtstag*, ed. H. Biesterfeldt and V. Klemm. Würzburg: Ergon Verlag, 2012, pp. 319–336.

———. 'La *taqiyya* et le jeûne du Ramadan: quelques réflexions ismaéliennes sur le sens ésotérique de la charia'. *Al-Qanṭara*, 34/2 (2013), pp. 357–386.

———. 'La transmigration des âmes. Une notion problématique dans l'ismaélisme d'époque fatimide', in *Unity in Diversity. Mysticism, Messianism and the Construction of Religious Authority in Islam*, ed. O. Mir-Kasimov. Leiden and Boston: Brill, 2014, pp. 77–110.

———. 'La naissance miraculeuse de l'Imam ismaélien: nourritures célestes et corps camphré', in *Acta Orientalia Belgica*, 28 (2015), ed. C. Cannuyer and C. Vialle, pp. 323–333.

———. 'Les racines docétistes de l'imâmologie shi'ite', in *L'ésotérisme shi'ite, ses racines et ses prolongements*, ed. Mohammad Ali Amir-Moezzi, Maria De Cillis, Daniel De Smet and Orkhan Mir-Kasimov. Turnhout: Brepols, 2016, pp. 87–112.

———. 'L'auteur des *Rasā'il Ikhwān al-Ṣafā'* selon les sources ismaéliennes ṭayyibites'. *Shii Studies Review*, 1 (2017), pp. 151–166.

———. 'Jeûner par le silence. L'interprétation ésotérique du ramadan selon l'auteur nuṣayri Maymūn b. Qāsim al-Ṭabarānī (m. 426/1034)', in *Affamés volontaires. Les monothéismes et le jeûne*, ed. Sylvio Hermann De Franceschi, Daniel-Odon Hurel and Brigitte Tambrun. Limoges: Presses Universitaires de Limoges, 2020, pp. 315–334.

———. 'The Demon in Potentiality and the Devil in Actuality: Two Principles of Evil according to 4th/10th Century Ismailism'. *Arabica*, 69 (2022), pp. 601–625.

———. ''Alī b. Abī Ṭālib et l'alphabet himyarite ou l'invention de l'écriture secrète ismaélienne', in *Acta Orientalia Belgica*, 36 (2023), ed. S. Holvoet and R. Veymiers, pp. 347–358.

Dussaud, René, *Histoire et religion des Noṣairîs*. Paris: Librairie Emile Bouillon, 1900.

Ebstein, Michael, *Mysticism and Philosophy in al-Andalus: Ibn Masarra, Ibn al-'Arabī and the Ismā'īlī Tradition*. Leiden and Boston: Brill, 2014.

———. 'Covenant (religious) pre-eternal', *EI3*.

EI2 = *The Encyclopaedia of Islam*, ed. H.A.R. Gibb et al. New ed., Leiden: Brill, 1960–2004.

EI3 = *The Encyclopaedia of Islam, Three*, ed. Gudrun Krämer et al. Leiden: Brill, 2007–.

EQ = *Encyclopaedia of the Qur'ān*, ed. Jane Dammen McAuliffe. Leiden: Brill, 2002–2006

EIr = *Encyclopaedia Iranica*, ed. E. Yarshater. London and New York 1982–.

Feki, Habib. 'Deux traités du Dâ'î Yéménite Ismaélien 'Alî Ibn Moḥammad Ibn Al-Walīd (VIIe/XIIIe siècle)'. *Annuaire de l'Ecole Pratique des Hautes Etudes*, 78 (1969), pp. 379–382.

———. *Les Idées religieuses et philosophiques de l'ismaélisme fâtimide. Organization et doctrine.* Tunis: Publications de l'Université de Tunis, 1978.

Firestone, Reuven. 'Thamūd'. *EQ*.

Freitag, Rainer. *Seelenwanderung in der islamischen Häresie.* Berlin: Klaus Schwarz, 1985.

Friedman, Yaron. *The Nuṣayrīs-'Alawīs, An Introduction to the Religion, History and Identity of the Leading Minority in Syria.* Leiden: Brill, 2009.

Gacek, Adam. *Catalogue of Arabic Manuscripts in the Library of the Institute of Ismaili Studies*, 2 vol. London: Islamic Publications, 1984.

Ghaemmaghami, Omid. *Encounters with the Hidden Imam in Early and Pre-Modern Twelver Shī'ī Islam*, Leiden and Boston: Brill, 2020.

Gillon, Fârès. 'Une version ismaélienne de *ḥadīṯ*s imamites. Nouvelles perspectives sur le traité II du *Kitāb al-Kašf* attribué à Ǧa'far b. Manṣūr al-Yaman (Xe s.)', *Arabica*, 59/5 (2012), pp. 484–509.

———. 'Aperçus sur les origines de l'ismaélisme à travers le *Kitāb al-Kašf* attribué au dā'ī Ǧa'far b. Manṣūr al-Yaman'. *Ishraq: Islamic Philosophy Yearbook*, 4 (2013), pp. 90–111.

———. 'Lumière et théophanie dans l'ismaélisme fâtimide: le cas du traité I du *Kitāb al-Kašf*. *Chronos*, 32 (2015), pp. 141–155.

———. 'Ismaili *Ta'wīl* of Religious Rites: Interpretation of Obligatory Prayer in Ja'far b. Manṣūr al-Yaman's *Riḍā' fī l-Bāṭin*'. *Shii Studies Review*, 6 (2022), pp. 224–252.

———. 'Du *tafsīr* chiite au *ta'wīl* ismaélien, l'évolution du commentaire personnalisé négatif dans la *da'wa*', in *Festschrift for M.A. Amir-Moezzi*, ed. O. Mir-Kasimov and Mathieu Terrier, forthcoming.

Gimaret, Daniel. *Dieu à l'image de l'homme. Les anthropomorphismes de la* sunna *et leur interprétation par les théologiens.* Paris: Éditions du Cerf, 1997.

Gleave, Robert. 'Quietism and Political Legitimacy in Imami Shi'i Jurisprudence: al-Sharīf al-Murtaḍa's Treatise on the Legality of Working for the Government Reconsidered', in *Political Quietism in Islam. Sunni and Shi'i Practice and Thought*, ed. Saud al-Sarhan. London: I.B. Tauris, 2020, pp. 99–128.

———. "Alī b. Abī Ṭālib'. *EI3*.

Goldziher, Ignaz, 'Spottnamen der ersten Chalifen bei den Schî'iten'. *Wiener Zeitschrift für die Kunde des Morgenlandes*, 15 (1901), pp. 321–334; repr. in idem, *Gesammelte Schriften*, ed. J. De Somogyi. Hildesheim, 1967–1970, vol. 4, pp. 291–305.

———. 'Schi'itisches', *Zeitschrift der Deutschen Morgenländischen Gesellschaft*, 64 (1910), pp. 529–533; repr. in idem, *Gesammelte Schriften*, ed. J. De Somogyi. Hildesheim, 1967–1970, vol. 5, pp. 210–214.

Goriawala, Mu'izz, *A Descriptive Catalogue of the Fyzee Collection of Ismaili Manuscripts*, Bombay: University of Bombay, 1965.

Gril, Denis, 'Dépôt divin', in *Dictionnaire du Coran*, ed. M.A. Amir-Moezzi. Paris: Robert Laffont, 2007, pp. 207–209.

Guyard, Stanislas. *Fragments relatifs à la doctrine des Ismaélîs.* Paris: Imprimerie Nationale, 1874.

Haider, Najam I. 'Camel, Battle of the'. *EI3*.

Haji, Hamid. 'Ja'far b. Manṣūr al-Yaman'. *EIr*.

Halm, Heinz, 'Zur Datierung des ismā'īlitischen "Buches der Zwischenzeiten und der zehn Konjunktionen" (Kitāb al-fatarāt wal-qirānāt al-'ašara) HS Tübingen Ma VI 297'. *Die Welt des Orients*, 8 (1975), pp. 91–107.

———. *Kosmologie und Heilslehre der frühen Ismā'īlīya: Eine Studie zur islamische Gnosis.* Wiesbaden: Franz Steiner, 1978.

———. 'Das 'Buch der Schatten': Die Mufaḍḍal-Tradition der Ġulāt und die Ursprünge des Nuṣairiertums. I. Die Überlieferer der häretischen Mufaḍḍal-Tradition'. *Der Islam*, 55 (1978), pp. 219–266.

———. 'Das 'Buch der Schatten': Die Mufaḍḍal-Tradition der Ġulāt und die Ursprünge des Nuṣairiertums. II. Die Stoffe'. *Der Islam*, 58 (1981), pp. 15–86.

———. 'Die Sīrat Ibn Ḥaušab: die ismailitische da'wa im Jemen und die Fatimiden'. *Die Welt des Orients*, 12 (1981), pp. 107–135.

———. *Die islamische Gnosis: Die extreme Schia und die 'Alawiten*. Zurich and Munich: Artemis Verlag, 1982.

———. 'Courants et mouvements antinomistes dans l'islam medieval", in *La notion de liberté au Moyen Age. Islam, Byzance, Occident*, ed. George Makdisi, Dominique Sourdel and Janine Sourdel-Thomine. Paris: Les Belles Lettres, 1985, pp. 135–141.

———. 'Der Treuhänder Gottes: Die Edikte des Kalifen al-Ḥākim', *Der Islam*, 63 (1986), pp. 11–72.

———. 'Les Fatimides à Salamya'. *Revue des Etudes Islamiques*, LIV (1986), pp. 133–147.

———. 'The Cosmology of the Pre-Fatimid Ismāʿīliyya', in *Mediaeval Isma'ili History and Thought*, ed. Farhad Daftary. Cambridge: Cambridge University Press, 1996, pp. 75–83.

———. 'The Isma'ili oath of allegiance (*'ahd*) and the 'sessions of wisdom' (*majālis al-ḥikma*) in Fatimid times', *Mediaeval Isma'ili History and Thought*, ed. Farhad Daftary. Cambridge: Cambridge University Press, 1996, pp. 91–115.

———. *The Empire of the Mahdi. The Rise of the Fatimids*, English translation by Michael Bonner. Leiden: Brill, 1996.

———. *The Fatimids and their Traditions of Learning*, London: I.B. Tauris, 1997.

———. 'Methods and forms of the earliest Ismāʿīlī *da'wa*', in E. Kohlberg, ed., *Shī'ism*. Aldershot: Ashgate Variorum, 2003, pp. 277–290.

———. 'D̲ja'far b. Manṣūr al-Yaman'. *EI2*.

———. 'Ebn Ḥawšab, Abu'l-Qāsim Ḥasan'. *EIr*.

Hamdani, Husayn F., *On the Genealogy of Fatimid Caliphs (Statement on Mahdī's Communication to the Yemen on the Real and Esoteric Names of his Hidden Predecessors)*. Cairo: American University at Cairo, 1958.

Hamdani, Abbas. 'An Early Fatimid Source on the Time and Authorship of the *Rasā'il Iḫwān al-Ṣafā*". *Arabica*, 26/1 (1979), pp. 62–75.

———, and François De Blois. 'A Re-examination of al-Mahdī's Letter to the Yemenites on the Genealogy of the Fatimid Caliphs'. *Journal of the Royal Asiatic Society*, 115 (1983), pp. 173–207.

Hawting, G.R. 'Muḥammad b. Abī Bakr'. *EI2*.

Hayes, Edmund. *Agents of the Hidden Imam: Forging Twelver Shi'ism 850-950 CE*. Cambridge: Cambridge University Press, 2022.

Hinds, Martin. 'Mu'āwiya I'. *EI2*.

Hodgson, Marshall G.S. 'How did the Early Shî'a become Sectarian?' *Journal of the American Oriental Society*, 75 (1955), pp. 1–13; repr. in *Shī'ism*, ed. Etan Kohlberg. Aldershot: Ashgate Variorum, 2003, pp. 3–15.

———. 'Ghulāt'. *EI2*.

———. 'Ḥud̲jd̲ja: in S̲hi'i terminology'. *EI2*.

Hollenberg, David. 'Interpretation after the End of Days: The Fatimid-Ismāʿīlī Ta'wīl (interpretation) of Ja'far ibn Manṣūr al-Yaman (d. ca. 960)'. PhD thesis, University of Pennsylvania, 2006.

———. 'Neoplatonism in pre-Kirmānīan Fatimid doctrine: A critical edition and translation of the prologue of the *Kitāb al-fatarāt wa-l-qirānāt*'. *Le Muséon*, 122/1–2 (2009), pp. 159–202.

———. 'The Empire Writes Back: Fatimid Ismaili *Ta'wīl* (Allegoresis) in the Mysteries of the Ancient Greeks', in *The Study of Shi'i Islam. History, Theology and Law*, ed. F. Daftary and G. Miskinzoda. London and New York: I.B. Tauris, 2014, pp. 135–147.

———. *Beyond the Qur'an. Early Ismāʿīlī Ta'wīl and the Secrets of the Prophets*. Columbia: University of South Carolina Press, 2016.

———. '*Anta anā wa-anā minka* ("You are me, and I am from you"): A Quasi-Nuṣayrī Fragment on the Intellect in the Early Ismāʿīlī Treatise *Kitāb Ta'wīl ḥurūf al-mu'jam*', in

Arabic Humanities, Islamic Thought. Essays in Honor of Everett K. Rowson, ed. Joseph E. Lowry and Shawkat M. Toorawa. Leiden: Brill, 2017, pp. 50–66.

Holtzman, Livnat. 'Anthropomorphism'. *EI3*.

Ivanow, Wladimir. 'Notes sur l'Ummu'l-kitâb des ismaéliens de l'Asie centrale'. *Revue des études islamiques*, 6 (1932), pp. 419–481.

Ivanow, W., *A Guide to Ismaili literature*. London: Royal Asiatic Society, 1933.

———. 'The Book of the Teacher and the Pupil', in W. Ivanow, *Studies in Early Persian Ismailism*. Leiden: Brill, 1948, pp. 85–113.

———. *Ismaili literature: A Bibliographical Survey*. Tehran, 1963.

Jeffery, Arthur, *The Foreign Vocabulary of the Qur'ān*. Baroda, 1938, repr. Leiden-Boston: Brill, 2007.

Keshk, K.M.G. "Amr b. al-ʿĀṣ'. *EI3*.

Kohlberg, Etan. 'The Term 'Rāfiḍa' in Imamī Shīʿī Usage'. *Journal of the American Oriental Society*, 99/4 (1979), pp. 677–679 (repr. in E. Kohlberg. *Belief and Law in Imamī Shīʿism*. Aldershot: Ashgate Variorum, 1991, article 4).

———. 'Some Imamī Shīʿī views on the *Ṣaḥāba*'. *Jerusalem Studies in Arabic and Islam*, 5 (1984), pp. 143–175 (repr. in E. Kohlberg. *Belief and Law in Imamī Shīʿism*. Aldershot: Ashgate Variorum, 1991, article 9).

———. 'Some Imamī Shīʿī views on *taqiyya*'. *Journal of the American Oriental Society*, 95 (1975), pp. 395–402 (repr. in E. Kohlberg. *Belief and Law in Imamī Shīʿism*. Aldershot: Ashgate Variorum, 1991, article 3).

———. '*Barā'a* in Shīʿi doctrine'. *Jerusalem Studies in Arabic and Islam*, 7 (1986), pp. 139–175.

———. 'Imam and Community in the Pre-*Ghayba* Period', in E. Kohlberg. *In Praise of the Few. Studies in Shiʿi Thought and History*, ed. A. Ehteshami. Leiden and Boston: Brill, 2020, pp. 187–212.

———. '*Taqiyya* in Shīʿī Theology and Religion', in *Secrecy and Concealment*, ed. H.G. Kippenberg and G.C. Stroumsa. Leiden, New York and Cologne: Brill, 1995, pp. 345–380.

———. 'Radjʿa', *EI2*.

Kraus, Paul. 'La bibliographie ismaëlienne de W. Ivanow'. *Revue des études islamiques*, 6 (1932), pp. 483–490.

———. 'Les dignitaires de la hiérarchie religieuse selon Gābir Ibn Ḥayyān'. *Bulletin de l'Institut français d'archéologie orientale*, 41 (1942), pp. 83–97.

———. *Jābir Ibn Ḥayyān. Contribution à l'histoire des idées scientifiques dans l'Islam*, 2 vol. Cairo: Imprimerie de l'Institut français d'archéologie orientale, 1942–1943.

Krinis, Ehud. *God's Chosen People: Judah Halevi's* Kuzari *and the Shīʿī Imām Doctrine*, English translation by Ann Brener and Tamar Liza Cohen. Turnhout: Brepols, 2014.

Lammens, Henri. 'al-Mughīra b. Shuʿba'. *EI2*.

Levi della Vida, Giorgio. 'Salmān al-Fārisī'. *EI2*.

Lewis, Bernard. *The Origins of Ismāʿīlism: A Study of the Historical Background of the Fāṭimid Caliphate*. Cambridge: W. Heffer and Sons, 1940.

———. 'Abu 'l-Khaṭṭāb', *EI2*.

Lindsay, J.E. 'Prophetic Parallels in Abu ʿAbd Allah al-Shiʿi's mission among the Kutama Berbers, 893–910'. *International Journal of the Middle East Studies*, 24 (1992), pp. 39–56.

Lory, Pierre. *Dix traités d'alchimie*. Paris: Sindbad, 1983.

———. *Alchimie et mystique en terre d'islam*. Paris: Verdier, 1989.

———. 'Esotérisme shiʿite et alchimie. Quelques remarques sur la doctrine de l'initiation dans le Corpus Jābirien', in *L'ésotérisme shiʿite, ses racines et ses prolongements*, ed. Mohammad A. Amir-Moezzi, Maria De Cillis, Daniel De Smet and Orkhan Mir-Kasimov. Turnhout: Brepols, pp. 411–422.

Madelung, Wilferd. 'Das Imamat in der frühen ismailitischen Lehre'. *Der Islam*, 37 (1961), pp. 43–135.

——. 'Bemerkungen zur imamatischen Firaq-Literatur'. *Der Islam*, 43 (1967), pp. 37–52.

——. 'The Fatimids and the Qarmaṭīs of Baḥrayn', in *Mediaeval Isma'ili History and Thought*, ed. F. Daftary. Cambridge: Cambridge University Press, 1996, pp. 21–73.

——. *The Succession to Muḥammad. A Study of the Early Caliphate*. Cambridge: Cambridge University Press, 1997.

——. 'Introduction', in *The Study of Shi'i Islam*, ed. F. Daftary and G. Miskinzoda. London and New York, 2014, pp. 3–16.

——. 'Early Imamī Theology as Reflected in the *Kitāb al-kāfī* of al-Kulaynī', in *The Study of Shi'i Islam. History, Theology and Law*, ed. F. Daftary and G. Miskinzoda. London and New York: I.B. Tauris, 2014, pp. 465–474.

——. Review of M. Brett, *The Rise of the Fatimids* (2001), *Journal of Islamic Studies*, 13/2 (2002), pp. 202–204.

——. 'Djābir al-Dju'fī'. *EI2*.

——. 'al-Ḥāmidī'. *EI2*.

——. 'Khaṭṭābiyya'. *EI2*.

——. 'Manṣūr al-Yaman'. *EI2*.

——. 'Manṣūriyya'. *EI2*.

——. 'Mughīriyya'. *EI2*.

——. 'Mukhammisa'. *EI2*.

——. 'Talḥa b. 'Ubayd Allāh'. *EI2*.

——. 'Talḥa b. 'Ubayd Allāh'. *EI3*.

——. 'Zaydiyya'. *EI2*.

——, and Paul E. Walker. *An Ismaili Heresiography. The "Bāb al-shayṭān" from Abū Tammām's* Kitāb al-shajara. Leiden, Boston and Cologne: Brill, 1998.

——, and Paul E. Walker. *The Advent of the Fatimids. A contemporary Shi'i Witness*. London and New York: I.B. Tauris, 2000.

——, and Paul E. Walker. *Affirming the Imamate. Early Fatimid Teachings in the Islamic West*. London and New York: I.B. Tauris, 2021.

Marquet, Yves. 'Quelques remarques à propos de *Kosmologie und Heilslehre der frühen Ismā'īlīya* de Heinz Halm'. *Studia Islamica*, 55 (1982), pp. 115–135.

——. 'La pensée philosophique et religieuse du Qāḍī al-Nu'mān à travers la *Risāla Muḏhiba*'. *Bulletin d'Etudes Orientales*, 39/40 (1987–1988), pp. 141–181.

——. *La philosophie des Iḫwān al-Ṣafā'*, Milan: Archè, 1999.

Massignon, Louis. 'Salmān Pāk et les prémices spirituelles de l'Islam iranien', in idem, *Opera Minora*, ed. Y. Moubarac. Beirut: Dār al-Ma'ārif, 1963, vol. 2, pp. 443–483.

——. 'Al-Muḥassin b. 'Alī'. *EI2*.

Massi Dakake, Maria. *The Charismatic Community: Shi'ite Identity in Early Islam*. Albany: State University of New York Press, 2007.

Meredith-Owens, G.M. 'Ḥamza b. 'Abd al-Muṭṭalib'. *EI2*.

Mir-Kasimov, Orkhan. 'The Word of Descent and the Word of Ascent in the Spectrum of the Sacred Texts in Islam', in *Controverses sur les écritures canoniques de l'islam*, ed. D. De Smet and M.A. Amir-Moezzi. Paris: Les Editions du Cerf, 2014.

——. *Words of Power. Ḥurūfī Teachings between Shi'ism and Sufism in Medieval Islam*. London and New York: I.B. Tauris with the Institute of Ismaili Studies, 2015.

Mirza, Sarah. ''Abd Allāh b. Rawāḥa'. *EI3*.

Miskinzoda, Gurdofarid. 'The significance of the *ḥadīth* of the position of Aaron for the formulation of the Shī'ī doctrine of authority', *BSOAS*, 78/1 (2015), pp. 67–82.

Modarressi, Hossein. *Crisis and Consolidation in the Formative Period of Shī'ite Islam: Abū Ja'far ibn Qiba al-Rāzī and his Contribution to Imāmite Shī'ite Law*. Princeton: Darwin Press, 1993.

Montgomery Watt, William. 'al-'Abbās b. 'Abd al-Muṭṭalib'. *EI2*.

——. ''Aḳaba', *EI2*.

Munt, Harry. 'Fadak'. *EI3*.

Newman, Andrew J. *The Formative Period of Twelver Shīʿism. Ḥadīth as Discourse Between Qum and Baghdad.* Richmond: Curzon Press, 2000.
Orthmann, Eva. '*Ẓāhir* und *bāṭin* in der Astrologie: Das *Kitāb al-Fatarāt wa-l-qirānāt al-ʿašara*', in *Differenz und Dynamik im Islam. Festschrift für Heinz Halm zum 70. Geburstag*, ed. H. Biesterfeldt and V. Klemm. Würzburg: Egon Verlag, 2012, pp. 337–358
Pellat, Charles. 'Fatra'. *EI2*.
———. 'Maskh'. *EI2*.
Poonawala, Ismail Kurban. *Biobibliography of Ismāʿīlī Literature*. Malibu, CA: Undena Publications, 1977.
———. 'Ismāʿīlī taʾwīl of the Qurʾan', in *Approaches to the History of the Interpretation of the Qurʾan*, ed. Andrew Rippin, Oxford, 1988, pp. 199–222.
———. 'The Chronology of al-Qāḍī al-Nuʿmān's Works'. *Arabica*, 65/1–2 (2018), pp. 84–162.
al-Qāḍī, Wadād, 'The Development of the Term *ghulāt* in Muslim Literature with Special Reference to the Kaysāniyya', in *Akten des VII. Kongresses für Arabistik und Islamwissenschaft*, ed. A. Dietrich. Göttingen: Vandenhoeck & Ruprecht, 1976, pp. 295–319; repr. in *Shīʿism*, ed. Etan Kohlberg. Aldershot: Ashgate Variorum, 2003, pp. 169–193.
Qutbuddin, Tahera. 'Idrīs 'Imād al-Dīn'. *EI3*.
Reckendorf, Hermann. ''Ammār b. Yāsir'. *EI2*.
Rippin, Andrew. 'Shuʿayb'. *EI2*.
Rob son, James. 'Abū Dharr'. *EI2*.
Rubin, Uri. 'Apes, Pigs and the Islamic Identity'. *Israel Oriental Studies*, 17 (1997), pp. 98–105.
Schaade, Arthur. ''Abd Allāh b. Rawāḥa'. *EI2*.
Schrier, Omert T. 'The Prehistory of the Fatimid Dynasty: Some Chronological and Genealogical Remarks'. *Die Welt des Orients*, 36 (2006), pp. 143–191.
Schwarb, Gregor M. 'Amr'. *EI3*.
Shahid, Irfan. 'Thamūd'. *EI2*.
Spies, Otto. 'Wadīʿa'. *EI1*.
Stern, Samuel Miklos. 'The earliest cosmological doctrines of Ismāʿīlism', in idem, *Studies in Early Ismāʿīlism*. Jerusalem/Leiden: Magnes Press/Brill, 1983, pp. 3–29.
———. 'Jaʿfar Ibn Mansūr al-Yaman's Poems on the Rebellion of Abū Yazīd', in idem, *Studies in Early Ismāʿīlism*. Jerusalem/Leiden: Magnes Press/Brill, 1983, pp. 146–152.
———. 'Ismāʿīlis and Qarmaṭians', in idem, *Studies in Early Ismāʿīlism*. Jerusalem/Leiden: Magnes Press/Brill, 1983, pp. 289–298.
———. 'Heterodox Ismāʿīlism at the time of al-Muʿizz', in idem, *Studies in Early Ismāʿīlism*, Jerusalem/Leiden: Magnes Press/Brill, 1983, pp. 257–288.
Straface, Antonella. 'The representations of *al-Jadd, al-Fatḥ* and *al-Khayāl* in the Ismaili literature. Some examples and further remarks', in *L'ésotérisme shiʿite, ses racines et ses prolongements*, ed. Mohammad A. Amir-Moezzi, Maria De Cillis, Daniel De Smet and Orkhan Mir-Kasimov. Turnhout: Brepols, 2016, pp. 423–440.
Strothmann, Rudolf. *Esoterische Sonderthemen bei den Nusairi. Geschichten und Traditionen von den Heiligen Meistern aus dem Prophetenhaus*. Berlin: Akademie-Verlag, 1958.
———. *Gnosis-Texte der Ismailiten. Arabische Handschrift Ambrosiana H 75*. Göttingen: Vandenhoeck & Ruprecht, 1943.
Tendler, Bella. 'Concealment and Revelation: a Study of Secrecy and Initiation among the Nuṣayrī-ʿAlawīs of Syria', Ph.D. thesis, Princeton University, 2012.
Tendler Krieger, B., 'Marriage, Birth and *bāṭinī taʾwīl*: A study of Nuṣayrī Initiation Based on the *Kitāb al-Ḥāwī fī ʿilm al-fatāwī* of Abū Saʿīd Maymūn al-Ṭabarānī'. *Arabica*, 58/1 (2011), pp. 53–75.
Tottoli, Roberto. ''Ād'. *EQ*.
Tucker, William F. *Mahdis and Millenarians. Shīʾite Extremistes in Early Muslim Iraq*. New York: Cambridge University Press, 2008.

Turner, Colin P. 'The "Tradition of Mufaḍḍal" and the Doctrine of the *Raj'a*: Evidence of *Ghuluww* in the Eschatology of Twelver Shi'ism?' *Iran: Journal of the British Institute of Persian Studies*, 44 (2006), pp. 175–195.

Van Ess, Josef. *Frühe mu'tazilitische Häresiographie: Zwei Werke des Nāšī'al-Akbar (gest. 293 H.)*. Beirut: In Kommission bei Franz Steiner Verlag, Wiesbaden, 1971; reed. 2003.

———. *Theology and Society in the Second and Third Centuries of the Hijra. A History of Religious Thought in Early Islam*. English translation by John O'Kane. Leiden and Boston: Brill, 2017–2019, 4 vol.

———. 'Tashbīh wa-tanzīh'. *EI2*.

Veccia Vaglieri, Laura. ''Alī b. Abī Ṭālib'. *EI2*.

———. 'al-D̲j̲amal'. *EI2*.

———. 'Fadak'. *EI2*.

———. 'G̲h̲adīr K̲h̲umm'. *EI2*.

Velji, Jamel. *An Apocalyptic History of the Early Fatimid Empire*. Edinburgh: Edinburgh University Press, 2018.

Vilozny, Roy. *Constructing a Worldview. Al-Barqī's Role in the Making of Early Shī'ī Faith*. Turnhout: Brepols, 2017.

Walker, Paul Ernest. 'The Ismaili Vocabulary on Creation'. *Studia Islamica*, 40 (1974), pp. 75–85.

———. 'Cosmic Hierarchies in Early Ismā'īlī Thought: the view of Abū Ya'qūb al-Sijistānī'. *The Muslim World*, 66/1 (1976), pp. 14–28.

———. 'The doctrine of metempsychosis in Islam', in *Islamic Studies presented to Charles J. Adams*, ed. Wael B. Hallaq and Donald P. Little. Leiden: Brill, 1991, pp. 219–238.

———. 'The Ismaili Da'wa in the Reign of the Fatimid Caliph Al-Ḥākim'. *Journal of the American Research Center in Egypt*, 30 (1993), pp. 161–182.

———. *Early Philosophical Shiism, The Ismaili Neoplatonism of Abū Ya'qūb al-Sijistānī*. New York: Cambridge University Press, 1993.

———. *Ḥamīd al-Dīn al-Kirmānī. Ismaili Thought in the Age of al-Ḥākim*. London and New York: I.B. Tauris, 1999.

———. *Orations of the Fatimid Caliphs. Festival Sermons of the Ismaili Imams. An edition of the Arabic texts and English translation of Fatimid* khuṭbas. London and New York: I.B. Tauris, 2009.

———. 'Techniques for guarding and restricting esoteric knowledge in the Ismaili *da'wa* during the Fatimid period', in *Sharing and Hiding Religious Knowledge in Early Judaism, Christianity, and Islam*, ed. Mladen Popovič, Lautaro Roig Lanzillotta and Clare Wilde. Berlin: De Gruyter, 2018, pp. 186–197.

———. 'Ismaili Polemics against Opponents in the Early Fatimid Period', in *Intellectual Interactions in the Islamic World. The Ismaili Thread*, ed. O. Mir-Kasimov, London and New York: I.B. Tauris, 2020, pp. 27–50.

Weaver, James. 'Mughīriyya'. *EI3*.

Wensinck, Arent Jan. ''Amr b. al-'Āṣ'. *EI2*.

———. 'Aṣḥāb al-Rass'. *EI2*.

Yazigi, Maya. 'Defense and Validation in Shi'i and Sunni Tradition: The Case of Muḥammad b. Abī Bakr'. *Studia Islamica*, 98/99 (2004), pp. 49–70.

Index of Qur'anic Verses

1) al-Fātiḥa
1:2 176, 224
1:6 99, 347, 358, 381

2) al-Baqara
2:1-2 99
2:1-3 72, 99
2:2 100, 460
2:3 100
2:5 72, 100
2:6 77
2:6-9 71, 76
2:7 77, 157
2:8 162
2:8-9 78
2:12 78
2:13 78, 148
2:16 78
2:24 234, 466
2:25 377
2:27 82
2:30-36 124
2:30 122
2:31 117, 124
2:31-33 117
2:34 117, 125, 360, 380
2:38 122
2:50 89
2:61 356
2:65 154
2:78-79 428, 445, 462
2:85 241
2:87 451
2:105 176
2:121 442
2:125 340
2:126 119, 241, 446
2:165 101
2:165-167 72, 101
2:166 101
2:167 101, 102
2:173 75
2:181 382
2:189 350, 365
2:190 211
2:191 112
2:197 320, 321, 346, 350, 352, 353, 354, 359, 364, 406, 414, 416, 419
2:205 111
2:205-207 111
2:206 111
2:207 111
2:208 97, 111
2:210 332
2:224 382
2:233 428, 436, 463, 464
2:239 345
2:255 173, 180, 188
2:256 82, 212, 325
2:257 177, 347
2:282 382
2:283 122

3) Āl ʿImrān

3:7	321, 358, 359, 363, 389
3:19	229
3:33-34	337
3:49	80, 118, 137, 235, 328, 330
3:67	96
3:96	378
3:96-97	321, 365, 366, 378
3:97	320, 329, 379, 380, 381
3:103	82, 212, 329
3:119	372, 375, 378
3:173	383
3:178	239
3:187	427, 435
3:191	344

4) al-Nisāʾ

4:6	367
4:10	272, 282
4:28	13
4:34	344
4:41	371
4:48	119
4:51	100, 101, 102, 358
4:54	183
4:59	351
4:64	330
4:69	321, 368, 370, 377, 378
4:140	223
4:157	412
4:160	434
4:171	9, 80, 82

5) al-Māʾida

5:3	75
5:6	351
5:54	113
5:64	176, 192
5:72	119
5:97	319, 320, 322, 329
5:110	80
5:120	304

6) al-Anʿām

6:1	74
6:12	366
6:14	116
6:26	355
6:28	213
6:46	446
6:50	243
6:53	358
6:59	72, 99, 374
6:68	177, 194
6:74	380
6:83	374
6:90	334
6:100	447
6:101	374
6:103	177, 303, 394
6:115	347, 366
6:150	451
6:153	431
6:157	447

7) al-Aʿrāf

7:12	117
7:29	332
7:30	177
7:54	172
7:85	85
7:142	92, 94, 142
7:155	246
7:172	123, 392
7:179	157, 372
7:180	177, 338, 377, 388
7:182	177

8) al-Anfāl

8:27	375, 376

9) al-Tawba
9:3 320, 331, 333, 339, 405, 418
9:6 373, 374
9:12 359
9:14-15 113
9:18 209
9:33 75, 114
9:70 85
9:90-94 234
9:100 432
9:114 323
9:129 174, 175, 176, 179

10) Yūnis
10:10 207, 224, 225, 267
10:17-18 428, 444
10:62 122

11) Hūd
11:7 179
11:17 442, 443
11:18 218
11:31 243
11:40 326
11:66 176
11:81 368
11:97-98 363

12) Yūsuf
12:24 105
12:41 370
12:46 357, 368, 370
12:50 110
12:76 370
12:99-100 357
12:101 116
12:106 177
12:108 380

13) al-Raʿd
13:2 266
13:15 225
13:33 428, 445
13:41 366, 378

14) Ibrāhīm
14:4 336
14:10 116
14:22 220
14:24 96
14:24-25 97
14:24-26 97
14:24-27 72, 96
14:24-30 68
14:25 344
14:25-26 97
14:26 97
14:27 98
14:28 100, 228
14:28-30 72, 100
14:29 100
14:30 100, 101
14:44 257

15) al-Ḥijr
15:40 117
15:42 117

16) al-Naḥl
16:15 467
16:21 256, 328
16:25 446
16:60 176, 344
16:64 443
16:68 103, 104, 259, 466
16:68-69 72, 103, 259, 261, 473
16:69 104, 259, 260, 261
16:90 427, 432, 433
16:91 76
16:92 427, 433, 461

16:101 362
16:115 75

17) al-Isrāʾ
17:23 366
17:26 432
17:35 378
17:49 222
17:50 158, 159
17:50-51 222
17:50-52 207, 221, 262, 267, 268
17:51 222, 223
17:52 223, 225, 262, 267
17:55 371
17:60 97
17:71 221, 224, 267
17:74 240
17:85 177
17:89 344
17:110 116

18) al-Kahf
18:9 173
18:31 368
18:46 377
18:49 369
18:50 354
18:57 381
18:82 277
18:104 177
18:105 212

19) Maryam
19:5-6 218
19:12 369
19:33 81
19:40 234
19:42-43 323
19:44 324
19:46 323
19:47 323
19:50 115
19:54-55 368
19:56-57 368
19:58 370
19:96 231
19:96-97 208, 231
19:97 232

20) Ṭāhā
20:4
20:5 174, 190
20:6 173
20:8 116
20:25-31 208, 231
20:48 358
20:82 241
20:85 461
20:85-87 110
20:87 461
20:95 461
20:105-107 428, 440
20:108 233
20:108-112 208, 233
20:109 235
20:110 233, 237
20:111 235
20:112 236, 237, 237
20:112-114 237
20:124 237
20:124-126 237
20:124-131 208, 237
20:125 238
20:127 238, 295
20:128 239
20:129 239
20:130 240, 295
20:131 240, 241
20:131-135 237
20:135 241, 323

21) al-Anbiyā'
21:10 243
21:18 109
21:22 176, 191
21:24 242, 242
21:25 180
21:30 175, 198
21:47 89
21:76 368
21:79 441
21:104 332
21:105 243
21:110 247

22) al-Ḥajj
22:3-4 244
22:9 160, 244, 245
22:10 245, 246
22:27 320, 340, 343, 345
22:37 344, 345
22:44 86
22:45 73, 115
22:46 372
22:61 381
22:75 373
22:78 88, 96, 113, 145

23) al-Mu'minūn
23:8 122
23:14 382

24) al-Nūr
24:35 79, 95, 96
24:36 210, 320, 334, 336, 337
24:36-37 210, 262, 334
24:40 73, 115

25) al-Furqān
25:23 99
25:27 109
25:27-29 109
25:27-31 109, 473
25:28-29 109, 228
25:29 109
25:30 110
25:31 87, 110, 151, 294
25:38 85
25:45 288
25:45-46 68, 207, 226, 230, 231
25:50 344
25:55 110
25:77 358

26) al-Shuʿarā'
26:193-197 320, 334, 335
26:193 349
26:194 336
26:195 336
26:196 336
26:197 336

27) al-Naml
27:16 183, 218
27:25 376
27:62 104

28) al-Qaṣaṣ
28:6 85
28:42 359
28:50 451, 454
28:76-82 85
28:78 358
28:88 172

29) al-ʿAnkabūt
29:1-2 110
29:1-3 110
29:3 110

29:33 85
29:45 433
29:46 353
29:47 443
29:49 88

30) al-Rūm
30:25 256
30:30 75
30:75 234

31) Luqmān
31:32 89

33) al-Aḥzāb
33:5 350
33:21 341
33:62 366
33:72 74, 122, 124, 125, 126, 467
33:72-73 107
33:73 108

34) Saba'
34:10 441
34:17 89
34:18 93
34:50 326, 365

35) Fāṭir
35:1 116
35:28 379
35:43 344

36) Yā-Sīn
36:12 430
36:67 154

37) al-Ṣāffāt
37:83 343
37:113 432
37:165-166 116

38) Ṣād
38:18-19 428, 441
38:67-68 88
38:75 350, 469

39) al-Zumar
39:19 223
39:46 116
39:60 359

40) Ghāfir
40:5 364
40:11 130
40:19 375, 376
40:24 85
40:36 85
40:78 115

41) Fuṣṣilat
41:6 410
41:6-7 108
41:42 322
41:54 240

42) al-Shūrā
42:11 116, 119
42:13 371
42:24 96
42:51 373

43) al-Zukhruf
43:45 372, 373
43:51-54 321, 354, 422
43:51 355
43:52 355, 422
43:53 355, 423
43:54 356

44) al-Dukhān
44:41 331
44:41-42 102
44:41-45 72, 102

44:42 102
44:43-45 102
44:51 102
44:52-54 72, 102
44:57 72, 102

45) al-Jāthiya
45:18 451
45:23 445, 451
45:27 115
45:29 369

46) al-Aḥqāf
46:9 243
46:12 428, 438, 439, 442, 462
46:35 371

47) Muḥammad
47:1 98
47:17 325
47:22 218
47:23 358

48) al-Fatḥ
48:12 100
48:25 98

49) al-Ḥujurāt
49:12 352, 421
49:13 236

50) Qāf
50:8 325
50:12 85

52) al-Ṭūr
52:1 214
52:1-6 84
52:1-8 72, 83
52:7-8 83
52:13 211, 263
52:46 331
52:48 369

53) al-Najm
53:13-17 119
53:18 119
53:23 429, 450
53:28-30 429, 430
53:32 382

55) al-Raḥmān
55:37 83, 163

57) al-Ḥadīd
57:3 240, 367
57:13 89, 350, 351, 415, 417
57:19 370
57:22 99

58) al-Mujādila
58:7 225
58:11 427, 436
58:19 363

59) al-Ḥashr
59:7 431
59:16 109
59:24 102, 116

60) al-Mumtaḥana
60:4 379
60:10 464
60:12 428, 437, 464

61) al-Ṣaff
61:6 93
61:7 430
61:9 75

62) al-Jumuʿa
62:2 428, 438, 461

66) al-Taḥrīm
66:6 234
66:7 234

67) al-Mulk
67:14 330
67:24 330
67:30 72, 103, 212

69) al-Ḥāqqa
69:17 179

70) al-Maʿārij
70:32 122
70:40 72, 82

72) al-Jinn
72:18 209, 262
72:75 247

74) al-Mudaththir
74:8 104
74:9-10 104
74:10 104

75) al-Qiyāma
75:15 234
75:20-23 106
75:20-25 106
75:24 106
75:25 107
75:26 107
75:29-30 107
75:29-34 106
75:31 107
75:32 107, 358
75:33-34 107

76) al-Insān
76:18 229

77) al-Mursalāt
70:30 68, 280
70:30-31 226, 227, 279, 288
70:31 229, 294
70:36 234

78) al-Naba'
78:1-3 88
78:12 440
78:12-20 428, 467
78:13 440
78:14 440, 468
78:15-16 440
78:17 440
78:18 441
78:19 441
78:20 441, 468

79) al-Nāziʿāt
79:28 349

81) al-Takwīr
81:15-16 86, 87

86) al-Infiṭār
82:6-7 78

83) al-Muṭaffifīn
83:9 173
83:20 173, 460
83:20-21 174, 183
83:29-30 358

85) al-Burūj
85:3 81
85:22 173

87) al-Aʿlā
87:2 382
87:3 383

89) al-Fajr
89:1 212
89:2 213
89:3 213
89:4 213
89:5 213
89:6-7 213, 264
89:6-8 214
89:6-12 215
89:7-8 214
89:9 214, 266
89:10 215
89:11-13 215
89:13 294
89:14 216
89:15 216
89:16 216
89:17 216, 281
89:17-18 281
89:17-19 286
89:18 217, 281
89:19-20 218
89:21 297
89:21-22 219
89:23 219, 220, 298
89:24 220
89:25-26 220
89:27-28 220

90) al-Balad
90:13 374

92) al-Layl
92:16 358

93) al-Ḍūḥā
93:6 282
93:6-9 272

95) al-Tīn
95:1 102
95:1-8 102
95:2 102
95:3 102
95:4 102
95:4-5 77, 158
95:5-6 103
95:6-7 103
95:8 103

96) al-ʿAlaq
13 358

107) al-Māʿūn
107:1 210, 211, 212
107:1-2 263
107:2 281
107:3 211, 281
107:4-5 212
107:6-7 212

112) al-Ikhlāṣ
112:1 310
112:2 188
112:2-3 304
112:3 304
112:4 304

114) al-Nās
114:5 355

Index of Names and Places

(Numbers in **bold** characters refer to pages in the translation of the *Kashf*.)

Aaron 64, 66, **87–8**, 110, 144–5, 151–4, 208, **232**, 398, 427, **431–4**, **439**, **443**, 449, 458–62
al-ʿAbbās 91, 273
ʿAbd Allāh b. Rawāḥa 273–5
ʿAbd Allāh b. Sabaʾ 10
ʿAbdān 25
ʿAbd al-Raḥīm b. Ṭayyib Khān 29
Abraham 84, **95–6**, **110**, **117–18**, 142, 145, 149, 165, **183**, 319–20, **323–4**, **335**, **337**, **340**, **342–3**, **371**, **379**, 398
Abū'l-ʿAbbās 26
Abū ʿAbd Allāh al-Shīʿī 24–6, 45, 271, 285, 385–6, 422, 424, 457, 471, 474
Abū Bakr / the First / ʿAtīq 13, 35, 63, 66, **73**, 85, **106–11**, 124–6, 139, 147–9, 151–3, 158, 160–1, 164–7, 208, **213**, 216, **219**, **220**, 228, **244–5**, 248–9, 252, 255, 263–7, 269–70, 286–7, 294–6, **354**, 387, 420, **477**
Abū Dharr 68, 90, 207, **226–8**, 248–9, 273–6, 278–80, 287, 299, 330, 396, 402
Abū Khālid 92, 273–5
Abū al-Khaṭṭāb (Ibn Abī Zaynab) **91–2**, 273–5, 482
Abū Ṭāhir al-Jannābī 457
ʿAdī 100
ʿAlī b. Abī Ṭālib 42, 71–2, 80, 86–7, **99–100**, **103**, **107**, **117–18**, 124–5, 135–6, 148, 187, 211–12, **214–15**, **217**, **221**, **223**, **237**, 255, 264, 267–8, 270, 273, 280, 283, 288, 294, 310, **354–5**, 389, 406, 409, 422–3, **429**, **432**, **435**, **439**, **442–3**, 448, 450, 460
ʿAlī b. al-Faḍl 25, 44
ʿAlī b. Muhammad b. al-Walīd 42
Amir-Moezzi, Mohammad Ali 7, 12, 15, 17, 139, 148, 155
ʿAmmār b. Yāsir 273–5
ʿAmr b. al-ʿĀṣ **215**, **217**
ʿAqaba 112, **242**
Asatryan, Mushegh 301, 311–2, 315
Aswad **90**, **92**, 273, 275
al-ʿAyyāshī, Abū al-Naḍr Muhammad b. Masʿūd 259–61

Badr al-Dīn al-Shaykh Ismāʿīl Jī 29–30
al-Bāqir, *see* Muḥammad al-Bāqir
Bar-Asher, Meir M. 2, 53, 480
Brett, Michael 476, 479

Daftary, Farhad 21–2
De Blois, François 39
De Smet, Daniel 150, 154, 417

Fadak **218**, 283, 286, **354**
Fāṭima 61, **95–6**, **116**, 165–6, 204, **213**, **218**, 276, 286, **327**, **329**, **354**, 388, 399, 404, 410
Fyzee, Ali Asghar 29, 33

Ghālib, Muṣṭafā 30, 32–3, 46–7

al-Ḥakīm (*see also* Muḥammad b. Aḥmad) **210**, **212**, **222**, **226**, **229**, **231**, **233**, **235**, **237–40**, **247**, 253–6, 272, 290, 292, 294, **323**, **331**, **342**, **344**, **350**, **352**, **357**, **367**, **374**, 418, 423, 457
Halm, Heinz 6, 9–10, 12, 61, 158, 166, 184, 198, 248, 251, 273, 275, 276, 296, 298, 398, 400, 405, 418, 448
Ḥamdān Qarmaṭ 25
Ḥamza b. ʿAbd al-Muṭṭalib **91–2**, 273
Ḥanẓala b. Asaʿd al-Shibāmī **91**, 273, 275
Hāshim b. ʿUtba b. Abī Waqqāṣ **103**
Hollenberg, David 47–8, 51, 59, 386, 474

Ibn Bābawayh, 'Shaykh Ṣadūq', Abū Jaʿfar Muḥammad 7, 155, 184–5, 187–9, 193, 205, 309–10
Ibn Ḥawshab Manṣūr al-Yaman 24–5, 43–4, 52, 108, 200, 266, 454
Ibn Mālik 44–5
Idrīs ʿImād al-Dīn 38, 44, 49, 189, 195, 204, 253, 455
Ifrīqiya 24–5, 44–5
Ismāʿīl Badr al-Dīn b. al-Shaykh Ādam Ṣafī al-Dīn 29–30, 34

Jābir b. Yazīd al-Juʿfī 80, 136, 166
Jaʿfar b. al-Ḥārith 273, 275
Jaʿfar b. Manṣūr al-Yaman 3, 5, 16–17, 24, 28–60, 145, 149, 153, 198, 447, 473–5, 477, 479–80
Jaʿfar al-Ṣādiq (Abū ʿAbdallāh) 9, 13–14, 19, 22–3, 42, 71–3, **77**, **79**, 90, **116–17**, **119**, 128, 135, 136, 139, 155, 166, 189, 195, 253, 296, 301, 309–10, 312–13, 321, **361**, 392–3, 412
Jawdhar 49
Joseph (Prophet) 61, **73**, **104–6**, 131, 141, 165, 261, 321, **357**, **368**, **370**, 470
Juḥfa **245**

Kādū b. Muʿārik al-Māwaṭī 26, **424–5**
Khālid b. al-Walīd 216
al-Kirmānī, Ḥamīd al-Dīn 48, 162, 196, 385, 413
Kraus, Paul 277–8
al-Kulaynī, Abū Jaʿfar Muḥammad b. Yaʿqūb 124, 136, 155, 187, 205, 394, 452

Mahdī (eschatological figure) 10–11, 17, 24–7, 44, 54, 66, 78, 111, 129, 143, 162–6, 250–1, 253, 264, 267–71, 290, 293–4, 296, 320, 339, 355, 361, 408, 414, 416, 419–24, **439–41**, 448–9, 455, 457, 463, 468, 471, 478–9
Madelung, Wilferd 22, 47, 62, 146, 252–4, 284, 292, 384, 397, 400, 405–6, 407
Massignon, Louis 22
al-Mahdī biʾllāh (1st Fatimid caliph) 4, 24–7, 45, 62, 166, 207, 250, 252–4, 269, 272, 284, 290, 298,

385–6, 400–1, 404–5, 408–9, 418, 422, 424–5, 457, 471
al-Majdūʿ, Ismāʿīl ʿAbd al-Rasūl al-Ujaynī 39
Makhzūm 100
al-Manṣūr biʾllāh, 3rd Fatimid caliph 27, 45, 49, 59, 475
Maryam (Mary) 41, 136, **327**, 398–9, 404
Al-Miqdād 68, 90, 207, **226–7**, 248, 273–6, 279–80, 287, 299, 396, 402
Muʿāwiya 85, 149, **215**, **217**, 270, **302**, 309
al-Muʾayyad fīʾl-Dīn Hibat Allāh al-Shīrāzī 39–40, 47, 146, 282–3, 385
Mufaḍḍal b. ʿUmar al-Juʿfī 9, 13–14, 89, 117, 121, 164, 166, 248, 305–6, 312–13
al-Mughīra b. Saʿīd 11
al-Mughīra b. Shuʿba **217**
Muḥammad (Prophet) 5, 17, 29–30, 44, 54, 61, 66, **73–4**, **88**, **90**, **92–4**, **96**, **99**, **101–3**, **108–11**, **114–15**, **117**, 119, 136, 139, 141–2, 144–8, 151–3, 164, 167, **174**, **176**, **178**, **183**, 189, 192, 194, 204, 207, **211–12**, **214**, **216–17**, **221**, **224–6**, **230–2**, **236**, **239–40**, **243**, 267–8, 272–3, 275–6, 281–2, 289–90, **322**, **324**, **327–8**, **333**, **335–6**, **350**, **355–6**, **361–3**, **372–3**, **383**, 393, 399, 405, 407, 410, 417, 420, 427–8, **431**, **434**, **438–9**, **442–3**, **447–9**, 451, 455, 459–62, 477, 479, 481
Muḥammad b. Abī Bakr 67, 90, **103**, 167, 204, 273, 275, 320, **324**, **379–80**, 398, 482
Muḥammad b. Aḥmad (Imam in Salamiyya) (*see also* al-Ḥakīm) 24–5, 44, 62, 252–4, 320, **328**, 385, 400–1, 405, 424
Muḥammad al-Bāqir 9, 80, 90, 136, 185–6, 274, 309, 452–3, 455
al-Muʿizz li-Dīn Allāh, 4th Fatimid caliph 4, 28, 47–50, 58–9, 166, 192, 253–4, 292, 475, 480
Mūsā al-Kāẓim 187, 274
al-Mustanṣir biʾllāh, 8th Fatimid caliph 41

Nahrawān (people of) **85**
Noah 13, **85**, **89**, **93**, **110**, 141–2, 149, **243**, **326**, **335**, **337**, **343**, **371**, 398–9, 419
al-Nuʿmān, al-Qāḍī Abū Ḥanīfa al-Tamīmī al-Maghribī 21, 40–1, 46–50, 198, 385, 409, 4454, 474–5, 482

Pharaoh 13, 149, 152–3, **215**, 320–1, **342**, **356–7**, **363**, 386, 388, 422–3, 459, 474, 477
Poonawala, Ismail Kurban 50

al-Qāʾim b. Amr Allāh, Abūʾl-Qāsim Muhammad, 2nd Fatimid caliph 4, 27, 45, 49, 62, 250, 284, 292, 319, **333**, 385, 404–5, 408, 424–5, 471, 474–5
Qanbar b. Kādān al-Dawsī 274
Qayrawān 25–6
al-Qummī, Saʿd al-Dīn b. ʿAbd Allāh 133, 159

Raqqāda 24, 26–7
Rushayd al-Hajarī **92**, 273–5

al-Ṣaffār al-Qummī 155
Safīna 92, 273–5

Salmān al-Fārisī **79**
Shaykh Ādam Ṣafī al-Dīn b. Ṭayyibshāh 29, 33–4
Shuʿayb (the Prophet) **326**
Shuʿayb (the Companion) 273
al-Sijistānī, Abū Yaʿqūb Isḥāq 48, 124, 146, 162, 191, 196–7, 205, 413, 417, 419
Strothmann, Rudolf 1, 28, 30–3, 35, 275, **304**
Sulaymān b. Ḥasan 34

Ṭalḥa 85
Taym 100, **228**

ʿUmar / the Second / Zufar 13, 63, 66, 73, 85–6, **109–11**, 125–6, 139, 147–9, 151–2, 159, 164–7, **214**, **216**, **232**, **238**, **241**, 244, 248, 252, 255, 265–7, 269–70, 294–6, **324**, **354**, 387, 477
ʿUthmān / the Third / Naʿthal 63, **85–6**, **90**, 149, 152, **215–6**, **232**, **241**, 249, 252, 255, 269–70, 387, 420
ʿUthmān b. Maẓʿūn al-Najashī 274

Yaḥyā b. Maʿmar al-Thumālī 274
Zurāra b. Aʿyun 302, 309

Index of Technical Terms

(Numbers in **bold** characters refer to pages in the translation of the *Kashf.*)

ʿahd (covenant, pact) **74**, 76 n.8, **82**, **92**, **105**, **106**, 106 n.126, **116**, 121–8, 131, 152, 296, **329**, **345**, **355**, **374**, 422, 433 n.339, **434**, **435**, **437**, 454, 465, 470

ahl al-bayt 255, 259, 278 n.201, **362**, **435**, 454, 455

ahl al-naṣb 114 n.154, **363**

ahl al-ẓāhir (people of exotericism) 97 n.95, **105**, 127 n.191, 131, 159, **350**, 415

amir al-muʾminīn (Prince of the Believers) **79**, **80**, **81**, **86**, **88**, **98–9**, **100**, **101**, **102**, **103**, **104**, **106**, **107**, **108**, **110**, **111**, **115**, **116**, **117**, **118**, **119**, **122**, 124, 125, 135, 141 n.242, 151,164, **173**, 204, **212**, **213**, **216**, **220**, **221**, **222**, **226**, **227**, **228**, **229**, **232**, **233**, **237**, **240**, **241**, **242**, **244**, **245**, **246**, **247**, 259, 270, 287, 288, 294, **323**, **324**, **325**, **329**, **355**, **363**, **379**, 398, 410, 423, **438**, 460

amīr al-naḥl 259–61

āya, pl. *āyāt* (sign) 17, 80 n.22, **88–9**, **104**, 119 n.167, **177**, 194, **230**, **237–8**, 238 n.81, **239**, **334–6**, **359–60**, **362**, **363**, **365**, **377**, **379**, **438–9**, **443–4**, **446–7**, 447 n.360, 451 n.373, 453

al-ʿayn al-ʿaẓīma (the Sublime *ʿayn*) 41, **327**, **332**, **333**, 334 n.44, 387–8, 399, 401, 403–5, 405 n.240, 406, 424

aẓilla (shadows) 11 n.24, 18, 125-126, **303**, 312

bāb, pl. *abwāb* (Gate) 8–9, 20, **74**, **75**, 75 n.6, **77**, **79**, **83**, **84**, 84 n.37, **89**, 90 n.65, 92 n.75, nn.77–80, 139, 144, 156, **173–5**, **178**, **180–1**, **183**, 190, 197, 199, 204, **221**, **224**, **227**, **229**, **232**, 238 n.81, **245**, 257, 258, 269, 273–5, 274 n.187, 277 n.198, 279–80, 288, **324**, 326 n.16, **327**, **332**, **335**, **338**, **342**, **348**, **350**, **351**, **357**, **362–3**, **370**, **377**, 389, 395–6, 397, 398, 407, 409, 417, **434**, **436**, **438**, **440–1**, **447**, 464, 465, 467–8, 469, 470

barāʾa / *tabarraʾa* / *barīʾ* (disavowment / to disavow, to dissociate from) 13 n.30, 15–16, 19 n.45, **75**, **119**, 127 n.190, 147–8, 152, **323**, **331**, **324**, **334**, **359**, **379**

bāṭin (esoteric) 14, 16, 17, 17 n.41, 48, 50, 53, 83 n.33, **84**, **93**, **94**, **97**, **105–6**, **107**, 129–30, 131–2, 136, 137, 139, 142, 143, 151, 152 n.282, 157, 159, 161, **175**, 190, 204, **210**,

211, **212**, 215 n.11, **217**, **218**, **220**, **221**, **223**, **224–5**, **226**, **232**, **236**, **241**, **245**, **246**, 256, 263–4, 265, 267–8, 271, 280, 281, 287, 323, 325 n.10, **327–8**, **329**, **330–1**, **333**, **335**, **336**, **339**, **341**, **343**, **345–6**, **346–7**, **348**, **349–52**, **353–4**, **355**, **357**, **362**, **367**, **373**, **374**, 374 n.130, **375–6**, **377**, **383**, 385, 387, 388, 389, 393, 399–400, 401, 402, 406–7, 410, 411, 412, 414, 414–19, 421, **429**, **430**, **437**, **441**, **446**, 448, 449, 451–2, 456, 459, 460–1, 465, 467, 468, 478, 479, 482

bayt (house) 29, 112 n.146, **117**, **176**, **329**, **362**, **365**

dāʿī, pl. *duʿāt* (Summoner) 3, 28, 29, 30, 32–4, 38, 42, 44, 48–9, 54, 63, **75**, 83 n.33, **104**, 104 n.117, **106**, 106 n.126, 127 n.190, 132, 137 n.228, 215 n.11, 219 n.24, **233–4**, 234 n.65, **236–7**, 238 n.81, **243**, 244 n.92, 251, 253, 257–61, 261 n.146, 282, 297, 298, **328**, 328 n.22, **332**, **339**, **343**, **345**, **348**, 349 n.69, **357–8**, 358 n.95, **359**, **362–3**, **367**, **369**, **370–1**, **377**, **378**, **379**, **380**, **381**, **382–3**, 386, 389, 396, 397, 400, 407, 409, 420, 423, **436–7**, **440**, **442**, **446–7**, 449, 454, 461, 462, 463–70, 470 nn.452–3, 471

daraja, pl. *darajāt* (degree) **76**, **77**, **78**, **241**, **342**, **345–6**, **362**, **370**, **372**, **374**, 413, **436**, **437**, **440**, 467

daʿwa (summons) 4, 16, 17, 21–8, 40–1, 43–4, 47–8, 51, 54, 58, 62, 64, 66, **77**, 83 n.33, **105**, 106 n.126, **113**, 125 n.183, 128–34, 138, 148, 157–8, 160–1, **171**, 187, 194, 198, 204, 207, **209**, **212**, **219**, 219 nn.24–5, **223**, **227**, **233**, **236**, 237 nn.74–5, 238 n.81, **242**, 242 n.86, 244 n.92, 245 n.96, 250–72, 280, 283–5, 287–90, 292, 293, 296–7, 299, 319, 321, **330–1**, **333**, 333 n.36, 334 n.44, **339**, **340–1**, **343**, **345**, **347**, **352–3**, 353 n.81, **362–3**, **369**, **370**, **376–7**, **378–80**, 381 n.146, **383**, 385–7, 389, 395, 397, 400–1, 403, 405–6, 407–8, 409, 413, 415, 419–25, 427, **438**, **439**, **440–1**, 442, 448–50, 454, 454 n.383, 460, 463–70, 474, 476–8, 481

dhikr (remembrance) **109**, 109 n.133, **210**, **219–20**, **228**, **237**, **242–3**, 243 n.90, **322**, **363**, **377**, **429–30**

ḍidd (antagonist), pl. *aḍdād* **77**, **82**, **102**

fatra (interval) **231**

ghuluww / *ghulāt* (exaggeration, exaggerators) 2, 5–20, 22–3, 41, 42, 60–3, 65, 67, 71, 76 n.9, **80**, 80 n.20, 84 n.37, 97 n.94, 98 n.99, 114 n.152, 121, 126 n.186, 127 n.191, 131 n.205, 133,136, 137, 139–40, 141–2 n.242, 143, 145, 150, 154–62, 163, 166–7, 185, 193, 248–52, 257, 261, 272–3, 276–7, 280–2, 286, 293, 295, 299, 303 n.11, 311–13, 332 n.32, **349**, 385, 387–8, 389, 391, 393, 394, 399, 400 n.217, 409–16, 411 n.269, 418, 424, 433 n.339, 470, 479, 480, 481–2

ḥadd, pl. *ḥudūd* (dignity, dignitary, degree, rank) 17 n.41, **106**, **171**, **173**, **175**, **178–9**, **180–1**, **183**, 194,

196, 198, 201, 202, 204, **236**, 246, 282, **304**, 314, **339**, **343**, 344 n.60, **345–6**, **348**, **354**, **368**, **375**, 395 n.189, 407, **438**, 469, 477
haykal, pl. *hayākil* (sacred form) 40–1, 40 n.96, **79–80**, 160, **246**, **332**, 334 n.44, **345**, **365**, 403, 424, 480
ḥijāb, pl. *ḥujub* (veil) **116**, **118**, 141, **215**, **227**, 277 n.198, **327**, **329**, 329 n.24, **334**, **335**, **336**, **337**, **340**, 341 n.55, **342**, **345**, **348**, **365**, **366–7**, **373**, **377**, **382**, **383**, 388, 389, 391, 399, 400 n.217, 401, 404, 424
ḥikma (wisdom) 92–3 n.81, 132, **209**, **215**, **216**, **227**, **233**, **236**, **239**, 282, 326 n.15, **337**, **342**, **345**, **347**, **349**, **354**, **360**, **365**, **366**, **370**, **374**, **376**, **382**, 422, **429**, **436**, **439**, 461
ḥujja, pl. *ḥujaj* (Proof) 25, 45, 54, 61, 62, 63, 69, 70, **74**, **75**, **83**, **84**, 84 n.37, **87**, **89–90**, 89 n.60, **92–4**, 93 n.82, 95, 95–6 n.91, **104**, 104 n.117, **105**, **106**, 125 n.183, **142**, **178**, 200, **210**, **211**, **214–15**, 215 n.11, **217**, 217 n.19, **219**, 219 n.24, **221**, 226 n.38, 227, 227 n.41, 230 n.56, 231 n.57, **232**, **233–4**, 238 nn.81–2, 239 n.83, 240, **243–4**, 243 n.91, **245**, 245 n.96, 253, 257, 258, 259–61, 266, 277 n.198, 279–81, 287, 288, 289, 295–6, 297, 298, 319, **324**, **326**, 326 nn.15–16, **327–31**, **332**, **339**, **342**, **345**, **347**, 347 n.64, **348–9**, 349 n.67, **354**, **355**, **357**, 361 n.106, 362, **365**, 366 n.117, **368**, **369**, **374**, **376–7**, **378**, **379**, **380**, 381 n.145, **382**, 385, 387, 388, 390–408, 397 n.202, 398 n.206, 409, 424, **429**, **434**, **437**, **438**, **440–1**, 441 n.351, **444**, **446–7**, 448, 449, 453–4, 459, 462, 463–70, 470 nn.452–3, 471, 474–5

ikhtiyār (choice) **246**, **330**, **339**, **346**, **357**, **371**, **373**, **380**, **382**, **429**, **431**, **435**, **444–5**, 451
ʿilm al-bāṭin (esoteric knowledge) 67, 130, 132, 136–7, 139, 151, 159, 161, **210**, **211**, **226**, 256, 287, **328**, **341**, **348**, **349**, **351–2**, **373**, **375**, **383**, 389, 399, 400, 406, 415, 416, **437**, **441**, 448, 449, 452, 465, 468, 478
ism, pl. *asmāʾ* (name) 12, **88**, 92 n.75, **116–17**, 136, 141, **172**, **177**, 185, 188, 193, 194, **210**, **229**, **231–2**, 273, 291, **304**, **306**, 313–14, 326 n.16, 336, 338, 338 n.49, **342**, **347**, **359**, **361**, **367**, **369**, **371**, **377–8**, 388, 388 n.170, 394–5, 403–4, 419, 433

janāḥ, pl. *ajniḥa* (wing) **83**, 83 n.33, 106 n.126, 442 n.352, 470 n.453
jārī (flow, flowing) 55 n.143, 89, **180–1**, 198–9, 198 n.91, 203, 365, 369, 372
Jibt **82**, **100–2**, 149, **358**

kālī **79** n.18, **84**, 139, 166
al-khalq al-jadīd (the new creation) 130, **327**, **330**, **377**, **383**, 402

maʿdin, pl. *maʿādin* (source, mine) **210**, 210 n.3, **220**, **332**, **335**, **377**, 379, 452
malāk, pl. *malāʾika* (angel) 83 n.33, 87 n.54, **108**, 108 n.130, 112 n.146, **116–17**, 122 n.173, 124–5, 125 n.183, 127 n.190, 179 n.39,

200, **219**, 219 nn.24–5, 224 n.35, **243**, 277 n.198, 297, **332**, **355–6**, **360**, **372–3**, **381**, 381 nn.145–6, 413–14, 423–4, 467 n.432

maʿnā (meaning) 92 n.75, **229**, 273, **304–5**, 314, 326 n.16, **333**, 333 n.38, 334 n.44, **337**, **342**, **347**, **359**, **366–7**, 388, 403–4, 424, 480

maqām, pl. *maqāmāt* (sacred station, position) **82**, 88 n.56, **97**, **102**, **104**, **106**, **108**, 125, 125 n.183, **209**, **210**, **211**, **214–17**, **221**, **222**, **224**, **225**, **226**, **227**, **244**, **246**, **247**, 263, 277 n.198, 283, 285, 292, **324**, **327**, **337**, **340**, 340 n.53, **343**, **346**, **347–8**, **354**, **360–1**, **362–3**, 362 n.109, **365–6**, **372**, **375**, **379**, **380**, 386, 389, 406, 411 n.269, **429**, **430**, **433**, **434**, **435**, **441**, **443**, **445**

maskh (metamorphosis; see also *musūkhiyya*) 9, 13, 18, 67, 154–62, 159 n.311, 162 n.321, 163, **246–7**, 248, 295, **325**, 412

maʿrifa (knowledge) 14, **102**, **231**, **241**, **242**, **339**, **341**, **344**, **346**, **359**, 393, 408

martaba, pl. *marātib* (rank) **107–8**, 124, 125, **346**, **348**, **360**, **362–3**, **371**, **372**, **377**, **436**

mawlā (master) 49, 91 n.74, 245 n.94, **305**, 331 n.31, **333**, **347**, **383**, **431**

mīthāq (alliance, pact) **74**, **82**, 121, 122 n.174, 123, 136, 272, **329**, **355**, **374**, 422, **434**, **435**

muʾmin (believer) **74**, 76 n.11, 87 n.54, 133 n.213, **100**, **108**, **114**, 160, 160 n.315, **177**, **210**, **211**, **217**, **220–1**, **225**, **232**, **233–4**, 234 n.64, **236–7**, 237 n.74, **241–2**, **243**, **245–6**, 259 nn.138, 139, n.141, 265, 281, 285, 298, **328**, 329 n.23, **345–7**, **349–53**, **362–3**, **370**, 374 n.129, **375**, **378**, **382**, 386–7, 392, 400, 413–15, 420–1, **430**, **436–8**, **440**, 464–8, 464 n.421, 465 n.423, 470 n.453

mutimm (Completer Imam) 40 n.96, 61, **93–4**, 94 n.85, 124, 142, 248, 258, 282 n.219, 289, 289 n.243, **336**, **340**, 340 n.51, **343**, **360**, **363**, **379**, 389, **436**

musūkhiyya (metamorphosis; see also *maskh*) 13, 67, **77–8**, 139, 151, 154–62, 165, 166–7, 250, 258, 261, 269–70, 279, 295 299, **325**, **364**, 480

mustafīd (receiver, beneficiary of knowledge) 132, 344 n.60, **381**, 404 n.421

mustajīb (respondent) 17 n.41, **370**, **378**, 470 n.453

al-nāṭiq al-qāʾim **209**

nikāḥ (coitus, penetration) **105**, 129, 131–2, 133 n.213, **236**, 236 n.72, 261, **343**

nuqabāʾ nāṭiq , pl. *nuṭaqāʾ* (speaking-prophet, speaker) 40 n.96, 64, **79**, **83**, **84**, 86 n.51, **93–4**, 94 nn.85–6, **96**, **99**, **100**, **118**, 139–40, 140 n.238, 142, 143, 147, 149–50, 153, 163–4, **183**, 184, 200–3, **209**, 214 n.9, 217 n.19, **219**, **221**, **226–7**, **230**, **231**, **238**, 238 n.82, **240**, **246**, 262, 277 n.198, 289–90, 291–2, 293, 295–8, 326 n.14, **327**, **329**, 329 nn.23–4, **331**, **333**, **335–6**, **338–9**, **340–1**, **343**, **347**, **355–7**, **359–61**, 361 n.106, **362–3**, **365**, **366**, **369**, **370**, **376**, **377**, **378**, **383**, 385–6, 389, 397–9, 401–6, 411 n.271, 415,

418–19, 422, 424, **432**, **436**, **439**, **441**, 448–9, 457, 459–61, 464, 468 n.438, 470 n.453, 477

qā'im (resurrector) 54, 61, 62, 66, 71, **81**, **82**, 82 n.26, **83–4**, 84 n.37, 86 n.51, 87, **88–9**, **90**, **101**, **103**, **104**, **107**, **109**, 111 n.139, **112–15**, 112 n.146, 114 n.152, 115 n.156, 160, 165, 203, 207, **209**, **213**, **219–21**, **227**, **230**, **233**, **235**, **240**, **245**, **246**, 252, 252 n.115, 255, 288, 291–3, 292 n.254, 294, 296–8, **329–30**, **338**, **359**, **363–4**, 404, 417, 419, 455, 467, 478–9
qā'im bi'l-sayf (bearer of the sword) **219**, **233**, **235**, **245–7**, 252, 291 n.252, 293–8, 299, **333**, 405

raqīb (guardian) **79**, 139
rutba, pl. *rutab* (degree) **342**, **354**, **362**, **365**, **368**, **383**, 422

sabīl (path) **77**, **82**, **98**, 99 n.101, **100**, **104**, **109**, **113**, **177**, **213**, **233**, **237**, **238**, **244**, **260**, 280, 282, 285, **324**, **339**, **348**, **358**, **365**, **380–1**, **431**, **432**, **434**, **439**, **445**, **446**, 451, 452, 453
ṣāḥib al-bāṭin (master of the esoteric) **217**, **225**, 280–1, **329**, 401, 407
ṣāḥib al-ḥaqq (master of Truth) **212**, **215**, **232**, **324**, **325**, **327**, **328**, **355**, **357**, **379**, 423
ṣāḥib al-sharī'a (master of the Law) 86 n.51, 140 n.238, **237**, **245**, **342**, **347**, **348**, **371**
ṣāḥib al-ta'wīl (master of the exegesis) 81 n.23, 93 n.82, 152, **217**, **221**, **222**, 281, **328**, 407, 450
ṣāḥib al-zaman (master of the Age) **78**, **88**, 124, 162, **219**, **231**, 270, 297, **342**, **364**, **377**, 478
ṣāmit (silent) **235**, 277 n.198, 297–8, **329**, **333**, **370**, **376**, 401–2, 406, 418, 460, 461
sayf (sword) **75**, **87**, **93**, **112–15**, **118**, **215**, **219**, **227**, 228 n.51, **229**, **233**, **235**, **240**, **245–6**, 252, 291 n.252, 294, 296–8, 329, **333**, **360**, **363**, **364**, **376**, **377**, 401, 405, 461, **469**
al-sayyid al-akbar (the greatest master) **76**, 76 n.9, 144, 167
shakhṣ, pl. *ashkhāṣ* (person) 14, 16, 141, 143, **331**, **332**, 332 n.34, **334**, 338 n.49, **342**, **350**, 389, 410–11, 411 n.270, 425
sharī'a, pl. *sharā'i'* (Law) 62, **78**, 86 n.51, **94**, 140 n.238, 204, **210**, **229**, **237**, **245**, 265 n.161, 288, 289, **327**, **329**, **334–5**, **337**, **339**, **342–3**, **347**, **348**, **352**, **362**, **371**, **375**, **376**, 386, 401–2, 406, 408–19, 418 n.299, 423, 436, 441, 460–1, 464
ṣirāṭ (way) **99**, 99 n.101, **241**, **323**, **339**, **347–8**, **358**, **376**, **381**, 408, **441**

Ṭāghūt **82**, **100**, **101**, **102**, 149, **177**, 195, **358**, 455
tanzīl (revelation) 53, **93**, 93 n.82, **94**, **97**, **98**, 98 n.98, 142, 145, 151–2, **222**, **223**, **225**, 245 n.95, 258, 265, 267, 268, 289, **322**, **332**, **335**, **349**, **351**, **355**, **373**, 374 n.130, 415, 416, 423, **429**, **436**, 451, 460, 462, 464
taqiyya (dissimilation, secrecy) 19–20, 19 n.44, 122, 127–8, 128 n.193, 142–3, 142 n.244, 143 nn.245–7, 150, 161, **232**, 253, 257,

324 n.9, **328**, **364**, 364 n.112, 392, 400, 422, 460, 463
taqṣīr / muqaṣṣir (falling short, shortcoming/er) **78**, 162–3, 163 n.325, **235**, 264, 265 n.161, **270**, **349**, **350**, **352**, **364**, 385, 387, 414–16
tarbiya (rearing, initiation) **236**, 278, **383**, **436**
taslīm (surrendering, submission) **225**, **230**, 322 n.3, **337**, **357**, **368**, **377**
ta'wīl (exegesis) 14 n.32, 17, 38 n.85, 48, 50–1 n.128, 51 n.130, 53–4, **81**, 93 n.82, **94**, 95 n.89, **98**, 98 nn.97–8, 127 n.191, 142 n.244, 152, 161, **217**, **221**, **222–3**, **225**, **244**, 245 n.95, **247**, 265, 266, 267, 268, 281, 282–3, **324**, **325**, **328**, **351**, **355**, **357**, **359**, 370 n.122, **373–4**, 374 n.130, 407, 415, 416, 422, **429**, **430**, **436**, 450, 451, 460, 462, 464
ta'yīd (divine assistance) 17 n.41, 198, **217**, **243**, **332**, **343**, **379**

wadīʿa, pl. *wadāʾiʿ* (deposit) 121–8, 121 n.171, **334**, **337**, **350**
waḥī (revelation, inspiration) **117**, 216, **243**, **332**, **335–7**, **343**, **349**, **356**, **366**, **373**, **379**, **429**
waṣī, pl. awṣiyā' (legatee) 40 n.96, **75**, **82**, **86**, **87–8**, 94 n.85, **95**, 95–6 n.91, **98**, **102**, 110 n.136, 114 n.152, **115**, 125 n.183, 136, 139, 144, 145, 146, 147, 149, 150, 189, **217**, **223**, **224**, **225–6**, **227**, **230**, **232**, **238**, 242 n.87, 245 n.95, 257–8, 265, 267–8, 280, 287, **324**, **325**, **335**, **351**, **355–6**, 361 n.106, **362**, **373**, **375**, **379**, **380**, 395–9, 415, 422–3, **429**, **430**, **431**, 431 n.337, **432**, 433 n.339, **435**, **437**, **439**, **441**, **443**, **444**, **445**, 449, 451, 452, 459, 461, 470 n.453, 477
waṣīṭa, pl. *wasāʾiṭ* (intermediary, mediator) **214**, 282, **337**, **372**, **377**, 389, 482
waṣiyya, pl. *waṣāyā* (legacy, testament) **82**, **93**, **217**, **221**, **222**, **360**, **431**, **432**, **435**, **443**, **445**

yatīm (orphan) 61, **90–2**, 92 n.76, 166, **210–11**, **216–17**, 248, 249, 251, 258, 263–4, 272–86, 299, 367 n.118, 395

ẓāhir (exoteric, apparent) 14, 16, 17 n.41, 48, 50, 53, 83 n.33, **93**, 93 n.82, 97 n.95, 104 n.119, **105**, 127 n.191, 131, 131 n.206, 142, 142 n.244, 143, 145, 151–2, 152 n.282, 159, 161, **173–5**, **180**, 190, 194, 204, **210**, **211**, **212**, **213**, **218**, 225 n.37, **237**, **246**, 264, 265, 265 n.161, 282, 296, 298, **323**, **328**, **329**, **333**, **336**, **339**, **341**, **345–6**, **350**, **351–2**, 352 n.80, **354**, **355**, **357**, **365**, **367**, **374**, 374 nn.130–1, **376**, **377**, 385, 387, 388–9, 393, 399, **405–6**, 410, 411, 411 n.271, 412, 414, 415–19, 423, **429**, **430**, **437**, **438**, **441**, **446**, 451, 461, 465, 468, 479